Praise for *Flex 3 in Action*

The code examples are the strength of this book—plentiful for almost every topic covered.
　　　　　　　　　　　—Andrew Grother, Triware Technologies, Inc.

Easy enough for the newbie, detailed enough for the veteran.
　　　　　　　　　　　—Ken Brueck, Move Network

This is a book you will not only want to read cover to cover but also keep on your desk as a reference for your day to day development needs.
　　　　　　　　　　　—Abdul Qabiz, reader

Does a great job of covering some of the history behind traditional web development and where Rich Internet Applications are headed.
　　　　　　　　　　　—Sami Hoda, eCivis Inc.

A user-friendly tutorial and reference.
　　　　　　　　　　　—Christophe Bunn, Kitry S.A.S.

An impressive amount of Flex content in a single volume.
　　　　　　　　　　　—Charlie Griefer, Amcom Technology

It's clear that the authors put a lot of time and effort into the book. The fact that it comes with an ebook for this version and the future Flex 4 in Action *is a nice bonus.*
　　　　　　　　　　　—A. Kapadia, Amazon reader

I'm a huge fan of Manning's In Action *series. This series caters to people who want more than a quick gloss-over.... Flex 3 in Action is a roll up your sleeves and get busy kind of book that makes it easy to get into Flex.*
　　　　　　　　　　　—Allan Mercado, Amazon reader

Flex 4 in Action

REVISED EDITION OF *FLEX 3 IN ACTION*

TARIQ AHMED
DAN ORLANDO

with JOHN C. BLAND II
and JOEL HOOKS

MANNING
Greenwich
(74° w. long.)

For online information and ordering of this and other Manning books, please visit
www.manning.com. The publisher offers discounts on this book when ordered in quantity.
For more information, please contact

Special Sales Department
Manning Publications Co.
180 Broad St.
Suite 1323
Stamford, CT 06901
Email: orders@manning.com

Manning Publications Co.
180 Broad St.
Suite 1323
Stamford, CT 06901

Development editor: Cynthia Kane
Copyeditor: Linda Recktenwald
Proofreader: Maureen Spencer
Typesetter: Dottie Marsico
Cover designer: Marija Tudor

ISBN 978-1-935182-42-9
Printed in the United States of America
1 2 3 4 5 6 7 8 9 10 – MAL – 15 14 13 12 11 10

brief contents

v

contents

vii

foreword to the first edition

The ability to create Rich Internet Applications (RIAs) has been around much longer than the term itself; since version 8, the Flash Platform has been a viable RIA platform. But it was initially geared toward designers using the environment from a creative perspective, which wasn't ideal for those coming from a pure development background.

If you were a Flash application developer, major hurdles still remained in your way. Delivering feature-laden rich applications in a productive and timely manner was difficult because you had to do most of the work yourself.

The challenge became clear and simple: provide a pure development environment that leveraged the ubiquity and capabilities of Flash yet catered directly to developers and their systems-development lifecycle. Give developers tools to be productive, and give them a framework that did most of the hard work for them so that they could focus their efforts on application logic. The solution to this challenge was Flex.

Flex has been on quite a journey since its release in March 2004 by Macromedia. That first version was followed by the more widely distributed version 1.5 later that year. Flex started as a server product and was billed as a way for developers to create applications on the Flash Platform.

This opened up a whole new world and helped light the fire for RIAs. As Flex-based RIAs began to gain traction, it proved that a demand existed for RIAs and that the general premise for the technological approach was sound. The next step would be to bring RIAs to the masses.

Now under the Adobe brand, the product made a huge jump with the release of Flex 2 in June 2006. Performance was greatly improved as a result of a language overhaul (ActionScript 3) and a major update to the Flash Player (V9).

The tooling switched to the Eclipse platform, which gave it instant credibility with programmers. Flex 2 saw the split of basic compilation and server-side data management. We also saw the first release of the free SDK for compiling Flex apps outside of the IDE. The server-side component evolved into Flex Data Services, now known as LiveCycle Data Services, which enabled real-time data sharing.

These changes helped legitimize the idea of RIAs by proving a desktop experience was possible inside of the browser. At this point, what RIAs needed most was community support.

Tariq saw the need for community support and was there from the very start. He began by creating the first portal and community dedicated to Flex—also known as Community Flex (CFLEX.Net).

CFLEX.Net aggregated tips, tricks, blog posts, events, and technical articles about how to get started with this new framework. Tariq was instrumental in contributing content to the early Flex community, and I owe many of my Flex skills to him.

Early on, Tariq grasped the importance of data services and how real-time data can help complete a Rich Internet Application. He's built everything from internal business-facing Flex applications to great consumer applications. He's seen and used everything the platform has to offer, which is one of many reasons he's an ideal author for a Flex book. I think it's long overdue that this recognized expert's work be bound and made portable.

The release of Flex 3 brings us to a new and exciting stage in the framework and the technology. Adobe open-sourced much of the Flex platform in an effort to be as transparent as possible and to incorporate valuable feedback (not to mention great code) from the community.

With the release of the Adobe AIR, developers can now use Flex to deploy desktop applications as well as browser-based applications.

Adobe has long been known for its great design tools. Flex 3 is the first release that allows designers using those tools to seamlessly collaborate with developers to create great-looking Flex applications. Numerous productivity enhancements in the framework and Flex Builder also make it easier for new developers to get started and scale their applications.

Regardless of your development background or experience with Flex, you'll find *Flex 3 in Action* to be an invaluable guide. There is something for everyone in this book. Tariq and his coauthors Jon and Faisal provide a must-have for any Flex library. This is to be expected from the star who has provided the Flex community with the must-have resource we all know and love, CFLEX.Net.

RYAN STEWART
PLATFORM EVANGELIST
ADOBE SYSTEMS, INC

preface

For many decades user experience was a generally low priority; up until the mid-2000s the term barely existed. It wasn't taught in software engineering university programs, and businesses weren't cognizant of user experience and design (also known as UXD).

Over the years, however, UXD has become a first-class citizen and a top priority, particularly for public-facing web applications. Supporting that are some awesome web-based technologies that allow developers to create these rich internet applications.

But it wasn't always so awesome. Back in the day (early 2000s) I'd been searching for a way to provide users with a better online experience. It took time before Google wowed everyone with the innovative Google Maps site, so for a long time users didn't know how much better things could be.

Through the years of using the web for document distribution, users' expectations devolved from the power of native desktop applications to the anemic ability of HTML applications. That's not a knock against HTML and the web; the web is perfect for what it does, which is deliver platform-neutral documents. Developers and companies focused on the web's ability to give them time-to-market rapid application development, and users accepted whatever was in front of them because, hey, that's how web applications are, right?

It bothered me that with every click, a backend system executed a lot of code to result in minimal UI changes. Even worse was the constant bombardment of database servers. For a technologist, the quick remedy to this is simple: Slap in more memory, load up on virtual machines, scale out horizontally with low-cost commodity servers, and call it a day. But I'm talking about the cost to the users. On their end, they were experiencing that annoying click-and-wait feeling that was common for web applications. In addition, UIs were limited. Sure, you could use JavaScript, but you could only go so far before you needed advanced skills. From an ROI perspective, it generally wasn't worth it.

At the time, Java applets and Flash were available, and they seemed to offer the potential to achieve what I was looking for. But applets failed as a solution; they were bloated, slow, and inconsistent across platforms. Flash was promising, but trying to produce enterprise business applications in a designer's environment proved to be more challenging than it was worth.

During my time in the Knowledge Management department at eBay, this challenge came up again. I needed a way to abstract the complexity of the data and make it simple for users to work in a visual environment.

Along came Flex in 2004 (V1 initially and V1.5 shortly after that). I was able to make a business case for using it, and our team delivered experiences at an entirely new level. At this point, I knew Flex would be big. It delivered the desktop power users needed while maintaining the development velocity that software teams required to survive.

As a believer in Flex, I made it a personal mission to help grow the Flex community. I created CFLEX.Net (www.cflex.net), believing that the bigger the community, the more it will reinvest in itself through knowledge and code sharing and in this way continue to boost the technology's adoption rate. If there's a strong support network, you take less of a risk in bringing a new technology into your organization.

For the early adopters of Flex, the learning curve was rough because only a limited number of books and other reading material were available. That changed with the release of Flex 2, when the number of resources dramatically increased.

I left eBay in late 2005 to join Amcom Technology and build and manage a team of developers. As with any new technology, experts in the field are hard to come by, so your best bet is to grow the skill. While training developers on Flex, I found that the current set of books didn't map to how they think and that obvious challenges were never addressed.

In continuing my mission of growing the community, I set out to write *Flex 3 in Action*, hoping it would help solve the learning challenges that everyday developers face. Instead of grouping topics based on feature categories, the book is structured according to the natural progression of creating an application. I focused on maximum simplicity by not introducing anything you don't need to know until it was needed and by using small code examples that are easy to absorb. I also found that people learn best when they're able to relate new things to things they already know, so whenever possible, I use analogies to how you'd do things in another technology.

With this Flex 4 version of the book, I brought on some industry heavy hitters (Dan Orlando, John C. Bland II, and Joel Hooks) to help take it to a higher level in order to provide you with a solid foundation of understanding. My hope is that by teaching you the keys to success, the Flex community will expand as a result, because you too will be able to share your knowledge and experience with those around you.

Now is the time to get into Flex. The community continues to grow, more and more third-party vendors are coming out with Flex-related technologies, and Flex user groups are popping up all over the place.

The RIA space is red hot with technologies and competition, but Adobe continues to prove it's a few steps ahead. We're in for some exciting times! HTML web applications will always have a place, but it's time to take your skills to another level, because the industry is moving forward with or without you.

Sit down, buckle up, and strap in for the ride!

TARIQ AHMED

acknowledgments

Although most developers want to believe that choices related to technology are premised on purity, capability, and supremacy, the reality is that in the end it boils down to business—and technology as a tool to help businesses achieve their goals. In this book I try to keep this perspective in mind, because a well-rounded view will help you be successful. I've learned about this perspective—and so much more—from my manager and mentor Steve McClary, president of Amcom Technology.

In this second incarnation the book was made possible and better with my fellow authors Dan Orlando, John C. Bland II, and Joel Hooks. While I focused on the basics, Dan teaches you about working with lists, reusability, custom components, architecture, how to work with back end systems, and how to snazzy up your apps with themes and skins. John demystifies events, and provides the in-depth lowdown on pop-ups and view states, as well as adding pizzazz using effects, and how to take advantage of drag and drop. Joel covers Flex charting, effective techniques and tools for debugging, wrapping up a project in preparation for deployment, and application architecture using the RobotLegs framework.

Of course, the crew at Manning are the silent heroes here; they make being an author as easy as possible. With their open and collaborative approach, they guided us along this journey; their professionalism and willingness to help made the process smooth and easy. They also made the experience a personal one—and that meant a lot to me. There are a lot of people to thank at Manning, starting with publisher Marjan Bace, acquisitions editor Mike Stephens, assistants Christina Rudloff and Megan Yockey, and review editor Karen Tegtmeyer, but special kudos to our development editor Cynthia Kane, and to the production team for the book (Linda Recktenwald, Maureen Spencer, Mary Piergies, and Dottie Marsico).

There were many reviewers who read the manuscript at different stages of its development and who provided us with invaluable insights and feedback. We'd like to thank Patrick Steger, Sara Plowright, Zareen Zaffar, Matt Smith, John Farrar, Niaz Jalal, Alex Salapatas, Nikolaos Kaintantzis, Doug Warren, Brian Curnow, Christophe Bunn, Phil Hanna, Rick Evans, Sopan Shewale, Jeremy Flowers, John Griffin, Peter Pavlovich, Norman Klein, Rick Wagner, Sean Moore, and Kevin Schmidt who did a final technical review of the manuscript shortly before it went to press.

Most importantly I thank my wife Juliana and daughter Zafira for being supportive of this project. Although I was physically around most of the time, I was often in another dimension, mentally. I know it was hard for them, and I want to thank them with all my heart for giving the opportunity to achieve this goal.

TARIQ AHMED

about this book

Flex is an event-driven, object-oriented application framework and programming language that lets you build compelling and fluid Rich Internet Applications (RIAs) that run in the Adobe Flash environment.

Historically, the priority in web application development has been feature velocity and time to market, at the cost of usability to the end user. Flex lets you maintain that centrally deployed rapid-turnaround model, but it gives you the power to achieve usability at the same time.

Someone coming into Flex faces unique challenges. First, many developers aren't used to an event-driven technology. They can understand it at a high level, but don't truly *get it* for a long time. Until that happens, you can't use the technology to its full capability; and, more important, you won't be able to work as productively.

The second challenge stems from the fact that many developers have been working in their current technology stack for many years. Because people go with what they know, they tend to copy what they did in HTML over into Flex. That will work, but you're limiting yourself creatively.

The third challenge is the complexity that comes as a result of Flex's power. It's not complicated *per se,* but a lot of web-application technologies are procedural and non-event-driven. The learning curve starts off slowly as you see the basic examples; but the moment you try to go one step further, it suddenly *feels* a lot harder.

Flex 4 in Action addresses these challenges and uses them as an underlying premise; it's what makes the book unique. With the first challenge, the book emphasizes the event-driven nature of Flex by periodically reminding you how to leverage the event objects. We also help you catch on more quickly by showing many ways of doing the same thing along with the advantages and disadvantages of each.

Addressing the second challenge, we don't negate your existing skills and we understand that you're probably coming from another web technology. We came from there, too, and we know the mental leap it takes to break out of a mold you're accustomed to. The book continuously provides suggestions how you can harness the power of a particular feature.

As far as the third challenge—complexity—is concerned, the mission of the book is to enable you to become an effective Flex developer in a short time. We do this through a combination of techniques that include using small examples you can relate to. We also leverage your existing skills by relating how you used to do things in other technologies with how you do them in Flex. The chapters are ordered in a logical progression of how you would go about building an application, starting with the easy stuff and ramping up your skills along the way.

You're in good hands, and we'll be your guide as you take your skills and career to the next level. The one thing we haven't figured out is how to deal with all the fanfare that you'll get from appreciative users. You'll have to figure that out on your own!

Roadmap

Chapter 1 introduces Flex. It defines the problem and the approach Flex takes to solving it. Playing off that, we give you the business case that you'll need to make in order to sell Flex to your department, customer, or clients. We describe how Flex works at a high level along with the concept of events, and where Flex sits in the overall suite of Adobe products.

Chapter 2 gets you started with building applications in Flex by introducing the toolset, environment, and languages. Events are fleshed out a bit more to ensure that your understanding continues to grow.

Chapter 3 is about Flex's core language: ActionScript. This powerful ECMAScript-compliant, object-oriented language is what makes Flex possible. The chapter reviews data types, operators, loops, conditionals, and so on. You won't get far without ActionScript, so it's worth learning about it early on.

Chapter 4 addresses the layout of an application. It covers how you position display objects, as well as use containers to group visual objects together.

Chapter 5 begins by teaching you how to capture user input via forms. Flex has form inputs similar to those in HTML, but it also has a number of inputs that move beyond how they are captured in HTML.

Chapter 6 continues the topics from chapter 5 by discussing how Flex's validators are used to validate user input. From a usability perspective, validating up front saves the user time and grief.

Chapter 7 flips things around by using formatters to format raw information (now that you have it). Often used alongside validators, formatters address the headache of having to format things yourself.

Chapter 8 explores the workhorse of Flex: list-based components. Lists are data-driven components that automatically build their display based on the data that they're pointed at.

Chapter 9 adds onto chapter 8 by delving into the next generation of list-based components, which are part of Flex 4's new Spark components.

Chapter 10 continues the topic of lists and focuses on how to customize them, from quick 'n' dirty approaches to using full-blown item renderers for customized display. Chapter 10 also introduces editors, which allow for inline editing.

Chapter 11 goes all out on events. By this point, we'll have introduced how to use events in a minimal way; but this chapter takes it to the next level by going deep into how they work.

Chapter 12 shows you how to add navigation to your application so you can give your users the ability to switch between features.

Chapter 13 covers the use of pop-up windows as an extension to application navigation. It describes how your application can communicate with the pop-up by sending information back and forth.

Chapter 14 explores the subject of application flow and discusses a unique Flex feature known as view states. This mechanism can save you a lot of time by configuring the different views in your application; you can then switch from one view to another easily.

Chapter 15 begins the subject of working with data, particularly with getting data to and from your application from a back-end service. This includes connecting to servers that support Flex's native binary protocol (AMF), XML over HTTP, and web services.

Chapter 16 covers objects and classes. Flex is an object-oriented language, after all. And although the comfort factor of sticking to its tag-based MXML language is nice, being aware of how ActionScript objects are created and used only adds to your powers.

Chapter 17 goes into detail about custom components, which is an area in which you'll spend a lot of your development time. Custom components are your primary vehicle to break your application into small, manageable, reusable pieces.

Chapter 18 wraps up application structure with an overview of Flex's reusability features such as sharing custom components across multiple projects and compiling shared libraries of functionality.

Chapter 19 takes application structure further by introducing formal architectural considerations, designing a Flex application, and utilizing the RobotLegs MVC framework as a means to accomplish a well architected application.

Chapter 20 begins the subject of customizing the experience. This topic includes using Flex's version of CSS styles, skinning, and themes. Images and fonts are also covered.

Chapter 21 dives into one of Flex's coolest features: effects. Effects add that "wow" factor to your application, and we also show how they can assist you in increasing usability.

Chapter 22 finishes our discussion of customization by showing you in detail how to use the drag-and-drop feature. This is a crowd favorite, but from the usability perspective you can save your users a few clicks by speeding up the workflow.

Chapter 23 is about charting. We review the various types of charts and give you advice about when to use each type. We also discuss the parts that make up a chart and how to customize it.

Chapter 24 covers testing and debugging. At this point, you're wrapping up the project and entering the QA cycle. Knowing how to debug applications and how to isolate issues is key. Flex comes with a number of built-in features, but we also review third-party tools.

Chapter 25 wraps up the project with the final steps. These involve adding print capabilities to your application, using wrappers to load your application, and developing a release plan to deploy a production build of the software.

Chapter 26 is a bonus add-on chapter, available online, which dives into working with XML. XML is a ubiquitous language; but Flex is the first to support the E4X syntax, which lets you work with XML as if it were a native Flex object. The chapter is available for download from the publisher's website at www.manning.com/Flex4inAction.

Code downloads and conventions

This book contains numerous examples of Flex, ActionScript, and XML code. All code examples can be found at the book's website: http://www.flexinaction.com as well as at the publisher's website: www.manning.com/Flex4inAction.

The following conventions are used throughout the book:

- *Italic* typeface is used to introduce new terms.
- `Courier/Fixed-Width` typeface is used for code samples, as well as elements, attributes/properties, function names, and class names. MXML components, when used by name, won't use this typeface in text unless they're referenced as part of an actual code snippet.
- **Bold** and *Italic face Courier/Fixed-Width* typeface is used to highlight portions within code.
- Code annotations accompany many segments of code. Certain annotations are marked with bullets such as ❶. These annotations have further explanations that follow the code.
- The > symbol is used to indicate menu items that should be selected in sequence.
- Code-line continuations use the ➥ symbol.

Author Online

Purchase of *Flex 4 in Action* includes free access to a private web forum run by Manning Publications where you can make comments about the book, ask questions, and receive help from the authors and from other users. To access the forum and subscribe to it, point your web browser to www.manning.com/Flex4inAction. This page provides information on how to get on the forum once you are registered, what kind of help is available, and the rules of conduct on the forum.

Manning's commitment to our readers is to provide a venue where a meaningful dialogue between individual readers and between readers and the authors can take place. It is not a commitment to any specific amount of participation on the part of the authors, whose contribution to the AO remains voluntary (and unpaid). We suggest you try asking the authors some challenging questions lest their interest stray!

The Author Online forum and the archives of previous discussions will be accessible from the publisher's website as long as the book is in print.

About the authors

TARIQ AHMED is an accomplished web application pioneer with over 15 years of experience introducing next generation web technologies to companies such as Bell Canada and REUTERS. He was first to introduce eBay to Adobe Flex, and saw it proliferate to other teams. As an Adobe Flex Community Expert, Tariq evangelizes the technology and supports the community, particularly through his Community Flex (CFLEX.Net) site and his personal blog (www.dopejam.com). He is currently the Manager of Product Development at Amcom Technology, managing a team of RIA Engineers and Business Intelligence Analysts.

DAN ORLANDO is a recognized RIA Architect, specializing in enterprise class Flex and AIR applications. Dan is often called on as a resource for information on topics involving bleeding edge technology platforms for radio interviews and print publications, which include: PHP Architect magazine, Flex and Flash Developer Magazine, Amazon Web Services Developer Connection, Adobe Developer Connection, IBM developerWorks, PHPBuilder.com, and many others.

JOHN C. BLAND II is founder of Katapult Media Inc. which focuses on software and web development using technologies such as ColdFusion, the Flash Platform, PHP, Java, the .NET Platform, and Objective-C (iPhone, Mac OSX, etc). Through Katapult, he works diligently on custom software and web products for small and large clients throughout the world. As a 2009 Adobe Community Expert, John continues to put back into the community which helped mold him into the developer he is today. John blogs regularly on his Geek Life blog: www.johncblandii.com.

JOEL HOOKS is a Flash Platform developer with experience in Actionscript 3, Flex, and Python. Joel spent the first 13 years of his professional career as a 3d animator and graphic designer working on computer based training applications from that perspective. His interest in programming goes as far back as "TELL TURTLE" and he has always been interested in the technological challenges related to developing software. With the introduction of Actionscript 3, Joel finally found a platform that allows him to architect useful tools while fully leveraging his experience as a visual artist. Joel is passionate about technology and enjoys exploring the landscape of frameworks, libraries, and tools that make his work constantly fun and challenging.

about the title

By combining introductions, overviews, and how-to examples, the *In Action* books are designed to help learning and remembering. According to research in cognitive science, the things people remember are things they discover during self-motivated exploration.

Although no one at Manning is a cognitive scientist, we are convinced that for learning to become permanent it must pass through stages of exploration, play, and, interestingly, retelling of what is being learned. People understand and remember new things, which is to say they master them, only after actively exploring them. Humans learn in action. An essential part of an *In Action* book is that it's example driven. It encourages the reader to try things out, to play with new code, and explore new ideas.

There is another, more mundane, reason for the title of this book: our readers are busy. They use books to do a job or solve a problem. They need books that allow them to jump in and jump out easily and learn just what they want just when they want it. They need books that aid them in action. The books in this series are designed for such readers.

about the cover illustration

The illustration on the cover of *Flex 4 in Action* bears the caption "An Armenian" and is taken from a collection of costumes of the Ottoman Empire published on January 1, 1802, by William Miller of Old Bond Street, London. The title page is missing from the collection and we have been unable to track it down to date. The book's table of contents identifies the figures in both English and French, and each illustration also bears the names of two artists who worked on it, both of whom would no doubt be surprised to find their art gracing the front cover of a computer programming book...two hundred years later.

The collection was purchased by a Manning editor at an antiquarian flea market in the "Garage" on West 26th Street in Manhattan. The seller was an American based in Ankara, Turkey, and the transaction took place just as he was packing up his stand for the day. The Manning editor did not have on his person the substantial amount of cash that was required for the purchase and a credit card and check were both politely turned down. With the seller flying back to Ankara that evening the situation was getting hopeless. What was the solution? It turned out to be nothing more than an old-fashioned verbal agreement sealed with a handshake. The seller simply proposed that the money be transferred to him by wire and the editor walked out with the bank information on a piece of paper and the portfolio of images under his arm. Needless to say, we transferred the funds the next day, and we remain grateful and impressed by this unknown person's trust in one of us. It recalls something that might have happened a long time ago.

The pictures from the Ottoman collection, like the other illustrations that appear on our covers, bring to life the richness and variety of dress customs of two centuries ago. They recall the sense of isolation and distance of that period—and of every other historic period except our own hyperkinetic present. Dress codes have changed since then and the diversity by region, so rich at the time, has faded away. It is now often hard to tell the inhabitant of one continent from another. Perhaps, trying to view it optimistically, we have traded a cultural and visual diversity for a more varied personal life. Or a more varied and interesting intellectual and technical life.

We at Manning celebrate the inventiveness, the initiative, and, yes, the fun of the computer business with book covers based on the rich diversity of regional life of two centuries ago, brought back to life by the pictures from this collection.

Part 1

Application basics

Your journey into Flex is about to begin. This part of the book is focused on getting you ramped up with the basics of making Flex applications.

Before the coding starts, we'll present a high-level overview of what Flex is, from its languages to its ecosystem, and show how the parts fit together. Building on what you learn, you'll set up your development environment so you can create and build Flex applications.

With the ability to compile and run Flex applications, the coding (a.k.a. the good stuff) begins with an overview of ActionScript—the core language of Flex. Progressively, you'll put together all the building blocks that make up the essence of every application from layout, to building and validating forms, to formatting data, to displaying lists of information.

Making the case 1

This chapter covers

- Solving problems with Flex
- Using RIAs and RWAs
- Comparing Flex to the competition
- Learning the Flex ecosystem

Why is Flex a great addition to your personal skill set or organization? With buzzwords flying all over, a nonstop stream of websites with missing vowels in their names, and the Web 2.0 space on fire, a hodgepodge of technologies leaves the common developer caught in the middle. It's vital to be able to defend the decision to move forward with Flex to both customers and management.

In this chapter, we talk about challenges that a web developer faces and how to solve them using Flex by Adobe. We also get into the mechanics of a Flex application and discuss the ecosystem as a whole. But before we get into that, we want to identify the problem that Flex solves, so let's begin with how the problem emerged with the proliferation of web applications.

1.1 *Why are web applications so prolific?*

Web applications are so prolific because the strength of the web is also its weakness. The original intent of the web was to be a lightweight information distribution

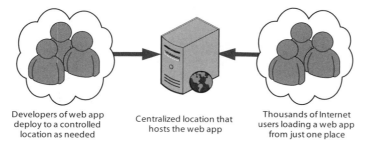

Developers of web app
deploy to a controlled
location as needed

Centralized location that
hosts the web app

Thousands of Internet
users loading a web app
from just one place

**Figure 1.1   The great
web advantage—
centralized deployment**

system: a simple and platform-neutral way (any OS, any hardware) to post documents on a server and retrieve them as easily.

This advantage of centralized deployment (figure 1.1) inherited by dynamic pages (such as web applications) provides such a strategic value in both a business (such as ROI) and development perspective that it makes the thought of developing old-school desktop applications difficult to justify.

Yes, desktop applications are rich and robust; you can do anything the OS permits. But their deployment model is a nightmare. The logistical complications of trying to get thousands, if not hundreds of thousands, of clients to run the precise version of your software at the exact same time are immense.

> **NOTE**   This may all feel obvious to some of you, but part of being successful with Flex is being able to articulate the business case to management and teammates. At the same time, knowing the problems that Flex solves helps you better understand the technology.

With the web, you can release enhancements and fixes as fast as you can code them. Now all your users can take advantage of the latest and greatest updates transparently.

Seems like a no-brainer, right? As you know, technologies quickly become obsolete, yet the centralized deployment model of web applications is so effective that we've continued to use its HTML 4 language since 1999 (HTML 5 is supposedly due by 2022).

During all this time, one critical element was overlooked: the user experience (figure 1.2). Users willingly gave up usability for the ubiquity of web applications. Ultimately, we trained ourselves and the users to accept this situation.

True, there was an emphasis in the web development community prior to the AJAX revolution to utilize JavaScript to improve usability by employing a more progressive approach, but the core of the usability problem lies in the historical roots of the web—its structure has been built around what was intended to be a documentation-distribution mechanism.

As a developer, you exert a significant amount of effort to restore some semblance of usability by transferring as much application logic as possible to the front end (client side) to mimic a client (desktop-like) experience.

The web was supposed to be platform agnostic, yet ironically the more you push logic to the client side, the more you struggle with browser incompatibilities. This is where rich internet applications (RIAs) come into play.

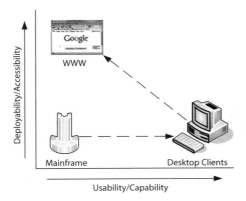

Figure 1.2 We took a great step backward in terms of usability for the sake of deployability. Mainframes provided horrific user experiences, but were easy to deploy based on their centralized model. Moving to desktop clients allowed for uncompromised usability, but they were a challenge to keep updated. Web applications took a step backward by having a high degree of deployment ease, but they sacrificed usability as a result.

1.2   The RIA solution

In this data-centric society, users and businesses depend on being able to work with information efficiently. Users want information quickly and easily. Businesses, from a customer-retention perspective, want to provide a better user experience than the competition and need the technology to ensure the workforce is functioning productively.

In a sense, you now have a paradox: users wanting a pleasant experience and businesses trying to achieve high-feature velocity and operational efficiency. This is the case with traditional technologies and the divide on which RIAs capitalize.

1.2.1   They all want it all

Users want to be able to access their data from whatever computer they're on. They also want to be able to do such trivial things as dragging and dropping. They want a rich, fluid graphical experience that incorporates sound and video. But they *don't* want to be constantly nagged to download the latest version.

Developers and software teams want it all too. Time-to-market is of high strategic value, whereas software development and maintenance are enormously expensive. Developers want to create software quickly and not worry about how to make it work on various platforms. They want the process of pushing out updates to be easy and fast.

Figure 1.3 summarizes who wins—and who loses—in each scenario.

But with problems or challenges comes opportunity, and RIAs seize this opportunity.

1.2.2   RIAs to the rescue

RIAs solve this problem by incorporating the best of both worlds. RIAs are a technology that gives businesses feature velocity and rapid deployment through the centralized internet deployment model while providing users a desktop-like experience (figure 1.4).

RIAs bring back usability by enabling developers to give their users a compelling and fluid experience with that feeling of a live application (versus completely reloading a page every time they click something). That's the core ingredient to providing users a sense of engagement.

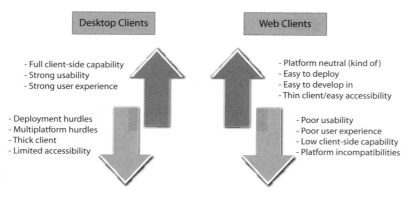

Figure 1.3   Pros and cons of desktop and web clients—choose the lesser of the evils. Desktop clients provide a high degree of experience, but it's difficult to keep all users synchronized to the same software version. Web applications are the opposite; you can push updates out all day long with ease, but this comes at a cost of usability.

At the same time, the deployment and accessibility model remains the same—users can load these applications from any machine and all be running the same version. The best part is true platform neutrality; the same application yields the same look and feel regardless of environment.

1.2.3   *How RIAs do it*

RIAs are able to accomplish this by not being an interactive document and thus having none of the restrictions of one. They do this via the use of a browser plug-in that acts as a local runtime engine. With a runtime engine available for various browsers and operating systems, you're able to achieve platform neutrality.

Because the RIA is a plug-in, it can piggyback onto the browser. Using the browser as a delivery mechanism gives the plug-in the high degree of deployability that web applications enjoy.

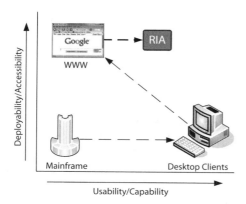

Figure 1.4   RIAs add the best of both worlds by combining the ease of deployment of web applications with the power of client-side usability. Who says you can't have your cake and eat it too?

1.3 The RIA contenders

The RIA space is hot right now, and contenders are standing in their respective corners. In one corner is the front-runner, Flex by Adobe, which faces Microsoft's Silverlight and Sun's JavaFX. From a technical perspective you could argue that AJAX is more of a rich web application (RWA) technology than a rich internet application technology, but because of the big advancements in the AJAX toolkit arena, it's worth adding to the list.

> **NOTE** RWA isn't a commonly used term but rather food for thought as to whether HTML and JavaScript natively support enough rich media to be considered a true RIA. And if not, shouldn't there be a term to make such a distinction?

Here's a brief summary of the major RIA contenders.

1.3.1 Flex by Adobe

First out of the gate, Adobe has maintained a fierce pace in expanding this platform. With Flex 4, Adobe made the framework open source; the software development kit (SDK) has been free since Flex 2, and the price point for the optional IDE is attractive.

Flex applications truly are rich *internet* applications; they're platform-agnostic, internet-deployed thin clients. Flex supports multiple transfer protocols such as text/XML, web services, RTMP/messaging, and the binary format known as Action Message Format (AMF). It also has a robust charting engine, can stream video natively, and do much more.

Flex has the following things going for it:

- It leverages the nearly ubiquitous Flash Player, which has a 98% penetration level.
- It uses the huge Flash ecosystem (existing forums, community, and knowledge).
- It's tightly integrated with other Adobe products from designer (Photoshop, Fireworks, Catalyst, and so on), to developer, to server (ColdFusion, Blaze DS, media streaming, and so forth).
- It has a four-year head start.
- It uses an open source framework and SDK.

On the downside:

- Although Flex's printing abilities are satisfactory, there's a lot of room for improvement (particularly with respect to report-style printing).
- Because the technology is still relatively new, the size of the community is relatively small compared to that of .NET and Java.

Although heated arguments in discussion forums erupt whenever technologies are compared, we'll next venture to Flex's main threat, Silverlight by Microsoft.

1.3.2   *Silverlight by Microsoft*

Microsoft isn't well known for being an early innovator, seemingly preferring to invest enormous amounts of capital to dominate only after others have invented market spaces. But once they set their minds on something, they're willing to do what it takes to win.

Microsoft released Silverlight 1.0 in September 2007, Silverlight 2.0 in October 2008, and Silverlight 4 in April 2010. They're moving at a blistering pace to capture as much market share as possible.

Comparing features of the Silverlight 4 technology with those of Flex 4 would be of little value because they're roughly on par with each other. The key differentiators are their respective ecosystems with their own distinct advantages.

Adobe dominates the design industry with their Creative Suite tools (Photoshop, Illustrator, Fireworks, and so on), and they have a new tool called Catalyst that can convert a Creative Suite image into a fully functioning Flex application.

Microsoft does have relatively lesser-known creative tools known as Expression and Blend, but on the server side they have a formidable arsenal. The .NET universe is a large one, and developing on the Silverlight platform allows you to tap into all things .NET (IIS.NET, SharePoint, and the like).

Adobe does have a server aspect to their business with ColdFusion, BlazeDS, Live-Cycle Data Services (LCDS), and their cloud computing initiatives. But compared to .NET, Microsoft has the edge. Granted, a Flex frontend could tap into a .NET backend. But the Silverlight environment makes it easy for developers familiar with .NET to be productive with a well-integrated development environment.

From a platform perspective, Silverlight is available on Windows and Mac OS X, along with browser plug-ins for Internet Explorer, Firefox, and Safari. Opera is unofficially available, and the Chrome plug-in is available only on the Windows version.

Flex, on the other hand, runs wherever Flash Player can be found, and that's all combinations of major OSes and browsers.

The bottom line is if you're already a .NET developer, you'll be able to leverage your existing code base and skill sets by going the Silverlight route.

1.3.3   *JavaFX by Sun Microsystems*

Sun had the opportunity to be the RIA leader with Java but failed to capitalize on it, rendering JavaFX pretty much a second attempt. JavaFX is also a latecomer to the game, with the first release having come out in March 2009, and as a result it has a lot of catching up to do.

JavaFX is in the fortunate position of being able to leverage the commanding ecosystem of the enormous Java community, but it's still too early to tell if the technology will be able to capitalize on it.

The big question going forward is, now that Oracle (which is a big adopter of Flex for the UI of various tools) owns Sun, what will they do with JavaFX? Time will tell!

1.3.4 AJAX—the last stand

Impressive results have been achieved using extremely advanced JavaScript and Dynamic HTML (DHTML) techniques in combination with the browser's XMLHTTP-Request function. But in the end, it's a last great effort to squeeze every possible ounce of application usability from a document platform.

Some amazing things have been done despite this limitation with AJAX toolkits such as Adobe's own Spry, EXT, YUI (by Yahoo), GWT (by Google), and the formidable jQuery. These JavaScript toolkits go to great efforts to enable you to develop highly interactive applications and are a good option for making web applications more usable.

NATIVE ABILITIES VERSUS HACKS

But consider this: What if you want a three-state check box? Figure 1.5 shows how Microsoft Excel uses this form element to present three possible states, whereas HTML's check box supports only two states (selected and unselected).

If you wanted to do this in HTML, you could fake it using a graphic, JavaScript, and some CSS. In contrast, an RIA engine such as Flex or Silverlight affords you the ability to extend the native check box to have three states.

Figure 1.5 In Flex, you can make a three-state check box like that of Microsoft Excel. In HTML, the option to extend components isn't available.

Take that even further and ask yourself if JavaScript can do the following:

- Play sound files natively?
- Decode a compressed video stream?
- Interact with devices such as a webcam?
- Create new user input controls?
- Transfer data natively in binary?
- Open, and maintain, a persistent network connection?

As we mentioned earlier, impressive innovations have resulted from this last-hurrah squeeze, but they've come at a price that's incurred by platform inconsistencies.

CROSS-PLATFORM ISSUES

If you've worked with JavaScript, you know it's a massive headache to support multiple browsers. Every browser has variations, such that if you utilize advanced AJAX/JavaScript techniques, the result would require a significantly increased quality-assurance cycle (figure 1.6).

This deficiency alone severely impairs the ability of a business or customer to achieve the

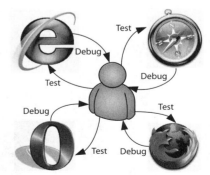

Figure 1.6 Don't forget to factor in the development costs of supporting multiple browsers when using AJAX.

desired return on investment (ROI); the biggest single cost of systems development is developer time.

AJAX COMMUNICATION LIMITS

AJAX supports just one thing: text over HTTP. Traditionally, that text has been in the form of XML, and the more recent trend is to use JSON to reduce client-side processing. In either case both are inefficient for transferring large amounts of information because of the verbose amount of text.

Try transferring 5,000 records using `XMLHTTPRequest` and then parsing them in JavaScript. That's exactly what Adobe's technical evangelist James Ward did, and you can see the results posted on his blog (http://www.jamesward.org/wordpress/2007/04/30/ajax-and-flex-data-loading-benchmarks/).

In figure 1.7, you can see how Flex—using its binary format, AMF3, versus XML or SOAP in AJAX—is up to 10 times faster. There are two reasons for this. First, as just mentioned, XML is verbose, which results in quite a bit of overhead in the message payload. Second, JavaScript is an interpreted language, whereas Flex is compiled to platform-neutral byte code.

Beyond speed, Flex's compact binary format offers other advantages. Less overhead means less demand on resources such as memory and network utilization.

NOTE Keep in mind that Flex and Flash do support simple transfer of textual data over HTTP and SOAP web services.

AMF3 provides a clear advantage, particularly for large-scale applications or applications that need to exchange large volumes of data.

The fact that JavaScript and HTML haven't had to evolve for many years is a true testament to their longevity. They've stood the test of time and will continue to thrive in some form or another for decades to come. This is because the web is great at what is does—distributing platform-neutral documents.

Web applications will have their place too, but the trend is clear that users are demanding more. True RIA technologies will take over where web applications leave off.

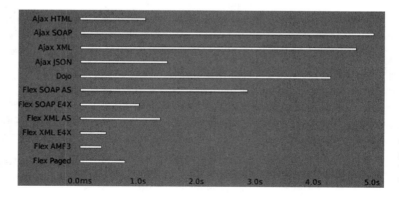

Figure 1.7 The speed of Flex's binary protocols versus the verbose approaches of AJAX

1.4 Becoming acquainted with Flex

Flex is a programmatic way (you use code) to make RIAs leverage the Flash platform. Flash is famous for interactive banner ads, cool animated portions of web pages, and interactive marketing experiences, which are often used for promotional sites.

Flex has a head start with its ability to leverage the widely recognized and mature technology of Flash Player, in addition to taking advantage of its widespread deployment. But it doesn't lock you out of the HTML world; you can have Flex interacting with web applications using JavaScript, while at the same time being a part of the large Adobe technology ecosystem.

1.4.1 Taking advantage of Adobe Flash

At the heart of Flex execution is Adobe Flash Player. This incredibly powerful, fast, lightweight, and platform-agnostic runtime engine is based on an object-oriented (OO) language called ActionScript. The experience is the same for Mac users as it is for Windows users—or users of any platform, for that matter (smart phones, PDAs, and so on).

The Flash Player on which Flex applications execute is capable of processing large amounts of data and has robust 2D graphical-rendering abilities and support for various communication protocols. Flash puts the *rich* in RIA by supporting multimedia formats such as streaming video, images, and audio.

The result is the ability to provide a rich desktop-like experience that allows developers to be innovative and creative. It also lets you present unique approaches to optimize the workflow for the end user.

WHY NOT DO IT IN FLASH?

Savvy Flash developers were making RIAs before Flex existed. But those coming from the development world and trying to get into Flash found it difficult to adopt the Flash mindset. Because Flash's roots are in animation (figure 1.8), its environment is based on timelines, layers, frames, frames per second, and so on. It's somewhat strange for someone with a development background based on lines of code to think of an application being a movie.

Even for seasoned Flash veterans, the cost of developing applications purely in Flash is significantly more than in other development environments (mostly due to the intensive work required to deal with change).

Although Flash and Flex can function as standalone applications, they can also interact with web applications by using JavaScript as a bridge between them.

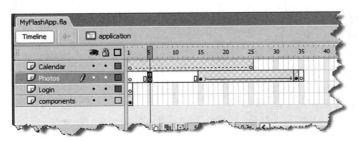

Figure 1.8 Flash has always been capable of making RIAs, but can you imagine coding based on time?

1.4.2   *Flex and JavaScript can play together*

If you've been developing HTML-based web applications and using JavaScript, as you get into Flex you'll notice that its ActionScript language looks incredibly similar.

That's because JavaScript and ActionScript are based on the ECMAScript standard. If you've used JavaScript extensively, you'll find comfort in familiarity. One interesting tidbit is that Flex's ActionScript was the first production language to adopt the current ECMAScript 4 standard.

In working with Flex you aren't locked into technology silos. It doesn't have to be all Flex or bust. Although RIAs and RWAs are different, Flex allows you to operate between technologies. To do this, Flex employs a feature called the External API, which enables JavaScript applications to communicate with Flex applications.

In the context of AJAX, Flex has an additional feature called the Flex-AJAX Bridge (a.k.a. FABridge) that makes it easy to integrate AJAX and Flex applications. If you have a significant investment in an existing AJAX application but would like to leverage Flex's capabilities, you can use Flex to generate interactive charts from your AJAX application.

> **NOTE** To learn more about harnessing the power of JavaScript, you might want to check out *Secrets of the JavaScript Ninja* by John Resig. See http://www.manning.com/resig/ for more information.

The harmony doesn't stop there; because Flex is made by Adobe, it also fits into a larger encompassing suite of technologies.

1.4.3   *The Flex ecosystem*

The amazing technology built into Flex isn't its only major advantage. Because it's part of a set of technologies from Adobe, your organization can achieve a smooth workflow from designer to developer to deployment. Figure 1.9 shows where Flex sits in relation to all of Adobe's other technologies.

In the land of regular web development, a lot of time is wasted bouncing between designers and developers. As you may know, designers use tools such as Photoshop to design the application, and developers laboriously slice up the images and generate CSS.

But in the Flex ecosystem, designers can export themes (skins), and developers can import them without tightly coupling the application to the design. And it keeps getting better. Catalyst, the most recent addition to the Adobe Creative Suite family, allows you to convert an image of an application (for example, from Photoshop) into a Flex application.

Another client technology that has garnered a lot of press and is directly related to Flex is AIR, which allows your Flex applications to run as native desktop applications.

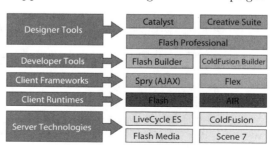

Figure 1.9   **Flex is part of a big technology stack.**

A BLURB ON AIR

AIR stands for Adobe Integrated Runtime. AIR allows you to go one step further by transforming your Flex RIAs into what we call rich desktop applications (RDAs). Although there's no official term for it, this type of technology is also known as a *hybrid desktop internet application.*

Because Flex is launched via the browser, for security reasons it's limited in its ability to do certain things, such as access data on hard drives or interact with peripherals like scanners. AIR liberates Flex applications from the browser and lets them execute directly on the desktop (figure 1.10), giving you the full desktop experience.

With AIR, you can perform functions such as these:

- Access cut-and-paste information from the operating system's clipboard
- Drag and drop from the desktop into the application
- Create borderless applications that don't require the square frame of a browser around them

AIR provides additional capabilities:

- Built-in database server
- Transparent and automatic software updates to ensure everyone is using the same version
- Built-in HTML rendering engine

It's a revolutionary platform. If you decide you want to take your Flex applications beyond the browser, check out Manning Publications' *Adobe AIR in Action* (Joey Lott, Kathryn Rotondo, Sam Ahn, and Ashley Atkins, 2007; ISBN: 978-1-933988-48-1).

A BLURB ON BLAZEDS

Mentioned in the Flex ecosystem is something called Adobe LiveCycle ES (Enterprise Suite). It's an engine similar to a workflow and business rules engine that allows companies to automate processes. The most publicly demonstrated use of this technology is automating the claims process for an insurance company.

Another popular use of LiveCycle is automating various government functions, because you can create triggers that execute subprocesses, ensure rules validation, and perform other such functions without having to write the code to do it.

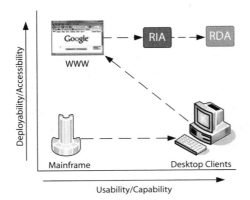

Figure 1.10   RDAs go that extra mile by achieving the desktop experience that RIAs aren't able to reach. RDAs exist outside the browser, and like a desktop application they have access to the operating system's clipboard and local filesystem.

Because LiveCycle ES is aimed at big enterprises, it comes with a hefty price tag. Fortunately there's its little brother BlazeDS, which is a trimmed-down version of Live-Cycle. It's a middle-tier server component that acts as a middleman between backend components and services (other server technologies like Java and .NET), as well as connectors to database servers and messaging technologies such as Java Message Service (JMS).

Its capabilities include the following:

- Transferring backend data to the Flex client using the binary AMF3 protocol.
- High-performance data transfer.
- Real-time data push using HTTP and AMF3. (It can notify your Flex application about new data, instead of your Flex application polling for new information.)
- Publish/subscribe messaging. This is achieved through a technique known as long polling, unlike its LiveCycle big brother, which supports the more advanced Real Time Messaging Protocol (RTMP).

TIP   Messaging-based applications are more network efficient when frequent updates are needed on many different items. For example, when making a chat application, an AJAX-based approach would periodically query for new information every few seconds. Using messaging, the chat client gets information pushed to it as it becomes available and not making unnecessary hits to the backend.

- Record set paging with a database. (It can stream 50 database records at a time or do the last/next 10 records from a query.)
- The best part is that it's free! As another piece of Adobe's open source software, this technology is available and can be distributed under the LGPL v3 license.

BlazeDS has been a major factor in the adoption of Flex in the Java community, because it allows Java developers to leverage their existing backend Java efforts by using BlazeDS as the bridge between Flex and the Java object.

1.5 *How Flex works*

At the heart of Flex is a free SDK that provides the framework for making Flex applications. In a nutshell, it's all the out-of-the-box libraries and the compiler.

1.5.1 *The Flex languages*

On top of that is the Eclipse-based IDE named Flash Builder. Instead of using the Flash editor to make Flash applications, you use Flash Builder.

Flex comprises two programming languages:

- The XML-based MXML tag language (No one knows what MXML stands for, but two popular assumptions are Macromedia XML and Magic XML.)
- The ActionScript scripting language

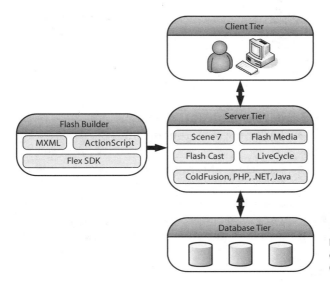

Figure 1.11   Use Flash Builder to compile your application, and then deploy it to a server.

When developing in Flex, you use both: MXML for primary layout of the application core (the visual components) and ActionScript to script out all the logic needed to drive your application.

Although it isn't particularly pertinent to our discussion at the moment, MXML is compiled behind the scenes into ActionScript. This means you can make a full-fledged Flex application using only ActionScript. (That's what it ends up being anyway.)

> **TIP**   New users struggle to determine when to use ActionScript and when to use MXML. A simple rule of thumb is to pretend HTML is like MXML, which allows you to visually lay out how you want your application to initially appear. Then, think of ActionScript as JavaScript—it adds the brains to your application. As you become comfortable with it, you'll find you can make entire applications using nothing but ActionScript.

Using the two languages, you create your application by compiling it into a single executable file that's then deployed onto a web server (figure 1.11).

Okay, I can tell you're itching to see some code, so check out the following listing, which has a simple example of how these two languages are related.

Listing 1.1   Example of a simple application

```
<?xml version="1.0" encoding="utf-8"?>
<s:Application xmlns:fx="http://ns.adobe.com/mxml/2009"
               xmlns:s="library://ns.adobe.com/flex/spark"
               xmlns:mx="library://ns.adobe.com/flex/mx">
  <fx:Script>
  <![CDATA[
   import mx.controls.Alert;
   public function handleEvent():void
```

```
    {
      mx.controls.Alert.show("Event handled");
    }
  ]]>
  </fx:Script>
  <s:Button label="Click on me" click="handleEvent()"/>
</s:Application>
```

❶ ActionScript for scripted logic

❷ MXML for layout

In figure 1.12 you can see what the code in listing 1.1 looks like: a pop-up alert window in the foreground with the background blurred out.

Even if you've never seen Flex code, this sample may feel somewhat familiar. One reason is that the tag-based MXML language ❷ is a derivative of XML. Another reason is that the script logic ❶ is similar to JavaScript.

Let's look at the typical lifecycle of the development process.

Figure 1.12 Using an event handler, the clicking of a button is intercepted.

THE DEVELOPMENT LIFECYCLE

This is what the Systems Development Life Cycle (SDLC) of a typical Flex application looks like:

1 Using Flash Builder or the SDK, build in your local development environment by writing MXML and ActionScript code.
2 When testing, use Flash Builder or the SDK to compile your code. Doing so generates the main output .swf file (often pronounced *swiff* file).
3 Use the browser to launch this file, invoking the Flash Player plug-in. Your application begins to execute.
4 A Flex application typically interacts with a server tier to exchange data.
5 When the application is ready to be released, the .swf file (and any accompanying files, such as images) is published to your production web server, where it's available to be invoked by your users via a URL.

For those who work with application servers like ColdFusion and PHP, note that you're not pushing the source files to production but rather a compiled application (similar to Java's .class files, but a Flex application also contains all the libraries needed for the application to work).

1.5.2 *Events, events, events*

It's all about events. Flex is an event-driven environment, which may be a big departure from what you're used to.

In traditional web development technologies, an event represents an action such as a user clicking a link or a submit button. The server responds, executing whatever function is required—in this case, displaying a web page or sending field data.

If you've been developing web applications, you've undoubtedly created JavaScript that responds to certain user gestures such as highlighting an item on a page by

Figure 1.13 Flex, like JavaScript, uses events that consist of triggers and handlers.

changing the background color of the item as the user moves the mouse over it (figure 1.13).

That's an event! But that term isn't used as much in traditional web applications because the majority of the application resides on the backend. As in the JavaScript example we just described, Flex is a client-side technology, meaning all the action occurs on the user's side.

A Flex application is driven entirely through events; something causes something to occur, and something else handles it when it occurs. The two main pieces of an event-driven application are these:

- *Event triggers*—Triggers cause events: the user moving the mouse over a button, the application loading, data coming back from a web service, and so on.
- *Event handlers*—Handlers respond to events: invoking a function that changes display characteristics, committing an input form, and so on; handlers are where the logic is.

Coming from a traditional web technology, you won't be used to thinking like this. We'll gradually introduce how events are used, but you'll need to let go of the web application notion of generating pages. With Flex, the application is already loaded; all you're doing is capturing events and responding accordingly.

1.5.3 *Limitations*

Flex isn't perfect and has limitations that are true for any browser plug-in based engine (such as Silverlight). But to be objective, it's worth being aware of these:

- Pop-up windows can exist only within the dimension of the player instance. This means that a pop-up can move around only within the area of the main application versus being a true pop-up that can move anywhere on the desktop. To break free of this limitation you'd have to convert your application to an AIR application (Silverlight refers to this as an out-of-browser application that's achieved via deployment configuration).
- Because Flash Player is a software install, many companies for support purposes standardize what's on the desktop. If your application relies on a minimum version of Flash Player (for example, a Flex 4 application won't run on the antiquated Flash Player 8), and the user is a corporate user who doesn't have permission to upgrade software on their desktop, there's a dependency on that organization's IT department to push a sitewide update to all users.
- Because you're loading an entire application, memory usage is something to watch for. In the book you'll learn about things like Runtime Shared Libraries that can help you manage that better, but this is an area that typically a web

developer rarely cares about because the user is usually working with only a page at a time.

- There's no access to local drives or the clipboard unless you go to AIR. This would be true for web applications as well, but this is a distinct advantage of desktop applications.

With that said, the rich, fluid, interactive and fast experience tends to enable users with higher productivity, and the pros outweigh the cons by a wide margin. Plus, with each version of Flex comes new capabilities; let's see what's new in Flex 4.

1.6   *What's new in Flex 4*

Since its inception, Flex technology has been evolving at an incredibly rapid pace. The product started as a pure server-side technology, modeling the conventions of most server-based web application technologies.

Flex 2 was a major overhaul of the language. Adobe split it into two portions: The client portion consists of the application framework and tools to compile a Flex application; the server portion is the data bridge. This has evolved into LCDS/BlazeDS. The Flex 2 overhaul also involved a technology rewrite—a one-time hit to provide an industrial-strength platform that could grow well into the future.

Flex 3 focused on developer tooling and maturing the framework to support larger-scale applications. On the IDE side they added a profiler for measuring memory and CPU usage within an application, refactoring abilities, and an initial attempt at design to developer workflow. On the framework side they added charting enhancements, persistent framework caching, and a power grid component called the Advanced DataGrid. There was also the introduction of Adobe AIR for allowing your Flex applications to run as desktop applications.

Now in its fourth version, Flex 4 focuses on three key areas. One area is developer productivity, which Flex 4 addresses by speeding up how fast you can create a typical CRUD (create, read, update, delete) application. A second area is the design-to-developer workflow by allowing designers and developers to work in tandem during the development process. And finally, data-centric development, where the process of hooking into backend systems now becomes much easier.

The designer-to-developer workflow, on any technology platform, has always been a challenging one because at the point where a designer hands over the graphics, the developer then starts chopping it up into pieces to make it functional. The problem is that if the design changes, the developer has to redo a lot of work as well as interpret the interaction because all the developer has is static images.

Adobe took a step back and redefined how the tools relate to each other. Instead of having an integration perspective where it's about getting one tool to integrate, the vision was updated to view it as a platform with Flash at the core. So it's not about just Flex; the whole platform (see figure 1.9) has evolved in unison.

With that said, here are some of the new goodies in Flex 4:

- A new class of visual components known as Spark components that replace the previous component set known as Halo components (also referred to as MX components). Spark components support Flex 4's new skinning abilities.

- Skinning is completely redone, allowing designers to have fine-grained control over the look and feel of all visual aspects. In Flex 3 you had to create programmatic skins if you really wanted to get serious, which no one did because it's too time consuming.

- A new graphics format called FXG that Flex, Flash, and Creative Suite will support. It's based on XML so you can easily define/create graphics in code.

- Data-centric development wizards and capabilities that let you quickly point at any backend service (ColdFusion, PHP, Web Service, and so on), and it'll figure out what all of the available functions are, what the parameters are, and what kind of information comes back. And then you can link it to data-centric components that can display and interact with the data.

- Along with data-centric development are other productivity boosters such as a faster compiler, getter/setter function generators, event coder generators, integrated FlexUnit support, tooltip documentation (mouse over some code, and a hover window shows the documentation about that function/tag), and a network monitor for watching communications over the wire.

- Layout and visual states have been overhauled to be easier to work with. Along those lines, Flash Player 10 introduces a new text layout engine that you can leverage in Flex (making it easier to lay out text).

These are the big at-a-glance features that are new Flex 4, but we'll get into a number of additional enhancements as the chapters progress.

1.7 Summary

You've seen that historically, usability has been sacrificed for the sake of rapid deployment and a semi-neutral platform, but it came at the cost of the user experience. Amazingly, users (including ourselves) became accustomed to it. When it came to web applications, we assumed that being limited was normal.

It was just a matter of time in our information-crazed lives until the cost of this sacrifice began to outweigh the benefits. Users were suffering, and businesses were paying the price in productivity and efficiency.

RIAs demonstrate that we can achieve the best of both worlds. On the development side, a centralized deployment model on a platform-neutral environment means enhancements can be made quickly. On the user side, we can provide a desktop-like experience, allowing for fluid and engaging experiences from any device that can access the application.

Flex entered this RIA scene, leveraging its ubiquitous cross-platform Flash Player by creating a programmatic way to make a Flash application. This programmatic approach uses Flex's core languages: the XML templating language (MXML) and its scripting language (ActionScript).

Now in its fourth major version, Flex maintains a lead in the RIA space, although Microsoft is working hard to catch up. But what Microsoft doesn't have is Flex's ecosystem—a large technology environment that encompasses the end-to-end workflow of software development. From designer to developer to deployment, Adobe offers the environments and tools for each phase of the game.

In the next chapter, we'll explain how to set up your development environment, become familiar with the language reference, and begin to learn how to make Flex applications.

Getting started 2

This chapter covers

- Touring the Flex tools
- Creating your first Flex application
- Understanding how MXML works
- Fitting ActionScript into the picture

To begin coding in Flex, you first need to set up a working environment. Flex comes with a free open source SDK that allows you to get started and create Flex applications, but serious developers prefer to use the Eclipse-based Flash Builder IDE.

We'll show you how to make the most of a limited budget by taking advantage of open source tools, and we'll spend a good part of this chapter going over the features of Flash Builder. Later, we'll present how to begin producing Flex applications.

As a Flex developer you're likely to spend most of your time in the Flash Builder tool. Before we jump in, you may want to ask yourself, "Can I get away with developing in Flex for free?"

2.1 Flex on the cheap

With Flex's free and open source SDK, there's nothing to stand in your way of making Flex RIAs. The SDK includes the compiler to convert source code into Flash .swf files, as well as the Flex framework to handle the guts of an application, and the core components, including visual components such as buttons.

Our goal is to make Flex simple and easy to get into, and we do that by filtering out the facets that are seldom used, keeping you focused on the areas that will make a difference in your ability to be a successful Flex developer.

When taking the SDK route, keeping things simple may be easier said than done because using the SDK is more complicated and involves more work than using Flash Builder. At the same time, if you're learning Flex on your own dime, perhaps to expand your skill set or to sell Flex to your organization (which hasn't yet bestowed its financial support), it's worth gaining insight into this free option.

NOTE Flash Builder is available as a 60-day free trial, which would allow you to conduct an evaluation to determine if it provides enough value to justify the price.

The purpose of this section is to give you a sense of what's involved in working with the SDK, from which point you can determine whether it's an approach you want to pursue. If you decide to go the SDK route, here's what your game plan is going to look like:

- *Set up a compile environment.* You can build applications via a command-line interface (an MS-DOS window, for example) by downloading the free SDK.
- *Set up an editing environment.* You can use a simple text editor, but you'll want an environment that maximizes productivity.

The first order of business is to prepare an environment that will allow you to convert your source code into a compiled application.

2.1.1 *Setting up the compile environment*

The Flex SDK comes in the form of a zip file that you download from an Adobe website. Download and deploy the files, and then configure your command-line environment.

1 The compiler needs the Java Runtime Environment (JRE version 1.4.2_06 or later). If you don't have this, you can obtain it at http://www.java.com/en/download/manual.jsp.

2 Navigate to the Flex SDK page on the Adobe website at http://opensource.adobe.com/wiki/display/flexsdk/. You'll find a download link that displays a page of various versions. Download the latest stable zip file under the Adobe Flex SDK column (approximately 103 MB).

3 Next, unzip the SDK zip file to a location of your choice. You may want to keep things simple and keep it near the root level (for example, c:\flex in Windows).

4 Check to see if you have Flash Player installed. If you do, congratulations—now throw it away! You'll want to replace what's likely the production Flash Player with the debug version of Flash Player.

5 Install the debug version of Flash Player. You'll find it in the runtimes/player folder (from the Flex SDK zip archive), and the install should replace the production Flash Player if it's installed. For you Windows folks, there are two main files:

– Install Flash Player 10 ActiveX.exe is the debug player for Internet Explorer.

– Install Flash Player 10 Plugin.exe is the debug player for other browsers such as Firefox.

– Run the one for the browser on which you plan to test and develop your Flex applications, though if you use both browsers there's no harm in installing the debug player for all browsers.

6 Add the bin folder to your system's path variable so that when entering command-line statements you don't need to provide the full path (see figure 2.1).

Figure 2.1 Add the Flex bin folder to your path to make life easier.

a In Windows, go to Control Panel > System > Advanced.

b Click Environment Variables.

c Edit the Path System variable.

d Append <installfolder>\bin to the end of the path (which is the folder you unzipped to, c:\flex in our example).

7 Verify that it works.

a Create a directory where you want to store your Flex projects, for example, c:\apps

b Create a directory called HelloWorld within c:\apps

c Create a text file inside c:\apps\HelloWorld\ called HelloWorld.mxml. (You can use Notepad to do this.)

d Type the following code in the HelloWorld.mxml file:

```
<?xml version="1.0" encoding="utf-8"?>
<s:Application xmlns:fx="http://ns.adobe.com/mxml/2009"
               xmlns:s="library://ns.adobe.com/flex/spark"
               xmlns:mx="library://ns.adobe.com/flex/mx"/>
```

e Open a command-line interface. In Windows, select Start > Run > cmd. Macintosh and Linux users will need to open a shell.

f Enter the following command:

```
mxmlc.exe HelloWorld.mxml
```

g If all goes well, you should see something similar to figure 2.2.

You should now have a new file called HelloWorld.swf in the same folder where HelloWorld.mxml is located. Double-click the new file, but don't be alarmed if it doesn't look like much. All it should do is display a bluish-gray background. The goal at this point is to verify that the compiler executes properly.

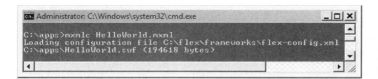

Figure 2.2   Testing to ensure you can compile a Flex application

Now that you know you're able to compile Flex applications, you can assume the SDK is properly installed. The next order of business is to set up an efficient way to work on the code.

2.0.1   Setting up the editing environment

Unless you're a huge fan of VI in Linux or Notepad in Windows, you'll want the best code editor that absolutely *no* money can buy. For Flex we recommend going with the popular Eclipse editor. You can find it at http://www.eclipse.org/.

Eclipse is an open source plug-in–based editor and IDE framework, meaning it does a good job of code editing but allows third parties to extend its capabilities through modules. The commercial Flex IDE (Flash Builder) is based on Eclipse; if you decide to purchase Flash Builder, you can download the Eclipse plug-in, adding its features to what you've already built.

Next, you'll want to get Aptana Studio, which comes in both commercial and freeware varieties. The problem with Eclipse by itself is that it doesn't know what Flex is, so by adding Aptana Studio you get the conveniences of code coloring/formatting, code completion, outlining, and error notifications. The free version is known as the Community Edition and can be downloaded at http://www.aptana.com/studio/.

With the SDK and the ability to compile a Flex application squared away, you can now edit code in a more fluid manner. The final task is to automate the process of building the applications so they aren't as command-line intensive.

2.0.2   Next steps (if you're still interested)

You're now at a point at which you have a bit of a vibe as to whether you feel comfortable with this command-line approach or you find it too much of a hassle. If you're comfortable with it, you'll want to look at the following techniques:

- Learning all the parameters that can be sent to the compiler. Refer to the MXMLC documentation online at http://cflex.net/go/flex4/mxmlc.
- Creating wrapper files (HTML files that launch your Flex application). See chapter 25 for more information on wrapper files.
- Using build scripts such as .bat files in Windows, or shell scripts in Linux and Mac OS X, to make it easier for you to perform compiling. For an example of shell scripts, look in the <installfolder>\samples folder for some Flex applications and their build scripts.

You have to hand it to the open source community; if you've encountered a common challenge, the odds are someone has created a tool to deal with it.

One particular challenge is automating repetitive tasks, and there's a neat tool that can help—appropriately named *Another Neat Tool* (Ant).

ANT + FLEX ANT TASKS

Born out of the Apache software project, Ant is a free and open source tool that makes scripting builds much easier. As a Java-based application that uses XML configuration files, it's platform neutral while at the same time fairly easy to learn and use.

Adobe has contributed a free-to-use Ant-based build mechanism called Flex Ant Tasks, and it comes standard with the SDK. You'll find it under the <installfolder>\ant folder of the SDK.

You won't need either Ant or Flex Ant Tasks to get started making Flex applications, but it's something to be aware of down the line. For more information on Ant, visit http://ant.apache.org.

If you want to look at Ant in more depth, there's a great book on this technology by Steve Loughran and Erik Hatcher (Manning Publications) titled *Ant in Action* (ISBN: 978-1-932394-80-1). This book can teach you how to get ramped up with Ant and maximize its strengths.

If you want to maximize your productivity in Flex, it would definitely be worth the investment to purchase Flash Builder. With features such as tag completion, code hinting, a built-in API reference manual, automatic importing of libraries, wizards, visual layout and styling, and automatic builds, Flash Builder is a lifesaver. In the game of software development, the number-one cost is resource time—or, more accurately, developers.

2.1 *Get serious with Flash Builder*

Flash Builder is a feature-rich Flex IDE for designing, developing, testing, and building Flex applications. If you skipped the previous section because you know you don't want to take that path, we briefly remind you that Flash Builder is based on the open source IDE framework and editor Eclipse (http://www.eclipse.org) and adds onto it as an Eclipse plug-in (so you can download Flash Builder as a plug-in to an existing Eclipse install or download Flash Builder and Eclipse as a single install).

> **NOTE** Flash Builder is currently available only for Windows and Mac. Adobe continually evaluates community interest in a Linux version but hasn't found sufficient interest to justify moving forward with such an initiative.

Why is it called Flash Builder and not Flex Builder? If you recall, in chapter 1 we mentioned that one of the shifts with Flex 4 was to recognize that Adobe views it all as the Flash platform (or ecosystem). In a move to minimize confusion over the difference between Flex and Flash, they renamed what used to be known as Flex Builder to Flash Builder. So Flex is an SDK and application framework for making Flash applications, and Flash Builder is the development environment.

But how much is this all going to cost? Let's find out!

2.1.1 *Product and pricing matrix*

Flash Builder is available in multiple versions at varying price points (see table 2.1). What you see online are the manufacturer's suggested retail prices. Purchasing from a value-added reseller may save you a couple of bucks, and if you work for an organization that has prenegotiated discounts with Adobe, you might be entitled to a better deal.

Table 2.1 Flash Builder and SDK pricing

Version	Price	Extras
SDK	$0	N/A
Standard	$249	Step-through debugger, code hinting/completion, code coloring, CSS editing, integrated API Reference, visual layout designer, data integration wizards, Creative Suite skin importing, automatic compiling, and much more
Premium	$699	Standard version features, plus memory and performance monitoring/profiling for identifying how your app uses memory and CPU, built-in unit-testing support, automated functional-testing support, and a network monitor to see how data moves to and from your app and the network
Education Standard	$0	Free for students and faculty
Education Premium	$349	

Note: For a detailed comparison see http://www.adobe.com/products/flex/upgrade/.

If you're learning Flex for personal interests and don't have any intention of applying it to a live project, there may not be an immediate value in purchasing the standard or professional version. You'll want to employ the Flex-on-the-cheap approach as described earlier.

Otherwise, there's no question that you or your organization will benefit from having the proper tool to do the job efficiently and productively.

> **TIP** If you find management is still hesitant because of the price, create a proof-of-concept interactive reporting dashboard that makes use of the chart component. One thing management finds irresistible is reporting and business intelligence.

If you want to explore Flash Builder 4 without risk, a 60-day trial version is available. That should be a sufficient amount of time to give it a good test run.

2.1.2 *Getting Flash Builder*

Flash Builder comes in two flavors: standalone and as a separate plug-in.

The standalone version comprises Eclipse and the plug-in, which are installed as a single product out of the box. The plug-in version is useful for those who already have Eclipse for other programming languages and want to add Flex development as part of their environment. In either case you can add more third-party plug-ins as you progress with your development experience.

If you don't have Flash Builder installed, download it by going to http:// www.adobe.com/products/flex/. If you install it without entering a serial number, you can use it for 60 days, after which time you'll need the serial number to continue.

With installation complete, you can launch the application and you're good to go! Next, we'll cover the features of Flash Builder.

2.2   *Exploring Flash Builder*

Flash Builder works on the basis of *projects*, which are collections of folders, files, and settings. Projects can be created, closed, imported, and exported (figure 2.3).

This is a different concept compared to other editors (for example, Dreamweaver) that use a full-file browser approach in which you navigate through file folders residing anywhere across your file system and network.

In Flash Builder, projects are made up of *assets*, which are the types of files nested within folders, usually located under the main project folder (though you can also link to folders in other locations) (see figure 2.3).

Using figure 2.3 as a reference, let's look at the basic Flash Builder layout.

THE WIZARDS (1)

This feature of Flex becomes incredibly useful when kick-starting projects from scratch. Not only does it help those who are new to Flex get set up quickly, but it also

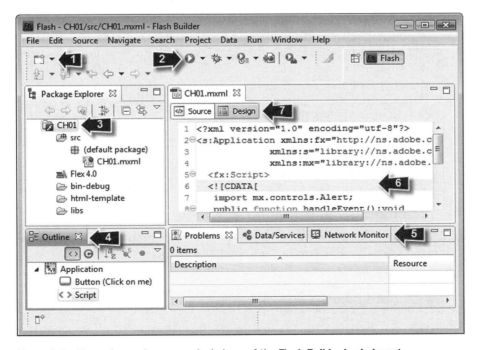

Figure 2.3   The major work areas and windows of the Flash Builder basic layout

comes in handy to the advanced Flex developer who wants to get going fast. Right out of the box, wizards, whose purposes range from creating an ActionScript class to generating a Flex CSS file, are available. But their most common use is to create Flex projects and custom Flex components.

APPLICATION LAUNCHER (2)

This button launches your application. Part of that process involves compiling any code you've written (if necessary), copying the latest compiled code to the output folder, and launching the application to the configured URL.

The two buttons to the right of it are similar but allow you to launch your application in Debug mode or in Profiling mode (allows you to monitor memory and CPU consumed by the application).

PACKAGE EXPLORER (3)

This lists all your projects, its assets, files, as well as linked resources such as additional libraries and directories.

An important feature to note here is you can configure the properties of your project by right-clicking the top-level project folder.

APPLICATION OUTLINE VIEW (4)

This is a different kind of navigator that dynamically builds a map of your application. It comes in handy when your application is large and you need to see how the pieces fit together. Selection of any of the items within the Outline view is mirrored in the source code editor, which will jump to the corresponding item.

BOTTOM PANE (5)

The bottom pane by default contains a number of views related to the status of your application; these include problems, data services, network monitor, and console.

The Problems view (the default) works hand-in-hand with the Editor view by pointing out any issues it encounters as you code. It displays any errors found in your application, along with the file and associated line number in which the error occurred.

The Data Services view allows you to configure integration with backend application services (for example, web services, PHP, ColdFusion), which allow you to quickly wire up components to pull data from them.

The network monitor is a handy tool for watching how raw traffic looks over the network connection so that if there are integration issues you can pinpoint what the issue is.

The Console view is used when testing your application. It displays warnings, alerts, and any other messages you specify and then saves them to a file called the *trace log*. Chapter 23 goes deeper into how to use the trace log.

SOURCE CODE EDITOR (6)

This is where all the action happens. The source code editor is where you write your code. It boasts nifty features such as color coding the text, real-time hover documentation regarding the components your cursor is currently on, and *code hinting*.

Code hinting is similar to an autocomplete feature because it attempts to anticipate what you want to type based on what you've already input. It then displays a list of possible match options from which you can select the remaining syntax. This helps speed up development, because you don't need to remember exact syntax.

SOURCE AND DESIGN VIEW TOGGLE (7)
These two tabs let you switch between the source code editor and the interactive design view. The Design view presents a WYSIWYG display of your application and certain visual elements while allowing you to control various properties of these visual elements such as color, transparency, size, and positioning.

2.3 Views and perspectives

We described a couple of views previously, and you'll notice Flash Builder is split into various sections, or panes. Each pane contains views; collections of views are called *perspectives.*

2.3.1 Out-of-the-box perspectives

During the course of developing a Flex application, there are three major perspectives in which you'll normally work: developing, debugging, and profiling (testing/ tuning). Perspectives are collections of views and panes that Flex supplies out of the box and are optimized for each of the major stages.

DEVELOPMENT PERSPECTIVE
The development perspective is a collection of views optimized for core development work: Outline, Problems, Console, and Navigator views.

DEBUGGING PERSPECTIVE
This perspective contains a collection of panes and views to help with debugging. Flash Builder will automatically switch to this perspective when you enter debugging mode (see chapter 23 for more information). The debugging perspective adds views that let you monitor the values of variables you're tracking, as well as the ability to control the execution of the application (pause, cancel, execute code line by line, and so on).

PROFILING PERSPECTIVE
The profiling perspective is similar to the debugging perspective in that it helps you isolate issues. This perspective leverages Flex's memory profiler capabilities by presenting information that allows you to track memory and performance usage. This information includes a memory usage chart, a list of functions that are being called, how often they're called, and how much time is spent inside each function.

2.3.2 Switching perspectives

You can change your perspective at any time by clicking Window > Perspective to see a list of the available perspectives, as shown in figure 2.4.

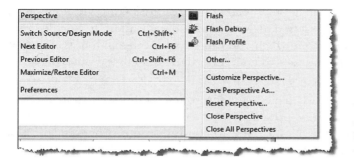

Figure 2.4 Flash Builder comes configured with three perspectives, but you can always add your own.

Figure 2.4 Over time you may find that you prefer a certain layout or require certain views, depending on the task at hand. The cool thing is Flex offers you a way to customize your own perspectives.

2.3.3 *Customizing perspectives*

You can add and move views around the various panes and then save the arrangement (along with any number of layouts) as a custom perspective.

MODIFY THE LAYOUT

Let's try modifying the layout. Follow these steps to get a feel for it:

1 Click and hold the mouse button on the Console tab, and drag the tab around the window.
2 You'll see a small black arrow in different locations as you move around (figure 2.5), indicating a potential place to drop the view.
3 Release the mouse button, and voila!

Rearranging the existing layout is a breeze, but you may want to display more information by adding views to the layout.

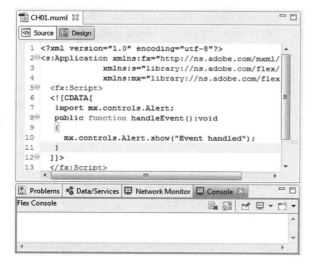

Figure 2.5 You can click and hold the mouse button to reposition a view.

ADD A VIEW TO THE LAYOUT

You can add new views to a perspective by following these steps:

1 Click Window at the top of Flash Builder. A number of views will appear such as the flex properties view; if you select other views you'll see the full list.

2 Select any one of these views, and it will appear inside the Flash Builder window.

3 Refer to the previous instructions to reposition the layout as needed.

Be sure to check out the other views option to display all the available choices. For example, if you're a ColdFusion developer, you might want to make use of the ColdFusion-specific views.

2.4 *Our first project—Hello World!*

As described earlier in the chapter, Flex applications are based on projects. When you're in Development mode, almost everything you do is contained within a project.

A project in Flash Builder is a collection of all the source code files, assets (images, MP3 files, and so on), and configuration settings. Let's get started creating our first project.

2.4.1 *Create the project*

Flash Builder comes with a collection of handy wizards that methodically step you through the processes. In particular, there's a new Flex Project Wizard that guides you through selecting the name of your project, where to store files, and even which back-end server technology is to be used by the application. We'll make use of this wizard right away by performing the following steps:

1 *Invoke the wizard selector.* In Flash Builder, click the top-left button to launch Flash Builder's wizard (figure 2.6).

2 *Select the Flex Project Wizard.* Select Flex > Flex Project Wizard and then click the Next button.

3 *Name the project.* You'll be prompted to provide a project name and application server type (figure 2.7). The project name can be anything you want, but let's call this one CH02, and select None for the application server type. Click Next to continue.

Figure 2.6   Click the wizard icon to launch the Flex Project Wizard.

NOTE In chapter 14, we'll talk about how to use the application server type feature. This Flash Builder option saves steps and makes it easier to connect to a backend system that supports Flash's binary communication protocol (AMF). Currently, the Flex Project Wizard supports ColdFusion, ASP.Net, Java 2 Platform, Enterprise Edition (J2EE), and PHP. We won't be using any of these protocols just yet, so select None for now.

4 *Configure the output directory.* This step allows you to select where you want the output directory to be created (figure 2.8).

Figure 2.7
The Flex Project Wizard

By default, it's located within your main project folder, but it can be located elsewhere if that's more convenient.

Flash Builder will publish the compiled debug version (necessary for testing) of your application to the specified folder. Chapter 24 covers the process of creating production builds in more detail.

TIP You're more than welcome to use a location of your choosing. This will likely be the norm as you become more comfortable with Flash Builder and standardize the location of projects within your organization. I prefer to have a root folder for all my software projects, and each of my Flex projects has a folder underneath that root.

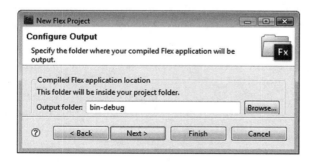

Figure 2.8 The specified output directory in which a debug version of your application is built and deployed

5 *Create the application.* Click the Next button to proceed to the last step. By default, the name you choose for your project is used as the name of your application's root folder and the name of the main Flex application file.

6 Click the Finish button at the bottom of the wizard window. Flash Builder will now initialize your project.

In this example, your project will reside in a folder called CH02, and the main file will be called CH02.mxml.

The project is now set up and ready for you to begin entering code.

2.4.2 Entering code

Once you click Finish, Flash Builder will automatically open the main project file, CH02.mxml, and it will look like that of listing here.

Listing 2.1 A rudimentary application

```
<?xml version="1.0" encoding="utf-8"?>
<s:Application xmlns:fx="http://ns.adobe.com/mxml/2009"
               xmlns:s="library://ns.adobe.com/flex/spark"
               xmlns:mx="library://ns.adobe.com/flex/mx"
               minWidth="1024" minHeight="768">
</s:Application>
```

Listing 2.1 shows the basic shell of an application that uses the MXML language to house the main elements of your application. This is good enough for now because all we want to do is verify that we can compile and execute the project.

2.4.3 Compile and run

Compiling and running a Flex project is as easy as clicking a mouse. On the Flash Builder toolbar, locate the green button with a right arrow (▶). Click the button; a new browser window should appear pointing to the file CH02.html. You'll be looking at a blank page, but you've officially made your first Flex application!

This HTML page is a wrapper to invoke your Flex application. It includes additional JavaScript to perform Flash Player version checking and set up the client-side environment in which your Flex application will run.

2.4.4 Making it real

In true Hello World! fashion, let's make one quick modification to the source code by going back to Flash Builder and adding in a <s:Button> tag, as shown here.

Listing 2.2 Hello World!

```
<?xml version="1.0" encoding="utf-8"?>
<s:Application xmlns:fx="http://ns.adobe.com/mxml/2009" xmlns:s="library://
    ns.adobe.com/flex/spark" xmlns:mx="library://ns.adobe.com/flex/mx"
    minWidth="1024" minHeight="768">
  <s:Button label="Hello World!" fontSize="40"/>
</s:Application>
```

Now, give it a run and see what happens. You should see
something similar to figure 2.9.

That wasn't too bad, was it? What you added was a button (no surprise there). Anything you can add via MXML is
categorized as a *component*. Visual components such as buttons are also known as *controls*. Flex comes with a lot of
components, but if you can't find what you want among
them, you can make your own as well (which is what chapter 17 is all about).

**Figure 2.9   Your first Flex
application! Congratulations,
you're now a Flex developer.**

In this example, we added our button programmatically, but Flash Builder has a
design side to it as well, which can help in prototyping and creating proof of concepts
quickly.

2.5   *Using design mode*

Flash Builder has an interesting feature called design mode that lets you visually create your application (see figure 2.3, item #7 to enable). Design mode allows you to
drag and drop visual components into the application, position them, and tweak their
properties (such as the background color).

Going back to the Hello World! example, click the Design button. This time you
should notice a couple more views on the right side of the window, titled States and
Flex Properties.

> **TIP**   A component is a reusable object you can invoke in your MXML. It's a
> way of making code reusable, similar to a Java class or a ColdFusion compo-
> nent (CFC). Components that are visual in nature are also known as controls.

Let's add to our application. Start by locating the Components view, which should be
displayed on the bottom left of Flash Builder (figure 2.10). If you expand the tree,
you'll see a catalog of all available components. Let's throw in a `Panel` component—you can keep doing this for as long as you want to continue laying out your
application.

You can then drag the Hello World! button into the panel. With your components
placed, we'll shift our focus to Flex properties. Selecting one component in the
Design mode displays all of that component's properties, which you can then edit in
the Flex Properties view.

You can use this to change visual characteristics of the component such as color,
transparency, and positioning. In its standard view, only a few characteristics are presented, but if you click the Category tab (figure 2.11), you'll gain access to every property available.

The biggest benefit of this graphical ability to design and build an application is
that of creating a proof of concept (POC). It's a great time saver when working with
customers and end users to interactively model how the application should appear
before you begin coding, because everyone is in sync with your ultimate goals.

Figure 2.10 Flash Builder's Design view allows you to visually lay out your application.

Although it's possible to build small applications entirely in design mode, its primary usefulness is in creating POCs, laying out your initial application, and adjusting visual properties to see how they will appear.

When you start working on real projects, the reality is you'll likely be doing straight-up coding as you would with any other language.

Flash Builder gives you powerful wizards to create projects. It has capabilities for mocking up layouts, and, as with any good integrated development environment, it has built-in help to make your coding experience all the more efficient.

2.6 Built-in reference and API documentation

Flex is an object-oriented language. In chapter 16 we delve into what object-oriented programming (OOP) is all about. But don't worry; leading up to that we'll progressively increase your understanding of its concepts as you work through the chapters.

An important factor in your ability to be productive as a Flex developer is how well you can leverage the Flex API Reference. We explore this in the following section.

2.6.1 Object-oriented languages and their APIs

One characteristic of object-oriented languages is that they tend to require the extensive use of an API Reference. This is because non-OO languages have variety of types and functions that are independent of one another. For example, with ColdFusion (a non-OO language) the `cfquery` tag returns a query structure that has some properties—end of story.

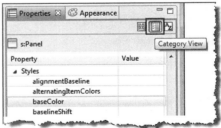

Figure 2.11 Use the Category view within the Flex Properties view to see all the component properties you can manipulate.

In object-oriented-languages land, we have objects, which contain functions (known as methods) and properties combined. We can keep extending one object from another, with each extension inheriting everything from the last (for example, animal > dog > pit bull).

What does all this have to do with help? Because you're dealing with so many objects, you'll find yourself needing to refer to the API Reference more frequently than in a non-OO language.

Throughout this book we periodically show you where in the API Reference you can go to find answers.

The more you become comfortable with the API Reference, the more efficient you'll become at coding in Flex.

2.6.2 *Accessing the API Reference*

Because you're just starting out, the API Reference isn't of much value yet. The only thing you need to do is make a mental note of how to access it as needed.

DYNAMIC HELP

The easiest way to use the API Reference is through Flash Builder's automatic Dynamic Help feature. To demonstrate how this works, try the following:

1 From the Flash Builder toolbar, select Help > Dynamic Help.
2 In the code editor, click anywhere within the `<s:Button>` line of code to position the cursor on that line.
3 A new pane appears (figure 2.12) on the right-hand side. In the first section are links to the API.
4 In this case a link to `spark.components.Button` is displayed, which is the formal location and definition of the button. Click it to see what the API Reference looks like for this component.

Having a live document search ready when you need it—and displaying relevant information—can help save time and isn't something too many IDEs can boast about. This isn't the only type of help available either. There's an awesome shortcut you'll want to memorize that brings up the API Reference immediately.

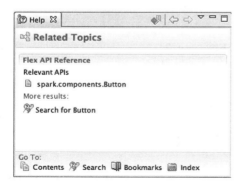

Figure 2.12 Dynamic Help automatically presents a link to the API Reference depending on where in your application the cursor is located.

HOVER HELP (ASDOC TOOLTIPS)

New to Flash Builder 4 is what Adobe calls ASDoc tooltips, although we like the descriptive *hover help* term because it's more self-explanatory.

You may have noticed this already, but if you click a component in the code editor, a document tooltip for that component shows up; pressing F2 after the hover help is displayed gives you a bit more information.

SHIFT+F2 HELP

Similar to the Dynamic Help approach, if you don't have the search pane already displayed, or you want to maintain what's currently shown under Dynamic Help, you can pull up the API Reference quickly using a hot key combination by following these steps:

1 In the code editor, click anywhere within the line of code that contains `<s:Button>`.

2 Press Shift+F2.

3 The API Reference for the button will appear.

It will take some time to develop the habit of using this key combination, but once you do, you'll be using it constantly.

At this juncture, all you've done is display the API Reference. Now you need to understand what you're looking at.

2.6.3 *Perusing the API Reference*

Let's look at the elements of an API Reference page. Having accessed the reference page of the button component using either Dynamic Help or the Shift+F2 technique, you should see something similar to figure 2.13.

Using the term *object* in a generic sense (versus the object-oriented nomenclature), here are brief descriptions of the five categories shown in figure 2.13:

- *Package*—Indicates to what directory the object belongs.
- *Class*—The particular object the API Reference page is describing.
- *Inheritance*—Who are the parents of this object? A child generally inherits the properties and functions of its ancestors. This is important to know, because being aware of what a parent object can do gives you insight as to what the child object can do as well.

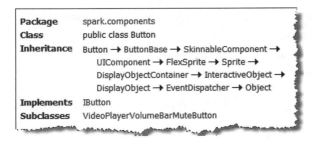

Figure 2.13 The first section of an API Reference page describes the world around a particular object.

- *Implements*—The lists of items here are called interfaces. These are like contracts to which the object agrees to adhere. Specifically, the object will implement the properties and functions/methods the interface demands.
- *Subclasses*—These are children of the object. This means that anything this object can do, the children can do as well.

The next portion of the API Reference page (not shown in figure 2.13) contains all the important pieces of information to which a Flex developer would regularly refer in order to manipulate an object or component. Following is a summary of those sections:

- *Properties*—Values you can retrieve and potentially set, such as width and height.
- *Methods*—Supporting functions, such as those that cause a component to redraw itself.
- *Events*—Actions to which objects will react (such as being clicked), that trigger the execution of specific instructions whenever the event occurs.
- *Styles*—Similar to CSS styles in HTML, these are stylesheet references.
- *Effects*—Used in conjunction with events to specify effects to be played. For example, if the mouse rolls over an object, you can specify a glowing effect to highlight that object.

Every API Reference page looks like this, and some even include examples of how to use an object or component. The key here is that once you get used to parsing the information and isolating the portion you need, you'll be able to flip back and forth between coding and the API Reference effortlessly.

2.7   *MXML and ActionScript in a nutshell*

Flex is based on MXML and ActionScript. As a result, when first learning Flex, it's often confusing to decide when to use one or the other, and new developers often ask themselves if they should be following some established best practice.

Let's start by taking a closer look at these two languages and explore this question a bit further.

2.7.1   *The structure of MXML*

In the previous example, you wrote a Flex application using pure MXML. MXML is a tag-based coding system derived from XML. Because of this heritage, it follows all the rules and conventions of XML, most notably:

- XML files, and therefore MXML files, require the XML declaration, which defines the version and character encoding.
  ```
  <?xml version="1.0" encoding="utf-8"?>
  ```
- XML files must have a top-level root tag (and corresponding closing tag at the end of the file).
- The language is case sensitive.

- Tags must have an opening tag and a closing tag.
  For example, `<myTag>...</myTag>`
  You can also use the shorthand version of `<myTag/>`.
- Tags must be nested properly.
  HTML is rather relaxed about this, but XML is strict and won't allow for such shenanigans.
  valid: `<a><b>...</b></a>`
  invalid: `<a><b>...</a></b>`
- Attribute values must be quoted.
  For example, `<tag attribute="value">`
- White space counts, which is worth noting for those of you coming from HTML-based applications because the rule is opposite to that of XML. HTML ignores consecutive repeating spaces, counting them as one.

If you've done a lot of work with XML, we're not breaking any new ground here. If you haven't, most of these conventions will feel like those rules that nag at an HTML developer.

> **NOTE** Flash Builder automatically indicates any violations of XML rules and won't let you compile until you've resolved any outstanding issues.

What it boils down to is keeping things clean, consistent, and structured.

2.7.2 How MXML and ActionScript relate

One point that puzzles some is why Flex is made up of two languages in the first place. Think of it this way: As a web developer you use HTML to describe your visual elements, such as tables, form inputs, and images. But these elements carry no functionality on the client side until you add JavaScript (to execute form validation, for instance).

It's the same in Flex. You use MXML to lay down your basic visual elements, as well as to define some nonvisual pieces, such as formatters and validators, and to access data services (we'll get into those a bit later).

> **TIP** Think of the relationship of MXML to ActionScript as similar to that of HTML to JavaScript.

In Flex you use ActionScript when you need to add functionality, decision making, interactivity, and business logic. As an example, let's go back to our Hello World! Flex project. But now we'll use ActionScript to modify it to appear as follows.

Listing 2.3 Using ActionScript and MXML together

```
<?xml version="1.0" encoding="utf-8"?>
<s:Application xmlns:fx="http://ns.adobe.com/mxml/2009"
               xmlns:s="library://ns.adobe.com/flex/spark"
               xmlns:mx="library://ns.adobe.com/flex/mx">
  <fx:Script>
    <![CDATA[
```

```
   import mx.controls.Alert;
 ]]>
</fx:Script>
<s:Button label="Marco" fontSize="40" click="Alert.show('Polo')"/>
</s:Application>
```

When you run the code in listing 2.3 and click the button labeled Marco, a pop-up alert will display (figure 2.14).

If you approach this with the mindset that Flex is to ActionScript as HTML is to JavaScript, it will make it easier to understand.

One mental hurdle web developers face comes as a result of having limited experience using client-side logic such as JavaScript. In traditional web technologies and web document models, most of the application logic resides on the server.

For example, ColdFusion folks are accustomed to using a tag-based language not only for the HTML but also for the logic:

```
<cfif itsAllGood>
  <b>It's all good</b>
</cfif>
```

The natural instinct when in Flex, therefore, is to code as in the following snippet:

```
<mx:if>...</mx:if>
```

Keep in mind that Flex is to ActionScript as HTML is to JavaScript model, and you'll be in good shape going forward. If ActionScript is to JavaScript, and JavaScript has events, you'd be correct in assuming that ActionScript also supports some kind of an event mechanism.

2.7.3 *Events are handled by ActionScript*

Flex is an event-driven application, which means everything occurs as a result of something happening. This is common with client-side technologies such as Flex. First you have something that triggers the event and then something that handles the event.

The device that handles the event is called (not surprisingly) an event handler and is implemented in ActionScript. If you refer to listing 2.3, you'll see that ActionScript was executed when the mouse button triggered the `click` event.

```
<s:Button label="Marco" fontSize="40" click="Alert.show('Polo')"/>
```

In the previous example, the specific event handler we wanted, `Alert.show('Polo')`, appears between quotation marks, but you can put any ActionScript event mechanism between them. Usually you call an event handler function to process all the logic you want executed when the event occurs.

ALMOST THE SAME AS IN JAVASCRIPT

This isn't any different than execution in JavaScript. JavaScript is used heavily to handle mouse-button and

Figure 2.14 ActionScript allows you to script in the logic and flow of your application.

mouse-over events. For example, you may need to validate data entered into a form before you send it to a server for processing.

Consider how this is done in the code presented in the following listing.

Listing 2.4   JavaScript, like ActionScript, is event driven.

```
<script language="JavaScript">
  img_over =new Image(); img_over.src ="over.gif";
  img_off=new Image();    img_off.src="off.gif";

  function handleOver()                    ❶ Mouse moving
  {                                           over target
    document.myImg.src=img_over.src;
  }

  function handleOut()                     ❷ Mouse moving
  {                                           off target
    document.myImg.src=img_off.src;
  }
</script>
<a href="#" onMouseOver="handleOver();" onMouseOut="handleOut();">
  <img name=myImg src="off.gif">
</a>
```

This is the classic mouse-over technique commonly used in JavaScript. You can see it makes use of two key events:

- onMouseOver—Caused by the mouse moving over a target ❶
- onMouseOut—Caused by the mouse moving off a target ❷

If you understand the way this is done in JavaScript and then look at the way this same functionality is implemented in Flex using ActionScript, you should feel right at home. The main difference that may jump out at you would be that events in Flex are represented as event objects.

ALMOST THE SAME, BUT ACTIONSCRIPT HAS AN EVENT OBJECT

JavaScript events are almost the same, but not quite. The main difference is Action-Script events also make available an event object.

All events are rooted from a generic top-level event object, and events add extra details through inheritance. What's cool about this is it allows you to easily write event handlers that are highly reusable because they can obtain the event's details through the event object and can be coded in a more flexible and generic fashion. The common details available through all event objects include the following:

- Where the event came from
- A reference or pointer to the data
- A indication of the type of the event (for example, a click versus a mouse-over)

To give you an idea of how that works, take a look at the following listing.

Listing 2.5   Using the event object makes event handlers more generic.

```
<?xml version="1.0" encoding="utf-8"?>
<s:Application xmlns:fx="http://ns.adobe.com/mxml/2009"
               xmlns:s="library://ns.adobe.com/flex/spark"
               xmlns:mx="library://ns.adobe.com/flex/mx">
  <fx:Script>
    <![CDATA[
    import mx.controls.Alert;
    public function clickHandler(clickEvent:Event):void       ⟵─── Accept event
    {
      Alert.show("Event Type:" + clickEvent.type +       ⟵─── Display event type
               " came from:" + clickEvent.currentTarget.id);     ⟵─┐
    }                                                    Display event source │
    ]]>
  </fx:Script>
  <s:Button id="Me" label="Handle Click" click="clickHandler(event)"/>   ⟵─┐
</s:Application>                                             Trigger the event │
```

Listing 2.5 demonstrates an event handler function being invoked when the user clicks the mouse button. When the mouse click occurs, an event object is created and passed along to the event handler (figure 2.15).

The event handler function has no idea what called it, but by using the event object it can find out any of the properties of the component that triggered the event, as well as what type of event it is.

This is extremely handy when you want to make an event handler reusable, because the handler doesn't need to know any specifics about how to access the related components.

Figure 2.15   Using the event object, a handler can access details such as from where the event came.

2.8   *Summary*

We've covered a lot of ground over the last two chapters, and things are going to ramp up quickly as we jump into more code. Before we do that, let's review a few things.

To those who may challenge your decision to use Flex because of its cost, you can counter with the fact that the Flex SDK is free, and by using the free Eclipse IDE and plug-ins you can get quite far in creating complete Flex applications. From a productivity perspective, the ROI realized by upgrading to Flash Builder (which is based on the Eclipse IDE) is easily justified and highly recommended.

Flash Builder's interface can be completely customized by the use of views, panes, and perspectives. Although there are default perspectives, you can alter the layout, add from the extensive catalog of views, and save them as new perspectives. This gives you a lot of freedom to customize how you work within the IDE.

Flash Builder comes with a catalog of wizards you can use to help perform all kinds of tasks, including creating a new project. The Flex Project Wizard will assist you in defining the main folder, its source directory, and where you want the compiled application to reside.

Flex is an object-oriented language, and because of that you'll need to become comfortable with the API Reference, more so than you would with a procedural language. This is because objects inherit from one another and contain built-in properties and functions. Knowing what an object's parents and children are lets you know their capabilities. Use the Dynamic Help and Shift+F2 features to assist you in that goal.

ActionScript is to MXML as JavaScript is to HTML. Use MXML to lay out your components and then add ActionScript for all the business logic. ActionScript and JavaScript are similar; they're both derived from the same scripting standard called ECMAScript, they're both client-side technologies, and they're both based on an event-driven model.

One key difference is that ActionScript creates an event object that an event handler can use to access almost everything it needs without needing to know about the source of the event.

In the next chapter, we'll jump right into ActionScript so we can add applicable logic going forward.

Working with ActionScript

3

In chapter 2 we introduced ActionScript. But what exactly can you do with it? As you'll soon see, quite a bit.

ActionScript is an extremely powerful object-oriented language about which you can dedicate entire books. In this chapter we'll focus on ActionScript's core concepts; obviously you'll need to be familiar with them before we get to the more powerful aspects of Flex itself. Speaking of which, you're probably anxious to get back into Flex, but tackling some ActionScript fundamentals will allow you to pick up the pace and move forward more quickly.

A fundamental concept in any programming language is that of comments, so we'll begin our discussion with how Flex supports documenting your code.

3.1   Comments

A basic construct of any programming language is the ability to document the mechanics of an application from within the code itself. You'll learn to do this through the use of comments.

From the perspective of implementation, a *comment* is a sequence of delimited text that's ignored by the Flex compiler. Flex's ActionScript language supports two popular formats: inline comments with regular code and block style with multiline comments.

3.1.1   Inline comments

The first comment type is the inline style, which you invoke using double forward slashes:

```
// one comment
var i:int;
var x:int; // another comment
```

As you can see, comments can exist on their own line or inline, alongside code. Using inline comments has limitations; the compiler recognizes the text following double forward slashes as a comment only until the end of the current line. A line return signals the end of the comment and the resumption of programmatic code.

3.1.2   Block comments

If you want to provide a much larger description using free-form text, you can use a multiline comment instead. Begin a multiline comment by typing a forward slash and asterisk (/*), and close it with the inversion (*/):

```
/*
   here is a chunk
   of text
*/
```

Commenting code serves two major purposes: It helps describe how the code works, and it assists in testing and debugging. With respect to documenting the code, it makes sense to use comments not only to be meaningful to other programmers but also to help keep track of what you've done for your own benefit. For debugging, you can temporarily comment out blocks of code to perform testing and diagnostics during the development process.

Let's move to variables, which allow you to gather and store information.

3.2   Variables

Variables are the basic building blocks of any programming language. They contain data you use to keep track of information, maintain the state of your application, and enable the user to manage data.

Although variables are common in all languages, their implementation varies from language to language. ActionScript may be a considerable departure from that with which you're currently familiar. ActionScript is based on a standard called

ECMAScript, which is the same standard on which JavaScript is based (though Action-Script follows a more recent version of ECMAScript).

3.2.1   Variable names

Variables have names and, as you may expect, there are rules to follow when creating them. Variable names may contain only letters, numbers, underscores, and the dollar sign. You can use any combination of those characters as long as the name doesn't begin with a number.

3.2.2   Strict data typing

Unlike JavaScript and ColdFusion, ActionScript uses *strict data typing*. This means when you declare a variable of a certain type, the value you assign it must be the same or a compatible type. Look at the following code snippet:

```
var myVar:Number;
myVar = "test"; //would result in an error
```

This code is invalid because you're trying to assign text to a variable that's expecting a numeric value.

3.2.3   Static versus dynamic type checking

Flex checks for type mismatches using two approaches known as *static* and *dynamic* type checking. Static type checking is performed during compile time, with the compiler ensuring the rules of typing are being maintained. Programmers coming from Java and C++ are accustomed to this method.

ActionScript can also perform dynamic type checking. With dynamic type checking, Flash Player examines your variable types during application execution. Of course, there are pros and cons to both approaches. One benefit of dynamic type checking is that it makes development more convenient because you can quickly prototype applications without having to cope with compiler warnings and errors.

By default, static is the mode that's used when compiling your application. You can change this via the Enable Strict Type Checking option found under Project > Properties > Flex Compiler.

Keep in mind that even if you turn Static mode off, during the execution of your application Flash Player still performs type checking; disabling Static mode skips the compile-time check.

Although it can be less of a nuisance to avoid compile-time checking, I recommend you save yourself some grief and leave Static mode on. In the long run you'll be better off looking into whatever the compiler is complaining about.

When creating a variable, you're creating an instance of a class, so let's briefly review what that's all about.

3.2.4 *Top-level classes*

Variables are instances of classes, which you, Java, C#, and PHP folks are already familiar with. For the ColdFusion readers, your CFCs are similar to classes. But regardless of your level of experience in this area, there are a few things worth noting.

A class is a collection of methods (functions) and properties, and classes are grouped into packages.

The Flex 3 SDK had a concept of primitive data types that by default were always available (meaning you didn't need to import them), and because they were primitives there was less overhead involved in using them.

With Flex 4 all the primitives are converted to classes and placed into something called the top-level package. From a coding perspective, there's little difference because the top-level package is included by default, and all of its classes are readily available.

Some of the classes that are part of this top-level package include:

```
Array       Boolean      Class      Date
int         Number       Object     String
uint        Vector       XML        XMLList
```

Traditionally, with most classes if you wanted to create an instance of that class, you'd follow a pattern along the lines of

```
import com.mypackage.MyClass;
var myVar:MyClass = new MyClass():
```

But with top-level classes you don't need to import the package because that's done by default, and some of them have a shortcut way of creating them. For example, although you could create a String via

```
var myString:String = new String("hello");
```

you can use the shortcut version to assign some text to a String variable:

```
var myString:String = "hello";
```

Here are a couple of more examples that you'll find handy:

```
var myString:String = "hello";
var myInt:int = -32;
var myUint:uint = 32;
var myNumber:Number = 32.32;
var myXML:XML = <root><node></node></root>;
var myObj:Object = {x:1,y:2,z:3};
var myArray:Array = ["item1","item2","item3"];
var myBool:Boolean = false;
```

We're almost finished with variables; the last thing to mention is special data types.

3.2.5   *Special data types*

Special data types are reserved words and values, meaning that if you were to name a variable one of these, you'd get an error. Table 3.1 provides a list of the special data types along with their descriptions.

Table 3.1   Special data types

Data type	Description
*	Used to indicate to the compiler that you'll set the variable's data type later.
void	Used in function declarations to indicate the function isn't returning any data.
undefined	Works hand-in-hand with void. The value of void is undefined.
null	Used by complex data types and Strings to indicate they currently have no associated value.
NaN	Not a number. Used by the Number data type to indicate it's currently not assigned to a numerical value.

To summarize, ActionScript variables are case sensitive, and you need to be sure their assigned values are compatible with their data types. ActionScript includes top-level classes, which are a collection of basic everyday variable types that don't need to be imported.

Now that you know how to make variables, you'll often have collections of them. This is when loops are useful to iterate over them (for example, arrays).

3.3   *Loops*

Loops are another fundamental construct all languages provide, in one variation or another. From a conceptual point of view, loops iterate over a range of numbers or a collection of items until a specified condition is no longer true.

In this section, we explore the types of loops ActionScript supports and how to use them, starting with the for loop.

3.3.1   *For (starting value; valid condition; increment)*

The standard for loop, common in most languages, lets you specify a starting value, stipulate the valid condition in which the loop will continue to iterate, and increment the starting value in accordance with what you specify:

```
for(var x:int=1;x<=10;x++)
  trace(x);
```

In this example, trace() outputs to a log file. The loop assigns the variable x a value of 1. It then performs its iteration, incrementing the x variable by 1 with each pass, until the variable's value equals 10. This type of loop comes in handy when you know how many times you need to perform a function, such as the number of items in an array.

3.3.2   *For (property names in array/object)*

If you have an array or an object, the `for..in` loop lets you iterate over all the items contained within that array or object by property name (which is a value contained in an object; for example, a person object might have a name property). This comes in handy when you're working with XML and XMLList objects.

```
var myArray:Array  = ["alpha","beta","chi"];
for(var i:String in myArray) {
  trace(i);
}
```

There's a catch—we're looping over property names, and in an array the property name is the array's index. This means the output for the previous example would be

```
0
1
2
```

In this case, the first index of an array would be 0. Because we're getting the index, we can obtain the values through the following:

```
var myArray:Array  = ["alpha","beta","chi"];
for(var i:String in myArray) {
  trace(myArray[i]);
}
```

The variable i is the zero-based index number of the items contained within myArray. When i is 0, it gets the first item in myArray.

Output:
```
alpha
beta
chi
```

Why is the variable i a String and not an int? In most cases, you'd receive an error if you tried using int because the `for..in` loop is returning property names, which are Strings. (In the second example, the Flash player is able to autoconvert to a number, because the index of an array is a number.)

The case for objects is similar; unlike arrays (which contain a sequence of items), objects have properties or attributes.

```
var myObject:Object = {firstName:'Jeff', lastName:'Smith'};
for(var i:String in myObject) {
  trace("Property: " + i + "=" + myObject[i]);
}
```

> **TIP** For you ColdFusion users, myObject[i] is similar to accessing a key in a structure as an associative array.

Output:
```
Property:firstName=Jeff
Property:lastName=Smith
```

This kind of loop has a variety of ways it can be used. If you only want the value of each item, you'll find the `for each..in` loop easier to use.

3.3.3   *For each (item in array/object)*

The `for each..in` loop iterates over arrays and objects, but instead of property names, it tests for the property's value.

```
var myObject:Object = {firstName:'Jeff', lastName:'Smith'};
for each(var i:String in myObject) {
  trace(i);
}
```

Output:
```
Jeff
Smith
```

This type of loop is a simplified version of the `for..in` loop. `for` loops work great when used against known quantities like arrays and objects, but when you want to keep looping until a condition is met, you need the `while` loop.

3.3.4   *While (condition)*

The `while` loop continues iterating until the specified condition is no longer true.

```
var x:int = 0;
while(x<5)
{
  trace('x is now ' + x);
  x=x+1;
}
```

Output:
```
x is now 0
x is now 1
x is now 2
x is now 3
x is now 4
```

Note that the `while` loop checks the condition at the start of the loop; if the condition isn't true upon the loop's initiation, no iterations will be performed.

3.3.5   *Do while (condition)*

The `do while` loop is the same as a `while` loop, with the subtle but important difference of the test condition being evaluated at the end of the loop instead of the beginning. This comes in handy if you need to run through a section of code at least once, regardless of the test condition's status. Use the `while` loop if you need to verify the condition is valid before engaging the loop.

```
var x:int = 5;
do
{
  trace('x is now ' + x);
```

```
    x=x+1;
} while(x<5);
```

Output:
```
x is now 5
```

The various types of loops provide you with all the control you'll need to iterate over a known set of quantities or while a condition is valid. The next building block to look at is conditional logic.

3.4 *Conditional statements (if statements and switches)*

Conditional statements are a fundamental piece of programming. ActionScript implements two forms of them, the `if` and `switch` statements, like most languages. Note the particular syntax here because ActionScript provides the same constructs as any other language.

3.4.1 *If..else*

When you need to check whether a condition has been met, such as whether the user has provided a password, `if..else` statements are your primary mechanism for doing so.

Here's a simple exercise to see how `if..else` works:

1　Create a new project in Flash Builder (for example, `"CH03"`).
2　Change the code to that presented in listing 3.1.
3　Test whether the `if..else` statement is doing its job by entering any password in the text input box generated by your code (figure 3.1) and then trying it without a password.

Listing 3.1　Using an `if..else` conditional statement to do a password check

```
<?xml version="1.0" encoding="utf-8"?>
<s:Application xmlns:fx="http://ns.adobe.com/mxml/2009"
               xmlns:s="library://ns.adobe.com/flex/spark"
               xmlns:mx="library://ns.adobe.com/flex/mx">
  <fx:Script>
    <![CDATA[
     import mx.controls.Alert;
     public function checkPassword():void
     {
        if(password.text.length < 1)             Referencing TextInput
          Alert.show("Missing Password!");     ◁┘ by name
        else
          Alert.show("Looks Good!");
     }
    ]]>
  </fx:Script>
  <s:Group>
    <s:layout>
      <s:VerticalLayout/>
    </s:layout>
```

```
      <s:TextInput id="password"/>
      <s:Button label="Check Password" click="checkPassword()"/>
    </s:Group>
</s:Application>
```

id used to assign a name

Curly braces are optional around the Alert code and not used in this case because there's only one line of code after if and else.

> **NOTE**   Because angle brackets mean something in XML, we use the CDATA directive, which allows us to use the left angle bracket in comparing the password's length while not breaking the XML structure of the document.

Figure 3.1 shows a simple text input box with a submit button created by the new code in listing 3.1.

Running our example with and without text generates the appropriate alerts.

When working with if statements, you don't necessarily need the else branch. In the previous example, if you want to pop the Missing Password! alert (but not display the Looks Good! message), you could use the if branch and omit the else section altogether.

Figure 3.1   A simple password-checking application verifies a password has been entered.

```
public function checkPassword():void
{
  if(password.text.length < 1)
    Alert.show("Missing Password!");
}
```

If you need to continue checking more conditions after the current condition has failed, you'll want to use the else if command. Let's assume you want to test for a missing password as one condition, check for a password containing too few characters as another, and allow anything other than the first two conditions as a third. Each condition will display the appropriate message to the user. The following listing shows how to configure the code.

Listing 3.2   Nesting multiple conditional statements

```
if(password.text.length < 1)
  Alert.show("Missing Password!");
else if (password.text.length < 5)
  Alert.show("Not Enough Characters!");
else
  Alert.show("Looks Good!");
```

You can continue adding as many else ifs as needed, but this can become unwieldy if there are many conditions to check. This is where the switch statement is a better alternative.

3.4.2   *Switch*

If you need to evaluate many conditions, it's often easier to use a switch statement instead of repeated else if commands. Listing 3.3 shows a switch statement evaluating a number of possible values.

Listing 3.3   Using a switch statement makes managing many conditions easy.

```
<?xml version="1.0" encoding="utf-8"?>
<s:Application xmlns:fx="http://ns.adobe.com/mxml/2009"
            xmlns:s="library://ns.adobe.com/flex/spark"
            xmlns:mx="library://ns.adobe.com/flex/mx">

  <fx:Script>
    <![CDATA[
      import mx.controls.Alert;
      public function moodCheck():void
      {
        switch(myMood.text)
        {
          case 'happy':
            Alert.show("Life is good isn't it?");      ⟵ Ends the
            break;                                         case block
          case 'sad':
            Alert.show("Some Prozac will cheer you up!");  ⟵ Default block
            break;                                            when no match
          default:
            Alert.show("Neither here nor there eh?");
        }
      }
    ]]>
  </fx:Script>

  <s:Group>
    <s:layout>
      <s:VerticalLayout/>
    </s:layout>
    <mx:TextInput id="myMood"/>
    <mx:Button label="Check your mood" click="moodCheck()"/>
  </s:Group>
</s:Application>
```

Using a switch statement makes the code naturally easier to read by grouping each condition in a case block, but there are a couple of syntax characteristics you'll want to keep in mind when using it:

- Don't wrap case blocks in curly braces.
- The end of each section requires a break statement.
- Instead of the case keyword, you can use default to catch anything that doesn't match any of the above.

To summarize, if, else, and switch statements are the basic way to add conditional logic to your application. Switching gears (get it?), we're going to cover another of the important fundamentals: arrays.

3.5   *Arrays*

An array is a variable that can store multiple values. For example, if you owned three houses and wanted to store information about the tenants living in each one, you could create one variable per occupant:

```
House1="John Doe";
House2="Michael Dorsay";
House3="Herald McGee";
```

The problem here is this pseudo code isn't scalable. With this approach you're required to know in advance how many variables you'll need (which isn't realistic in most real-world scenarios). If you were coding for hundreds (or thousands) of houses, it would require maintaining a lot of overhead.

An array is perfect for handling these kinds of situations:

```
HouseArray[1]="John Doe"
HouseArray[2]="Michael Dorsay"
HouseArray[3]="Herald McGee"
```

ActionScript supports three main types of arrays:

- *Indexed*—Use a number as a key for each value. This is useful when the values you need to store are based on some kind of sequence. For example, it would lend itself well to a queue of tasks that need to be executed in sequential steps, one-by-one.
- *Associative*—Use any kind of a key (usually a string) to associate values to the key. Associative arrays are useful when you want to make some kind of lookup mechanism. For example, you could use Social Security numbers as a key to store the name and details of the person associated with a specific number.
- *Multidimensional*—Arrays of arrays. Multidimensional arrays are useful when you need to use a combination of keys to store and retrieve information. Each dimension can be a mix of indexed and associative arrays. For example, you could use a two-dimensional array to store a grid of colors, using one dimension for the x coordinate and the second for the y coordinate.

Let's take a closer look at how indexed and associative arrays work (keep in mind that a multidimensional array is a combination of these).

3.5.1   *Indexed arrays*

This is the array that usually comes to mind. Indexed arrays store and allow access to data through a numerical index. To create one, you declare it as follows:

```
var houseArray:Array = new Array();
```

When you declare an array in this fashion, it contains no items, but you can add an extra parameter with which you can assign it an initial value.

```
var houseArray:Array = new Array(3);
```

Typically, in programmer's parlance, to load items into an array, you *push* and *unshift* them. To retrieve items, you *pop* and *shift* them off. To make life a bit easier, there's a multifunctional mechanism called a *splice* that lets you do both.

> **TIP** The index of the first item in an indexed array is 0, not 1, as would be your natural inclination to think. This isn't unique to ActionScript; many other modern languages (such as Java) adhere to this convention.

Here are the common array functions you can use:

- `push()`—Appends the item onto the end of the array.
  ```
  houseArray.push("John Doe");
  houseArray.push("Michael Dorsay");
  ```
- `unshift()`—Inserts the item onto the front of the array.
  ```
  houseArray.unshift("Herald McGee");
  houseArray.unshift("Jon Hirschi");
  ```
- `pop()`—Takes an item off the end of the array.
  ```
  houseArray.pop();
  ```
- `shift()`—Takes an item off the front of the array.
  ```
  houseArray.shift();
  ```
- `splice()`—Removes items from a position, and optionally inserts new items.

Most of these functions are self-explanatory, except the `splice()` function, which needs further explanation.

A CLOSER LOOK AT SPLICE()

Let's talk a bit more about the `splice()` function by looking at its parameters:

- *Parameter 1*—The index position in the array at which you want to start. Because the first item in an indexed array is 0, 1 would be the second item.
- *Parameter 2*—The number of items you want to take off, starting at the position defined in parameter 1. If you set this to 0, no items will be removed. If you set it to a higher value than there are actual items, it'll have the same effect as if you removed all items from the starting position.
- *Parameter 3*—Insert new items into the array starting at the position specified by parameter 1. This is done after items are removed (if any) as indicated in parameter 2.

Here's a brief example; The first line adds an item in the second position. The next line takes out the second item.

```
houseArray.splice(1,0,"Tariq Ahmed");
houseArray.splice(1,1);
```

Spicing it up a bit, this snippet starts at the fourth position, takes out two items, and adds three more:

```
houseArray.splice(3,2,"Ryan Stewart","Matt Chotin","Jeff Dougherty");
```

Although arrays are common in all languages, the `splice()` function is unique to ActionScript's implementation of this data type. Some languages also provide a shorthand way to initialize arrays. ActionScript provides a shorthand method as well, and we'll show you what it is.

SHORTHAND INITIALIZATION OF ARRAYS

You can take advantage of shorthand notation to initialize your arrays and set their starting values:

```
var houseArray:Array = new ["John Doe","Michael Dorsay","Herald McGee"];
```

In the previous code snippet, the square brackets indicate an array. The items contained in the array are separated by commas.

Now that you have a populated array, you'll want to be able to loop through it.

LOOPING THROUGH ARRAYS

To benefit from the full potential of arrays, you'll want to loop through their range of index values. The key to accomplishing that is the array's `length` property, which indicates how many items are contained within.

> **NOTE**   The `trace()` function is a simple logging mechanism for printing text to Flash Player's log file. We'll begin using it here as part of our demonstrations, but for more detailed information on the `trace()` function, see chapter 23.

When we talked about `for` loops, we mentioned that they're commonly used with arrays. Looking at listing 3.4, let's review a `for` loop used to iterate over each item in an array.

Listing 3.4   Listing 3.4 Looping through an array

```
var myFriendsArray:Array = ["John Doe","Marco Polo","Warren Jones"];
for (var i:int=0;i<myFriendsArray.length;i++)          ◁⌐ Determine
{                                                            array size
  trace(myFriendsArray[i]);          ◁⌐ Output to
}                                         log file
```

Listing 3.4 demonstrates how the array's `length` property is used to evaluate how many items it contains while progressively looping over each item.

You're not restricted to using numbers as a key to each item in the array. Another option is using a string for the key instead. We'll look at this next.

3.5.2   *Associative arrays*

The mechanics of an associative array are a little different in that you deal with keys instead of indices. For ColdFusion folks, you'll find comfort here, because the mechanism is exactly the same as ColdFusion's associative arrays (using a `Struct`).

As with indexed arrays, you create an associative array using the same method:

```
var carManufacturersByModel:Array = new Array();
```

But going forward, instead of pushing and popping, you assign values based on a textual string, as shown here:

```
carManufacturersByModel["xA"] = "Scion";
carManufacturersByModel["Viper"] = "Dodge";
carManufacturersByModel["IS350"] = "Lexus";
```

Then, to retrieve the value associated with the key, you access it using the key:

```
trace(carManufacturersByModel["xA"]);          ◁——— Output: Scion
trace(carManufacturersByModel["Viper"]);   ?       ◁——— Output: Dodge
trace(carManufacturersByModel["IS350"]);   ?           ◁——— Output: Lexus
```

Ultimately, you want to loop through all the items in the associative array, and to do this you'd typically use the reliable `for..in` loop.

```
for (var key:String in carManufacturersByModel)
{
  trace("Key:"+key);
  trace("Value:"+carManufacturersByModel[key]);
}
```

Output:
```
Key:Viper
Value:Dodge
Key:IS350
Value:Lexus
Key:xA
Value:Scion
```

Alternatively, if you want the values themselves and aren't interested in the corresponding keys, you can use the `for each..in` loop, as this snippet demonstrates:

```
for each (var manufacturer:String in carManufacturersByModel)
{
  trace(manufacturer);
}
```

Notice that the output in this case displays only the values of the items:

```
Lexus
Scion
Dodge
```

Do you sense something a little odd with this output? The order displayed (Lexus, Scion, Dodge) isn't the order in which the items were originally added (Scion, Dodge, Lexus). You'll need to keep in mind that items stored in an associative array are stored in a nonordered fashion—there's no predictability, so don't count on an order.

There's an alternate way to do all this by using the grandfather of all objects: the `Object`! Instead of creating an instance of an array, you can create an instance of an `Object`:

```
var carManufacturersByModel:Object = new Object();
```

For all intents and purposes, there isn't much difference except using an `Object` lets you use the shorthand way to populate the array-like data upon initialization.

```
var carManufacturersByModel:Object = {xA:"Scion",Viper:"Dodge",IS350:"Lexus"};
```

> **TIP** JSON is similar to ActionScript when it comes to associative arrays, except the keys don't need to be contained within quotation marks.

One bit of syntax to which new ActionScript users will need to adapt is using a colon for value assignment (`IS350:"Lexus"`). Don't worry; you'll get used to it. The last aspect of the associative array we'll cover is its support for dot notation.

DOT NOTATION

A nifty characteristic of associative arrays is that you can use a feature known as dot notation to access items within the array. It's another way of doing the same thing as the colon, but if you're accustomed to a particular coding style, you may prefer this format:

```
trace(carManufacturersByModel.xA);
trace(carManufacturersByModel.Viper);
trace(carManufacturersByModel.IS350);
```

Something to keep in mind if you use this style of notation is that ActionScript variables can't contain spaces, so although it's perfectly valid to use spaces in a key, you'd generate errors if you then tried to access a key containing spaces using dot notation.

```
carManufacturersByModel["Land Cruiser"]="Toyota";
trace(carManufacturersByModel.Land Cruiser);            ◁——— Error!
```

Dot notation in general is the syntax preferred by most Flex developers—it's faster to type and easier to read. On the topic of syntax, next we'll examine a number of other tidbits regarding the ActionScript language.

3.6   *ActionScript tidbits*

Every language supports certain characteristics, shortcuts, and nuances. In this section we'll briefly go over a collection of tidbits you'll want to know about when working with ActionScript, starting with curly braces.

3.6.1   *Braces*

When writing code blocks for scripts, such as functions, loops, switches, and `if` statements, you use curly braces to indicate to Flex all the code that falls under the switch control of those statements—*unless* the instruction after the statement comprises only one line.

Let's look at some examples, as in the following listing.

Listing 3.5 Listing 3.5 Examples of when curly braces are required or optional

```
for each (var manufacturer:String in carManufacturersByModel)
{
   trace(manufacturer);                    Braces optionally used
}
for each (var manufacturer:String in carManufacturersByModel)    Skip braces
   trace(manufacturer);
while(x<5)
{
   trace('x is now' + x);                  Braces required
   x=x+1;
}
if(x==5)
   trace(x);                               Braces not needed
else
{
   x=0;                Braces used
   trace(x);
}
```

These curly brace rules are the same as those prescribed by JavaScript, so you'll enjoy a bit of familiarity in that respect. You can skip the braces if there's only one line of code or only one line of code after the for...each statement. Braces are required if there's more than one line. Some people like using the curly braces even when it isn't required. This is mostly a matter of personal preference, and because there's no industry-adopted standard, feel free to use whatever approach you're most comfortable with.

3.6.2   *Logical operators and shortcuts*

Logical operators are special characters, or sets of characters, that have some kind of operational meaning to the compiler. Let's see what these are and how to use them.

++ AND —

To increase or decrease a number, the ++ and -- operators are quick and direct to the point, as the following code snippet demonstrates:

```
x=x+1;        ←—— You could do this!
x++;                      ←—— This is faster
x=x-1;        ←—— You could do this!
x--;                      ←—— This is faster
```

These two operators work on both sides of a variable; when the operator is on the left side, ActionScript will adjust the variable first before using its value in the rest of the statement, otherwise, it executes the statement as is and then applies the operator.

```
var x:int=0;                 Outputs 0;
trace(x++);                  increases the value!
trace(x);        ←—— Outputs 1
var y:int=0;                 Increases value;
trace(++y);                  outputs 1
```

Comparative operators, used to compare values, are similar to logical operators.

BASIC COMPARATIVE OPERATORS

When conducting a comparison for test purposes—in an `if` or `while` statement—there are several operators you can use to evaluate one value against another. Table 3.2 presents each operator and what it does.

Table 3.2 Operators for conducting comparisons

Operator	Description	Example
==	Determines whether one value is equal to another. Note that this is an equality comparison and not an identity comparison.	`if(x==y) trace("X and Y are the same");`
!=	Determines whether one value is not equal to another.	`if(x!=y) trace("X is not equal to Y");`
<	Determines whether one value is less than another.	`if(x<y)trace ("X is less than Y");`
<=	Determines whether one value is less than or equal to another.	`if(x<=y) trace("X is less than or the same as Y");`
>	Determines whether one value is greater than another.	`if(x>y) trace ("X is greater than Y");`
>=	Determines whether one value is greater than or equal to another.	`If(x>=y) trace ("X is greater than or equal to Y");`
!	The `not` operator takes the inverse of the value.	`var x:Boolean=false;` `if(!x)trace ("x is not true");`

Last, we have mathematical operators for performing computations.

MATHEMATICAL OPERATORS

When you need to manipulate numbers, create algorithms, or develop formulas, a group of mathematical operators is available to assist you. Table 3.3 lists these operators and their descriptions.

Table 3.3 Mathematical operators

Operator	Description	Example
*	Multiplication	`z = x * y;`
/	Division	`z = x/y;`

%	Modulus, the remainder of the first number divided by the second	`trace(9 % 3); // output 0`
		`trace(7 % 3); // output 1`

Table 3.3 Mathematical operators *(continued)*

Operator	Description	Example

+	Adds one value to another Note: This operator can be used with `Strings`. When used with `Strings`, the + operator joins text together.	`var z:int = 4 + 2; // z is 6`
		`var x:String="good"+"bye"; // x is "goodbye"`

To recap, there are different kinds of operators. Logical operators can act as shortcuts, comparative operators evaluate one item against another, and mathematical operators perform numerical manipulation.

The elements of code in which you'd normally contain all this logic are typically functions. Next, we'll look at what functions are and how operators work within them.

3.7 Sneak peek at functions, classes, and packages

When creating your applications, you'll eventually start splitting up your logic into smaller modules to enable reuse and simplify ongoing maintenance of your code. Chapters 17 and 18 will go much deeper into these organizational aspects of Action-Script, but for now let's take a peek at what this is all about.

A function is a way to encapsulate blocks of logic in such a way that the logic can be reused in a modular fashion by other elements. Once defined and properly packaged, functions can even be used by elements in other applications.

Recall from chapter 2, when you used the code repeated in listing 3.6, you were invoking a function of the `Alert` class called `show()`.

Listing 3.6 Making note of a function used in chapter 2

```
<fx:Script>
  import mx.controls.Alert;
</fx:Script>
<s:Button label="Marco" fontSize="40" click="Alert.show('Polo')"/>
```

To make functions reusable, they accept input parameters; in this example a single text parameter with the value `Polo` was passed along in `Alert.show()`. The `mx.control.Alert` itself is called a *class*, which is a self-contained collection of functions (a.k.a. methods) and variables. Instances of classes are usually referred to as objects.

NOTE Functions are also referred to as methods.

Again, referring to listing 3.6, we're using the function `show()` of the `Alert` class, which is part of a package called `mx.controls`. A *package* is a collection of classes. Does ActionScript let you make functions on our own? It does indeed, and you're about to learn how.

3.7.1 *Your own functions*

Declaring a function is easy and looks something like the illustration in figure 3.2.

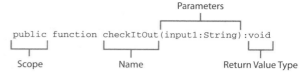

Figure 3.2   **This is what a function looks like in ActionScript.**

The first keyword (`public`) in figure 3.2 declares the *scope* of the function, which identifies who can access it. *Who*, in this context, is other code from within the same class/component (let's just say *object* for now) or code making use of the function from outside the class/component. Table 3.6 lists the available scopes.

Table 3.4   **Available scopes you'll encounter when working with functions**

Scope	Description
Public	Your object; anyone calling your object can access the function.
Private	Only your object can access the function.
Protected	Only your object and children of your object can access the function.

The second keyword (`function`), informs ActionScript you're declaring a function.

The third keyword is your function's name. It can be anything, as long as it doesn't start with a number, doesn't contain spaces, and doesn't contain nonalphanumeric characters (except the underscore (_) character).

The fourth keyword (between the parentheses) is a set of *typed parameters*. Earlier in this chapter, we discussed data typing, and this is an example of where that applies. This means you need to declare all the input parameters you're going to allow and what kind of variables you expect them to be (for instance, `int`s, `String`s, and so on).

The fifth keyword is the *return type*, which notifies anyone calling your function what kind of variable you're going to send back, for example, a `Number`, `Object`, or `Boolean`. In this case, nothing is being returned, so we used the keyword `void`.

Let's put this all together and make our own function.

CREATING YOUR OWN FUNCTION

Using what you've learned about functions, let's put it into action by creating your own, as shown in the next listing.

Listing 3.7   Creating your first function

```
<?xml version="1.0" encoding="utf-8"?>
<s:Application xmlns:fx="http://ns.adobe.com/mxml/2009"
               xmlns:s="library://ns.adobe.com/flex/spark"
               xmlns:mx="library://ns.adobe.com/flex/mx">

  <fx:Script>
    <![CDATA[
      import mx.controls.Alert;
      public function displayMe(input1:String):void
```

```
    {
        Alert.show(input1);
    }
  ]]>
</fx:Script>

<s:Group>
  <s:layout>
    <s:VerticalLayout/>
  </s:layout>
  <s:TextInput id="thisTextInput" text="try this"/>
  <s:Button label="Display It" click="displayMe(thisTextInput.text)"/>
</s:Group>
</s:Application>
```

After compiling and running the example, you'll see something similar to figure 3.3. Enter some text and click the Display It button. The text just entered will be passed along to a function.

Now let's examine what happened in more detail. You created an input box in which you can type text. When you clicked the Display It button, you told Flex to invoke our function named displayMe(), which captured the text entered into the input box as a variable and assigned that variable the name thisTextInput, using the id property.

Our function, which takes a single argument (the text from the input box), passed it along to Alert's show() function. In all this code, you likely noticed something new—the cryptic-looking <![CDATA[...]]>.

Figure 3.3 User-entered text is passed along to a function.

CDATA

Because Flex MXML files are XML-compliant, we're obliged to follow the rules of XML. CDATA instructs Flex Builder (and its compiler) to take the content within the square brackets ([]) as is and not try to process it as XML code.

In this case, you technically didn't need to use CDATA, because you wouldn't have broken any rules with the contents of your variable. But it won't take long before you find yourself handling data that uses the less-than (<) or greater-than (>) operator, and without that CDATA directive, Flex will think you're opening or closing an MXML tag.

It's always best practice to wrap a block of ActionScript within a CDATA directive.

One tedious aspect of working with functions is the amount of text used to call them from their packages. Fortunately, there's a way to ease that burden by importing the entire package.

IMPORTING PACKAGES

As you've seen so far, in order to use the Alert.show() function you first imported the mx.controls.Alert class. This is true for any class you wish to use (except for the top-level classes, which were covered earlier in section 3.2.4), for example:

```
import mx.collections.ArrayCollection;
var myAC:ArrayCollection = new ArrayCollection();
```

Alternatively, to import all of the classes in a package you use the * character in place of the specific class that you want. So, for example, to import all the collections in the collections package, you'd do it like so:

```
import mx.collections.*;
```

When you perform an import, whatever you imported is available only for that file (per each MXML file or ActionScript class). With each file you'd import the statement again, as necessary. This doesn't cost overhead, because Flex is merely pointing to the functionality, not making copies every time you invoke it.

The last piece to demonstrate is returning a value from the function to whatever invoked it.

RETURNING A VALUE

Taking things a bit further, let's return a data type. You'll notice in listing 3.8 that the function has been updated from void to String, meaning this function is declaring that it will return a text string.

Listing 3.8   Creating a function that returns a value of data type `String`

```
<?xml version="1.0" encoding="utf-8"?>
<s:Application xmlns:fx="http://ns.adobe.com/mxml/2009"
               xmlns:s="library://ns.adobe.com/flex/spark"
               xmlns:mx="library://ns.adobe.com/flex/mx">

  <fx:Script>
    <![CDATA[
      import mx.controls.Alert;
      public function textMerge(input1:String,input2:String):String
      {
        var x:String = input1 + input2;
        return x;
      }

    ]]>
  </fx:Script>

  <s:Group>
    <s:layout>
      <s:HorizontalLayout/>
    </s:layout>
    <s:TextInput id="value1"/>
    <mx:Label text="and"/>
    <s:TextInput id="value2"/>
    <s:Button label="Join The Two"
              click="Alert.show(textMerge(value1.text,value2.text))"/>
  </s:Group>
</s:Application>
```

Here, we have functions calling functions:

- When you click the button, Alert.show() calls textMerge(), passing the values of the two text inputs.

Figure 3.4 This function takes two separate pieces of text and returns them combined into one.

- `textMerge()`, in turn, joins the two `String`s together and returns the result to `Alert.show()`, which then displays the result (figure 3.4).

In all these examples, we've shown ActionScript inside MXML, similar to how JavaScript can be embedded within an HTML file. But this is just an option; the other option is separating it into individual files.

3.7.2 Separating ActionScript to individual files

Your ActionScript doesn't need to reside in your MXML files; you can split it into its own files. This makes it easier to maintain your code as your applications grow in size, as well as making your functions more reusable by allowing multiple applications to source in their logic.

To do this, pull out any ActionScript into a file, and save it with an `.as` extension, as demonstrated in the next listing.

Listing 3.9 myFunctions.as—ActionScript saved separately

```
public function textMerge(input1:String,input2:String):String
{
  var x:String = input1 + input2;
  return x;
}
```

In your main MXML file, you can source it back in, as follows.

Listing 3.10 Main MXML file sources the myFunctions.as file

```
<?xml version="1.0" encoding="utf-8"?>
<s:Application xmlns:fx="http://ns.adobe.com/mxml/2009"
            xmlns:s="library://ns.adobe.com/flex/spark"
            xmlns:mx="library://ns.adobe.com/flex/mx">
  <fx:Script source="myFunctions.as"/>              ❶ Import our functions
  <fx:Script>
    <![CDATA[
      import mx.controls.Alert;                       ❷ Import the Alert class
    ]]>
  </fx:Script>

  <s:Group>
    <s:layout>
      <s:HorizontalLayout/>
    </s:layout>
    <s:TextInput id="value1"/>
    <mx:Label text="and"/>
```

```
        <s:TextInput id="value2"/>                              Handle  ③
        <s:Button label="Join The Two"                      click event
                click="Alert.show(textMerge(value1.text,value2.text))"/>   ↵
    </s:Group>
</s:Application>
```

Note that because the `Button` is calling `Alert.show()` ③, you have to import the library ② in this same file, meaning that if you moved that `import` statement to the `myFunctions.as` ① file, it wouldn't be visible in the main MXML file ①. The import has relevance only for anything within the file that does the import.

We have only one more feature to cover, called data binding (or just binding), before we wrap up this chapter.

3.8   *Simple data binding*

ActionScript includes a feature that lets one item listen to the value of another. This is called binding. Not only does it help reduce the amount of code you need to write, but it also assists in making your applications more scalable by being able to easily abstract where information comes from or who is interested in it.

3.8.1   *Life without binding*

Let's take an example using the visual `TextInput` component in which you want to take its value and display it somewhere else. In this case, we'll use the `Label` component. From what you've learned so far, you could do it as shown in the following listing.

> **Listing 3.11   You can manually copy values from one place to another.**

```
<?xml version="1.0" encoding="utf-8"?>
<s:Application xmlns:fx="http://ns.adobe.com/mxml/2009"
              xmlns:s="library://ns.adobe.com/flex/spark"
              xmlns:mx="library://ns.adobe.com/flex/mx">
  <s:Group>
    <s:layout>
      <s:HorizontalLayout/>
    </s:layout>
    <s:TextInput id="myTextInput1"/>
    <s:Button label="Copy:" click="myTextInput2.text=myTextInput1.text"/>
    <s:TextInput id="myTextInput2"/>
  </s:Group>
</s:Application>
```

Listing 3.11 uses ActionScript to copy the `text` property of the `TextInput` component to the `text` property of the `Text` component (figure 3.5).

That's all fine and dandy, but Flex makes life easier with its binding abilities.

Figure 3.5   The value is copied from one variable to another.

3.8.2 Adding binding

Using binding you can do this automatically, as demonstrated in the next listing.

Listing 3.12 Using binding, you can do an automatic copy to a target.

```
<?xml version="1.0" encoding="utf-8"?>
<s:Application xmlns:fx="http://ns.adobe.com/mxml/2009"
               xmlns:s="library://ns.adobe.com/flex/spark"
               xmlns:mx="library://ns.adobe.com/flex/mx">
  <s:Group>
    <s:layout>
      <s:HorizontalLayout/>
    </s:layout>
    <s:TextInput id="myTextInput1"/>
    <s:TextInput id="myTextInput2" text="{myTextInput1.text}"/>
  </s:Group>
</s:Application>
```

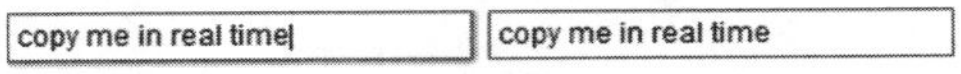

This would give you the dynamic implementation demonstrated in figure 3.6.

As you type in the text box, the characters appear in real time to the right of the input box because you've instructed the

Figure 3.6 Values are captured in real time using binding.

Text property on `myTextInput2` to listen to the `text` property of `TextInput`. But check this out: You can do it in both directions as well, so whichever one you're updating, it automatically propagates to the other. This is done with the following tweak to listing 3.12:

```
<s:TextInput id="myTextInput1" text="{myTextInput2.text}"/>
<s:TextInput id="myTextInput2" text="{myTextInput1.text}"/>
```

You can put any kind of expression within those curly braces, so you can do conditional expressions, calculations, and the like. As a quick example, this would use binding to join two `TextInput` values together:

```
<s:TextInput id="myTextInput1"/>
<s:TextInput id="myTextInput2"/>
<s:TextInput id="myTextInput3" text="{myTextInput1.text +
             myTextInput2.text}"/>
```

This approach works well if you know ahead of time what explicitly needs to be bound, but as your code gets more complex, you might want to manage your inter-element connections as separate elements within your MXML files. Fortunately, there's an easy way to do that through the use of the binding tag.

3.8.3 The binding tag

Another option to get binding happening is to externally wire up components using the `<fx:Binding>` tag, as the following snippet demonstrates:

```
<fx:Binding source="myTextInput1.text"
            destination="myTextInput2.text"
            twoWay="true"/>
<s:TextInput id="myTextInput1"/>
<s:TextInput id="myTextInput2"/>
```

These TextInputs will update each other in real time as the user makes changes, but the TextInputs themselves weren't explicitly instructed to do so. Note that the two-way binding was made possible by setting the twoWay property to true; otherwise it'll default to one way (from source to destination).

> **TIP**   To give you insight as to what's going on behind the scenes, Flex makes heavy use of the concept of events (see chapter 10). Events can be subscribed to by a listener, and the listener will be notified of these events as they're dispatched.

There's one last trick up our sleeves when it comes to binding, and that's the ability to enable binding on any ActionScript variable.

3.8.4   *Making ActionScript variables bindable*

All this is fine and dandy if you want to work with only these tags/components, but you're sure to create many ActionScript variables in your adventures with Flex, and as you may have guessed, there's a way to add binding to those as well.

To add binding to an ActionScript variable, we make use of a meta keyword called [Bindable].

> **TIP**   Meta keywords in MXML such as [Bindable] are used to describe additional properties of variables, components, and classes. Another popular use is to declare custom events a custom component will dispatch (covered in chapter 17).

By default, Flex doesn't assume everything is bindable—you need to explicitly instruct it as to what is bindable. Listing 3.13 explicitly authorizes Strings to be bindable.

Listing 3.13   Making your own bindable variable

```
<?xml version="1.0" encoding="utf-8"?>
<s:Application xmlns:fx="http://ns.adobe.com/mxml/2009"
               xmlns:s="library://ns.adobe.com/flex/spark"
               xmlns:mx="library://ns.adobe.com/flex/mx">
  <s:layout>
    <s:HorizontalLayout/>
  </s:layout>

  <fx:Script>
    <![CDATA[
      [Bindable]
      public var s:String="";
    ]]>
  </fx:Script>
```

```
    <s:TextInput id="myTextInput1"/>
    <s:Button label="Update my variable" click="s=myTextInput1.text"/>
    <s:TextInput id="myText" text="{s}"/>
</s:Application>
```

When you type data into TextInput and click the Update My Variable button, the value will be copied to the String variable. The Text component then displays the value of that String automatically. You might end up with something like figure 3.7.

Figure 3.7   Text is copied to a bindable variable, which is then displayed.

In a real-world application you'd have numerous components that use binding to listen to a variety of variables you configure and manage throughout the life of your application. The components react as the data changes but aren't concerned with the source of that data and information. A common scenario for this is retrieving data from some external source and storing the results locally in bound variables; visual components listening to those variables would display the information.

3.9   Summary

That was a lot of material to cover, and you should give yourself a pat on the back for powering through it. A lot of it is reference in nature, and you don't need to memorize it.

Construct-wise, many of the concepts are the same in ActionScript as they are in any other language, particularly when it comes to evaluating data, looping over information, and working with arrays.

Syntax-wise, ActionScript may vary considerably depending on what other languages you're accustomed to, but it should look familiar enough because ActionScript follows the ECMAScript standard, as does JavaScript (except ActionScript follows the most recent version).

One neat feature of Flex is data binding, which makes it easy to assign one variable to another and have those values automatically stay synchronized. This comes in handy because you don't need to write all the code necessary to copy values throughout your application.

Now that we've covered ActionScript, we can move forward into the features of Flex. In the next chapter you'll learn how to use the layout feature.

Layout and containers

This chapter covers

- Absolute and automatic layout
- Constraint-based layout
- Variable and fixed sizing
- Containers
- Dynamic layout with `Repeaters`

Now that you've been introduced to ActionScript and can manipulate visual effects, let the fun continue! In this chapter we talk about the visual building blocks and the types of containers you can use to quickly create layouts in a Flex application.

Containers are the foundation on which all your visual components rely. They make it easy for you to group and position collections of visual components. Layout is hosted within these containers but is limited to a specific set of components within a given container. Often referred to as child objects of the host container, these components can be anything from buttons, tables, and graphics to even other containers.

It might make it easier to think of a container as a box. You can place items (including other boxes) within the box and define where they're to be placed, with positioning specific to each item.

4.1 Spark versus Halo (MX)

Nope, we're not comparing video games, but we do need to call out an important aspect of developing in Flex 4. Halo components (also known as MX components) are the components (buttons, text fields, containers, and so on) that Flex 3 used exclusively, whereas with Flex 4 a new generation of such components called Spark components was introduced.

Flex 4 supports both at the same time, which has the benefit of allowing you to more easily migrate a Flex 3 application to a Flex 4 one. But from the onset it can be confusing because many, but not all, Halo/MX components have newer Spark equivalents.

It can be especially confusing because Spark components follow a different set of rules than Halo/MX components do when it comes to layout, positioning, and sizing. The key difference with Spark layout and related containers is that Spark containers allow you to change the layout algorithm, whereas Halo/MX components have their layout algorithm built in. So with Halo/MX you'd have to change the type of container being used if you wanted a different layout approach.

NOTE We'll focus primarily on Spark components going forward, because Halo/MX is likely to be phased out, and Spark affords the greatest flexibility. Not all Halo/MX containers have a Spark equivalent, unfortunately, so we'll cover those as well.

Layout is handled by way of the layout manager, which uses three stages to figure out the position and size of each visual component:

- *Commitment pass*—Looks at the property settings of all the components (for example, height and width properties). During this stage, each component has its commitProperties() method executed, which provides the layout manager the component's position/size-related properties. This pass is about finding out what each component is requesting its position and size to be.
- *Measurement pass*—Evaluates the default size of all components. It starts by looking at the deepest component (from a nesting perspective) and works its way out. This pass is about calculating the default or explicit size (when specified) of each component. Some of the variables that go into this calculation include summing the width of all inner child objects, thickness of borders, padding, and gaps between children. The layout manager asks each object to run its measure-Sizes() method to determine the default/explicit size.
- *Layout pass*—Now that the layout manager has gathered all the information from the previous passes, it lays out all the components by setting the position and size of each component. Unlike the measurement pass, it starts outward and works its way in to the deeply nested components. This pass calls each component's updateDisplayList() method in order for the component to refresh its display.

Each Spark container supports changing its layout approach to one of the following:

- *BasicLayout*—Also known as absolute layout, where you use x and y coordinates.
- *HorizontalLayout*—Components are positioned one after another horizontally in a single row.
- *VerticalLayout*—Components are positioned one after another vertically in a single column.
- *TileLayout*—Displays components in a grid-like form, creating as many rows and columns as necessary.

Sound a little daunting? The good news is that all components, both Spark and Halo/MX, have default behavior that allows Flex to do a fairly good job of positioning components automatically. So let's jump into it by starting with absolute layout.

4.2   Absolute layout

Absolute layout is a composition mode in which you control the exact position and size of elements you place within the container.

Containers implement positioning based on a two-dimensional coordinate grid. The top-left corner of any container represents the home coordinates of 0,0. Any item placed in the container is positioned in the grid relative to this point.

> **TIP**   In the Flex realm, the x coordinate starts on the left and the y at the top. As you increase the positive value of these properties, you move down and to the right.

One of the benefits of using absolute layout in a container is that it gives you fine-grained control of how objects are located and sized. Another benefit is that Flex (technically Flash Player) doesn't need to burn processing power calculating how items should look because you specify exactly where you want your controls to be. The cool thing is that you can mix and match by having one container use absolute layout, while others use automatic.

Let's get started by looking at a container with which you're already familiar—the `Application` container, which by default uses an absolute layout as shown in the following listing.

Listing 4.1   In absolute layout, the container doesn't waste effort arranging its children.

```
<?xml version="1.0" encoding="utf-8"?>
<s:Application xmlns:fx="http://ns.adobe.com/mxml/2009"
               xmlns:s="library://ns.adobe.com/flex/spark"          Prefix Spark
                                                                     components
               xmlns:mx="library://ns.adobe.com/flex/mx">
  <s:layout>                                                         Prefix Halo/MX
    <s:BasicLayout/>                           ❶ This is optional    components
  </s:layout>
  <s:Button label="Button 1"/>
  <s:Button label="This is Button 2"/>                Reference the
</s:Application>                                       Spark button
```

As we mentioned, the `Application` container by default uses an absolute layout, and to be more specific it uses the `BasicLayout` class. In the code we specified this `Basic-Layout` class ❶ because we wanted absolute positioning, but because it's the default for the `Application` container, we could have just as easily omitted those lines.

Run the application and look at the results, as shown in figure 4.1. Because we didn't explicitly specify coordinates, each button defaults to positioning itself at the top-left corner of the container (coordinates 0,0), resulting in the buttons overlapping one another.

Figure 4.1 The result of omitting coordinates when laying out items in absolute layout. These buttons overlap.

By explicitly providing values to the `Button`'s x and y properties, this situation is easily resolved. As shown in figure 4.2, adjusting the x property on Button 2 shifts that button to the right. The following snippet shows how to make the adjustment:

```
<s:Button label="This is Button 2" x="78" y="0"/>
```

As figure 4.2 demonstrates, specifically defining the coordinate fixes the problem nicely.

If you're coming from many years in the HTML world, you'll want to train yourself to be

Figure 4.2 Overlapping is fixed in absolute layout by explicitly defining a position.

aware of the more creative things you can do in Flex. For instance, in HTML if you caused an overlap such as you saw in figure 4.1, it would generally be considered a bug. The majority of web developers use HTML tables to lay out pages, which prevents overlapping from occurring. In Flex you can use overlap to your advantage.

It's up to your imagination; there's nothing to say that overlapping is bad, and you may well want to use the effect as part of your design. For example, as figure 4.3 demonstrates, you could have folder icons positioned slightly offset over each other to represent a folder structure or depth.

Figure 4.3 Programmatically, you can use absolute layout in innovative ways.

Another cool aspect of absolute positioning is that the x and y properties can also take negative values. This allows you to move an item out of the visual range, or screen of the container, hiding it until you're ready to display it. Let's try out this effect in the next listing.

> **Listing 4.2 Using a negative value in the x property to hide a component offscreen**

```
<s:Button id="button1"
        label="Show the other button"
        x="120" y="50"
        click="button2.x=155;"/>
<s:Button id="button2"
        label="Hello!"
        x="-100" y="80"/>
```

◁┐ **ActionScript updates x property**

Figure 4.4   The second button is always there. It's out of view until a change in its horizontal coordinate brings it in view.

Figure 4.4 shows how the button labeled Hello!—originally positioned out of view—appears after clicking Show the other Button. By manipulating these positioning properties, you can make UIs interactive.

> **TIP** The id attribute allows you to uniquely name an instance of a component (much the same as with HTML and JavaScript), which you can later use to access and manipulate the component's properties and functions. There's no industry-adopted naming convention, but many use prefixes that indicate the type of component, for example, "btnHello" to indicate a button. A common convention is to use something known as camel case, which uses lower-case letters in general and uppercase on the first letter of a new word (for example, myCoolVariable).

Absolute layout makes many assumptions regarding positioning. Some of these assumptions may or may not fit your requirements. For example, you assume the positions that you explicitly set sufficiently provide enough space for each component.

Alternatively, you can use the constraint approach, which determines positioning relative to certain anchor points.

4.3   Constraint-based layout

If supplying exact coordinates is impractical for your application, you can use a variation on absolute layout known as constraint-based layout. Instead of specifying x and y coordinates to position components relative to the container's top-left corner, constraint-based layout has you position items relative to the edges of the container or its center.

The advantage of this method is that you can configure components to maintain a relative position within the container, even if the user resizes the window.

To achieve the same results using fixed coordinates would require a considerable amount of coding in ActionScript to perform the calculations and update the component's x and y values in response to any changes in window size.

4.3.1   Basic constraints

Using the constraint-based approach, you need only tell Flex that you want your button to maintain a position 5 pixels from the bottom right of the window, and Flex handles all the behind-the-scenes work to hold that position for you.

- The top, bottom, left, and right properties of a component allow you to control the distance from the related edge.
- The horizontalCenter and verticalCenter properties control the distance from the center in their respective orientation.
- The baseline property lets you set the distance between the top edge of the component and its parent container.

Let's apply some of these properties with listing 4.3, which illustrates how to anchor a button to the bottom-right corner of the page. Figure 4.5 shows the result.

> **Listing 4.3 Positioning a button 5 pixels from the bottom-right corner of a window**

```xml
<?xml version="1.0" encoding="utf-8"?>
<s:Application xmlns:fx="http://ns.adobe.com/mxml/2009"
               xmlns:s="library://ns.adobe.com/flex/spark"
               xmlns:mx="library://ns.adobe.com/flex/mx">
  <s:layout>
    <s:BasicLayout/>
  </s:layout>
  <s:Button label="Hello!" bottom="5" right="5"/>
</s:Application>
```

Figure 4.5 Using constraint-based layout, this button is positioned relative to the bottom-right corner of the page.

As you can see in figure 4.5, regardless of window size or shape, the button maintains its position relative to the bottom-right corner of the page. If this weren't convenient enough, Flash Builder includes a feature that allows you to easily set constraints on components (figure 4.6).

1 In Flash Builder, click the Design View button to switch into Flash Builder's visual mode.

2 Click your `Button` component.

3 In the Properties window, scroll down to the Layout section.

4 Notice the check boxes along the top and left sides of the Layout window. You should see check marks in the farthest right and bottom check boxes.

5 Click the check boxes at random to see the effect each has on your button's position within the window.

For example, if you want your button to appear in the center of the page, you should click the center check boxes.

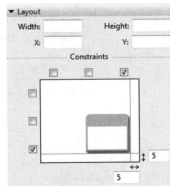

Figure 4.6 Design view in Flex Builder allows you to control constraints interactively.

TIP   Because Flash has its ancestry in an animation tool, the term *stage* is often used instead of *page*. Flex developers come in two varieties: traditional programmers and Flash developers and designers. You'll notice in discussion forums and blog postings that the folks who come from the Flash world tend to use the term *stage*. When you hear the phrase "centered on stage," it means an item is centered in a container or page.

When you want to fix the exact position of a component within a container—no matter the browser dimensions—use absolute layout. When you want a component to be able to move relative to a window's changing dimensions but stay within a specified distance of a browser's edge (or center), use constraint-based layout to handle this automatically.

If you find you prefer constraints but need more precise control, enhanced constraints can offer you extended flexibility.

4.3.2   *Enhanced constraints*

Enhanced constraints take the concept of constraints one step further by allowing you to arbitrarily create hidden horizontal and vertical guidelines against which you can position components. These guidelines are known respectively as constraint rows and constraint columns.

Guidelines expand your positioning options beyond the limits of the basic constraint-based layout, with which you can only designate the edges or center of the container as anchor points.

Constraint rows and constraint columns can be positioned within the container by three methods:

- *Fixed*—The position is determined by an absolute number (in pixels).
- *Relative*—The position is determined by a percentage, relative to the size of the container.
- *Content-sized*—Similar to relative constraint, with the exception that the position is based on the content (scaling up and down to accommodate the content). You'll see an example shortly, but this means the constraint column or row will be the size of its largest item.

Two tags are used to implement constraint guides, <mx:ConstraintColumn> and <mx: ConstraintRow>. Checking out the API Language Reference (see figure 4.7 for a snippet), you can see there are various properties for controlling the width and height, along with the minimum size the instance can be.

Enhanced constraint properties can be a little confusing at first. Instead of explaining

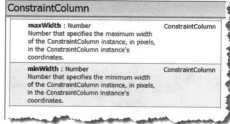

Figure 4.7   Using the API Language Reference, you see a number of properties for controlling the dimension and positioning of constraints.

all the rules and describing how Flex applies these properties, we'll first work through a couple of examples to help you understand them more clearly.

> **TIP** Because you're assuming layout control with constraints, they're almost exclusively used with the Halo/MX–based `Canvas` container. No Spark containers support enhanced constraints, although Spark components will work as expected with constraint columns and rows when placed within an MX container that uses such constraints.

The easiest way to remember how enhanced constraints work is to view them as a mechanism for splitting the container into sections. Let's look at examples of how you can do this.

TWO-COLUMN FIXED SLICE

Let's start by slicing a container into two sections. You'll use the `<mx:Constraint-Column>` tag to create two columns, as shown in the following listing.

Listing 4.4 Using two constraint columns to align a pair of buttons

```
<?xml version="1.0" encoding="utf-8"?>
<s:Application xmlns:fx="http://ns.adobe.com/mxml/2009"
               xmlns:s="library://ns.adobe.com/flex/spark"
               xmlns:mx="library://ns.adobe.com/flex/mx">
  <mx:Canvas width="100%" height="100%">
    <mx:constraintColumns>
      <mx:ConstraintColumn id="col1" width="200"/>
      <mx:ConstraintColumn id="col2" width="50" />
    </mx:constraintColumns>
    <s:Button label="Button 1" left="col1:0"/>
    <s:Button label="Button 2" left="col2:0"/>
  </mx:Canvas>
</s:Application>
```

Listing 4.4 produces two buttons: Button 1 is 200 pixels from the first constraint column; Button 2 is 50 pixels farther right than Button 1 (figure 4.8).

Here are a couple of items to note:

- You're telling each button's `left` constraint property to base itself on the `ConstraintColumn` position.
- The first portion of the syntax, `col1:0`, specifies the `ConstraintColumn` identified as `col1` as the `ConstraintColumn` you want to use, and the second portion instructs the button to offset 0 pixels in from that `ConstraintColumn`—meaning no offset.

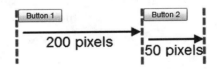

This example is fairly straightforward and is similar to creating a guide in a graphical tool to which you can align objects.

Figure 4.8 These buttons are aligned against named constraints.

TWO-COLUMN FIXED SLICE WITH BOTH LEFT AND RIGHT CONSTRAINTS

Next, you're going to make the width of a button scale to the width of the column in which it's placed. You accomplish this by specifying the `right` property constraint, while still using the original `ConstraintColumn`:

```
<mx:Button label="Button 1" left="col1:0" right="col1:0"/>
<mx:Button label="Button 2" left="col2:0" right="col2:0"/>
```

As figure 4.9 shows, the `left` property is set so the button lines up against the left side of the `ConstraintColumn`. Likewise, the button's right side lines up against the right side of the `ConstraintColumn`.

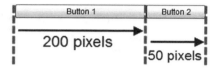

That wasn't too much of a stretch from the previous example (bad joke). Let's make things more interesting by adding rows.

Figure 4.9   These buttons are both configured to stretch their left and right edges to the constraints.

TWO-ROW MIXED SLICE WITH BOTH TOP AND BOTTOM CONSTRAINTS

You can construct your page vertically in a similar manner using a row-based approach. In listing 4.5, you position a pair of buttons, one above the other, using both a relative and a fixed `ConstraintRow`.

Listing 4.5   Create a relative- and a fixed-size constraint row

```
<?xml version="1.0" encoding="utf-8"?>
<s:Application xmlns:fx="http://ns.adobe.com/mxml/2009"
               xmlns:s="library://ns.adobe.com/flex/spark"
               xmlns:mx="library://ns.adobe.com/flex/mx">
  <mx:Canvas width="100%" height="100%">
    <mx:constraintRows>
      <mx:ConstraintRow id="row1" height="50%"/>       ◁── A relative size
      <mx:ConstraintRow id="row2" height="100"/>       ◁── A fixed size
    </mx:constraintRows>
    <s:Button label="Button 1" top="row1:0" bottom="row1:0"/>
    <s:Button label="Button 2" top="row2:0" bottom="row2:0"/>
  </mx:Canvas>
</s:Application>
```

This method affords you the ability to mix and match absolute and relative sizing approaches. Figure 4.10 illustrates the result of using the two together and highlights the following:

- Button 1 scales to 50% of the canvas height as the user resizes the browser.
- Button 2 always remains 100 pixels in height and begins vertically wherever Button 1 ends.

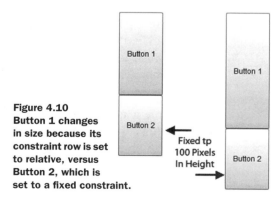

Figure 4.10 Button 1 changes in size because its constraint row is set to relative, versus Button 2, which is set to a fixed constraint.

To this point, we've presented separate column and row examples; now let's combine them in a new exercise.

TWO ROWS PLUS TWO COLUMNS WITH OFFSETS

If your application requires it, you can combine constraint rows and constraint columns. In listing 4.6, you do just that, but in addition, you make use of the offset parameter to see how it functions.

Listing 4.6   Create both constraint columns and rows.

```xml
<?xml version="1.0" encoding="utf-8"?>
<s:Application xmlns:fx="http://ns.adobe.com/mxml/2009"
               xmlns:s="library://ns.adobe.com/flex/spark"
               xmlns:mx="library://ns.adobe.com/flex/mx">
  <mx:Canvas width="100%" height="100%">
    <mx:constraintColumns>
      <mx:ConstraintColumn id="col1" width="100"/>
    </mx:constraintColumns>
    <mx:constraintRows>
      <mx:ConstraintRow id="row1" height="50"/>
      <mx:ConstraintRow id="row2" height="50"/>
    </mx:constraintRows>

    <s:Button label="Button 1" left="col1:0" right="col1:0"
                               top="row1:0" bottom="row1:0"/>
    <s:Button label="Button 2" left="col1:10" right="col1:10"
                               top="row2:0" bottom="row2:0"/>
  </mx:Canvas>
</s:Application>
```

Figure 4.11 displays how your buttons will appear when you run listing 4.6. By now, you've noticed you have a lot of creative freedom to mix and match these constraints to generate and control a variety of visual effects.

Looking at figure 4.11, you can see that we specified a value in the offset parameter for Button 2 that results in the button being squeezed 10 pixels from the right and left sides of the column.

Figure 4.11   These buttons are positioned using both column and row constraints.

Realistically, this is about as complicated a use of constraints as you're likely to see, although you can continue to design even more creative implementations if you like. The last approach we look at is content-sized constraints.

USING CONTENT-SIZED CONSTRAINTS

Content-sized constraints are enabled automatically by not supplying values to a constraint's `height` and `width` properties. Flex scales all items to the column width or row height, which themselves are based on the largest item in your container. Listing 4.7 shows how this is done.

Listing 4.7   Using content-sized constraints

```
<?xml version="1.0" encoding="utf-8"?>
<s:Application xmlns:fx="http://ns.adobe.com/mxml/2009"
               xmlns:s="library://ns.adobe.com/flex/spark"
               xmlns:mx="library://ns.adobe.com/flex/mx">
  <mx:Canvas width="100%" height="100%">
    <mx:constraintColumns>
      <mx:ConstraintColumn id="col1"/>
      <mx:ConstraintColumn id="col2"/>
    </mx:constraintColumns>
    <mx:constraintRows>
      <mx:ConstraintRow id="row1" height="50"/>
      <mx:ConstraintRow id="row2" height="30"/>
    </mx:constraintRows>
    <s:Button label="Button 1" left="col1:0" top="row1:0" width="200"  />
    <s:Button label="Button 2" left="col1:0" top="row2:0"/>
    <s:Button label="Button 3" left="col2:0"/>
  </mx:Canvas>
</s:Application>
```

This produces results similar to the HTML table trick of setting the column width to zero, which causes the column to shrink to the minimum size needed to accommodate an image. The difference is, with Flex it isn't a hack; you're in complete control, as figure 4.12 illustrates.

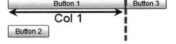

Buttons 1 and 2 use the same `ConstraintColumn`, but because Button 1 is the largest component in the container, the `ConstraintColumn` defaults to its width.

Figure 4.12   In a content-sized constraint, the column stretches to the size of the largest component within it.

YOU GET THE IDEA

The best thing you can do is experiment on your own. With so many constraint combinations available, it would take a separate chapter to cover them all. Give random combinations a try and see where they lead. There's yet one more feature to point out: You can manipulate constraint properties using ActionScript. For instance, you can change the size of your elements based on user interactions or a specific chain of events. (In chapter 14 we'll talk about how to use view states to achieve this efficiently.)

As powerful as constraints are, more work on your part is required to ensure your application has the look you want. If you don't particularly care about exact positioning, you always have the option of automatic layout.

4.4   *Automatic layout*

Automatic layout is a considerable departure from absolute layout, in which you explicitly determine the location and layout of elements within a container. With automatic layout, you're directing the container to position elements for you.

4.4.1 Using the layout classes

In section 4.1 we mentioned that there are four layout classes available to Spark containers, one of which we used for absolute layout (the BasicLayout class), and the remaining three (HorizontalLayout, VerticalLayout, and TileLayout) provide us with the automatic layout options.

Let's give it a shot in listing 4.8 by applying the HorizontalLayout class to the Application container.

Listing 4.8 Automatic horizontal layout used to place two buttons side by side

```
<?xml version="1.0" encoding="utf-8"?>
<s:Application xmlns:fx="http://ns.adobe.com/mxml/2009"
               xmlns:s="library://ns.adobe.com/flex/spark"
               xmlns:mx="library://ns.adobe.com/flex/mx">
  <s:layout>
    <s:HorizontalLayout/>            ⟵———  Layout class
  </s:layout>
  <s:Button label="Button 1"/>
  <s:Button label="Button 2"/>
</s:Application>
```

As expected, you can see in figure 4.13 that the buttons are side by side. As you'd expect, if you were to modify the code to use the VerticalLayout class instead, the buttons would be on top of each other.

Figure 4.13 Using the HorizontalLayout class positions the buttons automatically side by side.

This is obviously much easier than manually positioning components. But let's look at the TileLayout class, which arranges items in a grid-like fashion. Although each cell is equal in size, the TileLayout class provides a number of properties for controlling the dimension of the cells, the gap between them, count, orientation, and so on.

> **TIP** If you wanted to increase or decrease the space between the buttons in figure 4.13, you'd set the HorizontalLayout's gap property.

By default, the TileLayout class will lay out each item from left to right, row by row. So what if you want to have it go from top to bottom first and then go column by column? This is where the API Reference can help you find out your options.

1 If you had TileLayout in your code as such

```
<s:layout>
  <s:TileLayout/>
</s:layout>
```

you could then click Shift+F2 to pull up the API Reference on that component.

2 Under the Properties section, you'd see something called Orientation, which mentions that it controls the arrangement of elements.

3 Clicking that property then tells you that you can pass in "rows" or "columns" as values.

Cool—let's try it out. To make it a little more interesting, follow the same process to find a property called `requestedRowCount` that can advise the `TileLayout` class that you'd like a certain number of rows if possible. Listing 4.9 shows the result of what you're going to do.

Listing 4.9   Using the `TileLayout` class to form a grid of items

```
<?xml version="1.0" encoding="utf-8"?>
<s:Application xmlns:fx="http://ns.adobe.com/mxml/2009"
               xmlns:s="library://ns.adobe.com/flex/spark"
               xmlns:mx="library://ns.adobe.com/flex/mx">
  <s:layout>
    <s:TileLayout orientation="columns"            Top to
                  requestedRowCount="2" />         bottom

  </s:layout>                                       Two rows
  <s:Button label="One"/>                          please
  <s:Button label="Two"/>
  <s:Button label="Three"/>
    </s:Application>
```

The output from this experiment is shown in figure 4.14.

Nice! So here's a question for you: What do you think the output would look like if you changed the orientation to rows? It would almost look the same, except the first row would show buttons One and Two, and Three would start on the second line.

Figure 4.14   The `TileLayout` class used to arrange buttons in a grid

4.4.2   *Getting spaced out*

The `<mx:Spacer/>` component is another tool in your layout tool chest. The `mx` prefix on the tag does indicate it's a Halo/MX component, but you can mix it with both Spark and Halo/MX components and containers.

You can liken `Spacer` to an empty HTML column (`<td width="100%"></td>`) or the HTML `spacer.gif` trick, which was used for some time to distribute elements evenly. Using the API Language Reference, you see that the `Spacer` supports `width`, `height`, and minimum and maximum versions of those properties. These properties can contain a number (of pixels) or a percentage.

Let's use it to space three buttons, as shown in figure 4.15.

In listing 4.10, you instruct `Spacer` to use a 50% gap between the buttons, though it's not literally using 50% of the total visual space but rather evenly pushing the buttons apart as far as they can go (or contracting in size if they need to make space for the visual components).

Figure 4.15   The `Spacer` component can help you space components.

Listing 4.10   Use a `Spacer` to push two buttons apart

```
<?xml version="1.0" encoding="utf-8"?>
<s:Application xmlns:fx="http://ns.adobe.com/mxml/2009"
```

```
                  xmlns:s="library://ns.adobe.com/flex/spark"
                  xmlns:mx="library://ns.adobe.com/flex/mx">
  <s:layout>
    <s:HorizontalLayout/>
  </s:layout>
  <s:Button label="One"/>
  <mx:Spacer width="50%"/>
  <s:Button label="Two"/>
  <mx:Spacer width="50%"/>
  <s:Button label="Three"/>
</s:Application>
```

Whether you use automatic or absolute layout for your project, components themselves are capable of controlling their own size.

4.5 *Variable and fixed sizing*

Similar to HTML, but far beyond what HTML supports, all Flex visual components support variable and fixed sizing.

This is made possible by the width and height properties, which accept not only fixed values to define the element size in absolute numbers (in pixels) but also percentages that scale your item relative to the size of its host container.

4.5.1 *Variable sizing*

To demonstrate variable sizing, let's again use our workhorse Button component. If you want a button to scale proportionally to be 80% of the width of its parent container (the Application container), you can use the following code:

```
<s:Button label="My Button" width="80%"/>
```

This results in a button that spans 80% of the browser window's width, as shown in figure 4.16.

You can apply this technique to the vertical axis as well or both height and width properties at the same time. You can even mix in some constraints by centering it on the page by setting horizontalCenter="0" and verticalCenter="0".

That takes care of variable sizing. Now let's look at its counterpart—fixed sizing.

Figure 4.16 This button scales to 80% of the page based on the width setting.

4.5.2 *Fixed sizing*

Fixed sizing isn't much of a departure from variable sizing. You use the same parameters, except instead of specifying percentages, you use whole numbers to specify the dimensions of your component (in pixels).

To make your button 120 pixels wide and 80 pixels high, you'd use

```
<s:Button label="Hello!" width="120" height="80"/>
```

There's not much more to say about fixed sizing; it's extremely simple! Now that you can control the size and positioning of components and are familiar with the principles behind automatic layout, we'll explore the containers that utilize these features.

4.6   *Containers*

Containers are collections of components whose mission is to provide visual structure to your application. Their purpose is universal—to help you lay out your components visually rather than programmatically.

What changed significantly from Flex 3's Halo/MX containers to Flex 4's Spark containers is that with Halo/MX containers, the containers themselves provided different types of layout. For example Halo/MX has an `<mx:HBox/>` container that lays out items horizontally.

But with Spark, the responsibility for layout has moved to layout classes, as discussed in section 4.4. This allows any Spark container to use any of these layout classes. So with a Spark container it's less about layout and more about grouping items together. A loose (and I mean loose!) analogy would be that a Spark container is like an HTML `<div/>` tag, and the layout classes are like CSS being used to control the position of the `div` tags.

New to Flex 4, the following Spark containers are available to you:

- `Application`–Only one per application, it's the root container for your application.
- `Group`—A rudimentary container for grouping items together, by default it uses the `BasicLayout` class for absolute positioning. Its child `HGroup` and `VGroup` containers provide a shortcut for providing horizontal- and vertical-based layouts, respectively.
- `SkinnableContainer`—Similar to `Group`, but it supports the ability to be skinned (total control over the look).
- `Panel`—Based on the `SkinnableContainer`, it adds a title bar and frame.
- `DataGroup`—It's meant to group data (for example, arrays) that can be then rendered using something called an item renderer, which allows for customized display.
- `SkinnableDataContainer`—Similar to `DataGroup`, but it's a skinnable version.

Switching from nonskinnable to skinnable and vice versa is fairly painless because the main task is to rename the components you're using. The skinnable containers are heavier and carry the additional overhead needed to support skins, so if you don't plan on skinning, you should stick to the nonskinnable.

There are also a few Halo/MX containers that have no Spark equivalents, so we'll look at those as well.

4.6.1   *Application container*

You're familiar with the `Application` container, because you've been using it all along (`<s:Application/>`). It's special in the sense that all Flex applications require it to be the master starting container, and it replaces the Halo/MX `<mx:Application/>` container.

Another unique characteristic of this root container is the `preloader` property, which is the progress bar you see when launching a Flex application. By default it's turned on, but you can turn it off by setting its value to `false`.

Because this is the top-level object of your application, you can use it to house global variables and functions, allowing you to access them from anywhere within your application.

We'll take up the subject of custom components in detail in chapter 17, but briefly, custom components are a means to modularize your code. Listing 4.11 demonstrates how to invoke a custom component.

Listing 4.11 Invoking a custom component

```
<?xml version="1.0" encoding="utf-8"?>
<s:Application xmlns:fx="http://ns.adobe.com/mxml/2009"
               xmlns:s="library://ns.adobe.com/flex/spark"
               xmlns:mx="library://ns.adobe.com/flex/mx"
               xmlns:local="*">              ◁─┐ Define the
  <fx:Script>                                 ❶ local name space
    <![CDATA[
      [Bindable]
      public var myString:String = "hello";   ◁──── The message
    ]]>
  </fx:Script>                       ┐ Loads
  <local:CustomComponent/>          ◁┘ CustomComponent.mxml
</s:Application>
```

You have a publicly accessible variable (meaning anyone or anything can access it) in your main application file that carries a message. Let's use a custom component in a file we'll call CustomComponent.mxml located in the same directory as your main application file.

You may have noticed that your `Application` tag ❶ defines something called `local` with a wildcard for a path; this tells Flex that any component prefixed with `local` can be found in the root directory of the application.

With your custom component in place, and the Application container able to find it, your custom component will access the application's variables, as shown in this next listing.

Listing 4.12 CustomComponent.mxml—accessing the application's variables

```
<?xml version="1.0" encoding="utf-8"?>
<s:Group xmlns:fx="http://ns.adobe.com/mxml/2009"
         xmlns:s="library://ns.adobe.com/flex/spark"
         xmlns:mx="library://ns.adobe.com/flex/mx">
  <fx:Script>
    <![CDATA[
      import mx.core.FlexGlobals;
    ]]>
```

```
    </fx:Script>
    <s:Button label="{FlexGlobals.topLevelApplication.myString}"/>
</s:Group>
```

After running the application, you should end up with a button that says "hello." You can have many types of containers in your application and across all your files, but you'll have only one <s:Application/> container.

4.6.2 Canvas container

Canvas containers are the most basic type of container, but they're lightweight and not very robust. They're a Halo/MX-based component, and because of that you'd want to opt for the newer Spark-based containers (for example, group using the BasicLayout class).

The only reason you'd want to use the Canvas container would be if you wanted to use enhanced constraints, as described in section 4.3.2. Because you used it extensively earlier, we'll move on to the remaining Spark containers.

4.6.3 Group-based containers and SkinnableContainer

The Group container is a simple container that you pair with one of the layout classes. You used those layout classes in section 4.4.1 with the Application container, but you can just as easily use those with your Group container, as listing 4.13 demonstrates.

Let's step it up a notch by using two Group containers that lay out their items horizontally, while their parent Application container uses a vertical layout.

Listing 4.13 Using multiple containers for more complex layouts

```xml
<?xml version="1.0" encoding="utf-8"?>
<s:Application xmlns:fx="http://ns.adobe.com/mxml/2009"
               xmlns:s="library://ns.adobe.com/flex/spark"
               xmlns:mx="library://ns.adobe.com/flex/mx" >
  <s:layout>
    <s:VerticalLayout/>
  </s:layout>
  <s:Group>
    <s:layout>
      <s:HorizontalLayout/>
    </s:layout>
    <s:Button label="Button 1"/>
    <s:Button label="Button 2"/>
  </s:Group>
  <s:Group>
    <s:layout>
      <s:HorizontalLayout/>
    </s:layout>
    <s:Button label="Button 3"/>
    <s:Button label="Button 4"/>
  </s:Group>
</s:Application>
```

You can nest as well as mix and match containers and layout classes in any combination you'd like to achieve a desired layout. In this case, you end up with two rows of buttons, as shown in figure 4.17.

Figure 4.17 Two `Group` containers using horizontal layout coupled with an `Application` container using vertical layout

Alternatively, instead of specifying the layout class along with the `<s:Group/>` container, you could use the Group's child container `<s:HGroup/>` for horizontal layout or `<s:VGroup/>` for vertical layout. They provide you the convenience of not having to type out as much code.

The `SkinnableContainer` works the exact same way, and you could replace the Group container in listing 4.13 with the `SkinnableContainer`, and it would work and have the exact same result. The difference is that the `SkinnableContainer` allows you to apply a collection of look-and-feel information to it in the form of a skin.

We have an entire chapter dedicated to skins and themes, but to give you an idea of how this works, you create a separate skin file and then tell the `Skinnable-Container` to use it. There are two basic rules for a skin file:

- You have to provide support for all the states a component can be in. In this case, the `SkinnableContainer` can be in either a normal or disabled state. You can find this out by looking at the API Reference for the component you want to support (the `SkinnableContainer`), and by scrolling down to the skin states section you can see that it inherits the disabled and normal states.

- You have to define an additional container within the skin named `content-Group`. Everything will go inside this container (even though in this case you're creating a skin for another container).

Let's check it out by first creating a skin class called CoolSkin.mxml as shown in the following listing.

Listing 4.14 CoolSkin.mxml—a file that defines a skin class

```xml
<?xml version="1.0" encoding="utf-8"?>
<s:SparkSkin xmlns:fx="http://ns.adobe.com/mxml/2009"
    xmlns:mx="library://ns.adobe.com/flex/mx"
    xmlns:s="library://ns.adobe.com/flex/spark">

    <s:states>
        <s:State name="normal" />         Define
        <s:State name="disabled" />       supporting states
    </s:states>

    <s:Rect height="100%" width="100%">   Rectangle used
        <s:fill>                          in background
            <s:LinearGradient>
                <s:entries>
                    <mx:GradientEntry color="#92A1B9"/>
                </s:entries>
            </s:LinearGradient>
```

```
        </s:fill>
    </s:Rect>

    <s:Group id="contentGroup" left="5" top="5" right="5" bottom="5">
        <s:layout>
            <s:BasicLayout/>
        </s:layout>
    </s:Group>
</s:SparkSkin>
```

Content goes in here

Use constraints to add padding

You'll now make use of your skin. Notice in listing 4.15 how the SkinnableContainer specifies the skinClass property, which will load in the skin defined here.

Listing 4.15   A SkinnableContainer making use of a skin

```
<s:SkinnableContainer skinClass="CoolSkin">          ◁——— Skin specified
  <s:layout>
    <s:HorizontalLayout/>
  </s:layout>
  <s:Button label="Button 1"/>
  <s:Button label="Button 2"/>
</s:SkinnableContainer>
```

That was hard work! Okay, maybe not, but what's nice is that skin can be used on any number of components. Check out the id property; see how it's set to contentGroup? This is required because Flex will look for a container named contentGroup in order to know where to put the visual components associated with the skin.

MIGRATION TIP   The Group, HGroup, and VGroup containers replace Flex 3's Box, HBox, and VBox containers, which you can still use, but assume they'll be deprecated in future versions.

Figure 4.18 shows you the fruit of your labor; the container is now skinned with a square background.

Next we'll take a look at the child of a SkinnableContainer, the Panel.

Figure 4.18
SkinnableContainer with a skin class that defines a square background

4.6.4   *Panel container*

Definitely a crowd favorite, the Panel container is often used as a top-level container for the entire application (although you can have panels inside panels). What's neat about this container is it adds a title and status bar to the top of the window and by default draws a border around its child objects.

The Panel container by default uses the BasicLayout class, and because it's a child of the SkinnableContainer, it inherits all of its properties and abilities. In listing 4.16 you'll add an HGroup container inside of a Panel purely so that you can use constraints to add some padding from the Panel's edge; otherwise the buttons go right to the edge and don't look as aesthetically pleasing.

Listing 4.16   An HGroup inside a Panel is an easy way to add a margin from the edge.

```
<?xml version="1.0" encoding="utf-8"?>
<s:Application xmlns:fx="http://ns.adobe.com/mxml/2009"
               xmlns:s="library://ns.adobe.com/flex/spark"
               xmlns:mx="library://ns.adobe.com/flex/mx" >
  <s:Panel title="My Title">
    <s:HGroup top="5" bottom="5" left="5" right="5">      Constraints
      <s:Button label="Button 1"/>                        for padding
      <s:Button label="Button 2"/>
    </s:HGroup>
  </s:Panel>
</s:Application>
```

Figure 4.19 shows what this all looks like once loaded, and you can begin to see how an application takes its visual roots from the Panel container.

In addition to the cool border around it and the title area at the top, Panel containers can also support features such as a ControlBar.

Figure 4.19   A Panel container adds a title bar and border around its content.

4.6.5   *ApplicationControlBar container*

As their name implies, ApplicationControlBar containers add a control bar area to your application. Let's take a look.

The ApplicationControlBar container creates an area at the top of an application that's similar to the File menu of most desktop applications (for things like making edits, setting preferences, and so on). To use this container, you combine it with the Application container, as presented in the following listing.

Listing 4.17   ApplicationControlBar provides easy access to common functionality.

```
<?xml version="1.0" encoding="utf-8"?>
<s:Application xmlns:fx="http://ns.adobe.com/mxml/2009"
               xmlns:s="library://ns.adobe.com/flex/spark"
               xmlns:mx="library://ns.adobe.com/flex/mx" >
  <mx:ApplicationControlBar width="100%">
    <s:Button label="Back"/>
    <s:Button label="Forward"/>
    <s:TextInput width="60"/>
    <s:Button label="Search"/>
  </mx:ApplicationControlBar>
</s:Application>
```

In figure 4.20 you can see how you could use this to provide users with instant access to frequently used features of your application.

You might have noticed that the code uses an mx: prefix on the Application-ControlBar—this means that it's a Halo/MX component, and unfortunately there's no Spark equivalent of this container.

Figure 4.20
The `ApplicationControlBar`
container enables quick access to
frequently used features.

There's also a similar Halo/MX container called the `ControlBar`, which when paired up with a Halo/MX Panel container adds a border to the bottom of the `Panel` for putting things like cancel and save buttons. This container doesn't work properly with the Spark `Panel` container, so it's best to avoid it.

> **MIGRATION TIP**   The Spark-based `Panel` has the properties `controlBar-Content` and `controlBarLayout`, which allow you to achieve a similar effect to the `ControlBar`.

Previously we talked about the `Group` and `SkinnableContainer` containers. A similar set adds more flexibility if needed to customize the display of the data, and they're known as `DataGroup` and `SkinnableDataContainer`.

4.6.6 *DataGroup and SkinnableDataContainer*

On a surface level, these containers are quite similar to their `Group` and `Skinnable-Container` counterparts, but when we dig down deeper we find they add an additional bit of capability that allows them to take data and pair that up with an item renderer in order to display the data visually.

An item renderer is another component like the ones built into Flex (for example, buttons, text fields, or your own custom components) that gets called to utilize data on the fly.

In order to use one of these containers you'll need data, and that data is sent to the `DataGroup`'s or `SkinnableDataContainer`'s `dataProvider` property. This can be an array typically in the form of a collection (for example, an `ArrayCollection`), and it can contain anything such as strings, buttons, or graphics.

> **TIP**   For you ColdFusion folks, think of a collection as similar to an array of structures. Java folks might view it as similar to an `ArrayList` of `Hashmaps`.

You can use two item renderers that come with Flex with the `DataGroup` or `Skinnable-DataContainer` for the purpose of visualizing data:

- `spark.skins.default.DefaultItemRenderer`—Displays data as simple text.
- `spark.skins.default.DefaultComplexItemRenderer`—Displays data as components inside a `Group` container. This is effective only if the data contains visual components (buttons, images, and so on).

Let's try this out by creating an `ArrayCollection` variable with an array of strings in it as shown in the following listing.

Listing 4.18 Associating a `DataGroup`'s `dataProvider` with an array of strings

```
<fx:Script>
  <![CDATA[
    import mx.collections.ArrayCollection;
    [Bindable]
    public var someData:ArrayCollection =
        new ArrayCollection(["one","two","three"]);
  ]]>
</fx:Script>

<s:DataGroup
  dataProvider="{someData}"
  itemRenderer="spark.skins.default.DefaultItemRenderer">
    <s:layout>
      <s:HorizontalLayout/>
    </s:layout>
</s:DataGroup>
```

By default, the `DataGroup` uses the `BasicLayout` class, which if left as is would overlay each text item on top of the other. Instead you use a `HorizontalLayout` class to lay out the strings side by side.

MIGRATION TIP The `DataGroup` and `SkinnableDataContainer`, using a `Tile-Layout` class, replace the Flex 3 technique of using a repeater and the `Tile` container. A repeater in Flex 3 was a simple mechanism for looping over a collection of data (such as an array), which could be used to dynamically create child display objects in a container such as a `Tile`.

Similarly, in listing 4.19 you modify the code to create an array of buttons and use the `DefaultComplexItemRenderer` to show them as is.

Listing 4.19 Using an array of components to display

```
<?xml version="1.0" encoding="utf-8"?>
<s:Application xmlns:fx="http://ns.adobe.com/mxml/2009"
               xmlns:s="library://ns.adobe.com/flex/spark"
               xmlns:mx="library://ns.adobe.com/flex/mx" >

  <fx:Declarations>                              ⬳  Declare all
    <mx:ArrayCollection id="someData">         ❶ non-visual tags first
      <s:Button label="Button 1"/>
      <s:Button label="Button 2"/>
      <s:Button label="Button 3"/>
    </mx:ArrayCollection>
  </fx:Declarations>

  <s:DataGroup dataProvider="{someData}"
               itemRenderer="spark.skins.default.DefaultComplexItemRenderer">
    <s:layout>
      <s:TileLayout orientation="columns" requestedColumnCount="2"  />
```

```
      </s:layout>
    </s:DataGroup>
</s:Application>
```

Notice that you use an <fx:Declarations/> tag ❶, and this is because nonvisual tags (for example, the <mx:ArrayCollection/>) aren't allowed to be listed on their own if they aren't a property of the parent class/container (the Application container doesn't have an ArrayCollection property).

> **NOTE**   An ArrayCollection is an array on steroids, and like a variable containing data, it in itself isn't visual. You'll learn more about these in depth in chapter 8, where they're used heavily to populate lists and tables.

Because you're using the TileLayout class, you end up with something like figure 4.21, where your buttons follow a grid pattern.

Figure 4.21   A tiled layout of buttons using the DataGroup container

Using the SkinnableDataContainer would be the same process as you used going from Group to Skinnable-Container, where you replace the components in the code and apply a desired skin to control the look and feel.

4.6.7   *DividedBox, HDividedBox, and VDividedBox containers*

Although these containers are Halo/MX components, they're worth mentioning because they provide an extra bit of juice with their ability to provide user-controlled resizing. This is similar to HTML frames, where frame resizing is enabled.

The DividedBox container supports both horizontal and vertical (default) layout using the direction attribute. For a direct route you can use HDividedBox (horizontal layout) or VDividedBox (vertical layout).

Using the mouse pointer, you can click the divider's hotspot to resize the pane. This option permits users to customize their viewing space. In addition, you can nest them for some interesting and useful layouts.

In listing 4.20, a number of DividedBoxes are used to split portions of the application.

Listing 4.20   Making a dashboard with DividedBoxes

```xml
<?xml version="1.0" encoding="utf-8"?>
<s:Application xmlns:fx="http://ns.adobe.com/mxml/2009"
               xmlns:s="library://ns.adobe.com/flex/spark"
               xmlns:mx="library://ns.adobe.com/flex/mx" >
  <s:Panel title="Report Dashboard"
           verticalCenter="0"
           horizontalCenter="0"  >
    <mx:DividedBox direction="horizontal" width="100%">
      <s:VGroup height="100%">
        <mx:Text text="Categories" fontWeight="bold"/>
        <s:Button label="Finance" width="100%"/>
        <s:Button label="Operations" width="100%"/>
```

```
      </s:VGroup>
      <mx:VDividedBox width="50%" height="100%">
        <s:VGroup width="100%" >
          <mx:Text text="Finance Reports" fontWeight="bold"/>
          <mx:Text text="2008 Q1 Sales"/>
          <mx:Text text="2008 Q2 Sales"/>
        </s:VGroup>
        <s:VGroup width="100%" >
          <mx:Text text="2008 Q1 Sales" fontWeight="bold"/>
          <mx:Text text="North America: $2,832,132"/>
          <mx:Text text="Europe: $1,912,382"/>
        </s:VGroup>
      </mx:VDividedBox>
    </mx:DividedBox>
  </s:Panel>
</s:Application>
```

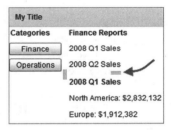

Figure 4.22   Divided boxes allow the user to customize the dimensions of the application.

This type of container is particularly useful when setting up drill-down displays, such as dashboards, which is exactly what you did.

If you have a lot of information to present in any of these divided sections (figure 4.22), this convenient mechanism allows the user to adjust how each section of real estate is allocated in order to see more of what's important.

Working with forms is always an aspect of any application, and there's a container for that too.

4.6.8   *Form container*

The purpose of the `Form` container is to make it easy to lay out a form in your application. Using the `Form` container is similar to creating forms in HTML, but in Flex the `Form` container has mechanisms to place labels beside each of your form input fields. Unlike HTML, which requires form elements to be contained within an HTML form tag, the Flex `Form` container is purely for layout, and it isn't necessary to have form items within the container.

An HTML form instructs the browser that all input elements inside the form tags are part of a collection of data to be sent to the server upon the trigger of a submit button. But with Flex, server-side communication is a completely different process, so there's no need for equivalent functionality to the HTML form element and submit button. A Flex form container is just like any other container in that all it does is layout.

The `Form` container holds a collection of three tags:

- `Form`—The main container
- `FormHeader`—An optional component for adding section headers
- `FormItem`—A component that lets you associate text with each form input field

Putting these together, listing 4.21 builds a form to capture user input.

```
<?xml version="1.0" encoding="utf-8"?>
<s:Application xmlns:fx="http://ns.adobe.com/mxml/2009"
               xmlns:s="library://ns.adobe.com/flex/spark"
               xmlns:mx="library://ns.adobe.com/flex/mx" >

  <mx:Form>
    <mx:FormHeading label="Contact Info"/>
    <mx:FormItem label="First Name">
      <s:TextInput/>
    </mx:FormItem>
    <mx:FormItem label="Last Name">
      <s:TextInput/>
    </mx:FormItem>
  </mx:Form>
</s:Application>
```

Figure 4.23 shows a basic login window, such as one you'd see in many applications. The form-related containers make it easy to create the pattern of field label and field input.

If you need more flexibility than the two-column approach of a form, check out the Grid container.

Figure 4.23 Form **containers make it easy to lay out input components and give each component a label.**

4.6.9   *Grid container*

The Grid container is similar to an HTML table in that there's a top-level grid tag to signal the start of the grid, a GridRow tag for entering rows, and a GridItem tag for entering data into each cell. Let's use the Grid container to build an MP3 player control panel in the following listing.

```
<mx:Grid>
  <mx:GridRow>
    <mx:GridItem>                            Create the
      <s:Button label="Rewind"/>            first row
    </mx:GridItem>
    <mx:GridItem>
      <s:Button label="Play"/>
    </mx:GridItem>
    <mx:GridItem>
      <s:Button label="Forward"/>
    </mx:GridItem>
  </mx:GridRow>
  <mx:GridRow>                              Create the
    <mx:GridItem colSpan="3">              second row
      <s:Button label="STOP" width="100%"/>
    </mx:GridItem>
  </mx:GridRow>
</mx:Grid>
```

If you want a cell to span more than one column (as in figure 4.24), you can use the `colSpan` attribute on any `GridItem`.

The `Grid` container is obviously simple, much like an HTML table, which makes it easy to arrange items in tabular format.

Figure 4.24 Control panel showing the layout abilities of the `Grid` container, which produces results similar to HTML tables

4.7 Summary

Flex's display is predicated on the concept of layout, and at a high level there are three approaches to this: absolute positioning, constraint-based layout, or automatic layout.

With absolute layout, you specify coordinates where components should be positioned, and with constraint-based layout, you anchor components relative to another dimension (such as the center of the browser). Automatic layout does all the heavy lifting for you by providing layout classes that support horizontal, vertical, and tiled layout algorithms.

You lay out components using containers, and Spark containers support these new layout classes. Alternatively, a few Halo/MX containers have no Spark equivalents that provide unique layout abilities such as the `Form` container.

Now that you know how to lay out an application, we can move forward by putting stuff inside those containers. What kind of stuff? Visual stuff—all the goodies that make up an application such as buttons, sliders, text inputs, combo boxes, and so on.

Displaying forms and capturing user input

This chapter covers

- Creating forms in Flex
- Using input components (controls)
- Capturing user input

Let's put your newly acquired understanding of layout and ActionScript to work and apply it to a fundamental operation of any application—capturing user input.

As mentioned in chapter 4, even though Flex offers a Form component, its use is optional and you'll find it functions best as a layout tool. In the land of Flex you're equipped with visual components (usually referred to as controls) that display information and accept user input. Alongside controls are events and event handlers that recognize and respond to user actions, such as clicking a mouse.

When event handler functions run, they access data from whatever source they've been instructed; there's no master Form tag that contains all the inputs as in HTML (see figure 5.1).

Remember, you're not restricted to the set of controls that comes with Flex. Unlike HTML, which limits your UI controls to the HTML specification and browser implementation, Flex encourages you to extend an existing control to add more functionality or create your own, completely new UI controls from scratch.

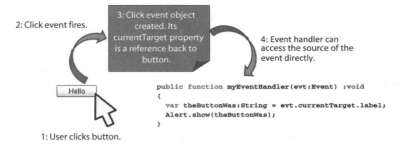

Figure 5.1 When a user interacts with a control, such as providing form-related input (in this case a button), you can configure an event handler (which is just a function) to handle the event. The event object provides a reference back to the source of the event via the `currentTarget` property, which allows the event handler function to access the source of the event directly.

NOTE Say goodbye to the notion of HTML Forms. The optional <Form> tag in Flex does nothing more than lay out UI components called controls.

One of the teaching approaches this book employs is to show many ways of doing the same thing. From example to example, we'll use an idea from the previous one but then change a portion of it to demonstrate an alternative. The alternatives aren't necessarily any better; they're just different. But more important they help you to think with the ActionScript mentality.

MIGRATION TIP Similar to what you saw in the previous chapter, Flex 4's new Spark components package provides controls that obsolete the previous Halo (a.k.a. MX) controls. And like containers, not all Halo controls have Spark equivalents. The main difference is that Spark components support a much more flexible approach to styling and skinning.

A core piece to that understanding is the invaluable `id` attribute, a handle to an MXML component that allows you to access the values contained by the `id` attribute. As we go through the catalog of user input controls, various examples will make use of this `id` attribute to access their values.

5.1 The id attribute

You were first introduced to the `id` attribute in chapter 2, but it's worth taking the time to review and expand what you learned. The `id` attribute can be used on any component, and you can access it the same way you would any other variable. It gives you a mechanism to uniquely name any instances of a component, which allows you to refer to the component explicitly using its unique identifier.

HTML Form tags also have `id` attributes that are similar in their role and use. Unlike HTML, MXML doesn't require you to use functions like JavaScript's `getElementByID()` to access an `id`. For example, this snippet shows how a function accesses the value of a control by using its `id` property.

```
<fx:Script>
  public function showit()
  {
    mx.controls.Alert.show('idMe is ' + idMe.text);
  }
</fx:Script>
<s:Label id="idMe" text="Hi mom"/>
```

When it comes to building forms, the id property is a convenient way to retrieve values from a target component; having introduced it, we'll use it in various examples as we explore the plethora of controls Flex provides.

5.2   Flex's catalog of controls

Text inputs, check boxes, radio buttons, and drop-down combo boxes. Yeah, Flex has them all, and so does any other UI technology. But a bunch more nifty controls come out of the box, such as the rich text editor, sliders, and the numeric stepper.

Getting right down to business, we start off with the most fundamental controls of them all, the text-based controls.

5.2.1   Text controls

The basic purpose for the UI of any application is to display text. Flex provides a variety of components that allow you to capture and display textual information. Table 5.1 presents these controls and their descriptions.

Table 5.1   Text controls for displaying and capturing

Control	Package	Description
Label	Spark	A simple control that displays textual information, where text can wrap. Replaces the Halo Text and Label controls.
RichText	Spark	Similar to Label, it has no scrolling, selection, or editing abilities. Does add the ability to render richly formatted text.
RichEditableText	Spark	Adds support for URL links, scrolling, selecting, and editing. No background, border, or scrollbars.
TextInput	Spark	Presents a single-line text entry field. This control is similar to the `<input type="text">` tag in HTML, and although it doesn't have scrolling, it does have a border and is skinnable. Replaces the Halo version.
TextArea	Spark	Presents a multiple-row text entry field by extending onto RichEditableText. Similar to the `<textarea>` tag in HTML. Supports scrolling, rich text, and graphics, is skinnable, and replaces the Halo version.
RichTextEditor	Halo	As the name implies, a robust editor that allows the user to format their text. This includes parameters like color, font, and text size. HTML doesn't offer a similar feature to RichTextEditor natively.

Let's start off with a simple case of using all of the controls mentioned in table 5.1, minus the `RichText` and `RichEditableText` controls. In listing 5.1 you have a simple user profile application that makes use of various text controls, and you'll use a `Panel` container to wrap around these components, which will make it look more professional (a.k.a. cool).

> **Listing 5.1   This code uses all the text-based control components.**

```
<?xml version="1.0" encoding="utf-8"?>
<s:Application xmlns:fx="http://ns.adobe.com/mxml/2009"
               xmlns:s="library://ns.adobe.com/flex/spark"
               xmlns:mx="library://ns.adobe.com/flex/mx">

  <fx:Script>                                            Display
    import mx.controls.Alert;                        ⟵   entered value
    public function showMsg(msg:String):void
    {
      Alert.show(msg);
    }
  </fx:Script>

  <s:Panel title="Profile" verticalCenter="0" horizontalCenter="0">
    <s:layout>
      <s:VerticalLayout/>
    </s:layout>

    <s:Label text="Enter your name" fontWeight="bold"/>
    <s:TextInput id="yourName" valueCommit="showMsg(yourName.text)"/>    ⟵

    <s:Label text="Profile Summary" fontWeight="bold"/>
    <s:TextArea id="aboutYou" textAlign="center" width="100%" height="40"
              valueCommit="showMsg(aboutYou.text)"/>                   ⟵

    <s:Label text="Enter your profile"
             fontWeight="bold"                          Send text value
             color="#ff0000"/>                            to showMsg
    <mx:RichTextEditor id="fullProfile" height="150"
              valueCommit="showMsg(fullProfile.text)"/>                ⟵
  </s:Panel>

</s:Application>
```

Try compiling and running the application and you'll see a display similar to figure 5.2.

Now let's look at what you've created and how it works. The `Label` component is used to display a descriptive label above each input control. To give you a sense of what `Label` can do, we've modified some of its styling properties. When a user enters a value and *commits* it—for example, by clicking Enter or Tab or an element such as a submit button—Flex will recognize this event and run the `showMsg()` function as instructed.

Moving on to `RichText` and `RichEditableText` (because we didn't use these yet), these components are a part of Flex's Spark primitives package and are a foundation piece for building more intelligent things. To use them you provide data by specifying the `content` attribute, which you can do as a property on the component itself or as a child tag.

The `content` attribute supports the following tags:

- `<p>` for a new paragraph
- `<span>` for styling a block of text
- `<br/>` for a single breakline

`RichText` itself has a number of style properties for setting the font size, weight, family, color, and so on. Think of the `span` tag as a way to override whatever the parent `RichText` sets. For example, in listing 5.2 you set the color to blue but then override the word *people* to be red and a heavier font.

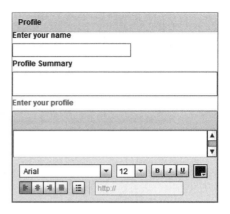

Figure 5.2   A user profile form constructed using Flex's text-based components

Listing 5.2   Using the `RichText` component

```
<s:Panel title="Howdy" verticalCenter="0" horizontalCenter="0" width="300">
  <s:layout>
    <s:VerticalLayout/>
  </s:layout>
  <s:RichText textAlign="center" color="#127892" width="100%">
    <s:content>
      Greetings
        <s:span fontWeight="bold"
                color="#ff0000">people</s:span>
        of<s:br/>
        <s:span fontSize="20">EARTH!</s:span>
    </s:content>
  </s:RichText>
</s:Panel>
```

Likewise, you increase the font size on the word *EARTH!*, which is evident in figure 5.3.

The `RichEditableText` component is much the same, except it allows the user to select the text and click hyperlinks, plus it adds scrolling if needed and the ability to edit the text. It's effectively a simpler version of `TextArea`. If you want to use it, try it out on the previous example except replace `RichText` with `RichEditableText`.

All of these text fields can be used to capture a broad range of data. You could even use them to capture a date. This would likely be your natural inclination when coming from an HTML background because there isn't a native date `Form` input available (the workaround is to use JavaScript to limit a text input field to store only dates). A better choice would be to use Flex's `Date` controls.

Figure 5.3   The `RichText` component supports styled text.

5.2.2 Date controls

When using HTML, a common technique to capture date-related input is to use the form's <input type="text"> tag, paired with a calendar image displayed directly after the tag. When invoked, a calendar appears in a pop-up window. When a user selects a date from the calendar, a bit of JavaScript is executed to copy the selected value to the input field.

Fortunately, there's an easier way to capture calendar-related data in Flex, which offers two date-based fields (table 5.2).

Table 5.2 Date-based controls

Control	Package	Description
DateChooser	Halo	Displays a small calendar similar to most HTML-based calendar selection widgets. A noteworthy feature is that you can control the display of ranges of dates as well as determine which ranges are selectable. This is quite useful if you want to block out dates such as holidays.
DateField	Halo	The input control that appears similar to the <input type="text"> tag/calendar image combination used in HTML. It allows the user to enter a date, or, if the icon is selected, it displays the DateChooser control.

The code in listing 5.3 demonstrates how to use both of these components.

Listing 5.3 Flex's two date-based components used to capture date information

```
<fx:Script>
  <![CDATA[
    public function showMsg(msg:String):void
    {
      mx.controls.Alert.show(msg);
    }
  ]]>
</fx:Script>
<s:Panel title="Profile" verticalCenter="0" horizontalCenter="0">
  <s:layout>
    <s:VerticalLayout/>
  </s:layout>
  <mx:DateField text="12/05/2010"                            Default the        Pass along
          id="thisDateField"                                 date               the value
          change="showMsg(thisDateField.selectedDate.toString())"/>

  <mx:DateChooser id="thisDateChooser"                       Limits range
          maxYear="2012" minYear="2010"                      of years
          selectedDate="{new Date(2010,10, 15)}"             Default
                                                             selectedDate
    change="showMsg(thisDateChooser.selectedDate.toString())">

  </mx:DateChooser>                                          Triggers calling
                                                             showMsg()

</s:Panel>
```

Notice how the id property's value is used to access the value of that component? The intention was merely to show you how the id property could be used; later in the chapter we'll show alternative ways to accomplish the same thing.

Did you also notice how the change event is used instead of valueCommit? The difference between these two specific events is that valueCommit is triggered when the user performs an action that indicates she's completed setting the value (for example, pressing the Enter key). The change event responds as the value changes, so feedback occurs in real time with each keystroke.

Compile and run the application, and you'll see the result of Flex's two date-based components, as illustrated in figure 5.4.

Figure 5.4   Flex's two date-based components displayed together

> **NOTE**   You'd think you could pass a simple date in the form of a string (for example, "10/15/2010") to a DateChooser, but unfortunately it's not that easy.
>
> If you pull up the Flex API Reference for this object, you'll see that selectedDate expects a Date object—in our example we're creating one on the fly and inline. The DateField also supports this attribute.

Just as Flex's date-based controls can be used more effectively to acquire calendar data than a text input box, Flex also has controls that are specific to capturing numeric values.

5.2.3   *Numeric controls*

Numeric controls are those that allow you to capture a number from the user. The user input controls presented in table 5.3 allow you to capture numeric data from the user. As you'd expect, they can be used for the more obvious tasks—such as obtaining someone's age—but thinking outside the HTML box, you can also use them to resize an image in real time, filter a set of data, or navigate to a section of the application.

Table 5.3   Controls used for capturing numeric values

Control	Package	Description
NumericStepper	Spark	A simple control that lets the user increment and decrement values. You can specify the minimum and maximum allowed values, as well as the unit size of the increment/decrement step.
Spinner	Spark	Almost the same as the NumericStepper, except it doesn't display a text input beside it to show the current value. It's meant to be paired up with something else or extended.

Table 5.3 Controls used for capturing numeric values *(continued)*

Control	Package	Description
HSlider	Halo	Allows the user to slide what's known as a *thumb* horizontally along a track. You can control the minimum and maximum allowed values, snapInterval increments (positions on the slide to which the thumb will snap), and visible increments (called *ticks*). You also have the option to set up more than one thumb if you want to allow the user to specify multiple values (for example, a range). A more primitive Spark version of this does exist.
VSlider	Halo	Identical to the HSlider, except the orientation of the track is vertical. A more primitive Spark version of this does exist.

Let's put these controls to work in listing 5.4 and capture some numbers.

Listing 5.4 Using Flex's Numeric input controls to capture values

```
<?xml version='1.0' encoding='UTF-8'?>
<s:Application xmlns:fx="http://ns.adobe.com/mxml/2009"
               xmlns:s="library://ns.adobe.com/flex/spark"
               xmlns:mx="library://ns.adobe.com/flex/mx">

  <fx:Script>
    <![CDATA[
      import mx.controls.Alert;
      public function showMsg(msg:String):void
      {
        Alert.show(msg);
      }
    ]]>
  </fx:Script>
  <s:Panel title="Profile">
    <s:layout>
      <s:HorizontalLayout/>
    </s:layout>
    <s:VGroup>
      <s:Label fontWeight="bold" text="How many kids do you have?"/>

      <s:NumericStepper id="kids"
                  minimum="0"
                  maximum="10"
                  stepSize="1"
                  change="showMsg(kids.value.toString())"/>

      <s:HGroup>
        <s:Label fontWeight="bold" text="Kids in college?"/>
        <s:Spinner minimum="0" maximum="10" id="collegeKids"/>
        <s:Label text="{collegeKids.value} in college"/>
      </s:HGroup>

      <s:Label fontWeight="bold" text="How long is your commute (mins)?"/>

      <mx:HSlider id="commuteTimeRange" minimum="0" maximum="180"
                  snapInterval="5"
                  tickInterval="15"
```

- **Too low for Octo-mom**
- **Increment/ decrement by 1**
- ❶ **Increments to snap the thumb to**
- ❷ **Space between each visual tick**

```
                      labels="[0 mins,180 mins]"          ◄── ❸ Labels at each end
                      thumbCount="2"                                                    ◄┐
                      change="showMsg(commuteTimeRange.values.toString())">              │
      </mx:HSlider>                                         This one has two thumbs      │
    </s:VGroup>
    <s:VGroup>                                                             ❹ Fewer ticks,
      <s:Label fontWeight="bold" text="How tall are you (cm)?"/> ┐          tighter
      <mx:VSlider id="yourHeight" minimum="0" maximum="300"      │          snap
                  tickInterval="50" snapInterval="1"           ◄─┘          spacing
                  labels="[0,50,100,150,200,250,300]"                              ◄─┐
                  change="showMsg(yourHeight.values.toString())"/>                   │
    </s:VGroup>                                              Seven evenly             │
  </s:Panel>                                                 spaced labels ❺ ─────────┘
</s:Application>
```

You can select in units of 5 ❶ and display markers every 15 units ❷. The display is two evenly spaced labels (one at each end) ❸. In the vertical slider ❹, the markers are farther apart than in the horizontal slider. Finally, you display seven evenly spaced labels ❺.

> **MIGRATION TIP** You may have noticed that we're using the Halo sliders in listing 5.4, and there are Spark equivalents of these. But we're making an exception by not using the newer Spark versions because they're primitive (meant to be built on). The Spark versions of these sliders don't have built-in support for interval labels and ticks, nor do they support multiple thumbs. The Spark versions are meant to be skinned, which will allow you to add on the interval ticks/labeling, but unless you care to do that, it's faster to use the Halo version.

After compiling and running the application, you'll see the results shown in figure 5.5. You've certainly never seen this collection of user input controls in HTML—they're not even that common among desktop applications.

Many developers fail to take full advantage of these components, usually because they come from an HTML background and aren't used to this level of utility. This is unfortunate, because you can use numeric-based components in ways more creative than simply capturing a value. You can use that value to provide real-time control to your end user. As another example, if you're designing a dashboard, you can have the display change in real time as the user moves a slider back and forth—effectively filtering data in and out.

Another traditional user input is the button, which often is used to submit a form, but Flex provides you a variety of buttons to choose from.

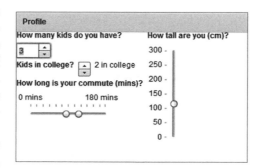

Figure 5.5 Flex's numeric-based components offer a unique way to capture values.

5.2.4 *Exploring Flex's buttons*

A whole section on buttons? When it comes to Flex, the answer is a resounding yes! Buttons from the user perspective look literally like a raised 3D graphic that's synonymous with buttons found in the physical life (think of the Power button on your TV). From a software perspective, they're a graphic that supports overlaid text and the user interaction of being clicked.

Flex goes beyond the plain-old button offered by HTML and adds a collection of interesting options (see table 5.4). Buttons are one of stalwarts of GUIs, but they can be a bit boring. Flex takes them to a higher level with a number of variations.

Listing 5.5 shows how to invoke all these button choices except for the pop-up ones, which we'll get to shortly.

Table 5.4 Flex offers an expanded range of button components.

Control	Package	Description
Button	Spark	The standard, all-purpose button for accepting a mouse-click interaction. Flex buttons have built-in support that lets you easily add an image into the button. In HTML you can use an image to create a `psuedo-Text+Image` button, but your text will be static. With Flex, the text remains dynamic.
ButtonBar	Spark	Dynamically generates a series of buttons based on an array. You could do the same thing by dynamically generating `Button`s on your own, but not only is a `ButtonBar` easier to implement, it adds some flair by rounding the edges of the outermost buttons to lend the appearance of a single menu bar, split into sections.
LinkButton	Halo	Flex's version of an HTML link. If you pull up the class reference for this object (in the Flex API Reference), you'll see it's a descendant of the `Button` but styled and extended to behave like an HTML link by having a transparent background and no border.
LinkBar	Halo	Similar to the relationship between a `Button` and a `ButtonBar`, the `LinkBar` is an easy way to create a series of `LinkButtons`.
ToggleButtonBar	Halo	Nearly identical to a `ButtonBar`, except it persists the selection—if you press one of the buttons, it stays down (and highlighted) until you change to another button. Think of it as a radio button with a label inside.
PopUpButton	Halo	A dual button that combines the functionality of two buttons—the left side acts like a normal `Button`; the right side invokes another UI object (anything derived from the `UIComponent` object). This is typically used to create a multiselection `Button` that looks like a `Button` and a `ComboBox` merged into one.
PopUpMenuButton	Halo	A descendant of the `PopUpButton`, it's geared to specifically create a drop-down menu.

Listing 5.5   A collection of `Button`-based components in action

```xml
<?xml version='1.0' encoding='UTF-8'?>
<s:Application xmlns:fx="http://ns.adobe.com/mxml/2009"
               xmlns:s="library://ns.adobe.com/flex/spark"
               xmlns:mx="library://ns.adobe.com/flex/mx">

  <fx:Script>
    <![CDATA[
      import mx.controls.Alert;
      import mx.collections.ArrayCollection;
      [Bindable]
      public var myArray:ArrayCollection = new
    ArrayCollection(['One','Two','Three']);
      public function showMsg(msg:String):void
      {
        Alert.show('You just clicked on ' + msg);
      }
    ]]>
  </fx:Script>
  <s:Panel title="Profile" width="360" height="240"
           horizontalCenter="0"
           verticalCenter="0">
    <s:layout>
      <s:HorizontalLayout/>
    </s:layout>

    <s:VGroup>
      <s:Button id="thisBtn" label="Button" click="showMsg('button')"/>

      <mx:LinkButton id="thisLinkBtn" label="LinkButton"
                     click="showMsg('linkbutton')"/>
    </s:VGroup>

    <s:VGroup>

      <s:ButtonBar id="thisBtnBar"
                   dataProvider="{myArray}"
      click="showMsg(ButtonBar(event.currentTarget).selectedItem)" />

      <mx:LinkBar id="thisLinkBar"
                  dataProvider="{myArray}"
                  itemClick="showMsg(event.label)" />

      <mx:ToggleButtonBar id="thisToggleBar"
                          dataProvider="{myArray}"
                          itemClick="showMsg(event.label)"/>
    </s:VGroup>

  </s:Panel>
</s:Application>
```

> **dataProvider populates display of components**

Being an OOP language, Flex tends to build upon itself, using some components as a foundation.

ButtonBar, LinkBar, and ToggleButtonBar are such a close family that from a mechanical perspective, aside from minor presentation differences, they're the same thing (see figure 5.6). More important is their use of dataProvider, which is a property that accepts array-like data to generate its display.

As with many applications, Flex makes arrays available, but you can also take advantage of its more powerful cousin, the ArrayCollection. In listing 5.5 you used

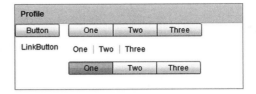

Figure 5.6 Flex has a number of Button-based components at your disposal.

ActionScript to create this ArrayCollection, which allows you to then bind the results to the various controls (note that a regular Array doesn't support binding).

The benefit of creating an ArrayCollection variable is the ability to decouple the logic it contains from the component that displays it. You can read in configuration data and populate variables accordingly.

> **NOTE** What's the difference between click and itemClick? Not much; itemClick adds label and index properties to make it convenient to know which button was clicked. Flex applications are event driven, and triggers cause an event to occur. Different components respond to all kinds of events. click refers to the mouse button being pressed (the trigger) on a Button component; itemClick is specifically which button (if you're using a component that has more than one). The itemClick is supported only by Halo controls, whereas the Spark ButtonBar uses the generic click event, so you have to use the currentTarget property to access the button that was pressed.

The previous examples covered all of the buttons except two: the PopUpButton and the PopUpMenuButton. As self-explanatory as they appear, in order for you to make proper use of them, some more explanation is required.

THE POPUPBUTTON AND POPUPMENUBUTTON

We're not playing favorites by giving these two Halo controls special attention. They're considered special cases, and as such, they do need a more thorough explanation.

Listing 5.6 illustrates a PopUpMenuButton in action.

Listing 5.6 Example of how to use a PopUpMenuButton

```
<?xml version='1.0' encoding='UTF-8'?>
<s:Application xmlns:fx="http://ns.adobe.com/mxml/2009"
               xmlns:s="library://ns.adobe.com/flex/spark"
               xmlns:mx="library://ns.adobe.com/flex/mx">

  <fx:Script>
    <![CDATA[
      import mx.controls.Alert;
      public function showMsg(msg:String):void
      {
        Alert.show('You just clicked on ' + msg);
      }
    ]]>
  </fx:Script>
```

```
<mx:PopUpMenuButton id="menuBtn"
                    dataProvider="{['One','Two','Three']}"
                    click="showMsg('left side')"
                    itemClick="showMsg('right side with ' + event.label)"/>
```

```
</s:Application>
```

Notice that this example makes use of both the `click` and `itemClick` events.

When you click the right secondary `Button` (figure 5.7), a drop-down menu appears, prompting you to select an item. When you make a selection, the `itemClick` event is triggered. But when you click the left side of the primary `Button`, the `itemClick` and `click` events fire, one after the other.

Figure 5.7 `PopUpMenuButton` is similar to a `Button` and a `ComboBox` wrapped into one.

This is useful when you need to differentiate between these two user interactions. For example, let's assume the drop-down menu defined in listing 5.6 contains a list of credit card brands (for example, Visa, MasterCard, and American Express). When the user changes the selection (`itemClick`), the credit card type is stored to a variable, but when the primary `Button` (`click`) is clicked, Flex submits the `Form`.

Let's move on to the father of the `PopUpMenuButton`: the `PopUpButton`. The `PopUp-Button` can perform the same tasks as `PopUpMenuButton` but possesses broader capabilities, which, naturally, take more code to implement.

`PopUpMenuButton` uses an element called `Menu` to generate the drop-down menu (another standard object with Flex). But `Menu` is the only thing `PopUpMenuButton` can display.

`PopUpButton` can display a greater variety of elements, but it doesn't default to any one in particular. This means it's considerably more flexible, but you do need to explicitly specify what `PopUpButton` is going to show.

To produce the same result as listing 5.6 using `PopUpButton`, the code would look like that in this next listing.

Listing 5.7   Using `PopUpButton` to display an optional menu

```
<?xml version='1.0' encoding='UTF-8'?>
<s:Application xmlns:fx="http://ns.adobe.com/mxml/2009"
               xmlns:s="library://ns.adobe.com/flex/spark"
               xmlns:mx="library://ns.adobe.com/flex/mx">

  <fx:Script>
    <![CDATA[
    import mx.controls.Alert;
    import mx.events.*;
    import mx.controls.Menu;
    public var menuItems:Object =                                     Create variable
      [{label:'One'},{label:'Two'},{label:'Three'}];                  with array-like
    public var thisMenu:Menu = Menu.createMenu(null,menuItems,false); menu values
    public function handleItemClick(event:MenuEvent):void
    {                                                                 Populate
      menuBtn.label = event.label;                                    Menu
    }                                                                 object
```

Create variable with array-like menu values

Populate Menu object

Set text label on button

Handle when menu item is clicked

```
            ]]>
        </fx:Script>
        <mx:PopUpButton id="menuBtn"
                        creationComplete=
                        "thisMenu.addEventListener('itemClick',handleItemClick);"
                        popUp="{thisMenu}"/>

    </s:Application>
```

Here are three points to note about listing 5.7:

- In most examples, the variable containing the information to be populated is an array. In the previous example, we used an object. If you recall from chapter 3, there's not much difference between them. In this context you could have declared `menuItems` an array instead of an object, and it would have worked as well.
- We introduced `creationComplete`. This event instructs `PopUpButton` to call extra code when its creation is finished.
- This extra code tells our `Menu` object (`thisMenu`) to listen for the `itemClick` event, and if that occurs, to call our event handler (`handleItemClick`) to manage it.

That seems like a lot more work, so why bother? After running the code in listing 5.7 it will look identical to the previous example's figure 5.7; the `Button` and drop-down menu appear nearly the same as those produced by `PopUpMenuButton`. Is it worth the effort? Yes. Unlike with `PopUpMenuButton`, the label in the `Button` doesn't default to the first item in the list.

The main difference between using `PopUpButton` and `PopUpMenuButton` is that with `PopUpButton` you're not restricted to using it for menus; you can use any visual element to interact with the user. If all you want is the drop-down menu effect, go with the `PopUpMenuButton`. If you need more control over the options you want to present to the user, leverage the flexibility of `PopUpButton`.

Along with buttons, the other common user input paradigm (in both desktop and web applications) is a `picklist`, which provides a selection list from which the user can choose one or more items.

5.2.5 Picklist controls

Picklists are controls that represent everything else—they present lists of options from which you can choose, and we've listed them in table 5.5.

Table 5.5 Flex's picklist controls

Control	Package	Description
CheckBox	Spark	The generic `CheckBox` control (identical in behavior to an HTML `CheckBox`). It's a descendant of the `Button`, except it's designed specifically for the purpose of being checked and unchecked. The most common use for a `CheckBox` is to provide a series of options from which the user can check (select) one or more of those options.

Table 5.5   Flex's picklist controls *(continued)*

Control	Package	Description
RadioButton	Spark	Similar to the CheckBox, except when grouped as a range of choices, the user can select only one. The RadioButton is also a descendant of Button.
DropDownList	Spark	This drop-down menu control displays the currently selected option, but when clicked it drops a display list of options from which to choose. ComboBox is the same as a <select> box in HTML, except unlike its HTML equivalent, you can allow the user to free-form edit the selected text. Although it appears to be based on Button, it isn't a descendant. Formerly known as the ComboBox in the Halo package, except it doesn't support inline editability.
ColorPicker	Halo	A sibling to ComboBox. It drops down a color menu, allowing the user to select from a color palette. You could use this to allow users to customize their desktop or as part of the application workflow (for example, a color selector with which visitors to an automobile manufacturer's website can view a vehicle's color options in real time).

To give you an idea of what these look like in action, we assembled a program fashioned on the concept of a user profile form in this next listing.

Listing 5.8   Examples of picklist controls

```
<?xml version='1.0' encoding='UTF-8'?>
<s:Application xmlns:fx="http://ns.adobe.com/mxml/2009"
               xmlns:s="library://ns.adobe.com/flex/spark"
               xmlns:mx="library://ns.adobe.com/flex/mx">
<fx:Script>
  import mx.controls.Alert;
  public function showMsg(msg:String):void
  {
    Alert.show(msg);
  }
</fx:Script>
<fx:Declarations>                              Declare nonvisual
  <s:RadioButtonGroup id="Spam"          ◁┘  components
                 itemClick="showMsg('User picked ' +    ❶ itemClick
                 event.currentTarget.selectedValue)"/>  ◁┘ event
</fx:Declarations>
<s:Panel width="400" height="150" title="Profile" horizontalCenter="0"
    verticalCenter="0">
  <s:layout>
    <s:VerticalLayout/>
  </s:layout>
  <s:HGroup>
    <s:Label text="Your hobbies:"/>
    <s:CheckBox id="cbVideoGames" label="Video Games"
                click="showMsg('Video Games is ' +
                cbVideoGames.selected)"/>
    <s:CheckBox id="cbFishing" label="Fishing"         Display value of CheckBoxes
                click="showMsg('Fishing is ' + cbFishing.selected)"/>  ◁┘
```

```
    </s:HGroup>
    <s:HGroup>

      <s:Label fontWeight="bold" text="Do you like spam:"/>

      <s:RadioButton id="rbYes" value="Yes" groupName="Spam"
                     click="showMsg('Yes')" label="Yes"/>
      <s:RadioButton id="rbNo" value="No" groupName="Spam"
                     click="showMsg('No')" label="No"/>
    </s:HGroup>

    <s:HGroup>
      <s:Label fontWeight="bold" text="Favorite car maker:"/>
      <s:DropDownList id="combo"
                  close="showMsg('Favorite car is ' +
                  event.currentTarget.selectedItem)" >
        <mx:ArrayCollection>
          <fx:String>Ferrari</fx:String>
          <fx:String>Porsche</fx:String>
          <fx:String>Hyundai</fx:String>
        </mx:ArrayCollection>
      </s:DropDownList>
      <s:Label fontWeight="bold" text="With the color of:"/>
      <mx:ColorPicker id="clr"
                  change="showMsg('Color ' +
                  event.currentTarget.selectedColor)"/>
    </s:HGroup>
  </s:Panel>
</s:Application>
```

❷ Click event fires

❸ Show changes in value

Inline data to populate CompboBox

Display the color

You present two CheckBoxes and display their value when clicked ❷. In your next step you create two grouped RadioButtons, which trigger two pop-up windows. First the click event ❸ on the RadioButton will fire, followed by itemClick event ❶. The RadioButtonGroup component is optional—use it when you need to call a single function regardless of which RadioButton is clicked. Note that because the <s:RadioButtonGroup/> tag is nonvisual, it needs to be grouped inside an <fx:Declarations/> tag.

After compiling and running the application, you'll see something similar to that of figure 5.8, which contains various questions using these picklist controls.

In comparing these components to their HTML form equivalents, there's not much of a departure in their general behavior—although the color picker stands apart as something completely different.

NOTE The term *picklist* isn't an official term associated with Flex; it's something we use as a category for these particular controls.

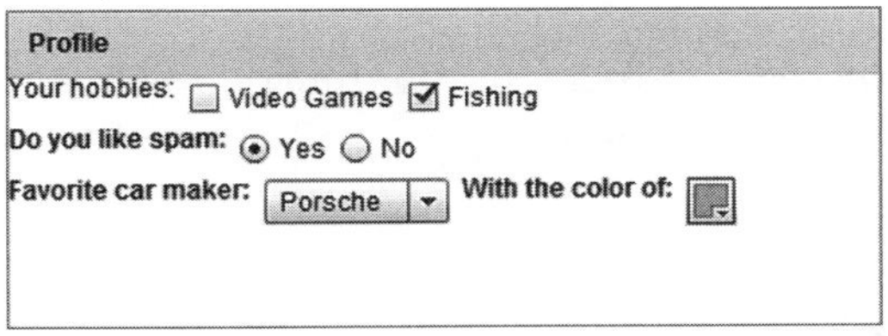

Figure 5.8 Take your pick! Picklist controls allow users to choose from a range of options.

Now having covered standard user input components (controls) along with usage examples, we need to take a deeper look at what your options are when interacting with the user and accessing any values they've provided.

5.3 Accessing the control's value

As with any programming language, there are many ways to carry out the same task. In the previous examples, we used the most straightforward techniques to make it easy to see what's going on in the background. Be aware that for each of these examples there are other (and perhaps better) ways to execute them.

5.3.1 Passing values to a function

The previous examples contain many instances of passing values to a function. Although our intention was to keep the examples streamlined and easy to understand, passing values to independent functions is a good technique to employ, because you relieve the logic that processes data from needing to know where the data came from.

This allows you to reuse that function and to change the implementation—for example, switching from a RadioButton to a CheckBox doesn't faze the function at all. This is what you observed with the showMsg function:

```
public function showMsg(msg:String):void
{
    Alert.show(msg);
}
```

When you call a function to which you pass the value, it's in response to a trigger that caused the event to occur. Each event has an event object to go along with it, which, by means of the currentTarget property, contains all kinds of goodies, including where the event came from.

This is what you're doing in the following code as you use currentTarget (in this case a reference to the RadioButtonGroup) to extract the selectedValue of the RadioButtonGroup:

```
<s:RadioButtonGroup itemClick="showMsg(event.currentTarget.selectedValue)"/>
```

But if you assign that control an id, you can reference it using that instead:

```
<s:RadioButtonGroup id="Spam"
    itemClick="showMsg(Spam.selectedValue.toString())"/>
```

Passing simple values is common in any language, but Flex, which is event based, provides an opportunity to tap into the event itself.

5.3.2 Passing events to a function

An inverse approach is to put more responsibility on the function by increasing its awareness of the data's origin. To do that, you can pass the entire event object, as shown in the following listing.

Listing 5.9 When the user clicks a control, you can pass the entire event object.

```
<fx:Script>
  import mx.controls.Alert;
  import mx.events.ItemClickEvent;                          ❶ Import the
  public function showMsg(anEvent:ItemClickEvent):void         event class
  {
    Alert.show(anEvent.currentTarget.selectedValue);
  }
</fx:Script>
<fx:Declarations>
  <s:RadioButtonGroup id="Spam"
                      itemClick="showMsg(event)"/>
</fx:Declarations>
```

As you can see, it's more involved, but it does simplify matters for the control that invokes the function. It only needs to pass the event object; the event handler function can independently process the event in whatever fashion is required. The key aspect to note is that you'll need to know the type of event that's being passed and execute an import of the class ❶.

You can determine this by displaying the component or control's class reference in the Flex API Reference (see chapter 2).

> **TIP** The quickest way to access the Flex API Class Reference (in this case to show the definition of the control) is to click the control in question and then press Shift+F2.

For example, in listing 5.9, you can determine that the event was an `itemClickEvent` object by following these steps:

1. In your code, click `RadioButtonGroup` and then press Shift+F2. The API Reference for this component will display.
2. We're using events, so scroll down to the Events section.
3. Select `itemClick` from the list (see figure 5.9).
4. The API Reference for the event itself will appear. The class will be listed under the Event Object Type area (see figure 5.10). In this example, it shows you need the `mx.events.ItemClickEvent` class.

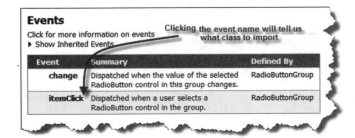

Figure 5.9 To learn more about a particular event, such as which class to import, select the event from the events list in the API Reference for a given component.

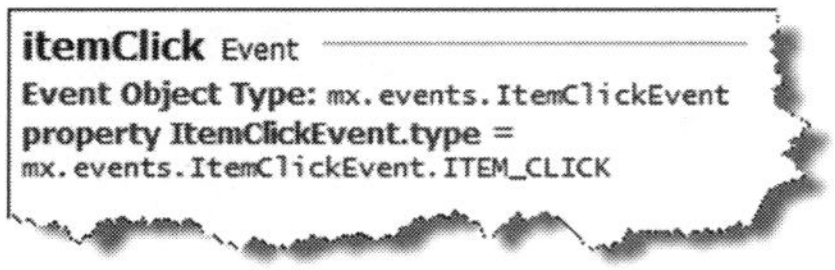

```
itemClick Event
Event Object Type: mx.events.ItemClickEvent
property ItemClickEvent.type =
mx.events.ItemClickEvent.ITEM_CLICK
```

Figure 5.10   When looking at an event in the API Reference, look at the object type to determine which class to import.

Initially, this approach takes the most amount of work to implement, but if you want a fast route, your function can directly access properties of the components to retrieve the values.

5.3.3   *Accessing properties directly*

Finally, the most tightly coupled approach—this requires your function to have specific knowledge of what it's accessing. This limits your function's reusability. Worse case, if the property it's accessing changes, the code could break down.

On the flip side, it's a convenient approach that doesn't require passing any data as you will see in the following listing.

Listing 5.10   This function accesses the value of the component directly

```
<fx:Script>
  import mx.controls.Alert;
  public function showMsg():void
  {
    Alert.show(Spam.selectedValue.toString());
  }
</fx:Script>
<fx:Declarations>
  <s:RadioButtonGroup id="Spam"
                      itemClick="showMsg()"/>
</fx:Declarations>
```

In this scenario, you can respond to an event on the input control if you want, but because you're accessing the value of the control directly, you can access it at any time, such as when a submit `Button` is pressed.

You can also use this technique in combination with any of the others previously mentioned. In listing 5.11 an event handler is used to validate the input value using a highly decoupled function that doesn't know where the value came from; at the same time, the submit `Button` is clicked on another function used to explicitly access a particular instance of the `TextInput`.

Listing 5.11   Combining techniques to access values of a control

```
<fx:Script>
  <![CDATA[
  import mx.controls.Alert;
  public function checkValue(inputValue:String):void      ◁─┐ Receives control's
  {                                                          value as passed
    if(inputValue.length < 5)                                parameter
      Alert.show("Are you sure there's not that much new?");
```

```
    }
    public function submitClicked():void          ⊲┐ Accesses
    {                                              │ control's
      Alert.show("User says:" + whatsnew.text + " is new.");  │ value directly
    }
    ]]>
</fx:Script>
<s:VGroup>
  <s:Label text="What's new?"/>
  <s:TextInput valueCommit="checkValue(event.currentTarget.text)"
               id="whatsnew"/>
  <s:Button label="Submit" click="submitClicked()"/>
</s:VGroup>
```

TIP Notice that `<![CDATA[ ... ]]>` was used inside the `<fx:Script>` block. This is because we're using a less than (`<`) character in ActionScript. In order to keep the examples short, we've been omitting this declaration, but it's always a good idea to declare it in your ActionScript blocks (refer to chapter 3 for a refresher).

Clearly, there's quite a bit of flexibility, but the question is, which technique is the way to go?

5.3.4 *Which approach to use*

Although purists may be adamant about how to implement functions that need to work with the values of controls, there's no hard-and-fast rule as to which approach works best. And as with any other programming language, the more time you invest upfront making your code reusable and easier to maintain, the less it will cost you in the long run.

In the end, there's no wrong way. It's a matter of evaluating factors, such as the size of the application, its life expectancy, and other issues. For example, if the goal of the application is to be a quick, one-off project or proof of concept, it may not warrant investing a lot of time concerning yourself with reusability issues.

5.4 *Summary*

Flex comes with a number of interface components known as controls. Some controls have equivalents in HTML, and many go far beyond their HTML equivalents.

For example, the `ColorPicker`, sliders, and the sheer variety of buttons offer tremendous freedom to be creative when building interfaces and forms.

Keep in mind that, unlike HTML, where a `<form/>` encapsulates a collection of form inputs, in Flex a form does nothing more than help lay out components. Those components don't necessarily need to be inside a `<s:Form/>` container.

There are a number of ways you can retrieve the value of user selections; you can do it in real time by leveraging events, or you can access the value as needed by using the `id` property of the component.

You now have the tools to create forms to capture input from the user and add the interactivity to access the values provided.

Capturing user input is one thing, but what about validating it? For instance, you may need to build an application that requires a user to enter a password made up of at least five characters. In the next chapter we'll take a look at how Flex validators can be used to undertake this, and much more.

Validating user input

6

This chapter covers

- Validation versus enforcement
- Pass-through validation
- Committed-value validation
- Scripted and real-time validation

Conducting client-side validation is a key strength of Flex. From a usability point of view, you want your application to do as much prevalidation as possible. This helps to avoid aggravating situations in which a user spends a fair amount of time filling out a large form and then clicks the submit button, only to find something is wrong with the input.

This is exactly the sort of thing that prevents an application from being fluid. In the HTML environment, JavaScript handles some data validation. How many times have you filled out a form, only to find out the username you've picked just happens to be taken?

Wouldn't it be nice to have all the validation done prior to submitting a form to avoid wasting time? Flex to the rescue! Flex provides a real-time validation mechanism that unobtrusively accomplishes that goal.

In this chapter, we look at how Flex handles validation and the different types of validators, such as those that verify the proper formatting of phone numbers and the structure of email addresses. Then we put them to use, employing several different approaches.

First, let's get a sense of Flex's approach to validation.

6.1   *Overview of validation*

Flex makes validating easy with built-in components to do the hard work for you and offers a number of approaches to invoke them. The following list explains common ways to validate user input:

- *Real-time validation*—With every keystroke or mouse interaction, the application checks to see that the data is input as expected or required.
- *Committed-value validation*—Similar to real time, except instead of evaluating every keystroke, the application waits until the user has filled out the field completely and commits the entry (for example, by pressing Enter or pressing Tab to change fields).
- *Pass-through validation*—Usually the result of hitting a submit button, this type of validation passes through all the form inputs to make sure everything is validated at once.
- *Scripted validation*—Using ActionScript you can dynamically create validators and even reuse the same validator on multiple elements.

In all of these cases you're controlling when the validation occurs. If you're not in compliance, Flex highlights the field (in an unobtrusive way) and displays a friendly mouse-over message indicating what the problem is (figure 6.1).

Keep in mind that we're not talking about automatic enforcement. Validation is about alerting both the user and the developer that certain criteria haven't been met. The developer needs to determine how to enforce the validation by prompting the user as to what needs to be done to comply with the application's requirements.

Now, let's look at what Flex has to offer with its built-in validators.

6.2   *Built-in validators*

Flex comes with a number of built-in validators. Each is a descendant of the parent validator class, so it carries a common set of properties, methods, and events.

The Flex team at Adobe extended the validator class to create preassembled validators that accommodate frequent validation scenarios. Each carries additional and unique properties relevant to its context.

Table 6.1 lists Flex's validators and describes what's unique about each. Keep in mind that each of them has the same capability as the parent (validator).

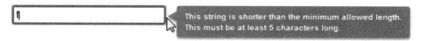

Figure 6.1   Flex implements validation by alerting the user in a friendly manner.

6.2.1 *Validator*

The parent of them all, Validator serves predominantly as a template for all other derived validators. Because the Validator component is rudimentary, its only purpose and capability is to check to see if the user provided a value to a given control (for example, a form input) to which the Validator is targeted.

Using the API Reference, you can see a number of properties that the Validator component supports, and because it's the parent to all other validators, all subsequent validators support this base set of properties (in addition to their own properties). To get a sense of what these properties look like, check out the properties of the Validator component, shown in table 6.1.

Table 6.1 Key properties and functions of the `Validator` component

Property	Type	Description
enabled	Boolean	true or false. Allows you to toggle whether validation is active.
required	Boolean	true or false. Is this a field in which the user is required to provide input?
requiredFieldError	String	If required is true, this is the message that's displayed to the user. If unspecified, it defaults to a general message.
source	Object	The object (for example, a TextInput) that you want to validate against.
property	String	The property (for example, the text property of the TextInput) of the source object that's checked to validate whether the value provided is compliant.
listener	Object	By default this is what the source is set to. When the property of the source doesn't validate, Flex highlights the source object, but if you want a different object highlighted, you can use the listener.
valid	Function	The name of a function you want to call if validation passes.
invalid	Function	The name of a function you want to call if validation fails.
trigger	Object	By default this is what the source is set to. It's the name of the object that will cause the trigger to occur (for example, an instance of a Button that a user would use to submit a form).
triggerEvent	String	The name of the event that you want to cause validation to execute based on the trigger (for example, a Submit button's click event). By default it looks for the valueCommit event (which is usually caused by the user moving to another field by pressing the Tab key or clicking elsewhere).

Listing 6.1 shows an example of the `Validator` component in action in its most basic form. Notice that the `Validator` component is nested inside a `Declarations` tag because it's a nonvisual tag.

Listing 6.1　A basic validator in action

```
<?xml version="1.0"?>
<s:Application xmlns:fx="http://ns.adobe.com/mxml/2009"
               xmlns:s="library://ns.adobe.com/flex/spark"
               xmlns:mx="library://ns.adobe.com/flex/mx">
  <fx:Declarations>
    <mx:Validator source="{username}" property="text" required="true" />
  </fx:Declarations>
  <s:VGroup horizontalCenter="0" verticalCenter="0">
    <s:Label text="Enter your username:"/>
    <s:TextInput id="username" />
  </s:VGroup>
</s:Application>
```

Nonvisuals to be declared

Intercepts `valueCommit` events

After compiling and running the code, you'll see an application similar to that shown in figure 6.2; click the input field where it asks you to enter your username.

Notice that as you move your mouse over the field, the focus changes. In addition, the field border turns red and a message pop-up appears informing the user the field is required.

The following is a summary of what happens:

- A change of focus, which occurs by moving from one UI piece to another (whether by clicking the mouse, pressing the Tab key, or pressing the Enter key), generally causes an input control to commit its value.
- Whatever is in the text field becomes committed; in this case, the text field is empty.
- The `triggerEvent` default is `valueCommit`. The validator is set to watch for the `valueCommit` event on the `text` property.
- When the `text` property of `TextInput` is empty, it causes the validation to fail and highlights the field in red.

Because all validators inherit from the parent `Validator` class, they all use this process. The difference is that they can each be configured to validate based on different criteria.

For example, the `StringValidator` can evaluate the number of characters entered versus the validator's simple `Boolean` (true/false) check.

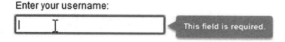

Figure 6.2　The `Validator` component highlights a field with a message when validation fails.

6.2.2　*StringValidator*

This is a general-purpose validator, which does all that its parent (the Validator) does but adds the ability to check whether a String is too short or too long. Using our friend the Flex API Reference, you'll find properties such as minLength, tooShort-Error, maxLength, and tooLongError that allow you to configure those thresholds and what you want to display to the user when they're crossed.

In listing 6.2 you use the StringValidator to check whether the input text contains at least 3 characters but no more than 20.

Listing 6.2　Using `StringValidator` to check character count

```
<?xml version="1.0"?>
<s:Application xmlns:fx="http://ns.adobe.com/mxml/2009"
               xmlns:s="library://ns.adobe.com/flex/spark"
               xmlns:mx="library://ns.adobe.com/flex/mx">
  <fx:Declarations>
    <mx:StringValidator
      source="{username}" property="text"
      minLength="3" maxLength="20"                          Used to trigger
      trigger="{submitButton}" triggerEvent="click"         validation
      tooShortError="Your username must be at least 3 characters"
      tooLongError="As if you'll remember that long of a username"
    />
  </fx:Declarations>
  <s:VGroup horizontalCenter="0" verticalCenter="0">
    <s:Label text="Enter your username:"/>
    <s:TextInput id="username" />
    <s:Button label="Submit" id="submitButton"/>
  </s:VGroup>
</s:Application>
```

In figure 6.3 you use the button click to trigger the validation.

You'll notice you did two things differently:

- By default the validator (in the generic sense) is going to listen for the triggering event to occur on the component it's validating (normally it would look for the user to commit the value in the TextInput). This was overridden by setting the trigger property to point to the button instead.
- By default, the triggering event is the valueCommit event. But because you're using a button, you want the validator to watch for the button's click event, rather than a press of the Enter or Tab key.

Figure 6.3　This `StringValidator` warns the user that the minimum required number of characters hasn't been entered into the field.

Using validators is pretty straightforward without a whole lot of pizzazz. They're utility oriented and have a narrow purpose, making them an easy-to-use mechanism.

Knowing that there are string-based validators, you'd be correct in assuming there's also a counterpart number-based validator.

6.2.3   *NumberValidator*

As its name implies, the NumberValidator caters to evaluating numerical information. It's so versatile that you can test to verify that the input value is neither too big nor too small, or perhaps that it should be an integer only, or that it doesn't contain negative numbers. The NumberValidator is also smart enough to recognize the separation between numbers in the thousands (for instance, 23,543,121.72).

> **TIP**   For internationalization, the NumberValidator provides the thousands-Separator and decimalSeparator properties.

With all the properties that are available, this is a flexible validator. In listing 6.3 you put it to work by making sure the value of the number entered by a user falls within the range of 5 and 110 and the number is an integer.

Listing 6.3   NumberValidator used to check a value and if the number is an integer

```
<?xml version="1.0"?>
<s:Application xmlns:fx="http://ns.adobe.com/mxml/2009"
               xmlns:s="library://ns.adobe.com/flex/spark"
               xmlns:mx="library://ns.adobe.com/flex/mx">
  <fx:Declarations>
    <mx:NumberValidator
      source="{age}" property="text" allowNegative="false"
      negativeError="I highly doubt you're that young!"
      minValue="5" maxValue="110" domain="int"
      trigger="{submitButton}" triggerEvent="click"/>
  </fx:Declarations>
  <s:VGroup horizontalCenter="0" verticalCenter="0">
    <s:Label text="Enter your age:"/>
    <s:TextInput id="age" />
    <s:Button label="Submit" id="submitButton"/>
  </s:VGroup>
</s:Application>
```

Figure 6.4 shows the results of entering a negative number; you should get a warning that the input provided is unacceptable.

The allowNegative attribute is redundant in the previous example. You can use it with no adverse effects; it would only indicate to the user (as shown in figure 6.5) that

Figure 6.4   NumberValidator used to check whether a user has typed in a realistic age

a negative number isn't allowed. Because we defined a minimum value, the user would have already been warned.

We've shown you how to validate strings and numbers. The next most popular components to validate are dates.

6.2.4 DateValidator

You guessed it! This helps you work with entries designed to receive calendar data. A neat feature of the DateValidator is that it accepts three separate input controls that store the month, day, and year (unlike other validators in which you target a single source).

You have the option of using the standard single source (for example, a Text-Input) that will store the number in the format mm/dd/yy or using a collection of input fields to capture each part of the date as separate items (month, date, and year), and you can then configure the DateValidator to understand which field represents which part of a date.

To demonstrate using a single source DateValidator, listing 6.4 checks a Text-Input to see if what's been entered is a valid date.

Listing 6.4 Using the `DateValidator` to validate a single-source input

```xml
<?xml version="1.0"?>
<s:Application xmlns:fx="http://ns.adobe.com/mxml/2009"
               xmlns:s="library://ns.adobe.com/flex/spark"
               xmlns:mx="library://ns.adobe.com/flex/mx">
  <fx:Declarations>
    <mx:DateValidator
      source="{birthday}" property="text" inputFormat="mm/dd/yyyy"
      allowedFormatChars="/"
      trigger="{submitButton}" triggerEvent="click"/>
  </fx:Declarations>
  <s:VGroup horizontalCenter="0" verticalCenter="0">
    <s:Label text="Enter your birth date:"/>
    <s:TextInput id="birthday" />
    <s:Button label="Submit" id="submitButton"/>
  </s:VGroup>
</s:Application>
```

In figure 6.5 you can see the DateValidator responds because December doesn't have 39 days. It even points out to the user where the error lies.

You take this example a bit further in listing 6.5 by splitting the date into separate fields using the advanced properties.

Figure 6.5 `DateValidator` doesn't like the date entered.

Listing 6.5   Advanced properties example

```xml
<?xml version="1.0"?>
<s:Application xmlns:fx="http://ns.adobe.com/mxml/2009"
               xmlns:s="library://ns.adobe.com/flex/spark"
               xmlns:mx="library://ns.adobe.com/flex/mx">
  <fx:Declarations>
    <mx:DateValidator
      monthSource="{month}" monthProperty="value"
      daySource="{day}" dayProperty="value"
      yearSource="{year}" yearProperty="text"
      trigger="{submitButton}" triggerEvent="click"/>
  </fx:Declarations>
  <s:HGroup horizontalCenter="0" verticalCenter="0">
    <s:Label text="Month:"/>
    <s:NumericStepper id="month" />
    <s:Label text="Day:"/>
    <s:NumericStepper id="day" />
    <s:Label text="Year:"/>
    <s:TextInput id="year" width="60"/>
    <s:Button label="Submit" id="submitButton"/>
  </s:HGroup>
</s:Application>
```

> Identifying a date split across multiple inputs

Let's put this to the test by entering all three sections—month, day, and year—of the date. This time, enter a bogus date, as shown in figure 6.6. A pop-up will prompt you to fix the problem.

The DateValidator is a convenient way to validate single text date entries or dates that are captured in separate fields.

> **TIP**   In a real-world application, you'd want to use the DateField or Date-Chooser controls to capture a date from the user.

Now that we've covered the basic validators, we'll look at other common use cases, starting with email validation.

6.2.5   *EmailValidator*

Verifying email addresses is a staple of any registration feature of an application, and in most web applications post validation is done on the server side. The EmailValidator is fairly thorough in its verification and checks everything, from making sure you have an @ sign to verifying there's a proper domain suffix.

The only properties you can configure are error messages. The reason for this is simple: An email is an email wherever you go, with a standardized naming structure and limited variations to that structure, so there's not much you'd need to prepare for to capture an address.

Figure 6.6   A DateValidator can be used to validate the separate form inputs that make up the complete date.

Putting this to work, listing 6.6 uses an `EmailValidator` to check whether an email address is formatted properly (no spaces, special characters, missing characters, and so on).

Listing 6.6 Verifying that what is entered is a properly structured email address

```
<?xml version="1.0"?>
<s:Application xmlns:fx="http://ns.adobe.com/mxml/2009"
               xmlns:s="library://ns.adobe.com/flex/spark"
               xmlns:mx="library://ns.adobe.com/flex/mx">
  <fx:Declarations>
    <mx:EmailValidator source="{email}" property="text"
                invalidCharError="You've got some funky characters"
                trigger="{submitButton}" triggerEvent="click"/>
  </fx:Declarations>
  <s:VGroup horizontalCenter="0" verticalCenter="0">
    <s:Label text="Email:"/>
    <s:TextInput id="email"/>
    <s:Button label="Submit" id="submitButton"/>
  </s:VGroup>
</s:Application>
```

Custom warning message

After compiling and running the application, try entering an email address with some invalid characters, and you should see the error message shown in figure 6.7.

Prevalidating an email address in real time isn't done too often in the web development world. The more complex the validation, the more developers are going to defer validating to the backend's server-side technology.

Email prevalidation is conducted infrequently in HTML+JavaScript, but what's even rarer is validating a credit card number on the fly.

6.2.6 *CreditCardValidator*

Now we're getting into some interesting validators that you don't come across in many programming languages. In this case we're talking about the `CreditCardValidator`, which uses the *Luhn mod10* algorithm (a simple checksum formula to validate numbers) to verify that the number and credit card type supplied by the user are a match.

This validator requires two input sources:

- Credit card type (Flex supports American Express, Diners Club, Discover, MasterCard, and Visa.)
- Credit card number

Its properties are focused on providing the ability to check for formatting characters, number (no number provided, bad number provided, and so on), and type.

Figure 6.7
The `EmailValidator` flags this address, because there's an invalid space character within it.

In listing 6.7, instead of hardcoding many of the properties, you allow the user to select the credit card type. Then, using data binding, you update the appropriate property on the `CreditCardValidator`.

Listing 6.7   Using data binding to know which type of credit card to validate

```
<?xml version="1.0"?>
<s:Application xmlns:fx="http://ns.adobe.com/mxml/2009"
               xmlns:s="library://ns.adobe.com/flex/spark"
               xmlns:mx="library://ns.adobe.com/flex/mx">
  <fx:Declarations>
    <mx:CreditCardValidator
      cardNumberSource="{cardNumber}"
      cardNumberProperty="text"                    Card type set
      cardTypeSource="{cardType}"                  dynamically
      cardTypeProperty="selectedItem"              using binding
      trigger="{submitButton}"
      triggerEvent="click"/>                       Trigger on the
  </fx:Declarations>                               button click
  <s:VGroup horizontalCenter="0" verticalCenter="0">
    <s:DropDownList id="cardType" width="150">
      <mx:ArrayCollection>
        <fx:String>American Express</fx:String>
        <fx:String>Visa</fx:String>
        <fx:String>Diners Club</fx:String>
        <fx:String>Discover</fx:String>
        <fx:String>MasterCard</fx:String>
      </mx:ArrayCollection>
    </s:DropDownList>
    <s:Label text="Card Number:"/>
    <s:TextInput id="cardNumber"/>
    <s:Button label="Submit" id="submitButton"/>
  </s:VGroup>
</s:Application>
```

Let's test this by running the application and inserting four blocks of four digits to represent a credit card number. Unless you type a valid Visa number, you'll get a warning similar to that of figure 6.8.

While we're on the subject of online transactions, what about validating currencies? If your system accepts international orders, the next step would be to verify the value of currency conversions.

**Figure 6.8
`CreditCardValidator`
used to pair up a credit card
type and credit card number**

6.2.7 *CurrencyValidator*

If you've written applications for the international market, you understand the extra effort involved to encompass the many different ways in which people around the world express the same thing.

The CurrencyValidator provides some relief because it's designed to help you validate an expression containing currency. It's similar to the NumberValidator because it allows you to check for decimal-point precision, minimum and maximum values, decimal separator, and so on. But it adds the understanding of currency symbols and their position.

In listing 6.8, we use a CurrencyValidator to verify that numbers have only two decimal places.

Listing 6.8 Using a `CurrencyValidator` to make sure money values are correct

```xml
<?xml version="1.0"?>
<s:Application xmlns:fx="http://ns.adobe.com/mxml/2009"
              xmlns:s="library://ns.adobe.com/flex/spark"
              xmlns:mx="library://ns.adobe.com/flex/mx">
  <fx:Declarations>
    <mx:CurrencyValidator
      source="{income}" property="text" allowNegative="false"
      negativeError="You pay your employer?"
      precision="2" precisionError="Just 2 decimals please."      ◁─┐ Accept only
      trigger="{submitButton}" triggerEvent="click"  />               two decimal
  </fx:Declarations>                                                   places
  <s:VGroup horizontalCenter="0" verticalCenter="0">
    <s:Label text="How much do you make?"/>
    <s:TextInput id="income" />
    <s:Button label="Submit" id="submitButton"/>
  </s:VGroup>
</s:Application>
```

In figure 6.9 you can see there's a problem with the amount of money entered in response to the prompt (although you may feel the error is that you don't make enough money). In this scenario the validation failed because the user entered three digits to the right of the decimal point, triggering our custom error message to pop up.

Similar to the CurrencyValidator's role in international trade, PhoneNumberValidator facilitates global communication by validating international telephone numbers.

Figure 6.9 This example fails validation because the **CurrencyValidator** is configured to check for two decimal places only.

6.2.8   *PhoneNumberValidator*

This is a simple validator indeed—you either type in a proper number or you don't. It can recognize numbers originating internationally, as well as in North America.

You need only look for two things: The number must contain at least 10 digits, and any formatting characters you use must be valid (defaults to the expected dashes, plus signs, and parentheses).

Listing 6.9 is a simple example that checks to see if the number entered validates a typical phone number.

Listing 6.9   Checking whether the phone number entered is a valid format

```
<?xml version="1.0"?>
<s:Application xmlns:fx="http://ns.adobe.com/mxml/2009"
               xmlns:s="library://ns.adobe.com/flex/spark"
               xmlns:mx="library://ns.adobe.com/flex/mx">
  <fx:Declarations>
    <mx:PhoneNumberValidator
      source="{phone}" property="text"
      trigger="{submitButton}" triggerEvent="click"  />
  </fx:Declarations>
  <s:VGroup horizontalCenter="0" verticalCenter="0">
    <s:Label text="What number can we reach you at?"/>
    <s:TextInput id="phone" />
    <s:Button label="Submit" id="submitButton"/>
  </s:VGroup>
</s:Application>
```

Compile and run the application, but in this case, enter both valid and invalid phone numbers to observe how the validator interprets your input, as shown in figure 6.10.

Trying to write your own phone number validator would be quite cumbersome, if for no other reason than there are so many ways phone numbers are structured. But if you ever come across a situation in which you need to check something these validators don't support, there's always the general, all-purpose, regular expression validator at your disposal.

6.2.9   *RegExpValidator*

RegEx (regular expressions) goes back decades, and still its simple yet powerful language has almost no limits. The validator in this case compares a RegEx expression against a value to determine whether a match has been found (and therefore is valid). Using the expression property along with the optional RegEx flags property (which

Figure 6.10   The `PhoneNumberValidator` is used to verify that only properly formatted phone numbers are entered.

can be used to ignore case, conduct a global search, and the like), you can define the pattern to match.

For example, if you want to validate that the user entered a Social Security number (SSN), you can test whether the text entered matches the SSN pattern using a `RegEx` pattern, as shown in the following listing.

Listing 6.10   `RegExpValidator` matches text against a `RegEx` pattern

```
<?xml version="1.0"?>
<s:Application xmlns:fx="http://ns.adobe.com/mxml/2009"
               xmlns:s="library://ns.adobe.com/flex/spark"
               xmlns:mx="library://ns.adobe.com/flex/mx">
  <fx:Declarations>
    <mx:RegExpValidator source="{ssn}" property="text"
                    flags="gmi"                                       ⟵ Global, multiline, ignore case
                    expression="\d\{3\}.\d\{2\}.\d\{4\}"              ⟵
                    noMatchError="Your SSN is unrecognized."
                    trigger="{submitButton}"                          SSN RegEx pattern
                    triggerEvent="click"/>
  </fx:Declarations>
  <s:VGroup horizontalCenter="0" verticalCenter="0">
    <s:Label text="Social Security Number:"/>
    <s:TextInput id="ssn" />
    <s:Button label="Submit" id="submitButton"/>
  </s:VGroup>
</s:Application>
```

Looking at figure 6.11, you can see that the result is like any other validator, except that behind the scene, the `RegExpValidator` works a little differently. This is because regular expressions are rooted in pattern matching (versus validation).

Figure 6.11   A regular expression used to validate an SSN

You can use this ability to see how many hits were successful matches of that pattern and where they're located in the `String`. To do this you need to employ a little Action-Script to create a validation event handler, as follows.

Listing 6.11   Using `RegExpValidator` to find all the matches on the pattern

```
<?xml version="1.0"?>
<s:Application xmlns:fx="http://ns.adobe.com/mxml/2009"
               xmlns:s="library://ns.adobe.com/flex/spark"
               xmlns:mx="library://ns.adobe.com/flex/mx">
  <fx:Script>
  <![CDATA[
    import mx.events.ValidationResultEvent;              ⟵ Import necessary libraries
    import mx.validators.RegExpValidationResult;
    import mx.controls.Alert;
    private function handleValidation(event:ValidationResultEvent):void
```

```
    {
      var oneResult:RegExpValidationResult;
      for (var i:int = 0; i < event.results.length; i++)
      {
        oneResult = event.results[i];
        Alert.show("Found a match at Index:" +
          oneResult.matchedIndex +
          "\nOn the characters of:" + oneResult.matchedString
          ,"RegEx Results",Alert.NONMODAL);
      }
    }
  ]]>
  </fx:Script>
  <fx:Declarations>
    <mx:RegExpValidator source="{test}" property="text" flags="gmi"
                        valid="handleValidation(event)"
                        expression="m[ai]n" noMatchError="I don't like it!"
                        trigger="{submitButton}" triggerEvent="click"/>
  </fx:Declarations>
  <s:VGroup horizontalCenter="0" verticalCenter="0">
    <s:Label text="Try me:"/>
    <s:TextInput id="test" />
    <s:Button label="Submit" id="submitButton"/>
  </s:VGroup>
</s:Application>
```

Annotations in the code:
- **Evaluate each match** — `var oneResult:RegExpValidationResult;`
- **Loop over each pattern match** — `for (var i:int = 0; i < event.results.length; i++)`
- **Use temporary variable for convenience** — `oneResult = event.results[i];`
- **Display information about match** — `Alert.show("Found a match at Index:" + ...`

In the previous example, a couple of valid pattern matches are returned (figure 6.12), and then using ActionScript we loop through all the matches.

Regular expressions are so powerful that if you could only have one validator, you could use `RegExpValidator` to replace almost the entire set of validators offered by Flex. But for many developers, `RegEx` patterns aren't their cup of tea.

6.2.10 *SocialSecurityValidator*

In the previous example, you used a `RegExpValidator` to validate an SSN, but lo and behold, Flex happens to have a validator specifically crafted for the numerical identifier.

Operationally, this is a straightforward validator that expects a series of digits and a separator in the format of xxx-xx-xxxx. In addition, the `SocialSecurityValidator` lets you specify the delimiter character (a dash or space by default), and it adheres to the SSN rule that the first three digits can't be 000.

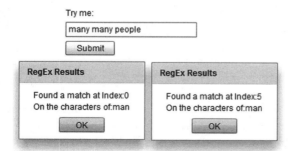

Figure 6.12   The submitted text pattern results in two matches found by the regular expression.

Compare listing 6.11, which uses a regular expression, to listing 6.12, which uses the `SocialSecurityValidator`.

Listing 6.12 `SocialSecurityValidator` alerts user if SSN is improperly formatted.

```
<?xml version="1.0"?>
<s:Application xmlns:fx="http://ns.adobe.com/mxml/2009"
               xmlns:s="library://ns.adobe.com/flex/spark"
               xmlns:mx="library://ns.adobe.com/flex/mx">
  <fx:Declarations>
    <mx:SocialSecurityValidator
      source="{ssn}" property="text"
      trigger="{submitButton}" triggerEvent="click" />
  </fx:Declarations>
  <s:VGroup horizontalCenter="0" verticalCenter="0">
    <s:Label text="Try me:"/>
    <s:TextInput id="ssn" />
    <s:Button label="Submit" id="submitButton"/>
  </s:VGroup>
</s:Application>
```

After you compile and run the application, any input that doesn't match the expected SSN pattern will trigger an error message, as shown in figure 6.13.

Figure 6.13   Busted! The `SocialSecurityValidator` detected that the value entered isn't a valid SSN.

We are almost finished with the built-in validators; the last one to go is the `ZipCodeValidator`.

6.2.11   *ZipCodeValidator*

Finally, the `ZipCodeValidator`. It's a simple convenience validator that lets you check to see if a U.S. Zip Code or a Canadian postal code has been properly entered. For Zip Codes, it accepts either the 5-digit format or the 5+4 format. To control whether you're validating Canadian or American, use the `domain` property, which can be either `US Only`, `US`, or `Canada`. The remaining properties listed in the API Reference allow you to override the default error messages for the various errors that could occur (invalid characters, wrong length, and so on).

Listing 6.13 shows how a `ZipCodeValidator` is used to check whether the user input matches the Zip Code format.

Listing 6.13 Trying out the `ZipCodeValidator` to test for U.S. ZIP Codes

```
<?xml version="1.0"?>
<s:Application xmlns:fx="http://ns.adobe.com/mxml/2009"
               xmlns:s="library://ns.adobe.com/flex/spark"
```

```
                    xmlns:mx="library://ns.adobe.com/flex/mx">
  <fx:Declarations>
    <mx:ZipCodeValidator
      source="{zipcode}" property="text" domain="US Only"
      trigger="{submitButton}" triggerEvent="click"/>
  </fx:Declarations>
  <s:VGroup horizontalCenter="0" verticalCenter="0">
    <s:Label text="What's your Zip Code (US Only)?"/>
    <s:TextInput id="zipcode" />
    <s:Button label="Submit" id="submitButton"/>
  </s:VGroup>
</s:Application>
```

This is another validator with which you'll want to experiment. Entering an invalid Zip Code causes a warning to appear, as illustrated in figure 6.14. Here, a Canadian postal code is entered when only U.S. Zip Codes are permitted.

Figure 6.14   The `ZipCodeValidator` has been configured to check only for Zip Codes, so this Canadian postal code fails.

Because the `ZipCodeValidator` has been configured to validate for Zip Codes only, entering a Canadian postal code won't work (though the validator is capable of accepting both via the `domain` property).

That wraps up all of the available out-of-the-box Flex validators. Next we'll look at the different approaches toward employing validation.

6.3   *Real-time validation*

To validate in real time, or, to put it another way, to catch input mistakes as they happen, requires that you "listen" for each change that occurs when data is input.

To do that, you want to monitor the `change` trigger event, as illustrated in the following listing.

Listing 6.14   Using the `change` event, you can validate in real time.

```
<?xml version="1.0"?>
<s:Application xmlns:fx="http://ns.adobe.com/mxml/2009"
               xmlns:s="library://ns.adobe.com/flex/spark"
               xmlns:mx="library://ns.adobe.com/flex/mx">
  <fx:Declarations>
    <mx:StringValidator source="{address}"
                        minLength="5"
                        property="text"
                        trigger="{address}"                    Use change event to
                        triggerEvent="change"/>                trigger validation
  </fx:Declarations>
  <s:VGroup horizontalCenter="0" verticalCenter="0">
```

```
    <s:Label text="What's your address?"/>
    <s:TextInput id="address"  />
    <s:Button label="Submit" id="submitButton"/>
  </s:VGroup>
</s:Application>
```

In listing 6.14, the moment the user starts typing, the field turns red until the minimum required number of characters (five) has been entered. It's an effective way to keep the user typing until the minimum requirement has been met, but it might also be annoying. To avoid leaving a bad taste in the user's mouth, it may be more appropriate to validate when the user commits the value.

6.4 *Committed value validation*

This is a slight variation on real-time validation using change. Instead of validating on every keystroke, you might prefer to validate as the user commits their value. This can occur when the Tab, Enter, or any of the arrow keys is pressed or the mouse is clicked on another component.

In order to do this you need to change the triggerEvent from change to value-Commit:

```
<mx:StringValidator source="{address}" minLength="5" property="text"
            trigger="{address}" triggerEvent="valueCommit"/>
```

It adds a nice flavor of interactivity, but there may be cases where you want to delay validation yet further until a few fields are filled out. This is when you want to use pass-through validation.

6.5 *Pass-through validation*

Pass-through validation is the more passive approach in which you delay conducting the validation of inputs. In many web applications it's fairly common to let the user fill out the entire form and validate before committing any values to a database.

The submit button is the usual paradigm in such a case, and to make that happen you change the trigger and triggerEvent attributes so they don't default to wherever the source is pointed, but instead to the click event of a button instance.

In an actual form, you'd have many inputs that would have their validators engage on that button click.

Listing 6.15 demonstrates how multiple validators are set up to check various Text-Input fields, but notice how they're all configured to listen for the click event from the submit button.

Listing 6.15 Using a submit button to validate form fields

```
<?xml version="1.0"?>
<s:Application xmlns:fx="http://ns.adobe.com/mxml/2009"
            xmlns:s="library://ns.adobe.com/flex/spark"
            xmlns:mx="library://ns.adobe.com/flex/mx">
  <fx:Declarations>
```

```
<mx:StringValidator source="{username}"
                    property="text"
                    minLength="6"
                    trigger="{submitButton}"
                    triggerEvent="click"/>

<mx:EmailValidator source="{email}"
                   property="text"
                   trigger="{submitButton}"
                   triggerEvent="click"/>
</fx:Declarations>
<s:VGroup horizontalCenter="0" verticalCenter="0">
  <s:Label text="Enter your email:"/>
  <s:TextInput id="email"/>
  <s:Label text="Enter your username:"/>
  <s:TextInput id="username" />
  <s:Button label="Submit" id="submitButton"/>
</s:VGroup>
</s:Application>
```

Validators set up for form fields

Validate on button click

Input form fields have validators

This and the previous examples make use of automatic events, meaning they respond without manual assistance at the triggering of the event. But you can validate a value whenever you want using scripted validation.

6.6   *Scripted validation*

All the validators presented thus far have an ActionScript equivalent to provide maximum convenience and control.

You'd typically use the ActionScript version when you want to reuse the same validator to check many values. Those values don't need to be user input controls; you can use them to validate anything.

Listing 6.16   Using ActionScript to validate values at will

```
<?xml version="1.0"?>
<s:Application xmlns:fx="http://ns.adobe.com/mxml/2009"
               xmlns:s="library://ns.adobe.com/flex/spark"
               xmlns:mx="library://ns.adobe.com/flex/mx">
  <fx:Script>
  <![CDATA[
    import mx.validators.EmailValidator;
    import mx.validators.StringValidator;
    import mx.controls.Alert;
    import mx.events.ValidationResultEvent;
    public var emailVal:EmailValidator = new EmailValidator();
    public var stringVal:StringValidator = new StringValidator();
    public function validateForm():void
    {
      var valResult:ValidationResultEvent;
      stringVal.source = username;
      stringVal.property = "text";
      stringVal.minLength=6;
      emailVal.source = email;
      emailVal.property = "text";
```

Import needed ActionScript classes

❶ Use two validator

❷ Use two TextInputs

❸ Invoke validateForm() function

```
      valResult = emailVal.validate();                      Validate email
      if(valResult.type == "invalid")               4      address
      {
        Alert.show("Please fix your Email address.");
      }
      else
      {
        valResult = stringVal.validate();                   Check
        if(valResult.type == "invalid")             5      username
        {
          Alert.show("Please fix your Username.");
        }
      }
    }
  ]]>
  </fx:Script>
  <s:VGroup horizontalCenter="0" verticalCenter="0">
    <s:Label text="Email:"/>
    <s:TextInput id="email"/>
    <s:Label text="Enter your username:"/>
    <s:TextInput id="username" />
    <s:Button label="Submit" id="submitButton" click="validateForm()"/>
  </s:VGroup>
</s:Application>
```

In listing 6.16, we have two validators ❶ aimed at the two TextInputs ❸. When the submit button is pressed, the validateForm() function is invoked ❷. The email address is validated first. ❹ If it's okay, validateForm() moves to the next input field to check the username ❺.

We've covered the types of validators and how they can be utilized, but we have a couple of parting tips to share before we wrap up this chapter.

6.7 Validation tidbits

For the most part, validation is clear cut, but there are a few more items to cover to round out your understanding of how validators work.

6.7.1 Does a validator always check all criteria?

What if the user types in something that fails to meet more than one of the requirements? Will all of the error messages show? No. Flex runs through its laundry list, checking one thing after another, and then the moment one of the tests fails, it stops on that issue.Validating what was entered vs. criteria matching

To best understand validators, keep in mind that although they can be used to verify that values entered are of a certain type—for example, what was entered is a date, or a credit card number, or telephone number—they can also be used for the more important task of determining whether the value matches certain criteria, such as checking to ensure a date entered by the user is within a certain time frame.

Events

Click for more information on events

▼ Hide Inherited Events

Event	Summary	Defined By
↑ activate	[broadcast event] Dispatched when the Flash Player or AIR application gains operating system focus and becomes active.	EventDispatcher
↑ add	Dispatched when the component is added to a container as a content child by using the addChild() or addChildAt() method.	UIComponent
↑ added	Dispatched when a display object is added to the display list.	DisplayObject

Figure 6.15 Use the API Reference to learn which events are available to use as a `triggerEvent`.

6.7.2 Controlling what triggers validation

To keep things simple we labeled some high-level approaches to validation (for instance, real-time validation), but using the `trigger` and `triggerEvent` properties you can cause validation to initiate off any event you want.

In our examples, we used the `id` of a button for the `trigger` and its corresponding `click triggerEvent`.

How do you know what events are available for you to use? In Flex Builder you can view components in which you're interested via the API Reference, which you can access by clicking Help > Search or clicking the component and pressing Shift+F2.

> **TIP** Another approach is to allocate an area within your Flex Builder workspace for a dynamic help view (see chapter 2), which will automatically display the reference.

Scroll down to the section titled Events. Anything you see listed (figure 6.15) is fair game. For example, you could save the user a click by using the button's `mouseOver` event as a trigger.

You'll find that knowing how to quickly look up information in the API Reference is an important element and fact of life when developing Flex applications. Each of these validators has unique properties, and each component you can validate on has various events that can be used to trigger a validator. All of this information is readily available in the API Reference.

6.8 Summary

Validation is a valuable mechanism for providing a positive experience to your users by minimizing the amount of back-and-forth activity between their client device and a server. By validating on the client side, you add usability by reducing the time it takes to fill out a form. There's also something in it for you and your backend systems, because you'll be relieving some of the server's workload by providing data that has been prevalidated on the frontend.

Flex comes with an impressive collection of out-of-the-box validators that range from basic text and numerical validators to more specialized ones that can validate SSNs and phone numbers. If none of those match your needs, you can use the regular expression validator to match not only a pattern but all occurrences of that pattern in the text.

You can employ validation in different ways: in real time to check every keystroke as it's entered, as soon as the user has committed the value, or all your fields at one time by triggering off the click of a submit button.

You don't have to limit yourself to automatic events, such as clicks. You can use ActionScript to programmatically create a validator on the fly and test it against some specified data.

Once you've validated your fields, a common thing to do then is format them nicely. In the next chapter we'll look at how this can be done using Flex's formatters.

Formatting data

This chapter covers

- Formatting raw data with Flex's built-in formatters
- Types of formatters
- Real-time formatting and scripted formatting
- Dealing with formatting errors

Formatters are a class of objects that take raw data and transform it into a presentable visual format. From a usage perspective, they're comparable to validators in that similar mechanisms are employed to implement them. Formatters can be configured to function in two modes:

- *Real-time*—Formatting is conducted on the fly automatically via data binding.
- *Scripted*—Using ActionScript you can create instances of formatters explicitly when needed and process the data accordingly.

The most important thing to know is that formatters are incredibly easy to use. Raw data is fed in and structured, and legible content is delivered back. In this chapter we show you how to use the built-in formatters that come with Flex and all the ways they can be applied.

> **NOTE** Formatters work only with raw, unformatted data. If you use a formatter on a user-editable field, be sure any formatted data is removed from the input before attempting to process it again. For example, if you have a

form that allows users to update their phone number, and you default the value to the current phone number in the system in a formatted manner and they make an update, you'd strip away all nonnumeric characters before giving it to the formatter again. Otherwise, the formatter will give you an error saying that it's not happy with the data given to it.

Formatters can function independently and can be used across a range of scenarios. One common case is to retrieve data from a server (a database, for instance) and send that to a formatter in order to present it in an organized, readable fashion. This is usually done over the internet, but we don't want to waste a lot of time in this chapter dealing with connectivity issues, so to keep things simple we'll use static XML to simulate this data.

Let's start with the built-in formatters.

7.1   Built-in formatters

Flex provides a number of built-in formatters that get you going quickly. Each is a descendent from the master `Formatter` class and by default carries a common set of properties, functions, and events.

As Adobe did with validators, these descendants are focused on formatting data in specific contexts, and they have unique properties to address each of these scenarios. This is where the API Language Reference lets us know of these available properties.

We'll list all the formatters, starting with the parent class, and show how they work. Note that each can do what the parent (formatter) can do.

7.1.1   Formatter

`Formatter` is a parent object and serves as a template for its family of more specialized formatters. As a base class, its utility is limited, but as shown in table 7.1, it does define one key function.

Table 7.1   The key function of all formatters

Function	Description
format	Takes in an object that needs to be formatted and returns a `String` with the result.

`Formatter` also has an important property (table 7.2) that's used to determine the source of a format problem.

Other formatters may have additional configuration properties, but the usage is the same.

Table 7.2   The key property of all formatters

Property	Type	Description
error	String	Use this property when trying to isolate a format problem. You'll know an error has occurred when the `format()` function returns an empty `String`.

7.1.2   *NumberFormatter*

No doubt, the most popular formatter is `NumberFormatter`, which handles numerical presentation details, such as decimal point precision and designating the character to use for thousands separation.

TIP   ColdFusion provides a similar `NumberFormat()` function.

Table 7.3 presents a list of the additional properties included as part of `Number-Formatter`.

Table 7.3   Additional properties of `NumberFormatter`

Property	Type	Description
decimalSeparatorFrom	String	Specifies the character to be used as the decimal separator for the input data. The default is a period (.).
decimalSeparatorTo	String	Specifies the character to be used as the decimal separator for the formatted result. The default is a period (.).
precision	Number	Sets the level of precision (number of decimal places) to be presented in the formatted result. The default setting (−1) instructs the formatter to ignore this property and use the same precision as was used for the input.
rounding	String	Allows you to round off a decimal result. Available options are `up`, `down`, and `nearest`. The default value is `none`. Using `nearest`, the formatter will round up or down to the next full integer (whole number) based on which is closer.
thousandsSeparatorFrom	String	Specifies the character to be used as the thousands separator for the input data. The default is a comma (,).
thousandsSeparatorTo	String	Specifies the character to be used as the thousands separator for the formatted result. The default is a comma (,).
useNegativeSign	Boolean	`true` (default) or `false`. When `true`, a minus sign is used to indicate a negative value. `false` specifies that the number will be displayed within parentheses (accounting style).
useThousandsSeparator	Boolean	`true` (default) or `false`. Determines whether a thousands separator is to be used. If `true`, the thousands separator will be included in the output, represented by the character specified in the `thousandsSeparatorTo` property.

Let's create our first example by using the Number-Formatter to take in a raw number with four decimals and reformat it to display only two-decimal accuracy (figure 7.1). Listing 7.1 shows how this is done.

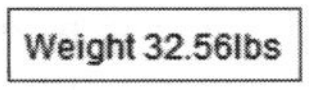

Weight 32.56lbs

Figure 7.1 `NumberFormatter` used to format this weight

Listing 7.1 Using a `NumberFormatter` to format a number to two decimal places

```xml
<?xml version="1.0" encoding="utf-8"?>
<s:Application xmlns:fx="http://ns.adobe.com/mxml/2009"
               xmlns:s="library://ns.adobe.com/flex/spark"
               xmlns:mx="library://ns.adobe.com/flex/mx">
  <fx:Declarations>
    <fx:XML id="myData">
      <root>
        <forsale>
          <item name="weight" value="32.5698" />       ⟵—— Raw data
        </forsale>
      </root>
    </fx:XML>
                                                          ⎫ Define a
    <mx:NumberFormatter id="fmtNumber" precision="2"/>  ⟵┘ NumberFormatter
  </fx:Declarations>
                                                          Format the raw data ⎤
  <s:Label
    text="Weight {fmtNumber.format(myData.forsale.item.@value)}lbs"/>  ⟵┘
</s:Application>
```

Notice that the number (32.5698) was truncated, but recall from table 7.3 that we can use the `rounding` property to round off that return value. The absence of the `rounding` property in listing 7.1 results in the default of no rounding. If you want the output to round up, you'd override the default as follows:

```xml
<mx:NumberFormatter id="fmtNumber" precision="2" rounding="up"/>
```

`NumberFormatter` has a couple of additional error messages (beyond those of the generic formatter) that are specific to its context. These messages are listed in table 7.4.

Table 7.4 Error messages of `NumberFormatter`

Error message	Description
Invalid Value	The value provided doesn't match what the formatter was expecting. For example, nonnumeric characters were provided.
Invalid Format	A combination of parameters doesn't make sense. This can be the result of incorrect property settings, such as specifying an unsupported value for rounding.

These error messages appear in the `error` property of `NumberFormatter`, which in this case would be `fmtNumber.error`. As a programmer, you can use these values to check whether the formatter is unhappy and why and then do something about it.

Now that we've looked at `NumberFormatter`, you may already be visualizing how you could use it to process dollar amounts (or any other denomination). And although you could ostensibly use it for monetary presentation, you'll find that `NumberFormatter` has a close sibling known as `CurrencyFormatter` that specializes in performing such tasks.

7.1.3   *CurrencyFormatter*

Given raw numerical information, `CurrencyFormatter` organizes the data to present it in a recognizable monetary expression by inserting a predefined currency symbol and thousands separators, if needed.

TIP   For you ColdFusion folks, this is similar to `DollarFormat()`.

`CurrencyFormatter` supports all the same properties as the `NumberFormatter` but includes two additional currency-specific attributes, as shown in table 7.5.

Table 7.5   `CurrencyFormatter`'s two additional properties

Property	Type	Description
alignSymbol	String	Instructs where in the output string to place the currency symbol. Options are `left` (default) or `right`.
currencySymbol	String	Specifies which currency symbol to use in the output string. The default symbol is the dollar sign (`$`).

Putting the `CurrencyFormatter` to work, we find it's nearly the same as the `NumberFormatter` (listing 7.2), but it automatically adds the currency symbol, as shown in figure 7.2.

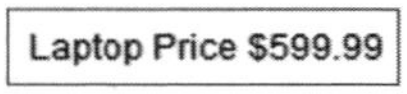

Laptop Price $599.99

Figure 7.2   `CurrencyFormatter` automatically adds the currency symbol for you.

Listing 7.2   `CurrencyFormatter` used to display a price

```xml
<?xml version="1.0" encoding="utf-8"?>
<s:Application xmlns:fx="http://ns.adobe.com/mxml/2009"
               xmlns:s="library://ns.adobe.com/flex/spark"
               xmlns:mx="library://ns.adobe.com/flex/mx">
  <fx:Declarations>
    <fx:XML id="myData">
      <root>
        <forsale>
          <item name="Laptop" price="599.99" />
        </forsale>
      </root>
    </fx:XML>
    <mx:CurrencyFormatter id="fmtCurrency" precision="2"/>
  </fx:Declarations>
  <s:Label text="Laptop Price
              {fmtCurrency.format(myData.forsale.item.@price)}"/>
</s:Application>
```

`CurrencyFormatter` also shares the same error messages with its sibling `Number-Formatter`. Refer to table 7.4 to review those messages.

Moving away from numbers, formatting dates is a ubiquitous requirement in almost all applications. Next, we'll look at how to work with them using `DateFormatter`.

7.1.4 DateFormatter

`DateFormatter` is probably the most heavily used of all formatters. As its name implies, it provides control over how dates appears in your output. Table 7.6 presents the key property this formatter supports (in addition to the properties it inherits from the main `Formatter` class).

Table 7.6 Key property of `DateFormatter`

Property	Type	Description
formatString	String	A pattern mask to apply to the date

That's it! One property that makes use of a *pattern mask*, a sequence of characters that instructs the formatter of the order in which the parts of the date are presented and how to separate those parts. The pattern mask, `formatString`, can take a multitude of combinations, and table 7.7 presents a summary of the characters you can use in it.

Table 7.7 Formatting characters used in `DateFormatter`'s `formatString` property

Character	Description/Examples
Y	Year: YY—Two-digit year. Example: 08 YYYY—Four-digit year. Example: 2008
M	Month: M—One-digit minimum. Examples: 8 and 12 MM—Two-digit minimum. Examples: 08 and 12 MMM—Three-character month. Examples: Aug and Dec MMMM—Full month name. Examples: August and December
D	Day of Month: D—One-digit minimum. Examples: 6 and 22 DD—Two-digit minimum. Examples: 06 and 22
E	Day of Week (0 = Sunday): E— One-digit. Example: 0 EE—Padded with a zero. Example: 00 EEE—Three-character name. Example: Sun EEEE—Full name. Example: Sunday
A	AM/PM
J	Hour of the day in 24-hour format, where 0 is the first hour: J—One-digit minimum. Examples: 4 and 18 JJ—Two-digit minimum. Examples: 04 and 18

Table 7.7 Formatting characters used in `DateFormatter`'s `formatString` property *(continued)*

Character	Description/Examples
H	Hour of the day in 24-hour format, where 1 is the first hour: H—One-digit minimum. Examples: 4 and 12 HH—Two-digit minimum. Examples: 04 and 12
K	Hour of the day in 12-hour format, where 0 is the first hour: K—One-digit minimum. Examples: 0 and 11 KK—Two-digit minimum. Examples: 00 and 11
L	Hour of the day in 12-hour format, where 1 is the first hour: L—One-digit minimum. Examples: 1 and 12 LL—Two-digit minimum. Examples: 01 and 12
N	Minute: N—One-digit minimum. Examples: 5 and 55 NN—Two-digit minimum. Examples: 05 and 55
S	Second: S—One-digit minimum. Examples: 2 and 56 SS—Two-digit minimum. Examples: 02 and 56
Misc. format characters	Nested between any of the other `DateFormatter` properties, you can specify any other characters you wish to use in your presentation. Common characters are commas, dashes, forward slashes, and spaces.

As with other formatters, these include error messages, as shown in table 7.8.

Table 7.8 Error messages of `DateFormatter`

Error message	Description
Invalid Value	`DateFormatter` didn't recognize the data as a date. It accepts either a `Date` object or a **String** object that contains a date.
Invalid Format	A noncompliant format was entered into `formatString`.

Although `DateFormatter`'s `format()` function can take the date as a string, it can also take a date object, as demonstrated in the following listing.

Listing 7.3 `DateFormatter` can format strings with dates and date objects

```
<?xml version="1.0" encoding="utf-8"?>
<s:Application xmlns:fx="http://ns.adobe.com/mxml/2009"
               xmlns:s="library://ns.adobe.com/flex/spark"
               xmlns:mx="library://ns.adobe.com/flex/mx">
  <fx:Script>                                              Date represented
    <![CDATA[                                              as String
      [Bindable]
      public var sDate:String = "12/01/08 12:42";      ◁┘
      [Bindable]                                            Date object to
                                                            be formatted
      public var dDate:Date = new Date("12/01/08 12:42");  ◁  cases
```

```
      ]]>
    </fx:Script>
    <fx:Declarations>
      <mx:DateFormatter id="fmtDate" formatString="MM.DD.YY"/>
    </fx:Declarations>
    <s:VGroup verticalCenter="0" horizontalCenter="0" horizontalAlign="center">
      <s:Label text="Formatting the Date as a String:
                {fmtDate.format(sDate)}" />
      <s:Label text="Formatting the Date as a Date object:
                {fmtDate.format(dDate)}" />
    </s:VGroup>
  </s:Application>
```

One `DateFormatter`
used in both cases

The formatter in this example isn't directly bound to any specific variable—an instance is created and it's reused as necessary to format both `String` and `Date` objects, as shown in figure 7.3.

Formatting the Date as a String:	12.01.08
Formatting the Date as a Date object:	12.01.08

Figure 7.3 A single `DateFormatter` is used to format both `Strings` and `Date` objects.

In the previous examples we used XML data, and to show you something different we used other data types. But you certainly can use XML data if you'd like.

USING XML WITH THE DATEFORMATTER

Listing 7.3 used variables as the data to format, but applying the same approach to XML data doesn't return the expected results, as shown in the following listing.

Listing 7.4 You'd think this works, but it doesn't.

```
<fx:Declarations>
  <fx:XML id="myData">
    <root>
      <info>
        <item lastvisit="12/01/08 12:42"/>
      </info>
    </root>
  </fx:XML>
  <mx:DateFormatter id="fmtDate" formatString="MM.DD.YY"/>
</fx:Declarations>
<s:Label
  text="{fmtDate.format(myData.info.item.@lastvisit)}" />
```

This doesn't work because Flex internally transforms XML into a collection of high-level objects—neither specifically a `Date` nor a `String` (which is what the format function expects).

But this is a simple fix by wrapping a `String` around the variable as follows:

```
<s:Label text="{fmtDate.format(String(myData.info.item.@lastvisit))}" />
```

This technique is known as *casting*, which lets you convert (cast) one type of data into another.

You'll be using the `DateFormatter` quite a bit in your Flex applications. The main thing to remember is that this formatter is slightly different in that it can accept not only a textual `String` but also a `Date` object.

Another aspect that makes the DateFormatter somewhat special is its format-String property, which offers significant control in how the date is displayed. This property is shared by PhoneFormatter, which we'll explore next.

7.1.5 *PhoneFormatter*

PhoneFormatter is particularly useful if you're storing phone numbers—in a database, for example—in plain digits only, but you want to present them in commonly recognized forms.

In terms of its behavior, it's similar to DateFormatter in that you have a format-String to specify the display pattern to apply to the number, and its format() function accepts two types of objects: a String and a Number.

Table 7.9 contains a list of the available properties supported by PhoneFormatter.

Table 7.9 Properties of `PhoneFormatter`

Property	Type	Description
formatString	String	A pattern to apply the phone number.
areaCode	Number	Allows you to specify an area code if a 10-digit phone number is entered. If set to -1, this property will be ignored. The default value is -1.
areaCodeFormat	String	Defines how the area code should be presented. Defaults to (###).
validPatternChars	String	A list of valid characters allowed in the formatString. The pound sign (#), is used to indicate placement of a digit. Default characters are +, (,), #, and -.

PhoneFormatter properties supply a broad range of formatting flexibility. Between the default characters and those you can define explicitly, you can create virtually any pattern for your output. Table 7.10 presents a few examples.

Table 7.10 Examples of patterns that can be used for the `formatString` property

Pattern	Input data	Result
###-###-####	2099109872	209-910-9872
(###)-###-####	2099109872	(209)-910-9872
###.###.####	2099109872	209.910.9872
#-###-###-####	12099109872	1-209-910-9872
+##-########	6569362267	+65-69362267

Figure 7.4 illustrates an example of applying a PhoneFormatter to an unformatted phone number; using the formatString you can make it show the way you want.

Contact Phone:	(201) 667-9872

Figure 7.4 A nicely formatted phone number thanks to the `PhoneFormatter`

Listing 7.5 shows how the `PhoneFormatter` was used to display these raw phone number digits.

Listing 7.5 `PhoneFormatter` used to format raw, unformatted phone digits

```
<?xml version="1.0" encoding="utf-8"?>
<s:Application xmlns:fx="http://ns.adobe.com/mxml/2009"
               xmlns:s="library://ns.adobe.com/flex/spark"
               xmlns:mx="library://ns.adobe.com/flex/mx">
  <fx:Declarations>
    <fx:XML id="myData">
      <root>
        <contactlist>
          <item name="contact" phone="2016679872" />
        </contactlist>
      </root>
    </fx:XML>
    <mx:PhoneFormatter id="fmtNumber" formatString="(###) ###-####"/>
  </fx:Declarations>
  <s:Label text="Contact Phone:
           {fmtNumber.format(myData.contactlist.item.@phone)}"/>
</s:Application>
```

If you encounter any problems, be sure to refer to the `error` property of the `Phone-Formatter` to see if an issue occurred. If there's an error, it'll be one of those in table 7.11.

Table 7.11 Error messages of the `PhoneFormatter`

Error message	Description
Invalid Value	This formatter accepts either a `String` or a `Number`; anything else will result in this error. In the case of a `String`, the number of characters has to match the number of characters in the `formatString`; otherwise, you'll get this error.
Invalid Format	Indicates an error in `formatString`. This could be caused by either invalid input characters or the area code not containing three digits.

One important rule to which you need to adhere is that `PhoneFormatter` expects the number of digits in your input data to match the number of pound signs you specify in the `formatString`.

7.1.6 *ZipCodeFormatter*

The `ZipCodeFormatter` is useful when formatting U.S. Zip Codes or Canadian postal codes. Although there's not a lot of formatting involved with Zip Codes, it does give you some added convenience when dealing with 5+4 Zip Codes, as well as when you want to separate each three-part block of the Canadian postal codes.

Table 7.12   The main property of `ZipCodeFormatter`

Property	Type	Description
formatString	String	The pattern mask to apply to the Zip Code or Canadian postal code. The mask you apply must be a known pattern for Zip or postal code representation. Defaults to #####.

Table 7.12 lists the main property available in `ZipCodeFormatter`.

For U.S. Zip Codes you must indicate either five pound symbols (#) or nine. Canadian postal codes must always have six.

If you defined a nine-digit format but only five digits are input, `0000` will be displayed for the additional four digits of the 5+4 portion of the Zip Code. Conversely, if your input data contains nine digits but `ZipCodeFormatter` is expecting only five, the additional four digits of the 5+4 portion of the Zip Code will be ignored.

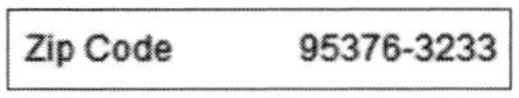

Zip Code	95376-3233

Figure 7.5   Zip Code formatted using the `ZipCodeFormatter`

Let's use the now-familiar `formatString` in listing 7.6 to format a Zip Code with the 5+4 format. After running the example, you should see something similar to figure 7.5.

Listing 7.6   Using the `ZipCodeFormatter` to format a 5+4 Zip Code

```xml
<?xml version="1.0" encoding="utf-8"?>
<s:Application xmlns:fx="http://ns.adobe.com/mxml/2009"
               xmlns:s="library://ns.adobe.com/flex/spark"
               xmlns:mx="library://ns.adobe.com/flex/mx">
  <fx:Declarations>
    <fx:XML id="myData">
      <root>
        <contacts>
          <item name="John Doe" zipcode="953763233"/>
        </contacts>
      </root>
    </fx:XML>
    <mx:ZipCodeFormatter id="fmtZip" formatString="#####-####"/>
  </fx:Declarations>
  <s:Label text="Zip Code
          {fmtZip.format(myData.contacts.item.@zipcode)}"/>
</s:Application>
```

Any errors encountered are usually related to a mismatch between the number of characters entered as input and the number of characters expected by `ZipCode-Formatter`. Table 7.13 lists those errors and their message descriptions.

If the `ZipCodeFormatter`, or any of the other formatters you've just seen, doesn't meet your needs, you can always take advantage of the general-purpose `SwitchSymbolFormatter`.

Table 7.13 Error messages for the `ZipCodeFormatter`

Error message	Description
Invalid Value	This can occur if the input value doesn't match the number of digits `ZipCodeFormatter` expects. In a U.S. Zip Code, only numbers are allowed, and a Canadian postal code must have six characters.
Invalid Format	Indicates an error in `formatString`. This could be caused by an invalid input character, or the pattern itself isn't a recognized format.

7.1.7 *SwitchSymbolFormatter*

`SwitchSymbolFormatter` is a generic, catchall device for presenting data that doesn't fall neatly into Flex's predefined formatters. It stands apart from the other formatters in that it has no contextual understanding of the type of data it's manipulating, making its use somewhat limited.

This formatter is for those who want to get into advanced Flex development and create their own custom formatter (by extending it and adding additional logic; see chapter 17 for more on that). The `SwitchSymbolFormatter` is the foundation for doing that.

Because of this, an MXML component version doesn't exist, but for fun we can make use of it anyway by using the ActionScript version. See table 7.14 for a list of available functions you can use.

Table 7.14 Functions of the `SwitchSymbolFormatter`

Function	Description
SwitchSymbolFormatter	The constructor (default function). It accepts a character value that indicates the character you're using as a placeholder for digits. Defaults to the pound symbol (#).
formatValue	Takes a combination of a format `String` and a reference to a `Source` object that contains text to format. The format `String` is anything you want, but for each digit in the `Source` object there has to be a corresponding pound symbol (#), unless you specify a different digit indicator.

It's hard to visualize what this formatter does until you see it in action. Take a look at listing 7.7, which uses a `SwitchSymbolFormatter` to process and format raw data.

Listing 7.7 Formats an eight-digit number to be split by a dash

```
<?xml version="1.0" encoding="utf-8"?>
<s:Application xmlns:fx="http://ns.adobe.com/mxml/2009"
               xmlns:s="library://ns.adobe.com/flex/spark"
               xmlns:mx="library://ns.adobe.com/flex/mx">
  <fx:Script>
    <![CDATA[
      import mx.formatters.SwitchSymbolFormatter;
```

Import the class

```
        public var fmtSymbol:SwitchSymbolFormatter                    Create instance
                 = new SwitchSymbolFormatter("#");                    of formatter
        public function formatMe(rawData:String):String
        {
          return fmtSymbol.formatValue("####-####",rawData);          Format raw data
        }                                                             on demand
      ]]>
    </fx:Script>
    <fx:Declarations>
      <fx:XML id="myData">
        <root>
          <workorders>
            <item name="Fix something" id="99818382" />              Raw data
          </workorders>
        </root>
      </fx:XML>
    </fx:Declarations>                                                Call formatting
    <s:Label verticalCenter="0" horizontalCenter="0"                 function on data
      text="Work Order: {formatMe(myData.workorders.item.@id)}"/>
</s:Application>
```

Because this is a high-level formatter, SwitchSymbol-
Formatter has no unique error messages. Figure 7.6
shows a number formatted with SwitchSymbolFormatter.

Work Order: 9981-8382

Now let's explore different ways you can leverage the
formatters you've seen so far.

**Figure 7.6   The eight-digit
number was formatted using a
SwitchSymbolFormatter.**

7.2   *Real-time formatting*

This isn't the official term for it, but it's the approach we've been using for all of the
examples in this chapter thus far (except for the SwitchSymbolFormatter), in which
the formatter's format() function has been invoked on the fly.

For example, these snippets format phone numbers in real time:

```
<mx:PhoneFormatter id="fmtPhone" formatString="###-###-####"/>
<s:Label text="Contact Phone: {fmtNumber.format("1112223333")}"/>
```

It's nothing fancy, but it's easy to use and gets the job done. The limitation is there
isn't any kind of specific business logic embedded within it. If you want to add custom
logic as part of the process, you'll need to move on to scripted formatting.

7.3   *Scripted formatting*

Whether you call it scripted or dynamic formatting, this approach involves using
ActionScript to process input on a more granular level.

Although there are many variations to this approach, they all involve using a function to handle the formatting.

7.3.1   *Using a function with a formatter component*

In this variation we pass the value that we need to format, and we receive back the formatted result from the function. The function itself makes use of an MXML formatter
component that's been previously created.

Because the formatter isn't tightly coupled to, or aware of, the source of the information, this approach is practical in that it makes your function more reusable. At the same time it's still fairly easy to use.

In listing 7.8 a function is invoked when formatting is necessary. It contains some custom logic to change the formatString on the fly.

Listing 7.8 Using ActionScript with a static formatter to format if and when needed

```
<?xml version="1.0" encoding="utf-8"?>
<s:Application xmlns:fx="http://ns.adobe.com/mxml/2009"
               xmlns:s="library://ns.adobe.com/flex/spark"
               xmlns:mx="library://ns.adobe.com/flex/mx">
  <fx:Script>
    <![CDATA[
      [Bindable]
      public var rawPhone:String = "2223333";          ⟵── Raw data
      public function formatThis(plainText:String):String
      {
        //We can add some extra business logic if we want.
        //For example, changing the formatString on the fly
        //depending on the size of the text.
        if(plainText.length == 7)                        Add extra
          fmtPhone.formatString = "###-####";            business
        else                                             logic
          fmtPhone.formatString = "###-###-####";
        return(fmtPhone.format(plainText));
      }
    ]]>
  </fx:Script>
  <fx:Declarations>
    <mx:PhoneFormatter id="fmtPhone"/>
  </fx:Declarations>                                     ❶ Format
  <s:Label text="{formatThis(rawPhone)}"/>               ⟵┘  function
</s:Application>
```

From the perspective of the code that needs something to be formatted, this approach is nearly as easy as the real-time formatting method. It calls the format function, formatThis() ❶, as needed. But you're able to isolate your reusable logic into a function.

One limitation to this approach is that you need to know what kind of formatter you're going to use at the outset. Although you could create an MXML instance of each type of formatter and access each accordingly, it would probably be easier to use the ActionScript version of a formatter to create an instance as needed.

7.3.2 Using a function with a formatter class

Each formatter has an ActionScript class equivalent. This affords you the option of not requiring an MXML component to be packaged along with it. This makes it easier to create a self-contained function that doesn't rely on the user ensuring that an MXML formatter component exists (as shown here).

Listing 7.9   Create an instance of a `PhoneFormatter` on the fly using ActionScript

```
<?xml version="1.0" encoding="utf-8"?>
<s:Application xmlns:fx="http://ns.adobe.com/mxml/2009"
               xmlns:s="library://ns.adobe.com/flex/spark"
               xmlns:mx="library://ns.adobe.com/flex/mx">
  <fx:Script>
    <![CDATA[                                   Import the
      import mx.formatters.*                    formatters

      [Bindable]
      public var rawPhone:String = "2223333";
      public function formatThis(plainText:String):String
      {
        var fmtPhone:PhoneFormatter = new PhoneFormatter();
        if(plainText.length == 7)
          fmtPhone.formatString = "###-####";
        else
          fmtPhone.formatString = "###-###-####";
        return(fmtPhone.format(plainText));
      }
    ]]>
  </fx:Script>
  <s:Label text="{formatThis(rawPhone)}"/>
</s:Application>
```

In the previous listing, you create a PhoneFormatter object on the fly every time the function is called. This new formatter would then be deleted when the function completes execution. With this approach there's a bit of extra overhead, so if you know a particular formatter will be used often, it might be better to declare it once outside the function, as demonstrated in the following:

```
import mx.formatters.*
public var fmtPhone:PhoneFormatter = new PhoneFormatter();
```

The drawback here is the formatter would exist whether you're using it or not.

Because it's modular, you can continue expanding this reusability. For example, you could pass formatString along with the String to be formatted as follows.

Listing 7.10   This custom formatting function also accepts a formatting pattern

```
<?xml version="1.0" encoding="utf-8"?>
<s:Application xmlns:fx="http://ns.adobe.com/mxml/2009"
               xmlns:s="library://ns.adobe.com/flex/spark"
               xmlns:mx="library://ns.adobe.com/flex/mx">
  <fx:Script>
    <![CDATA[
      import mx.formatters.*
      public var fmtZip:ZipCodeFormatter = new ZipCodeFormatter();

      public function formatThis(plainText:String,
                                 formatString:String):String
      {
        fmtZip.formatString = formatString;
        return(fmtZip.format(plainText));
```

```
            }
        ]]>
    </fx:Script>
    <s:VGroup horizontalCenter="0" verticalCenter="0">
        <s:Label text="U.S. Zip Code: {formatThis('95376','#####')}"/>
        <s:Label text="Canadian Postal Code: {formatThis('K1E2X5',
                    '### ###')}"/>
    </s:VGroup>
</s:Application>
```

As the output in figure 7.7 shows, using the Action-Script approach affords you extensive flexibility. You can continue innovating this way indefinitely. For example, you could invoke a different kind of formatter depending on the data type—you get the idea.

The last thing we need to discuss is how to deal with the possible errors you may encounter when working with formatters.

U.S. Zip Code: 95376
Canadian Postal Code: K1E 2X5

Figure 7.7 Using ActionScript, a single function was used to create a `ZipCodeFormatter` where the formatting `String` was passed as a parameter.

7.4 Working with formatting errors

Another benefit of using the scripted approach is that you have an opportunity to address problems. As described previously, the formatters have an error property, which you can use as an alert that a problem has occurred.

If all goes well, the error property will be blank, but if an issue is encountered, it will be presented as an error code (either `Invalid value` or `Invalid format`). When this occurs, the formatted value will also be set to blank, as shown in this next listing.

Listing 7.11 Use the error property to check if a problem occurred during formatting

```
<?xml version="1.0" encoding="utf-8"?>
<s:Application xmlns:fx="http://ns.adobe.com/mxml/2009"
               xmlns:s="library://ns.adobe.com/flex/spark"
               xmlns:mx="library://ns.adobe.com/flex/mx">
    <fx:Script>
        <![CDATA[
            import mx.formatters.*;
            import mx.controls.Alert;
            public function formatThis(plainText:String):String
            {
                var fmtPhone:PhoneFormatter = new PhoneFormatter();
                var formattedString = fmtPhone.format(plainText);
                if(fmtPhone.error == "Invalid value")          ◁─┐ Check if there's
                {                                                   an error
                 Alert.show('The value you entered is invalid.');
                }
                else if(fmtPhone.error == "Invalid format")
                {
                    Alert.show('The value you entered is invalid.');
                }
                return(formattedString);        ◁─┐ Empty String if
            }                                        problem occurred
```

```
    ]]>
  </fx:Script>
  <s:Label text="{formatThis('222')}"/>
</s:Application>
```

When working with formatters, it's always a good idea to check the error property soon after you invoke the format() function, because it gives you a chance to deal with any issues that may have occurred.

7.5   Summary

Formatters are similar to validators, with the two often being used hand-in-hand to first validate data and then format any output to be displayed.

Flex comes with a number of predefined formatters that can make your development chores easier. These Flex formatters have been specifically designed to handle data that typically comes from a backend system, such as a database, but likely isn't in a presentable format for the user to comfortably view.

Formatters can be used in a number of ways, from real-time formatting that uses a static formatter to ActionScript-based approaches that give you the flexibility to inject custom logic.

Don't forget to check the error property though, because you can't guarantee that the formatter was able to successfully work with the data.

In the next chapter we move on to lists, which are a major workhorse of Flex applications. Often these lists are used to display the data results from a backend system, and as you'll see, formatters and lists are often used in conjunction with each other to carry out that task.

MX DataGrids, Lists, and Trees

This chapter covers
- Using `List`-based components from the MX library
- Using `List`-based components to display flat data
- Using `List`-based components to display hierarchical data
- Handling user interactions with `List`-based components
- Retrieving selected items from `List`-based components

`List`-based components are a powerful part of your RIA arsenal, and some consider them the workhorse of an application. `Lists` handle the bulk of the work involved with displaying data and provide many of the conveniences that enhance the usability of Flex applications, such as sortable columns and word wrapping.

Let's say, for example, that you're given a project requirement that requires you to have the initial user interface up and running in a short period of time. You can drag and drop a couple of MX `List`-based components onto the stage from Design view, wire up the bindings from within the IDE (a new feature in Flash Builder 4, described further in chapter 15), and be up and running with a functional prototype for your client in a relatively short amount of time.

8.1 MX List genealogy

As discussed in chapter 2, Flex is a declarative framework for the object-oriented ActionScript 3.0 language, and it's important to be aware of how objects within the framework are related. When it comes to List-based components in the MX library, the top dogs are the MX ListBase and AdvancedListBase classes (which extend ScrollControlBase, which then subclasses UIComponent). Because these are base classes, you don't use them directly. Instead, they act as the foundation for the MX List-based controls.

ListBase and AdvancedListBase provide support for attributes such as width and height, how many rows are to be displayed, and the basic display of information. They also handle user interactions by triggering events (for example, an item being selected). The diagram in figure 8.1 demonstrates these relationships.

Looking at figure 8.1, you can see that whatever the List component is capable of doing, so too is the Tree component, through inheritance. They're all derived from the same foundation, so you can leverage all of the core properties that are abstracted in the base classes.

8.1.1 ListBase and AdvancedListBase's properties

Because all MX List and Tree components are derived from ListBase and AdvancedListBase, each will include the properties of those objects. That's quite a few properties to cover all at once, so we'll save some for later. For now, let's look at the most commonly used properties, which are listed in table 8.1.

The list of properties is lengthy, but remember that List-based components are often the visual workhorse of a Flex application, and they must include enough configurable and flexible options to carry out their tasks.

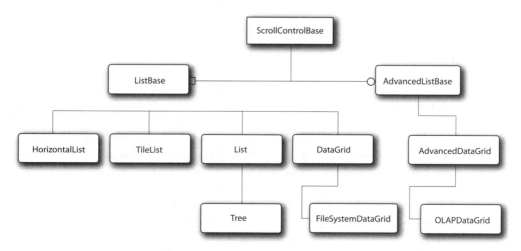

Figure 8.1 The List-based family of MX components and how they're related

Keep in mind that Flex is an event-driven environment as well, so knowing which events are available for `List`-based MX components is just as important.

Table 8.1 Common properties supported by MX `List`-based components

Property	Type	Description
columnCount	Number	Number of columns to be displayed.
columnWidth	Number	Width of the columns.
dataProvider	Object	Object containing the data to be displayed.
iconField	String	Fieldname, if any, that contains a reference to an icon. By default `Lists` look for a field called icon and use it if available.
iconFunction	Function	Optional function name you'd like to run for each icon. This can be used for formatting the icon.
labelField	String	Field name that contains a value to be displayed in the column.
labelFunction	Function	Optional function name you can call for each record. The function determines how the label is formatted and displayed.
lockedColumnCount	Number	Number of columns that always remain in view as the user scrolls horizontally. Used by `DataGrid` and `AdvancedDataGrid`.
lockedRowCount	Number	Similar to `lockedColumnCount` but applies to rows. Lets you specify how many rows at the top of a table are always in view as the user scrolls vertically.
rowCount	Number	Number of rows to display.
rowHeight	Number	Height of each row in pixels.
selectable	Boolean	Value that indicates whether you're allowing items to be selected by the user. Options are `true` (default) and `false`.
selectedIndex	Number	Row that has been selected (if any), if the component is selectable.
selectedIndices	Array	Array of all the selected indices; used when multiple selection is allowed.
selectedItem	Object	Link to the item that's currently selected. You can use this to access all the values pertaining to that row.
selectedItems	Array	Array of `selectedItems` for use when multiple selections are allowed.
variableRowHeight	Boolean	Value indicating whether each row can dynamically adjust its height to fit the content. Set this to `true` if you're allowing `wordWrap`. Options are `true` and `false` (default).
wordWrap	Boolean	Value indicating whether word wrapping is turned on. Options are `true` and `false` (default).

8.1.2 MX ListBase events

Just as the ListBase class carries with it a minimum set of properties that are inherited by its children, the events of the ListBase class are also inherited by the classes that extend it (see table 8.2). You can specify a function name or any ActionScript code you'd like to run when that event occurs. This function is referred to as the event handler. Later in this chapter, we'll explain how to use these events in greater detail.

Table 8.2 Events that are common to List-based components

Property	Type	Description
change	Event	Triggers when the user selects a new row
dataChange	Event	Triggers when the data changes
itemClick	Event	Triggers when a user clicks a column
itemDoubleClick	Event	Triggers when a user double-clicks a column
itemRollOut	Event	Triggers when the user moves the mouse off an item
itemRollOver	Event	Triggers when the user moves the mouse over an item

List-based components would be boring if you didn't populate them with something. Let's look at where that data comes from and how you get it into a List-based component.

8.2 Understanding collections and the dataProvider

You were introduced to the dataProvider in chapter 5. This is one of the fundamental properties of a List-based component, so we're going to dive into it in detail here.

Most components that display a series of data items are powered by a dataProvider object, which encapsulates a for loop that runs on the supplied data collection, assigning an object from the collection to the next item renderer (more on item renderers in chapter 10) in sequential order. Sometimes you might hear this type of component referred to as a *data-driven control*. Although there may be some processing that occurs behind the scenes, the only thing you have to worry about is telling the component the name of the variable that holds the data that you want it to present.

You can do this many ways. Let's look at a few examples of how you can feed information to the dataProvider property so it can be consumed by a data-driven control.

8.2.1 Feeding the dataProvider

A variable can be in the form of a lower-level object such as an Array, Boolean, or String, but it's usually most beneficial to feed a dataProvider with a data type that extends ListCollectionView, such as an ArrayCollection.

Think of a collection as an array on steroids, complete with built-in sorting functionality and filtering capabilities, among other things. It also provides a universal plug-and-play interface to any object that's capable of consuming a `dataProvider` by abstracting the complexities of the data-interaction process.

The best part about collection objects is that they fire off a `dataChange` event whenever any part of the data within the collection changes. This means that any components that are binding to the collection listen for this event automatically so they can update their own visual state whenever a change of data within the collection occurs. This is a bindable event too, so other components can listen for it and perform some type of processing or action when the event is dispatched. Another key advantage of a collection is that if its status changes, the collection broadcasts an event indicating what has changed. Anything that's listening for that event will respond accordingly.

The low-level objects don't support this automatic change notification; if they're altered, anything using them (to drive a display, for instance) won't be aware that a change has occurred.

8.2.2   *Types of collections*

The different types of collections all support a common set of base capabilities, which each type extends further with context-specific features:

- `ArrayCollection`—The celebrity of collections. `ArrayCollection` is based on an `Array`.
- `XMLListCollection`—A wrapper around XML and `XMLList` objects that adds the standard collection features.
- `GroupingCollection`—Used explicitly by the `AdvancedDataGrid` to group data together.

These collections are used to drive anything that supports the `dataProvider`, of which `List`-based components are a key user.

8.2.3   *Users of collections*

As you just learned, `List`-based components are the prime users of collections. Table 8.3 shows which MX components are fueled by a collection object being passed to a `dataProvider`.

Table 8.3   Components that can use a collection for their `dataProvider`

AdvancedDataGrid	Menu
ButtonBar	MenuBar
Charting components including Legends	OLAPDataGrid
ColorPicker	PopUpMenuButton
ComboBox	Repeater
DataGrid	TabBar
Datefield	TileList
HorizontalList	ToggleButtonBar
LinkBar	Tree
List	

You now know the benefits of collections and that these advanced array-like objects can be used as the `dataProvider` for many data-driven components. Next, you'll learn how to use them.

8.3   *Initializing collections*

You can use two methods to initialize a collection. The first is the MXML approach via the associated tag, as follows:

```
<mx:ArrayCollection id="myAC">
  <fx:Object label="Dan Orlando" data="dorlando" />
  <fx:Object label="Tariq Ahmed" data="tahmed" />
  <fx:Object label="John C Bland II" data="jcbland" />
</mx:ArrayCollection>
```

Alternatively, you can initialize a collection purely in ActionScript by importing the class and then declaring a variable instance, as shown in the following listing.

> **Listing 8.1   This `ArrayCollection` is initialized using pure ActionScript**

```
<fx:Script>
  <![CDATA[                                    Import
    import mx.collections.ArrayCollection;      ArrayCollection
                                                when using ActionScript

    public var myAC:ArrayCollection  = new ArrayCollection([
      { label:"Dan Orlando", data:"dorlando" },
      { label:"Tariq Ahmed", data:"tahmed" },
      { label:"John C Bland II", data:"jcbland" }
    ]);
  ]]>
</fx:Script>
```

Let's quickly parse the ActionScript version:

- Start by assigning the variable `myAC` to a new instance of an `ArrayCollection`.
- The `ArrayCollection`'s *constructor* (the function that executes when an object is created) accepts an array of information to use for initial population.
- The square brackets [ ] are a shorthand notation for creating an array (see chapter 3), which is what that constructor expects.
- The curly braces { } are a shorthand notation for creating an object. In listing 8.2, you're creating an array of objects, where each object contains two fields (`label` and `data`).
- You can have as many fields as you want.

NOTE   You can assign your fields any names you desire, but by default components that use a `dataProvider` assume the field containing the display value is called *label* and the field containing data is called *data*. In the interest of convenience, it's nice to take advantage of these defaults; but if your fields are named something else, it's easy to instruct the components as to what field names they need to find.

In this example, the data is hardcoded into the initialization. In most real cases, you'll need to dynamically populate the collection after it's initialized.

8.4   *Populating collections*

Usually, `List`-based components are populated dynamically by pulling in data from a middle-tier application server (for example, from ColdFusion, returning a query).

In chapter 14, we'll explain that process in detail; in a nutshell, you retrieve XML data over an HTTP connection, or call a WebService function, or use a RemoteObject (Flex's binary data-transfer mechanism), to pull in the data—for example, from Cold-Fusion, LCDS, AMFPHP in PHP, and so on. When that data is returned, you convert it to a collection for which your `List`-based component is listening, whereupon it displays the information accordingly.

At this point, let's keep it simple and use static mechanisms to populate our collections. In the following sections, we'll show you a few techniques.

8.4.1   *List*

The `List` is a lightweight component for displaying a listing of information. It's a single-column approach to presenting information.

INVOKING A LIST

You can create and populate a `List` component many ways. Let's start with listing 8.2, which demonstrates the simplest method.

Listing 8.2   Using a `ComboBox` component to display a single column of names

```
<?xml version="1.0" encoding="utf-8"?>
<s:Application xmlns:fx="http://ns.adobe.com/mxml/2009"
               xmlns:s="library://ns.adobe.com/flex/spark"
               xmlns:mx="library://ns.adobe.com/flex/mx"
               height="300" width="400">

   <mx:List id="myFriends" x="10" y="10">
      <fx:String>Ely Greenfield</fx:String>
      <fx:String>Ryan Stewart</fx:String>
      <fx:String>Serge Jespers</fx:String>
   </mx:List>

</s:Application>
```

If you compile and run the application, you'll see a `List` component similar to that in figure 8.2, which contains a single-column list of names. Note that there's no column header and that mousing over any of the items causes the background color to change automatically.

Pretty easy, right? This example uses a shorthand approach to populate the list's `dataProvider`; you'd use this approach only if you wanted to hardcode the display (which is fine for making proof of concepts).

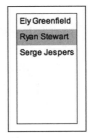

Figure 8.2   An MX `List` component used to display names

Realistically, you wouldn't couple the data so tightly to your code. You want to separate them so your `List` component is told where to look for the information but not how that information is populated. This way, if you need to change how your collection is managed, your `List` isn't affected.

Using only MXML, let's update the example to separate the data into an Array-Collection and then use that to feed the list's `dataProvider`; see the following listing.

Listing 8.3 Using an `ArrayCollection` to drive the display of a `List` component

```
<?xml version="1.0" encoding="utf-8"?>
<s:Application xmlns:fx="http://ns.adobe.com/mxml/2009"
               xmlns:s="library://ns.adobe.com/flex/spark"
               xmlns:mx="library://ns.adobe.com/flex/mx">
  <fx:Declarations>
    <s:ArrayCollection id="myAC">
      <fx:Object label="Ely Greenfield"/>
      <fx:Object label="Ryan Stewart"/>
      <fx:Object label="Chet Haase"/>
    </s:ArrayCollection>
  </fx:Declarations>

  <mx:List id="myFriends" dataProvider="{ myAC }" />        ◁── Binding
                                                                dataProvider
</s:Application>                                                 to myAC
```

Why does this example use an array of objects when the original `List` example used `<mx:String>`? You could use the following approach:

```
<fx:String>Dan Orlando</fx:String>
```

But a `String` holds only that one value, and in a real application you'll most likely be working with multiple fields.

Another option is shown in listing 8.4, which uses the ActionScript class of Array-Collection to populate it with a group of objects.

Listing 8.4 Populating the `List` using ActionScript

```
<?xml version="1.0" encoding="utf-8"?>
<s:Application xmlns:fx="http://ns.adobe.com/mxml/2009"
               xmlns:s="library://ns.adobe.com/flex/spark"
               xmlns:mx="library://ns.adobe.com/flex/mx">
  <fx:Script>
    <![CDATA[
    import mx.collections.ArrayCollection;          Same bindable
                                                     ArrayCollection
    [Bindable]                                   ◁── in ActionScript
    public var myAC:ArrayCollection = new ArrayCollection([
                                { label:"Dan Orlando" },
                                { label:"Tariq Ahmed" },
                                { label:"John C Bland II" }
                                ]);
    ]]>
    </fx:Script>
    <mx:List id="myFriends" dataProvider="{ myAC }" />
</s:Application>
```

That's straightforward. But unless your data always has a field called *label*, you need a way to identify that label more uniquely.

SPECIFYING A LABEL

In the real world, your data is probably representative of the columns of the database in which it's stored. With all these columns being returned, you need to tell the List which field to use as the display, by specifying the labelField.

Listing 8.5 takes the previous example one step further by incorporating this concept and informing the List which column to display via the labelField.

> **Listing 8.5   Using the `labelField` to tell the `List` which column to present**

```
<?xml version="1.0" encoding="utf-8"?>
<s:Application xmlns:fx="http://ns.adobe.com/mxml/2009"
               xmlns:s="library://ns.adobe.com/flex/spark"
               xmlns:mx="library://ns.adobe.com/flex/mx">
<fx:Script>
 <![CDATA[
    import mx.collections.ArrayCollection;
    [Bindable]
    public var myAC:ArrayCollection  = new ArrayCollection([
        {name:"Dan Orlando", email:"dan@domain.com",
                    url:"http://danorlando.com"},
        {name:"Tariq Ahmed", email:"tariq@domain.com",
                    url:"http://www.flexinaction.com"},
        {name:"John C Bland II", email:"john@domain.com",
                        url:"http://www.johncblandii.com/"}
    ]);
    ]]>
 </fx:Script>

    <mx:List id="myFriends" dataProvider="{ myAC }" labelField="name"/>

</s:Application>
```
**Specify the
`labelField`**

Now you know how to invoke the List component, populate it with a collection, and specify which column in the collection is to be used for display purposes. At this point, the List displays in a vertical format; but what if you want to view it in a horizontal orientation?

8.4.2   *HorizontalList*

The default layout orientation for a List component is vertical (the content displays from top to bottom). If you're the type of person who likes to be accurate, you can refer to this as a *vertical list*. As luck would have it, the vertical list has a counterpart, known as the HorizontalList; it functions exactly like the default List, except that its orientation is horizontal.

Revisiting listing 8.5, let's change the List to a HorizontalList (listing 8.6) and see how it affects the output.

Listing 8.6   Switching from `List` to `HorizontalList`

```
<?xml version="1.0" encoding="utf-8"?>
<s:Application xmlns:fx="http://ns.adobe.com/mxml/2009"
               xmlns:s="library://ns.adobe.com/flex/spark"
               xmlns:mx="library://ns.adobe.com/flex/mx">
 <fx:Script>
  <![CDATA[
   import mx.collections.ArrayCollection;
   [Bindable]
   public var myAC:ArrayCollection  = new ArrayCollection([
        {name:"Dan Orlando", email:"dan@domain.com",
                 url:"http://danorlando.com"},
        {name:"Tariq Ahmed", email:"tariq@domain.com",
                 url:"http://www.flexinaction.com"},
        {name:"John C Bland II", email:"john@domain.com",
                 url:"http://www.johncblandii.com"}
   ]);
  ]]>
 </fx:Script>
  <mx:HorizontalList id="myFriends"
                     dataProvider="{ myAC }"
                     labelField="name" />
</s:Application>
```

Change `List` to `HorizontalList`

After compiling and running the application (figure 8.3), you can see that Horizontal-List is identical to List—except it does its job sideways.

A common use of this component is to present images side by side in applications such as product selectors or thumbnails in a photo viewer.

Dan Orlando Tariq Ahmed John C Bland

Figure 8.3   The `HorizontalList` is identical to the `List`, except it presents a horizontal layout.

8.4.3   *TileList*

TileList is similar in concept to its sibling List, but instead of a single column it creates a grid of equal-size *tiles* that contain your display items. There are no column headers or anything to sort. TileList comes in handy if you want to display a visual catalog.

DIRECTIONS

TileList populates and displays its contents either horizontally (the default) or vertically. The primary difference between the two is how scrollbars are used:

- *Horizontal direction*—Horizontal direction builds from left to right, adding new rows as needed. If the grid is made up of more rows than can be displayed in a single view, a vertical scrollbar appears.
- *Vertical direction*—Vertical direction builds top to bottom, creating new columns as needed. If the grid contains more columns than can be displayed on the screen, a horizontal scrollbar appears.

If you want to control the number of columns or rows, check out the `columnCount` and `rowCount` properties, respectively.

INVOKING A TILELIST

Let's take our trusty `List` example and modify it from a `List` to a `TileList` (listing 8.7) to see how the data is presented now.

Listing 8.7 Using a `TileList`

```
<?xml version="1.0"?>
<s:Application xmlns:fx="http://ns.adobe.com/mxml/2009"
               xmlns:s="library://ns.adobe.com/flex/spark"
               xmlns:mx="library://ns.adobe.com/flex/mx">
  <fx:Script>
    <![CDATA[
      import mx.collections.ArrayCollection;
      [Bindable]
      public var myAC:ArrayCollection  = new ArrayCollection([
            {name:"Dan Orlando", email:"dan@domain.com",
                        url:"http://danorlando.com"},
            {name:"Tariq Ahmed", email:"tariq@domain.com",
                        url:"http://www.flexinaction.com"},
            {name:"John C Bland II", email:"john@domain.com",
                        url:"http://www.johncblandii.com"},
            {name:"Joel Hooks C", email:"joel@domain.com",
                        url:"http://www.joelhooks.com"}
    ]);
    ]]>
  </fx:Script>
  <mx:TileList id="myFriends" dataProvider="{myAC}" labelField="name"/>
</s:Application>
```

Create data collection and make `Bindable`

Set data provider to bindable collection

Compile and run the application, and you'll see the `ArrayCollection` laid out as shown in figure 8.4.

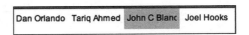

As you can see, by default `TileList` lays out items left to right. To control that behavior, add the `direction` property and set it to `vertical` (see figure 8.5).

Figure 8.4   This `TileList` defaults to a horizontal direction. It adds one item after another until the end of the row, where it begins a new line.

You'll notice in figures 8.3 and 8.4 that John's name got cut off (sorry John!). This happens because the default width of the column isn't sufficient to accommodate the data you're displaying. This is easily corrected by setting the `columnWidth` property to a value that fits your longest item, like so:

```
<mx:TileList x="0" y="0" id="myFriends"
             dataProvider="{myAC}"
             labelField="name"
             columnWidth="150" />
```

TILELIST VERSUS TILE

Hold it! Isn't this just like the `Tile` component you saw in chapter 4? Yes, it's similar; but there are basic tradeoffs to consider.

As a general guideline, `TileList` is usually the more logical way to go. Using a `TileList` consumes less memory and produces a faster initial response, because it renders only the viewable portion of the data. As you scroll to bring more items into view, they must be rendered on the fly, causing a momentary blank spot in their place (hint: one way of mitigating this is to display a little swirling loader icon until the item is rendered), increasing the lag time between scroll movement and a repainted window. The benefit is that from a memory perspective, the `TileList` is generating the minimum number of objects needed to display on the screen (versus generating all of them, regardless of whether they're on the screen). The drawback can be usability if the contents of the `TileList` are complex and numerous, which makes the application feel sluggish. Another way to mitigate this might be to cache a certain number of items in anticipation of the movement so they're shown immediately. But this is a somewhat advanced technique, so it may be worth consulting with another (preferably senior-level) programmer ahead of time in order to work out any potential issues you may encounter.

In contrast to the way item renderers are handled by `List`-based components, a `Tile` renders all children at once, whether it's within the dimensions of the stage's current viewport or not. If you have a decent number of items to be rendered, be careful if you go this route, because the stage won't paint itself until every display object (including all those renderers!) has completed the component lifecycle (see chapter 17 for more on this) and is ready to be displayed. On a slower connection, this could take a long time. On the plus side, once the render is complete, scrolling is seamless, with the only real limitation now being the hardware resources available (for example, scrolling fast will make CPU usage go up a lot because graphics rendering unfortunately can't be offloaded to the graphics processor, and so the Flash Player is limited to a single thread on the main CPU to render everything on the stage).

8.4.4   *DataGrid*

Everyone's favorite display component, the `DataGrid` is your go-to component when you need to display tabular information such as the results of a database query. Most web developers have flocked to this component to substitute for HTML-like tables. Technically, the `Grid` component is closer to an HTML table, but the `DataGrid` makes life so easy it's addictive.

Table 8.4   Additional properties of the `DataGrid` component

Property	Type	Description
resizeableColumns	Boolean	Determines whether the user is allowed to resize the column. Applies to all columns. Options are `true` (default) and `false`.
sortableColumns	Boolean	Determines whether the user is allowed to sort the columns. Applies to all columns. Options are `true` (default) and `false`.

DataGrid offers features such as sortable columns and user-interchangeable columns—the user can arrange the order of columns. It's similar to the List component but includes multiple-column formatting and column headers.

Everything we discussed about the List also applies to the DataGrid. Table 8.4 lists a couple of additional properties DataGrid supports that are specific to its multicolumn nature.

Next let's see how to invoke a DataGrid.

INVOKING A DATAGRID

Referring to the genealogy tree of List-based components, the DataGrid is a close sibling to List. As demonstrated in listing 8.8, invoking a DataGrid is similar to invoking a List.

Listing 8.8   Invoking a `DataGrid`, which is similar to invoking a `List`

```
<?xml version="1.0"?>
<s:Application xmlns:fx="http://ns.adobe.com/mxml/2009"
               xmlns:s="library://ns.adobe.com/flex/spark"
               xmlns:mx="library://ns.adobe.com/flex/mx">
 <mx:DataGrid id="dg" width="500" height="200" >
  <mx:dataProvider>
    <fx:Object name="Tariq Ahmed" email="tariq@domain.com"/>
    <fx:Object name="John C Bland II" email="john@domain.com"/>
    <fx:Object name="Dan Orlando" email="dan@domain.com"/>
  </mx:dataProvider>
 </mx:DataGrid>
</s:Application>
```

The output of listing 8.8 (shown in figure 8.5) illustrates differences that should stand out when compared to previous examples. For starters, a DataGrid includes a header row and is made up of multiple columns.

Try the DataGrid's user-friendly features. Click the column titles to sort a column; click and hold the divider line between the columns and move it left and right to resize them; finally, try clicking and holding a column title and dragging to change its position.

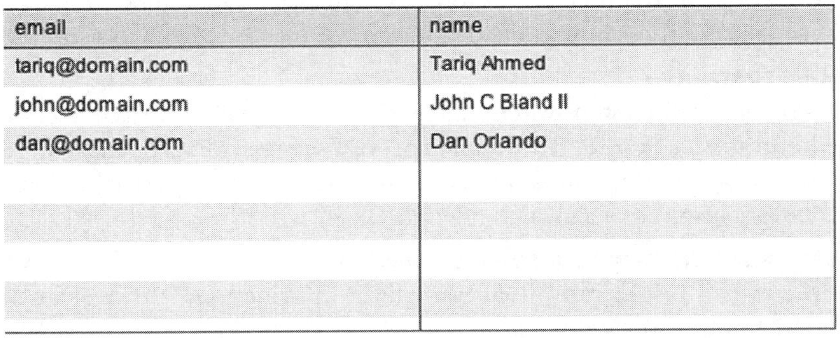

email	name
tariq@domain.com	Tariq Ahmed
john@domain.com	John C Bland II
dan@domain.com	Dan Orlando

Figure 8.5   The first look at a `DataGrid` reveals a sortable header row and resizable columns.

As with a List, your dataProvider is populated externally (refer to section 8.2). Borrowing from the previous ActionScript example, you bind your dataProvider to a variable that contains the information (see the following listing).

Listing 8.9   Using an `ArrayCollection` to feed the `DataGrid`'s `dataProvider`

```
<?xml version="1.0"?>
<s:Application xmlns:fx="http://ns.adobe.com/mxml/2009"
              xmlns:s="library://ns.adobe.com/flex/spark"
              xmlns:mx="library://ns.adobe.com/flex/mx">
  <fx:Script>
  <![CDATA[
  import mx.collections.ArrayCollection;
  [Bindable]
  public var myAC:ArrayCollection  = new ArrayCollection([
      {name:"Dan Orlando", email:"dan@domain.com",
                  url:"http://danorlando.com"},
      {name:"Tariq Ahmed", email:"tariq@domain.com",
                  url:"http://www.flexinaction.com"},
      {name:"John C Bland II", email:"john@domain.com",
                  url:"http://www.johncblandii.com"}
  ]);

  ]]>
</fx:Script>
 <mx:DataGrid id="dg" width="500" height="150" dataProvider="{myAC}" >
   <mx:columns>
     <mx:DataGridColumn dataField="name"
                        headerText="Contact Name"
                        width="300" />
     <mx:DataGridColumn dataField="email"
                        headerText="E-Mail"
                        width="200" />
     <mx:DataGridColumn dataField="url"
                        headerText="Web Site"
                        width="200" />
   </mx:columns>
 </mx:DataGrid>
</s:Application>
```

To support and control the DataGrid's extra display capabilities, you can use yet another set of properties. In particular, you can control the ability to sort.

CONTROLLING SORTABILITY

sortableColumns is the main switch that allows you to enable or disable column sorting for the entire DataGrid. To disable sorting, set sortableColumns to false. To enable or disable sorting on a per-column basis, set the sortable property on DataGridColumn to true or false as needed.

SPECIFYING COLUMN TITLES WITH DATAGRIDCOLUMN

The DataGrid is a bright individual; with little information, it can glean the field-names as the titles for the columns.

But as demanding coders, we always want more—and in this case, we want to be able to control a lot more. To grant that control, Flex provides a tag called the `DataGridColumn` that works in conjunction with `DataGrid`.

You can use the `DataGridColumn` tag to control attributes such as these:

- Column width
- Column header or title
- Word wrapping within a column
- Inline editing
- Instructions for handling mouse clicks in a column

Let's give `DataGridColumn` a try by using it to label each column's header in a more human-consumable manner; see the following listing.

Listing 8.10　With `DataGridColumn` you can control attributes such as column titles.

```
<?xml version="1.0"?>
<s:Application xmlns:fx="http://ns.adobe.com/mxml/2009"
               xmlns:s="library://ns.adobe.com/flex/spark"
               xmlns:mx="library://ns.adobe.com/flex/mx">
  <fx:Declarations>
    <s:ArrayCollection id="myAC">
        <mx:Object name="Tariq Ahmed" email="tariq@domain.com"/>
        <mx:Object name="Dan Orlando" email="dan@domain.com"/>
        <mx:Object name="John C Bland II" email="john@domain.com"/>
    </s:ArrayCollection>
  </fx:Declarations>
  <mx:DataGrid id="dg" width="500" height="150" dataProvider="{myAC}">
    <mx:columns>
      <mx:DataGridColumn dataField="name"
                         headerText="Contact Name" width="300"/>      Defines title
      <mx:DataGridColumn dataField="email"                            and width
                         headerText="E-Mail" width="200"/>            for column
    </mx:columns>
  </mx:DataGrid>
</s:Application>
```

Figure 8.6 shows the results. Mission accomplished—and you use only two of the many properties `DataGridColumn` supports. To see the full range, check out table 8.5.

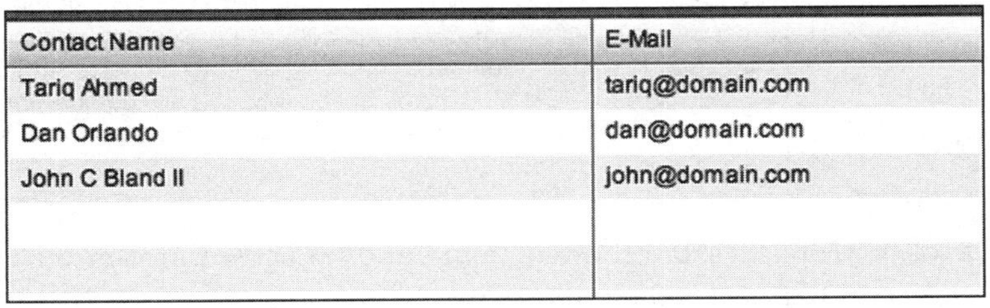

Contact Name	E-Mail
Tariq Ahmed	tariq@domain.com
Dan Orlando	dan@domain.com
John C Bland II	john@domain.com

Figure 8.6　Using the `DataGridColumn`, each column now has a specified title and width.

Table 8.5   Properties of the `DataGridColumn`

Property	Type	Description
`dataField`	String	Indicates which field in your dataset is represented by the selected column.
`headerText`	String	Indicates the column title.
`headerWordWrap`	Special	Permits word wrapping for a column title. Options are `true` (word wrap enabled) and `false` (disabled). If no value is entered, defaults to the `wordWrap` property setting in the `DataGrid` component.
`labelFunction`	Function	If a function name is specified, passes the raw data to the function and displays the text that comes back. Useful for formatting raw data.
`minWidth`	Number	Specifies minimum width of a column.
`resizeable`	Boolean	Value that specifies whether the user is permitted to resize columns. Options are `true` (default) and `false`.
`sortable`	Boolean	Value that specifies whether the user is permitted to sort a column. Options are `true` (default) and `false`.
`sortCompareFunction`	Function	Adds the custom logic necessary to enable `DataGrid` to sort columns based on specified criteria such as numbers, dates, and so on. By default, the `DataGrid` uses a basic string comparison.
`sortDescending`	Boolean	Indicates the default sort order. Options are `true` (descending) and `false` (default, ascending).
`visible`	Boolean	Value that specifies whether the column is displayed. Options are `true` (default) and `false`.
`width`	Number	Specifies the width of the column. Can be given as a fixed number (in pixels) or a percentage of the window in which the column appears. If no columns have their width set, `DataGrid` distributes all columns evenly; if some are set and others aren't, the remaining unallocated space is distributed evenly among the unspecified columns.
`wordWrap`	Special	Similar to `headerWordWrap`, but specific to the column's content. If you provide any value, content wraps; otherwise, it defaults to the `wordWrap` property setting in `DataGrid`. If you enable `wordWrap`, be sure the `DataGrid`'s `variableRowHeight` property is set to `true`.

It seems like a lot of properties, but they come in handy because `DataGrids` are among the most versatile and heavily used components.

As popular as the `DataGrid` and `List` are, their usefulness is specific to flat data. To present hierarchical data, you need to use `Trees`.

8.4.5 *Tree*

The concept of a Tree goes back as far as visual operating systems and is something you've undoubtedly had experience with (Windows Explorer and Apple's Finder are great examples). A descendent of the List, a Tree becomes vital when you need to display hierarchical data; files and folders of an operating system are the most obvious examples.

HIERARCHICAL DATA

Because of the nested nature of the display, it makes sense that your data needs to be structured accordingly. One form of data happens to be structured as such—XML. In Flex 3, the XML and XMLList objects were somewhat redundant, so it's important to know that Flex 4 does away with the XML object in favor of XMLList and XMLListCollection.

As a rule, an XMLList can only be declared within the <fx:Declarations/> tags. The snippet that follows introduces an XMLList object within the Declarations tag:

```
<fx:Declarations>
  <fx:XMLList id="myXML">
    <friends>
      <friend name="Dan Orlando"/>
      <friend name="John C Bland II"/>
      <friend name="Tariq Ahmed"/>
    </friends>
  </mx:XML>
</fx:Declarations>
```

An XMLList can also pull in data from a separate file by using the source attribute:

```
<mx:XMLList source="my.xml" id="myXML"/>
```

The XMLListCollection has the responsibility of wrapping an XMLList object like an ArrayCollection does an Array, adding the functionality of the ICollection implementation. The following code snippet demonstrates how to go about this:

```
<mx:XMLListCollection id="myXMLCollection">
  <mx:XMLList id="myXML">
    <friends label="Friends">
      <friend label="Elad Elrom"/>
    </friends>
    <families label="Family">
      <family label="Laura Orlando"/>
    </families>
  </mx:XMLList>
</mx:XMLListCollection>
```

You'll want to use collections if you're expecting the data to change, because doing so signals any component to whose dataProvider the collection is bound that it needs to refresh its display.

INVOKING A TREE

Creating a Tree is simple once you have the data that drives it. Let's start with the basics of invoking a Tree; listing 8.11 creates a folder structure of contacts.

Listing 8.11   Feeding the `Tree` XML data

```
<?xml version="1.0"?>
<s:Application xmlns:fx="http://ns.adobe.com/mxml/2009"
               xmlns:s="library://ns.adobe.com/flex/spark"
               xmlns:mx="library://ns.adobe.com/flex/mx">
<fx:Declarations>
  <mx:XMLListCollection id="myXMLCollection">
    <fx:XMLList id="myXML">
      <friends label="Friends">                          ⊲┐
        <friend label="Tariq Ahmed"/>                      │
        <friend label="John C Bland II"/>      Top-level nodes
        <friend label="Ryan Stewart"/>         turn into top-level
        <friend label="Joel Hooks"/>           folders
      </friends>                                           │
      <families label="Family">                          ⊲┘
        <family label="Laura Orlando"/>
        <family label="Doug Orlando"/>
      </families>
    </fx:XMLList>
  </mx:XMLListCollection>
</fx:Declarations>

<mx:Tree dataProvider="{myXMLCollection}"        Tells Tree to
         labelField="@label"                     look for label
         width="300" height="200" />       ⊲

</s:Application>
```

The compiled application in figure 8.7 shows the output. The top-level nodes are represented by folders, and final nodes display a file icon. Any item that has child nodes also includes an expand/collapse icon that can be toggled to show the hierarchy.

The `Tree` has no idea what field or attribute needs to be displayed. Because it relates to XML data, you need to tell the `Tree` which attribute among the XML nodes contains the display field by specifying `@label` (or whatever the appropriate attribute is).

Up to now, you've been learning about the display of MX `List`-based components. Now it's time to learn about interaction with these components. Many of the `List`-based components from the MX library have respective Spark equivalents, and it's always recommended to use the Spark version if one exists. But one important component that didn't get ported to Spark is the `DataGrid`. With that in mind, we'll focus a lot of our attention in the next section on interacting with the `DataGrid` specifically. We'll also go into much further depth on interacting with `List`-based components in chapters 9 and 10.

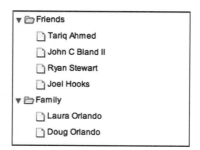

Figure 8.7   The output of a `Tree` component is reminiscent of an OS's file-folder display.

8.5   *Interacting with MX List-based components*

In Flex, ordered sets of data are versatile, and applications use them in unique and interesting ways. The other role `Lists` play is furnishing the user with a means to interact with your application through a component that supports a wide variety of interaction types.

The examples you'll see in this section use the `itemClick` event, but you can use the other events that you'll learn about as easily. For example, if you want to use the `change` event, specify `change` instead of `itemClick`—it's that simple. You can even use both; you may want to execute some logic every time a click occurs, along with the separate logic needed to signal a move from a previously selected row.

By default, when you click a cell, you're clicking the entire row. This isn't as noticeable in a `List`, because it comprises only one cell. But in a `DataGrid`, you'll notice that when you mouse over a row, the entire row becomes highlighted. This highlight is the result of an event that's fired off when the user selects the item.

8.5.1   *List events*

Events are the drivers behind Flex's interactivity; actions trigger events, and event handlers execute a response to those actions. Not all events are relevant to `Lists`, but those with which you need to concern yourself are listed in table 8.6.

Table 8.6   Table events that can be used to handle interaction with `List`-based components

Event	Description
click	Occurs when the user clicks a component. This is a high-level event that's universal to many applications in Flex.
doubleClick	Fires when the mouse button is pressed twice.
itemClick	Indicates which row and column were clicked.
change	Occurs when the user clicks a different row than the current selection.

Implementation of these events is similar to the techniques described in previous chapters. You can leverage them several ways. Some methods are quicker to put into use, whereas others result in greater code reusability by decoupling the dependent logic.

8.5.2   *Passing the event to a function*

Listing 8.12 instructs the `DataGrid` to call some ActionScript (in this case, a function) that passes along the event object that's created as part of the process.

Listing 8.12   Handling a user interaction by passing the event object to a function

```
<?xml version="1.0"?>
<s:Application xmlns:fx="http://ns.adobe.com/mxml/2009"
           xmlns:s="library://ns.adobe.com/flex/spark"
           xmlns:mx="library://ns.adobe.com/flex/mx">
```

```
<fx:Script>
 <![CDATA[
  import mx.collections.ArrayCollection;
  import mx.events.ListEvent;
  import mx.controls.Alert;

  [Bindable]
  public var myAC:ArrayCollection  = new ArrayCollection([
    {name:"Dan Orlando", email:"dan@domain.com"},
    {name:"John C Bland II",  email:"john@domain.com"}
  ]);

  public function contactDataGrid_clickHandler( event:ListEvent ):void
  {
    Alert.show( "You clicked on row:" + evt.rowIndex + " and col:" +
              evt.columnIndex + "." +
              "Which is for " + event.currentTarget.selectedItem.name
              );
  }

 ]]>
</fx:Script>
 <mx:DataGrid id="contactDataGrid" width="500" height="150"
           dataProvider="{ myAC }"
           itemClick="contactDataGrid_clickHandler( event )">
   <mx:columns>
    <mx:DataGridColumn dataField="name"
                     headerText="Contact Name"
                     width="300" />
    <mx:DataGridColumn dataField="email" headerText="E-Mail" width="200"/>
   </mx:columns>
 </mx:DataGrid>
</s:Application>
```

Display Alert box with specific info

Event handler function

Item name accessed

Figure 8.8 illustrates what happens when a row in the `DataGrid` is clicked. As you instructed it to do in listing 8.12, the function displays information pertaining to the selection's row and column that were clicked.

To break it down, let's focus on this piece:

```
itemClick="contactDataGrid_clickHandler(event)".
```

Here, you instruct the application to run the specified event handler function whenever `contactDataGrid` dispatches an `itemClick` event. The event argument is passed

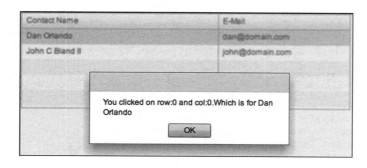

Figure 8.8 A function displaying details about the row on which a mouse click occurred

in the constructor because the handler function will need it to access information about the interaction (for example, where it came from, the data that's attached to the dispatching item, and so on).

This function in turn accepts the event object as its parameter and accesses various properties pertaining to it. When you use this approach, the main property in which you're interested is `currentTarget.selectedItem`.

The `currentTarget` property is a reference, or pointer, to whatever item the event is related to. From an advanced perspective, it's a little more complicated than that; but from a new developer's viewpoint, it's the thing you clicked. In this case, it means `currentTarget` points to your `DataGrid`.

Going one level deeper, now that you have a reference to the `DataGrid`, you access the `selectedItem` property, which contains a reference to the data in the row with which it's associated. By continuing to drill down, you can access the specific data fields on that row:

```
evt.currentTarget.selectedItem.name
```

Mind you, you're not limited to accessing displayed data; you can access any field that's providing the data. You can do so even if you have many more fields:

```
{name:"Tariq Ahmed", email:"tariq@domain.com", domain:"www.dopejam.com"}
```

And for the moment, you're displaying only the name and email fields. You still have access to the domain field in the `selectedItem`:

```
evt.currentTarget.selectedItem.domain
```

Similar to `selectedItem` is `selectedIndex`. It's a number that informs you which row was clicked (0 is the first row).

8.5.3 Passing data to a function

Another approach is to pass only the event in which you're interested, versus the entire event object. This technique offers a slight advantage in that it makes the recipient function more reusable: The function doesn't need to know that the data is part of an event's payload or need to rely on making assumptions regarding the source of the event.

In some circumstances, you may want your function to have specific knowledge about the event. But let's say you want to add a bit of abstraction. The following snippet shows how you can do this:

```
<mx:DataGrid id="dg" width="500" height="150" dataProvider="{ myAC }"
          itemClick="handleClick( event.currentTarget.selectedItem )">
  <mx:columns>
    <mx:DataGridColumn dataField="name"
                       headerText="Contact Name" width="300" />
    <mx:DataGridColumn dataField="email"
                       headerText="E-Mail" width="200" />
  </mx:columns>
</mx:DataGrid>
```

When you click an item, your function is invoked along with a reference to the item clicked. This lets you access the various properties of the object:

```
public function handleClick( data:Object ) : void
{
  Alert.show("Name:" + data.name + ",Email:" + data.email);
}
```

The drawback to this approach is that the function has no reference to the component that caused the event. Without this information, the function can't carry out chores such as changing the component's color to red if a problem occurs.

8.5.4   Accessing the selected row directly

A more straightforward approach is to access the component directly. The advantage of this approach (other than it being simpler to implement) is that you can easily access any of the properties specific to that type of component (in this case, a DataGrid):

```
<mx:DataGrid id="dg" dataProvider="{myAC}" itemClick="handleClick()"> (...)
```

Notice that you don't pass anything in your itemClick handler. The function then accesses the values directly:

```
public function handleClick():void
{
    Alert.show("Name:" + contactDataGrid.selectedItem.name + ", Email:" +
               contactDataGrid.selectedItem.email);
}
```

It's a simple technique, but it does the job, and you benefit from ease of maintenance with respect to the function—it doesn't care who called it or why it was called.

8.5.5   Binding to a selected row

This is the simplest approach. By using Flex's binding feature, you can display or store the selected item without having to use event handlers. This snippet shows how to use this technique without a function, by binding the current selection to an item that calls for the value:

```
<mx:DataGrid id="contactDataGrid" width="500" height="150"
               dataProvider="{myAC}">
  <mx:columns>
    <mx:DataGridColumn dataField="name" headerText="Name" width="300" />
    <mx:DataGridColumn dataField="email" headerText="E-Mail" width="200"/>
  </mx:columns>
</mx:DataGrid>
<mx:Label text = "The selected person is { + dg.selectedItem.name +
                 dg.selectedItem.email + }." fontSize="16" />
```

Here you're able to show more information about the selected person at the bottom of the window.

That wraps things up for us in terms of the MX List-based components. For the next chapter, its time to bring in the big guns: Spark list controls!

8.6 Summary

List-based components are undoubtedly a crucial part of many Flex applications and the visual workhorse of displaying data with Flex. Part of this is due to lists being a common UI paradigm. Most of the Flex applications you'll build will interact with a middle tier and database tier, both of which run on a server. You'll eventually be making requests for data to the server tiers, but we'll get into that more in chapter 15.

As you learned in this chapter, once the data is displayed, the last piece of the puzzle is handling user interactions. You have many options to accomplish this—you can pass entire event objects to an event-handler function, you can pass only the data, or the data can be retrieved by the function directly. For simple cases, you can take advantage of data binding.

In the next chapter, we'll continue by discussing list customization and the new List-based classes that come with the Spark library.

Using the
Spark List controls

This chapter covers

- How to use Flex 4 List-based components included in the Spark library
- The Spark List-based component class hierarchy
- Spark List customization
- Spark List component architecture
- Interactivity with Spark List-based components

In chapter 8, you learned that List-based components are often the engines that drive your Flex applications. You also learned how to quickly and efficiently utilize and customize the prebuilt List-based components that come with the Flex MX library. In this chapter, you'll learn about the List-based features and functionality that ship with the Spark library, which is new to Flex 4. You'll start by learning about the Spark List-based component architecture, and then you'll learn how to leverage the new List-based Spark functionality in your Flex 4 applications.

The Spark library that ships with the Flex 4 SDK caters to requirements that are more demanding in terms of design and functionality because it provides more opportunity for scalability. For example, let's say you're the senior user experience designer on your Flex team for a high-profile game-changing RIA application. The

UI designs came from the number-one design firm in the world, and they require a level of customization that's among the most complex that you've ever seen. This is the kind of situation where the Spark library comes in handy.

Spark includes an alternative architecture for `List`-based components that's largely centered on building advanced, custom `List`-based components. This chapter primarily focuses on the out-of-the-box components that are packaged with the Spark library in the Flex SDK.

9.1 Spark List genealogy

As you learned in chapter 8, `List`-based components in the MX library are derived from the `ListBase` and `AdvancedListBase` objects. In Spark, a `List`-based component extends the Spark `ListBase` class located in the `spark.components.supportClasses` package. The Spark `ListBase` class extends the `SkinnableDataContainer` class. It's important to understand that although both the MX and the Spark libraries have a class called `ListBase`, these are two completely different classes, which reside in two separate libraries.

9.1.1 Identifying the proper component using namespaces

Flex automatically knows which one to use through the use of namespaces. For example, by instantiating a new list with `<mx:List/>`, the MX version of the `List` component will be used, along with the MX `ListBase` class. But by instantiating a new list with `<s:List/>`, the Spark version of the `List` component will be used and so will the Spark `ListBase` class. In ActionScript, you can tell your application which one to use via your `import` statements. If you want to use the MX `List` component, import `mx.controls.List`. In contrast, assuming you want the Spark `List`, import `spark.components.List`. Although `<mx:List/>` will work, the Flex team makes it clear that you should use the Spark version of any component assuming there is one is available. If you start typing the code `<mx:List/>`, the Flash Builder 4 code-hinting feature will tell you that you should use `<s:List/>` instead. This is a handy little feature because in the event that you are not sure whether a particular component is supported in Spark, you can start by typing the characters `<mx:`, and if a Spark version is available, it will automatically recommend that you use it instead.

If you feel like your head is spinning already, don't worry. As you continue reading this chapter, this will all begin to make sense. It's a noteworthy point that by default, `List`-based components from the MX library can coexist with those that belong to the Spark library within a given application provided that the respective namespaces are declared at the root tag of the document.

9.1.2 Item renderers with Spark List-based controls

In both MX and Spark, `List` extends `ListBase`. In MX, `ListBase` extends `Scroll-ControlBase`, which extends `UIComponent`. In contrast, Spark `ListBase` extends the Spark `SkinnableDataContainer` class, which is responsible for displaying data items using item renderers.

Data items can be simple data types, such as `String` and `Number` of objects, or more complex data types, such as `Object` and `XMLNode` objects. This is where item renderers come into play. Item renderers may already be a familiar concept if you've worked with the MX list-based components in Flex 3. If this is a new concept for you though, you'll be happy to know that we'll discuss the concept of item renderers in further detail in the next chapter, on customizing `List`-based controls. Figure 9.1 shows you three Spark `List`-based controls and how they're subclassed.

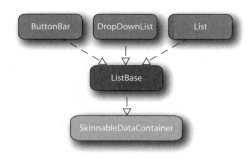

Figure 9.1 The relationship of Spark `List`-based components and their base classes. The three Spark `List`-based components are derived from the `SkinnableDataContainer` class.

9.2   *Spark List-based controls*

It's noteworthy to point out that creating a custom `List`-based component in Flex 4 is easier than with previous versions of the Flex SDK. The best way to accomplish this is by extending either the Spark `ListBase` class or the `SkinnableDataContainer` class. When a custom component extends the Spark `ListBase` class, the following properties can be declared as MXML tags: `dataProvider`, `labelField`, `labelFunction`, `requiresSelection`, `selectedIndex`, `selectedItem`, and `useVirtualLayout`. If the component extends directly from the `SkinnableDataContainer` class, these properties are still available as attributes but can't be declared as MXML tags.

9.2.1   *The ButtonBar control*

As shown in figure 9.2, the `ButtonBar` control is similar in functionality to the MX `ToggleButtonBar`.

The `ButtonBar` is technically a `List`-based control in Spark because it extends the `ListBase` class. A menu is easy to create using the Spark Button-Bar control, as shown in the following listing.

Figure 9.2 The Spark `ButtonBar` control is similar to the MX `ToggleButtonBar`. Because it's `List`-based, its buttons can be generated using a simple `ArrayCollection` as the `dataProvider`.

Listing 9.1   Implementing a `List`-based menu with the `ButtonBar` control

```xml
<?xml version="1.0" encoding="utf-8"?>
<s:Application xmlns:fx="http://ns.adobe.com/mxml/2009"
 xmlns:s="library://ns.adobe.com/flex/spark"
 xmlns:mx="library://ns.adobe.com/flex/mx"
 minWidth="1024" minHeight="768">
  <s:layout>
```

```
      <s:VerticalLayout paddingLeft="20" paddingTop="20"/>
   </s:layout>
   <s:ButtonBar>
      <mx:ArrayCollection>
         <fx:String>Button One</fx:String>
         <fx:String>Second Button</fx:String>
         <fx:String>Button Three</fx:String>
         <fx:String>Last Button</fx:String>
      </mx:ArrayCollection>
   </s:ButtonBar>
</s:Application>
```

◁─┐ **Buttons are set with an
   ArrayCollection**

You may be wondering why the `ButtonBar` control is considered `List` based, whereas other controls that are similar in functionality aren't. Because the control extends the `ListBase` class, the array of buttons within the `ButtonBar` is created from a `for` loop that's abstracted in the `ButtonBar` class. This means that you can use any object that implements the `ICollectionView` interface as the `dataProvider` to create a `Button-Bar`. This includes all of the collection objects discussed in chapter 8. The example in listing 9.2 uses an `ArrayCollection` object to declare the array of buttons within the `ButtonBar` list.

A `ButtonBar` can also be dynamically populated using an object that's passed to the application from another data source, such as a ColdFusion web server or an external XML file.

> **TIP** The `ButtonBar` is a handy component. Consider using it as an alternative to the `TabNavigator` when you need to control a `ViewStack`. This gives you the freedom to place the `ButtonBar` and `ViewStack` anywhere on the stage without them being bound to each other.

9.2.2 *The Spark List control*

Properties of `List`-based components are easily defined with MXML tags, as listing 9.2 demonstrates. When the Spark `List` control is declared, it's followed by declaration of the `<s:dataProvider/>` property. Because `dataProvider` is the default property of a Spark `List`-based control, the `<s:dataProvider/>` tag could be removed from the code in listing 9.2, as it is in listing 9.1, and it will still work. If Flex sees a data collection, it will automatically wrap the data in the `dataProvider`.

With Flex 4, most component properties can be declared using MXML tags. For example, in listing 9.2, the Spark List component is immediately followed by the declaration of the `dataProvider`. The same thing can be done for other common properties such as `labelFunction`, `labelField`, and `itemRenderer`.

Listing 9.2 Using the Spark List control

```
<?xml version="1.0" encoding="utf-8"?>
<s:Application xmlns:fx="http://ns.adobe.com/mxml/2009" xmlns:s="library://
    ns.adobe.com/flex/spark"
xmlns:mx="library://ns.adobe.com/flex/mx"
xmlns:comp="com.danorlando.components.*"
```

```
minWidth="600" minHeight="450">
   <s:layout>
      <s:VerticalLayout gap="1" useVirtualLayout="true" />
   </s:layout>
      <s:List>
         <s:dataProvider>
            <mx:ArrayCollection>
               <fx:String>Menu Item 1</fx:String>
               <fx:String>Second Menu Item</fx:String>
               <fx:String>Third Menu Item</fx:String>
               <fx:String>Fourth Menu Item</fx:String>
               <fx:String>Last Menu Item</fx:String>
            </mx:ArrayCollection>
         </s:dataProvider>
      </s:List>
</s:Application>
```

◁─┐ **dataProvider is
default if not declared**

BINDING THE DATA PROVIDER USING THE DECLARATIONS TAG

Spark List-based controls receive data in much the same way as the MX List-based controls. Refer to chapter 8, sections 8.2 and 8.3, for more information on the data-Provider property and using collections. All of the methods of data binding described in chapter 8 on MX List-based controls also apply to Spark List-based controls, but the Flex 4 SDK includes an additional way of binding data to a List control. Listing 9.3 shows how the <fx:Declarations/> tag can be used to bind data to a Spark List-based control. Notice that the dataProvider for the List control is set to listItems, which is the id of the ArrayCollection that was declared inside the <fx:Declarations/> tags.

Listing 9.3   Binding the dataProvider of a List control

```
<?xml version="1.0" encoding="utf-8"?>
<s:Application xmlns:fx="http://ns.adobe.com/mxml/2009"
   xmlns:s="library://ns.adobe.com/flex/spark"
   xmlns:mx="library://ns.adobe.com/flex/mx"
   minWidth="1024" minHeight="768">
    <s:layout>
       <s:VerticalLayout paddingLeft="20" paddingTop="20"/>
    </s:layout>
   <fx:Declarations>
      <mx:ArrayCollection id="listItems">
         <fx:String>Menu Item 1</fx:String>
         <fx:String>Second Menu Item</fx:String>
         <fx:String>Third Menu Item</fx:String>
         <fx:String>Fourth Menu Item</fx:String>
         <fx:String>Last Menu Item</fx:String>
      </mx:ArrayCollection>
   </fx:Declarations>
   <s:List dataProvider="{listItems}"/>
</s:Application>
```

◁─┘ **Declare list
and bind data**

9.2.3 The DropDownList control

Just as with other Spark `List`-based controls, the data for the list is specified by using `dataProvider`. It doesn't have to be declared, though, because it's the default property, as shown in the following listing.

Listing 9.4 Implementing the `DropDownList` control

```
<?xml version="1.0" encoding="utf-8"?>
<s:Application xmlns:fx="http://ns.adobe.com/mxml/2009"
 xmlns:s="library://ns.adobe.com/flex/spark"
 xmlns:mx="library://ns.adobe.com/flex/mx"
 minWidth="1024" minHeight="768">
  <s:layout>
     <s:VerticalLayout paddingLeft="20" paddingTop="20"/>
  </s:layout>
  <s:DropDownList width="200">                    DropDownList is
     <mx:ArrayCollection>                          implemented the
       <fx:String>Item One</fx:String>            same as ButtonBar
       <fx:String>Second Item</fx:String>
       <fx:String>Item Three</fx:String>
       <fx:String>Last Item</fx:String>
     </mx:ArrayCollection>
  </s:DropDownList>
</s:Application>
```

You'll also notice from listing 9.4 that the `width` property was set to 200 as an attribute of the `DropDownList` tag rather than as a separate MXML declaration. The `width` property can't be declared with MXML; it can only be set as an attribute of the respective component tag.

SETTING THE DROPDOWNLIST PROMPT

When you first work with the `DropDownList` control, you'll immediately notice that there is no default selected item when the control is initialized. As a result, you end up with what appears to be an empty drop-down list, as shown in figure 9.3.

Figure 9.3 The `DropDownList` control in its closed state. As you can see, the label field is empty by default.

In most situations, you'll want to display some text to let the user know what they should do with it. For example, you may want to enhance the usability of the interface by displaying instructions to the user instead of just a blank rectangle, as shown in figure 9.4.

The code for adding the user prompt to your `DropDownList` is shown in listing 9.5. As you can see, this is easily accomplished by setting the `prompt` property.

Figure 9.4 The `DropDownList` control with the `prompt` property set. This gives you the ability to provide instructions to the user for enhanced usability.

Listing 9.5   Use the `prompt` property of `DropDownList` control for enhanced usability.

```
<?xml version="1.0" encoding="utf-8"?>
<s:Application xmlns:fx="http://ns.adobe.com/mxml/2009"
 xmlns:s="library://ns.adobe.com/flex/spark"
 xmlns:mx="library://ns.adobe.com/flex/mx"
 minWidth="1024" minHeight="768">
  <s:layout>
     <s:VerticalLayout paddingLeft="20" paddingTop="20"/>
  </s:layout>
  <s:DropDownList width="200"
    prompt="Select an Item">                    ◁┐ Use prompt for
      <mx:ArrayCollection>                          │ initial display
        <fx:String>Item One</fx:String>
        <fx:String>Second Item</fx:String>
        <fx:String>Item Three</fx:String>
        <fx:String>Last Item</fx:String>
      </mx:ArrayCollection>
  </s:DropDownList>
</s:Application>
```

Obviously, the `DropDownList` in figure 9.4 is preferable to the one in figure 9.3 because usability is enhanced when you provide instructions on how to use the control in the initial label text. In this case, you're telling the user, "Select an item." This brings us to Spark `List`-based component interaction.

9.3   *Interacting with Spark List-based components*

`List`-based component interaction with Spark is similar to MX `List`-based component interaction because Spark controls come from the same `UIComponent` base class that's in the MX library. But there are some new events to be aware of that are specific to Spark `List`-based components.

9.3.1   *Default event dispatching on item selection*

User interaction with Spark `List`-based components is similar to that of the `List`-based components provided in the MX library. The major differences are the names of the events and the timing of when they're dispatched. For example, when an item is selected in a MX `List`-based component, `ListEvent.CHANGE` and `ListEvent.ITEM_CLICK` events are fired. In Spark, the selection of a `List` item results in three different events being fired: `selectionChanging`, `itemFocusChanged`, and `selectionChanged`; see table 9.1.

Table 9.1   Events of `List`-based components specific to the Spark library `ListBase` class

Event	Class	Type
selectionChanged	IndexChangedEvent	SELECTION_CHANGED
itemFocusChanged	IndexChangedEvent	ITEM_FOCUS_CHANGED
selectionChanging	IndexChangedEvent	SELECTION_CHANGING

9.3.2   *The IndexChangedEvent object*

The event object for all three of these events is `IndexChangedEvent`. In addition, an `itemFocusChanged` event is also dispatched after the focus changes from one data item to another. The event object for `itemFocusChanged` is also an `IndexChanged-Event`. The third `IndexChangedEvent` is fired when a new item is selected, called the `selectionChanging` event. This last event is dispatched before the currently selected data item changes. This event gives you the ability to call the `preventDefault()` method in the event handler to prevent the selection from changing.

> **TIP**   If you want to perform processing on the item before the selection moves to the new item, or if you want to prevent an item from being selected entirely, set a listener and an event handler on `selectionChanging`.

9.4   *Understanding Flex 4 List-based component architecture*

If you're confused by the component architecture with Flex 4 and the Spark library, don't be alarmed. The key to understanding Spark components is to first understand that Spark components are built on the same infrastructure as MX components.

9.4.1   *Class hierarchy*

The Flex 4 Spark library builds upon the MX library of Flex 3, which allows for (mostly) seamless backward-compatibility and simple portability of applications from the Flex 3 SDK over to Flex 4 with minimal hassle. This is demonstrated by the class hierarchy displayed in figure 9.5. In Flex 3, you'd usually extend the `UIComponent` class when creating a custom component. This is because `UIComponent` encapsulates the base functionality of a Flex component because of the classes it's derived from through inheritance. With Spark, `UIComponent` may still be the best option for custom components that are unique, but in order to take advantage of the Spark architecture when creating custom `List`-based components, consider subclassing either `ListBase` or `Skinna-bleDataContainer`. Let's look at the Spark-specific classes for `List`-based components in further detail to understand why you might want to do this.

9.4.2   *New Spark classes for List-based components*

For `List`-based components, the Spark library adds four additional classes, which appear above the `UIComponent` class in figure 9.5 and are identified by boldface type. The primary objective of these four classes is to separate design from behavior, allowing themes, styles, and FXG skins to be created and assigned to a component separate from its internal functionality and state management. This

Separating concerns

The separation of design from behavior played a significant role in the evolution of web design during the late 1990s and early 2000s through the proliferation of the W3C CSS standard. It's worth pointing out that Flex 4 potentially marks a significant step forward in the evolution of rich internet application (RIA) by following a similar path in this regard.

also allows skins to be dynamically instantiated and assigned at application runtime as objects or entities that are separate from the component object.

Most of the Spark components are derivatives of the SkinnableComponent object, but that doesn't necessarily mean they're direct subclasses of SkinnableComponent. The Spark List-based components, for example, contain several layers of abstraction, as figure 9.5 demonstrates. The class that extends SkinnableComponent, however, depends on the type of component. Because a list is a container of data elements, the next class in the chain is the SkinnableContainerBase class, followed by SkinnableDataContainer, and then finally the List-Base class. Table 9.2 provides a simpler way of understanding the purpose of these new classes.

If this is all beginning to make sense, then great! I wouldn't be doing my job, though, if I didn't keep you on your toes. With that in mind, you can forget about getting comfortable—for now anyway—because I'm about to throw you a curve ball.

9.5   *Building custom List-based components on Spark Architecture*

The truth is, there's more to it than it may seem at first glance. The diagram in figure 9.6 provides a good visualization of what I mean. The Group class is also an important piece of the Spark library because it provides an

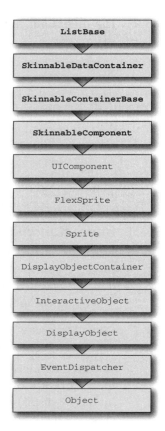

Figure 9.5   Class hierarchy of a Flex 4 List-based component

Table 9.2   Spark List-based component classes

Class name	Subclass	Purpose
SkinnableComponent	UIComponent	Adds the functionality for assigning a skin class that's a separate class that extends Skin, outside the component
SkinnableContainerBase	SkinnableComponent	Base class for container components; includes functionality for internal state management of container components
SkinnableDataContainer	SkinnableContainerBase	Base class for skinnable components that hold data content; includes item renderer functionality
ListBase	SkinnableDataContainer	Adds full MXML property declaration support

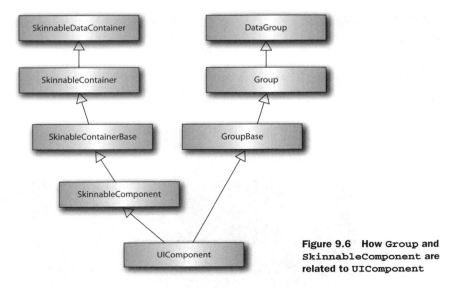

Figure 9.6 How Group and SkinnableComponent are related to UIComponent

alternative for developing custom components that don't carry the load of the skinning features and are more lightweight as a result.

9.5.1 Understanding the Group and SkinnableContainer classes

The Group container will take any components that implement the IUIComponent interface as children and any components that implement the IGraphicElement interface. Use this container when you want to manage visual children, both visual components and graphical components, but you don't want it to be skinnable. If you want to apply a skin, use the SkinnableContainer instead.

It's important to understand that SkinnableContainer and Group are still abstract classes, which should be directly extended only in special cases. More often than not, there's another class that extends the abstract class, adding more functionality that you can use in your custom component. For List-based Spark components, these are the SkinnableDataContainer and the DataGroup classes. Because this chapter is on List-based components, you'll build two custom List-based components from the Spark library, one based on the Spark List class, which extends ListBase, and the second based on the DataGroup class, which extends Group.

9.5.2 Building a custom Spark List component

The sample code provided in listing 9.6 demonstrates a number of facets that have been discussed so far in this chapter, including handling Spark List-based events, using an itemRenderer with Spark, setting the dataProvider, and internal state management. The result is an "unfolding image gallery" comprising a list of image titles; when one is selected, the respective image is displayed, as shown in figure 9.7.

Figure 9.7   The visual result of the component code shown in listing 9.6

The component's code shown in listing 9.6 is primarily MXML with a single Action-Script function to handle the `selectionChanging` event. Notice that the component extends the `Panel` container, which holds the custom `List` control. For the sake of simplicity, the only abstraction here is between the component and the application that declares the component, shown in listing 9.7. Other than the application file being separated from the component, everything is declared inline in the component code.

Listing 9.6   Custom Spark `List` component MXML code (MyCustomList.mxml)

```
<?xml version="1.0"?>
<s:Panel title="Spark List Component Example"
   xmlns:fx="http://ns.adobe.com/mxml/2009"
   xmlns:s="library://ns.adobe.com/flex/spark"
   width="75%" height="75%"
   horizontalCenter="0"
   verticalCenter="0">

  <fx:Script>
    <![CDATA[
    import mx.events.IndexChangedEvent;
    private function selectionChangingHandler(evt:IndexChangedEvent):void
    {
```

```
            var item:* = list.dataProvider.getItemAt(evt.newIndex);         ◁──────┐
            if (item.type != "travel")                                    getItemAt
            {                                                          method switches
               evt.preventDefault();      ◁──┐                        selectedIndex
            }                              preventDefault()
         }                                halts propagation
    }
  ]]>
</fx:Script>

<s:VGroup left="20" right="20" top="20" bottom="20">
  <s:SimpleText text="Select a title to see the image."/>
  <s:List id="list"
      selectionChanging="selectionChangingHandler(event);"     ◁────┐
      width="100%" height="100%" lineHeight="22">
    <s:layout>                                          Handler function declared
       <s:VerticalLayout/>                                 on selectionChanging
    </s:layout>
    <s:itemRenderer>                             ◁──┐  Item renderer
      <fx:Component>                                    declared inline
         <s:ItemRenderer>
            <s:states>                           ◁──┐  States
               <s:State name="normal" />              declared inline
               <s:State name="hovered" />
               <s:State name="selected" />
            </s:states>
            <s:Rect left="0" right="0" top="0" bottom="0">
               <s:fill>
               <s:SolidColor color="0x999999" alpha="0"
                  alpha.hovered="0.2"
                  alpha.selected="0.4" />
               </s:fill>
            </s:Rect>
            <s:SimpleText id="titleLabel" text="{data.title}"/>
            <s:BitmapImage horizontalCenter="80" id="img"
               source="{data.image}"
               includeIn="selected" />            ◁──┐  includeIn allows for
         </s:ItemRenderer>                              defining respective state
      </fx:Component>
    </s:itemRenderer>                           ───┐  dataProvider
    <s:dataProvider>                            ◁──┘  declared inline
      <s:ArrayList>
         <fx:Object type="travel" title="San Francisco"
            image="images/san_fran.jpg" />
         <fx:Object type="travel" title="San Francisco Lightrail"
            image="images/san_fran_lighrail.jpg" />
         <fx:Object type="travel" title="San Francisco Carriage"
            image="images/san_fran_carriage.jpg" />
      </s:ArrayList>
    </s:dataProvider>
  </s:List>
 </s:VGroup>
</s:Panel>
```

Listing 9.7   MXML code for custom Spark List component (SparkListApp.mxml)

```
<?xml version="1.0" encoding="utf-8"?>
<s:Application xmlns:fx="http://ns.adobe.com/mxml/2009"
    xmlns:s="library://ns.adobe.com/flex/spark"
    xmlns:mx="library://ns.adobe.com/flex/mx"
    minWidth="1024" minHeight="900" xmlns:local="*">
  <s:layout>
    <s:BasicLayout/>                                    MyCustomList
  </s:layout>                                           declared in
  <local:MyCustomList id="list" />            ◁──┘     main application
</s:Application>
```

As previously stated, the component code in figure 9.6 holds all information about the component, including style information, skinning, the item renderer, and even the data provider for the purpose of simplicity.

> **TIP**   Custom components can add up quickly, and it's wise to organize components into different packages, such as containers, controls, and item-Renderers. A custom component will almost always fall into one of these three categories.

It's important to point out that you should consider the Spark component architecture and the intentions of the Flex SDK team with regard to best practices during application development. This means the skin and states should be abstracted into a ListSkin class, the data provider should be pulled from an external source rather than being embedded within the component, and the item renderer should also be abstracted into its own class and placed in a separate package named itemRenderers; see the following listing.

Listing 9.8   A custom MXML List-based component built from the DataGroup class

```
<?xml version="1.0" encoding="utf-8"?>
<s:DataGroup xmlns:fx="http://ns.adobe.com/mxml/2009"       DataGroup
    xmlns:s="library://ns.adobe.com/flex/spark"             must have
    xmlns:mx="library://ns.adobe.com/flex/mx"               itemRenderer
    itemRenderer="spark.skins.default.DefaultItemRenderer">  ◁──┘
  <s:layout>                              ◁──┐ Declare layout
    <s:VerticalLayout gap="1" />               within component
  </s:layout>
  <s:dataProvider>                        ◁──┐ Declare list's
    <s:ArrayCollection>                        dataProvider
      <fx:String>First Data String</fx:String>
      <fx:String>Data String Two</fx:String>
      <fx:String>Last Data String</fx:String>
    </s:ArrayCollection>
  </s:dataProvider>
</s:DataGroup>
```

9.6 *Summary*

In this chapter you learned about the three Spark List-based controls, Spark List-based component architecture, and how to build custom Spark List-based components.

Working with List-based components in the Spark library is generally a pleasurable experience as a result of the separation between the view logic and behavior of the component that comes with the addition of the Spark SkinnableComponent, SkinnableContainerBase, SkinnableDataContainer, and the ListBase set of classes. The key to speeding up your development workflow is to take the time to learn, understand, and practice using the additional features and functionality that the Spark library provides in Flex 4.

List customization

10

This chapter covers

- The `labelField` property
- Label functions
- Overriding `itemToLabel`
- Item renderers and editors
- Combined item editor and item renderer
- Advanced item renderers
- Filter functions

In the previous two chapters, you learned about the various types of `List`-based components in Flex. In this chapter, you'll build on this knowledge by learning how to customize these `List`-based components.

When it comes to visual Flex components, `List`-based components are typically the workhorses of a Flex or Adobe Integrated Runtime (AIR) application. Consequently, a large portion of development in Flex tends to focus on the presentation of, and interaction with, `List`-based components.

10.1 *Customizing data display*

In your Flex application development, it's likely that at some point you will need a high level of control over the presentation of your list content beyond aesthetics.

This includes adding interactive capabilities that enable the user to work with the content. The best way to start working with List-based components is by learning how to map data fields from a collection of objects such as an ArrayCollection or XMLList-Collection and then learning how to manipulate that data with label functions. As you may have guessed, this is what you'll be doing in the sections that follow.

10.1.1 *The labelField property*

When working with List-based controls, the single most important attribute besides the dataProvider is the labelField. This property tells the control which property in the object assigned to it by the dataProvider it should care about, especially if a label function is used. For example, let's say you make a call to a service that returns an array of contact objects, which is then wrapped in an ArrayCollection by the function that's assigned to handle the result of the service request. Each contact object contains the following properties: firstName, lastName, email, and phone. But let's assume you want your list to display only the email address value of each object. In this case, your List declaration would probably look something like this:

```
<s:List id="myList"
        dataProvider="{contactCollection}"
        labelField="email" />
```

It would be nice if the data always came to you formatted exactly how you wanted it to be displayed, but that's rarely the case. This is where label functions come in handy.

10.1.2 *Label functions*

Let's take a moment to reset the stage now; you're calling a service that returns an array of objects (which is then typed to an ArrayCollection by the result handler), just as you were before for the labelField, and you've reached a point where you need to do more than just show the data in the same form as it was when you received it.

This time you have a Spark ButtonBar component on the stage that must generate a new button for each contact object. As if that weren't enough, you also have to display the respective contact's first and last names on the button! Well, don't panic just yet, because this is a walk in the park if you use the labelFunction property, as shown in the following listing.

> **Listing 10.1 The labelFunction allows you to process the data before displaying it.**

```
<?xml version="1.0" encoding="utf-8"?>
<s:Application xmlns:fx="http://ns.adobe.com/mxml/2009"
    xmlns:s="library://ns.adobe.com/flex/spark"
    xmlns:mx="library://ns.adobe.com/flex/mx">
    <s:layout>
        <s:VerticalLayout/>
    </s:layout>
  <fx:Script>
    <![CDATA[
        private function concatenateName(item:Object):String
```

Label function ➊ called by List to process items ⊲┘

```
        {
            return item.firstName + " " + item.lastName;
        }
    ]]>
</fx:Script>

<s:ButtonBar id="buttonBar"
    labelFunction="concatenateName">
    <mx:ArrayCollection>
        <fx:Object firstName="Tariq"
                   lastName="Ahmed"
                   email="tahmed@flexinaction.com"
                   phone="544-235-2425" />
        <fx:Object firstName="John"
                   lastName="Bland"
                   email="jbland@flexinaction.com"
                   phone="555-343-5567" />
        <fx:Object firstName="Dan"
                   lastName="Orlando"
                   email="dorlando@flexinaction.com"
                   phone="343-246-4639" />
    </mx:ArrayCollection>
</s:ButtonBar>
</s:Application>
```

◁ **Merges two fields and returns `String`**

❷ **Label function requested by `List`** ◁

◁ ❸ **Data used to populate `List`**

> ## Performance optimization tip
> You may suffer from performance repercussions if you use `labelFunction` for data processing on a list that's constantly receiving updates. Each time a `dataChange` event is fired off from the `dataProvider` binding, the `labelFunction` must loop through and process all of those label fields before it redraws the list with the updated data. Depending on how much processing you have going on in your label function, the user could experience a brief moment of "application stalling" (even though it's processing, it looks like it stalled). The important things are to be mindful of how much processing you're doing in your formatting functions and to know how many `dataChange` events are *really* getting fired off at any given moment by profiling the application.

In the code sample shown in listing 10.1, the `concatenateName` function is responsible for doing the label formatting for each data object contained in the list ❶. By specifying this function for the `labelFunction` property ❷, the `List`-based component automatically passes the data item to `concatenateName` before displaying it so that it can be processed by the function ❸, which then returns the `String` that's to be displayed for the respective object.

The result of the code from listing 10.1 is shown in figure 10.1.

Label functions operate by instructing a column in a `List` to call a function on each row of data. Whatever that function returns will be the value to display.

Figure 10.1   The resulting button labels display the first and last names together.

> **They're not just for Lists!**
> Many elements support label functions, such as data tips in charting components and even form controls like `ComboBox` and `DateField`. Keep in mind as we progress that even though the specific focus of this chapter is customizing `Lists`, as it relates to label functions, the same operating principles apply to these non-`List` components as well.

10.1.3 Types of label functions

You have the option to select from two types of label functions: One is intended for lists made up of a single column, such as List, HorizontalList, TileList, and Tree; the other is designed for multicolumn List-based components, including DataGrid, AdvancedDataGrid, PrintDataGrid, FileSystemDataGrid, and OLAPDataGrid.

The only difference between the two types of label functions is the form of their arguments, as you're about to see.

SINGLE-COLUMN LABEL FUNCTION

In a single-column label function, you accept one parameter—a reference to the current record (or row) of information within your data. You access whatever data fields you need and return a String:

```
public function fullName( rowItem:Object ) : String
{
    return rowItem.firstName + ' ' + rowItem.lastName;
}
```

Conversely, if you're presenting a component made up of more than one column, you need a multicolumn label function.

MULTICOLUMN LABEL FUNCTIONS

Multicolumn label functions perform like their single-column stable mates, with the exception of taking an additional parameter—a reference to the column to determine which column you're pointing to. Listing 10.2 shows what this looks like.

Listing 10.2 Using a label function with multicolumn `List`-based components

```
public function formatDate(rowItem:Object,column:DataGridColumn) : String
{
    var retVal:String = "";
    if(column.dataField == "dtJoined")
      retVal = dFmt.format(rowItem.dtJoined);
    else if(column.dataField == "dtLogin")
      retVal = dFmt.format(rowItem.dtLogin);

    return retVal;
}
```

The best examples of components that would use this function are the DataGrid and the AdvancedDataGrid, because they're the most commonly used components that contain both rows and columns.

10.1.4 Using a multicolumn label function

In this next example, we have data files that contain information regarding members of a hypothetical organization—perhaps an online forum or a blog. The data includes date and time fields that maintain information about when each member joined, as well as a field for when they last logged in. For the moment, we're not interested in the time portion, only the date, so we'll use a label function to pass that raw data through a formatter (listing 10.3) and display the result.

Listing 10.3 Using a label function to support a multicolumn `DataGrid`

```
<?xml version="1.0"?>
<s:Application xmlns:fx="http://ns.adobe.com/mxml/2009"
               xmlns:s="library://ns.adobe.com/flex/spark"
               xmlns:mx="library://ns.adobe.com/flex/mx"
               backgroundColor="white">
    <s:layout>
        <s:VerticalLayout/>
    </s:layout>

    <fx:Script>
        <![CDATA[
            import mx.collections.ArrayCollection;
            [Bindable]
            public var myAC:ArrayCollection  =
                new ArrayCollection([{ name     : "Dan Orlando",
                    username : "dorlando",
                    dtJoined : "01/02/2008 12:32:55",
                    dtLogin  : "02/20/2010 13:33:22" },
                { name     : "Tariq Ahmed",
                    username : "tahmed",
                    dtJoined : "03/12/2007 05:44:32",
                    dtLogin  : "07/09/2010 14:44:23" },
                { name     : "John C Bland II",
                    username : "jbland",
                    dtJoined : "06/16/2009 05:41:04",
                    dtLogin  : "04/09/2010 11:14:23" }
                ]);

            public function formatDate(row:Object, col:DataGridColumn):String
            {
                var retVal:String = "";
                if( col.dataField == "dtJoined" )
                    retVal = dFmt.format( row.dtJoined );
                else if(col.dataField == "dtLogin")
                    retVal = dFmt.format( row.dtLogin );
                return retVal;
            }
        ]]>
    </fx:Script>

    <fx:Declarations>
        <mx:DateFormatter id="dFmt" formatString="MM/DD/YY"/>
    </fx:Declarations>
```

1 Data has date with time fields

2 If joined field, only return date

3 If date login field, return date portion

Date-only formatter

```
<mx:DataGrid id="dg" width="500" height="100" dataProvider="{myAC}">
  <mx:columns>
    <mx:DataGridColumn dataField="name"    headerText="Name"/>
    <mx:DataGridColumn dataField="username" headerText="Username"/>
    <mx:DataGridColumn dataField="dtJoined" headerText="Joined"
                       labelFunction="formatDate"/>

    <mx:DataGridColumn dataField="dtLogin"
                       headerText="Last Login"
                       labelFunction="formatDate"/>
  </mx:columns>
</mx:DataGrid>
</s:Application>
```

Two columns use label function

The `ArrayCollection` variable with the name `myAC` serves as the `dataProvider` for the `DataGrid`. As you can see, the date and time are provided in the form of a string that has obviously already been formatted by some external source ❶. More than likely, the server-side code did some manipulation of the string before storing it to the database, so now we must change it to something we can use. The `formatDate` function is set as the `labelFunction` for the respective `DataGridColumn` objects to carry out this task. The function contains a conditional, which states that if the data field being processed is the date the user joined, then set the return value to only the date portion of the `dtJoined` field ❷; otherwise, set the return value to only the date portion of the `dtLogin` field ❸.

After the application is run, the two date-related fields, which are supplied with raw date and time information, are nicely formatted to show only the date and ignore the time.

Keep in mind the following points about this example:

- You can't pass parameters to the label function—Flex automatically passes a reference of the row and column.
- You use the column data to determine which column is being used, to ensure you're formatting the appropriate value.

This label function is a little more involved compared to the less-complex single-column label function. With that said, let's review some situations where the use of label functions is ideal and discuss how they should be implemented.

10.1.5 Uses for label functions

The following are some common uses for label functions:

- Concatenating data fields of an object to create and display them as a single `String`
- Formatting raw data
- Converting raw data to human-readable format

Here's another use case for label functions and an exercise you might want to try out: Run a conditional in the body of the label function (prior to the `return`) to evaluate

> **"Humanizing" raw data**
>
> Label functions are most useful for converting raw data into a human-readable format. By far the greatest example of this is the infamous Unix date conversion dilemma, in which dates are returned as the number of milliseconds that transpired since 12:00 a.m. on January 1, 1970. I always find this humorous because it does almost sound like a joke. I remember the first time I was told about this, I really thought the person was trying to play a trick on me!

the data passed to the row, but instead of formatting the data so you can show it, display a custom result that's based on the conditional statement. For example, you can run a date comparison and present a "Past Due" message if a payment due date has been exceeded.

10.1.6 *The bigger picture*

Let's take a moment to step back and look at the big picture here and what you're trying to accomplish by learning about list customization. It's important every so often to take a snapshot of where you're at and where you're going and what the result will be. As my baseball coach used to say, "If you can see the forest for the trees, you'll never take your eye off the ball."

By learning list customization techniques, you'll be able to manipulate the display of data in ways that may be hard to imagine right now (video item renderers in 3D, anyone?). In addition, you may not have noticed that although chapter 8 focused solely on MX lists and chapter 9 on Spark lists, you're using the two interchangeably now without much regard for what component library they come from. With that in mind, it's logical to ascertain that you're learning how to determine the solution based on the *context* of the situation. You'll continue down this path in the next section, where you'll transition to one of my favorite things to talk about: item renderers!

10.2 *Item renderers*

Label functions are easy to use, but that ease comes with the inherent limitation of not being able to do much more than you did in the previous pair of examples. What if you needed to do more than return and display formatted text?

This is where item renderers come into play. They give you fine-grained control over the display of data items. Flex identifies three types of item renderers: regular, inline, and drop-in. We'll start by showing an example of how a basic item renderer might be used in a simple Flex 4 application before getting into more complex item-renderer goodness.

10.2.1 *Spark MXML item renderers*

One sweet little perk that the Flex 4 Spark library brought along with it is a native `ItemRenderer` object that can be declared as the root node of a custom MXML item renderer. This is an example of a regular item renderer. The following listings demonstrate the use and implementation of this nifty little addition to Flex.

Listing 10.4   Utilizing the Spark `ItemRenderer` object

```
<?xml version="1.0" encoding="utf-8"?>
<s:ItemRenderer xmlns:fx="http://ns.adobe.com/mxml/2009"
            xmlns:s="library://ns.adobe.com/flex/spark"
            xmlns:mx="library://ns.adobe.com/flex/mx" >

    <s:layout>
        <s:VerticalLayout/>
    </s:layout>

    <s:SimpleText id="label" paddingBottom="3"
                paddingTop="20" paddingLeft="25"
                text="{ data.labelText }" />

    <s:BitmapImage id="img" source="{ data.imgSource }"/>

</s:ItemRenderer>
```

◁─┐ **ItemRenderer as root node in ❶ MXML**

Listing 10.4 is the code for the item renderer MXML component and is based on the Spark `ItemRenderer` object ❶. Then, listing 10.5 demonstrates the implementation.

Listing 10.5   Spark item renderer object implementation

```
<?xml version="1.0" encoding="utf-8"?>
<s:Application xmlns:fx="http://ns.adobe.com/mxml/2009"
            xmlns:s="library://ns.adobe.com/flex/spark"
            xmlns:mx="library://ns.adobe.com/flex/mx" >

    <s:SkinnableDataContainer itemRenderer="TileGroupIR">
        <s:layout>
            <s:HorizontalLayout/>
        </s:layout>

        <mx:ArrayCollection>
            <fx:Object labelText="Kitty"
                    imgSource="assets/IMG_0325.JPG"/>
            <fx:Object labelText="Baseball"
                    imgSource="assets/IMG_0359.JPG"/>
            <fx:Object labelText="4th of July"
                    imgSource="assets/IMG_0425.jpg"/>
            <fx:Object labelText="July 4th Fun"
                    imgSource="assets/IMG_0426.JPG"/>
        </mx:ArrayCollection>

    </s:SkinnableDataContainer>

</s:Application>
```

◁─┐ **itemRenderer declared as ❶ argument**

Each data object gets a renderer

Looking at Listing 10.5, you'll notice a tag called `itemRenderer` that is set on the `SkinnableDataContainer` object ❶. You can simply insert the name of the `Item-Renderer` object you created as a string value and Flex will locate and implement it into the data component for you. If the ItemRenderer exists in a different package, be sure to specify the relative path using dot notation. In this case, instead of just saying

Figure 10.2   The result of our simple item renderer

`TileGroupIR` for the value of `itemRenderer`, you might instead declare the value as `com.fx4ia.chapter10.components.itemRenderers`.

The result of the code in listing 10.5 is shown in figure 10.2, which is a static film reel with picture titles displayed above each picture.

10.2.2   MXML item renderers in Spark with MX components

We're now going to accomplish the same thing using a `HorizontalList` component from the MX library. The following example demonstrates how you can combine elements of both the MX and Spark libraries without worrying about conflict, although the implementation is a bit different. Let's look at this next listing.

Listing 10.6   The MXML item renderer code for the `HorizontalList` implementation

```
<?xml version="1.0" encoding="utf-8"?>
<mx:Canvas xmlns:fx="http://ns.adobe.com/mxml/2009"          ◁── Canvas as
           xmlns:s="library://ns.adobe.com/flex/spark"        ❶ root node
           xmlns:mx="library://ns.adobe.com/flex/mx"
           height="350" width="355" >

  <s:VGroup>                                                  ◁── Spark VGroup
                                                              ❷ inside MX Canvas
    <s:SimpleText id="stext" paddingBottom="3"
                  paddingTop="20" paddingLeft="25"
                  text="{ data.labelText }" />

    <s:BitmapImage id="img" source="{ data.imgSource }" />

  </s:VGroup>
</mx:Canvas>
```

Looking at the code in listing 10.6, you can see that this item renderer's root object is the `Canvas` container from the MX library ❶, instead of the Spark `ItemRenderer` object. In this instance, we're using the `Canvas` container because the `List`-based component that uses the item renderer comes from the MX library. As a demonstration of how well MX and Spark components work together, we use a Spark `VGroup` container to house the Spark `Label` and `BitmapImage` controls within MX's `Canvas` container ❷. Listing 10.7 demonstrates the use of this `Canvas`-based item renderer.

Listing 10.7 The MX HorizontalList component with item renderer in Flex 4

```xml
<?xml version="1.0" encoding="utf-8"?>
<s:Application xmlns:fx="http://ns.adobe.com/mxml/2009"
               xmlns:s="library://ns.adobe.com/flex/spark"
               xmlns:mx="library://ns.adobe.com/flex/mx"
               minWidth="1024" minHeight="768" >

    <s:layout>
      <s:VerticalLayout/>
    <mx:HorizontalList id="hList" x="10" y="10"
                    width="100%" height="100%"
                    itemRenderer="HListIRExample" >

      <mx:dataProvider>
        <mx:ArrayCollection>
          <fx:Object labelText="Kitty"
                     imgSource="assets/IMG_0325.JPG"/>
          <fx:Object labelText="Baseball"
                     imgSource="assets/IMG_0359.JPG"/>
          <fx:Object labelText="4th of July"
                     imgSource="assets/IMG_0425.jpg"/>
          <fx:Object labelText="July 4th Fun"
                     imgSource="assets/IMG_0426.JPG"/>
        </mx:ArrayCollection>
      </mx:dataProvider>

    </mx:HorizontalList>

</s:Application>
```

- ❶ Spark **Application** object as root node
- ❷ MX `HorizontalList` declared in Spark `Application`
- ❸ `itemRenderer` property declares renderer object

As you can see in listing 10.7, the `HorizontalList` component from the MX library ❷ is declared within the Spark library's `Application` object ❶. Furthermore, the MX-style item renderer shown in listing 10.7 is declared for the `itemRenderer` property of the `HorizontalList` ❸. Figure 10.3 displays the result.

When creating custom item renderers, you can consider either the Spark or MX implementation. But you get the benefits of the Spark component architecture, namely skinning and reusability, only by using Spark. Furthermore, in contrast to Flex 3, version 4 makes it possible for you to do anything in MXML that you can do in ActionScript with few exceptions. If you're already a Flex developer, however, it may take some time to get used to Flex 4 and the idea of doing everything with MXML. Until then, it's perfectly fine to use ActionScript for more complex components.

Figure 10.3 Item renderer implementation with a `HorizontalList` in Flex 4

FLEX 4 TIP   If you want to create a Spark item renderer in MXML, but you don't want to use the ItemRenderer object as the root object node of your MXML file, you can use Group, BorderContainer, SkinnableComponent, SkinnableContainer, HGroup, VGroup, or just about any other Spark container. The way to make this work is by implementing the IListItemRenderer (for List-based renderers) or IDropInListItemRenderer or IItemRenderer if you don't need the added list functionality.

Flex uses the Label control as its default item renderer. This doesn't do much other than render text that has been provided to it. When you specify an item renderer, you're overriding the default with your custom renderer.

Let's look at how this is accomplished:

- Flex creates an instance of the renderer for each object in the collection.
- As each renderer is created, the creationComplete event is triggered.
- A listener function for creationComplete checks the next object to see if a renderer has been created yet for it. If not, it creates a new one and sets its data property to the data object itself, so any necessary values that are called can be extracted as needed.

Yes, it's that simple, although there's one slight catch.

ONE LITTLE CAVEAT

For performance reasons, Flex reuses existing rows—if you have 1,000 objects to display, it won't generate 1,000 rows all at once; instead, it will generate the number of rows that are needed just for display on the current screen, which in this case is one. This means you might notice a slight lag time in how quickly the bitmaps of each set of four images are drawn, because they weren't already loaded prior to the scroll event occurring.

To avoid this problem, do the following:

- Continue to use the creationComplete event to initialize the renderer. For example, the myAC ArrayCollection may not be populated yet. Alternatively, you could override the data setter as well. For more information on using overrides, consult chapters 17 and 18.
- Use the dataChange event to check whether you should load the next and previous rows.
- Override the following methods of the UIComponent class: invalidateDisplay-List, updateDisplayList, invalidateProperties, updateProperties, and updateDisplayList. Be sure to make the call to super on each one, but also include the logic to create the previous and next rows for when the user scrolls the mouse wheel, but with their respective visible properties set to false.

Listing 10.8 shows the improved item renderer.

Listing 10.8   More robust item render that resets itself as the data changes

```xml
<?xml version="1.0" encoding="utf-8"?>
<mx:HBox xmlns:fx="http://ns.adobe.com/mxml/2009"
         xmlns:s="library://ns.adobe.com/flex/spark"
         xmlns:mx="library://ns.adobe.com/flex/mx"
         width="100%"
         creationComplete="initDisplay()"
         dataChange="checkEmail()" >
```
⟵ Calls function to initialize itself

⟵ Calls function to reset display

```xml
    <fx:Script>
        <![CDATA[

        import flash.net.*;

        private function initDisplay() : void
        {
            emailButton.visible = false;
        }
```
⟵ Initializes button to be invisible

```xml
        private function checkEmail() : void
        {
            if( data.email.length > 0 )
                emailButton.visible = true;
            else
                emailButton.visible = false;
        }
        public function sendMail() : void
        {
            var u:URLRequest = new URLRequest( "mailto:" + data.email );
            navigateToURL( u, "_self" );
        }
        ]]>
    </fx:Script>
```
⟵ Adjusts visibility as data changes

```xml
    <s:Button id="emailButton"
              visible="false"
              label="Send Email"
              click="sendMail()"/>

</mx:HBox>
```

This approach is the most commonly used because reusing item renderer instances can save gobs of memory that would otherwise be hogged by the application. An additional added benefit is that by decoupling your item renderer component, you can now use it anywhere else in your application with ease. Believe it or not, the regular type of item renderer is the most complex of the three. The following is a brief description of the other two types of renderers.

10.2.3   Creating an inline item renderer

With inline item renderers, the renderer is no longer decoupled as a separate component but is instead coded as a child of the parent container using the <item-Renderer/> MXML tag. This approach is convenient when rapidly prototyping a proof-of-concept interface but isn't best practice when developing an application that will go to production

Listing 10.9 shows how to set up an inline item renderer, which involves nothing more than copying the logic directly into your code and nesting it within the appropriate tags.

Listing 10.9   `DataGrid` column with an inline item renderer

```
<mx:DataGrid id="dg" width="500" height="100" dataProvider="{myAC}">
    <mx:columns>
        <mx:DataGridColumn headerText="Name">
            <mx:itemRenderer>
                <mx:Component>
                    <mx:Text text="{data.firstName} {data.lastName}"/>
                </mx:Component>
            </mx:itemRenderer>
        </mx:DataGridColumn>
        <mx:DataGridColumn headerText="Email" itemRenderer="myRenderer"/>
    </mx:columns>
</mx:DataGrid>
```

This method can be quite convenient. But if you think it's simple, the drop-in item renderer takes even less effort.

10.2.4 *Using drop-in item renderers*

Flex provides a number of components that can be used as drop-in renderers. Let's look at how you can use one of them—the `Image` component—to perform the same tasks as an item renderer but with less effort (see the following listing).

Listing 10.10   Drop-in item renderer that renders an image in a column

```
<?xml version="1.0"?>
<s:Application xmlns:fx="http://ns.adobe.com/mxml/2009"
        xmlns:s="library://ns.adobe.com/flex/spark"
        xmlns:mx="library://ns.adobe.com/flex/mx"
        backgroundColor="white" >

  <mx:Script>
    <![CDATA[
        import mx.collections.ArrayCollection;          ⎤ Make data
                                                        ⎦ bindable
        [Bindable]
        public var myAC:ArrayCollection  = new ArrayCollection([
            { name : "Dan Orlando",
                    thumbnail : "assets/dan.jpg" },          ◁
            { name : "Tariq Ahmed",  thumbnail : "assets/tariq.jpg" },
            { name : "John C Bland", thumbnail : "assets/john.jpg" },
        ]);
                                                            name and
    ]]>                                                     thumbnail
  </mx:Script>                                            for each object

  <mx:DataGrid id="dg" width="250"                 ⎤ Component bound
        height="100" dataProvider="{ myAC }">      ⎦ to data collection
```

```
  <mx:columns>
      <mx:DataGridColumn headerText="Name" dataField="name" />
      <mx:DataGridColumn headerText="Picture" dataField="thumbnail"
          itemRenderer="mx.controls.Image" />
  </mx:columns>
  </mx:DataGrid>
```

⟵ **Call for drop-in**
item renderer

```
</mx:Application>
```

Hopefully you found the code shown in listing 10.10 to be pretty straightforward. Simply put, you're specifying an ArrayCollection, binding it to the dataProvider of a Flex DataGrid, and telling each DataGridColumn within the DataGrid which field it should care about.

> **TIP** If you want the images to be larger, you need to set the rowHeight property for the DataGrid to the specific size. If you want it to scale to the full size of the image, set variableRowHeight="true".

Table 10.1 contains the full list of the components you can use as drop-in item renderers.

Table 10.1   Components that support the drop-in item renderer

Component	Default property	Notes
Button	selected	Displays a button. Unfortunately, you can't control the button's associated label.
CheckBox	selected	
DateField	selectedDate	
Image	source	Use the List-based component's rowHeight or variableRowHeight property if you want the image to be larger than the default height of the row.
Label	Text	
NumericStepper	Value	
Text	Text	By default, you're already using this.
TextArea	Text	
TextInput	Text	

Be aware of the default properties for these components because those components look for this field in your dataProvider. For example, consider what would happen if your DataGrid were configured as follows:

```
<mx:DataGridColumn headerText="Picture" itemRenderer="mx.controls.Image"/>
```

The Image component will assume you have a field in your data called source. This is demonstrated in the ArrayCollection:

```
public var myAC:ArrayCollection  = new ArrayCollection([
    { name : "Dan Orlando",  source : "assets/dan.jpg" },
    { name : "Tariq Ahmed",  source : "assets/tariq.jpg" },
```

```
        { name : "John C Bland", source : "assets/john.jpg" },
    ]);
```

Referring back for a moment to listing 10.10, notice that the field was called `thumbnail`. This means you explicitly specified the `dataField` as a target for the component. This instructs the component to use what you've specified instead of the default.

The item renderer provides a high degree of control and logic over the display of information in a cell. But what if your list customization requirement calls for the user to be able to *edit* the data? Not to worry; this is where you can use a similar feature called an *item editor.*

10.3   *Item editors*

A renderer enters an editable state when two conditions are met:

- Editing has been enabled.
- The user has triggered the edit event (usually a single or double click).

We'll start by explaining how to enable the editing process that causes an item editor to appear on the stage, followed by a discussion on creating custom item editors and associating events that capture and pass the data that the user provides. By the time you're finished with this section, you'll be ready to dig into the real meat of customizing list components in the section that follows: building advanced item renderers!

10.3.1 *Enabling item editing*

By default the editing feature is disabled for item renderers. To begin the edit process, you set the `editable` property to `true`, which then allows the user to click an item renderer and alter the data within it.

To do this, first set the component to be editable with `editable = true`. This setting can apply to the entire component, just a cell, or just a column. When the user focuses on an item that can be edited by clicking it or by pressing the Tab or Enter key, the item renderer is temporarily swapped out and replaced by the item editor. The item editor interacts with the user to capture new data. It then self-terminates on certain user actions, such as pressing Enter or Tab or clicking out of the cell. As the item editor terminates, the respective value is updated in the display. More important, the original variable that provided the data (the property to which the `dataProvider` is pointing) is also updated with the new value, and the corresponding `dataChange` event is fired for anything that may be listening for it. Listing 10.11 presents a minimalist approach.

Listing 10.11 Simple way to leverage item editors

```
<?xml version="1.0"?>
<s:Application xmlns:fx="http://ns.adobe.com/mxml/2009"
               xmlns:s="library://ns.adobe.com/flex/spark"
               xmlns:mx="library://ns.adobe.com/flex/mx">

  <fx:Script>
```

```
    <![CDATA[
        import mx.collections.ArrayCollection;

        [Bindable]
        public var myAC:ArrayCollection   = new ArrayCollection([
                { name : "Dan Orlando",  email : "Dan@iscool.com" },
                { name : "John C Bland",  email : "John@iscool.com" },
                { name : "Tariq Ahmed",  email : "tariq@iscool.com" }
            ];

    ]]>
</fx:Script>

<mx:DataGrid id="dg" width="150" height="100"
            dataProvider="{ myAC }"
            editable="true" >
  <mx:columns>
      <mx:DataGridColumn headerText="Name"
                        dataField="name" />
      <mx:DataGridColumn headerText="EMail"
                        dataField="email"
                        editable="false" />
  </mx:columns>
</mx:DataGrid>

</s:Application>
```

Defaults all columns to be editable

Overrides `DataGrid`'s editable setting

When the user clicks an individual's name (figure 10.4), the cell becomes editable, and the user can change the value.

Would you care to guess what the default item editor is for most `List`-based components? If you said `TextInput`, you'd be right. But you're by no means restricted to only its use; you're free to change it and create your own custom item editors just like you can with item renderers.

10.3.2 *Creating an item editor*

Creating an item editor is similar to creating an item renderer, but there are some additional properties that you can configure:

- You can create a separate MXML file that can be invoked by anything that wants to use it.
- You can create a public variable that can be used by the `List`-based component to know where the new value is stored. Be sure this variable is a data type compatible with the original data (numbers to numbers, strings to strings, dates to dates, and so on).
- When the item editor is initiated, you should default your form input to whatever the current value is (along with the public variable).

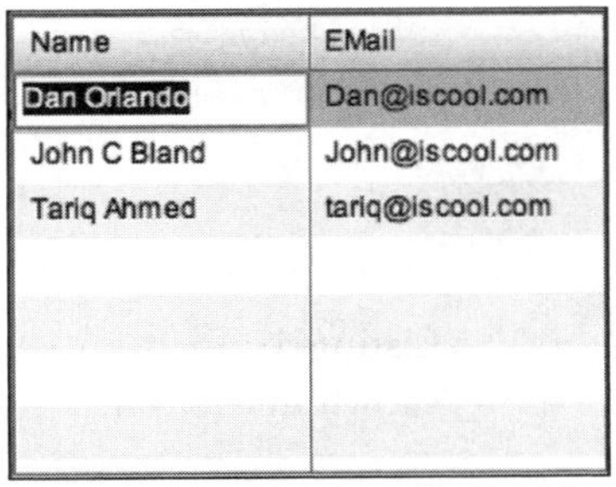

Name	EMail
Dan Orlando	Dan@iscool.com
John C Bland	John@iscool.com
Tariq Ahmed	tariq@iscool.com

Figure 10.4 Setting the `editable` field allows the user to edit data in the cells of the respective column.

Listing 10.12 puts this into play with a custom item editor; listing 10.13 is a consumer of this item editor.

Listing 10.12   MyEditor.mxml: custom item editor

```
<?xml version="1.0" encoding="utf-8"?>
<mx:HBox xmlns:fx="http://ns.adobe.com/mxml/2009"
        xmlns:mx="library://ns.adobe.com/flex/mx"
        creationComplete="init()">

  <fx:Script>
    <![CDATA[
      import mx.collections.ArrayCollection;

      [Bindable]                                    Variable read by
      public var newEmployeeType:String;            List-based component

      [Bindable]
      private var typeAC:ArrayCollection  =
                      new ArrayCollection([
                            { type : "Employee" },
                            { type : "Customer" }
      ]);
      private function init() : void               Initializes return
      {                                             variable to that of
          newEmployeeType = data.type;             current value

          for( var i:int = 0; i < typeAC.length; i++ )    Loops through
          {                                               ComboBox's values
              if( typeAC[i].type == data.type )           and defaults to
                  myCB.selectedIndex = i;                 current value
          }
      }

      private function myCB_changeHandler() : void
      {                                             On change,
          newEmployeeType = myCB.selectedItem.type; update value
      }
      ]]>
    </fx:Script>
    <mx:ComboBox id="myCB"
                    dataProvider="{ typeAC }"
                  labelField="type"
                    change="myCB_changeHandler()" />
</mx:HBox>
```

Listing 10.12 is an example of a custom item editor, which is then used in the code shown in the following listing.

Listing 10.13   HelloWorld.mxml: uses the custom item editor for a column

```
<?xml version="1.0"?>
<s:Application xmlns:fx="http://ns.adobe.com/mxml/2009"
              xmlns:s="library://ns.adobe.com/flex/spark"
  <fx:Script>
    <![CDATA[
```

```
        import mx.collections.ArrayCollection;

        [Bindable]
        public var myAC:ArrayCollection  = new ArrayCollection([
            { name:"John C Bland", email:"john@iscool.com", type:"Customer" }
             { name:"Tariq Ahmed", email:"tariq@iscool.com", type:"Employee" }
             { name:"Dan Orlando", email:"dan@iscool.com", type:"Customer" }
            ]);
    ]]>
</fx:Script>

<mx:DataGrid id="dg"
             width="350" height="200"
             dataProvider="{myAC}"
             editable="true">
    <mx:columns>
        <mx:DataGridColumn headerText="Name"
                           dataField="name" />
        <mx:DataGridColumn headerText="EMail"
                           dataField="email"
                           editable="false" />
        <mx:DataGridColumn headerText="Type"
                           dataField="type"
                           editorDataField="newEmployeeType"
                           itemEditor="myEditor" />
    </mx:columns>
</mx:DataGrid>

</s:Application>
```

Identifies variable that contains new value (points to `editorDataField="newEmployeeType"`)

Instructs column to use custom item editor (points to `itemEditor="myEditor"`)

All of this boils down to two simple things: First, you initialize the item editor to make sure it's displaying the right data type; second, you pass the result of the user's selection. Note how the editor-DataField property is used to indicate which variable in the item editor should be used to populate the DataGrid when the user finishes editing. Although the process can be reduced to those two steps, you can leverage a number of events that are triggered along the way, which is exactly what you'll learn about next.

10.3.3 *Item editing events*

Flex fires off a number of events during the editing process, which you can intercept in order to add business logic or parameters, clean up routines, or add checkpoints. These events include the following:

- itemEditBeginning—Dispatched as the item-editing process is about to begin. It occurs as a result of the user clicking the mouse button on a cell, pressing Enter while over a cell, or pressing the Tab key to move from one cell to the next. Typically, this is used to add business logic to determine if you're going to begin cell editing.

- itemEditBegin—Occurs directly after itemEditBeginning, when the data is about to be passed to the item editor. As a result, it's an opportunity to manipulate the data if you need to.

- itemEditEnd—Occurs when the user has triggered the end of the item-editing process. The item editor still exists but is about to be destroyed. This is a point at which you can compare the original value with the new value, as well as conduct any additional validation.

You can handle any of these events in the List-based component, as we'll demonstrate shortly. But first, let's get the lowdown on the event object that's generated when these events occur.

The event that you get is relative to the specific List-based component you're using:

- ListEvent is used by any of the Spark or MX List-based components.
- DataGridEvent is used by the DataGrid in addition to using ListEvent events.
- AdvancedDataGridEvent is used by the AdvancedDataGrid in addition to using ListEvent events.

Each event object has some unique properties; but they have many things in common, particularly those listed in table 10.2.

Keep in mind that you don't need to handle any of these events—you can let them all pass through as is. Alternatively, you can pick and choose which events you want to handle.

Thus far, we've treated item renderers and item editors as two separate components, even though they have a lot in common. It's often useful to have the renderer

Table 10.2   Properties of the event object

Property	Type	Description
columnIndex	Number	Index of the column, starting at 0.
currentTarget	Object	Reference to the component that generated the event. For example, if you had a HorizontalList named myHList from which the cell-editing process was initiated, the currentTarget would link back to myHList.
itemRenderer	Object	Reference to the itemRenderer used in the cell currently being edited. You can use this to determine the current value of the cell (before editing began).
reason	String	Read only. Action that caused the itemEditEnd to occur (if it occurred at all). Values include cancelled (user cancelled editing), newRow (user moved onto a new row), newColumn (user moved to the next column on the same row), and other.
rowIndex	Number	Related row of the cell being edited.
type	String	Type of event that occurred.
dataField	String	Data field related to the column being edited. Specific to DataGrid/AdvancedDataGrid.
preventDefault	Function	Function you can call to interrupt the chain of event dispatching.

and editor as the same component, and that's exactly what you're going to learn how to do next.

10.3.4 *Combining forces: rendererIsEditor*

It's possible to create a hybrid component from the item renderer and item editor. You may want to do this if you need to employ a single component that can switch states from read-only to read-write and vice versa.

For example, it's common for many web mail programs to display a check box beside each mail item to let users select all the email they want to bulk process. This is a good approach when you need to make many updates quickly.

Let's borrow from an earlier example (listing 10.12), in which we used a ComboBox to change the user type, and create an always-on edit field. Using listing 10.13 as your starting point, find the following code segment:

```
<mx:DataGridColumn headerText="Type" dataField="type"
          editorDataField="newEmployeeType" itemEditor="myEditor"/>
```

Change those lines to the following:

```
<mx:DataGridColumn headerText="Type" dataField="type"
    rendererIsEditor="true" editorDataField="newEmployeeType"
    itemRenderer="myEditor"/>
```

The result of these changes causes the ComboBox to be activated and remain on for all rows, effectively providing the convenience of an in-place editor that's on all of the time.

This technique is useful for data entry in applications in which you need to stay in edit mode because data is constantly being changed or needs to be changed quickly. As an example, help desk personnel may need to change data on the fly during a conversation, and having to double-click a cell to make the data editable would be far from user friendly for these help desk personnel.

When the DataGrid doesn't suffice for the application you're building, the enhanced functionality built into the AdvancedDataGrid may come in handy. These item renderers and editors that you've seen so far serve well for general purposes, but more advanced versions cater specifically to the AdvancedDataGrid.

10.4 *Advanced item renderers*

The AdvancedDataGrid supports item renderers as any other List-based component does, but it takes rendering to a higher level. The AdvancedDataGrid can work with item renderers that can span multiple columns and use multiple item renderers on the same column, as well as item renderers that can insert additional rows—the latter being used if you need to summarize or categorize sequences of data.

You can do an amazing variety of things based on those capabilities. In this section, you'll see some examples of advanced item renderers. By the time you finish reading this, you'll be an expert on item renderers and item editors! Let's start with the most fun Flex component of them all: the AdvancedDataGridRendererProvider.

10.4.1   *The AdvancedDataGridRendererProvider*

AdvancedDataGridRendererProvider is probably the longest named component in Flex! It makes custom item rendering possible in an AdvancedDataGrid. Table 10.3 lists its properties.

Table 10.3   Properties of the `AdvancedDataGridRendererProvider`

Property	Type	Description
column	Object	References an AdvancedDataGridColumn. Using binding, you specify the id of the column to which this advanced renderer refers. For example, you can use the field {myCol} instead of columnIndex. This property lets you reference a column by its name.
columnIndex	Number	Similar to Column, but you can reference columns numerically. The first column starts at 0.
columnSpan	Number	Similar to the colSpan property of an HTML table; specifies the number of columns you wish to span. This is an optional property that carries a default value of 1. Setting to 0 spans all columns.
dataField	String	Determines which field in your data provider should be used by this item renderer (if any). An optional property.
renderer	Component	Name of the item renderer to be invoked. Required.
rowSpan	Number	Similar to the rowSpan property of an HTML table; specifies the number of rows you wish to span. An optional property. Default value is 1.

You furnish AdvancedDataGridRendererProviders with these properties as part of the `<mx:rendererProviders/>` tag, which can be nested within the MXML declaration of AdvancedDataGrid. Listing 10.14 shows an example of this structure.

Listing 10.14   Advanced renderers nested at the same level as columns

```
<mx:AdvancedDataGrid>
    <mx:columns>
        <mx:AdvancedDataGridColumn dataField="col1"/>
        <mx:AdvancedDataGridColumn dataField="col2"/>
      Etc...
    </mx:columns>
    <mx:rendererProviders>
        <mx:AdvancedDataGridRendererProvider [properties]/>
        <mx:AdvancedDataGridRendererProvider [properties]/>
      Etc...
    </mx:rendererProviders>
</mx:AdvancedDataGrid>
```

Listing 10.14 is a high-level overview of this concept. In terms of implementation, it's all about referencing the column to which an advanced item renderer is applied.

10.4.2 Referencing the column

You can reference a column two ways: using the column's `id` property or specifying the column's position.

REFERENCING BY ID

Use the `column` property if you want to use a named approach to specify the column to which the renderer applies. Listing 10.15 binds on the column called `nameCol`.

Listing 10.15   Applying an advanced item renderer using a column name

```
<mx:AdvancedDataGrid dataProvider="{myAC}">
    <mx:columns>
        <mx:DataGridColumn id="nameCol" headerText="Name"
            dataField="name"/>
    </mx:columns>
    <mx:rendererProviders>
        <mx:AdvancedDataGridRendererProvider column="{nameCol}"
            renderer="myRenderer"/>
    </mx:rendererProviders>
</mx:AdvancedDataGrid>
```

This is the way to go if you feel you may reposition a particular column; the item renderer will continue to work regardless of where you move its target column.

REFERENCING BY INDEX

If you want to reference by the position of the column, use the `columnIndex` property instead. For example, listing 10.16 instructs the `AdvancedDataGridRendererProvider` to apply itself to the first column.

Listing 10.16   Applying an advanced item renderer to the first column

```
<mx:AdvancedDataGrid dataProvider="{myAC}">
    <mx:columns>
        <mx:DataGridColumn id="nameCol" headerText="Name"
            dataField="name"/>
    </mx:columns>
    <mx:rendererProviders>
        <mx:AdvancedDataGridRendererProvider columnIndex="0"
            renderer="myRenderer"/>
    </mx:rendererProviders>
</mx:AdvancedDataGrid>
```

The advantage of this approach becomes clear if you need to have an item renderer that's based on the position of the column. For example, an item renderer may be used for column 2, regardless of that column's content. Or, you can dynamically set a variable and use it to set the `columnIndex`.

Identifying which column an advanced item renderer is linked to is the basic use case, but you can also use it to span multiple columns.

10.4.3 *Spanning columns*

To span columns, use the `columnSpan` property. You can use `columnSpan` in much the same way as you would the HTML <td> tag, which has a similar property named `colspan`. Listing 10.17 demonstrates how to use `columnSpan` by instructing an advanced item renderer to span two columns, starting at the second column.

> **Listing 10.17 Using an advanced item renderer to span two columns**

```
<?xml version="1.0"?>
<s:Application xmlns:fx="http://ns.adobe.com/mxml/2009"
               xmlns:s="library://ns.adobe.com/flex/spark"
               xmlns:mx="library://ns.adobe.com/flex/mx">
<fx:Script>
    <![CDATA[
        import mx.collections.ArrayCollection;
        [Bindable]
        public var myAC:ArrayCollection  = new ArrayCollection([
          { name:"John C Bland", email:"john@iscool.com", type:"Customer" }
          { name:"Tariq Ahmed", email:"tariq@iscool.com", type:"Employee" }
          { name:"Dan Orlando", email:"dan@iscool.com", type:"Customer" }
        ]);
    ]]>
</fx:Script>
<mx:AdvancedDataGrid width="350" height="120" dataProvider="{myAC}">
    <mx:columns>
        <mx:AdvancedDataGridColumn headerText="Name" dataField="name"/>
        <mx:AdvancedDataGridColumn headerText="Email" dataField="email"/>
        <mx:AdvancedDataGridColumn headerText="Type" dataField="type"/>
    </mx:columns>
    <mx:rendererProviders>
        <mx:AdvancedDataGridRendererProvider columnIndex="1"
            columnSpan="2" renderer="myRenderer"/>
    </mx:rendererProviders>
</mx:AdvancedDataGrid>
</s:Application>
```

When you run this application, the email column for each person continues into the adjacent column; by using an advanced item renderer, you're able to have the email field span two columns. This comes in handy when you want to extend the cell's width if there's no data for the cell to its immediate right. If you've ever used Microsoft Excel, you've seen this functionality in action because that's how cells work by default.

Now, let's say you have hierarchical data to which you want to add a summary row. The question is, what if you have to span an entire row?

10.4.4 *Spanning an entire row*

To span an entire row, set the `columnIndex` to 0. This technique isn't particularly useful if you're working with flat data, because you're effectively creating a single column. But it can come in handy if you have hierarchical data to which you want to add a summary row, as demonstrated in this next listing.

Listing 10.18 HelloWorld.mxml: spanning rows with hierarchical data

```
<?xml version="1.0"?>
<s:Application xmlns:s="library://ns.adobe.com/flex/spark"
               xmlns:mx="library://ns.adobe.com/flex/mx">
<fx:Declarations>
  <mx:XMLList id="myXML">
      <friends name="Friends">
          <friend name="Dan Orlando" email="dorlando@domain.com">
              <info>
                  <summary>
                      47 emails sent in the last 24hrs
                  </summary>
              </info>
          </friend>
          <friend name="John C Bland II" email="jbland@domain.com">
              <info>
                  <summary>
                      12 emails sent in the last 24hrs
                  </summary>
              </info>
          </friend>
      </friends>
  </mx:XMLList>
</fx:Declarations>
<mx:HierarchicalData source="{myXML}" id="myHD"/>
<mx:AdvancedDataGrid dataProvider="{myHD}" width="300">
    <mx:columns>
        <mx:AdvancedDataGridColumn dataField="@name"
            headerText="Contacts"/>
        <mx:AdvancedDataGridColumn dataField="@email"
            headerText="Email"/>
    </mx:columns>
    <mx:rendererProviders>
        <mx:AdvancedDataGridRendererProvider dataField="summary"
            columnIndex="0" columnSpan="0" renderer="myRenderer"/>
    </mx:rendererProviders>
</mx:AdvancedDataGrid>
</s:Application>
```

The code for the item renderer that's used for the grid is simple:

```
<?xml version="1.0" encoding="utf-8"?>
<s:Label xmlns:s="library://ns.adobe.com/flex/spark"
         width="100%"
         text="{data.summary}" />
```

Spanning an entire row is particularly useful when paired with hierarchical data. Also keep in mind that the renderer itself is exactly the same, whether it's used as a normal item renderer or as an advanced item renderer.

Let's say you're building a dashboard for a client to show sales in various countries. To conserve bandwidth, the client wants you to make only one call to the server on startup and load all the data into the application as opposed to making multiple service calls. When the applications loads, you have a huge collection of data with no context. Luckily, you can use *filter functions* to give context to the data and give your dashboard components the data providers that they need, as you'll see next.

10.5   Filter functions

Filter functions aren't specific to `List`-based components. They're part of the built-in functionality of collection objects. Filter functions let you filter subsets of information contained in collections of data. One of the most common uses is in conjunction with `List`-based components. Instead of laboriously creating temporary arrays to hold subsets of data, you can let the collection do all the work for you.

Let's assume for your dashboard that you want to allow the user to control what's displayed based on specified criteria. Listing 10.19 uses a filter function to provide that capability.

Listing 10.19   Controlling a dashboard display with a filter function

```
<?xml version="1.0"?>
<s:Application xmlns:fx="http://ns.adobe.com/mxml/2009"
               xmlns:s="library://ns.adobe.com/flex/spark"
               xmlns:mx="library://ns.adobe.com/flex/mx">
    <fx:Script>
        <![CDATA[
            import mx.collections.ArrayCollection;
            [Bindable]
            public var salesAC:ArrayCollection  = new ArrayCollection([
            {name:"Canada",revenue:295323},
            {name:"United States",revenue:982832},
            {name:"England",revenue:109283},
            {name:"Brazil",revenue:12495},
            {name:"India",revenue:597232},
            {name:"China",revenue:682011}              Does record ❶
            ]);                                       match criteria?

            public function filterFunc(item:Object):Boolean
            {
                if(item.revenue >= salesRange.values[0] && item.revenue <=
                    salesRange.values[1])
                    return true;                             Record
                else                                         matches
                    return false;          Record
            }                              doesn't match
                                                        ❷ Applies
            public function filterSales():void             filter
            {
                salesAC.filterFunction=filterFunc;      Sets
                salesAC.refresh();                      ArrayCollection's
            }                  Applies records          filterFunction
        ]]>                    that match on          ❸ property
    </fx:Script>            ❹ filter function
    <mx:Panel width="400" height="300" title="Sales Dashboard">
        <mx:HSlider change="filterSales()" id="salesRange"
            width="100%" thumbCount="2"
            labels="['0','250000','500000','750000','1000000']"
```

```
            tickInterval="50000" height="50"
            maximum="1000000"/>
        <mx:DataGrid id="dg" width="100%" height="100%"
            dataProvider="{salesAC}">

                <mx:DataGridColumn headerText="Country"
                                    dataField="name"/>
                <mx:DataGridColumn headerText="Revenue"
                                    dataField="revenue"/>
            </mx:columns>
        </mx:DataGrid>
    </mx:Panel>
</s:Application>
```

⬅ **Lets user filter**
⑤ range of values

There's quite a bit going on in listing 10.19, so let's walk through it. First, the HSlider ⑤ is used to capture the range of values to filter via the user. When the HSlider's values change, the filterSales function ❷ is called. Next, filterSales tells the salesAC ArrayCollection to use filterFunc ❸ as its filter function. Then, filterSales calls salesAC.refresh ❹, which signals salesAC to check every record with filterFunc. Finally, filterFunc checks ❶ whether the record currently being evaluated is within the value range of the HSlider.

If you run the code, you'll see that only the sales revenue from countries that are within the specified slide range is displayed. As you move the sliders, the content within the DataGrid changes in response by using the filter function.

You just learned how to filter data behind the scenes by using the filterFunction property to call a function that will process the data that will populate your component. This opens up the opportunity to use the component that's best suited for a particular application without being limited by its built-in functionality for data processing.

10.6 Summary

When you begin working with List-based components, you can throw a lot of data at them and have that data displayed with little effort on your part. This chapter corralled all the independent pieces you'll need to confidently begin taking on the challenge of customizing List-based components. In the later chapters of this book, you'll learn how to harness this power even further when we talk about best practices with design patterns for ultimate scalability.

In this chapter, you first learned to use a label function to customize the display in a List-based component. Label functions are easy to initialize and work well when combined with a formatter, but they're limited in what you can do with them.

Your main tool is the item renderer, which gives you maximum flexibility over display logic. Complementary to item renderers are item editors, which let users perform inline editing. Both item renderers and editors come with a number of events that let you tap into the editing process to further inject your own business logic and checkpoints.

The Flex SDK includes advanced List-based components (such as the Advanced-DataGrid), which support all the same item renderers but in more advanced ways (for instance, spanning multiple columns).

In the traditional web application world, when a user changes selection criteria (such as date ranges, sales figures, and geographical regions), the web application requeries the service or database for an updated set of data. With Flex, you can spare unnecessary round trips to web services by loading all the data up front and storing it in memory (assuming that this is logistically reasonable and you're not trying to load billions of records at once), and then use filter functions to parse your information on the client side.

We've used events to support various interactions; in this chapter, we looked at events that accompany item editors. We've also been reminding you regularly that Flex is an event-driven application framework. Now that you've been introduced to various cases demonstrating how events are used, it's time to look further into the mechanics of how they work.

Part 2

Application flow and structure

Part 1 focused on putting together the core blocks of an application. Part 2 moves forward with the application's wiring and structure.

Flex is an event-based environment. Although part 1 discussed the basic mechanics of using events, the next nine chapters go into much more depth about how the event model works and how you can make your own events. You'll use the power of events to add navigation and interactivity to your Flex applications.

A Flex application isn't much use without a backend system to exchange data with. You'll learn about the mechanisms available to transfer data back and forth as part of application flow.

That data may come in the form of XML, which the Flash Player is adept at handling. With Flex's support for ECMAScript for XML (E4X), you can use ActionScript to work with XML as if it were a native ActionScript data type.

Once you have both the building blocks and the flow of an application under your belt, the application structure will be the key to making your code manageable, maintainable, and reusable. Flash Player supports a number of ways to achieve this, so we'll end this part of the book by discussing how to encapsulate logic into modular pieces.

11

Events

Events are central to understanding how to work with Flex and how to create compelling, well-designed applications. Events are a powerful tool and one of the main features of the Flash Player.

Events are deceptively simple, but at the same time, they're an extremely powerful communication mechanism for your applications. We've mentioned several times that Flex is built around an event-driven framework. Events are the central nervous system within your applications, with information flowing in and out of them, up and down, and side to side. We don't mean to be melodramatic, but if you don't understand events, Flex becomes a terrible chore and ActionScript 2.0 begins to look sexy again.

Let's begin by introducing the event system and describing its all-important role in a Flex application. Next we explore integrating native and custom events in an application while gaining an understanding of event nuances.

11.1 *The event system*

When working with web technologies such as ColdFusion, .NET, ASP, PHP, PERL, and Python, information is transmitted on a *request* and *response* basis, or what is called *synchronous requests*. In this model, remote servers wait for requests from clients (users) and then gather and process information relevant to the request. They build the appropriate response and send the data back to the client, at which point the transaction is over—until the client requests the next transaction. Figure 11.1 shows a request from your laptop, over the internet, to the web server (where the site is held), and back to your computer. Between steps 1 and 2 there is latency, or a delay, because of the time it takes to travel from your location to the location of the server. The same goes for step 3 to step 4.

Flash Player employs a different paradigm. Instead of sending out requests and receiving responses, Flash Player makes requests and then listeners patiently wait and *listen* for asynchronous events. When a listener hears an event, it performs the task it was designed to do and then waits again for the next event to occur.

Figure 11.2 shows an example of a profile manager with a form and the resulting information as two separate components. In phase 1, the top graphic, the "Your information" pod registers as a listener for update events from the "Update your information" component. At this point nothing happens until the update event is dispatched, and the rest of the application is still available for interaction. Once the user enters some information and clicks the Update button, an event is dispatched and anything listening for this event will be notified, as shown in phase 2, the bottom graphic. Notice that all of this interaction happens within the application and without returning to the server.

In Flash Player, events are constantly fired in response to a variety of user inputs and system notifications. The main instigator for these events is the user. By clicking a mouse button, moving the mouse, or selecting an item from a drop-down menu, the user is unwittingly setting off events, which trigger the application to respond accordingly.

With Flash Player applications, the difference is in the user-transparent operations that take place in the background. This gives you the ability to fire off tasks asynchronously, in parallel, none of which are dependent on each other, allowing for transparent activities to go on behind the

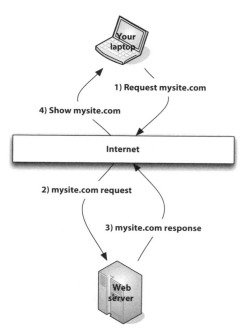

Figure 11.1   Example of a synchronous request

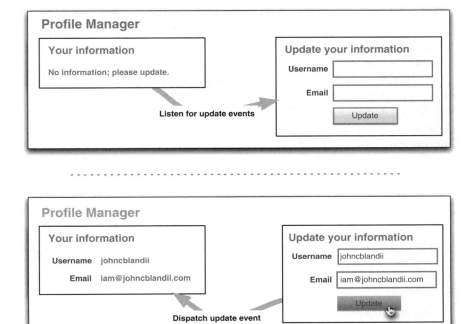

Figure 11.2   Example of event listening

scenes while your application interacts with and provides feedback to the user in real time (versus having code execute synchronously, or sequentially, while the user waits for it to complete).

In addition, when requests for new information are made, they're sent to the target server, and the application carries on with other tasks or patiently waits. The response will be processed whenever the result comes back, whether that happens to be in five seconds or five minutes.

In contrast, when making a request to a web server, an HTML page viewed using a web browser shows the page in a vertical manner from the top of the page to the bottom of the page, unless JavaScript is used to asynchronously update the page after the page has loaded.

We'll get into how this works in a moment; before we do, let's look at how the Flash Player event system is similar to another system you already know well: "I'll call you. Don't call me."

11.1.1   Event system—the Hollywood Principle

Components and classes, also known as dispatchers or targets, need to communicate and pass data to each other through the event system. To illustrate this more clearly, we can draw a parallel between the event system and the Hollywood Principle, which states, "Don't call me. I'll call you."

Think of a person calling you asking to borrow money. You tell them you'll contact them with an answer after checking your bank account. This is the Hollywood Principle, which is nothing more than an asynchronous request, in tech terms. Consider the following example.

Your Flex application is supposed to load data from the server, but while the data loads you want to show some cute, animated message to the user. The data-loading component would be you on the phone, the application would be the person in need, and the cute, animated message would be you dancing to "Footloose" in your mirror while checking your bank balance.

The request has been made. The amount of time between the request and the resulting call back is undetermined, so you could be dancing for a while, but once you've checked your account and have an answer, you're ready to inform the caller of your answer.

This is exactly how Flex applications are developed and why events are critical: Dispatchers receive requests and dispatch events accordingly but not necessarily immediately.

11.1.2 *Event-delivery system*

It's important to know the pathway events take within a Flex application, because this pathway determines which components receive the events and which don't.

Events originate from the dispatcher, traverse the display tree vertically to the application root and then to the stage, and are sent back down to the dispatcher, as shown in figure 11.3.

The event goes through the parent tree (and any components that are specifically listening to it), which has implications for which components receive notifications about events. For example, as shown in figure 11.3, a component's parent typically receives event notifications; children and siblings don't receive notifications.

From an application perspective, when a component dispatches an event, that event can either *bubble* or not bubble. If the event bubbles, it traverses up the parent

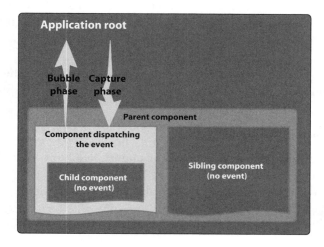

Figure 11.3   The event flow from component to root and back to component

chain to the application root, passing by every parent in the chain. Each parent can listen for application events at its own level and rebroadcast those events as needed, stop the propagation, or call methods to take specific action.

This is the real power behind the Flash Player event system: the ability to create custom events and pass them around. Tying into the event system allows for maximum decoupling of logic and maximizes the components that can use that logic, which in turn affords maximum code reuse.

Now that you've learned a bit about how the application passes events around, let's break down the event's journey from start to finish by exploring sending and receiving events.

11.2 Sending and receiving events

A Flash Player event is made up of the following core properties (see table 11.1).

Table 11.1 Core event properties

Property	Description
Event.target	Event dispatcher.
Event.currentTarget	Component currently containing and inspecting the event or the dispatcher.
Event.type	A string name that identifies the type of event, such as a click event (clicking a button), a mouse event (moving the mouse), or a select event (selecting an item). Events come in many types, and each type includes unique items, but each event has the generic types mentioned here.
Event.eventPhase	Current phase of the event.

NOTE In the Target phase currentTarget has the same value as target, the dispatcher, but in the Capturing and Bubbling phases currentTarget is different.

Each portion of the event journey—from dispatcher to parents to stage and back again—can be divided into phases. Events have only three phases, depending on where they are in the process, as shown in table 11.2.

NOTE The Bubbling and Capturing phases travel through parents but never through the children of the dispatcher.

Table 11.2 The different event phases

Phase	Description
Capturing	Event travels from the stage through the parents to the dispatcher.
Bubbling	Event travels from the dispatcher through the parents to the stage.
Target	Occurs only when the event has reached its target object or the dispatcher and relates only to the one object, target, or dispatcher.

You can determine which phase you're in by using the event object's eventPhase property. This property contains an integer that represents one of the following Event constants:

- Event.CAPTURING_PHASE:uint = 1
- Event.AT_TARGET:uint = 2
- Event.BUBBLING_PHASE:uint = 3

Best practice
When you're referring to or monitoring these phases, you can use either the number or the constant, although it's considered best practice to use constants wherever possible to make your code easier to read and manage.

Other events and custom classes can contain other properties as well, as you'll see in section 11.3, but at minimum they include these properties.

Let's examine what happens with a simple click event generated by pressing a mouse button, as shown in listing 11.1. Copy and paste listing 11.1 into a new file named mxmlAndScriptBlock.mxml and then run it.

Listing 11.1   Event listening with MXML and an ActionScript event listener

```
<?xml version="1.0" encoding="utf-8"?>
<s:Application xmlns:fx="http://ns.adobe.com/mxml/2009"
               xmlns:s="library://ns.adobe.com/flex/spark">
  <fx:Script>
    <![CDATA[
      import mx.controls.Alert;
      protected function onClick(event:Event):void{
        Alert.show(event.target.label + " clicked", "Event Test");
      }
    ]]>
  </fx:Script>
  <s:Button label="Button 1" click="onClick(event)" />
</s:Application>
```

When you click the button, a click event is generated and the onClick listener is called. In the onClick listener, you show an alert. The alert's message is the target item's label, event.target.label, with " clicked" appended.

NOTE   Remember, event.target references the dispatcher, so label is a property of the target, which in this case is a Button component.

Listing 11.1 uses a script block to manage the click event. This can also be done without a script block. Listing 11.2 uses inline MXML to show the same alert.

Listing 11.2   Event listening with inline MXML

```
<s:Button label="Button 1">
  <s:click>
    <![CDATA[
```

```
        Alert.show(event.target.label + " clicked", "Event Test");
    ]]>
  </s:click>
</s:Button>
```

Listing 11.2 uses the same button but makes the event listening occur inline. This has advantages and disadvantages. Ultimately, it boils down to your preference, but keep in mind that an inline event listener can't be used by multiple dispatchers. In the case where multiple `Button` components need to call the same method, this approach would fail miserably.

Although these examples do the event adding in MXML, you aren't restricted to working in that environment. You can do the same thing in ActionScript by using the `addEventListener()` function.

11.2.1 Adding event listeners in ActionScript

Using the `addEventListener()` function provides more fine-grained control over the events and is the only way in ActionScript to listen for dispatched events. One huge reason for adding event listeners in ActionScript is that event listeners added in MXML can't be removed. We cover this in more detail later, but keep it in mind for now as a big win in the ActionScript-approach column.

If you need to listen for an event in the capture phase, rather than the bubbling and target phases, you must add the listener using the ActionScript method. As a handy reference guide, we've included the main attributes of an event listener in table 11.3.

Let's take the previous MXML application from listing 11.1 and use ActionScript to register the listener. Listing 11.3 shows how you add an event listener on a previously instantiated display object using ActionScript.

Table 11.3 Event listener properties and method arguments

Property	Type	Description
type	String	(Required) The type of event for which to listen. You can define the event type as a `String` or use best practices and use the event type constant defined on every event object.
listener	Function	(Required) The function to call when the event is dispatched.
useCapture	Boolean	(Optional) The phase in which to listen. If `true`, the listener listens for the event during the capture phase. The default value is `false` (uses the bubbling or target phase).
priority	Integer	(Optional) When the listener is called. The higher the number, the sooner it's called. The value can be negative; the default value is `1`.
weakReference	Boolean	(Optional) How quickly the event listener object is picked up and destroyed by the garbage collector. `true` means it's discarded sooner. The default value is `false`, which prevents garbage collection from destroying the listener (performance at the cost of memory).

Details on using weakReference

weakReference is a hot topic in the ActionScript community pertaining to the proper way of managing application performance and memory. Many developers rely heavily on using weakReference, whereas others rely on removing all listeners. The arguments on both sides are solid, and it all boils down to personal preference. Find out what works best for you and your applications.

Relying on weakReference isn't always ideal. This waits for the garbage collector to pick up the "trash" for you. In most cases, this is fine, but your objects may not disappear instantly as you desire.

Ideally, every event listener you add should be removed before destroying the object. This provides a clean entry and exit for the object without having to play roulette with your memory.

The best practice is to use both.

Listing 11.3   Click event example using ActionScript

```
<?xml version="1.0" encoding="utf-8"?>
<s:Application xmlns:fx="http://ns.adobe.com/mxml/2009"
               xmlns:s="library://ns.adobe.com/flex/spark"
               applicationComplete="init()">
  <fx:Script>
  <![CDATA[
    import mx.controls.Alert;

    protected function init():void{
      button1.addEventListener(MouseEvent.CLICK, onClick);     ◁── Sets onClick
                                                                    to run when
                                                                    click event
    protected function onClick(event:Event):void{                   occurs
      Alert.show(event.target.label + " clicked", "Event Test");
    }
  ]]>
  </fx:Script>
  <s:Button id="button1" label="Button 1" />
</s:Application>
```

As demonstrated in listings 11.1 and 11.3, the main difference between the MXML and ActionScript methods for adding a simple event listener involves the use of addEventListener.

When the button is clicked, it dispatches a click event, which activates and passes the click event to onClick(). With the ActionScript method, you need an intermediary function to add the event listener to the button.

In listing 11.3, this is handled by init(), which is called when the Application issues the applicationComplete event. This event is the last event dispatched in the Application startup and is called when the Application is fully initialized and added to the display list.

NOTE If you add an event listener for the capture phase, passing `true` as the third parameter of `addEventListener`, of a button's click event, it listens only during the capture phase. Remember, the capture phase is the way down from the top-level application, as shown in figure 11.3. If you need to listen to both the capture phase and the bubbling phase, you must add a second event listener, omitting or passing `false` as the third `addEventListener` parameter.

You've probably already gathered this, but most actions in Flex have corresponding events for which you can listen by using the event listeners; you can then respond as needed. This is the communication and nervous system of your Flex application. Even setting variables can cause events to be broadcast. This type of event dispatch is called *binding*.

NOTE When adding listeners, a serious consideration for `weakReference` is required. If you think the object will ever need garbage collection and you aren't going to explicitly remove all event listeners from the object, use `weakReference`. Don't use `weakReference` on local objects (objects created in a method and then destroyed) because the garbage collection occurs automatically, which could cause your listeners not to fire if they're garbage collected before your expected event.

11.2.2 Binding events

Binding in Flex is carried out in the event system. When you bind a variable, you're establishing a dedicated listener that picks up on change events issued from the variable or object to which it's bound (for more about binding, refer to chapter 3).

Whenever you create a binding to a variable, you register an event listener to respond to any changes that occur in that variable. When binding in MXML, the updating takes place behind the scenes, as demonstrated in the following listing.

Listing 11.4 MXML binding

```
<?xml version="1.0" encoding="utf-8"?>
<s:Application xmlns:fx="http://ns.adobe.com/mxml/2009"
               xmlns:s="library://ns.adobe.com/flex/spark">
  <s:layout>
    <s:HorizontalLayout />
  </s:layout>
  <fx:Script>
    <![CDATA[
      [Bindable]                                    [Bindable] means
      protected var _labelText:String = "Label before event";   watch this variable
    ]]>
  </fx:Script>

  <s:Button id="myButton" label="Change Label!">
    <s:click>
      <![CDATA[
        _labelText = "Label " + Math.round(Math.random()*10);
      ]]>
    </s:click>
  </s:Button>
```

```
      </s:Button>
      <s:Label id="myLabel" text="{_labelText}"/>
    </s:Application>
```

Compare the code in listing 11.4 to what's required to accomplish the same thing in ActionScript (listing 11.5). This ActionScript version relies on a class called Change-Watcher, which monitors any changes in the value of a property to which you have it bound. If a change occurs, ChangeWatcher triggers the necessary events to watch that value. It's much like an event listener object in that it listens for specific events from a property.

Listing 11.5 ActionScript binding using ChangeWatcher

```
<?xml version="1.0" encoding="utf-8"?>
<s:Application xmlns:fx="http://ns.adobe.com/mxml/2009"
               xmlns:s="library://ns.adobe.com/flex/spark"
               applicationComplete="init()">
  <s:layout>
    <s:VerticalLayout/>
  </s:layout>
  <fx:Script>
    <![CDATA[
      import mx.events.PropertyChangeEvent;              Necessary imports to
      import mx.binding.utils.ChangeWatcher;             dynamically bind variables

      protected var _watcher:ChangeWatcher;

      protected function init():void{
        toggleWatch();
      }
      protected function toggleWatch():void{             Verifies the
        if(_watcher && _watcher.isWatching()){           watcher is active
          _watcher.unwatch();
          toggleButton.label = "Watch";          Removes
        }else{                                    watched variable
          _watcher = ChangeWatcher.watch(inputField,"text",onTextChange);
          toggleButton.label = "Stop Watching";
        }                                              Tells ChangeWatcher
      }                                                 to detect changes
      protected function onTextChange(event:Event):void{
        myLabel.text = inputField.text;
      }
    ]]>
  </fx:Script>
  <s:Button id="toggleButton" label="Watch Text" click="toggleWatch()"/>
  <s:TextInput id="inputField" text="start text"/>
  <s:Label id="myLabel" />
</s:Application>
```

This method isn't as easy as other ActionScript approaches or even the shortest ActionScript approach, but it's more flexible. Upon receipt of the application-Complete event from the application, you toggle the watcher. Because _watcher is null at startup, the first if statement in toggleWatch fails, causing the else block to run. The else block binds to changes on the inputField's text property by calling the `ChangeWatcher.watch()` method, which acts as the factory method for `Change-Watcher`; an instantiated `ChangeWatcher` object is returned when you call the `watch()` method.

This method takes inputs for the object you want to watch and a property of the watched object that's listened to (in this case, you're watching the `text` property of `inputField`). The third property specifies which function to call when this event is triggered—in this case, `onTextChange()`.

If you look back at the `addEventListener()` method, you'll see that this approach acts in a similar manner. With the `addEventListener()` method, you're listening to the entire object; with the method presented in listing 11.5, you're watching a specific object property. Changes made to the object property trigger the event listener.

When you type anything in the text input, `ChangeWatcher` automatically listens for those updates and executes the listening method. Each time you press a key, you send out an event that's monitored by `ChangeWatcher`. As demonstrated in listing 11.5, your binding event can be as simple as copying the user input value into the `myLabel` component, or it can be as complex as you need it to be.

Another benefit of this implementation is the ability to remove a binding from an object. You can't remove the binding in MXML. As shown in listing 11.5, using Action-Script, when the `toggleWatch` is called and `_watcher.isWatching()` is true, the bind event is removed using `_watcher.unwatch()`, causing future property changes to not call the event listener.

If you look at the toggle method, the `toggleButton`'s label is changed to reflect the current watch state of `_watcher`. This could be done using multiple buttons or by listening to other types of events as well. This approach is for user interface simplicity.

NOTE `ChangeWatcher.watch()` also has a `weakReference` argument. Use this argument in the same instances and for the same reasons as you would `addEventListener()`.

The `BindingUtils` class also allows binding through ActionScript, but it's only a wrapper around `ChangeWatcher`. Using `BindingUtils.bindProperty` or `BindingUtils.bindSetter`, you can set up a `ChangeWatcher` binding. It's a helper class to condense the lines of code necessary to bind objects in ActionScript. The following line of code is similar to calling `ChangeWatcher.watch()`:

```
BindingUtils.bindProperty(myLabel, "text", inputField, "text");
```

Table 11.4 lists a few of the benefits of the different approaches to data binding.

Table 11.4 Benefits of using each binding approach

	MXML Binding*	**ChangeWatcher**	**BindingUtils**
Ability to toggle on/off	No	Yes	Yes
Call methods on change	No	Yes	Yes
Two-way binding	Yes	No	No

* This includes the simple { } and @{ } syntax as well as using `<fx:Binding />`.

11.2.3 *Removing event listeners*

You've just seen the unwatch() method in action, which lets you stop monitoring a variable for changes. When using event listeners, you have the same type of capability. If an event listener was added at runtime in ActionScript, you'd be able to remove it using the removeEventListener() method. unwatch() merely uses removeEvent-Listener to stop the events from dispatching. If you look at the underlying code for the ChangeWatcher class, you'll notice on roughly line 500 the following statement:

```
host.removeEventListener(p, wrapHandler);
```

Take a look at listing 11.6 (testingForListeners.mxml) to see how to remove event listeners.

Listing 11.6 Example of adding and removing events

```
<?xml version="1.0" encoding="utf-8"?>
<s:Application xmlns:fx="http://ns.adobe.com/mxml/2009"
               xmlns:s="library://ns.adobe.com/flex/spark">
  <s:layout>
    <s:VerticalLayout/>
  </s:layout>
  <fx:Script>
    <![CDATA[
      protected function toggleListeners():void{
        if(box.hasEventListener(MouseEvent.CLICK)){
          log("Listeners removed");
          box.removeEventListener(MouseEvent.MOUSE_OVER, onEvent);    ◀── Removes
          box.removeEventListener(MouseEvent.MOUSE_OUT, onEvent);         event
          box.removeEventListener(MouseEvent.MOUSE_MOVE, onEvent);        listeners
          box.removeEventListener(MouseEvent.CLICK, onEvent);
        }else{
          log("Listeners added");
          box.addEventListener(MouseEvent.MOUSE_OVER, onEvent);       ◀── Adds
          box.addEventListener(MouseEvent.MOUSE_OUT, onEvent);            event
          box.addEventListener(MouseEvent.MOUSE_MOVE, onEvent);          listeners
          box.addEventListener(MouseEvent.CLICK, onEvent);
        }
      }

      protected function onEvent(event:Event):void{                   ◀── Event
        log("Event triggered: " + event.type);                          handler
      }

      protected function log(text:String):void{
        logField.text = text + "\n" + logField.text;
      }
    ]]>
  </fx:Script>
  <s:Button label="Toggle Listeners" click="toggleListeners()" />
  <s:Group id="box">
    <s:Rect width="200" height="50">
      <s:fill>
        <s:SolidColor color="0x979797" />
      </s:fill>
    </s:Rect>
```

```
    </s:Group>
    <s:TextArea id="logField" width="400" height="400" />
</s:Application>
```

Listing 11.6 shows how to test an object to determine if a particular event listener was added and then remove the listeners or add them back accordingly so the same listener isn't added multiple times. Run the code and you'll see output similar to figure 11.4.

> **NOTE** `removeEventListener()`, in listing 11.6, uses only two arguments, but it's important to note the third parameter. The third argument is `use-Capture`, which is `false` by default. When an event listener is added for the capture phase, to remove it you must pass `true` as the third argument.

`toggleListeners()` introduces a new method: `hasEventListener(type:String): Boolean`. This method checks the target object for existence of the passed-in event type. If the listener hasn't been added to the target object, the event listener is added; otherwise, it's removed, toggling the existence of the listeners.

For logging purposes, you can add and remove four different types of events. This allows you to see the different events trigger accordingly.

Knowing how to add and remove event listeners is the starting point to building a great application. Adobe didn't stop with allowing internal events. In the next section, we cover dispatching and creating custom events. This will give you ultimate control over events and enable you to dynamically determine when events are sent out and what data these events should carry.

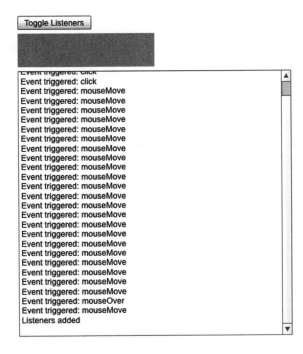

Figure 11.4   Output from listing 11.6

Removing MXML event listeners

It's important to remember that removing event listeners works only on events added using the ActionScript method of defining an event listener; listener functions added using the MXML format are permanently attached to the object. For example, you can't remove an event listener added using the MXML script shown in the following snippet:

```
<s:Button label="Toggle Listeners" click="toggleListeners()" />
```

If you think you might need to remove the event listener at some point, use the `add-EventListener()` method.

11.3 *Custom events*

Part of what makes events so powerful is the ability to create your own custom events and use them to communicate within your application. By sending out events when data changes or when the user initiates some action, like clicking a button, you decouple an application's logic from the objects that use it. This is critical because it creates a more modular structure, allowing changes to a component without affecting other parts of your application.

Imagine dispatching an event from two separate unrelated classes. Each class has a property containing the data we need, but both classes have different property names. `ClassA` has a property named `someData` and `ClassB` has a property named `content`. When the event is dispatched, calling `event.target.someData` throws an error if the dispatcher is `ClassB`. By passing the data in the event, the listener no longer cares which target dispatched it as long as the event contains the proper data. This eliminates the listener from having to determine which class is the dispatcher, only to determine the name of the class. Also keep in mind that if the listener does use the dispatcher's property to access the data, the listener now is tightly coupled to the dispatcher, so changes to the expected property name means changes to the listener as well.

This is where and why custom events shine.

11.3.1 *Dispatching custom event types*

All objects implementing the `flash.events.IEventDispatcher` interface can dispatch events, which include all display objects as well as other nondisplay classes. Typically, you achieve this in your custom nondisplay classes by extending `flash.events.EventDispatcher`. You'll see this in section 11.3.2. For now, let's focus on the basics of dispatching a custom event type.

Consider the following snippet:

```
dispatchEvent(new Event("complete"));
```

It performs two distinct operations:

- A new event class is instantiated to handle and hold the information.
- The event of type `"complete"` is dispatched using the `dispatchEvent()` function call.

When dispatching events with custom types, try your best to utilize an already available event constant (Event.COMPLETE, Event.CHANGE, and so on) or create your own static constants. You won't get beat up in a dark alley if you don't, but we're aiming to write solid, reusable code, right? To do so you can create static constants on the dispatcher or, if you want to be in the cool crowd, create a custom event class with constants. Doing so will allow you to write code capable of being used in multiple applications or even in multiple places within the same application. This also allows you to pass custom data with the events.

11.3.2 Creating custom events

Dispatching a custom event type is easy, but, as noted earlier, it won't get you any closer to stardom with other skilled developers or, more importantly, help reduce your application maintenance. Custom events give you full control over what data is sent with an event, the event types, default values, and so on.

To demonstrate, let's create a simple real-world example of adding event dispatching to a custom nondisplay class. Our application will load an XML file and display the results in a list. The focus is on the event dispatching though, not the user interface.

Start by creating a new ActionScript class named DataLoader in a packaged named net (see figure 11.5). This class will handle all of the data loading and parsing. Copy the code from listing 11.7 into the new class.

Listing 11.7 net.DataLoader class

```
package net{
  import events.ContentEvent;

  import flash.events.ErrorEvent;
  import flash.events.Event;
  import flash.events.EventDispatcher;
  import flash.events.IOErrorEvent;
  import flash.events.SecurityErrorEvent;
  import flash.net.URLLoader;
  import flash.net.URLRequest;

  import mx.collections.ArrayCollection;

  public class DataLoader extends EventDispatcher{          ⤆ Extend
    protected var _loader:URLLoader;                             EventDispatcher
                                                                 class
    public function DataLoader(){
      super();

      _loader = new URLLoader();
      _loader.addEventListener(Event.COMPLETE, onComplete);
      _loader.addEventListener(IOErrorEvent.IO_ERROR, onError);
      _loader.addEventListener(SecurityErrorEvent.SECURITY_ERROR, onError);
    }

    public function load(url:String):void{
      _loader.load(new URLRequest(url));
    }
```

```
protected function onComplete(event:Event):void{
  var users:ArrayCollection = new ArrayCollection();
  for each(var user:XML in XML(_loader.data).user){
    users.addItem(user.@name + " - " + user.@site);
  }

  var ev:ContentEvent = new ContentEvent(ContentEvent.DATA_BACK);
  ev.users = users;                                              Create and dispatch
  dispatchEvent(ev);                                          complete custom event
}

protected function onError(event:ErrorEvent):void{
  var ev:ContentEvent = new ContentEvent(ContentEvent.DATA_ERROR);
  ev.error = event.text;                                         Create and dispatch
  dispatchEvent(ev);                                             error custom event
  }
 }
}
```

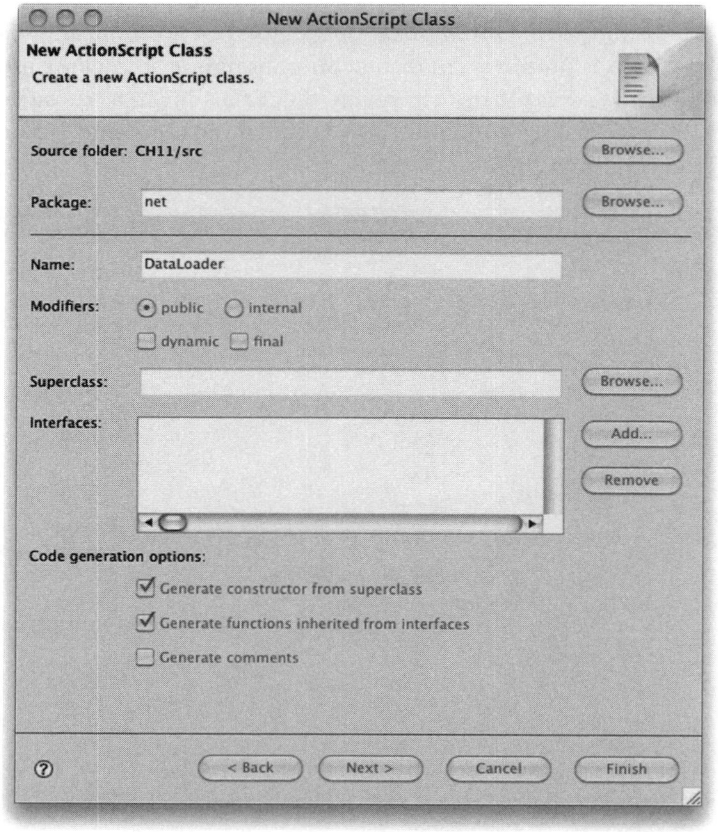

Figure 11.5 Use the New ActionScript Class Wizard to create the DataLoader class.

The DataLoader is simple. In the constructor an instance of the URLLoader is created with events tied to the instance to monitor the Event.COMPLETE, IOError-Event. IO_ERROR, and SecurityErrorEvent.SECURITY_ERROR events. From here the class does nothing until the load() method is called, which uses the loader to load the content.

Once the content is loaded, the onComplete() method handles the data parsing; then you get into dispatching the custom event:

```
var ev:ContentEvent = new ContentEvent(ContentEvent.DATA_BACK);
ev.users = users;
dispatchEvent(ev);
```

Notice that the only difference from dispatching the events as you have before is the assignment of the users property. The event type is referenced from a static constant of the custom event, and you're still passing the event object to dispatchEvent().

The onError() method dispatches an event in the same way. You create the event, passing in the custom type, in this case ContentEvent.DATA_ERROR, set the error property, and dispatch the event. Typically you want the onError method to redispatch the ErrorEvent using the clone() method. We discuss ways of improving this class at the end of this section.

Create a new ActionScript class named ContentEvent in the events package, and copy listing 11.8 into the class.

Listing 11.8 events.ContentEvent–The custom event for content

```
package events{
  import flash.events.Event;

  import mx.collections.ArrayCollection;

  public class ContentEvent extends Event{
    public static const DATA_BACK:String = "dataBack";      │ Event constants used
    public static const DATA_ERROR:String = "dataError";    │ for event references

    public var users:ArrayCollection;                        │ Custom data
    public var error:String;                                 │ properties

    public function ContentEvent(type:String, bubbles:Boolean=false,
     cancelable:Boolean=false){
      super(type, bubbles, cancelable);
    }
  }
}
```

This is a bare-minimum custom event class. It's important to note the constants. These are the event types, and the names are completely up to you. Normally better names would be chosen, like COMPLETE and ERROR, but it's a great way to introduce event-naming constructs.

The format of event names should be in all caps with an underscore (_) between words. The values of the constants are also completely up to you, but camel case is suggested. We'll cover why in the metadata section.

Event name conflicts can and do occur. If ContentEvent had an event named COMPLETE (versus DATA_BACK) and the DataLoader dispatched the event, the listener could also be triggered by dispatching Event.COMPLETE. In these cases some developers choose to name their events with full names, for example, events.Content-Event.DATA_BACK. This breaks the metadata constructs and disables MXML event access in some cases, but when done right, it completely ensures the listeners are called only for the specific event and no other events. This is especially important when listening to the Bubbling and Capture phases or when using Flex frameworks like Mate (http://mate.asfusion.com) or Swiz (http://swizframework.org).

> **Best practice**
>
> When building custom events, it's best to leave the constructor alone. Some developers like to change the constructor arguments to include type but leave out bubbles and cancelable. This will only confuse other developers new to your code.

One thing the ContentEvent class is missing is the clone() method. We previously noted that the class is the bare minimum, and it is. All of your custom events should always override the Event.clone() method. If the method isn't overridden and the event is cloned, the custom data won't make it into the clone, which means the clone won't match the original event.

All the method does is create a new instance of itself and set the new instance properties to match the current properties, essentially a clean copy of the event. Here's the clone() method as it would be implemented in the ContentEvent class:

```
override public function clone():Event{
    var event:ContentEvent = new ContentEvent(type, bubbles, cancelable);
    event.users = users;
    event.error = error;
    return event;
}
```

At this point the DataLoader class is complete. For now the class does exactly what you need: load data and dispatch complete and error events. The next step is to build the application.

Create a new MXML application in the (default package) named Users-View.mxml and copy listing 11.9 into the file.

Listing 11.9 UsersView application

```
<?xml version="1.0" encoding="utf-8"?>
<s:Application xmlns:fx="http://ns.adobe.com/mxml/2009"
               xmlns:s="library://ns.adobe.com/flex/spark"
               width="300" height="200"
               applicationComplete="init()">
  <s:layout>
    <s:BasicLayout/>
```

```
    </s:layout>
    <fx:Script>
      <![CDATA[
        import mx.controls.Alert;
        import events.ContentEvent;                          Create
        import net.DataLoader;                            listeners for
        protected function init():void{                    DataLoader
          var dataLoader:DataLoader = new DataLoader();
          dataLoader.addEventListener(ContentEvent.DATA_BACK, onData);
          dataLoader.addEventListener(ContentEvent.DATA_ERROR, onError);
          dataLoader.load("data/content.xml");      ◁┐ Initiate load
        }                                               │ request
        protected function onData(event:ContentEvent):void{
          userList.dataProvider = event.users;      ◁┐ Set list data
        }                                               │ to result
        protected function onError(event:ContentEvent):void{
          Alert.show(event.error, "Error!");        ◁┐ Show alert
        }                                               │ on errors
      ]]>
    </fx:Script>
    <s:List id="userList" width="100%" height="100%" />
</s:Application>
```

The application starts with the applicationComplete event, as shown previously, to call the init() method. This is where you instantiate a local instance of the Data-Loader class, add event listeners for the ContentEvent.DATA_BACK and Content-Event.DATA_ERROR events, and then tell it to load the data/content.xml file, which is shown in the following snippet:

```
<?xml version="1.0" encoding="UTF-8"?>
<users>
    <user name="John C. Bland II" site="http://www.johncblandii.com" />
    <user name="Tariq Ahmed" site="http://www.dopejam.com" />
    <user name="Dan Orlando" site="http://www.danorlando.com" />
    <user name="Joel Hooks" site="http://www.joelhooks.com" />
</users>
```

Once the data load is complete, the onData method is called, and you update the userList component to display the results. That's it. Your display is super simple, and all of the underpinnings are handled in separate classes. The beauty here is the Data-Loader can change to loading content via internal dummy data, Flash Remoting (AMF), SQLite (via Adobe AIR), and so on, and your UserView application won't have to be touched beyond the URL to load the content.

You can't leave out the onError method. Even though the DataLoader listened for two events (IOErrorEvent.IO_ERROR and SecurityErrorEvent.SECURITY_ERROR), your application had to worry about only one: ContentEvent.DATA_ERROR. When an error occurs, the onError method shows a simple alert displaying the event.error property as the message of the alert. Again, the underlying code can change to display any type of message, but your application stays the same. DataLoader could choose to use localized text, display a generic message, or display an error from the server. The possibilities are endless, but the changes to your application are nil.

Now that you've seen how to dispatch custom events, let's look at how to improve our events with metadata.

11.3.3 *Adding event metadata to custom dispatchers*

An important part of completing the dispatch of events—particularly when using custom components and classes—is adding metadata to dispatchers, to take advantage of code hinting in Flash Builder.

It's not necessary to add metadata, but doing so adds convenience by giving you the ability to see events as properties in MXML or to get code hints in ActionScript. Listing 11.10 shows how to add metadata to the `DataLoader` class from listing 11.7.

> **Listing 11.10   Event metadata `DataLoader` class**

```
package net{
  ...
  [Event(name="dataBack", type="events.ContentEvent")]
  [Event(name="dataError", type="events.ContentEvent")]
  public class DataLoader extends EventDispatcher{
    ...
  }
}
```
Event metadata for all errors dispatched by the `DataLoader`

The `name` attribute is required and refers to the property value, not the static constant of the class. Don't use `DATA_BACK` as the name. Instead, use the value of `DATA_BACK`, which is `dataBack`. This is where constant values are critical for code hinting. If the constant's value isn't in CamelCase, Flash Builder won't properly interpret which static constants are available from the event class referenced in the `type` attribute.

The `type` attribute references the event class. If the event class is `flash.events.Event`, the `type` attribute isn't required.

Why is this important? We're glad you asked! Figure 11.6 shows the before and after screenshots for code hinting in ActionScript.

To demonstrate the effectiveness for an MXML implementation, create a new MXML application named UserView2.mxml and copy listing 11.11 into the file.

Figure 11.6   Before (left) and after (right) the custom metadata

Listing 11.11 `UserView` implementing `DataLoader` in MXML

```
<?xml version="1.0" encoding="utf-8"?>
<s:Application xmlns:fx="http://ns.adobe.com/mxml/2009"
               xmlns:s="library://ns.adobe.com/flex/spark"
               xmlns:net="net.*"
               width="300" height="200"
               applicationComplete="init()">
  <fx:Script>
    <![CDATA[
      import mx.controls.Alert;
      import events.ContentEvent;
      protected function init():void{
        dataLoader.load("data/content.xml");
      }

      protected function onData(event:ContentEvent):void{
        userList.dataProvider = event.users;
      }

      protected function onError(event:ContentEvent):void{
        Alert.show(event.error, "Error!");
      }
    ]]>
  </fx:Script>
  <fx:Declarations>
    <net:DataLoader id="dataLoader" dataBack="onData(event)"
                    dataError="onError(event)" />
  </fx:Declarations>
  <s:List id="userList" width="100%" height="100%" />
</s:Application>
```

> **DataLoader implemented in MXML**

The main change is that `DataLoader` is now instantiated in MXML with the `dataBack` and `dataError` events shown as MXML properties. This isn't possible without metadata on the `DataLoader` class.

It's important to note how to add metadata in an MXML component. The exact same event metadata is used with a slight change, as shown in the following code:

```
<fx:Metadata>
  [Event(name="eventName", type="EventClass")]
</fx:Metadata>
```

NOTE Adding class-level metadata also improves your documentation when using ASDoc.

Using events with custom dispatchers as we've presented in this chapter lets you retain loose coupling. Your components don't need to know about each other, and the parent windows can control their behavior and manage interactions. You'll find out more about custom components in chapters 17 and 18.

Our last stop on the event train is how to stop the event, pun intended.

11.3.4 *Stopping event propagation*

During any event phase (capture, target, or bubbling), you can use the event's stop-Propagation() and stopImmediatePropagation() methods to discontinue the event from broadcasting to any other components. The two methods are virtually identical, differing only in whether other event listeners on the same component are allowed to receive the event.

For example, if the event.stopPropagation() method is used on an event, it discontinues propagation after all other event listeners on a given component have finished responding to the event. If you were to use the event.stopImmediate-Propagation() method, event propagation would be terminated before it was delivered to any other events, even if they were listening on the same component.

When used in conjunction with the priority attribute of the event listener (set when adding the event listener), you can create a function to be the first responder to the event. This can be an effective gating mechanism to evaluate an event and cease propagation if necessary to any other event listener on a given component (see the following listing).

Listing 11.12 Stopping propagation

```xml
<?xml version="1.0" encoding="utf-8"?>
<s:Application xmlns:fx="http://ns.adobe.com/mxml/2009"
               xmlns:s="library://ns.adobe.com/flex/spark"
               applicationComplete="init()">
  <fx:Script>
    <![CDATA[
      import mx.controls.Alert;
      public function init():void{
        button.addEventListener(MouseEvent.CLICK, onClick);      ← Adds event listener with high priority
        box.addEventListener(MouseEvent.CLICK, onParentClick);
      }
      public function onClick(e:Event):void{
        Alert.show("AS event. Calling stopPropogation.","First Event");
        e.stopPropagation();                                      ← Stops propagation— second event fires
      }
      public function onButtonClick(e:Event):void{
        Alert.show("MXML Click Event.", "Second Event Listener");
      }
      public function onParentClick(e:Event):void{
        Alert.show("You should never see this alert.", "Parent Event");   ← Event never reaches parent
      }
    ]]>
  </fx:Script>
  <s:HGroup id="box" width="100%">
    <s:Button id="button" label="Fire Event" click="onButtonClick(event)"/>
  </s:HGroup>
</s:Application>
```

You interrupt the propagation of the event at the button level. Normally, this event would travel through all the functions, triggering all three alerts. But after the first event, you call the `stopPropagation()` method. When you run the example, the first two events—those listening directly to the button—will run, but the parent event listening to box won't receive the event and therefore won't run.

If you change the `stopPropagation()` method to `stopImmediatePropagation()`, you'll see only the first alert. The `stopImmediatePropagation()` method terminates any and all delivery of the event beyond the first event listener. Discontinuing the propagation of events is an effective way to handle your event flow, depending on the circumstances. This is true when you have custom components sending out custom events.

You've learned the event flow (phases), how to start and stop listening (adding and removing event listeners), how to create custom events, and how to build your own event dispatchers. Dive into events as much as you can. They're crucial to the completion of great applications and key portions of the available Flex frameworks.

11.4   Summary

This chapter focused on the events system and how this system is used in Flash Player as well as Flex specifics, namely binding. The events system is arguably the most important upgrade from ActionScript 2.0 to ActionScript 3.0.

If you're coming from a web development background, learning asynchronous events is a paradigm shift from the standard request/response model of creating web applications. The events system is the core of this shift. Everything you do through Flex in some way touches upon the events system. When you key into an application's events, you can free your objects to behave independently, to the point where they don't need awareness of the application.

Now that you've tackled the events system, we'll move on to discuss application navigation, building on your event knowledge while continuing to improve your application's structure, functionality, and portability.

Application navigation

This chapter covers

- Components that facilitate navigation
- Assembling data to drive navigation components
- Interacting with navigation components

We've explored application flow and structure through custom and native application events. Events provide a clear way of communicating between different parts of the application. An important aspect of application development is the ability to move from one functional area of the application to another. We borrow from a real-world metaphor and refer to this activity as *navigation*. Just as with navigation in the real world, it's important to maintain familiarity with navigation components. In this chapter, we'll look at the following components that you'll use to add navigational features to your application:

- Menu
- MenuBar
- ViewStack
- ButtonBar
- TabNavigator
- Accordion

Before we can delve into how to use each of these components, we need to prepare the data they'll use. Like so many tasks, this can be done many ways; we'll explore the options along with their pros and cons.

12.1 *Preparing the menu data*

Drop-down menus have been a part of basic navigation since the innovation of the GUI; they add an easy way to display an application's features and selection lists without taking up a lot of your window's valuable real estate—they remain conveniently hidden until you need them. Drop-downs also reduce user fatigue and effort because the menu appears at the location where the user clicks a button, tab, or heading.

Using HTML to create drop-down menus from scratch is tricky because you need to deal with layering, Z-indices, overlapping form elements, cross-browser compatibility issues, and quite a bit of JavaScript and DHTML (particularly if you want context-driven menus). Many third-party products are available that abstract the complexity of implementing drop-downs in HTML, but the complexity is still there in the background. Fortunately, Flex offers easier solutions.

Putting aside the issues surrounding ease of use, we need to address how to prepare the data you intend to present in your menus. The information that populates cascading menus is usually hierarchical in nature, so your data needs to reflect this.

You can provide data to menus in many ways, each with advantages and disadvantages. We explore using arrays, array collections, model objects, and different XML data approaches. Let's look at the options at your disposal.

12.1.1 *Nested arrays*

Nested arrays are made up of one or more levels of arrays. They simulate a tree-like structure of data, which you can program in ActionScript.

Nested arrays offer economical memory usage. But their syntax can seem complicated; changes in the underlying data aren't automatically reflected visually because nested arrays aren't collection-based objects, which dispatch update events.

Listing 12.1 demonstrates how you can set up and use a nested array.

Listing 12.1 Preparing a nested array

```
protected var menuData:Array =          <-- Instantiates array
  [
    {
      label:'New',
        children: [{label:'Task'},{label:'Request'},{label:'Person'}]    <┐
    },                                                           Nested array ❶
    {
      label:'Import',
        children: [{label:'Image'},{label:'Document'},{label:'Project'}]  <┘
    }
  ];
```

In listing 12.1, a couple of lines of code ❶ start with the declaration `children:`. These lines define two nested arrays inside the primary `menuData` array. This declaration instructs a `Menu` object to treat the data contained in these subarrays as nested information.

TIP   By default, menus look for nested arrays named `children`.

The problem with using arrays is they're a simple type of object, and because they aren't members of the collection family, changes to the underlying data aren't automatically broadcast to other objects designated to listen. If your data is going to change after the initial menu `dataProvider` assignment, this is where upgrading to a collection-based object can be more advantageous—particularly the `Array-Collection`.

12.1.2   *Nested array collections*

Nested array collections function nearly the same way as nested arrays, except that you employ the `ArrayCollection` class. These array collections automatically broadcast data changes. The `ArrayCollection` class takes an array, or `null`, as the first argument.

As listing 12.2 illustrates, we can use the `menuData` array from listing 12.1 and pass that to the `ArrayCollection`.

Listing 12.2   Preparing an `ArrayCollection`

```
import mx.collections.ArrayCollection;              ◁─┐ Imports
protected var menuData:Array =          ◁─┐ Nested    ArrayCollection class
  [                                          array data
    {
      label:'New',
        children: [{label:'Task'},{label:'Request'},{label:'Person'}]
    },
    {
      label:'Import',
        children: [{label:'Image'},{label:'Document'},{label:'Project'}]
    }
  ];
                                                   Instantiates
                                                   ArrayCollection
protected var menuCollection:ArrayCollection =
                    new ArrayCollection(menuData);       ◁─┘
```

Listings 12.1 and 12.2 are similar, but in listing 12.2 we import the `ArrayCollection` class, create the nested array, call the `ArrayCollection` constructor, and initialize an instance of it with the nested `menuData` array.

Arrays and array collections work well in the ActionScript environment, but the syntax can be challenging to visualize when multiple levels are involved. If you prefer using MXML, you can also nest in MXML, which might look a bit more familiar, as shown in the following listing.

Listing 12.3 Preparing an `ArrayCollection` in MXML

```
<s:ArrayCollection id="menuCollection">
<fx:Array>
  <fx:Object label="New">
    <fx:children>
      <fx:Array>
        <fx:Object label="Task" />
        <fx:Object label="Request" />
        <fx:Object label="Person" />
      </fx:Array>
    </fx:children>
  </fx:Object>
  <fx:Object label="Import">
    <fx:children>
      <fx:Array>
        <fx:Object label="Image" />
        <fx:Object label="Document" />
        <fx:Object label="Project" />
      </fx:Array>
    </fx:children>
  </fx:Object>
</fx:Array>
</s:ArrayCollection>
```

Listing 12.3 is the same as listing 12.2 except it's written in MXML. Notice that the hierarchy follows the indenting. This is considerably easier to read.

NOTE The `fx:Object` from listing 12.3 doesn't have a native property named `fx:children`. Because the `Object` class is `dynamic`, you can create any property with any name you'd like, so `fx:children`, `fx:generalhospital`, and `fx:allmychildren` are all valid.

Creating an `ArrayCollection` in MXML is convenient and easy on the eyes, but it comes with extra overhead. You can also use `fx:Model` in MXML, which will be similar and will use less overhead.

12.1.3 Models

The next way you can set up navigation data is with models. Models are a type of data bearing a striking resemblance to XML but are actually nested low-level objects. They can be used as a parking lot to hold data that needs to be processed later. For example, you can use models to temporarily hold the values for a form.

Models offer several advantages:

- Although a model appears similar to XML, behind the scenes Flex converts the data into nested low-level objects. This provides some convenience with respect to syntax, because you're working with native ActionScript objects.
- You can easily script and visualize the code structure because of its XML-like nature.
- You can implement binding with little effort.

- Models contribute minimally to application overhead (they're low-level objects).
- You can pull in data from a separate file using the `source` property.

On the downside, models must conform to a specific syntax to be compatible with components that display hierarchical data in nested structures, such as menus.

Listing 12.4 shows an example of using a model.

Listing 12.4 Creating a model to drive a menu display

```
<fx:Model id="menuData">
 <menuinfo>
    <menuitem label="Task">
      <children label="Request"/>
      <children label="Person"/>
    </menuitem>
    <menuitem label="Import">
      <children label="Image"/>
      <children label="Document"/>
      <children label="Project"/>
    </menuitem>
  </menuinfo>
</fx:Model>
```

You can change the node names—`menuinfo` and `menuitem`—to whatever you prefer. But if you want to create deeper node levels, you must declare them as `children`.

Models let you benefit from XML-like convenience, but they're not XML. You'll come across circumstances in which there's no substitute for the real thing. It's time to bring XML into the game.

12.1.4 XML component and class

Flex's XML capabilities are rooted in the `XML` class; as you'll see in chapter 15, XML in Flex is an extremely powerful tool. The tree-like nature of the data needed to drive menus is a natural for XML. This approach is similar to using models in terms of ease of writing and reading.

Using XML offers several benefits:

- XML is available in MXML (`<fx:XML>`) and an ActionScript class.
- Unlike models, you can name all your nodes whatever you want—you're not restricted to the top levels, and nested levels don't have to be named `children`.
- The XML component is a more intelligent object, providing supporting functions for manipulating and searching the XML: E4X.
- You can pull in data from a separate file using the `source` property.

As with a nested array, an XML component isn't a collection-based object, so changes in underlying data aren't automatically propagated throughout the event system.

In listing 12.5, the model from listing 12.4 is converted into an XML component.

Listing 12.5 Converted model to XML

```
<fx:XML id="menuData">
  <menuinfo>
    <menuitem label="Task">
      <submenu label="Request"/>
      <submenu label="Person"/>
    </menuitem>
    <menuitem label="Import">
      <submenu label="Image"/>
      <submenu label="Document"/>
      <submenu label="Project"/>
    </menuitem>
  </menuinfo>
</fx:XML>
```

Listing 12.5 uses the arbitrary submenu instead of the children node name required by other types of data.

Similarly, you can code this in ActionScript, as the next listing demonstrates.

Listing 12.6 Using the XML ActionScript class to create menu data

```
<fx:Script>
  <![CDATA[
    protected var menuData:XML= <menuinfo>
                                 <menuitem label="Task">
                                   <submenu label="Request"/>
                                   <submenu label="Person"/>
                                 </menuitem>
                                 <menuitem label="Import">
                                   <submenu label="Image"/>
                                   <submenu label="Document"/>
                                   <submenu label="Project"/>
                                 </menuitem>
                               </menuinfo>;
  ]]>
</fx:Script>
```

XML is a great match for driving menus with tree-structured data. But you need to factor in the overarching XML rule that all XML documents must have a single root node.

Fortunately, you have options to get around this. In Menu components, you can indicate a starting point, or you can use an XMLList component instead.

12.1.5 *XMLList component*

The next way to set up data is using an XMLList. An XMLList component is much like an XML component, but its primary purpose is to store fragments or sections of data extracted from an XML-based document. When you use XMLLists with menus, they offer all the advantages of XML—and you can work with multiple roots. XMLLists also provide more supporting functions for working with and manipulating data.

On the other hand, because an XMLList component isn't a collection-based object, changes in the underlying data aren't automatically propagated.

Let's try an `XMLList` component by modifying the menu data from listing 12.6; see the following listing.

Listing 12.7   Using an `XMLList` component to configure menu data

```
<fx:XMLList id="menuData">
  <menuitem label="Task">
    <submenu label="Request"/>
    <submenu label="Person"/>
  </menuitem>
  <menuitem label="Import">
    <submenu label="Image"/>
    <submenu label="Document"/>
    <submenu label="Project"/>
  </menuitem>
</fx:XMLList>
```

Listing 12.7 demonstrates that there are multiple root nodes. This isn't a monumental difference, but it's another option available to you.

We continue to mention the disadvantage of not being a collection. Recall how arrays suffer from this limitation, but array collections can be used as alternatives. Likewise, the `XML` class has an alternative `XMLListCollection` component and class.

12.1.6 *XMLListCollection component and class*

The `XMLListCollection` acts like a wrapper by encapsulating existing XML and adding the capabilities of a collection. It offers all the benefits of XML but is collection based, so changes to underlying data are automatically transmitted to components designated to listen—in this scenario, the `Menu` component. `XMLListCollection` is available in MXML and ActionScript class varieties, and it can be used to wrap existing XML. It's a powerful object, so it's heavier than the lightweight objects mentioned earlier—but can be well worth it.

You can use the `XMLListCollection` in a variety of ways, all of which have it act as a wrapper around existing XML data. Let's explore some of these variations. Listing 12.8 shows how the `XMLListCollection` is used to wrap an existing `XMLList` in order to populate itself with data.

Listing 12.8   `XMLListCollection` component wrapped around an `XMLList`

```
<s:XMLListCollection id="menuData">
  <fx:XMLList>
    <menuitem label="Task">
      <submenu label="Request"/>
      <submenu label="Person"/>
    </menuitem>
  </fx:XMLList>
</s:XMLListCollection>
```

Listing 12.9 takes a different approach by indirectly wrapping an existing XML component via the `source` property.

Listing 12.9 XMLListCollection component sourcing XML

```
<fx:XML id="config">
  <configData>
    <appData>
      <appName name="My Application"/>
    </appData>
    <menuData>
      <menuitem label="Task">
        <submenu label="Request"/>
        <submenu label="Person"/>
      </menuitem>
    </menuData>
  </configData>
</fx:XML>
<s:XMLListCollection id="menuData"
                     source="{config.menuData.menuitem}"/>
```

The beauty of listing 12.9 is that the XML can be stored in a separate XML configuration file, which pares down your XMLListCollection to only the data needed to drive your menu:

```
<fx:XML id="config" source="config.xml" />
<s:XMLListCollection id="menuData" source="{config.menuData.menuitem}"/>
```

In listing 12.10, we switch to an XMLListCollection class instead of MXML.

Listing 12.10 XMLListCollection class used to source XML

```
<fx:Script>
  <![CDATA[
    import mx.collections.XMLListCollection;
    protected var menuData:XMLListCollection =        Instantiate
      new XMLListCollection();                         XMLListCollection
    protected function init():void{
      menuData.source = config.menuData.menuitem;     Set
    }                                                  XMLListCollection
  ]]>                                                  source
</fx:Script>
<fx:Declarations>
                                                       Create XML instead
  <fx:XML id="config" source="config.xml" />           of config.xml
</fx:Declarations>
```

Using ActionScript, you can declare an instance of the XMLListCollection and set up the source to point to the source of the XML information. The source can be an instance of the XML and XMLList classes, whether from ActionScript or MXML.

We've explored all of the core options for preparing data, and as you can see, you have many options available to configure the data for your menus and menu bars. A general rule is to never force an approach, and the small plethora of data options proves this rule true, yet again. You should use the option that works best for your particular scenario. Without covering every argument, we're going use the XMLList-Collection for the remaining examples in this chapter as you learn how to use the Menu component.

12.2 *Working with menus*

We've explored the different data options, and we're now ready to begin adding navigation to our application. As we move forward, we'll explore the following components:

- Menu
- MenuBar
- ViewStack
- ButtonBar
- TabNavigator
- Accordion

A menu creates a single-column window of user-selectable choices or options. Menus can contain other menus (to any number of levels), each opening, or *cascading*, to reveal yet more choices to the user.

The main points we'll be exploring as you learn how to work with menus are

- Creating menus
- Positioning menus
- Customizing menus
- Interacting with menus

Remember, our goal is to add navigation to our application, and so far we've covered the data side. We'll continue with the most essential step: creating a basic menu.

12.2.1 *Creating a menu*

Menus can be created using ActionScript or MXML. Listing 12.11 shows how to create a menu using MXML and an XMLListCollection as the dataProvider.

Listing 12.11   Creating a menu from scratch

```
<?xml version="1.0" encoding="utf-8"?>
<s:Application xmlns:fx="http://ns.adobe.com/mxml/2009"
               xmlns:s="library://ns.adobe.com/flex/spark"
               xmlns:mx="library://ns.adobe.com/flex/halo">
  <s:layout>
    <s:VerticalLayout gap="0" />
  </s:layout>
  <fx:Declarations>                                         Declarations is new to
    <mx:XMLListCollection id="menuData">                    Flex 4; see note below
      <mx:source>                                           Data to
        <fx:XMLList>                                         drive menu
          <menuitem label="Tasks">
            <submenu label="Add Request"/>
            <submenu label="Add Person">
              <submenu label="Customer"/>
              <submenu label="Employee"/>
            </submenu>
          </menuitem>
        </fx:XMLList>
```

```
        </fx:XMLList>
      </mx:source>
    </mx:XMLListCollection>
  </fx:Declarations>
  <s:Button label="Display Menu" click="menu.show()"/>
  <mx:Menu id="menu" showRoot="true" labelField="@label"
        dataProvider="{menuData}" />
</s:Application>
```

| Button shows menu on click event

| Menu instance

NOTE The <fx:Declarations> tag has been introduced in Flex 4 to better support FXG and improve consistency between MXML and FXG for handling nondefault, nonvisual property declarations. Visual children are allowed inside the <fx:Declarations> tag, but they'll be instantiated as if they were nonvisual and won't be added to a container via addChild().

Listing 12.11 contains a button used to show the menu. By default a Menu instance is hidden until told otherwise. In the button's click event handler, we call menu.show(), which, as you guessed, shows the menu. Because the application has a VerticalLayout with a gap of 0 pixels, the menu will show directly under the button (see figure 12.1).

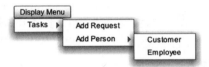

Figure 12.1 A hierarchical menu appears when you click the Display Menu button.

To get the menu data to display properly, you need to tell the menu which property in the dataProvider to use as the label. Because we're using XML, this is specified as @label. The @ sign is used to denote the label attribute of the XML node. If instead you were using an array collection, you wouldn't use the @ declarative.

You can also create a Menu using ActionScript:

```
var menu:Menu = Menu.createMenu(null, menuData,true);
```

The createMenu() function takes three parameters, which are described in table 12.1.

Listing 12.11 uses a VerticalLayout to position the menu, but you don't have to use a specific layout to control the positioning. Now that you know how to generate a basic menu, the next thing we'll look at is how to position it.

Table 12.1 Parameters to the Menu.createMenu() function

Parameter	Type	Description
parent	DisplayObjectContainer	(Optional) A container that the PopUpManager uses to place the Menu control in. The Menu control may not be parented by this object.
mdp	Object	The data provider for the Menu control.
showRoot	Boolean	A Boolean flag that specifies whether to display the root node of the data provider.

12.2.2   *Positioning the menu*

So far you've created your menu in MXML and called `menu.show()` without passing any arguments to the `show()` method. The `show` method has optional arguments: `xShow` and `yShow`. You can explicitly control the positioning of your menu by supplying x and y coordinates to the `show()` function, as follows:

```
menu.show(10,20);
```

Recall from chapter 4 that coordinates are defined relative to the upper-left corner of the current window. In this snippet, by specifying 10 for the x coordinate and 20 for the y coordinate, you define a position 10 pixels from the left edge of the window and 20 pixels from the top edge.

We wish we could throw around big words and show a bunch of code examples to look smarter than we are but…. Well, positioning is a breeze, and `menu.show(xShow, yShow)` is all there is to it. There's more you can do to your menu, though. You can improve your menu functionally and visually through customized menu items.

12.2.3   *Customizing menu items*

Look at almost any software that uses a menu and you'll notice several different styles of menu items. Some menu items have graphics/icons, check boxes, or radio buttons and can be enabled or disabled at different times. Wow, can I do those things with Flex? We're glad you asked. Yes!

The data driving your menu items can contain additional display instructions for the menu. For a list of available menu item attributes and descriptions, see table 12.2.

Table 12.2   Available menu item attributes

Attribute	Type	Description
enabled	Boolean	Specifies whether the user can select the menu item (`true`) or not (`false`). If not specified, Flex treats the item as if the value were `true`. If you use the default data descriptor, data providers must use an `enabled` XML attribute or object field to specify this characteristic.
groupName	String	(Required, and meaningful, for `radio` type only.) The identifier that associates radio button items in a radio group. If you use the default data descriptor, data providers must use a `groupName` XML attribute or object field to specify this characteristic.
icon	Class	Specifies the class identifier of an image asset. This item isn't used for the `check`, `radio`, or `separator` types. You can use the `checkIcon` and `radioIcon` styles to specify the icons used for radio and check box items that are selected. The menu's `iconField` or `iconFunction` property determines the name of the field in the data that specifies the icon or a function for determining the icons.

Table 12.2 Available menu item attributes *(continued)*

Attribute	Type	Description
label	String	Specifies the text that appears in the control. This item is used for all menu item types except separator. The menu's labelField or labelFunction property determines the name of the field in the data that specifies the label or a function for determining the labels. (If the data provider is in E4X XML format, you must specify one of these properties to display a label.) If the data provider is an Array of Strings, Flex uses the String value as the label.
toggled	Boolean	Specifies whether a check or radio item is selected. If not specified, Flex treats the item as if the value were false and the item isn't selected. If you use the default data descriptor, data providers must use a toggled XML attribute or object field to specify this characteristic.
type	String	Specifies the type of menu item. Meaningful values are separator, check, or radio. Flex treats all other values, or nodes with no type entry, as normal menu entries. If you use the default data descriptor, data providers must use a type XML attribute or object field to specify this characteristic.

Listing 12.12 gives you a grand tour by demonstrating how to use everything at once.

Listing 12.12 Customizing a menu's display

```
<?xml version="1.0"?>
<s:Application xmlns:fx="http://ns.adobe.com/mxml/2009"
 xmlns:s="library://ns.adobe.com/flex/spark"
 xmlns:mx="library://ns.adobe.com/flex/halo">
  <s:layout>
    <s:VerticalLayout gap="0" />
  </s:layout>
    <fx:Script>
      <![CDATA[
        [Bindable]                                          Image to be used
        [Embed(source="assets/icons/user.png")]            as icon in menu
        public var userIcon:Class;
      ]]>
    </fx:Script>
  <fx:Declarations>
    <mx:XMLListCollection id="menuData">            Menu data
      <fx:XMLList>
        <menuitem label="Tasks">                          Adds      Displays
          <submenu label="Add Request" enabled="false"/>  menu      icon
          <submenu type="separator"/>                     separator beside
          <submenu label="Add Person" icon="userIcon">              item
            <submenu label="Customer" type="radio" groupName="persons"/>
            <submenu label="Employee" type="radio" groupName="persons"
                    toggled="true"/>
                                                    Displays radio button
          </submenu>
          <submenu label="Auto Update" type="check" toggled="true"/>
        </menuitem>
                                                    Displays
      </fx:XMLList>                                  check box
```

```
      </mx:XMLListCollection>
    </fx:Declarations>
      <s:Button label="Display Menu" click="menu.show()"/>
    <mx:Menu id="menu" showRoot="true"
      labelField="@label"
            iconField="@icon" dataProvider="{menuData}" />
  </s:Application>
```

Indicates label
and icon fields

Figure 12.2 shows the results when you run listing 12.12.

As you can see, it's relatively painless to customize the display. Play around with these options at your leisure to build your menu according to your needs. You can build pretty menus all day, but they aren't any good if they don't do anything. We need to explore how to handle user interactions.

Figure 12.2   Using the additional display-control attributes, you can customize a menu's appearance.

12.2.4 *Interacting with menus*

Displaying a menu is only half the picture (pardon the irresistible pun). Just as important is how you handle all the events generated when a user interacts with the menu. Ideally, these handlers should provide an intuitive interaction flow that's familiar to the user (within the context of your application) while providing immediate feedback.

In addition to a wide array of events that are provided by the Menu class ancestry, specific events are available at the menu level for selection changes, at the menu's submenu level, and at the item level. For a complete list of events, please consult the Flex 4 Language Reference.

The events specifically defined by the Menu class are dispatched as MenuEvent types. MenuEvents carry information providing enough about the user's interaction to guide the handler function.

Listing 12.13 combines these properties and passes the event to a function, which can then use the data.

Listing 12.13   Handling menu user interactions

```
<?xml version="1.0" encoding="utf-8"?>
<s:Application xmlns:fx="http://ns.adobe.com/mxml/2009"
               xmlns:s="library://ns.adobe.com/flex/spark"
               xmlns:mx="library://ns.adobe.com/flex/halo">
  <s:layout>
    <s:VerticalLayout gap="0" />
  </s:layout>
  <fx:Script>
    <![CDATA[
      import mx.events.MenuEvent;
      private function onMenuClick(event:MenuEvent):void{
        var item:XML = XML(event.item);
        lastEvent.text = "Selection: " + item.@label +
```

Creates
reference to
selected item data

Shows item
@label property

```
                                    ", Position: " + event.index +        ◁─┐
                                    " Type: " + item.@personType;      ◁─┐   │
            }                                                Shows item │ Shows item
        ]]>                                              @personType  │ index in menu
    </fx:Script>                                           property   │
    <fx:Declarations>
        <mx:XMLListCollection id="menuData">
            <fx:XMLList>
                <menuitem label="Tasks">
                    <submenu label="Add Request" enabled="false"/>
                    <submenu label="" type="separator"/>
                    <submenu label="Add Person" icon="userIcon">
                        <submenu label="Customer" type="radio" groupName="persons"
                                 personType="32"/>
                        <submenu label="Employee" type="radio" groupName="persons"
                                 toggled="true" personType="57"/>
                    </submenu>
                    <submenu label="Auto Update" type="check" toggled="true"/>
                </menuitem>
            </fx:XMLList>
        </mx:XMLListCollection>
    </fx:Declarations>
    <mx:Button label="Display Menu" click="menu.show()"/>
    <mx:Menu id="menu" showRoot="true" labelField="@label" iconField="@icon"
             dataProvider="{menuData}" itemClick="onMenuClick(event)" />    ◁─┐
    <mx:Spacer height="10" />                                                  │
    <mx:Label id="lastEvent"/>                              Sets itemClick to │
</s:Application>                                          onMenuClick handler │
```

After you click a menu item, the `itemClick` event fires and calls the `onMenuClick()` function. Using the event argument (`event:MenuEvent`), you can determine where the item came from, what position in the menu the item occupied, and all the data behind that item. To showcase this data, you set the `text` property on the `lastEvent` `Label` to display the `@label`, `index`, and `@personType`, as shown in figure 12.3.

Compile and run the example. You should see something similar to figure 12.3.

NOTE Because the item data is XML, to access any of the attributes you must use the `@` attribute syntax (for example, `item.@personType`). If you used nested objects, arrays, or array collections, you wouldn't need to use this syntax.

Using the `MenuEvent` object allows you to create reusable functions to handle any number of menus in your application.

This is the first step in your journey of adding navigation to an application. The `Menu` component has provided a well-formatted and highly usable menu, but it does have a limitation: When processing XML data, it can handle only a single root node. But fear not; its cousin, the menu bar, takes matters to the next level.

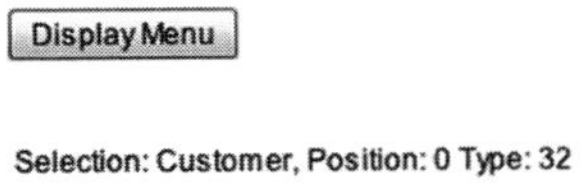

Display Menu

Selection: Customer, Position: 0 Type: 32

Figure 12.3 Clicking the button and selecting a menu item outputs information extracted from the **MenuEvent** object.

12.3   *Using a menu bar*

The menu bar expands upon the menu by allowing for multiple top-level cascading. Menus are positioned side by side, a common layout in most applications. It's a nonintrusive mechanism that lets users navigate the features and capabilities of your application, while maintaining their existing page.

Aside from the obvious visual distinctions, the primary difference between a menu and a menu bar is that a menu bar isn't meant to be a pop-up mechanism. It's designed to allow your Flex applications to offer the same kind of menu functionality common to desktop applications.

12.3.1   *Creating a menu bar*

Listing 12.14 creates a simple menu bar. Note the top-level placement of each top-level node.

Listing 12.14   Creating a simple menu bar

```
<?xml version="1.0" encoding="utf-8"?>
<s:Application xmlns:fx="http://ns.adobe.com/mxml/2009"
               xmlns:s="library://ns.adobe.com/flex/spark"
               xmlns:mx="library://ns.adobe.com/flex/halo">
  <fx:Declarations>
    <s:XMLListCollection id="menuData">
      <fx:XMLList>
        <menuitem label="File">
          <submenu label="New">
            <submenu label="Project"/>
            <submenu label="Request"/>
          </submenu>
          <submenu label="Print"/>
        </menuitem>
        <menuitem label="View">
          <submenu label="Users"/>
          <submenu label="Reports"/>
        </menuitem>
      </fx:XMLList>
    </s:XMLListCollection>
  </fx:Declarations>
  <mx:MenuBar id="menuBar" labelField="@label" dataProvider="{menuData}" />
</s:Application>
```

After compiling and running the code in listing 12.14, you'll see a rudimentary menu bar resembling figure 12.4.

As you did with the menu, let's fine-tune the menu bar's position and then customize it a bit.

12.3.2   *Positioning the menu bar*

Positioning a menu bar is no different than positioning any other component: The layout rules are determined by the

Figure 12.4   A rudimentary menu bar in action

parent container's layout and/or the x and y properties. The following snippet would set the menu bar position 10 pixels from the left and 20 from the top:

```
<mx:MenuBar id="menuBar" x="10" y="20" labelField="@label"
             dataProvider="{menuData}" />
```

Again, positioning is terribly simple, so we won't spend any more time than needed. As with menus, you have the option to customize your menu bars.

12.3.3 *Customizing items in the menu bar*

The items in menus and menu bars follow the same rules and access the same properties, which means you can add separators, radio buttons, check boxes, and icons to a menu bar exactly the same way you do a menu.

Listing 12.15 uses an XML structure to customize the output, similar to the earlier menu example.

Listing 12.15 Using special attributes in XML data to customize a menu bar

```
<?xml version="1.0" encoding="utf-8"?>
<s:Application xmlns:fx="http://ns.adobe.com/mxml/2009"
               xmlns:s="library://ns.adobe.com/flex/spark"
               xmlns:mx="library://ns.adobe.com/flex/halo">
  <s:layout>
    <s:VerticalLayout />
  </s:layout>
  <fx:Script>
    <![CDATA[
      [Bindable]
      [Embed(source="assets/icons/user.png")]
      public var userIcon:Class;
    ]]>
  </fx:Script>
  <fx:Declarations>
    <s:XMLListCollection id="menuData">
      <fx:XMLList>
        <menuitem label="File">
          <submenu label="New Task">
            <submenu label="Add Request" enabled="false"/>
            <submenu type="separator"/>
            <submenu label="Add Person" icon="userIcon">
              <submenu label="Customer" type="radio" groupName="persons"/>
              <submenu label="Employee" type="radio" groupName="persons"
                       toggled="true"/>
            </submenu>
            <submenu label="Auto Update" type="check" toggled="true"/>
          </submenu>
          <submenu label="Print"/>
        </menuitem>
        <menuitem label="View">
          <submenu label="Users"/>
          <submenu label="Reports"/>
        </menuitem>
      </fx:XMLList>
```

```
    </s:XMLListCollection>
  </fx:Declarations>
  <mx:MenuBar id="menuBar" labelField="@label" iconField="@icon"
            dataProvider="{menuData}" />
</s:Application>
```

After compiling and running the application, you'll see a customized menu bar, as shown in figure 12.5.

As with the earlier menu example, you now need to add the ability for the menu bar to interact with the user.

Figure 12.5   A customized menu bar

12.3.4 *Handling user interactions with menu bars*

The same events that apply to menus also apply to menu bars. For your convenience, table 12.3 lists those events.

Event	Description
change	The user changed the current selection.
itemClick	The user clicked an enabled menu item.
itemRollOut	The mouse pointer moved off a menu item.
itemRollOver	The mouse pointer moved over a menu item.
menuHide	A menu or submenu closed.
menuShow	A menu or submenu opened.

Table 12.3   Menu bars share the same events as menus.

The events listed in table 12.3 (of the MenuEvent ActionScript class) have the same properties and values as their menu counterparts. Those properties appear again in table 12.4.

Listing 12.16 shows how to handle the selection and display of a menu item.

Table 12.4   The properties of a MenuEvent in a menu bar

Property	Type	Description
item	Object	The row of data with which the menu item is associated.
index	Number	The index of the menu/submenu item.
label	String	The field in the data that contains the label to display. If the field is an attribute of an XML node, prepend it with the @ declarative.
menu	Object	A reference to the menu that created the event. Not applicable in the case of a menu bar.
menuBar	Object	A reference to the menu bar that created the event. Not applicable in the case of a menu.

Listing 12.16 Handling a user's selection of a menu item

```
<?xml version="1.0" encoding="utf-8"?>
<s:Application xmlns:fx="http://ns.adobe.com/mxml/2009"
               xmlns:s="library://ns.adobe.com/flex/spark"
               xmlns:mx="library://ns.adobe.com/flex/halo">
  <s:layout>
    <s:VerticalLayout />
  </s:layout>
  <fx:Script>
    <![CDATA[
      import mx.events.MenuEvent;
      private function onMenuClick(event:MenuEvent):void{
        var item:XML = XML(event.item);
        lastEvent.text = "Selection: " + item.@label +
                         ", Position: " + event.index;
    }
    ]]>
  </fx:Script>
  <fx:Declarations>
    <s:XMLListCollection id="menuData">
      <fx:XMLList>
        <menuitem label="File">
          <submenu label="New Task">
            <submenu label="Add Request" enabled="false"/>
            <submenu type="separator"/>
            <submenu label="Add Person" icon="userIcon">
              <submenu label="Customer" type="radio" groupName="persons"/>
              <submenu label="Employee" type="radio" groupName="persons"
                       toggled="true"/>
            </submenu>
            <submenu label="Auto Update" type="check" toggled="true"/>
          </submenu>
          <submenu label="Print"/>
        </menuitem>
        <menuitem label="View">
          <submenu label="Users"/>
          <submenu label="Reports"/>
        </menuitem>
      </fx:XMLList>
    </s:XMLListCollection>
  </fx:Declarations>
  <mx:MenuBar id="menuBar" labelField="@label" iconField="@icon"
              dataProvider="{menuData}" itemClick="onMenuClick(event)" />
  <mx:Spacer height="10" />
  <mx:Text id="lastEvent"/>
</s:Application>
```

Compile and run the application, and you'll see something similar to figure 12.6. Clicking items in the menu bar causes the display to be updated with information about the item that was clicked.

Selection: Customer, Position: 0

Figure 12.6 Clicking the button and selecting a menu item outputs information extracted from the `MenuEvent` object.

Interacting with a menu bar should be familiar because you did the same thing with the menu. Keep in mind that the menu bar is a collection of menu components. Earlier we covered creating a single menu, and we've now covered creating a collection of menus in a menu bar. We also know how to interact with a menu, or menu bar, but we haven't done anything particular with the interactions. To continue our goal of implementing application navigation, our next stop covers navigation containers, starting with view stacks.

12.4   *Using view stacks*

A view stack is an interesting mechanism for navigating within your application. It operates by layering each of its child containers on top of each other. Think of a view stack like a deck of playing cards; you can select one card from the deck at any given point in time.

A view stack is a relatively uncomplicated mechanism compared to Flex's other navigation containers. This simplicity can come in handy if you need to produce innovative displays with easily swapped containers.

The one seemingly downside is that a view stack doesn't possess any built-in UI controls to facilitate navigation. This is something you'll need to include in your code, but thankfully Flex makes this easy.

12.4.1   *Creating a view stack*

Listing 12.17 shows a simple example of using the ViewStack component.

Listing 12.17   Creating a simple view stack

```
<?xml version="1.0" encoding="utf-8"?>
<s:Application xmlns:fx="http://ns.adobe.com/mxml/2009"
               xmlns:s="library://ns.adobe.com/flex/spark"
               xmlns:mx="library://ns.adobe.com/flex/halo">
  <mx:ViewStack id="stack" width="100%"                        Create the
    height="100%">                                             ViewStack
    <s:NavigatorContent label="TVs" width="100%" height="100%">
      <s:Label text="TV Content" />
    </s:NavigatorContent>                                Add child labeled TVs
    <s:NavigatorContent label="Cameras" width="100%" height="100%">
      <s:Label text="Camera Content" />
    </s:NavigatorContent>                           Add child labeled Cameras
    <s:NavigatorContent label="Computers" width="100%" height="100%">
      <s:Label text="Computer Content" />
    </s:NavigatorContent>                                 Add child labeled
  </mx:ViewStack>                                              Computers
</s:Application>
```

NOTE   If you run listing 12.17, it will say "TV Content" in the top-left corner of your application. You won't see any of the other child containers because they aren't on the top of the stack.

Each of the child containers is a `NavigatorContent`. In order to use a Spark component in a `ViewStack` component, which is still a Halo component, the child has to be a `NavigatorContent` container. Because the `NavigatorContent` is a container, it has a `layout` property. It's an equivalent to `Group`.

Why not use `Group`? You're asking the right questions today. The `ViewStack` children need deferred instantiation, giving you, the developer, control over the creation of a child containers' children. `Group` isn't a deferred instantiation component like `NavigatorContent`.

Why didn't they give `Group` deferred instantiation? Great question! Deferred instantiation comes with particular performance repercussions, which means the `Group` container would have a bunch of extra junk—yes, that's the technical term, used only in particular scenarios. The idea behind the `Group` container is for it to be a lightweight container, so Adobe decided to keep it that way and provide a similar container for deferred instantiation: `NavigatorContent`.

NOTE Deferred instantiation is available in most containers, which navigation components either extend or implement.

For the sake of demonstration, the inner containers in listing 12.17 have a simple `Label` component. Next, you'll begin populating your containers with more specific content.

You can break an application into smaller segments called *custom components*. At the core of this technique, each container in a view stack is saved as a discrete MXML component file. Listing 12.18 shows a custom MXML component named TVView.mxml for use in the view stack (chapter 17 goes into custom components in detail).

Listing 12.18 TVView.mxml – Custom `ViewStack` component

```
<?xml version="1.0" encoding="utf-8"?>
<s:NavigatorContent xmlns:fx="http://ns.adobe.com/mxml/2009"
                    xmlns:s="library://ns.adobe.com/flex/spark"
                    xmlns:mx="library://ns.adobe.com/flex/halo"
                    width="100%" height="100%">
  <s:Panel title="TVs" width="100%" height="100%">          ◁── Set up Panel
    <s:layout>
      <s:VerticalLayout paddingLeft="20" paddingTop="20"
                        paddingRight="20" paddingBottom="20" />
    </s:layout>
    <s:HGroup width="100%" enabled="false">          ◁─┐ Add simple
      <s:TextInput width="100%" />                      │ horizontal search form
      <s:Button label="Search for TVs"/>
    </s:HGroup>
    <mx:HRule width="100%" />
    <mx:Spacer height="10" />                          ┐ Simple message
    <s:Label text="There are no TVs available." />    ◁─┘ to user
  </s:Panel>
</s:NavigatorContent>
```

Listing 12.19 shows, from the application, that you assign the subdirectory that contains your custom components an XML namespace, and you're good to go.

Listing 12.19   Using TVView.mxml as a container in the view stack

```
<?xml version="1.0" encoding="utf-8"?>
<s:Application xmlns:fx="http://ns.adobe.com/mxml/2009"
               xmlns:s="library://ns.adobe.com/flex/spark"
               xmlns:mx="library://ns.adobe.com/flex/halo"
               xmlns:views="views.*">                        Maps stacks
  <mx:ViewStack x="20" y="20" width="400" height="200">      subdirectory
    <views:TVView />                                          to views folder
    <views:ComputersView />         Adds custom components
  </mx:ViewStack>                   to ViewStack
</s:Application>
```

To recap, you've generated three files, two of which are custom components residing in a subdirectory called views. Figure 12.7 shows the chapter's file structure.

This last approach makes things easier to read and, more importantly, lets you conveniently separate your components' functionality into their own set of files in a modular fashion. Compare this approach to the tightly coupled structure of the previous examples.

You still need to add the ability to switch between stacks.

12.4.2   *Adding navigation to the view stack*

Navigation isn't automatic—you need to include instructions that manage which container in the view stack is currently visible.

Prior to Flex 4 you could use the TabBar, ButtonBar, and LinkBar components to add navigation. Because Flex 4 provides amazing skinning capabilities, you can style the Button-Bar to your liking, so TabBar and LinkBar don't

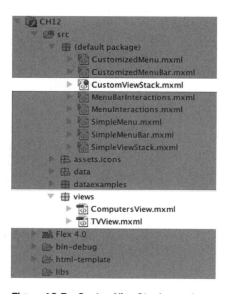

Figure 12.7   CustomViewStack.mxml contains a view stack that invokes the custom components resident in the views subfolder. All other files/folders are blacked out to highlight the exact files.

exist in Flex 4. Chapter 20 will go into more detail on skinning components.

To tie a ButtonBar to a ViewStack, set the dataProvider property to the id value of your ViewStack, as shown in the following listing.

Listing 12.20   Adding navigation to a view stack

```
<?xml version="1.0" encoding="utf-8"?>
<s:Application xmlns:fx="http://ns.adobe.com/mxml/2009"
               xmlns:s="library://ns.adobe.com/flex/spark"
               xmlns:mx="library://ns.adobe.com/flex/halo"
```

```
                  xmlns:views="views.*">
  <s:layout>
    <s:VerticalLayout paddingLeft="20" paddingTop="10" paddingRight="20" />
  </s:layout>

  <s:ButtonBar dataProvider="{stack}" />

  <mx:ViewStack id="stack" width="400" height="200">
    <views:TVView label="Buy TVs" />
    <views:ComputersView label="Buy Computers" />
  </mx:ViewStack>
</s:Application>
```

dataProvider is name of view stack

Navigation provided by `ButtonBar`

NOTE To manually add or remove items from a `ButtonBar`, use `addItem` and `removeItem` on the `ButtonBar`'s `dataProvider`.

Now that you've added navigational capabilities to the view stack, you can switch between stacks with the click of a mouse, as illustrated in figure 12.8.

NOTE The `ButtonBar` buttons display their labels based on the `label` property of each stack.

Figure 12.8 A `ButtonBar` is used to switch between stacks in a view stack.

Using the default properties of display components allows you to easily assemble a stack, but you always have the option to take control of component attributes if you prefer.

DO IT YOURSELF

If you need more component control, adding custom navigation features isn't much more difficult than using default attributes. Two key properties furnish this control:

- `selectedIndex`—The numeric position of a container in the view stack, where the first position is index 0
- `selectedChild`—The `id` property of a given container in the view stack

Listing 12.21 creates two buttons that let you switch views.

Listing 12.21 Programmatically controlling which stack is visible

```
<?xml version="1.0" encoding="utf-8"?>
<s:Application xmlns:fx="http://ns.adobe.com/mxml/2009"
               xmlns:s="library://ns.adobe.com/flex/spark"
               xmlns:mx="library://ns.adobe.com/flex/halo"
               xmlns:views="views.*">
  <s:layout>
    <s:VerticalLayout paddingLeft="20" paddingTop="10" paddingRight="20" />
  </s:layout>
```

```
<s:HGroup>
  <s:Button label="TVs">
    <s:click>
      <![CDATA[
      stack.selectedIndex = 0;            Set the selected
      ]]>                               ⤶ stack by index
    </s:click>
  </s:Button>
  <s:Button label="Computers">
    <s:click>
      <![CDATA[
      stack.selectedChild = computers;    Set the selected
      ]]>                               ⤶ stack by child id
    </s:click>
  </s:Button>
</s:HGroup>

<mx:ViewStack id="stack" width="400" height="200">
  <views:TVView label="Buy TVs" />
  <views:ComputersView id="computers" label="Buy Computers" />
</mx:ViewStack>
</s:Application>
```

Keep in mind the `selectedChild` property is associated with the `id` of the container, not its label.

> **TIP** Be creative: There are many ways you can add custom navigation beyond the customary gang of buttons. For example, you can use images, radio buttons, combo boxes, text links—whatever you can imagine.

Figure 12.9 shows listing 12.21 in action.

Flex makes it easy to take control and add your own custom navigation to a view stack. This comes in particularly handy when you integrate custom logic into your application to create context-sensitive stacks.

Being able to control which stack is selected is one form of control. Another is reacting to a selection, or finding out which stack is currently selected.

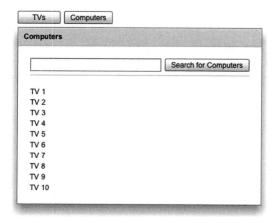

**Figure 12.9   Custom buttons
controlling the stack navigation**

12.4.3 Handling user interactions with view stacks

ViewStack is a child component of the Container class, and as such it inherits all the properties of the container. But because you don't interact with the view stack directly, only one event is of any interest: change, which detects selection changes.

The change event generates an IndexChangedEvent event with the properties listed in table 12.5.

Table 12.5 Properties of IndexChangedEvent

Property	Type	Description
newIndex	Number	Specifies the index number of the new selectedIndex
oldIndex	Number	Indicates the previous index number of the selectedIndex
relatedObject	Object	References the container to which the newIndex is pointed

Listing 12.22 shows the old and new indexes as well as the new index's container label.

Listing 12.22 Working with the view stack's index property

```
<?xml version="1.0" encoding="utf-8"?>
<s:Application xmlns:fx="http://ns.adobe.com/mxml/2009"
               xmlns:s="library://ns.adobe.com/flex/spark"
               xmlns:mx="library://ns.adobe.com/flex/halo"
               xmlns:views="views.*">
  <s:layout>
    <s:VerticalLayout paddingLeft="20" paddingTop="10" paddingRight="20" />
  </s:layout>
  <fx:Script>
    <![CDATA[
      import mx.controls.Alert;                              Imports
      import mx.events.IndexChangedEvent;              ⊲── event class    Receives
      protected function                                                  IndexChangedEvent
    onChange(event:IndexChangedEvent):void{             ⊲──              object
        var related:Object = event.relatedObject;
        Alert.show("Old Index: " + event.oldIndex.toString() +
                   "\nNew Index: " + event.newIndex.toString() +
                   "\nLabel of new Selection: " + related.label);
      }
    ]]>
  </fx:Script>

  <s:ButtonBar dataProvider="{stack}" />
                                                          Calls onChange
  <mx:ViewStack id="stack" width="400" height="200"       when selection changes
              change="onChange(event)">            ⊲──
    <views:TVView label="Buy TVs" />
    <views:ComputersView label="Buy Computers" />
  </mx:ViewStack>
</s:Application>
```

Any further interactions would be with the component used to control the view stack—which in this example happens to be the ButtonBar. ButtonBar also has a change event of type `IndexChangeEvent`. Notice that it isn't `IndexChangedEvent`. There's a difference in the name but not much else. Understand that this doesn't relate to which item was selected but to which button was selected within the `Button-Bar`. You can use the change event in the same way as listing 12.22. We used a `Button-Bar` for navigation, but at times you may want tabbed navigation, which also comes as an out-of-the-box implementation in Flex.

12.5   TabNavigator

So far we've covered menus and view stacks. The next item from our list of navigation components to explore is the `TabNavigator`. Tabbed navigation has always been a part of GUI navigation and has survived the test of time as a navigational paradigm in all types of applications. Tabbed navigation makes efficient use of limited screen space by allowing users to choose what's currently visible in that space.

In listing 12.22, you accomplished this task using a button bar to control a view stack. But you can achieve the same result using the `TabNavigator` component. The `TabNavigator` component is a descendent of a view stack with a tab bar incorporated directly into it.

12.5.1   Creating a tab navigator

A tab navigator works by making a tab for each container within it. Listing 12.23 demonstrates how easily you can generate tabs using the `TabNavigator` component.

Listing 12.23   Using a tab navigator to created tabbed navigation

```
<?xml version="1.0" encoding="utf-8"?>
<s:Application xmlns:fx="http://ns.adobe.com/mxml/2009"
               xmlns:s="library://ns.adobe.com/flex/spark"
               xmlns:mx="library://ns.adobe.com/flex/halo"
               xmlns:views="views.*">
  <mx:TabNavigator width="200" height="100">
    <s:NavigatorContent label="TVs" width="100%" height="100%">      Tab I
      <s:Label text="TV Content" />
    </s:NavigatorContent>
    <s:NavigatorContent label="Cameras" width="100%" height="100%">  Tab 2
      <s:Label text="Camera Content" />
    </s:NavigatorContent>
    <s:NavigatorContent label="Computers" width="100%" height="100%"> Tab 3
      <s:Label text="Computer Content" />
    </s:NavigatorContent>
  </mx:TabNavigator>
</s:Application>
```

The compact bit of code in listing 12.23 produces the results shown in figure 12.10.

NOTE   The title for each tab is specified via the `label` property of each child container.

Just as with the view stack, to use Flex 4 containers, such as `Group`, you need to wrap the content in a `NavigatorContent`

Figure 12.10   A tab navigator creates a tab for each container within it.

container or use a custom component. This is because TabNavigator is a subclass of ViewStack, so it inherits ViewStack's properties and then goes on to offer even more functionality.

Because of this lineage, handling user interactions is similar to doing so in a ViewStack.

12.5.2 *Handling user interactions with a tab navigator*

Because TabNavigator is a child object of ViewStack, you borrow from the view stack's properties:

- selectedIndex—The position of the selected tab (starting from 0)
- selectedChild—The id of the selected tab

Likewise, the change event is the same as that for a view stack (for example, the Index-ChangedEvent event): It fires when the tab selection changes (see this next listing).

Listing 12.24 Responding to tab changes in a tab navigator

```
<?xml version="1.0" encoding="utf-8"?>
<s:Application xmlns:fx="http://ns.adobe.com/mxml/2009"
               xmlns:s="library://ns.adobe.com/flex/spark"
               xmlns:mx="library://ns.adobe.com/flex/halo"
               xmlns:views="views.*">
  <s:layout>
    <s:VerticalLayout paddingLeft="20" paddingTop="20" />
  </s:layout>
  <fx:Script>
    <![CDATA[
      import mx.controls.Alert;
      import mx.events.IndexChangedEvent;

      protected function onChange(event:IndexChangedEvent):void{
        Alert.show("Changed to Tab Index " + event.newIndex +
                   "\nLabel: " + tabs.selectedChild.label);
      }
    ]]>
  </fx:Script>
  <mx:TabNavigator id="tabs" width="200" height="100"
                   change="onChange(event)">
    <s:NavigatorContent label="TVs" width="100%" height="100%">
      <s:Label text="TV Content" />
    </s:NavigatorContent>
    <s:NavigatorContent label="Cameras" width="100%" height="100%">
      <s:Label text="Camera Content" />
    </s:NavigatorContent>
    <s:NavigatorContent label="Computers" width="100%" height="100%">
      <s:Label text="Computer Content" />
    </s:NavigatorContent>
  </mx:TabNavigator>
</s:Application>
```

Compiling and running the application displays an alert window (figure 12.11) whenever the tab selection changes. The alert also posts which index is selected and the associated label for the tab.

This is the same process you executed with the view stack, which also used its change event. The problem with this approach is that the function is explicitly told which tab navigator is involved. As we continue our never-ending quest for code reusability, we're driven to employ a more modular technique.

Figure 12.11 Using the change event, you can tell which tab was selected.

Tabs and menus have their purpose and are proven stalwarts of the common UI paradigm. The accordion navigator isn't as common but can be as useful.

12.6 Accordion

When Flex and its implementation of the Accordion component first appeared, the web-application world was taken aback, because it was such a fresh approach to navigating an application. Although Flex wasn't the first to introduce this type of navigation (Outlook 2003, Flash sites, and so on had it before Flex), it was unheard of in the traditional web application scene. Today, the accordion has become an accepted option thanks to AJAX toolkits that make implementation so easy, such as Adobe's Spry.

12.6.1 Creating an accordion

Creating an accordion is much like creating a tab navigator, but instead of each child container displaying as a tab, it displays a section divider. Coding an accordion is similarly easy, as listing 12.25 illustrates.

Listing 12.25 Creating an accordion navigator

```
<?xml version="1.0" encoding="utf-8"?>
<s:Application xmlns:fx="http://ns.adobe.com/mxml/2009"
               xmlns:s="library://ns.adobe.com/flex/spark"
               xmlns:mx="library://ns.adobe.com/flex/halo"
               xmlns:views="views.*">
  <mx:Accordion width="200" height="100">
    <s:NavigatorContent label="TVs" width="100%" height="100%">
      <s:Label text="TV Content" />
    </s:NavigatorContent>
    <s:NavigatorContent label="Cameras" width="100%" height="100%">
      <s:Label text="Camera Content" />
    </s:NavigatorContent>
    <s:NavigatorContent label="Computers" width="100%" height="100%">
      <s:Label text="Computer Content" />
    </s:NavigatorContent>
  </mx:Accordion>
</s:Application>
```

Accordions follow the same construction pattern as view stacks and tab navigators by placing containers within them. Using the same content as the tab navigator from listing 12.24 and the view stack from listing 12.17 produces figure 12.12.

Now let's see how to populate an accordion.

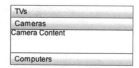

Figure 12.12 Accordion navigator with three sections

12.6.2 *Populating an accordion*

Whatever you can put inside a container, you can use to populate an accordion. For example, you can display thumbnails in each section as part of photo album application.

BREAKING DOWN A FORM

If you need to format a large form, using an accordion is a great way to break it into smaller, more digestible pieces. For example, a loan application may look similar to that shown in figure 12.13.

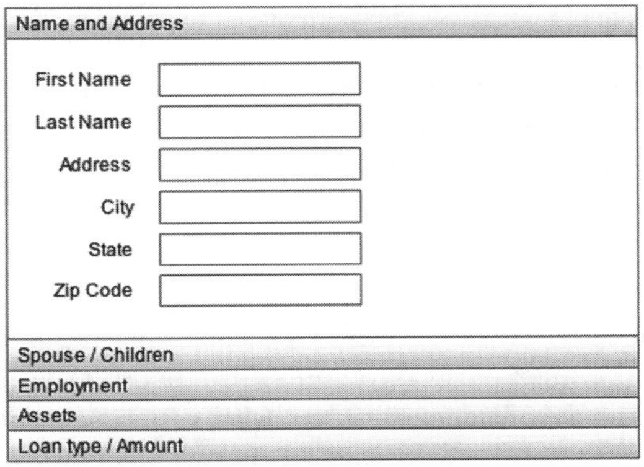

Figure 12.13 An accordion used to break up a large form into sections

To keep the code manageable, see figure 12.14, which contains a code snippet showing how the accordion breaks up the form.

This accordion example employs a `Form` to create a clean vertical layout. You continue repeating this pattern of configuring a container to create each accordion panel.

But don't limit yourself to forms. You can put anything you want inside an accordion, including lists. Lists are another popular content choice for accordion sections. You can embed a `DataGrid`, a `List`, or even a `Tree` component within an individual section.

Forms and lists are two of the most common uses for accordions, but you can add any other mechanisms you can think of. For example, if you have a complex directory

```
1  <?xml version="1.0" encoding="utf-8"?>
2  <s:NavigatorContent xmlns:fx="http://ns.adobe.com/mxml/2009"
3                      xmlns:s="library://ns.adobe.com/flex/spark"
4                      xmlns:mx="library://ns.adobe.com/flex/halo">
5    <mx:Form>
6      <mx:FormItem label="First Name">
7        <s:TextInput />
8      </mx:FormItem>
9      <mx:FormItem label="Last Name">
10       <s:TextInput />
11     </mx:FormItem>
```

Figure 12.14 The accordion has containers inside it, with each container representing a section of the form.

structure, you can use a tree inside each accordion section to separate the directory into smaller, more easily read subsections.

The only thing left to consider is how to handle user interactions with an accordion.

12.6.3   *Handling user interactions with an accordion*

We're going to give your eyes a rest: Everything we wrote about handling user interactions with the tab navigator applies to the accordion as well—you already know what to do. But as a quick reminder, you use `selectedIndex` or `selectedChild` to set or determine which accordion section is selected and then react to the user via the `change` event.

In most cases, the majority of user interactions are with components within containers versus the accordion (or the tab navigator) itself.

We've now covered the core set of navigation tools.

12.7   *Summary*

You have many options to provide navigation to your user, and the best part is that these options are all easy! No complicated DHTML or complex JavaScript is required to create desktop-like experiences. For the most part, it's all out-of-the-box functionality.

Flex provides the common UI navigation paradigms with which most users are familiar, particularly drop-down menus and tab navigation. But to mix things up a bit, you can get serious and use the tab navigator's parent, the view stack, and use buttons (or any other graphic) to switch from one stack to another. To experience unique navigation, explore the accordion navigation component.

Except for menus, which follow their own model, all other navigation components follow the paradigm of placing containers inside each other for each item to display or navigate. Menus tend to represent tree-like (hierarchical) data, and there are many ways you can assemble the data to drive a menu. For the most part, you'll want to stick with XML, because it lends itself to hierarchical data structures.

You can be creative with navigation components, using different components interchangeably or customizing them with images.

Continuing with the theme of application navigation, chapter 13 teaches you how to provide pop-up windows. This includes how to exchange data with pop-ups and how to customize the experience.

Introduction to pop-ups

This chapter covers
- Creating a pop-up window
- Sizing and positioning pop-ups
- Communicating with a pop-up window
- Closing pop-up windows
- Using alerts

The previous chapter showed you how to wire the navigation for an application and the different approaches you can use. When you construct an application, your design will likely call for a pop-up or editing window. Flex offers a convenient mechanism in the *pop-up manager* to help you create, delete, position, close, and destroy windows. When you're choosing the type of pop-up window to add to your application, it's a good idea to plan ahead and determine what the purpose of the pop-up will be and what you'll need to do in the pop-up window. In this chapter we cover the different ways of creating and managing pop-ups as well as simple ways to style them.

13.1 *Creating your first pop-up*

Every pop-up window is created and manipulated through the pop-up manager. The `PopUpManager` class handles the initialization of the window and manages window layering within the application, which relieves you of the responsibility of avoiding placement conflicts. The pop-up manager is simple to use and doesn't carry many properties to configure. This section covers the creation and destruction of pop-up windows.

13.1.1 *First things first: create your title window*

Several options are available to you for creating a pop-up. Each option requires at least one window file that's used for the display of the window. The pop-up manager calls this window and renders it in a layer above any existing layers. Additional new pop-up windows are created similarly and placed above other open pop-up or alert windows. When the top window layer is closed, the next-highest window regains prominence. This continues until the last pop-up is closed, leaving the main layer, which is the parent application layer.

Listing 13.1 introduces the `TitleWindow` component, which enables all this to take place.

Listing 13.1   SimplePopupWindow.mxml: `TitleWindow` component in action

```
<?xml version="1.0" encoding="utf-8"?>
<mx:TitleWindow xmlns:fx="http://ns.adobe.com/mxml/2009"
                   xmlns:s="library://ns.adobe.com/flex/spark"
                   xmlns:mx="library://ns.adobe.com/flex/halo"
                   width="400" height="100" layout="vertical"
      showCloseButton="true"
         close="closeMe()">
  <fx:Script>
    <![CDATA[
      import mx.managers.PopUpManager;

      protected function closeMe():void{
        //we will write this code later in the chapter
      }
    ]]>
  </fx:Script>
    <s:Group>
        <s:Label text="Hello there!  I'm a simple popup window." />
    </s:Group>
</mx:TitleWindow>
```

When creating a pop-up window, you have a choice of the container component on which to base the pop-up (a.k.a. a *base tag*). One of the most common—and easiest to use—tags is `TitleWindow`, which contains window-specific functionality (close button, title, and the like). You can also use `Group`, `HGroup`, `VGroup`, or other common containers.

Once you've configured `TitleWindow` as your base component window tag, you can add any other MXML or ActionScript tags. Listing 13.1 uses the `Label` component to display a simple text message on the screen. The component is wrapped in the `Group` container to allow it as a child of `TitleWindow`, a Halo component. As you progress, we'll cover the remaining portions of the code.

> **MIGRATION TIP** In order to add children to a Halo container, the child must extend `UIComponent`. Flex 4 primitives and other non-`UIComponent`-based components can be wrapped in a `Group`, which extends `UIComponent`.

Now, let's look at how to present this window to the user via the `PopUpManager`.

13.1.2 *Using PopUpManager to open the window*

With your pop-up window text complete, let's put it to work by creating the code to use it. Follow these steps:

1 Create a project in Flash Builder called CH13.
2 Create a package called `windows` under CH13's src folder.
3 Create a new MXML component called SimplePopupWindow.mxml in the windows package.
4 Copy listing 13.1 into the new SimplePopupWindow.mxml file.
5 Create a testSimplePopup.mxml file in the (default package), and copy the contents of listing 13.2 into it.

> **TIP** A *package* is what Flash Builder calls a folder containing source files.

Listing 13.2 generates the pop-up window shown in figure 13.1, which opens the pop-up as soon as the application loads.

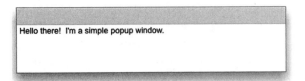

Figure 13.1   A basic pop-up window showing a simple text message and an empty title

---

Listing 13.2   testSimplePopup.mxml: showing a pop-up window

```
<?xml version="1.0" encoding="utf-8"?>
<s:Application xmlns:fx="http://ns.adobe.com/mxml/2009"
               xmlns:s="library://ns.adobe.com/flex/spark"
               xmlns:mx="library://ns.adobe.com/flex/halo"
               applicationComplete="openSimpleWindow()">
    <fx:Script>
        <![CDATA[
            import mx.core.IFlexDisplayObject;
            import mx.managers.PopUpManager;          Looks in
            import windows.SimplePopupWindow;         windows folder

            protected var simpleWindow:SimplePopupWindow;
            protected function openSimpleWindow():void{
                simpleWindow = new SimplePopupWindow();
                PopUpManager.addPopUp(simpleWindow, this, false);
```

```
            PopUpManager.centerPopUp(simpleWindow);
        }
    ]]>
    </fx:Script>
</s:Application>
```

This is the most commonly used and simplest mechanism for calling a new pop-up window. An instance of the `SimplePopupWindow` component is created and stored in the `simpleWindow` protected variable so you can interact with it, which we'll show you how to do a little later in this chapter.

The first argument in the `addPopUp()` method is an instance of the component you want to pop up. `this`, the second argument, indicates the parent of the pop-up is the component that launched the window, in this case `Application`. The final argument determines whether the window should be *modal*. Modal windows constrain the user to clicking only within the confines of the pop-up window and don't permit clicks beyond the borders of the modal background. Because the pop-up parent is the main application, attempts to click anywhere outside the pop-up are ignored.

> **TIP** It's important to know that the pop-up's parent can be any child display object of `Application` and the pop-up would be a child of that display object versus the `Application`.

Now that you've seen how to create a pop-up, you need to know how to close it when the user is finished with it.

13.1.3 *Closing the pop-up*

In figure 13.2, you'll notice an *X* in the upper-right corner of the pop-up window. As you already know, this is the universally recognized *close* button used by the vast majority of web and desktop applications.

The close button is available as an option when you use a `TitleWindow` tag. You can access this option through `TitleWindow`'s `showCloseButton` property, which accepts either `true` or `false` as a value, as shown in listing 13.1. When you set the `showClose-Button` property to `true`, the X button in the corner of the pop-up will display. When the button is clicked, `TitleWindow` dispatches a `close` event that can be used as a trigger by components designated to listen for it. In listing 13.1, the `TitleWindow`'s `close` event calls the `closeMe` function.

The following snippet illustrates the full `closeMe()` method used to remove the pop-up from view:

```
protected function closeMe():void{
    PopUpManager.removePopUp(this);
}
```

Just like the `addPopUp` function, the `removePopUp` function can be used to reference any child object. For instance, the main `Application` could listen for the `close` event from `SimplePopupWindow` and manage the closing. In this instance, this would be replaced with `simpleWindow`, the pop-up's variable name.

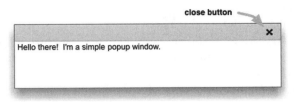

Figure 13.2 Notice the close button in the upper-right corner of the pop-up window.

Opening and closing a pop-up allows you to create your own custom pop-up windows to alert the user of a change, get information from them, or fulfill any myriad of needs. The pop-up we created is in the upper-left corner of the application. The next thing to look at is controlling the position of the pop-up.

13.2 Controlling the window location

When you first launch a window, you may see that it's not automatically positioned in the middle of the screen. You need to give your pop-up layout instructions, or it will appear in the upper-left corner of the parent object in which it was created. We'll now show you how to automatically center pop-ups and manually control a pop-up location.

13.2.1 Using the centerPopUp() method

PopUpManager contains a centerPopUp() method to center (to no surprise) the location of a pop-up window. The centerPopUp() method takes a single argument of type IFlexDisplayObject, which is any visual component—it's the name of a pop-up window, as the following line describes:

```
PopUpManager.centerPopUp(IFlexDisplayObject);
```

IFlexDisplayObject can be any pop-up window variable you define. For example, when you created the window, the pop-up was stored in the simpleWindow variable. To apply this to the previous example, you could do something like this:

```
protected function openSimpleWindow():void{
    simpleWindow = new SimplePopupWindow();
    PopUpManager.addPopUp(simpleWindow, this, false);
    PopUpManager.centerPopUp(simpleWindow);
}
```

Because simpleWindow is declared as a SimplePopupWindow, which implements IFlexDisplayObject through inheritance, as discussed in chapter 2, you can pass it directly to centerPopUp.

The centering method operates somewhat counterintuitively. Initially, most Flex coders assume that centering a pop-up means it will display in the center of the browser window. This isn't the case. Centering a pop-up window establishes a position over the center of the parent object in which you created the pop-up. If your parent object occupies a small area in the upper-right corner of the browser window, the centerPopUp() method will center the pop-up over that window, not the middle of the screen as defined by the main browser window.

The easiest strategy to deal with the placement issue is to name a parent as close to the application root as possible and define this parent with the largest view possible within the window space. Or, you can have your main application perform all the window openings (for example, you can dispatch events the main application can listen for and create pop-ups accordingly).

In most cases, using `centerPopUp()` works fine for noncritical window positioning. In the majority of circumstances, it's all you'll need to manage the placement of your windows.

13.2.2 Calculating window placement

Centering a window is easy, but you can get fancy with manipulating the position and dimensions of a pop-up. Let's demonstrate by creating another pop-up in your src/windows directory called MoveWindow.mxml. Also create another test application in the (default package) called testMoveWindow.mxml and set it as the default application. In this project (see figure 13.3), the pop-up has buttons to move, on click, the pop-up to each corner of the window or to the center.

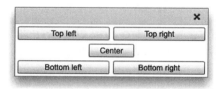

Figure 13.3   MoveWindow.mxml: clicking the buttons manipulates the x and y coordinates to reposition this pop-up.

Although the manual method of placing windows on a screen gives you more control over the exact location of the window, it requires more calculation and greater attention to where you position the window. Listing 13.3 presents the code snippet used to determine where the window is currently located and its dimensions (which you'll later manipulate to move the pop-up to each of the four window corners). The variables x and y correspond to the horizontal and vertical coordinates, respectively.

Listing 13.3   Accessing a pop-up's position and dimensions

```
var currentX:Number = x;
var currentY:Number = y;
var currentWidth:Number = width;
var currentHeight:Number = height;
```

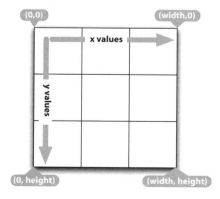

Figure 13.4   Visualizing the positioning parameters of a pop-up

Imagine the window as a grid with lines running up and across the window, as illustrated in figure 13.4. X and y are points on that grid for the window or whatever object you're measuring. In listing 13.3, x and y are points on the grid.

X and y are points that are available in every object that can be displayed on the screen, and they match up to the current location of the object on the screen; the x and y values identify any single point on the screen.

If you evaluate the x and y properties of a newly created window without any positioning applied to it, you'll see the window has an x value of zero (0) and a y value of zero (0) (see the upper-left corner of figure 13.4). Combining these values with the height and width of the window, you can arrive at the placement of the object on the screen.

Leveraging that as the premise for moving a pop-up window, listing 13.4 shows how to use the dimensions of the pop-up against the dimensions of the parent component (which is the main application in this case) to calculate a new position for the window. To make it more interesting, we add 10 pixels of *padding* from the edges.

Listing 13.4   MoveWindow.mxml: manipulating the pop-up's position

```xml
<?xml version="1.0" encoding="utf-8"?>
<mx:TitleWindow xmlns:fx="http://ns.adobe.com/mxml/2009"
                xmlns:s="library://ns.adobe.com/flex/spark"
                xmlns:mx="library://ns.adobe.com/flex/halo"
                width="300" layout="vertical" showCloseButton="true"
                close="closeMe()">
  <fx:Script>
    <![CDATA[
      import mx.managers.PopUpManager;

      protected function closeMe():void{
        PopUpManager.removePopUp(this);
      }

      protected function moveWindow(location:String):void{
        var newX:Number = 0;
        var newY:Number = 0;
        var padding:Number = 10;
        if(location == "center"){
          PopUpManager.centerPopUp(this);
          return;
        }
        if(location.indexOf("bottom") > -1)
          newY = (parent.height - this.height)-padding;
        if(location.indexOf("top") > -1)
          newY = padding;
        if(location.indexOf("left") > -1)
          newX = padding;
        if(location.indexOf("right") > -1)
          newX = (parent.width - this.width)-padding;
        move(newX,newY);
      }
    ]]>
  </fx:Script>
  <s:HGroup width="100%">
    <s:Button label="Top left" width="100%"
              click="moveWindow('topleft');"/>
    <s:Button label="Top right" width="100%"
              click="moveWindow('topright');"/>
  </s:HGroup>
  <s:VGroup width="100%" horizontalAlign="center">
```

Annotations:
- **Method to determine location** → `protected function moveWindow(location:String):void{`
- **Random amount of padding** → `var padding:Number = 10;`
- **newY set to bottom minus padding** → `newY = (parent.height - this.height)-padding;`
- **newY set to top plus padding** → `newY = padding;`
- **newX set to left plus padding** → `newX = padding;`
- **newX set to right minus padding** → `newX = (parent.width - this.width)-padding;`
- **Move pop-up to determined location** → `move(newX,newY);`

```
  <s:Button label="Center" click="moveWindow('center')" />
</s:VGroup>
<s:HGroup width="100%">
  <s:Button label="Bottom left" width="100%"
            click="moveWindow('bottomleft');"/>
  <s:Button label="Bottom right " width="100%"
            click="moveWindow('bottomright');"/>
</s:HGroup>
</mx:TitleWindow>
```

As we mentioned earlier, when you're calculating and setting window placement by coordinates, it's particularly important to remember that all coordinate calculations are relative to the size and location of the parent object—not the coordinates of the main window.

The issues surrounding window location become important when you're dealing with modal windows. As a worst-case scenario, if you define a modal window that appears outside the visible screen, it renders the application unusable because the user can't close the window or click anywhere else on the screen to release the modal window's control of the application unless you build in some other close mechanism, such as a keystroke.

Implementing a keystroke close mechanism

To implement a keystroke close mechanism, you can use an event listener on the keyboard.

Example:

```
stage.addEventListener(KeyboardEvent.KEY_UP, onKeyUp, false, 0, true);
...
protected function onKeyUp(event:KeyboardEvent):void{
    if(event.keyCode == Keyboard.ESCAPE) close();
}
```

This is a simple example of listening for a keystroke and, when the escape key is released, calling the close() method to remove the pop-up.

Specifying the location of pop-up windows in your application is a critical visual and functional responsibility. The next aspect we'll look at is sending and receiving data from a pop-up.

13.3   *Data integration with pop-ups*

In this section, you'll take your knowledge of pop-ups one step further by learning how to retrieve data inside the pop-up (usually information the user enters on a form) or send information to a pop-up. To set up the example, you'll create a user login pop-up, as shown in figure 13.5.

Figure 13.5 This pop-up window accepts user input and saves it to a variable that will be retrieved later.

Let's start by creating a new MXML component called LoginWindow.mxml in the src/windows folder. Enter the code shown in the following listing.

Listing 13.5 LoginWindow.mxml: pop-up that captures user login information

```
<?xml version="1.0" encoding="utf-8"?>
<mx:TitleWindow xmlns:fx="http://ns.adobe.com/mxml/2009"
                xmlns:s="library://ns.adobe.com/flex/spark"
                xmlns:mx="library://ns.adobe.com/flex/halo"
                title="Login" showCloseButton="true" close="closeMe()">
  <fx:Metadata>
  [Event(name="loggingIn")]
  </fx:Metadata>
  <fx:Script>
    <![CDATA[
      import mx.managers.PopUpManager;

      public static const LOGGING_IN:String = "loggingIn";      ⟵  Static event
                                                                    constant name
      [Bindable]                                                    Getter for
      private var _username:String = "";                            username
      public function get username():String{ return _username; }  ⟵

      [Bindable]                                                    Getter for
      private var _password:String = "";                            password
      public function get password():String{ return _password; }  ⟵

      public function closeMe():void{
        PopUpManager.removePopUp(this);
      }                                                           Dispatch
                                                                  LOGGING_IN
      protected function sendLogin():void{                        event
        dispatchEvent(new Event(LOGGING_IN));                   ⟵
        closeMe();
      }
    ]]>
  </fx:Script>                                         Input field bound to
  <mx:Form>                                            username variable
    <mx:FormItem label="Username">
      <s:TextInput id="usernameField" text="@{_username}" />   ⟵
    </mx:FormItem>
    <mx:FormItem label="Password">
      <s:TextInput id="passwordField" displayAsPassword="true"
                   text="@{_password}" />          ⟵  Input field bound to
    </mx:FormItem>                                     password variable
    <mx:FormItem>
      <s:Button label="Log In" click="sendLogin()" />
    </mx:FormItem>
  </mx:Form>
</mx:TitleWindow>
```

The LoginWindow is a simple pop-up much like ones we created previously. The user interface consists of a form with two input fields and an action button. We're taking advantage of two-way data binding to store the user input in the _username and _password variables, respectively. There's also a getter for each property so an outside component or application can access the data. Later we'll look into making the component a black box.

Once the user clicks the Log In button, a new event is dispatched telling all listeners the user clicked the Log In button. To let other components know of the `loggingIn` event, custom metadata is added for the `loggingIn` event, which is stored in the static `LOGGING_IN` variable. This, as noted in previous chapters, is a great coding practice so that changing the event name doesn't silently affect the entire application. Once the event is dispatched, the pop-up is removed from the display but not destroyed.

One of the greatest advantages of storing pop-ups in component variables is that the window can be reused and all of its state values are retained. To test the Login-Window, create a new MXML application in the (default package) named testLogin-Popup.mxml. Copy the code from listing 13.6 into the file.

Listing 13.6   Using a component object as a window

```xml
<?xml version="1.0" encoding="utf-8"?>
<s:Application xmlns:fx="http://ns.adobe.com/mxml/2009"
               xmlns:s="library://ns.adobe.com/flex/spark"
               xmlns:mx="library://ns.adobe.com/flex/halo"
               applicationComplete="init()">
  <fx:Script>
    <![CDATA[
        import windows.LoginWindow;
        import mx.managers.PopUpManager;

        protected var loginWindow:LoginWindow;          ⟵ Variable to store pop-up instance

        protected function init():void{
          loginWindow = new LoginWindow();              ⟵ Creates pop-up instance
          loginWindow.addEventListener(LoginWindow.LOGGING_IN, onLogin,
            false, 0, true);
        }                                               Adds LoginWindow.
                                                        LOGGING_IN event listener
        protected function openLoginWindow():void{
          PopUpManager.addPopUp(loginWindow, this, true);   ⟵ Opens pop-up
          PopUpManager.centerPopUp(loginWindow);            ⟵ Centers pop-up
        }

        protected function onLogin(event:Event):void{
          userInfo.text = "User info: " + loginWindow.username +    Updates
                          " (" + loginWindow.password + ")";        user info
        }
    ]]>
  </fx:Script>

  <s:Label id="userInfo" horizontalCenter="0" verticalCenter="-20" />

  <s:Button horizontalCenter="0" verticalCenter="0" label="Login"
            click="openLoginWindow()" />
</s:Application>
```

In listing 13.6, the `init` method is called when the `applicationComplete` event is dispatched. The window is initialized and a reference stored in the `loginWindow` variable. An event listener is then added for the custom `LoginWindow.LOGGING_IN` event. At this point the application is initialized and awaiting user input.

Users have the option of clicking the Log In button. When the button's `click` event dispatches, the `onLogin` method is called, which opens the window through the `addPopUp` function. The application is again waiting on user input to proceed. Once the user enters her information and the `LOGGING_IN` event is dispatched, `onLogin` is called, which updates the `userInfo` field to show the new information through a simple string update.

After testing the login once, open the window again by clicking the same button, and notice that your form fields have retained their value. The majority of the time for a login window, the form fields would be cleared after a validated login attempt has been made.

Any windows not generated and stored in a component variable are re-created and initialized every time the window is opened. This approach can be both good and bad, depending on how you intend to use the window. On one hand, your application can benefit from the object maintaining its state if it's to be displayed often; on the other hand, storing the window and its constituent data can be a drain on memory resources—particularly if the window is used only once. There's no magic bullet for every pop-up need. Be sure you assess the pop-up requirement(s) and choose an approach accordingly.

If you have a previously initialized object, the process of reinitializing it wipes out any stored data. Using the `addPopUp()` method, you can display and hide the window repeatedly without affecting the data inside. This is an important distinction between `addPopUp` and `createPopUp`, particularly as you get into extracting user-edited data from a window without using a custom event, as you'll see later in the chapter.

13.3.1 Getting data out of your pop-up window

When you're first getting started with Flex, most developers have the impulse to include a data service, such as `WebService`, `RemoteObject`, or `HTTPService`, to communicate user-entered form data to a server directly in the pop-up. This approach is a quick way to integrate data but is not reusable and can quickly become a maintenance headache if your backend web service changes or you need multiple components to call the same service.

There are several ways to capture form data. You can dispatch a custom event with the values stored in the event object itself or present the data as public variables or a getter and then send out an event to notify the parent application the information is available to process. We covered dispatching an event and accessing getters directly in the previous example. In the following sections, we show you how to dispatch the custom event.

13.3.2 Sending custom events with data

Event listeners are objects that respond to events generated by the window. These events can be either custom events or system-type events generated by the application. For more information about events and how to use them, we recommend reviewing chapter 11. The following snippet shows event listeners registered on the login window object:

```
loginWindow.addEventListener(LoginWindow.LOGGING_IN, onLogin,
        false, 0, true);
```

In this scenario, an event listener is configured for the loginWindow object. This event listener will monitor for the custom events to be dispatched and react to them by gathering user-supplied information from the dispatched event. To demonstrate, create a copy of LoginWindow.mxml and name it LoginWindow2.mxml. In the copy you'll change the application to receive the data from the event versus from the component itself.

The first thing you want to do is delete the username and password getters. This provides the black-box effect mentioned earlier. Now the _username and _password variables are closed to external access. You'll change the sendLogin() method to dispatch a custom event, but first you must create your custom event class. Create an ActionScript class in a new package named events and copy the code from listing 13.7 into the class.

Listing 13.7   Custom LoginEvent

```
package events{
    import flash.events.Event;
    public class LoginEvent extends Event{
        public static const LOGGING_IN:String = "loggingIn";
        public var username:String;
        public var password:String;

        public function LoginEvent(type:String, bubbles:Boolean=false,
                                cancelable:Boolean=false){
            super(type, bubbles, cancelable);
        }
    }
}
```

LoginEvent.as is a basic custom event with two properties: username and password. You'll store the login information in these variables prior to dispatching the event. The main application will then reference the properties from the event rather than from the component itself.

Notice the static variable LOGGING_IN, as you previously saw in the first version, LoginWindow.mxml. Remember, custom events should house the information about the events available for dispatch. Remove the static LOGGING_IN variable from the LoginWindow2.mxml because you'll reference the event name from your custom event. Now you need to tweak the metadata.

Previously the metadata didn't reference the event type. If you recall, when a metadata type isn't specified, the default type is flash.events.Event. Add the type parameter to the Event metadata to reference the new LoginEvent class:

```
<fx:Metadata>
    [Event(name="loggingIn", type="events.LoginEvent")]
</fx:Metadata>
```

The new login window is almost complete. You need to adjust the `sendLogin` method to dispatch your new custom event as well as store the data in the event properties. Change the `sendLogin` method to use the following snippet:

```
protected function sendLogin():void{
        var event:LoginEvent = new LoginEvent(LoginEvent.LOGGING_IN);
        event.username = _username;
        event.password = _password;
        dispatchEvent(event);
        closeMe();
}
```

This snippet dispatches a custom event with the specific data from the window stored in the event's properties. Now any listener can access the data from the event, as we'll explain in more detail in the next section.

13.3.3 *Getting data out*

To test your new LoginWindow2 component, create a copy of testLoginWindow.mxml and name it testLoginWindow2.mxml. Be sure to set the new application as the default application. You have only a few minor adjustments to make to prepare the application for the custom event.

The first thing you need to do is change all references to `window.LoginWindow` to `window.LoginWindow2`. In the `init` method, change the event listener to use the `LoginEvent.LOGGING_IN` constant:

```
loginWindow.addEventListener(LoginEvent.LOGGING_IN, onLogin,
        false, 0, true);
```

Also adjust the `onLogin` event handler to expect a `LoginEvent` argument instead of the `Event` argument and use the event properties instead of the window's properties:

```
protected function onLogin(event:LoginEvent):void{
        userInfo.text = "User info: " + event.username +
                        " (" + event.password + ")";
 }
```

Run the application, and you'll notice it acts exactly the same as the previous example. It may make you question why use component properties versus event properties. The event-based approach is the suggested way to manage data between your application and the component or object dispatching the event. This keeps your application from requiring a specific login component, for instance, in order to function. By utilizing a custom event, the application doesn't care where the user information originated. The `LoginEvent` houses the data, and the application flows normally regardless of the originating component being a pop-up window or a simple component in the display list.

Another question may arise: Why not access the usernameField and password-Field directly in the component? We strenuously caution against taking this approach. It violates best-practice object-oriented coding principles by strongly coupling your application to a specific component as well as a specific component's elements. For instance, LoginWindow2 might change the username field to be a drop-down list of users, which isn't likely, but let's explore the idea. In this case, the application will have to be updated to work with the changes made to the login component.

The better way to pull your data out of a window is via the user-triggered event. When the event is fired and an event handler is called, it doesn't matter what the internal component looks like but that the event has the data you expect and need. The login component can be a drop-down list, data grid, or anything else, as well as completely change the name of the internal elements without affecting any other portion of the application. A loosely coupled application is the goal, and the event approach gets you there.

Beyond receiving data from a pop-up, you can also send data to the component.

13.3.4 *Sending data to the window*

To send data in, generally the easiest and simplest method is to call a public method or setter on the window to which to pass the data. To demonstrate, let's create a portion of a user management system. Start by creating a new MXML component named UsersWindow.mxml in the windows package. Copy the code from listing 13.8 into the component.

Listing 13.8   UsersWindow pop-up component

```
<?xml version="1.0" encoding="utf-8"?>
<mx:TitleWindow xmlns:fx="http://ns.adobe.com/mxml/2009"
                xmlns:s="library://ns.adobe.com/flex/spark"
                xmlns:mx="library://ns.adobe.com/flex/halo"
                title="User Manager ({_users.length} users)"
                width="400" height="300" showCloseButton="true"
                close="closeMe()" creationComplete="init()">
  <fx:Script>
  <![CDATA[
    import mx.managers.PopUpManager;

    [Bindable]
    private var _users:Array;
    public function get users():Array{ return _users; }
    public function set users(value:Array):void{
      _users = value;
    }

    protected function init():void{
      if(isPopUp) PopUpManager.centerPopUp(this);       ◁─┐ Automatically
    }                                                        center pop-up
    protected function closeMe():void{
      PopUpManager.removePopUp(this);
    }
```

```
        ]]>
    </fx:Script>
    <mx:DataGrid id="usersList" width="100%" height="100%"          Bind grid to
            dataProvider="{_users}" />                          ◁─┘ _users array
</mx:TitleWindow>
```

Listing 13.8 has a familiar pop-up component. There is the normal closeMe method, but you made a change. Instead of having the main application control the positioning, inside the init method, called in the creationComplete event phase, the component centers itself. Because this component could be used elsewhere, instead of it being a pop-up, you do a check against the isPopUp (Boolean) variable. If the value is true, you use the PopUpManager to center the pop-up.

> **NOTE** isPopUp is a variable available to any component extending UIComponent. The variable is set to true by the PopUpManager. In all other scenarios, the value will be false.

You also have a _users property with a getter and setter. Because you're using data binding for the DataGrid's dataProvider, the setter merely updates the _users property. The TitleWindow's title property is set to a custom string. The title is to read "User Manager (# users)," where the number of users is updated through data binding on the _users.length property. This gives a simple yet great visual cue to the user, signifying the number of users in the list.

The UsersWindow is complete and ready for implementation. To test the pop-up, copy the code from listing 13.9 into a new MXML application named testUsers-Window.mxml.

Listing 13.9 User management application

```
<?xml version="1.0" encoding="utf-8"?>
<s:Application xmlns:fx="http://ns.adobe.com/mxml/2009"
            xmlns:s="library://ns.adobe.com/flex/spark"
            xmlns:mx="library://ns.adobe.com/flex/halo"
            applicationComplete="init()">
    <fx:Script>
    <![CDATA[
        import windows.UsersWindow;
        import mx.managers.PopUpManager;
                                                             Variable to store
        protected var _usersWindow:UsersWindow;          ◁─┘ pop-up instance

        protected function init():void{                     Creates pop-up
            _usersWindow = new UsersWindow();            ◁─┘ instance
        }

        protected function openWindow():void{
            PopUpManager.addPopUp(_usersWindow, this, true);   ◁─┐  Opens
            generateData();                          ◁─ Generates    │ pop-up
        }                                               dummy data
        protected function generateData():void{
            var users:Array = new Array();
```

```
      var totalRecords:uint = Math.round(Math.random()*100);
      var name:String;
      for(var i:uint = 0; i < totalRecords; i++){
        name = "User" + i.toString();
        users.push({name: name, email: name + "@domain.com"});
      }
      _usersWindow.users = users;                    ◁┐  Sets pop-up
    }                                                  │  users property
  ]]>
</fx:Script>

<s:Button label="View Users" horizontalCenter="0" verticalCenter="0"
          click="openWindow()" />
</s:Application>
```

The majority of this application should look familiar. It mimics the previous test applications. One button opens the window created in the `init` method. The main difference here is you're generating dummy data in the `generateData` method.

The `generateData` method is purely for testing purposes. It creates an array, loops a random number of times based on `totalRecords`, and adds a generic object to the array with two properties: `name` and `email`. Once the loop is complete, the data is passed to the `_usersWindow.users` property. From there it's up to the pop-up to display the data accordingly. Normally this data would come from a data call or would be already available by way of a previous data call.

> **NOTE**   In listing 13.9 you use a generic object, but in a real application you'd want to use a custom object with `name` and `email` properties. You'll learn more about objects in chapter 16.

Your main application is created and ready to go, so you can test it. Run the application and open the window. You'll see the grid filled with data, and the title of the window will show the number of users listed. Close the window and open it again. The number of users will vary accordingly, because of the random number of users you're generating.

You now have a good understanding of pop-up windows as well as how to work with windows using `PopUpManager`. We'll move on to another type of pop-up window you've most likely already seen and used: alerts.

13.4   *Using alerts*

The `Alert` class is a specialized type of class designed to rapidly create a specific type of pop-up window. You've already had some exposure to alerts by going through the examples in the book. Alerts let you quickly advise users about important information (generally errors) and messaging back values. If you're familiar with JavaScript, the `Alert` class is similar to `alert()`. You're going to see how to show simple alerts, similar to JavaScript alerts, and then explore ways to adjust the alert buttons and style.

13.4.1   *Creating a simple alert*

Creating an alert is as easy as pie. The following snippet constructs an alert with code you've likely already used by now:

```
import mx.controls.Alert;
Alert.show("Hello World!");
```

Undoubtedly, that's a simple alert. The only item required to make an alert pop up is the message to be communicated to the user. Figure 13.6 shows the output of this code.

The alert in figure 13.6 and the previous snippet perform only one action; you can't do much more with it except click OK to close the window.

This limited interactivity is sufficient for communicating an error and directing a user to some other location to address the problem, but the user can't interact with the alert. This isn't the end of the story; you can do much more with alerts.

Figure 13.6   An alert issuing a simple "Hello World!" message. Click OK to close the window.

13.4.2   *Doing more with alerts*

Alerts in general are like pop-up windows. You can perform most of the same tricks with them: listen to and move events, change transparency, and so on.

But alerts are more specialized entities than pop-ups—you can add or remove buttons and set an icon. In addition to providing a message for the alert, you can also manipulate the following properties in the `Alert.show` method, in argument order:

- Title
- Flags: buttons (Yes, No, OK, Cancel) or nonmodal
- Owning object
- Custom close handler method
- Icon class
- Default button flag

Any of these properties can be specified or omitted.

13.4.3   *A more advanced alert*

A one-button-fits-all approach to alerts doesn't work for every occasion. Consider the scenario in which you want to prompt a quick agreement from the user, perhaps to confirm that she wants to save a file or configuration before moving to a new screen.

To do this, you may want to display a small confirmation dialog asking her if she wants to save changes before closing a window. Listing 13.10 creates an alert containing multiple buttons.

Listing 13.10   Setting up a more advanced alert

```
<?xml version="1.0" encoding="utf-8"?>
<s:Application xmlns:fx="http://ns.adobe.com/mxml/2009"
               xmlns:s="library://ns.adobe.com/flex/spark"
               xmlns:mx="library://ns.adobe.com/flex/halo"
               applicationComplete="init()">
  <fx:Script>
    <![CDATA[
      import mx.controls.Alert;
      import mx.events.CloseEvent;

      protected function init():void{
        Alert.show("Do you want to save your changes?", "Save Changes",
          Alert.YES|Alert.NO, this, onAlertClose);     Show alert
      }

      protected function onAlertClose(event:CloseEvent):void{
        //we will write this code later in the chapter     Handle
      }                                                      close event
    ]]>
  </fx:Script>
  <s:Label id="statusField" horizontalCenter="0" verticalCenter="0" />
</s:Application>
```

In this case, the pop-up is created with the Alert.show() method, in which you can include message and title information. To add more buttons, you can use the Alert static variables to indicate which buttons to show. In listing 13.10, Alert.Yes presents a Yes button and Alert.No displays a No button.

Figure 13.7   An alert message showing Yes and No buttons. You have a choice of what to do.

You can code the button callouts in any order, but it won't affect the order in which the buttons are displayed in the alert. The alert buttons always appear in the following order: OK, Yes, No, Cancel. Figure 13.7 shows the output of the code from listing 13.10.

In listing 13.10, the alert close handler, onAlertClose, is called when the user clicks any button. With alert windows, clicking any button automatically closes the window and fires a CloseEvent.

You can respond to this event by comparing the event.detail value against the static values on the alert object. For example, the following snippet updates the onAlertClose method from listing 13.10 and tests whether the event.detail value is equal to Alert.YES. This snippet shows the alert handler code for figure 13.7:

```
protected function onAlertClose(event:CloseEvent):void{
  if(event.detail == Alert.YES)
    statusField.text = "You answered Yes";
  else
    statusField.text s= "You answered No";
}
```

NOTE It's considered good practice to use the object static variables whenever possible, because doing so makes your code easier to read and understand. Also, should those values ever change, you'll need to change them in only one place. For example, consider which is easier to understand: `Alert.YES` or `1`. Intrinsically, they mean the same thing; but `Alert.YES` is much easier to read.

The new `onAlertClose` method handles the `close` event fired from the alert window and updates the `statusField.text` property to show a result. The way you handle an alert close won't change, but what you do with the result will. For instance, to respond to an alert window, you always listen for `CloseEvent` and evaluate the result of the close event to determine which button was clicked.

What can and does frequently change is the appearance of the alert window, which lends itself to a fair amount of rework.

13.4.4 Pimp this alert

You can select from a variety of appearance options for your alert window. You can resize it, change the labels on the buttons, and include an icon in the alert window. Listing 13.11 combines all these options in one tricked-out message.

Listing 13.11 Launching the pimped-out alert

```
<?xml version="1.0" encoding="utf-8"?>
<s:Application xmlns:fx="http://ns.adobe.com/mxml/2009"
               xmlns:s="library://ns.adobe.com/flex/spark"
               xmlns:mx="library://ns.adobe.com/flex/halo"
               applicationComplete="init()">
  <fx:Script>
  <![CDATA[
    import mx.events.CloseEvent;
    import mx.controls.Alert;
    [Embed(source="assets/warning.gif")]
    [Bindable]
    protected var _iconWarning:Class;

    protected function init():void{
      var alert:Alert;
      Alert.buttonWidth = 150;
      Alert.okLabel = "Disneyland"
      Alert.yesLabel = "Kennedy Space Port";          Assigns custom
      Alert.noLabel = "Six Flags";                     button labels
      Alert.cancelLabel = "Marine World";
      alert = Alert.show("Where do you want to go today?", "Destination",
                  Alert.OK| Alert.YES | Alert.NO| Alert.CANCEL,
                      this, onAlertClose, _iconWarning, Alert.YES);   ◁┐
      alert.height = 150;                                           Uses embedded
      alert.width = 700;                                            image as icon
      Alert.okLabel = "OK";
      Alert.yesLabel = "Yes";              Resets labels
      Alert.noLabel = "No";                to default values
      Alert.cancelLabel = "Cancel";
    }
```

```
      protected function onAlertClose(event:CloseEvent):void{
        //we will write this code later in the chapter
      }
    ]]>
  </fx:Script>
</s:Application>
```

You can set the labels for each of the buttons by using the buttonLabel property (one for each button). Setting the buttonWidth property allows you to determine the size of the buttons. Unfortunately, it's a one-size-fits-all situation; whatever size you choose in Alert.buttonWidth applies to all the buttons in that window.

In listing 13.11, you also embed an image and use the image as the icon in the pop-up. The Alert class lets you set an icon alongside the alert message. In addition, you can designate which button displays as the default selection. In this example, you set Alert.YES (the last argument in the Alert.show call) as the default button. You can see what the pimped-out alert looks like in figure 13.8.

Figure 13.8 Pimped-out alert with a custom icon, custom button labels, and a default button

Listing 13.11 also sets the returned result from the Alert.show function to an object typed as an Alert. Once the alert has opened, it acts similarly to a standard pop-up. You can do nearly everything to an alert window you can do with a normal pop-up window, including changing its height, width, position, and transparency.

To establish which button was clicked, listen for the close event and trap the value using the event.detail value, as in listing 13.12.

It's also important to remember to change the button labels back to their original values if you've changed them, as shown in listing 13.11. The majority of the time it's probably best to reset the labels right after the alert is shown so subsequent alerts will display the appropriate labels, unless the new labels are expected to change application-wide.

Listing 13.12 Pimped-out alert handler

```
protected function onAlertClose(event:CloseEvent):void {
  var message:String = "Woohoo!  Looks like we're going to ";
  switch (event.detail)    {
    case Alert.YES :                                              Updates
      status.text = message + Alert.yesLabel;                     status text
    break;
```

```
     case Alert.NO :
       status.text = message + Alert.noLabel;
     break;
     case Alert.OK :
       status.text = message + Alert.okLabel;
     break;
     case Alert.CANCEL :
       status.text = message + Alert.cancelLabel;
     break;
   }
}
```

Updates
status text

Changing the look and feel of the alert is one way you can furnish your application with a little extra sophistication. By default the alert will follow the application's theme, but it's not strictly necessary to change the alert display much at all. Just know that it's possible to completely customize your alert visuals. In most cases, programmers show a Yes/No or OK type of alert because it's quick and easy and a modal way of interacting with the user. Now that you've seen how you can modify alert messages, you can include some of these extras to give your application polish.

13.5   *Summary*

Many applications use pop-up windows in some form or another. Pop-up windows can be easy to manage if you remember a few things:

- Creating a pop-up can be done with or without a companion MXML component, but it's most often easier using an MXML component.
- Storing a pop-up in a variable is an effective way of maintaining window state even when the window is closed.
- A window can have public properties and public functions, which can both be used to set and retrieve data from the window, but it's best to use custom events where possible.
- Pop-up placement in the application depends on the location and placement of the parent of the pop-up. In most cases, you should try to use a parent as close to the root as possible, or at least a component that has the widest visible range on the screen. Your application needs may vary though.
- You can modify alerts to include an icon image and up to four buttons with custom labels. Using the `closeEvent` along with the `event.detail` item lets you determine which button was clicked.
- Alert windows act like pop-up windows. Most of the actions you expect on a pop-up window can also be done on an alert, including moving, resizing, and varying the interface.

You've made it through another chapter, and we're happy you've stuck with us this far. You've learned how to create custom pop-up windows and use the `Alert` class. The next chapter builds on the component functionality we presented here and adds view states, which allow you to modify the visual state of your components (including pop-up windows).

Implementing view states

This chapter covers

- Understanding view states
- Using view states in Flex
- Bringing it together

In previous chapters, you learned about controls, containers, layouts, and various other features incorporated within Adobe Flex and how you can use these tools to build RIAs.

In this chapter, we'll explore another important feature: view states. With view states, you can build RIAs that impart a polished and satisfying user experience. Before we jump into Flex-specific view state features, let's discuss the concept of view states in general.

14.1 Understanding view states

An RIA's UI consists of different views. Traditional websites consist of stateless, or static, pages (such as HTML pages).

Views can take on different visual appearances and representations depending on the conditions in which they're presented. An example of a condition is a user input, such as picking an item from a drop-down list or clicking a button. Other examples include your application responding to a request sent to a server or the result of an algorithm. A simple application might have only one view with some states, whereas complex applications might have several views, each with different states.

A view state can be defined as a particular visual appearance, behavior, and representation for a view (UI).

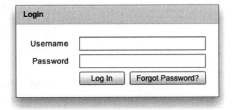

Figure 14.1 **Default view state of a login form**

Views have at least one state, which is known as the default or base state of the view. You can define any number of additional states depending on your requirements.

To illustrate the concept further, let's look at a real-world example. Figure 14.1 shows the login form from chapter 13. The illustration shows the default (base) state of the login form (view).

Figure 14.2 **Forgot Password view state of a login form**

Figure 14.2 shows a different state of the login form that displays when the user clicks the Forgot Password? button shown in figure 14.1.

Figures 14.1 and 14.2 are one view: `LoginView`. The view consists of two different states: `login` and `password`. A view consists of states, whether it's one state or multiple.

View states can be used for many other scenarios, such as these:

- A search view that shows results in a different state than the search form
- A layout-personalization view that lets users customize their application's appearance by defining different layouts as different states
- A view that shows user data in one state and then allows editing in different states

This is a basic introduction to view states. In the remainder of the chapter, we'll explore view states in detail and their related features in Adobe Flex. Don't worry if you're not a states guru yet. As we move forward, views and states will make more sense.

14.2 View states in Flex

In Flex, each application, custom component, or view has at least one state, which is known as the *default* view state. You can define additional states by adding a state to the `states` property.

The default state is the original state of the components you code into your application. Other states modify that original state by setting properties or removing or adding child objects. The following snippet demonstrates how you can define two additional states:

```
<s:states>
  <s:State name="somestate" />
  <s:State name="state2" />
  <s:State name="state3" />
</s:states>
```

The previous snippet creates three states: somestate, state2, and state3. Flex 4 sets the default state to the first state in the list. In this case, somestate is the default state. If state3 were first in the list, it would be the default state. You can also control the default state by using the currentState property of any view (the view being the application or custom component). At this point, we've only created a state by name, which ultimately means nothing until the state is referenced. It may feel like we're going to give a boring geography lesson, but all of this state talk starts getting interesting shortly.

Table 14.1 shows view state–related properties for mx.core.UIComponent.

Table 14.1   View state–related properties of the mx.core.UIComponent class

Property	Type	Description
states	Array	An array of state objects. This is populated to create more view states or read from to find available states.
currentState	String	The current view state name. The default value is ' ' or null (default view state).
currentCSSState	String	The current state used for CSS pseudo selectors. The default value is the same as the currentState property.

To change a view's state, you set the value of the view's currentState property to the name of the new state. currentCSSState is covered later in the book when we explore styling, in chapter 20.

Views also automatically send out events to notify listening components of view state changes, as well as before the view state changes. Table 14.2 lists the generated events when the view changes state. By listening for these events, your components can respond as needed. For more information about listening for events, see chapter 11.

Table 14.2   View state-related events of the mx.core.UIComponent class

Property	Type	Description
currentStateChanging	StateChangeEvent	This event is dispatched after the currentState property has been changed but before the view state changes. This event can be used to validate the change request or to perform actions before the state changes. It can also be used to prevent the state from changing.
currentStateChange	StateChangeEvent	This event is dispatched when the view's state has been changed.

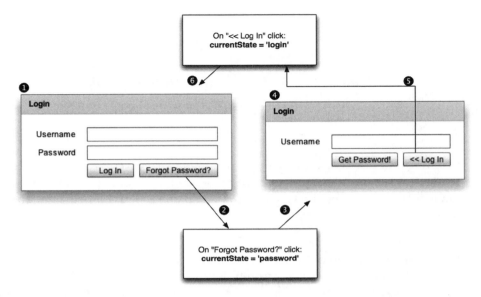

Figure 14.3   State change illustration

Figure 14.3 shows the flow between the two states in figures 14.1 and 14.2. Keep in mind this is the same component but with two different states toggled by the click of a button.

With a little background story under our belts, we can dig a little deeper and even get into some code!

14.2.1   *Working with properties*

If you have any experience with states in Flex 3, we're about to blow your mind! States in Flex 4 are completely different in an amazingly great way. To illustrate how to implement states, we're going to step through a lot of code to showcase how to change properties, event handlers, and state groups; add and remove children; and manage state events. We finish off with a real example built in part from figure 14.1.

Listing 14.1 starts us off with a simple example showing two buttons set to toggle the application state.

Listing 14.1   Changing properties with states

```
<?xml version="1.0" encoding="utf-8"?>
<s:Application xmlns:fx="http://ns.adobe.com/mxml/2009"
               xmlns:s="library://ns.adobe.com/flex/spark"
               xmlns:mx="library://ns.adobe.com/flex/halo">
  <s:layout>
    <s:VerticalLayout />
  </s:layout>
  <s:states>
    <s:State name="orange" />          State declaration
    <s:State name="black" />           named orange    State declaration
                                                       named black
```

```
  </s:states>                                         Orange button changes
  <s:HGroup>                                            state to orange
    <s:Button label="Orange" click="currentState = 'orange'" />
    <s:Button label="Black" click="currentState = 'black'" />
  </s:HGroup>                                         Black button
  <s:Rect width="200" height="200">    ◁── 200x200 rectangle   changes state
    <s:fill>                                             to black
      <s:SolidColor color.black="#000000" color.orange="#de7800" />   ◁
    </s:fill>                                    Rectangle's fill, color
  </s:Rect>                                    changed by state
</s:Application>
```

In listing 14.1, there are two states: orange and black. The two buttons have click events set to change the currentState property of the Application. When either button is clicked, changing the Application's state, the Rect's color changes with the following line of code:

```
<s:SolidColor color.black="#000000" color.orange="#de7800" />
```

Let's break this line down a bit. The SolidColor class has a color property. This property can be set as you normally would, but with states you can conditionally set the property based on which state is selected, using the following syntax: property. state="value". Figure 14.4 shows the changes from state to state. The left side of the figure shows the original state, orange, and the right side shows the second state, black. Keep in mind the image is pieced together, but they're indeed the same application.

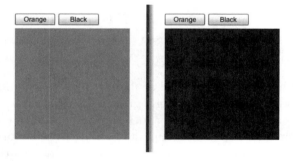

Figure 14.4 Two different states from listing 14.1

To drill this home a bit more, let's see another example of changing properties based on state change. Listing 14.2 is the same basic concept from listing 14.1 with a slight change.

Listing 14.2 Changing more properties with states

```
<?xml version="1.0" encoding="utf-8"?>
<s:Application xmlns:fx="http://ns.adobe.com/mxml/2009"
               xmlns:s="library://ns.adobe.com/flex/spark"
               xmlns:mx="library://ns.adobe.com/flex/halo">
  <s:layout>
    <s:VerticalLayout />
  </s:layout>
  <s:states>
```

```
  <s:State name="orange" />
  <s:State name="black" />
</s:states>
<s:HGroup>
  <s:Button label.orange="Black"
    label.black="Orange">
    <s:click>
      <![CDATA[
      currentState = (currentState == 'orange' ? 'black' : 'orange');
      ]]>
    </s:click>
  </s:Button>
</s:HGroup>
<s:Rect width.orange="200" height.orange="200"
      width.black="150" height.black="150">
  <s:fill>
    <s:SolidColor color.black="#000000" color.orange="#de7800" />
  </s:fill>
</s:Rect>
</s:Application>
```

State declarations

Button with different label per state

Click handler to toggle events

Rectangle width/height for orange state

Rectangle width/height for black state

Rectangle's fill, color changed by state

Before digging into the code, look at figures 14.5 and 14.6, which show the two separate states.

From listing 14.1 the main visual change in listing 14.2 is the use of one button instead of two and the size of the rectangle in the orange state. The following line of code from listing 14.2 sets up the label property to change per each state:

```
<s:Button label.orange="Black" label.black="Orange">
```

When the Application's currentState is set to orange, the label will read "Black" and vice versa for the black state. This creates a simplistic toggle button. The event handler for the button checks the currentState property and changes it depending on the current value:

```
<s:click>
  <![CDATA[
  currentState = (currentState == 'orange' ? 'black' : 'orange');
  ]]>
</s:click>
```

There's a better way of handling state-specific events, but we'll cover that next. The last change from listing 14.1 is in the width and height properties of the Rect:

```
<s:Rect width.orange="200" height.orange="200"
      width.black="150" height.black="150">
```

Figure 14.5 Listing 14.2's orange state

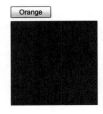

Figure 14.6 Listing 14.2's black state

Notice here there's a specific width and height for the two states. When the state is orange, the `Rect` is resized to 200x200, and it's resized to 150x150 when in the `black` state. The `Rect`'s fill color changes in the same way as in listing 14.1, so nothing new there.

So far we've explicitly set the values for the orange state, but we didn't have to. Take, for instance, the following snippet, which is another way of changing the `Rect` size:

```
<s:Rect width="200" height="200"
        width.black="150" height.black="150">
```

What's different? The initial `width` and `height` are set, but there are no specific settings for the orange state, right? Technically, the previous two snippets are the exact same. orange is the default state, because it's first in the list of states, so any property set not explicitly referencing a state is a default state property. In the case of the previous snippet, changing the `currentState` property to orange, `""` (empty string), or `null` will all resize the `Rect` to 200x200. Which way is best entirely depends on your application's needs. The previous examples are simple, so either one works, but there are cases where explicit state changes are needed. As we move forward you'll see a swap between explicit state changes and implicit, utilizing the default state.

We have a good start here at getting used to the state syntax. There are a lot of examples to dig into though. To continue our journey we'll explore state-specific event handlers.

14.2.2 *Working with event handlers*

In the previous section we looked at setting properties for states, which also showed us the new states syntax. Flex 4 doesn't stop with properties though. When using states, you can also set specific event handlers based on the selected state. Listing 14.3 builds on listing 14.2 and showcases how to use state-specific events.

Listing 14.3   Using state-specific events

```
<?xml version="1.0" encoding="utf-8"?>
<s:Application xmlns:fx="http://ns.adobe.com/mxml/2009"
               xmlns:s="library://ns.adobe.com/flex/spark"
               xmlns:mx="library://ns.adobe.com/flex/halo">
  <s:layout>
    <s:VerticalLayout />
  </s:layout>
  <s:states>
    <s:State name="orange" />                         State
    <s:State name="black" />                          declarations         Different label
  </s:states>                                                              per state
  <s:Button label.orange="Black" label.black="Orange"
            click.orange="currentState='black'"                           State click
            click.black="currentState='orange'"/>                         handlers
  <s:Rect width.orange="200" height.orange="200"                          Rectangle
          width.black="150" height.black="150">                           dimensions per state
    <s:fill>
```

```
        <s:SolidColor color.black="#000000" color.orange="#de7800" />
      </s:fill>
    </s:Rect>
</s:Application>
```

Rectangle's solid fill,
color changed by state

This listing provides little new from the previous listings. There's a button toggling the `Application`'s state from `orange` to `black` and vice versa. In each state the `Rect`'s fill color is changed from the color #de7800 to #000000. The big difference here is the `click` handler for the `Button`. Let's look specifically at the button code:

```
<s:Button label.orange="Black" label.black="Orange"
          click.orange="currentState='black'"
          click.black="currentState='orange'"/>
```

The `Button`'s `label` changes the same way as before, but you now see that the `click` handler also uses the same syntax as the state-specific properties: `event.state="value"`. The same rules applicable to state-specific properties apply here as well. With that said, you can also write the button code as such:

```
<s:Button label.orange="Black" label.black="Orange"
          click="currentState='black'"
          click.black="currentState='orange'"/>
```

Remember, orange is our default event, so we don't necessarily have to explicitly set the orange event handler. The button code could also utilize event handlers in a script block. The event handler value is presently using inline ActionScript, which is perfectly fine at times. Listing 14.4 shows the exact same code but with a script block rather than inline ActionScript.

> **Listing 14.4 Using state-specific events with a script block**

```
<?xml version="1.0" encoding="utf-8"?>
<s:Application xmlns:fx="http://ns.adobe.com/mxml/2009"
               xmlns:s="library://ns.adobe.com/flex/spark"
               xmlns:mx="library://ns.adobe.com/flex/halo">
  <s:layout>
    <s:VerticalLayout paddingLeft="20" paddingTop="20" />
  </s:layout>
  <s:states>
    <s:State name="orange" />
    <s:State name="black" />
  </s:states>
  <fx:Script>
    <![CDATA[
      protected function onOrangeClick(event:MouseEvent):void{
        currentState='black';
      }

      protected function onBlackClick(event:MouseEvent):void{
        currentState='orange';
      }
    ]]>
  </fx:Script>
```

Event handler for
orange click state

Set the currentState
to black

Set the currentState
to orange

Event handler
for black click
state

```
<s:Button label.orange="Black" label.black="Orange"
        click.orange="onOrangeClick(event)"
        click.black="onBlackClick(event)"/>
<s:Rect width.orange="200" height.orange="200"
        width.black="150" height.black="150">
  <s:fill>
    <s:SolidColor color.black="black" color.orange="#de7800" />
  </s:fill>
</s:Rect>
</s:Application>
```

Click event for orange state

Click event for black state

Visually there will be no difference when listing 14.4 runs versus listing 14.3. The end result, visually, is shown in figures 14.2 and 14.3, but how we get there has changed from listing 14.2. The main difference is in the event handlers. Instead of using inline ActionScript, each click event calls a related event handler, essentially doing the same thing as the inline ActionScript from listing 14.3. As a last example of another way to write state-specific events, consider the following:

```
<s:Button label.orange="Black" label.black="Orange">
  <s:click.black>
    <![CDATA[
    currentState='orange';
    ]]>
  </s:click.black>
  <s:click.orange>
    <![CDATA[
    currentState='black'
    ]]>
  </s:click.orange>
</s:Button>
```

This approach is the same as that of listing 14.2, but instead of using one event handler, it's broken into two. Notice that the syntax is a bit different: `<namespace:event.state />`. This syntax can be used for any child node of the `Button` component.

We're looking pretty good so far. We've covered properties and events. Our next step is to look into state groups, which provide a way to create a collection of states to manipulate the view for multiple states with one reference.

14.2.3 *Utilizing state groups*

For those of us who effectively used states in Flex 3, `basedOn` was a great friend to have. It allowed us to build states based on other states. This was useful, but compared to the Flex 4 implementation, you'll consider it a ghetto hack.

State groups provide a clean way of setting up a group of states, allowing you to reference them as states for state-specific properties, events, and the like. The syntax is the same as for properties or events: `<property of event>.<state or group>="value"`. This may not make sense yet, but hold out for a few more paragraphs and it'll all come together. To create a state group, you reference the group in the specific state declaration, like so:

```
<s:states>
  <s:State name="orange" stateGroups="box" />
  <s:State name="black" stateGroups="box" />
  <s:State name="green" stateGroups="circle" />
  <s:State name="blue" stateGroups="circle" />
</s:states>
```

These declarations build on the states from previous examples. You created two separate state groups: box and circle. The stateGroups property of the State component is a comma-separated list. This means you can have a state be a part of multiple groups. For instance, you could make the orange state part of the groups box and circle, if you so desire. The following snippet shows how to have a state participate in multiple groups:

```
<s:State name="orange" stateGroups="box,circle" />
```

Before we look into examples of using groups, you have to understand the difference between a group and a state.

- A state is a true state. This means you can set the currentState property to a state in order to adjust your view in any way. Look back at figure 14.3. Notice how the state is changed only when currentState is set to the state login or password.

- A group isn't a state but more a way to lessen the amount of MXML required to switch states. Listing 14.5 showcases an example of using state groups by building on our previous listings.

Listing 14.5 Using state groups

```
<?xml version="1.0" encoding="utf-8"?>
<s:Application xmlns:fx="http://ns.adobe.com/mxml/2009"
               xmlns:s="library://ns.adobe.com/flex/spark"
               xmlns:mx="library://ns.adobe.com/flex/halo">
  <s:layout>
    <s:VerticalLayout />
  </s:layout>
  <s:states>
    <s:State name="orange" stateGroups="box" />      States in
    <s:State name="black" stateGroups="box" />       box group
    <s:State name="green" stateGroups="circle" />    States in
    <s:State name="blue" stateGroups="circle" />     circle group
  </s:states>
  <s:Button label.orange="Black" label.black="Green"
          label.green="Blue" label.blue="Orange"
          click.orange="currentState='black'"
          click.black="currentState='green'"
          click.green="currentState='blue'"
          click.blue="currentState='orange'"/>
  <s:Rect width="200" height="200"                    Rectangle
          visible="false" includeInLayout="false"     to show in
          visible.box="true" includeInLayout.box="true">  box group
    <s:fill>
```

```
      <s:SolidColor color.black="#000000" color.orange="#de7800" />
    </s:fill>
  </s:Rect>
  <s:Ellipse width="200" height="200"
           visible="false" includeInLayout="false"
           visible.circle="true" includeInLayout.circle="true">
    <s:fill>
      <s:SolidColor color.green="green" color.blue="blue" />
    </s:fill>
  </s:Ellipse>
</s:Application>
```

Ellipse to show in circle group

The Button should look familiar. It toggles the Application's state to the next state in the list and changes the label accordingly. The Rect still has the same fill colors, but you need to toggle the visibility because you only want to show the Rect when current-State is a box group state. This is where you utilize the group box.

The Rect has two properties specific to the box group: visible and includeIn-Layout. Because you're using a VerticalLayout you have to remove the Rect from the layout if you want the space consumed by another component. Notice the syntax for changing the visibility when the currentState belongs to the box state: visible. box="true". It looks exactly like a state, but you never see currentState="box" in the code. The current state group is determined by which state is selected and to which groups the selected state belongs.

Previously you used the orange state interchangeably with a default value of the Rect's properties, but this time the default value for visible and includeInLayout would be false for the orange state. Wait, orange is in the box group, so how does that work? We're glad you asked. In plain English, the Rect visibility would read as such: For every state not included in the box state group, hide this component, and for every state included in the box state group, show this component.

Figure 14.7 shows the result of listing 14.5.
Figure 14.7 shows all of the states separated by lines. The first two states belong to the box group and the latter to the circle group. Both the Ellipse and the Rect do the same exact thing, hide for a specific state group, and Flex determines the appropriate group based on the currentState's stateGroups list.

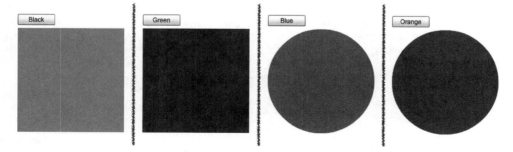

Figure 14.7   Simultaneous look at views in listing 14.5

Groups rock! You'll see them more as we move into other sections. Our next stop is adding and removing components. Adding and removing components allows you control over when components are created and destroyed.

14.2.4 *Adding and removing components*

In the last section you learned how to utilize state groups, and in the example you removed elements from the stage with `visible` and `includeInLayout`. It worked great and your application successfully stepped through the states, but there's a better way. In this section we're going to look at how you can include and exclude components by building on the previous examples.

Adding and removing components can be tricky business. The big gotcha is in knowing whether the element is available when you need it—in code, that is. If you don't have an element available and try to access it, you'll get a runtime error. You also have to determine whether you truly want the element removed or whether you want it hidden from the display, as you did in the previous section. A general rule is to create components only when you need them and destroy them when you don't need them. It's truly a case-by-case scenario, so choose wisely depending on your application needs.

To add or remove an element, you use the `includeIn` and `excludeFrom` properties. They're both comma-delimited lists of states, but they can't be used together. The following snippet shows how you can include and exclude elements in specific states:

```
<s:Button includeIn="myState" />
<s:Button includeIn="yourState" />
```

Wait, this lists only `includeIn` and not `exclude`, so how are you excluding anything? You're getting there. Listing 14.6 showcases how you can achieve listing 14.5 using `includeIn` rather than toggling visibility.

Listing 14.6 Using `includeIn`

```
<?xml version="1.0" encoding="utf-8"?>
<s:Application xmlns:fx="http://ns.adobe.com/mxml/2009"
               xmlns:s="library://ns.adobe.com/flex/spark"
               xmlns:mx="library://ns.adobe.com/flex/halo">
  <s:layout>
    <s:VerticalLayout />
  </s:layout>
  <s:states>
    <s:State name="orange" stateGroups="box" />
    <s:State name="black" stateGroups="box" />
    <s:State name="green" stateGroups="circle" />
    <s:State name="blue" stateGroups="circle" />
  </s:states>
  <s:Button label.orange="Black" label.black="Green"
            label.green="Blue" label.blue="Orange"
            click.orange="currentState='black'"
            click.black="currentState='green'"
```

```
                 click.green="currentState='blue'"
                 click.blue="currentState='orange'"/>
    <s:Rect width="200" height="200" includeIn="box">
      <s:fill>
        <s:SolidColor color.black="black" color.orange="#de7800" />
      </s:fill>
    </s:Rect>
    <s:Ellipse width="200" height="200" includeIn="circle">
      <s:fill>
        <s:SolidColor color.green="green" color.blue="blue" />
      </s:fill>
    </s:Ellipse>
</s:Application>
```

Include **Rect** in box group

Include **Ellipse** in circle group

Listing 14.6 is the same code as for listing 14.5, but notice that it's short a few lines, specifically where `visible` and `includeInLayout` took up four lines themselves. You removed four whole lines of code by replacing those lines with a simple `includeIn`. It reads: Include the `Rect` in all state groups `box` and exclude it from any other state not in the `box` group. You could also use `excludeFrom` for the `Rect` and `Ellipse` by swapping the values, like so:

```
<s:Rect width="200" height="200" excludeFrom="circle">
  <s:fill>
    <s:SolidColor color.black="black" color.orange="#de7800" />
  </s:fill>
</s:Rect>
<s:Ellipse width="200" height="200" excludeFrom="box">
  <s:fill>
    <s:SolidColor color.green="green" color.blue="blue" />
  </s:fill>
</s:Ellipse>
```

Notice the opposite is true in this snippet. You tell the `Rect` to not show up in the `circle` group but to show up for all other states or groups; in this case `box` is the only other group. The same is true for the `Ellipse`. The code is now cleaner and easier to read. You went from setting two properties eight times for two components to setting one property twice for two components. Again, you have to keep in mind your needs. `includeIn` and `excludeFrom` both destroy and create the target element accordingly. If you need the element around all of the time, consider using the previous section code or creation/destruction policies.

Creation and destruction policies allow you to determine when your component is created and/or destroyed. Listing 14.7 is a twist on listing 14.6 so you can see when elements are created by using creation and destruction policies.

Listing 14.7   Using creation and destruction policies

```
<?xml version="1.0" encoding="utf-8"?>
<s:Application xmlns:fx="http://ns.adobe.com/mxml/2009"
               xmlns:s="library://ns.adobe.com/flex/spark"
               xmlns:mx="library://ns.adobe.com/flex/halo"
               applicationComplete="init(event)">
```

```
<s:layout>
  <s:VerticalLayout paddingLeft="20" paddingTop="20" />
</s:layout>
<s:states>
  <s:State name="orange" stateGroups="box" />
  <s:State name="black" stateGroups="box" />
  <s:State name="green" stateGroups="circle" />
  <s:State name="blue" stateGroups="circle" />
</s:states>
<fx:Script>
  <![CDATA[
    protected function init(event:Event):void{
      log(event);
      trace(boxElement, circleElement);
    }
    protected function log(event:Event):void{
      trace(event.target.id, event.type);
    }
  ]]>
</fx:Script>
<s:Button label.orange="Black" label.black="Green"
          label.green="Blue" label.blue="Orange"
          click.orange="currentState='black'"
          click.black="currentState='green'"
          click.green="currentState='blue'"
          click.blue="currentState='orange'"/>
<s:Group id="boxElement" includeIn="box"
         itemCreationPolicy="deferred"           ⟵  Set
         itemDestructionPolicy="auto"                itemCreationPolicy
         creationComplete="log(event);"              property
         addedToStage="log(event);"              |  Log events
         removedFromStage="log(event);">         ⟵  Log removedFromStage
  <s:Rect width="200" height="200">                 event
    <s:fill>
      <s:SolidColor color.black="black" color.orange="#de7800" />
    </s:fill>
  </s:Rect>
</s:Group>
<s:Group id="circleElement" includeIn="circle"  ⟵  Set
         itemCreationPolicy="immediate"              itemCreationPolicy
         itemDestructionPolicy="never"               property
         creationComplete="log(event);"          |  Log events
         addedToStage="log(event);"
         removedFromStage="log(event);">         ⟵  Log removedFromStage
  <s:Ellipse width="200" height="200">              event
    <s:fill>
      <s:SolidColor color.green="green" color.blue="blue" />
    </s:fill>
  </s:Ellipse>
</s:Group>
</s:Application>
```

There are a few changes to this listing from listing 14.7. First, you wrapped the Rect and Ellipse in their own Group so you could access the policies. Second, you added policies to each group, and you're calling the log method for a few events so you can see when elements are created and destroyed. Visually there are no changes. To see what happens you can look at the trace log as you change states. Your initial application state yields the following traces:

```
boxElement creationComplete
boxElement addedToStage
Including2 applicationComplete
Including2.ApplicationSkin3._ApplicationSkin_Group1.contentGroup.boxElement
    - circleElement
```

Notice that the first trace is the boxElement being created and then added to the stage. This happens immediately because the selected state is orange, which is in the box group. The next two lines are custom traces from Including2, the name of our Application, which shows the application complete event and traces the boxElement and circleElement. Notice that the boxElement has a parent component and circleElement doesn't. boxElement has a parent because it has been added to the stage, but circle doesn't, but it does exist because of the creation policy you set: itemCreationPolicy="immediate". This tells the Application to create this child element immediately, allowing you access to the element on startup. If the creation policy was set to deferred, the element would be created only when it's needed. As you move to the next state, the trace shows the following:

```
_Including2_Button1 click
boxElement removedFromStage
boxElement addedToStage
```

The first trace is the button click. Next, the boxElement is removed from the stage and then added back to the stage. Remember, you're changing states here and using includeIn, so while the state changes, the element is removed and then added back in. Keep this in mind when using addedToStage as a trigger for certain functionality. The next state is a part of the circle group, so you'll see a few more lines:

```
_Including2_Button1 click
boxElement removedFromStage
circleElement addedToStage
circleElement creationComplete
```

The button click changes the state to green, and you can see that the boxElement is removed from the stage and then the circle is added and creation complete is dispatched. The circleElement is now visible and the boxElement is gone. If you traced boxElement, it would show null because it has been fully removed. This is important because your code can no longer reference boxElement if it has been destroyed. We'll discuss the destruction in a second, but for now let's move to the final state:

```
_Including2_Button1 click
circleElement removedFromStage
circleElement addedToStage
```

There's nothing new here. The button is clicked and the circleElement is removed and then added. You've reached the end of the states, but you're going to go to one more state, the beginning state orange, to see what happens to circleElement:

```
_Including2_Button1 click
circleElement removedFromStage
boxElement addedToStage
boxElement creationComplete
```

This is the exact opposite from what happened when going from the box group to circle. There's a huge difference, though. You set the circleElement item-DestructionPolicy to never, so tracing circleElement here doesn't show null. This means the object was created, but it was not and never will be destroyed, so it's always available. If your code calls for the elements to always be around, use never as your destruction policy.

Table 14.3 shows the available values for each policy.

Table 14.3 Available policies

Policy	Values	Description
itemCreationPolicy	deferred immediate	Create the element only when it's needed. Create the element immediately.
itemDestructionPolicy	auto never	Let Flex determine when to destroy. Never destroy the element.

We've now covered adding and removing, including when elements are created and destroyed, but sometimes you might want to move an element from one parent to another instead of deleting it. Think of an application with horizontal and vertical looks. When the application moves from horizontal to vertical, you may want to move a graphic from one parent to another in order to position it properly in the view. This is called *reparenting* and is our next stop.

14.2.5 Reparenting components

To reparent an element you can use ActionScript: newParent.addChild(myElement);. That's easy enough, but maybe you want to be the cool kid on the playground who uses as little ActionScript as possible, if such a playground exists. You can achieve reparenting by using a new state class: Reparent. It might seem a little odd at first, but think of Reparent as a placeholder class. Listing 14.8 shows Reparent in action.

Listing 14.8 Reparenting elements

```xml
<?xml version="1.0" encoding="utf-8"?>
<s:Application xmlns:fx="http://ns.adobe.com/mxml/2009"
               xmlns:s="library://ns.adobe.com/flex/spark"
               xmlns:mx="library://ns.adobe.com/flex/halo">
  <s:layout>
    <s:VerticalLayout paddingLeft="20" paddingTop="20" gap="20" />
  </s:layout>
  <s:states>
    <s:State name="boxLeft" />                    State
    <s:State name="boxRight" />                   declarations
  </s:states>
```

```
<s:HGroup>
</s:HGroup>
<s:HGroup gap="20">
  <s:VGroup id="left" width="200" height="200">
    <s:Label text="Left" />
    <s:Button id="button" includeIn="boxLeft"
            label="box &gt;&gt;"
            label.boxRight="&lt;&lt; box"
            click.boxLeft="currentState='boxRight'"
            click.boxRight="currentState='boxLeft'"/>
    <s:Rect id="boxElement" width="200" height="200"
            includeIn="boxLeft">
      <s:fill>
        <s:SolidColor color="#de7800" />
      </s:fill>
    </s:Rect>
  </s:VGroup>
  <s:VGroup id="right" width="200" height="200">
    <s:Label text="Right" />
    <fx:Reparent target="boxElement" includeIn="boxRight" />
    <fx:Reparent target="button" includeIn="boxRight" />
  </s:VGroup>
</s:HGroup>
</s:Application>
```

Parent I
(left side)

Button to
toggle state

Rect to move
between sides

Parent 2
(right side)

boxElement
placeholder

Button
placeholder

Let's look at this visual before we step through the code. Figure 14.8 shows the initial state of our application.

As figure 14.8 shows, your initial view consists of a label, the toggle button, and the orange rectangle. What you need to look at is the use of includeIn for the rectangle. You're telling Flex you want to include the rectangle in the boxLeft state, meaning you're excluding it from all other states including boxRight. When the button is clicked, the rectangle will be removed from the stage and, depending on the destruction policy, deleted, but because you have a Reparent component targeting the box, the element is removed from boxLeft and added to boxRight. The same goes for the button because it's included in boxLeft and has a Reparent included, boxRight. Let's look at the Reparent code by itself in the following snippet:

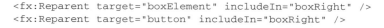

```
<fx:Reparent target="boxElement" includeIn="boxRight" />
<fx:Reparent target="button" includeIn="boxRight" />
```

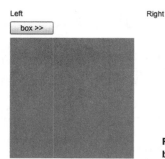

Figure 14.8   Initial view with the button and box on the left

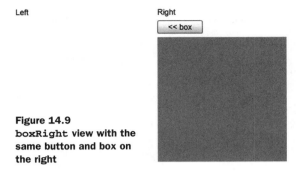

Figure 14.9
boxRight view with the same button and box on the right

What's happening here is state specific. In plain English, the above says: When the currentState changes to boxRight, move the boxElement and button to this parent. Where you put the Reparent component is where the target will show up, and it will show when one of the states listed in includeIn is active. Figure 14.9 shows the boxRight state.

> **NOTE** Always keep in mind the use case for a Reparent. The idea is to change the parent of a component when you enter a different state. This means you can't have the component in two places at once, so all Reparent instances must reference a different state from the one the component already resides in. In simpler terms, you can't Reparent a component into two separate parents within the same state.

Reparenting is definitely different than Flex 3, if you used it, but as you can see, it's much cleaner and pretty easy to implement. We've shown how to add and remove as well as reparent. At times we may need a little more detail on when a state is changing. We can do so by exploring state events.

14.2.6 State events

Everything to this point has been sort of autopilot on states. You changed states and your app responded, but you didn't do anything with the state changes. Even though you didn't, you absolutely could listen for state changes and respond accordingly, as shown in the following listing.

Listing 14.9 Listing for state events

```
<?xml version="1.0" encoding="utf-8"?>
<s:Application xmlns:fx="http://ns.adobe.com/mxml/2009"
               xmlns:s="library://ns.adobe.com/flex/spark"
               xmlns:mx="library://ns.adobe.com/flex/halo"
               currentStateChange="log('change: '+currentState);"
               currentStateChanging="log('change: '+currentState);">
  <s:layout>
    <s:VerticalLayout />
  </s:layout>
  <s:states>
```

Handle state change ◁

Handle the state changing ◁

```
    <s:State name="orange"
            enterState="log('--orange enter')"
            exitState="log('--orange exit')" />
    <s:State name="black"
            enterState="log('--black enter')"
            exitState="log('--black exit')" />
  </s:states>
  <fx:Script>
    <![CDATA[
      protected function log(text:String):void{
        logElement.text += text + "\n";
      }
    ]]>
  </fx:Script>
  <s:HGroup>
    <s:Button label.orange="Black" label.black="Orange"
            click.orange="currentState = 'black'"
            click.black="currentState = 'orange'" />
  </s:HGroup>
  <s:Rect width="300" height="200">
    <s:fill>
      <s:SolidColor color.black="#000000" color.orange="#de7800" />
    </s:fill>
  </s:Rect>
  <s:TextArea id="logElement" width="300" height="150" />
</s:Application>
```

Handle orange's enter and exit states

Handle black's enter and exit states

On the Application we're listening for two events: currentStateChange and current-StateChanging. Table 14.2 provides detailed descriptions of the two events, but what happens during both events is that you log some text plus the currentState property so that you can see when they happen and what the state is at the time of each event.

Each state declaration also listens for the enterState and exitState events. These events tell you when a specific state is entered or exited, respectively. The visuals in the application are the same as before but with a slightly wider rectangle and a TextArea for logging. Figure 14.10 shows the application after changing from orange (default state) to black and back to orange.

Notice the initial changing log. It shows currentState as null, and then immediately you see that the orange state is entered, and finally the Application is fully in the orange state, so the change event is dispatched. At this point your application is in the orange state and all state events are done. When you click the button to change to black, notice that the first event is a changing event and it shows that the

Figure 14.10 Application after three state changes

currentstate is orange. Next you see that the orange state is exited, and you enter the black state, rounding it off with a final change showing that the new value for currentState is black. After a third button click you see the same thing but opposite, switching from black to orange. You're not doing anything within your event handlers, but as you can see, you have knowledge, from a code perspective, of all of the levels of your application when going through state changes. You can build on this and use it to save the user's current state in a shared object, database, and so on, so the next time they open your application they return to the proper state.

State events are no different from any other event. They provide a window into the state-changing process and allow you full control over your application during state changes. You can use the events to store the view's last state so returning users can start in their last location or trigger a new data call to grab new information. Your states skill set is ready for primetime now. In the next section you take your newfound knowledge and build a mock real-world application.

14.3 Bring it together

We've covered all of the state functionality: changing properties, event handlers, state groups, adding and removing children, and managing state events. Everything so far has shown simple examples for you to build on yourself. We don't want to leave you without showing a real-world example, so let's explore how you can utilize states in a sample real-world application. Listing 14.10 shows your application's code.

Listing 14.10 Real-world state example

```
<?xml version="1.0" encoding="utf-8"?>
<s:Application xmlns:fx="http://ns.adobe.com/mxml/2009"
               xmlns:s="library://ns.adobe.com/flex/spark"
               xmlns:mx="library://ns.adobe.com/flex/halo"
               xmlns:views="views.*"
               applicationComplete="init()">
  <s:layout>
    <s:VerticalLayout paddingLeft="20" paddingTop="20" />
  </s:layout>
  <s:states>
    <s:State name="login" stateGroups="loggedOut" />         ◁┐  State declaration for
    <s:State name="computers" stateGroups="loggedIn" />          loggedOut group
    <s:State name="info" stateGroups="loggedIn" />           ┐  State declarations
    <s:State name="tv" stateGroups="loggedIn" />             │  for loggedIn
  </s:states>                                                 │  group
  <s:Panel includeIn="loggedOut" title.login="Get in there!">  ◁┐
    <s:layout>                                                      Login view
      <s:VerticalLayout />
    </s:layout>
    <mx:Form>
      <mx:FormItem label="Username">
        <s:TextInput />
      </mx:FormItem>
      <mx:FormItem label="Password">
        <s:TextInput />
```

```
        </mx:FormItem>
      </mx:Form>
      <mx:ControlBar>
        <s:Button label="Login" click="currentState='computers'"/>
      </mx:ControlBar>
    </s:Panel>
    <s:HGroup includeIn="loggedIn">                    ←—— Application menu
      <s:ButtonBar dataProvider="{contentStack}" />
      <s:Button label="log out" color="black" click="currentState='login'"/>
    </s:HGroup>
    <mx:ViewStack id="contentStack" includeIn="loggedIn">    ←┐  ViewStack
      <views:ComputersView label="Computers" />                │  showing content
      <views:InfoForm label="Info" />
      <views:TVView label="TVs" />
    </mx:ViewStack>
</s:Application>
```

This application should look a little familiar. It uses a similar `login` component to figure 14.1, without the Forgot Password? button, and the `ViewStack` and `ButtonBar` are from chapter 12. Your states are defined in groups based on the current user "session" status, logged in or out. For brevity, you're faking a real login, so the Login button changes the state to the computer's state, which shows the user as logged in. Once you're logged in, the menu

Figure 14.11   Initial application view

and `ViewStack` show. This provides you with three buttons for the `ViewStack` and a Log Out button, which sends you back to the `login` state.

The application should be pretty readable for you by now. It uses a combination of what you've learned to this point, from this and other chapters, to showcase how you can use states in your application. Figure 14.11 shows the initial application view, and figure 14.12 shows the logged-in state.

This is still a simple example, but you can see now where you can tie in user authentication, change states, and see the full application with the user logged in. The syntax is enormously easier than that of Flex 3, leading to much cleaner, leaner, and more readable code. You're now equipped and ready to utilize states. Congratulations on beginning to utilize MXML to its fullest!

14.4   Summary

States are a great asset to your development toolbox. You can use states to manipulate component properties, set specific click

Figure 14.12   View in the computer's state

handlers, add and remove objects from the display, control when elements are created and/or removed from the display list, move objects between parents, and control each phase of your states through events. If you're coming from a world of Flex 3 states, you've probably moved Adobe up your Christmas list to a higher spot. In the next chapter you'll learn how to integrate data services into your application.

Working with data services

15

This chapter covers

- Data-centric development with Flash Builder
- Connecting to web services
- Using `HTTPService` and `WebService` components
- Understanding Action Message Format (AMF)
- Communication with Java EE using BlazeDS
- ColdFusion communication
- Communicating with PHP via Zend_AMF
- Setting up your development environment for a seamless client/server workflow

Integrating an RIA client application with its corresponding server-side application services can be a daunting task the first time you do it, so if you don't have much experience in this area, strap in tight because you're going to be spending about the next hour or so getting the crash course in RIA data communications. By the time you've finished with this chapter, you'll have a level of confidence that's felt by experts in the field, and you'll be considered a top resource in your workplace for enterprise data communications for RIA.

316

Client/server RIA communication gets easier the more you do it. Understanding the inner workings of how a Flex application communicates with data services will provide you with the knowledge to be able to connect a Flex or AIR application to any server-side technology, even if you don't know the server-side language being used. This is a highly sought-after skill set that you'll be able to add to your arsenal upon completing this chapter.

15.1 Accessing server-side data

RIA architects often find themselves bewildered when faced with the dilemma of choosing a web service infrastructure. Knowing the technology that's available in this area is critical, because the wrong decision could be catastrophic. Table 15.1 is a high-level overview of the services that are available to you and can be used as a reference when making infrastructure design decisions.

Table 15.1   Web service protocol matrix

Communication Server support	Application	Benefits
HTTP (includes REST and RPC hybrids)		
- All	Simple widget-based applications; speed and real-time UI updates aren't required.	Easy implementation via the `HTTPService` object; RPC hybrid protocols can be invoked using `RemoteObject`.
SOAP/WSDL		
- All	Data aggregation from external web services.	Easy implementation; pull data from multiple outside resources regardless of platform.
AMF		
- BlazeDS & LiveCycle Data Services (LCDS): Java, - .NETZend: PHP - AMFPHP: PHP - WebOrb: .NET, Ruby, PHP	Approaching enterprise level; speed is important; data is usually pulled from server by polling.	Binary data compression makes communications 12 times faster; strong data typing; multiplatform support.
RTMP		
- LiveCycle Data Services (LCDS), - Flash Media Server (FMS)	Enterprise level, messaging, instantaneous UI updates; data can be pushed to the client; streaming media content; data-intensive RIAs.	Integrates into existing J2EE infrastructure; document management, rapid data transfer, clustering, data tracking, syncing, paging, and conflict resolution.
Flash Remoting		
- Native to ColdFusion	Robust, enterprise platform for client/server Flex communications; native.	Seamless integration with the Flash platform; removes the need for an intermediate code library to do data type mapping and data serialization.

Table 15.1　Web service protocol matrix *(continued)*

Communication Server support	Application	Benefits
JSON		
- All (JavaScript data objects are serialized and transferred in binary form.)	AIR applications that use AJAX or Flex applications that use the `ExternalInterface` API.	Easy implementation with the `HTTPService` object; part of the AS3CorLib library.

TIP　Note that you must place a cross-domain policy file at the root of the domain in order to use the HTTPService object. If you aren't familiar with the cross-domain policy, the Adobe Developer Connection has a good resource at the following web address: http://www.adobe.com/devnet/articles/ crossdomain_policy_file_spec.html.

Table 15.1 is a basic protocol matrix that provides a starting point for knowing when to use each of the technologies available for Flex data communications along with the benefits that can be gained for each of them.

15.1.1　Using the HTTPService object

Because the `HTTPService` object uses the same request-response paradigm as your Internet browser does when it displays web content, it can be used to invoke operations on any server-side technology with `GET` and `POST`. It doesn't require an intermediate code library for socket-level serialization and parsing as other data communication protocols do. Listing 15.1 illustrates how the `HTTPService` object is declared in MXML so it can be invoked later to run a search query on the Yahoo! search engine.

Listing 15.1　The `HTTPService` object declared in MXML notation

```
<mx:HTTPService
    id="yahooHTTPService"
    url="http://search.yahooapis.com/WebSearchService/V1/webSearch"
    method="GET"                              ⊲──── Request can be GET or POST
    makeObjectsBindable="true"                ⊲──── Makes result object bindable
    result="responseHandler(event)"           ⊲──── Declare the method to handle the result
    fault="httpFaultHandler(event)"           ⊲──── Declare a method to handle a fault
    showBusyCursor="true">                     ⊲──── Show busy cursor while in progress
</mx:HTTPService>
```

Before the service is invoked, a request object is set up so the necessary arguments can be sent with the service call; see the following listing.

Listing 15.2　Calling the `HTTPService` from ActionScript

```
<fx:Script>
  <![CDATA[

  import mx.rpc.events.ResultEvent;
  import mx.rpc.events.FaultEvent;
```

```
public function sendHttpRequest():void {
    var requestObj:Object = new Object();
    requestObj.appid = new String("YahooDemo");
    requestObj.query =
        new String("Flex in Action");
    requestObj.results = new int(2);
    yahooHTTPService.request = requestObj;
    yahooHTTPService.send();
}

private function
    responseHandler(e:ResultEvent):void {
    trace("Received a result: " + e.result);
}

private function
    httpFaultHandler(e:FaultEvent):void {
    trace("Received a Fault: " + e.message);
}
    ]]>
</fx:Script>
```

1 Generic object created to send with request

2 Service variables passed into object

3 Generic object passed to property

4 `HTTPService.send()` method called

5 Response handler

6 Fault handler

As shown in listing 15.2, the function sendHTTPRequest() invokes the HTTPService object. Before that happens, though, a generic object called requestObj is created **1** and the variables appid, query, and results are passed to it **2**, which the Yahoo! service will expect to find on the generic object when it receives the request. The requestObj is then passed into the HTTPService.request property **3**, and finally the HTTPService.send() method is called **4**.

In addition, the functions named responseHandler and faultHandler (**5 6**) are implemented to catch the event that's triggered by the service's response to the request. As you can see in the Alert.show that's called in the body of the response-Handler function, the data that's returned from the server can be accessed through the generic ResultEvent.result property. Any data type can be passed through this property, including value objects (or data transfer objects if you come from the world of Java or .NET development). You've learned all about the HTTPService object, which makes this an excellent opportunity to introduce you to the WebService object, as you'll see in the next section.

15.1.2 Consuming web services with the WebService component

Web Service Description Language (WSDL) is a standard format for describing SOAP- and RPC-based web services. This type of data consumption is great for mash-up-style applications, because many online services have adopted the Simple Object Access Protocol (SOAP) standard, but this is generally the slowest way to transfer data because it carries a lot of overhead with it. On the other hand, SOAP is similar to HTTP in that it's supported by just about every server-side platform.

Setting up web service integration in Flex is easy and takes only a few lines of code. For example, if you wanted to use the <mx:WebService> tag to connect to the weather web service, it would look like the code in the following listing.

Listing 15.3   Using the `WebService` component

```
<mx:WebService id="weatherService"                    Declare the WSDL document location  ❶
    wsdl="http://www.webservicex.net/WeatherForecast.asmx?WSDL"
    fault="wsdlFault(event)">
      <mx:operation name="GetWeatherByZipCode"                  Multiple operation
          result="weatherResponse(event)"                  ❷ declarations within
          fault="weatherFault(event)"/>                        a WebService
      <mx:operation name="GetWeatherByPlaceName"
          result="weatherResponse(event)"
          fault="weatherFault(event)"/>
</mx:WebService>
```

The `<mx:WebService>` tag contains the necessary information to point the Flex application to the WSDL document ❶. When the `<mx:WebService>` tag is initialized, it parses the WSDL document and extracts the information it needs to generate Flex objects with which you can interact with the web service.

The `operation` tags ❷ define the various operations that are used with this web service. In this case, the `GetWeatherByZipCode` and `GetWeatherByPlaceName` operations are defined and ready for you to invoke in the same way as you did earlier with the `HTTPService` object. Each operation has a handler defined to deal with the response from the service request.

TIP   In some cases, a web service you'd like to connect to may use methods that are reserved words in Flex. In these situations, you can use the `WebService.getOperation("nameOfOperation")` function to get a handle for the operation.

Flex removes the responsibility of translating SOAP XML packets into usable objects by abstracting the functionality for parsing SOAP packets within the `WebService` class. You can obtain the data object that's created after parsing is completed from the generic object `ResultEvent.result` after parsing of the data packets has completed and the `ResultEvent` is fired and captured by your result handler function.

15.2   *Action Message Format in action*

As you saw back in table 15.1 at the beginning of the chapter, the Action Message Format is a robust communication protocol that's quickly becoming the preferred method of communication among RIA developers because of its open technology, speed, and native support for the Flash virtual machine.

To show how fast AMF is, Adobe senior technical evangelist James Ward wrote a Census RIA Benchmark application. He's been updating it over the course of the last couple of years with new features and has included as many ways of transferring data as the community has been able to throw at him. Despite stiff competition from some serious community challengers, the AMF protocol remains the reigning champion. Figure 15.1 provides a screenshot of the application, which can be found at http://www.jamesward.com/census/.

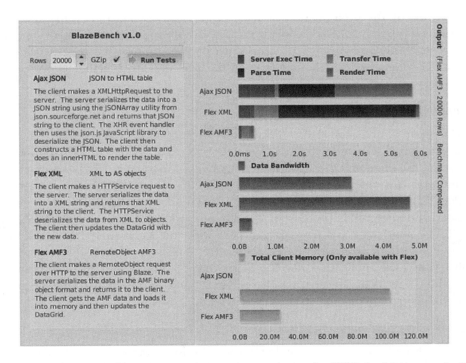

Figure 15.1 James Ward's benchmark illustrates how impressive AMF is for data communication.

Comparing data transfer times is truly a dose of reality. In figure 15.1, I set the number of rows to retrieve to a minimum of 500 (from 5,000) and turned off GZIP compression, and then I ran benchmarks only on data transfer mechanisms that are comparable to AMF3.

Upon running the same benchmark on any of the cases that involved SOAP, my browser usually hung after about 90 seconds. It then displayed a message that the server was taking a long time to respond, prompting me to tell it whether I wanted to continue waiting or not. This was appalling, and yet I found it to be quite humorous at the same time. Spend a few minutes with the Census RIA Benchmark application, and I guarantee that you'll think twice about your choice of communication protocol the next time you build an enterprise Flex application.

AMF presents you with a number of choices with regard to its implementation, but the options are usually narrowed by your choice of server-side technology. In the next sections, we'll do a brief roundup of the technologies available at the time of this writing.

15.2.1 Open-source AMF

In December of 2007, Adobe announced that AMF would become an open protocol, which immediately led to the development of a number of code libraries, many of which mimicked the data transfer capabilities with ColdFusion via Flash Remoting.

Opening up the protocol was the icing on the cake for most Flash platform developers. It was already speedier than anything else, and its support is native to the Flash virtual machine. The number of open source code libraries that were developed soon after is evidence of this. Getting to know the tools that are available for data communication with AMF is simple.

15.2.2 AMF with PHP

The open source AMFPHP project began in January of 2008, right after AMF went open source. It included a fairly steep learning curve for developers who were new to Flex at the time, and there was little documentation to go by, resulting in a lot of trial and error for determined PHP RIA programmers. Thankfully, Adobe formed a strategic alliance with Zend Technologies in Q308, and the Zend_AMF module was developed and integrated into the PHP Zend framework by a friend of mine, Wade Arnold.

The Zend_AMF module is easy to work with and is currently the ideal solution for data communication between Flex and PHP, especially if you're using Flash Builder for your Flex application development. One of the greatest new features of Flash Builder 4 is its ability to turbocharge your workflow by automating the process of hooking up data services, as you'll see in section 15.3.

15.2.3 AMF and ColdFusion

At the time of this writing, the beta of ColdFusion 9 was just released along with the first-ever ColdFusion development tool made by Adobe, called CFBuilder. Not surprisingly, AMF is most effective when working with ColdFusion because it has native support for the AMF format. That means that when running a Flash platform RIA application on the client with ColdFusion data services on the server, you have native support for the fastest available data-transfer mechanism on both the client and the server.

The result is a rich, web-based application that operates as if it's running native to the local desktop. More specifically, massive amounts of data can be captured, filtered, organized, processed, and displayed in a human-readable graphical summation in less than a second. It was merely a few years ago that this kind of query would be run by a research technician, who would then get up and go have lunch and come back 45 minutes later only to find that the query was not complete yet.

15.2.4 BlazeDS

Adobe open-sourced the AMF specification in tandem with the release of BlazeDS, an open source Java application that can be used for integrating Java and Flex via AMF. With BlazeDS, developers can invoke methods on preexisting plain old Java objects (POJOs), Spring Services, EJBs, and other Enterprise Java implementations. Blaze can also be hooked into JMS and Hibernate for applications that require messaging. Java application servers supported by BlazeDS include Tomcat, WebSphere, WebLogic, JBoss, and ColdFusion.

15.2.5 LiveCycle Data Services

BlazeDS was an offspring of LiveCycle Data Services ES. It's logical to assert that BlazeDS is the baby sibling of LCDS. The target market for LCDS is primarily large-scale enterprise environments consisting of large server farms. Considering the cost of a single LCDS license, it's no wonder that most small businesses and entrepreneurial developers view LCDS as out of reach. As with BlazeDS, LCDS is a Java-based implementation of AMF and offers additional advantages that are conducive to the needs of the enterprise. The cost is typically justified by the level of support that comes with the package.

15.2.6 Additional technologies

Other technologies that have surfaced over the last couple of years include WebOrb, AMF.NET, AMFPHP, and RubyAMF. But the three that stand out among the rest in the RIA arena are Zend_AMF, ColdFusion Remoting, and BlazeDS for Java EE. We'll be focusing on those technologies for the remainder of this chapter.

You're now armed with the background knowledge that you'll need to embark on your next mission: learning to build data-centric AMF applications using Flash Builder.

15.3 Building data-centric applications with Flash Builder

The data-centric development (DCD) features that ship with Flash Builder were created to shave a significant amount of development time for data-driven Flex applications and are undoubtedly my personal favorite of all the new Flash Builder features.

The first thing to point out with regard to the highly anticipated data-centric development features included in Flash Builder 4 is that the workflow generally remains the same regardless of the server-side technology being used. In a moment we'll walk through this workflow. I'll point out differences in the workflow that are dependent on the server-side technology being used as we walk through the examples.

Development time is cut down by implementing a series of DCD wizards that guide you through the process of connecting to your server-side code and transferring strongly typed data objects, otherwise known as *value objects*. While you're guided through the wizards, code is being generated in the background for you. The following example demonstrates how you can truly streamline your workflow for connecting to data services without even leaving the design view of the Flash Builder IDE!

15.3.1 Setting up the right environment

When developing RIA applications, your integrated development environment (IDE) should reflect both the client and server-side platforms you're working with. Table 15.2 provides a list of recommendations for how you can configure your environment based on your choice of server-side platform.

The concept of the IDE matrix shown in table 15.2 is to be able to do both client and server-side development without leaving the Eclipse environment. This will streamline your workflow and save you a lot of time.

Table 15.2   Eclipse IDE configuration matrix for data-driven Flex 4 RIA development

PHP	Eclipse PDT + Flash Builder 4 plug-in	Zend Studio + Flash Builder 4 plug-in
J2EE/Blaze/LCDS	Eclipse for Java + Flash Builder 4 plug-in	Eclipse for Java EE + Flash Builder plug-in
ColdFusion	CFEclipse + Flash Builder 4 plug-in	CFBuilder + Flash Builder 4 plug-in
WSDL	Flash Builder 4 + WDT Eclipse plug-in	WDT Eclipse + Flash Builder 4 plug-in
.NET	Flash Builder 4 + WDT Eclipse plug-in	WDT Eclipse + Flash Builder 4 plug-in

HTTP, RPC, AMF, and SOAP, oh my!

With Flex and Flash Builder 4, there's no need to be overwhelmed by the choice in protocol for your data communications. Flash Builder 4 takes care of most of this for you behind the scenes when you use the DCD wizards and tries to use Action Message Format for data communications whenever possible because of its superior transfer speeds, among other things.

15.3.2 *Establishing connection to the server*

Because the Flex framework is based on a Model-View-Controller architecture, it's usually in your best interest to maintain consistency by using MVC methodology in your application as well. In this section, we'll focus on using the Flash Builder GUI to generate the code for the model layer of your application. But first you need to establish a connection to your server-side application layer.

> **TIP** The data-centric development workflow built into the Flash Builder 4 IDE is almost identical between integrating with PHP and integrating with ColdFusion services.

You have two scenarios for connecting to a data service: Either you're trying to connect from a project that already exists, or you're starting fresh with a new project.

In the first scenario, you have an existing project that you'd like to connect to a data service. This is easily done by selecting the Connect to Data/Service link from the Data/Services panel in Flash Builder, as shown in figure 15.2.

In the second scenario, you can set up the connection to the server during creation of a new Flash Builder project. As shown in figure 15.4, the New Project Setup Wizard includes a drop-down menu that allows you to select an application server for configuration during the project setup process. The options are None/Other, .NET, J2EE, ColdFusion, and PHP.

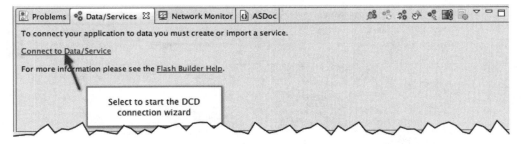

Figure 15.2   Select Connect to Data/Service from the Data/Services panel to start the DCD wizard. You're then greeted with the window shown in figure 15.3, which lists all of the service types that you can connect to.

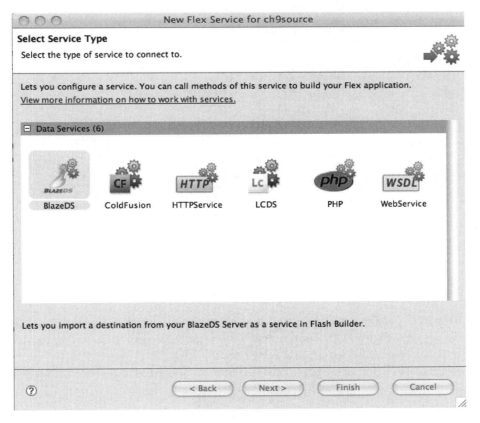

Figure 15.3   Select from the list of available service types.

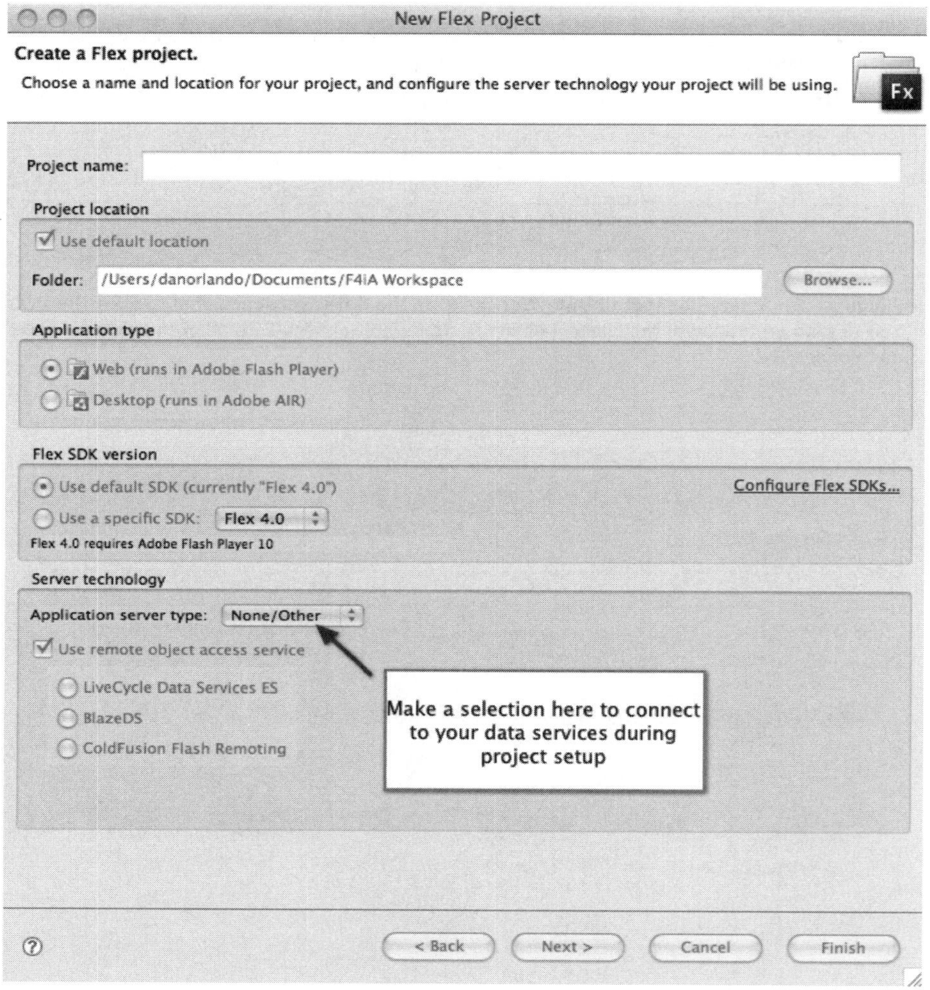

Figure 15.4   Use the drop-down menu to set up the application server when creating a new project in Flash Builder.

Regardless of the scenario, you'll end up in the same place, the server configuration dialog box. Figure 15.5 demonstrates the server configuration dialog window after I selected PHP as the application server type.

Regardless of the server type, Flash Builder is concerned about two things here:

1   The endpoint URI that it should connect to
2   Validating that it's able to connect successfully

After you enter the necessary parameters in the configuration fields, the button labeled Validate Configuration will be enabled. The wizard won't allow you to continue until you successfully validate your server configuration. You'll know when

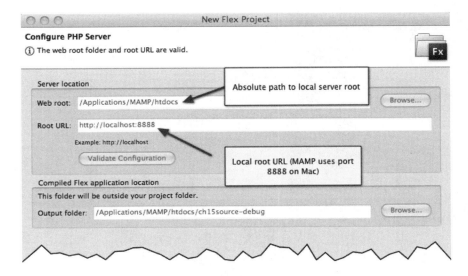

Figure 15.5 Configuring a local PHP server for DCD in Flash Builder

validation is successful because you'll see a friendly message at the top of the window, as shown in figure 15.5.

> **NOTE** If you're working with PHP on the server side, and Flash Builder sees that you don't yet have the Zend Framework installed, it will ask you if you want it to be installed. This is done so you can take advantage of the benefits of AMF through the Zend_AMF module. Make sure you select Yes if you're prompted with this message.

Now you're ready to have some fun as you learn how to autogenerate your services right from Flash Builder!

GENERATING SERVICES

One of the neatest things about the DCD features in Flash Builder 4 is the ability for the application to generate basic services for you containing standard CRUD operations for a specified database table. It also includes other handy operations such as retrieving paged result sets (20 at a time, for example).

If you've already created your database schema, Flash Builder can read the schema of a specified table and generate all the code you should need for a basic service from it. If that table contains many fields, the amount of time that this can save is immeasurable.

The process of generating a service stub begins by selecting the Click Here to Generate a Sample link under the PHP Location field, as shown in figure 15.6. If the code for your service has already been written, however, you can use this window to specify the name and location of the service so it can be introspected by Flash Builder.

The dialog box that appears next in the sequence is displayed in figure 15.7. To take full advantage of the built-in DCD features, make sure you've first created a data-

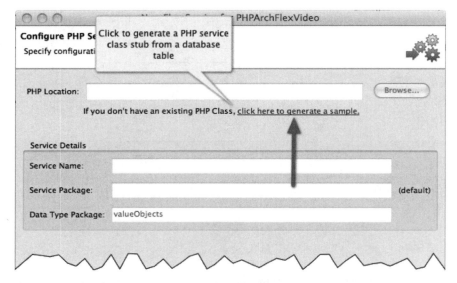

Figure 15.6   Service stubs can be generated right from the service configuration dialog box.

base and a table with fields inside your database. Then, make sure that Generate from Database is already selected when the sample service generator window opens. Fill in the rest of the parameters according to your database configuration, and click the Connect to Database button. You'll begin to see the magic happen.

Assuming all of your input parameters were correct and Flash Builder connected to the database you specified, you'll notice that all of a sudden the Table drop-down menu populates with all of the tables in your database. The next thing you need to do is select the table that you want to use to generate the service stub. Now click OK, and let the games begin!

The first thing you might think is that Flash Builder took on a mind of its own, and you may wonder what just happened when it's finished. Here's a rundown of what happened in those few tenths of a second:

- A package was added to your src folder.
- A services folder appeared under the libs folder.
- The service class was generated and opened up in the main editing pane of the Eclipse IDE or the default editor on your system if it isn't Eclipse for that file type.
- The class was introspected by Flash Builder, and all of its methods were displayed in the Data/Services panel.
- An abstract class was created in the project that contains methods to easily call each of the service's operations.
- An empty class was also created that makes the call to the super (abstract) class. The empty class is where you should place any custom code you might need.

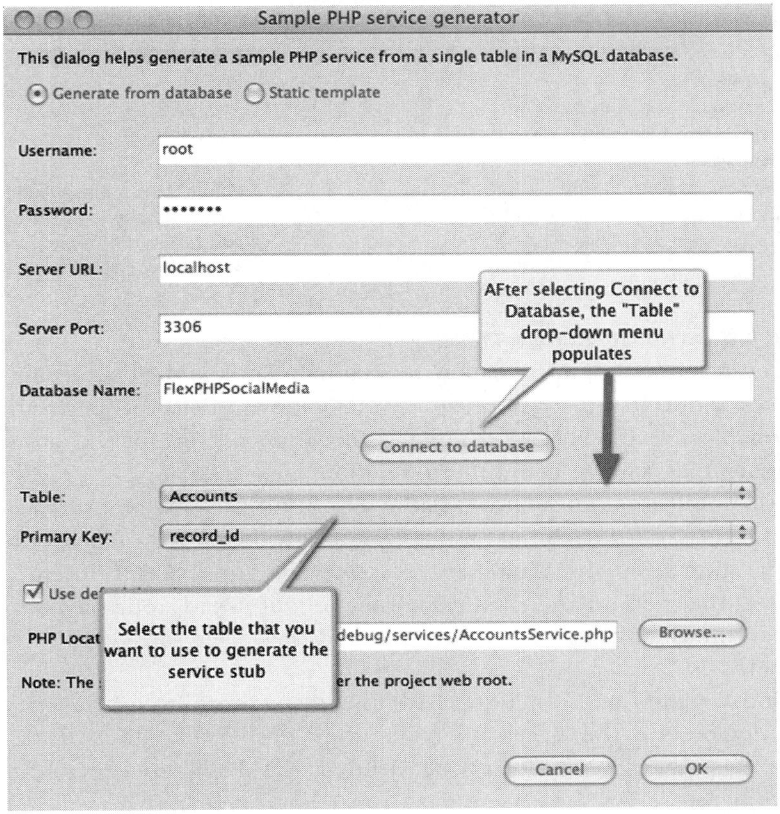

Figure 15.7 The database table names appear in a drop-down menu after the Connect to Database button is clicked.

If you're working in the full version of Flash Builder without having installed the necessary editor for your service code into the IDE, Flash Builder opens the generated service with whatever the default application is for that file type (most likely Adobe Dreamweaver, if it's installed on your local machine).

> **MIGRATION TIP** The important thing to understand is that the old paradigm that was used with previous versions of the Flex SDK—where value objects were created on the server side to correspond with value objects on the client side— has changed significantly. More specifically, you don't need to create a strongly typed PHP object that corresponds with your ActionScript objects (unless you want to!). With that said, for basic CRUD services, little coding is needed in the autogenerated PHP service other than what's already there. Configure your database connection parameters and table names accordingly.

Now that you've generated a service stub, it's time to configure your send and return types. Keep in mind that you've accomplished all of this, and you still haven't left the Flash Builder design view!

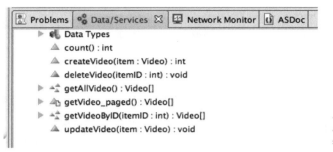

Figure 15.8 Flash Builder automatically sets the send and return data types upon service introspection.

CONFIGURING DATA SEND AND RETURN TYPES

Before you even start configuring data types manually, look at the data typings in your Data/Services panel. If you set the type in your database fields properly, then Flash Builder probably already set your data types for you, as it did for the project that's shown in figure 15.8. This is yet another incredible time-saver!

Your Flash application must know what to expect for the data object types that will be sent and returned for each operation. To configure your data types, either right-click an operation from the Data/Services pane and then click Configure Return Type, or select the method and then click the configure send/return type icon from the toolbar of the Data/Services pane. You should then see a window that looks similar to figure 15.9.

As previously mentioned, you don't have to code your own value objects anymore. You can autogenerate the necessary code when you invoke the `getAllItems()` method. In the past, when an array of strongly typed objects came back in the response from the server, it was standard practice to type the data as a bindable `ArrayCollection` declared at the top of the class and then bind the list or data grid to that `ArrayCollection` variable. You can still do things this way if you want to, but it's worth letting Flash Builder handle this for you because it makes the workflow so much faster. Figure 15.10 demonstrates how to enable autodetection of data return types.

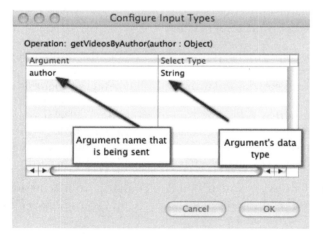

Figure 15.9 In the Configure Input Types window, you configure the parameters that will be sent with the request when the operation is invoked.

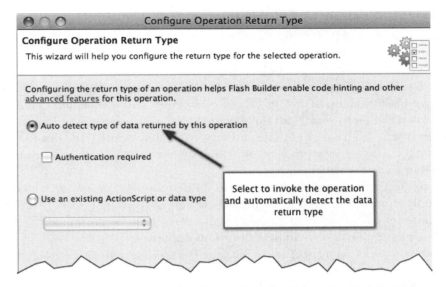

Figure 15.10   Return types can be automatically detected by letting Flash Builder invoke the operation.

The value objects that Flash Builder generates are more like value objects on steroids, in that they do a whole lot more than wrap a bunch of values for strong data typing between the client and server. For example, the return type set for getAllItems() is a User object, even though it's a collection of User objects. This is because the autogenerated result handlers are smart enough to know the difference between a single User object that's returned versus a collection of User objects. You don't have to type the result to an ArrayCollection and go through the whole typing, binding, and object-mapping process as you would have done with the old Flex Builder. Things like class mapping also made the process even more difficult. Luckily, that's all in the past.

So far you've been creating this data-centric application without leaving the design view of the Flash Builder IDE, which is pretty neat. Continuing with this theme, you'll learn how to perform drag-and-drop data binding in a moment. But before we move into drag-and-drop data binding, we'll take this opportunity to build on your data services skill set and knowledge base by showing you how to work with some of the other server technologies available.

It's important to know how to work with a diverse range of server-side technologies because you never know what you'll be working with on the server side for your next project. For example, in the last three months alone, the projects I've been involved with include WebOrb AMF for C#.NET, BlazeDS, LCDS, Tomcat/JBoss, Zend_AMF for PHP, AMFPHP, AMF.NET/C#, and a custom AMF server framework written in C++ for its increased multithreading capabilities. The more server-side technologies you can integrate your Flex applications with, the less you'll ever have to worry about finding work.

15.4   *Data-centric Flex with ColdFusion*

If you're already a PHP developer and are curious about ColdFusion, Flash Builder 4 makes it especially easy to get started. Adobe has finally added a fully supported development tool specifically for ColdFusion development to its IDE palette, called CFBuilder. From a Flex development standpoint, the coolest thing about CFBuilder is that, like Flash Builder, CFBuilder is built on Eclipse. This means that CFBuilder can be installed right into your Flash Builder IDE as a plug-in, as shown in figure 15.11, so you can handle both the client-side and server-side development of your RIA applications without leaving your primary IDE. There's never been a better time to start using ColdFusion with Flex than now.

To set up a new Flex project for use with ColdFusion services, select ColdFusion for the Application Server Type in on the first screen of the New Project Setup Wizard, and choose the Flash Remoting radio button. You'll then be prompted to set up the server configuration as you did in the previous example.

The purpose of figure 15.12 is to reiterate the point that the process of getting set up with data services is generally the same regardless of server technology. Figure 15.12 should look familiar because it's nearly identical to figure 15.5, where you configured and validated a PHP server. In this case, however, you're configuring the project for use with ColdFusion data services.

After completing the New Project Setup Wizard, select Connect to Data/Service, as you did earlier. The next pop-up window will look like figure 15.13, where you're presented with the option of setting up a ColdFusion service (Flash Remoting, in this case), `HTTPService`, or `WebService`.

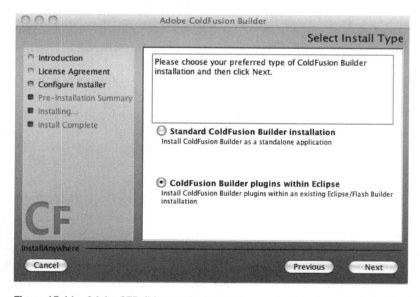

Figure 15.11   Adobe CFBuilder can be installed as a plug-in to your Flash Builder 4 IDE.

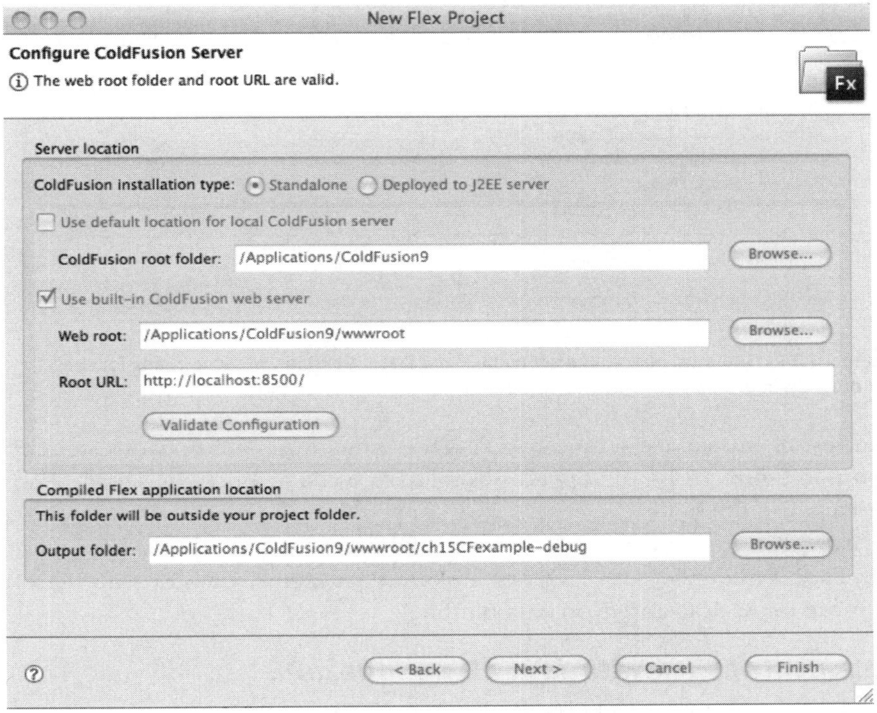

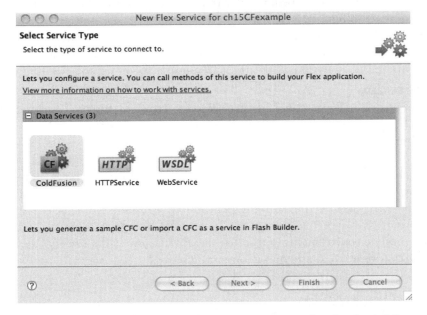

Figure 15.12   Configuring a Flex project for ColdFusion data services

Figure 15.13   Selecting ColdFusion in this case lets you take advantage of the built-in Flash Remoting.

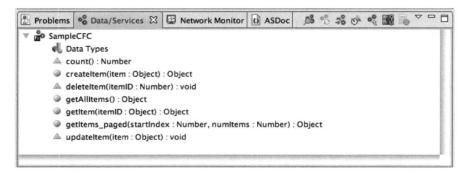

Figure 15.14   The stub operations show up in the Data/Services window, ready for drag-and-drop binding.

The rest of the service setup process is the same as for the previous example, and as shown in figure 15.14, the operations that are available once the service stub is generated are also the same.

Now that you've taken a look into ColdFusion-specific data-centric development with Flash Builder, let's take a quick look into data-centric Java EE with BlazeDS before we move on to drag-and-drop data binding.

15.5   *Data-centric Flex with Java EE and BlazeDS*

For development of the client-side Flex application, setting up a Flex project for use with J2EE web applications is as simple as selecting J2EE from the Application Server Type drop-down menu when prompted with the first window of the New Project Setup Wizard, as shown in figure 15.15.

After selecting J2EE, you're given the option of using either LiveCycle Data Services or BlazeDS. For this example, choose BlazeDS because it's powerful, the code is open source, and, best of all, it takes only about 15 minutes to get up and running with it.

SETTING UP BLAZEDS

Release builds of BlazeDS come in three flavors: Turnkey, Binary Distribution, and Source. The quickest way to get up and running is to deploy the Turnkey download. Release builds of BlazeDS are available from the Adobe Open Source website at http://opensource.adobe.com/wiki/display/blazeds/Release+Builds. In addition, Adobe evangelist Sujit Reddy G has a great post on setting up BlazeDS at http://sujitreddyg.wordpress.com/2009/04/07/setting-up-blazeds/. The BlazeDS documentation that's provided on the Adobe Open Source website also includes step-by-step instructions.

The moment you've been waiting for has finally come. It's time to tie together everything you've learned and make something useful!

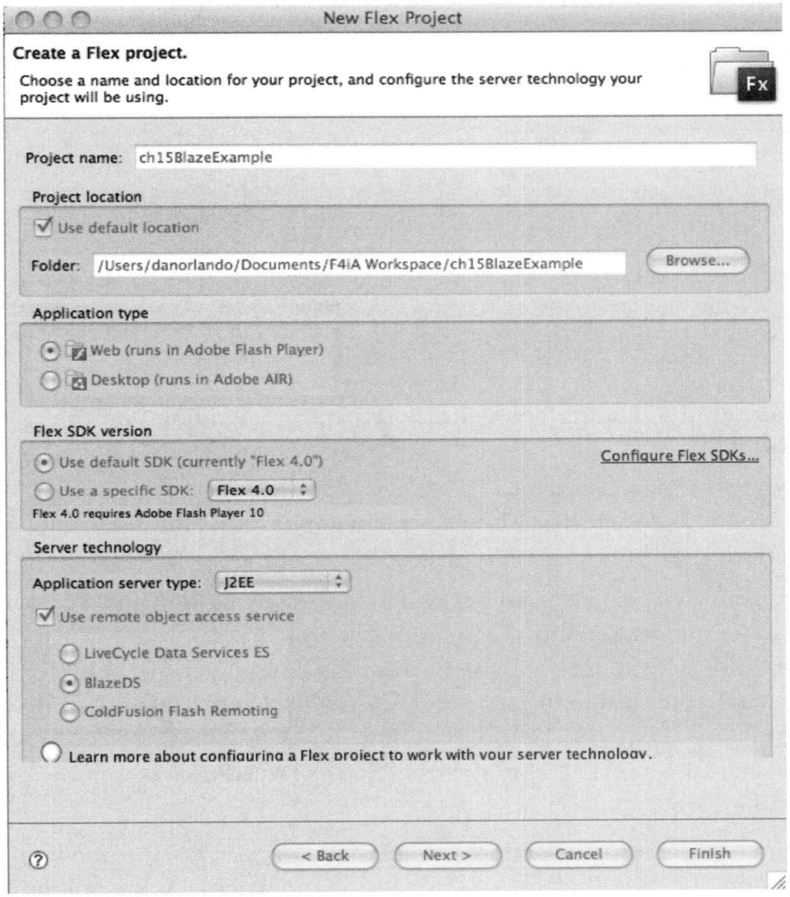

Figure 15.15 Setting up a new Flex project for use with J2EE and BlazeDS

15.6 *Binding the model to the view*

A data model is no good without a means of visualizing it. In the MVC design pattern, the model is the collection of data that's retrieved from the server side by invoking operations from a service, the view is the display of such data, and the controller is the code responsible for binding the model and the view together. In theory, this sounds great, but in practice, writing all of the code for this can be tedious and boring. Enter drag-and-drop data binding.

15.6.1 *Drag-and-drop data binding*

One of the coolest things about Flash Builder 4 is the ability to drag and drop operations from the Data/Services panel onto list-based components in design view,

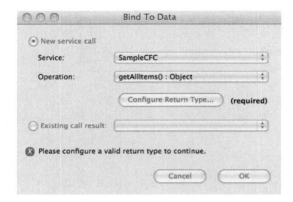

Figure 15.16 If you see this window, you need to go back and configure your return types.

effectively creating a binding between the respective operation and the component you dropped it on.

THREE SIMPLE STEPS TO DATA BINDING

Make sure you're in design view with your main application MXML file selected in the main window.

1 First, grab a VDividedBox and drag it to the stage. Set its X and Y values both to 0, and set the height and width properties to 100%.

2 Next, grab a DataGrid component from the components list and drag it to the stage so that it's inside the VDividedBox. Set its X and Y values both to 0 as well. Then set its width to 100% and its height to 30%.

3 Now select the getAllItems() method in the Data/Services window and drag it onto the DataGrid.

If you did not set the return type for your methods yet, you'll see a pop-up that looks similar to figure 15.16. Otherwise, you should immediately see the column headers autopopulate with the field names, and the number of columns should change based on the number of fields you have.

Assuming you followed the instructions in the previous section on connecting to a local database and you have data in your database, you should be able to run the application at this point. The DataGrid will display the data from your database when the application is initialized.

What if it didn't work?

A good way to pinpoint errors is to go back and invoke the methods through the return type configuration for each operation again. The error responses that come back are surprisingly detailed and will usually tell you exactly what the problem is and where it occurred (I managed to find and fix a couple of forgotten semicolons in PHP in less than a minute this way!). The Network Monitor will also come in handy during your experimentation endeavors, which we discuss shortly.

15.6.2 *Generating a Master-Detail form*

One thing is for sure: Drag-and-drop data binding is ultra cool, but generating a Master-Detail form without having to write a single line of code is even cooler!

Start by right-clicking your `DataGrid` component in design view, and select Generate Details Form. As demonstrated in figure 15.17, the window that's displayed should have Master-Detail selected as well as the Make Form Editable check box selected. Uncheck this box if you want the details of the selected item to be displayed as text fields, but you don't want the values of the selected item to be editable.

Next, select the check box labeled Make a New Service Call to Get Details. Make sure that the correct Service is selected, and for the Operation menu, select the `get-ObjectByID()` method, as shown in figure 15.17. Then click Next. The next window displayed should look similar to figure 15.18.

The Property Control Mapping window that's displayed (figure 15.18) provides you with the opportunity to unselect any fields that you don't want shown in the Master-Detail form. You can also leave a field selected and select Text for the control, which means it will display but won't be an editable item. A unique identifier field is a good example of this type of situation, which is illustrated in figure 15.18, where video_id is the unique identifier for each record. If you've been following along with a specific project of your own, you should be able to run it at this point with all the features and functionality available. Remember, *you accomplished all of this without even leaving the Flash Builder design view!*

Figure 15.17 Be sure to use the correct configuration settings for your Master-Detail form.

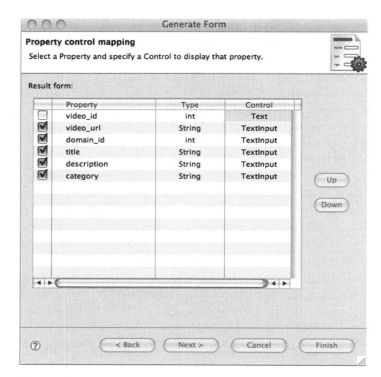

Figure 15.18   Property control mappings of the Generate Master-Detail Form Wizard

Those of you who are fairly new to Flex will certainly appreciate this, but veteran Flex programmers may want to dig a little deeper and find out what's going on behind the scenes, which is what we do in the next section.

15.6.3 *Flash Builder code review*

You accomplished a lot without looking at any of the code that was being generated behind the scenes, so now might be a good time to check up on Flash Builder and make sure it's still writing quality code. Listing 15.4 is the full set of code that should have been generated in the main MXML application file that you were working in this whole time.

Listing 15.4   DCD code generated by Flash Builder in main application file

```
<?xml version="1.0" encoding="utf-8"?>
<s:Application xmlns:fx="http://ns.adobe.com/mxml/2009"
               xmlns:s="library://ns.adobe.com/flex/spark"
               xmlns:mx="library://ns.adobe.com/flex/halo"
               minWidth="1024" minHeight="768"
                xmlns:videoservice="services.videoservice.*"
               xmlns:valueObjects="valueObjects.*">
  <fx:Script>
    <![CDATA[
      import mx.events.ListEvent;
      import mx.events.FlexEvent;
```

```
import mx.controls.Alert;
```

Function for populating the `DataGrid`

```
protected function
   dataGrid_creationCompleteHandler(event:FlexEvent):void
{
  getAllVideoResult.token = videoService.getAllVideo();
}
```

Function for when `selectedItem` is changed

```
protected function
   dataGrid_changeHandler(event:ListEvent):void
{
  getVideoByIDResult.token =
    videoService.getVideoByID(dataGrid.selectedItem.video_id);
}
```

Manual code **❶** modification for selected item

```
]]>
</fx:Script>
```

Service declarations placed within `<fx:Declarations/>`

```
<fx:Declarations>
  <s:CallResponder id="getAllVideoResult"/>
  <videoservice:VideoService id="videoService"
    fault="Alert.show(event.fault.faultString + '\n'
    + event.fault.faultDetail)"
    showBusyCursor="true"/>
  <valueObjects:Video id="video"
    domain_id="{parseInt(domain_idTextInput.text)}"/>
  <s:CallResponder id="getVideoByIDResult"
    result="video = getVideoByIDResult.lastResult[0] as Video"/>
</fx:Declarations>
<mx:DataGrid x="10" y="10" id="dataGrid"
```

Begin `DataGrid` code

```
    creationComplete="dataGrid_creationCompleteHandler(event)"
    dataProvider="{getAllVideoResult.lastResult}"
    change="dataGrid_changeHandler(event)">
  <mx:columns>
    <mx:DataGridColumn headerText="video_id"
        dataField="video_id"/>
    <mx:DataGridColumn headerText="video_url"
        dataField="video_url"/>
    <mx:DataGridColumn headerText="domain_id"
        dataField="domain_id"/>
    <mx:DataGridColumn headerText="title"
        dataField="title"/>
    <mx:DataGridColumn headerText="description"
        dataField="description"/>
    <mx:DataGridColumn headerText="category"
        dataField="category"/>
  </mx:columns>
</mx:DataGrid>
<mx:Form>
```

Begin Master-Detail form code

```
  <mx:FormItem label="Video_url">
    <s:TextInput id="video_urlTextInput"
        text="@{video.video_url}"/>
  </mx:FormItem>
  <mx:FormItem label="Domain_id">
    <s:TextInput id="domain_idTextInput"
        text="@{video.domain_id}"/>
  </mx:FormItem>
```

```
      <mx:FormItem label="Title">
        <s:TextInput id="titleTextInput"
            text="@{video.title}"/>
      </mx:FormItem>
      <mx:FormItem label="Description">
        <s:TextInput id="descriptionTextInput"
            text="@{video.description}"/>
      </mx:FormItem>
      <mx:FormItem label="Category">
        <s:TextInput id="categoryTextInput"
            text="@{video.category}"/>
      </mx:FormItem>
    </mx:Form>

</s:Application>
```

The code generated by Flash Builder wasn't too shabby. One thing had to be manually changed though. The change handler function ❶ for the data grid needed the video ID value set manually from `itemID` to `dataGrid.selectedItem.video_id`.

If you're paying attention, you may notice something else missing as well. There isn't a control or a function for updating the selected item! You should still be able to run the application at this point, but changing values in the Master-Detail form won't have any effect on the database record.

To address this, switch back to design view, drag a button component to the stage, then drag the `updateVideo()` method from the Data/Services panel to it, and voila! Congratulations, you've completed your Flash Builder DCD CRUD service application!

15.7 *Summary*

In this chapter you learned about the many ways of communicating with the outside world from your Flex 4 applications. You also gave the new Flash Builder 4 data-centric development features a spin and learned how to speed up your workflow ten-fold by doing so.

Although the code-generating features for data-centric development with Flash Builder are incredibly useful and can save huge amounts of time during development, you should be aware of a couple of caveats as a conscientious developer. First, at the time of this writing, the DCD features don't support any of the microarchitecture frameworks for enterprise Flex development (discussed in chapter 19). It's worth noting, however, that there's a good possibility we'll see third-party plug-ins that add DCD support for use with the Swiz and Mate frameworks in the not-so-distant future. The second caveat is the general idea of generated code. In theory, it sounds like the be-all end-all to programming in general, but in practice, this is hardly the case. It's important to analyze and review any code that has been generated for you by the IDE and make sure it's consistent with what you're trying to accomplish.

In the next chapter, you'll learn about the concepts of objects and classes, which will be a nice lead-in for chapter 17 on building custom components with Flex 4.

Objects and classes

16

This chapter covers

- OO concepts
- Implementing OO concepts using ActionScript classes
- Creating your own classes
- Packages

You should now be equipped with enough knowledge of ActionScript to use it to respond to events, add user interactivity to your application, and manipulate properties. Now it's time to take those skills to the next level.

In this chapter, we explore a fundamental feature of Flex: objects and classes. We also delve into some OO theory. What you'll learn will save you considerable development time and render your software easier to maintain.

By the end of this chapter, you'll have learned how to create objects and classes, invoke and destroy them, and extend those that already exist. This may seem like we're putting a lot on your plate, but it won't take more than 30 minutes to learn, and upon completion, you'll have created a fully functional OO program.

16.1   OO theory in five minutes

Flex is an OO-based application. Therefore, having some understanding of OO programming will be tremendously beneficial toward taking Flex and your designs to a higher plane and resolving issues more quickly. Most important, expanding your knowledge of OO programming will provide the foundation for creating reusable code.

In the following sections, we explore the basic concepts of programming using objects and classes. This is arguably the most important branch of computer programming in which you'll engage. Understanding objects and classes will help you quickly learn many other programming languages, such as C#, C++, and Java.

16.1.1   The relationship between objects and classes

To help you clearly understand objects, we'll set up a brief mental exercise. Instead of conceptualizing theory, let's use the common, everyday reality.

Stop for a moment and look around. You'll notice that your surroundings are full of objects: a car, a television, a computer—even this book. Each object has a certain function or role to fulfill. Objects also have characteristics, such as their color or size.

Some objects rely on other objects—a computer relies on a CPU object—whereas other objects are independent. For example, your computer isn't dependent on this book. If you understand this analogy, that's half of the battle. The rest is implementation.

An object is a self-contained widget. It knows about itself and is aware of its capabilities. Objects display a bipolar personality in that

- They generally care only about themselves (how rude!).
- They make it easy for others to use them by doing the hard work behind the scenes (how nice!).

Now you have a cursory idea of what an object is, but what about a class?

WHAT ARE CLASSES?

In pure OO theory, only objects exist. But throughout this book, you've probably noticed we've been using the terms *objects* and *classes* interchangeably. OO theory is just theory: It has no notion of implementation. Flex has to turn that theory into reality, so, like most OO languages, Flex implements the concepts by using classes as a template (a blueprint, if you will) with which to create objects. More succinctly, objects are *instances* of classes.

For example, if you had a class called `Human` and an instance of that human named `Derek Douville`, then `Derek Douville` would be an object.

16.1.2   Objects have properties and methods

An object knows about itself and its capabilities through two features:

- Properties
- Methods (or, as they're also known, functions)

Going back to the `Human` class, figure 16.1
shows how a human possesses various properties. Some of the properties in an instance of
`Human` are set only once—`Place of Birth`, for
example—whereas other properties can
change constantly, such as `Mood`. Likewise,
your human is capable of various functions,
including eating and sleeping.

Human Class	
Properties	**Functions/Methods**
- Age	- Eat
- Height	- Sleep
- Place of Birth	- Code
- Mood	- Laugh

Figure 16.1 The `Human` class has properties
that define it and various functions of which
it's capable.

Although you as a human have properties
such as your age, and you have functions such as secretly eating ice cream in the middle of night, that doesn't mean you want the whole world to know about it. This is
where *scope* comes into play.

PROPERTIES AND METHODS HAVE SCOPE

The purpose of scope is to control who has access to what. For example, your human
needs to keep its Social Security number (SSN) property closely guarded to avoid the
number becoming publicly known. But in certain circumstances, a method may need
to be provided to make use of the number, such as a method to apply for credit. Using
scope, you can keep this SSN private from the outside world and use methods within
that class to work with it.

Similarly, this scope applies to methods. A human can provide public methods
such as a function to do work, which an external boss object can invoke. There may
also be private methods that the human wants to use internally and that no one else is
allowed to use (for example, a method to pick one's nose). Flex supports the following scopes for properties and methods.

- *Private*—Methods and properties are available only to this class.
- *Public*—Methods and properties are available everywhere.
- *Protected*—Methods and properties are available in the same class or any class
  that extends from it.
- *Internal*—The default. Methods and properties are available to classes in the
  same package.
- *Static*—Methods and properties can be used without an instance of a class.

What if you want to make an object that does everything a human does, and more?
You can copy all the methods and properties and then add the additional properties
and methods. A problem arises when you have to make a change common to both:
You'll need to make that same change in two places. Fortunately a mechanism called
inheritance solves this problem.

16.1.3   *Inheritance*

An object can inherit attributes and characteristics from another object. This allows
the properties and methods of one class—also known as the *base* or *parent* class—to be
passed on to the child object. You can continue to add more properties and methods
to those inherited from the parent.

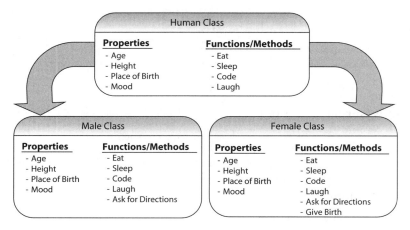

Figure 16.2 Subclasses inherit all of the parent's attributes, but you can add more.

In Flex, a well-known custom component called `promptingTextInput` is available in the `FlexLib` package (http://code.google.com/p/flexlib/). This child of the `Text-Input` component has been extended to provide not only the native abilities of `Text-Input` but also the additional ability to prompt the user for input by means of a message, such as *please enter a value.*

Some OO languages (including Flex) refer to this action as *extending a class.* Building on the analogy, you could take the `Human` class and extend it to make `Male` and `Female` subclasses (see figure 16.2). Each of those subclasses can have unique properties and functions of its own. More significantly, they can have the same functions but implement them differently.

For example, if both `Female` and `Male` have an `askForDirections` function, `Female`'s version of that function will return a sequence of instructions that can be used to successfully navigate to the desired location, whereas the `Male` class will return nothing (asking for directions isn't something it supports).

Using inheritance, you can save a lot of time by eliminating the need to define properties and attributes in each child object you create. Inheritance is about how objects can relate to each other, but it's good practice to ensure that objects regardless of their lineage are able to stand on their own in terms of purpose and functionality. This process is called *encapsulation*, and it's useful for reusing code.

16.1.4 *Encapsulation and coupling*

The principle of encapsulation is key to reusable code. Encapsulation defines an object that exists in a self-contained environment, or *module.* The object doesn't need to know about the workings of the overall application in which it resides. Likewise, the application doesn't need to know how the object works.

The more you adhere to that rule, the more reusable your code will be, because the elements that form your application aren't dependent on the *knowledge* of how each other works. An object's goal is to tend to its own tasks within its self-contained world.

If you want other code elements to be able to work with your object, you need to expose methods and properties that abstract the object's inner workings from the calling code. This way, you can change aspects of the object, but the calling code still works unperturbed, and vice versa.

As an illustration, let's assume you have an object that needs a piece of information from elsewhere in the application in order to perform its task—for this example, we'll assume the information to be UserID. If your object were to reach outside itself directly into the main application to gather UserID, it would need to know what UserID is, what it looks like, and where to find it. You could provide that information to your object by giving it explicit instructions (hardcoding), but then any changes to UserID or the object would render those instructions useless and require you to update them manually (figure 16.3 demonstrates this concept).

Your object is now dependent on knowing specifically how and where to acquire a value. This breaks the object's encapsulation (it can no longer ignore the outside world) and makes it *tightly coupled* to the application around it.

The better approach is to make your objects *loosely coupled* by passing values between them in such a way that your object (and everything else with which it interacts) doesn't know or care where UserID came from. It knows to take the information passed to it and process it according to instructions.

In the world of ActionScript 3/Flex 3, everything is an object. From panels, to formatters, to user input components, everything follows the concept of OO programming.

This is true for both MXML components (for example, <s:Panel/>) and Action-Script classes, such as ArrayCollection. More important, anything you create in MXML is converted to ActionScript classes.

Enough with the theory; let's dive in and play with some objects!

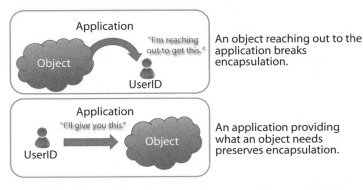

Figure 16.3 Demonstrating the concept of encapsulation. In the first instance, an object reaching out breaks encapsulation by assuming it knows where information resides, resulting in a fragile application that can break easily. In the second case, encapsulation is preserved because the object doesn't know or care where UserID is coming from.

16.2   *Playing with objects*

We've always espoused the premise that you won't learn something until you physically use it. You've been introduced to most of this material throughout the previous chapters, but let's look into the mechanics behind it. Time to roll up your sleeves and get your hands dirty!

In this section we take a closer look at objects by deconstructing the bits and pieces that are involved in invoking an object and the meat that makes up an object (its methods and properties).

16.2.1   *A closer look at objects*

To begin, you'll create a generic starting point by performing the following steps:

1   Create a Flex project called CH16.
2   Open the file CH16.mxml.
3   Create an `<fx:Script>` block in which to place your ActionScript code.

With these steps complete, your code should resemble that of the following listing.

Listing 16.1   Shell application

```
<?xml version="1.0" encoding="utf-8"?>
<s:Application xmlns:fx="http://ns.adobe.com/mxml/2009"
               xmlns:s="library://ns.adobe.com/flex/spark"
               xmlns:mx="library://ns.adobe.com/flex/mx">
  <fx:Script>
    <![CDATA[

    ]]>
  </fx:Script>
</s:Application>
```

You're under way. Next, let's add a simple object.

ADDING A PRIMITIVE OBJECT

You'll create an instance of an object through which you can explore the process of adding an object—in this case, a primitive. A *primitive* object is an object that possesses only rudimentary capabilities.

Within the `<fx:Script/>` block, add the line shown in figure 16.4.

You've now created a *new* object called myObj. The new operator following the variable definition, myObj:Object, informs the ActionScript compiler that you're creating a new *instance* of this object class.

Now that you've created an object, let's open it up and see what's inside.

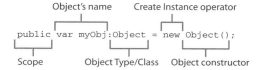

Figure 16.4   **The common pattern of creating an instance of an object. Scope controls who can access the instance, the name allows you to reference it, the class declares its type, and the constructor initializes the object.**

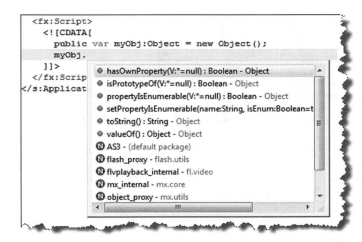

```
<fx:Script>
  <![CDATA[
    public var myObj:Object = new Object();
    myObj.
  ]]>
</fx:Scrip
</s:Applicat
```

- ● hasOwnProperty(V:*=null) : Boolean - Object
- ● isPrototypeOf(V:*=null) : Boolean - Object
- ● propertyIsEnumerable(V:*=null) : Boolean - Object
- ● setPropertyIsEnumerable(name:String, isEnum:Boolean=t
- ● toString() : String - Object
- ● valueOf() : Object - Object
- Ⓝ AS3 - (default package)
- Ⓝ flash_proxy - flash.utils
- Ⓝ flvplayback_internal - fl.video
- Ⓝ mx_internal - mx.core
- Ⓝ object_proxy - mx.utils

Figure 16.5 Inserting a period after an instance prompts Flash Builder to list the known public properties and methods associated with the object.

TAKING A PEEK

An easy way to view the makeup of this object is to type myObj on a new line and add a period directly after it. Flash Builder displays a list of associated properties and methods, as shown in figure 16.5.

Figure 16.5 shows a number of methods at the top of the list, which are the functions that perform some kind of logic. Other objects may also present a list of properties; for example, many visual objects have width and height properties.

Properties can act as a form of communication with an object. They can be used both to configure an object and to ascertain its attributes (its current state). For example, the Array object has a property known as length, which indicates how many items are currently in the array.

As mentioned earlier, along with properties are an object's methods, which are the workhorse of an object. Let's delve deeper into what methods are all about.

16.2.2 *Methods of objects*

Each ActionScript class includes methods. They perform the actions defined for them by programmers and developers. Let's spend a few moments looking at some of the methods associated with an Array class.

As you did earlier with a simple object, create a new array variable called myArr:

```
var myArr:Array = new Array();
```

Again, by using the new operator, you create a new instance of the Array class. On the next line, type myArr. (remember to add the period). You should see something similar to figure 16.6.

Flash Builder displays a list of methods and properties associated with myArr. The items followed by parentheses are the methods. Included among them are concat(), every(), and forEach().

```
var myArr:Array = new Array();
myArr.
```

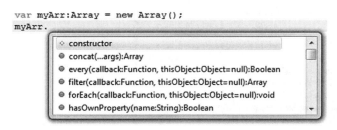

Figure 16.6   Flash Builder's autosuggest feature displays a number of methods.

The primary mission of an object is to make programming easier. If you glance down the list, you'll notice some useful methods that help carry out that mission. The Flex team wrote these methods specifically for interacting with the `Array` object. For example, the array methods, `split()` and `push()`, do the following:

- `split()`—Splits an array into smaller pieces
- `push()`—Adds onto the array

Remember, objects don't concern themselves with the world around them. As a result, their methods don't know much about that environment either. To communicate with methods and give them the information to perform their tasks, you need to pass them parameters.

16.2.3 *Method parameters*

You can communicate with methods via *arguments*, or, as they're also known, *parameters*. Look again at the list of methods for `Array`. Notice the text within the parentheses that follows the structure: `text:ObjectName`.

When you enter data into the parentheses, you're passing parameters, or arguments, to the method. If you want to add a new value to an array, you supply it as follows:

```
myArr.push("some Value");
```

The data, `"some Value"`, is passed to the method, which does with it whatever it has been instructed to do—remember, in OO, what the object does, and how it does it, is irrelevant to other parts of the code. As it relates to this example, `"some Value"` is added as the parameter to `Array`.

Not only can methods take information, but they can also pass it back by returning a result.

16.2.4 *Methods return information*

Methods can also communicate information or data back to the object that sent it via a mechanism known as a *return* value. Referring back to the Flash Builder autosuggest feature, you'll see that along with presenting the parameters each method takes, the list also indicates what's returned from the method. For example, you can see back in figure 16.6 that the method `concat()` returns another array.

Objects are the fundamental building blocks behind a class. Let's take the information you've learned about objects and apply it to creating a class of your own.

16.3 *Creating a class*

We'll begin the study of classes by creating a simple math program that calculates the area of a given shape. You'll draw the shapes using your own class. You'll also create the methods to perform the area computation.

16.3.1 *Creating the class file*

For this example, create a dedicated project by following these steps:

1 Select File > New > Project.
2 Name the project Shapes.
3 Click Finish.

Next, following these steps, create an ActionScript class file (see figure 16.7):

4 Select File > New > Create New ActionScript Class.
5 Fill out the fields in the dialog box to match the information shown in figure 16.7, but don't click Finish yet. First, let's take a few moments to learn more about the New ActionScript Class Wizard.

Figure 16.7 Flash Builder's New ActionScript Class Wizard guides you through the process of creating a class by specifying what package it's a part of, its name, and a few other attributes. It will then create the file containing skeletal code that you can fill in.

You've created the project and a simple class. Let's look in detail at what you entered in the dialog box.

16.3.2 Specifying a package

The first field you filled in defines the class package. A *package* organizes similar classes into folders. This is a more effective strategy than placing your classes in the top-level source folder. A package helps you develop applications faster and more efficiently by providing a mechanism to keep your elements organized.

Everyone has personal preferences regarding the package name, but most developers adopt reverse-domain notation, which is the domain name in reverse (for example, com.mycompany) and any further identifiers you deem necessary.

For example, a package named com.mycompany.sales.management indicates a folder structure of com/mycompany/sales/management.

This exercise uses com.flexinaction.shapes. You use shapes as the group name because this folder contains all the shape classes you create.

NAMING CLASSES

The next input is self-explanatory: the name of the class. You can choose any name you like, but we recommend the name be relative to the *purpose* of the class. In this case, you're creating a rectangle, so use the name MathRec. When you create class names, it's always best practice not to use the same name as another class in your project.

16.3.3 Class modifiers

Class modifiers let you control what other application elements can access the class. You set the class modifiers using a pair of radio buttons (located below the Name field) labeled Public and Internal.

Modifiers determine how *sociable* a class is with other classes in the application. If you choose the Public modifier, this permits the class to be accessed by other classes and your application. If you set the class to Internal, it can be accessed only by other classes from within the same package. You can use these four scope modifiers:

- *Public*—Any code can use this class.
- *Internal*—The default. Other classes within the same package are allowed to use this class.
- *Dynamic*—An optional modifier that you can use with the Public or Internal modifier, which lets you add properties during runtime.
- *Final*—An optional modifier that you can use with the Public or Internal modifier, which prevents other classes from extending this class.

Why choose one over another? This is an architectural decision you must make when designing your application. Some factors that can influence your decision are these:

- Do you want other classes accessing this class?
- What are the security implications of exposing the class?
- Is the class meant to support only other classes of which it's aware?

This gives you a synopsis of classes and how to create objects to do your bidding. But how can you incorporate a preexisting object into your application? The next section shows you how to *extend* classes.

16.3.4 Superclasses: extending a class

No, a superclass isn't a class from the planet Krypton. A superclass is a way to extend the methods and properties of one class by including those of another class. For example, let's assume your application has two classes: class A and class B. Class A has 20 methods, and class B has 10. By instructing class B to extend class A, you make class B incorporate the methods from class A but keep those it possessed prior to extension. The extended class B has 30 methods.

You'll use the `mx.core.UIComponent` class to extend your area-calculating class because it's part of the Flex core and is related to visual objects on the screen—a great match for what you want to do (make shapes). You'll see shortly how to change or extend the class programmatically, not by means of the wizard.

> **TIP** Superclasses are also known as *parent* or *base* classes.

An *interface* is similar to a class but not as robust.

16.3.5 Interfaces

Without being too technical, let's just say that an interface is a predefined template that catalogues the necessary methods and properties that a class must implement in order to comply with the interface. For example, if you're making a collection of shape classes (square, circle, triangle, and so on), all of which have formulas for calculating the area or perimeter, you can use an interface to enforce that they all have methods to support each formula.

An interface serves as a contract with a class—a contract stating that the class will implement the methods defined by the interface. You could try making a `Shape` superclass with `area` and `perimeter` methods that are overridden by specific subclasses (such as a `Circle` class), but this may not be the best approach. This is because the area formula for a circle varies from that of a square, so the `Shape`'s `area` method is of little value at the cost of overhead.

The problem you're trying to solve is making sure all types of shapes employ certain methods. Interfaces work great because they solve this problem and are lightweight in the process (they carry no implementation).

Let's put some of this theory into action by creating a class and using it.

16.3.6 Looking at your class

For those of you who follow directions to the letter, you can now click the Finish button in the New ActionScript Class Wizard and watch Flash Builder create the code shown in this next listing.

Listing 16.2   Basic class structure

```
package com.flexinaction.shapes                    The package
{                                                  ❶ identifier
  import mx.core.UIComponent;
  public class MathRec extends UIComponent                      The public
  {                                                             ❷ modifier
    public function MathRec()
    {                                ❸ The UIComponent
        super();
    }
  }
}
```

The package identifier ❶

The public modifier ❷

The UIComponent ❸

Much of what you see is probably familiar to you by now:

- The package identifier ❶ is followed by the name of the package you entered.
- The public modifier ❷ is assigned the class so it can be accessed by other classes and the application itself.
- The UIComponent ❸ class is extended by the MathRec class.

NOTE Throughout this chapter, we've been talking about methods, yet the code in listing 16.2 presents functions. Confused? Don't be. *Function* is another name for a method. *Method* is the term used by those in the programming and development community, but both terms refer to the same thing.

In listing 16.2, you create a function called MathRec(). Coincidentally, this happens to be the name of the class as well. Whenever an instance of a class is created, Action-Script automatically generates a default method for that class (hence, the same name). The mechanism that executes this is known as a *constructor*.

Within this method resides another method named super(), which is a way to call the parent's (superclass) constructor. In this example, because you extend from UIComponent, super() calls the UIComponent's constructor (which initializes the object). You don't need to have a constructor, and you can realize a slight performance boost by omitting it, but it's best practice to include one.

In the next section, you'll learn how to impart unique characteristics to your class by adding *properties*.

16.4   *Working with properties*

Now that you've created your class, you need to get down to the business of drawing the shape. But before you do, you need to consider a few use cases. For instance, what if the user prefers a red rectangle instead of blue? Or, what if the user wants a big rectangle rather than a small one? It's easy for the user to input values to effect the changes, but how will the class know about these modifications, and how will it accommodate them?

16.4.1 Adding properties

Returning to an earlier analogy, in the real world you can change aspects of the environment around you by passing instructions, or information, to the appropriate resource. For example, you can instruct a builder to create a rectangular shape of a specific length and width and further instruct that the rectangle be painted red.

You can do the same thing with classes by creating variables to hold the specification data. In the line beneath the class identifier, create these three private variables:

- _color of type uint
- _height of type int
- _length of type int

The underscore character at the beginning of each variable is a common industry convention for naming private variables. You don't need to do this, but it helps to visually identify privately scoped variables in your code.

After you add your new variables, the code should appear as shown in the following listing.

Listing 16.3 A class with private properties defined

```
package com.flexinaction.shapes
{
  import mx.core.UIComponent;
  public class MathRec extends UIComponent
  {
    private var _color:uint = 0x000000;
    private var _length:int = 10;
    private var _height:int = 20;
    public function MathRec()
    {
      super();
    }
  }
}
```

NOTE Why wasn't the whole new Object() thing done with these int and uint variables? These are top-level classes and get special treatment by allowing for such shortcuts.

These variables are the properties of the class; now let's add some methods.

16.4.2 Adding geter/setter methods

We could have taken the easy way out and defined our new properties as public, allowing the outside world to access and manipulate them. There would be nothing wrong with doing this, but to properly and efficiently program with Flex, it's best to use an alternate mechanism to provide access to those variables: *getter* and *setter* methods.

These are special methods that have only one role: access the variable and change it. This approach provides a controlled way to access variables and change them internally without interfering with the calling code.

First, you'll create setter methods to set the three variables. The setter method follows a simple pattern:

```
public function set yourPropertyname(value:DataTypeOfProperty):void{
    this._propertyname = value; }
```

You use the `public` identifier at the beginning of the line to define the setter method as accessible to the other classes and the main application. You use the `function` identifier to create the method and then add the special keyword `set` to indicate this is a setter method.

The property name should be assigned with an eye toward avoiding confusion about what you're setting and getting. The name can be whatever you prefer, but it's best to use the same name as your private variables. Next, the value and data type of the parameter you want to pass are specified within parentheses. The `:void` designation indicates that this function won't return a value. Finally, code within the curly braces will be executed. Listing 16.4 shows some examples.

Listing 16.4   Examples of setter functions

```
public function set color(value:uint):void
{
  this._color = value;
}


public function set Reclength(value:int):void
{
  this._length = value;
}


public function set Recheight(value:int):void
{
  this._height = value;
}
```

The syntax of `this.`, which precedes the variable name, is an option you can use when referring to variables in the class. Like the underscore character, it makes the code easier to read and clearly identifies where that variable is coming from (in this case, the class).

Next, you'll configure the three getter functions so you can provide access to the variable. The syntax is similar, except you use the keyword `get` instead of `set`, as shown in this next listing.

Listing 16.5   Examples of getter functions

```
public function get color():uint
{
  return this._color;
}
```

```
public function get Reclength():int
{
  return this._length;
}

public function get Recheight():int
{
  return this._height;
}
```

The key difference between a getter function and a setter function is that instead of passing values, a getter function returns values.

16.5 Creating methods for your class

With the getter and setter methods in place, it's time to draw the rectangle and add the required methods to calculate the area and perimeter. ActionScript comes with a number of drawing classes; among them is a rectangle class you can easily employ in the application.

Create a new method called `DrawRectangle()`, and enter the code from the following listing.

Listing 16.6 Method to draw a rectangle

```
public function DrawRectangle():void
{                                                    ① Clear stage
  this.graphics.clear();                                          ② Set line color
  this.graphics.lineStyle(1,_color);
  this.graphics.drawRect(120,120 ,_length,_height);
}                                                    ③ Draw rectangle
```

Whenever you call this method, it will do the following:

- Clear the stage ① of any other rectangles.
- Set the line color ② to the color specified via the private variable `_color` (defaulted to black in the class definition).
- Draw the rectangle ③ at coordinate `120,120` on the screen using the `_length` and `_height` variables.

Using the constructor-generated default method, you call the `DrawRectangle` function. This causes a default rectangle to be created when an instance of this class is created. Your code should look as shown in the following snippet:

```
public function MathRec()
{
  super();
  DrawRectangle();
}
```

Now that you have the shape drawn, you'll create helper methods to calculate the area and perimeter. Listing 16.7 presents the functions needed to perform the calculations.

Listing 16.7   Supporting methods

```
public function getArea():int
{
  return (this._length * this._height);          ⟵——— Area = base * height
}

public function getPerim():int
{
  return ((2*(this._height)) + (2*(this._length)));   ⟵——— Calculates perimeter
}
```

Let's put the application to work. Try entering values in the height and length input fields, and watch the results, as illustrated in figure 16.8.

Listing 16.8 presents the complete code used to invoke an instance of the class we created, set its properties, and then invoke its methods to draw a rectangle.

Listing 16.8   CH16.mxml: using the class you created

```
<?xml version="1.0" encoding="utf-8"?>
<s:Application xmlns:fx="http://ns.adobe.com/mxml/2009"
               xmlns:s="library://ns.adobe.com/flex/spark"      Adds
               xmlns:mx="library://ns.adobe.com/flex/mx"        myRectangle
               initialize="addElement(myRectangle);" >       ⟵┘ to application
  <fx:Script>
    <![CDATA[                                          Imports    Creates an
      import com.flexinaction.shapes.MathRec;       ⟵┘ class     instance of
                                                               ⟵┘ MathRec
      public var myRectangle:MathRec = new MathRec();
      private function drawMyRectangle():void
      {
        myRectangle.Recheight = Number(inputHeight.text);    | Setter
        myRectangle.Reclength = Number(inputLength.text);    | functions
        myRectangle.DrawRectangle();                  ⟵——— Invokes public method
        outputArea.text = myRectangle.getArea().toString();   | Getter
        outputPerim.text = myRectangle.getPerim().toString(); | functions
      }
    ]]>
  </fx:Script>
  <s:Button x="365" y="207" label="Draw Rectangle" click="drawMyRectangle()"/>

  <s:Label text="Enter Length:" x="29" y="181"/>
  <s:TextInput x="29" y="207" id="inputLength" width="50"/>

  <s:Label text="Enter Height:" x="197" y="181"/>
  <s:TextInput x="197" y="207" id="inputHeight" width="50"/>

  <s:Label text="Area of Rectangle:" x="197" y="237"/>
  <s:Label id="outputArea" x="197" y="263"/>
  <s:Label text="Perimeter of Rectangle:" x="29" y="237"/>
  <s:Label id="outputPerim" x="29" y="263"/>

</s:Application>
```

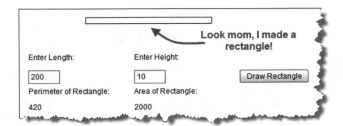

Figure 16.8   Using the `Rectangle` class that we created, our application allows the user to enter the dimensions, and the object will do the work of drawing the rectangle.

As you learned earlier, when you want to use an object, you must first import the class. This is what you do when you import the `MathRec` class using the `import` statement, as shown in the following extract from listing 16.8:

```
import com.flexinaction.MathRec
```

The `drawMyRectangle()` method converts the height and length values specified by the user to numbers and then sets the parameters in the `MathRec` class using the setter functions.

Putting it all together, you now have a class that, once instantiated as an object, has properties that can be set and retrieved (dimensions of a rectangle) and methods that do work (in this case the drawing of a rectangle).

16.6   *Summary*

Regardless of what you do in Flex, it all boils down to ActionScript. It may not be something you're used to if you're coming from a tag-based language like HTML, but over time you'll become more comfortable with it. Along with that comfort will come the power to harness ActionScript classes.

You can spend months learning about OO programming, only to find yourself struggling with its vast number of theories and advanced techniques. But in the time it took for you to read this chapter, you successfully learned the ins and outs of basic OO programming, which will dramatically extend your Flex development skills.

This knowledge will form the foundations that will enable you to create well-designed applications that have self-contained, reusable objects. In the next chapter, we'll continue to enhance your understanding of reusability through the use of custom components.

Custom components

This chapter covers

- Making your own custom components
- Using existing components as a base
- Passing parameters to custom components
- Retrieving values from custom components
- Employing getter and setter functions
- Broadcasting events from a custom component
- Creating ActionScript components
- Componentizing

You've come a long way in a short amount of time so far. You now know enough to create a standard Flex application!

You can capture and validate input from the user, interact with backend data services to get and transmit data, and format and display information. These are all great things to know, but unless you plan to have all your code in one huge file, you need to know how to break your application into smaller, reusable pieces.

This is where custom components come into play. Although this isn't the only option for making code reusable, it's one of the few de facto standards because of ease of implementation and the benefits that are gained from components. This chapter covers the basics of creating and utilizing custom components and tackles ways of getting your components to communicate with each other.

We'll start off by taking a look at how components are handled in Flex 4 and the Spark architecture, followed by a discussion on types of components and the difference between simple and composite. We'll then take a deep dive into advanced Spark-based components and how you can achieve maximum code reuse by building and implementing them into your own projects.

17.1 Understanding Flex 4 components

You've used components since the start of this book. They range from controls like the simple `Button` that accepts actions from the user to container components like the `VBox`. Custom components either add to or override functionality that already exists within the Flex framework. They're created by extending the same base classes as the default components that are part of the Flex framework. More specifically, `UIComponent` can be thought of as the granddaddy of all visual Flex components.

In this section you'll learn about the underlying foundation of the Spark component architecture in Flex 4. Most important, you'll learn key facets that are specific to the Flex 4 Spark architecture. This will get you on your way toward building your own collection of Spark-based components that take advantage of Spark architecture.

17.1.1 Spark component architecture

If you've been a Flex developer for a little while now, or you've used a different language or framework for user interface development, you may have heard of something called *Model-View-Controller*, or MVC which is an architectural design pattern often used to build user interfaces. MVC is continuously evolving, spawning new and innovative implementations to create more scalable applications on a regular basis. This evolutionary process runs in parallel to the evolution of best practices for Flex in the enterprise. Figure 17.1 shows the overall structure of a Flex 4 enterprise application.

Chapter 19, on architecture, discusses how the layers shown in figure 17.1 work together. In this chapter, you'll learn about skins and components, the second and third levels of the application architecture, which are illustrated in figure 17.2. As previously mentioned, the evolution of best practices with Flex evolves at

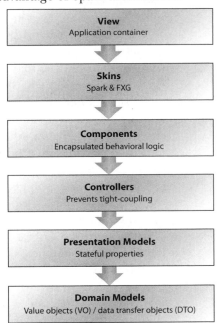

Figure 17.1   Example of an organizational structure of a typical Flex 4 enterprise application

about the same rate as architectural design patterns. This is because the two are closely related. The Spark component architecture is a good example of the positive changes that occur as a result of this evolutionary process.

As you saw a moment ago, there are two pieces to a Spark component: the skin and the component class that contains the behavioral logic for the component. According to the Flex 4 documentation:

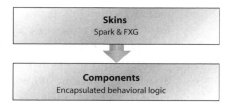

Figure 17.2   Application layers that compose the Spark component architecture

> *The general rule is any code that is used by multiple skins belongs in the component class, and any code that is specific to a particular skin implementation lives in the skin.*

Let's put all this theory into practice by looking at some real-life situations.

17.1.2   The many flavors of custom components

Creating a custom component means extending a preexisting class that either directly or indirectly extends one of the Flex framework classes. For example, imagine three 2010 Ford Mustangs side by side. The first is the base Mustang Coupe with the standard V6 engine. The second is the Mustang GT with a 4.6-liter V8, upgraded wheels, and some other upgrades. The third is a Shelby Cobra, sporting 510 horsepower, premium sound, a navigation system, and a number of additional sexy upgrades. The GT and Cobra both extend the Coupe. In other words, the GT and Cobra inherit the properties of the Coupe, overriding some of those properties as well as adding in some of their own, so that they may include the additional amenities that the GT and Cobra have to offer.

Besides inheriting the properties of the base Mustang V6 Coupe, the Cobra has another little secret. The Cobra is a subclass, or extension of, the GT. Because GT extends Coupe, Cobra inherits the properties of both the GT and the standard Mustang and overrides the Coupe's properties in favor of the GT's properties where applicable. As if that wasn't already confusing enough for you, the Cobra then overrides certain properties of the GT so it can add its own features to the package. How could the Cobra and the GT inherit the properties of the standard Mustang if the engines are different? The answer is that the GT overrides the engine property of the standard Mustang, and the Cobra overrides the engine of the GT. The relationship between these three automobiles is illustrated in the simple class diagram shown in figure 17.3.

When you extend classes in the Flex framework, you inherit the properties, functions, events, and styles from the class you're extending (also referred to as *subclassing*). This makes code a lot more manageable and is one of the fundamental characteristics of object-oriented programming and code reusability. Let's look at two different component types.

SIMPLE VERSUS COMPOSITE

There are two major types of custom components: simple and composite. A simple custom component usually extends a single, preexisting component within the Flex framework.

The fun doesn't stop there though. When developing Flex applications, you'll find it valuable to group simple components together, keeping your application better organized. You can create components that group disparate components in what's called a composite component, which is a container that holds any number of additional components inside it, which you'll see later in the composite component example.

MXML VERSUS ACTIONSCRIPT

When developing custom components, you have the option of creating your component in either MXML or ActionScript. In most cases, either one will do. The main advantage of MXML is that you can usually write the code necessary using fewer lines. In my experience, the biggest problem that I've seen in regard to writing MXML components is the inability of the developer to differentiate between code that's interdependent with either the application, the stage, or other components (doesn't belong) and code that's entirely self-contained to that component only (does belong).

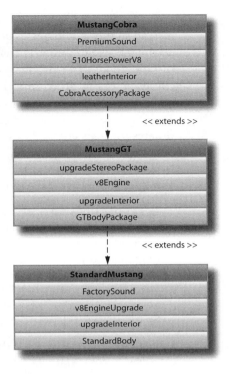

Figure 17.3   Automobiles are a good metaphorical example of inheritance. Notice how the classes labeled `MustangGT` and `MustangCobra` inherit certain properties of the `StandardMustang`, while adding to or overriding other parts of it.

This antipattern is due to the abuse of the `<Script/>` tag in MXML and the ability to embed ActionScript on an MXML object property, putting ActionScript code where you'd normally place a binding. Here's a wonderful example of such code, taken directly out of an enterprise production Flex application:

```
<mx:CheckBox id="filteredCheckBox"
    enabled="{(_pm &amp;&amp; _pm.viewState ==
    DashboardReportsViewStates.READY) &#124;&#124;
    (_pm.isDataExisting &amp;&amp;
    !_pm.data.DashboardData.TestingStarts.weAreInDraftState)}" />
```

A number of antipatterns are being used in this code sample, and in case your memory of HTML character codes is a little vague, `&#124;` is the pipe character, which is defined twice to signify the `or` conditional. Why the character codes? Well, conditionals like this weren't meant to be applied in MXML—or in XML for that matter! Therefore, conditional arguments like greater than, less than, the ampersand, and the pipe aren't supported without being placed in a `CDATA` wrapper. In order to get around this, the creative developers who wrote the code used the HTML character codes instead so they could get away with shoving their conditional logic into properties that accept a boolean value. The conditions will always equate to either `true` or `false`, but this method is error prone, not to mention messy and confusing to any developer who comes across it. Most important, there are dependencies in the previous code that make the composite component that holds this `CheckBox` impossible to reuse. For example, the code `!_pm.data.DashboardData.TestingStarts.weAreInDraftState` violates the *Law of Demeter* by traversing the display list to get an argument. This kind of code can't be unit tested with any kind of accuracy.

Ultimately, the result is a breakdown of the MVC design pattern and an inconsistent application structure that's hard for other developers to follow.

> **BEST PRACTICES TIP**   Use MXML for your custom components *only* if you have a clearly defined set of patterns and practices that's accepted and commonly known by every person writing code in that application. For example, if everyone knows and appropriately codes according to a certain set of design principles, such as the Presentation Model pattern, the code will be organized the same way regardless of whether components are written in MXML or Action-Script. This emphasizes the value of the Spark architecture. For example, with Spark, it's a lot clearer how to keep the design code separate from the model.

I must emphasize the point that in Flex 4 *anything* you can do with ActionScript you can also do in MXML. The biggest issue for Flex 3 coders is breaking old habits, and trust me when I say that I'm no exception. For example, I've developed custom components using ActionScript for so long that it has been challenging to get used to the fact that MXML is just as powerful now in Flex 4. Ultimately, MXML is broken down to basic ActionScript when it's compiled anyway. If you have ever reverse-engineered a SWF file that was developed with Flex, you know that you'll never find any of the original MXML that was written for the application.

Whether you decide to use ActionScript or MXML for component development in Flex 4 is a matter of personal preference, although you could save considerable time by writing your composite components with MXML. An excellent example of this is a shipping information form. It's useful to have a reusable shipping form component because it can be used for many applications. With Spark, this can be created to be fully skinnable depending on the context of the application—and all in about 10 minutes. It's worth noting here that in chapter 18 on code reusability, you step through the process of building a single component that's skinned several different ways so you can see for yourself how this process works in action.

> **MIGRATION TIP**   In Flex 3, MXML composite components were usually based on the Flex `Canvas` container from the Halo library (which by the way is now referred to as the MX library). In Flex 4, MXML composite components most often are based on one of the following abstract base classes: `MXMLComponent`, `SkinnableComponent`, `Group`, `DataGroup`, `SkinnableContainer`, `Skinnable-DataContainer`, `BorderContainer`, or `ItemRenderer`.

If you want to use Flash Builder's Design view (which got a major overhaul from the "slightly less useful" Design view that shipped with Flex Builder 2 and 3), you're still not going to be able to do so when coding display objects in ActionScript. This may not be a problem for you if you prefer to stay in code view the entire time you work on an application.

Regardless of whether you code in AS or MXML, if you're using the Flex framework, it's extremely advantageous for you to know about the Flex component lifecycle. This will allow you to know when to override the abstracted methods that are built into the Flex framework as well as make calls to them so you can take full advantage of the code that's already been written for you.

In MXML, you have the option of overriding methods of UIComponent such as commitProperties() and updateDisplayList() from within the <fx:Script/> tag if you need to (and there are certainly plenty of cases where you'll need to). We'll talk more about all of that in a moment. The bottom line is that finding the formula that works best for you comes with a lot of practice (and, unfortunately, a lot of mistakes). The important thing is that you know enough about each to make an informed decision.

Now that you've learned about the options available, the first custom component you'll build is of the *simple* type.

> **TIP** When it comes to making a custom component, your goal should be to make it simple for other developers to use your component (even if it's complicated inside). This is referred to as *encapsulation*. You'll get some tips on how to achieve this goal throughout this chapter.

17.2 *Creating simple custom components*

At the most fundamental level, a viewable component (one that's added to the display list of your application) can be categorized according to the purpose that it serves. This can be broken down into three categories: controls, containers, and item renderers.

CONTROLS

The first custom component that you'll build is an extension of the Flex ComboBox. This falls under the control category because it affects the *application state*. This brings up an important point: The use of the term *states* to refer to different sections of a Flex application sometimes causes confusion with *application state* as used as a general computer programming term. A change in application state generally refers to some effect on the model, whether it be the presentation model or the domain model of the application. In the ComboBox example, the control can initiate an action or sequence of actions when the selected value is changed, which has an effect on application state because the view (presentation) model or the data (domain) model has been altered in some way.

CONTAINERS

Categorizing container components is easy because the container's job is to hold one or more controls. For example, I had to create a lightweight container component for a project. The container I made was a subclass of the Spark Group object, and the only thing that it did was draw a repeating set of vertical and horizontal lines using the drawing API.

ITEM RENDERERS

This is another easy one to categorize because item renderers share the common characteristic of being an object that repeats inside a container but with different data for each instance. Its display is dependent on the data (or listData) property that's passed to it by its parent. A simple example is the Label that's used as the default item renderer in a list-based component. Note that any control or container is categorized as an item renderer if it's being repeated for each item in a data collection that's passed to its parent. The homegrown ComboBox you'll build in the next section demonstrates this.

17.2.1   *Build your own simple ComboBox*

Let's walk through a simple example. Say your application is geocentric, meaning that pieces of information carry location data. As a result, several forms in the application require the user to specify an address, complete with the state or province in which they reside. For the sake of usability, let's say you have functionality on the server side to determine the user's location based on their IP address and to communicate the country they're in to the client-side Flex application. If the server tells the Flex application that the user is in the United States, you want to display a drop-down menu of states for them to select from when they encounter an address form, as figure 17.4 demonstrates.

Figure 17.4 is a good example of a simple custom Combo-Box control that shows a listing of states when clicked and allows selection of a state to be submitted as a data object. In listing 17.1, you're presented with the code for the component shown in listing 17.3. As you'll see, this component is highly reusable, because it's often needed when creating an address submission form.

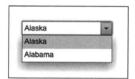

Figure 17.4   This custom component uses a ComboBox to present a list of states.

Listing 17.1   USStatesComboBox.mxml: ComboBox-based custom component

```xml
<?xml version="1.0" encoding="utf-8"?>
<s:ComboBox xmlns:fx="http://ns.adobe.com/mxml/2009"
            xmlns:s="library://ns.adobe.com/flex/spark"
            xmlns:mx="library://ns.adobe.com/flex/mx"
            dataProvider="{this.statesCollection}">

    <fx:Declarations>
        <s:ArrayCollection id="statesCollection">
            <fx:Object stateCode="AK" label="Alaska"/>
            <fx:Object stateCode="AL" label="Alabama"/>
            <!-- the rest of the US states -->
        </s:ArrayCollection>
    </fx:Declarations>

</s:ComboBox>
```

❶ Binds to the data collection

❷ Nonviewable objects go in `<fx:Declarations/>`

❸ Data collection for the drop-down

As listing 17.1 shows, we use the `dataProvider` property of the `ComboBox` to bind the list of states to the component ❶. Notice that the data collection is created within the `<fx:Declarations/>` tag ❷. This is extremely important: In Flex 4, any objects that aren't directly part of the display list must be specified within `<fx:Declarations/>`. This is where our states data collection must be declared for the U.S. states `ComboBox` example ❸.

Wouldn't it be awesome if any part of your application could display this list by calling a single line of code? Okay, that's a loaded question, but as you can see in the main application file provided in listing 17.2, it really does only take one line of code to make this happen.

Listing 17.2   Main application file for USStatesComboBox.mxml

```
<?xml version="1.0" encoding="utf-8"?>
<s:Application xmlns:fx="http://ns.adobe.com/mxml/2009"
               xmlns:s="library://ns.adobe.com/flex/spark"
               xmlns:mx="library://ns.adobe.com/flex/mx"
               xmlns:control="com.fx4ia.view.components.controls.*"
               minWidth="955" minHeight="600">          Declaration of custom
                                                        ◁─┘ ComboBox component
    <control:USStatesComboBox id="states" />

</s:Application>
```

Listing 17.2 demonstrates how the component is instantiated with MXML in a Flex application. One advantage of extending preexisting Flex user interface components is that anyone who uses it will know its general properties and behaviors as a result of inheritance. In this case, if they know your simple custom component is based on a `ComboBox`, then they also know your component supports the same properties, events, styles, and functions as the Flex `ComboBox` control. Now let's look at simple Spark components.

17.2.2   Simple Spark components

A visual object on the stage is considered a Spark component when it inherits the Spark component architecture by extending a Spark visual component base class. These include the following:

- `SkinnableContainer`
- `SkinnableDataContainer`
- `Group`
- `DataGroup`
- `MXMLComponent`
- `ItemRenderer`
- `SkinnableComponent`
- Any Spark library component (for example, a Spark `List`)
- `UIComponent`

If you're familiar with Flex 3, you may be wondering about the last item in the list, UIComponent. Even with the Spark library, it's still technically accurate to state that all visual components in Flex are subclasses of UIComponent. Therefore, if a component that subclasses UIComponent instantiates a Group, SkinnableContainer, or SkinnableComponent object to hold a set of display objects, then we refer to it as a Spark composite component. Use caution if you must take this approach, because you may be causing a needless performance hit by nesting containers. Most of the time, subclassing a Spark-specific base class such as SkinnableComponent or Group will suffice, as you'll see in the examples that will come later and in chapter 18. Before we dive into the examples, though, it's time for some discussion on skins and how the Skin object fits into this picture.

> **MIGRATION TIP**   Beware! One of the biggest compatibility issues that haunted the Flex 4 beta releases involved placing Spark components inside a Canvas container. The problem reared its ugly head in some unusual ways, even after it was thought to have been resolved. In one of my own experiences, the problem caused compile errors within Flash Builder beta of type unknown and source unknown. The source of the problem turned out to be a SkinnableContainer that was instantiated inside a Canvas. The moral of the story here is, if you find yourself debugging and feeling like you're chasing a ghost, consider checking your application to see if you have any Canvas objects before you start banging your head against the wall. If you do have any, try changing them to Group objects. If that doesn't fix the problem, I still suggest leaving the Group in place of the Canvas because I've generally found the Group container to be more reliable and functional than Canvas.

17.3 *Skinning with the Spark Skin object*

As mentioned earlier in this chapter, the clear separation of display logic is one of the most important and valuable facets of the Spark library. Imagine you just built an application with a set of five custom components. If your five components each extend one of the classes listed earlier from the Spark library, you can create an unlimited number of skins for each of your five custom Spark-based components and keep them organized in an entirely separate package or library. You can then declare a different default skin for each instance of the same component or even swap skins on the fly by triggering an event during runtime from a user-initiated behavior or sequence. Isn't that cool? Listing 17.3 is an example of a Spark skin component.

Listing 17.3   Example of a skin for a Spark Button

```xml
<?xml version="1.0" encoding="utf-8"?>
<s:Skin xmlns:fx="http://ns.adobe.com/mxml/2009"
    xmlns:mx="library://ns.adobe.com/flex/mx"
    xmlns:s="library://ns.adobe.com/flex/spark"
    xmlns:ai="http://ns.adobe.com/ai/2008"
    xmlns:d="http://ns.adobe.com/fxg/2008/dt"
    minWidth="21" minHeight="21">
    <fx:Metadata>
      [HostComponent("spark.components.Button")]
```

Skins *always* extend Skin in Flex 4

Namespace declaration for Illustrator graphics

Namespace declaration for FXG graphics

```
    </fx:Metadata>
    <s:states>
      <s:State name="up"/>
      <s:State name="over"/>
      <s:State name="down"/>
      <s:State name="disabled"/>
    </s:states>
  <!-- FXG exported from Adobe Illustrator. -->
  <s:Graphic version="1.0" viewHeight="30"
    viewWidth="100" ai:appVersion="14.0.0.367" d:id="mainContainer">
    <s:Group x="-0.296875" y="-0.5" d:id="firstGroup"
    d:type="layer" d:userLabel="Group One">
  <s:Group d:id="secondGroup">            ◁─┐ Group object
      <s:Rect x="0.5" y="0.5" width="100"        │ followed by design
        height="30" ai:knockout="0">
      <s:fill>
      <s:LinearGradient x="0.5" y="15.5" scaleX="100" rotation="-0">
        <s:GradientEntry color="#ffffff" ratio="0"/>
        <s:GradientEntry ratio="1"/>
      </s:LinearGradient>
      </s:fill>
        <s:stroke>
          <s:SolidColorStroke color="#0000ff" caps="none"
            weight="1" joints="miter" miterLimit="4"/>
        </s:stroke>
      </s:Rect>
    < /s:Group>
    </s:Group>
  </s:Graphic>                               ┐ Label declaration
    <s:Label id="labelElement" horizontalCenter="0"   │ followed by style
      verticalCenter="1" left="10" right="10"    ◁─┘ information
      top="15" bottom="2">
    </s:Label>
  </s:Skin>
```

When you create Spark components, you'll usually create two classes for every component. The component class holds behavioral logic, such as events that are dispatched by the component, a loosely coupled model (no dependencies!), skin parts that are implemented by the skin class, and view states as defined in the skin class.

The skin class, on the other hand, is responsible for managing the visual appearance of the component and visual subcomponents, including how everything is laid out and sized. It must also define the view states, graphics, and how to display specific items on the stage with regard to layout and measurement.

MIGRATION TIP FXG stands for Flash XML Graphics and, in essence, does for MXML what CSS did for HTML. But FXG has quite a bit more power under the hood, so although its relationship to Flash and Flex components can be loosely compared to the relationship between CSS and HTML, it doesn't make logical sense to compare FXG directly to CSS. Many of the limitations imposed on CSS don't exist with FXG. Although it may seem strange to compare FXG to CSS, FXG theoretically accomplishes the same thing that CSS does: It creates a separation of concerns between the model and the view. This makes it easier to create components that can be quickly and easily integrated into any application without even having to look at the component's code base.

17.3.1 *Using metadata to bind component skins*

The component and skin classes must both contain certain metadata in order for them to work properly together.

The component class must

- Define the skin(s) that correspond to it
- Identify skin parts with the [SkinPart] metadata tag
- Identify view states that are supported by the component using the [SkinState] tag

The skin class must

- Use the [HostComponent] metadata tag to specify the corresponding component
- Declare view states and define the appearance of each state
- Define the way skin parts should appear on the stage

Let's look at the three essentials of a skin component in further detail, starting with the SkinState metadata tag.

> **MIGRATION TIP**   Note that skin parts must have the same name in both the skin class and the corresponding component class or your application will show compile errors or throw runtime errors.

17.3.2 *Custom component view states*

The view states that are supported by a component and its corresponding skin must be defined by placing a [SkinState] tag for every view state. These tags are placed directly above the class declaration, as shown in the following listing.

Listing 17.4   View states are defined directly above the class statement.

```
package
{
   import spark.components.supportClasses.SkinnableComponent;

   [SkinState("default")]                    SkinState tags
   [SkinState("hover")]                      precede the class
   [SkinState("selected")]                   declaration
   [SkinState("disabled")]
   public class SkinStateExample extends SkinnableComponent
   {
      public function SkinStateExample()
      {
         super();
      }
   }
}
```

You can now control the state of the component by setting the currentState property with the component declaration in MXML, as shown in this next listing.

Listing 17.5 Controlling custom component state

```
<?xml version="1.0" encoding="utf-8"?>
<s:Application xmlns:fx="http://ns.adobe.com/mxml/2009"
    xmlns:mx="library://ns.adobe.com/flex/mx"
    xmlns:s="library://ns.adobe.com/flex/spark"
    xmlns:MyComp="myComponents.*">
  <s:layout>
    <s:VerticalLayout/>
  </s:layout>
  <s:Label text="Login or Register"
    fontSize="14" fontWeight="bold"/>
  <MyComp:SkinStateExample currentState="default"/>    ◁┘
</s:Application>
```
> Use **currentState** to set the component's state

Although states are defined in a component's implementation class and controlled in the skin, skin parts are defined in the MXML skin and controlled by the implementation class.

17.3.3 Defining skin parts

The importance of the [SkinPart] metadata tag is another critical facet of understanding the relationship between component classes and skin classes in the Spark architecture. As you'll see in a moment, this metadata tag is especially useful for creating custom components.

The implementation of the SkinPart metadata is simple. First, you define skin parts in the same way as you'd declare objects in a standard MXML file. For example, if one of your skin parts was a Spark Button with an id property of myButton, you'd define it with the following code:

```
<s:Button id="myButton" width="100" height="20" x="0" y="0" />
```

Next, you declare the skin parts in the component using the [SkinPart] metadata tag. Make sure that the variable is typed the same as what you just defined in the MXML skin and that the id of the object in the MXML skin matches the name of the variable in the component. The component code for the myButton skin part that you just saw is illustrated in the following listing.

Listing 17.6 SkinPart tag binds component variables to MXML skin part definitions.

```
public class CustomComponent extends SkinnableComponent
{
    public function CustomComponent()
    {
        super();
    }

    [SkinPart(required="true")]
    public var myButton:Button;
}
```
> SkinPart metadata binding on the **myButton** variable

Notice the use of the `required` property after the `SkinPart` metadata tag is declared. Make sure you declare this property because `required` is—pardon the pun—required.

You've now learned two of the three essentials to Spark skinning. The third essential element is tying the component implementation to the skin using the `HostComponent` metadata.

> **WARNING** In order for your skin part bindings to work, you must type the respective variable the same as the MXML object definition, and the variable must be named the same as the `id` attribute that's set on the respective MXML object definition.

17.3.4 *Declaring the host*

The last of the three essentials to using skins with custom Spark components is the declaration of the host component in the skin. To accomplish this, you use the `[Host-Component]` metadata tag. An excellent example of this was provided in the example skin at the beginning of this chapter, in listing 17.3, and is provided again for you as the following code snippet:

```
<fx:Metadata>
    [HostComponent("spark.components.Button")]
</fx:Metadata>
```

You now know how to make a simple custom component. Next up are composite components.

17.4 *Composite components*

A composite component is a container that encapsulates multiple additional components. A composite component is like a computer. In its entirety, the computer is referred to as a Macintosh, Hewlett Packard, Dell, or IBM computer, for example. But if you were to open up the case of the computer, you would likely find a processor component made by Intel or AMD, a motherboard made by another manufacturer, RAM made by a different manufacturer, and so on. The company that packages all of these components into a functional computer system stamps their label on the machine, but the system comprises many parts that are vastly different from each other, just like the parts of a composite component.

> **TIP** You might hear other developers refer to the root node of an MXML composite component as a *wrapper*. Similarly, you may also hear the superclass of an ActionScript composite component referred to as the component's wrapper. If an ActionScript custom component extends a base class like `UIComponent` or `SkinnableComponent` rather than a container class, then usually the first child that's added in the `createChildren()` method is referred to as the component wrapper.

By the time you finish reading this section, you'll know how to create composite components that adhere to the Halo library convention, as well as composites that adhere to the conventions of the Spark library.

17.4.1 *Halo versus Spark*

Once upon a time in Flexland, there was a library called Halo. All of the little Flexland component villagers had their own unique names, except for one—a lowly skin that also bore the honorable name Halo. In Flexland, such a thing was an atrocity that caused mass confusion among all the little villagers. Okay, so this isn't a fairy tale and there's no such thing as Flexland, but the name Halo got slapped on both the Flex 3 component library and the default component skin used by Flex 3 applications, causing these two things to be referenced interchangeably (this should sound familiar—Flex the framework and Flex Builder—two different things referenced interchangeably as if they were one and the same). The inherent issue with this became obvious when Spark was introduced, and then there were namespace issues. One thing led to another until Halo the library was finally dubbed MX (ah, the sweet sound of simplicity).

> **MIGRATION TIP** You may have noticed by now that I bring up the story of how the Flex 3 Halo component library became the Flex 3 MX component library a number of times throughout several chapters in this book. Simply put, you need to drill this into your brain in order to be effective at building Flex 4 applications, especially if you did any work with the public beta 1 and/or beta 2 releases of Flash Builder. Both of them still used *Halo* rather than *MX* in the namespaces, and a lot of the language still has to be updated accordingly in the massive amount of documentation that exists for Flex.

In Flex 3, the container that holds the children of a composite component is usually any of the Flex layout components that implement the IContainer interface. Examples of containers used to house Flex 3 composite components include Canvas, HBox, VBox, TitleWindow, Panel, HDividedBox, and VDividedBox. The layout functionality that's encapsulated within these components made them ideal for holding a bunch of controls together in a Flex 3 application.

In Flex 4, you have more control over container layout if you need it; otherwise, you can let the container handle layout for you as you did with the MX components. Table 17.1 provides a breakdown of the Spark container objects and how they relate to the MX containers with similar functionality.

Table 17.1 Six of the Spark container classes and their relationship to the respective components in the MX component library

Spark container	Subclass	Description	Related MX container
Group	GroupBase	Base container class for visual elements	Canvas
HGroup	Group	Group that uses the HorizontalLayout	HBox

Table 17.1 Six of the Spark container classes and their relationship to the respective components in the MX component library *(continued)*

Spark container	Subclass	Description	Related MX container
VGroup	Group	Group that uses the VerticalLayout	VBox
TileGroup	Group	Group that uses the TileLayout	Tile
BorderContainer	SkinnableContainer	Container catering to the styling of its surrounding border	(n/a)
DataGroup	GroupBase	Base container class for data items	(n/a)

The Flex 4 Spark library ships with a set of specific layout classes. This means that not only does Spark decouple the design of a component using separate skin classes as you just learned, but it also decouples the layout from the design and the behavior!

17.4.2 *Spark layout classes*

If you come from the world of web design, then it might make sense to view Spark architecture as somewhat similar to using best practices when developing websites. More specifically, modern websites often have page layout defined in an XHTML file, design in a separate CSS file, and behavior in a separate JavaScript file. This is an example of *separation of concerns*. Table 17.2 lists the classes contained in the spark.layouts package.

Table 17.2 Layout classes in the Spark library

Class name	Description
BasicLayout	Implements absolute positioning and is used most often. It allows explicit positioning or constraint-based positioning of the container's children.
HorizontalLayout	Encapsulates the same layout functionality that's abstracted into the Halo HBox and HDividedBox containers, where all children are placed next to each other in a horizontal row with a small gap between each child of the container. It also self-adjusts its own height property according to the tallest child.
VerticalLayout	Does the same thing as HorizontalLayout, but vertically instead of horizontally. It's equivalent to the functionality that was seen in Flex 3 with the VBox and VDividedBox containers.
TileLayout	The fourth layout class that can be declared in MXML, it lays out its children into both columns and rows. It encapsulates the functionality that's abstracted into the Halo Tile container.

The layout definition of a component, module, or application should be declared first when instantiating a container, as shown in the next listing.

Listing 17.7 Define the layout immediately after the root in an MXML file

```
<?xml version="1.0" encoding="utf-8"?>
<s:Application xmlns:fx="http://ns.adobe.com/mxml/2009"
               xmlns:s="library://ns.adobe.com/flex/spark"
               xmlns:mx="library://ns.adobe.com/flex/mx"
               width="500" height="500">
    <s:Group id="myGroup">
        <s:layout>                                        Layout
            <s:VerticalLayout/>                           declared first
        </s:layout>
        <s:Button width="50" minWidth="25"/>
        <s:Button width="100%" minWidth="30"/>
    </s:Group>
</s:Application>
```

As listing 17.7 points out, you must declare the layout of the container before declaring anything else that you want to fit inside that container. In this case, we're using a group and specifying that we want it to have a vertical layout. It would be a lot easier to use `<s:VGroup/>` instead, but you'll need to use this method when basing your custom components on objects with no predefined layout, such as `SkinnableContainer`.

You'll now take what you learned about the Spark layout classes and apply it to a custom MXML composite component that extends the `VGroup` class.

17.4.3 Creating MXML composite components

For our composite component example, you'll be making a reusable address form using the `VGroup` container. The result is shown in figure 17.5.

The component shown in figure 17.5 uses the Spark `VGroup` container to house a number of controls for the address form. Listing 17.8 shows the code that produces this composite component.

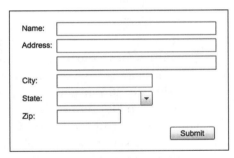

Figure 17.5 A composite component reusable address form

Listing 17.8 AddressFormVGroup.mxml: custom composite component

```
<?xml version="1.0" encoding="utf-8"?>                Component is
<s:VGroup xmlns:fx="http://ns.adobe.com/mxml/2009"   based on VGroup
          xmlns:s="library://ns.adobe.com/flex/spark"
          xmlns:mx="library://ns.adobe.com/flex/mx"
          xmlns:control="com.fx4ia.view.components.controls.*"
          width="325" height="220"                   Namespace for
          paddingLeft="10" paddingTop="10">           custom controls
    <s:HGroup verticalAlign="middle" gap="18">
        <s:Label text="Name:"/>                       HGroup containers
        <s:TextInput id="nameInput" width="250" />    to align controls
    </s:HGroup>
    <s:HGroup verticalAlign="middle">
        <s:Label text="Address:"/>
```

```
      <s:TextInput id="address1Input" width="250" />
   </s:HGroup>
   <s:HGroup verticalAlign="middle">
      <mx:Spacer width="48"/>
      <s:TextInput id="address2Input" width="250" />
   </s:HGroup>
   <s:HGroup verticalAlign="middle">
      <s:Label text="City:"/>
      <mx:Spacer width="18"/>
      <s:TextInput id="cityInput" width="150" />
   </s:HGroup>
   <s:HGroup verticalAlign="middle">
      <s:Label text="State:"/>
      <mx:Spacer width="10"/>
      <control:USStatesComboBox id="statesComboBox"
         width="150"/>                                      ⟵  Your custom
   </s:HGroup>                                                   ComboBox
   <s:HGroup verticalAlign="middle">                            control
      <s:Label text="Zip:"/>
      <mx:Spacer width="21"/>
      <s:TextInput id="zipInput" width="100" />
   </s:HGroup>
   <s:HGroup>
      <mx:Spacer width="225"/>
      <s:Button id="submitButton" label="Submit" />
   </s:HGroup>
</s:VGroup>
```

It's evident from the code in listing 17.8 that this is nothing more than an ordinary address form. You may also have noticed that it doesn't look a lot different from a Flex 3 form, aside from the changes in MXML tag names. Most important, notice that we're using the HGroup and VGroup containers just as you might use HBox and VBox to build a form in Flex 3 (assuming you didn't use <mx:FormItem/> objects instead, which you could alternatively do here as well).

The key to taking full advantage of custom composite components is breaking things into small, reusable pieces. With composites, you have more control over layout and positioning, but keep in mind that users have no ability to expect or predict anything about your composite other than what you make available. The onus is on you to provide enough public properties so the calling code can make the modifications it needs to without the developer having to crack open the code for your component and hack it to make it work the way they need it to.

As discussed in the beginning of this chapter, decoupling the display of the component through skinning is an excellent start to making your components reusable. But it's through ActionScript that you truly reach the promised land of building powerful and reusable custom components, as you're about to see.

Now that you've learned how to create both simple and composite components in Flex 4, you're ready to learn how to create advanced Flex 4 components.

17.5 Creating advanced Flex 4 components

As we mentioned previously, everything we've shown you so far can also be done through ActionScript. Although MXML allows for rapid, tag-based component development, many feel that creating custom components with ActionScript provides enough control for maximum reusability. By the time you finish this section on creating custom components, you'll be able to evaluate the options for yourself and decide whether you agree.

17.5.1 Using ActionScript to build the state selector

Let's start by creating a state-selector custom component, but this time you'll be using ActionScript instead of MXML to create it. The ActionScript code for the component is illustrated in the following listing.

Listing 17.9   CBStatesScripted.as: ActionScript U.S. state selector

```
package                              ◁──❶ Package declaration
{
  import flash.events.Event;

  import mx.controls.ComboBox;                ❷ Import and
                                                 extend class
 public class cbStatesScripted extends ComboBox
 {
    [Bindable]
    private var _selectedValue:String="";

    public function cbStatesScripted()       ◁──❸ Create constructor
    {
      super();            ◁──❹ Call super function
    }

    public function setItem(evt:Event):void        ◁──┐
    {
      selectedValue=selectedItem.stateCode;
    }
                                                        Add custom
    public function get selectedValue():String   ◁──❺ properties
    {                                                   and
      return _selectedValue;                            methods
    }

    [Bindable]
    public function set selectedValue(statecode:String):void  ◁──┘
    {
        _selectedValue = statecode;
        for(var x:int=0;x<this.dataProvider.length;x++)
          if(this.dataProvider[x].stateCode == _selectedValue)
            this.selectedIndex = x;
    }
  }
}
```

Here's the step-by-step process:

1 Create a file called CBStatesScripted.as.

2 The main block is encapsulated by a `package` declaration ❶. A `package` indicates a directory and is a way to group multiple ActionScript classes together. You're using the same directory as the main MXML file; later we'll talk about how you can structure custom components.

3 Import the ActionScript class you're basing the component on (in this case, a `ComboBox`), and create a class of your own that extends it ❷.

4 The constructor function ❸ has the same name as the class. It's called automatically by Flex when it creates instances of this class.

5 The call to the `super` class is called to make sure the constructor of the parent class is executed ❹ (the `ComboBox`'s class constructor).

6 Add the custom properties and methods that are unique to this class ❺.

7 Everything else remains the same, except that in order to invoke it you'd use `<local:CBStatesScripted/>` instead of `<local:USStatesComboBox>`, to instantiate the class in MXML.

This technique is a little more work, but one of the advantages is that you can override the functions from the parent class. So how do you know when to override a function of the class that you're subclassing? Not to worry, because you're about to find out.

17.5.2 *Knowing when to override*

One of the most important aspects of custom component development is knowing when to override the methods that are involved in the component lifecycle. The more complex your custom component is, the more of a necessity it is to override these functions so you can define new properties, dispatch new events, and perform any additional customizations that are required. The methods that are encapsulated in the `UIComponent` class that you can override in the implementation of your custom Spark component are these:

- `createChildren`
- `commitProperties`
- `measure`
- `updateDisplayList`
- `partAdded` and `partRemoved`
- `getCurrentSkinState`

These methods are placed in a queue when they're called so that display objects get the necessary updates on a single redraw of the stage when the next `render` event occurs. This is done through a technique known as *invalidation*, and it prevents massive resource overconsumption in a Flex application.

Why invalidating is so important to Flex

Enterprise data-analysis dashboards are excellent examples of where the invalidation technique becomes critical to the performance of a Flex application. In data-analysis dashboards, several graphs are often displayed at once. In addition, applications that make use of an AMF implementation such as BlazeDS or Zend_AMF get new data by *polling* the server for data changes at specified time intervals (usually every other second). In a case such as this, multiple display objects are constantly calling their invalidation routines so they can be redrawn on the next render event. Flex keeps track of the objects on the stage that have invalidated themselves so they all get redrawn and updated at the same time during the rendering of each frame. Without using this technique, data-analysis dashboards would not be possible with Flex because such an application would immediately come to a screeching halt as soon as the application started polling the server for data.

Let's look at what happens after the constructor of a component is called upon object instantiation and when invalidation methods are called on an object in the display list. This is referred to as the *component lifecycle* and is demonstrated in figure 17.6.

Understanding the component lifecycle is easiest when you imagine it in three stages: creation, invalidation, and validation.

CHILDREN CREATION

The createChildren method is where you should instantiate all subcomponents as necessary and make any calls to addElement or addChild. For example, the Flex NumericStepper control includes two Button objects and a TextInput as children of the component.

INVALIDATION PHASE ROUTINES

Each time addElement() or addChild() is called, the component enters the invalidation phase. Using the NumericStepper as an example, it wouldn't make sense to run the validation-and-rendering process three separate times just because it encapsulates three components. It makes more sense to add the children all in one pass, then render them all at once, which significantly reduces resource consumption. The specific invalidation method or methods that are called depend on what was affected by the new addition. For example, if one of the three NumericStepper children was to be resized, it would call its invalidateSize() method so the LayoutManager could resize it if necessary and keep the component's children within the bounds of the parent container.

Each invalidation routine has a corresponding validation routine, with the exception of invalidateSkinState(), which is called when the value of the state property in a component changes. The invalidation routines and their corresponding validation routines are as follows:

- invalidateProperties() : commitProperties()
- invalidateSize() : measure()
- invalidateDisplayList() : updateDisplayList()

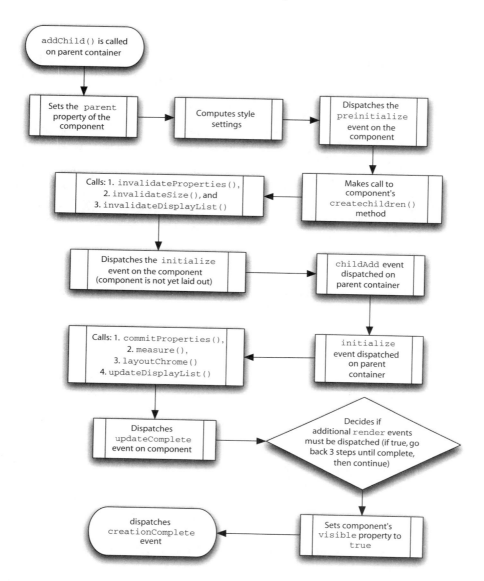

Figure 17.6 Lifecycle of the UIComponent, which begins when the call to addChild() is made

COMMITPROPERTIES()

The validation phase works differently from the invalidation phase. Invalidation routines can be called many times, and the sequence in which they're run doesn't matter. The validation phase must follow a specific flow of commands, as shown in figure 17.7. As figure 17.7 illustrates, the call to commitProperties is the first of the validation routines, and it's scheduled when a call to invalidateProperties occurs. Visual properties are often implemented on a component using getters and setters. You can place a call to `invalidateProperties` in every setter that has to do with the visual display of a component or its data. By calling `invalidateProperties`, you're telling the application that the next time it renders the screen to redraw that component because its properties changed. This allows Flex to queue the screen rendering, updating all elements and properties in a single redraw, effectively managing resource consumption.

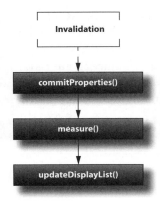

The result is a smoother-flowing application. Whenever you need a component to rerender itself because its properties changed, call `invalidate-Properties`. But it's important to note

Figure 17.7   Illustration of the validation phase of a Flex component, which begins the respective invalidation routines, which "dirty" boolean flags to let Flex know that it must run validation on the object, beginning with `commitProperties()`, then `measure()`, and finally `updateDisplayList()`

that unless you're implementing your own custom display properties into the component, Flex will make the call to `invalidateProperties` for you any time you set a layout property on a component, such as height and width or registration point (x and y) on a component. Flex also calls this method automatically as a result of certain Flex events, such as the `dataChange` event.

MEASURE()

The `measure()` routine calculates the new dimensions of a Flex display object when the `invalidateSize()` method is called #4. But `invalidateSize()` registers the component with the `LayoutManager` class provided that the component has a parent. It also sets a boolean flag to `true` when it's invalidated, so if the invalidation method is called again during the same invalidation cycle, it won't register itself multiple times with the `LayoutManager`. For example, if you were to set the height and width of a button, then set the font for the button label to a bigger size, the height and width of the button are set yet again. If it weren't for the `invalidateSizeFlag`, the component would register itself four times with the `LayoutManager`, which would then place it into the queue to be processed and redrawn four separate times on the next `render` event. The result would be a lot of unnecessary overhead. Using this design, however, you can call `invalidateSize()`many times during the invalidation phase, and `measure()` is still called only once when it moves to validation.

UPDATEDISPLAYLIST()

The `updateDisplayList()` method is scheduled when the `invalidateDisplayList()` method is called. The `invalidateDisplayList` method is often called at the end of a `commitProperties()` override. This method is called automatically whenever a call is made to the `addElement()` or `addChild()` methods. It's responsible for sizing, positioning, and displaying children components on the stage.

PARTADDED() AND PARTREMOVED()

The partAdded() and partRemoved() methods are called when a skin part is created or destroyed, respectively. The most common reason for overriding these methods is to add event listeners on partAdded and then remove those listeners on partRemoved. The name of the skin part can be used to reference it in the partAdded and partRemoved methods, as seen in this next listing.

Listing 17.10 Sample implementation of partAdded() and partRemoved()

```
override protected function partAdded(partName:String,
                                      instance:Object) : void
{
  super.partAdded(partName, instance);
  if(instance == myComboBox) {                        ① Check if instance id
    myComboBox.addEventListener("change", onChange);     is myComboBox
  }                                                   ⟵ Add listener for
}                                                     ② change event

override protected function partRemoved(partName:String,
                                        instance:Object) : void
{
  super.partRemoved(partName, instance);
  if(instance == myComboBox && myComboBox.hasEventListener("change")) {
    myComboBox.removeEventListener("change", onChange);  ⟵ Remove listener
  }                                                   ③ for change event
}
```

It's easy to see how these methods could come in handy from the sample implementation provided in listing 17.10. In this implementation, you're able to intercept the call to partAdded() and check to see if the instance id of the object that was passed is myComboBox ①. If it is, you put an event listener for the change event on it, so that your own onChange method can be called when the component's value changes ②.

Because you manually added the listener to the component when it was added to the stage, you must also manually remove it before the automated garbage collection is run on it. The partRemoved() method allows you to take care of this ③.

GETCURRENTSKINSTATE()

When building your custom components, you can use the getCurrentSkinState() method to set the view state on a skin class. The following code demonstrates how this is done:

```
override protected function getCurrentSkinState():String {    ① Set state var
  var state:String = "default";                                  to "default"
  if (_alignment == "left") {
    state = "ShiftLeft";                  ⟵              ⟵ SetCheck if private var
  }                               ③ Set state based on  ② _alignment=="left"
  return state;                      value of _alignment
}                     ⟵
              ④ Return state string
```

You may not immediately recognize what's happening here at first glance, but it's pretty interesting once you realize what getCurrentSkinState() is doing in the previous code. Because the hypothetical component has only two states, and the initial state of the component is called `"default"`, we know that the state of the component will always be set to `default` unless `_alignment == "left"` is true.

Knowing this, you write the method to first declare the variable `state` and set it to `"default"` ❶. A check is then run to see if the private variable `_alignment` is set to `"left"` ❷. If it is, then the value of the state variable is changed to `"ShiftLeft"` ❸. The value of the `state` variable is then returned ❹.

Now that you've learned the basics of creating advanced components, let's focus on the process of creating an advanced visual Spark component with Flex 4.

PRACTICE MAKES PERFECT

You'll quickly get the hang of building advanced custom components by using the following simple four-step process as a guide:

1 Begin by creating the component's skin class. This is typically done in MXML. Refer to the previous section on creating component skins for an example.

2 Create an ActionScript class that extends `SkinnableComponent`.

3 Place the code from listing 17.10 after the class constructor method.

4 Add your custom properties, methods, styles, events, and metadata, as shown in the examples throughout this chapter.

Now that you know how to create a custom component, you'll want your components to be able to communicate with each other and the main application. Therefore, component communication will be the last topic of discussion for this chapter. Then, you'll start off in chapter 18 by putting what you learned from this chapter into practice when you create an advanced custom composite component with multiple skins.

17.6 *Get your components to communicate*

Rather than show you all of the different ways data can be passed within an application, we'll instead primarily focus on methodologies that support *loose coupling* and are also consistent with the core design patterns and methodologies that the Flex framework is built on. More specifically, we'll mostly look at how data binding and events can be used to get your components communicating with each other. This will lead you nicely into chapter 18, where I'll show you some interesting design patterns for communication between objects that will make your life a lot easier by making your code reusable.

17.6.1 *Use getters and setters as property proxies*

The notion of using getters and setters to declare properties of a component is quite simple. Let's say you've created a custom ActionScript control component that use a `Tree` in place of the default list for a `ComboBox`. In addition, every node in the tree must have a `CheckBox` associated with it. Before you move any further, you already know that you'll need to access the `Tree` component and you'll need a variable to hold the data collection for the component as well. Listing 17.11 demonstrates how you can accomplish this in a simple four-step process.

Listing 17.11 Implementation of property proxies in four easy steps

```
private var _treeSelector:Tree;                                    Declare
private var _treeDataCollection:ICollection;                       private variable      Write getter
                                                                                         function
public function get treeSelector():Tree {                                                skeleton
   return this._treeSelector;                 Write getter/setter
}                                             function
                                                                           Write getter
public function get treeDataCollection():ICollection {                     function skeleton
   return _treeDataCollection as ICollection;
}                                                         Write getter/setter
                                                          function
public function set treeDataCollection(collection:ICollection):void {
   this._treeDataCollection = collection;
}                                                          Write setter
                                                           function skeleton
```

Using this method, the data for this component can now be set in MXML with the code shown in the next listing.

Listing 17.12 Setting the `treeDataCollection` property on the custom component

```
<?xml version="1.0" encoding="utf-8"?>
<s:Application xmlns:fx="http://ns.adobe.com/mxml/2009"           Declare
               xmlns:s="library://ns.adobe.com/flex/spark"        namespace for
               xmlns:mx="library://ns.adobe.com/flex/mx"          custom Tree
               xmlns:controls="com.f4ia.view.components.controls.*"
               minWidth="1024" minHeight="768">
   <fx:Declarations>                                    Flex 4
      <mx:ArrayCollection id="collection">              <fx:Declarations/>
        <fx:Object>Item One</fx:Object>               ❶ implementation
        <fx:Object>Item Two</fx:Object>
        <fx:Object>Item Three</fx:Object>          Data collection
      </mx:ArrayCollection>                         ❷ for Tree
   </fx:Declarations>
   <controls:TreeSelector id="tree"                ❸ TreeSelector
       treeDataCollection="{collection}"/>            declared and bound
</s:Application>                                        to collection
```

You may have noticed that we did something a little differently than the typical Action-Script implementation that you may have seen in past Flex 2 and Flex 3 examples for binding data collections. Instead, we used the `<fx:Declarations />` tag ❶ and created the `ArrayCollection` using entirely MXML ❷. In this case, the `ArrayCollection` only acts as a storage unit for the `Tree`'s data collection and is capable of being visible without a corresponding display object that requires it as a data provider.

When the custom `TreeSelector` component is declared, the property proxy implementation demonstrated in listing 17.13 allows `treeDataCollection` to be declared as an attribute of `TreeSelector`, which can then be directly bound to the `ArrayCollection` using its `id` attribute ❸.

If you've been developing with Flex 2 and 3, you may be more comfortable using ActionScript for binding data collections, which is still an option. We'll look at that next.

17.6.2 *Binding variables to component properties*

Keep in mind that calling code can pass a bound value rather than set a static property value. Similarly to how you use binding for the dataProvider of many List-based components, you can support it in your own components:

```
<mx:List dataProvider="{myArrayCollection}"/>
```

In the example of the TreeSelector, the component's only purpose is to present data. It doesn't know or care about where the data comes from, only that the data meets a certain set of requirements, that the data collection object that's passed to it implements the Flex ICollection interface. Listing 17.13 demonstrates how to bind the attribute of an MXML object to a data object created with ActionScript.

Listing 17.13   Binding an AS variable to an MXML attribute

```
<?xml version="1.0"?>
<?xml version="1.0" encoding="utf-8"?>
<s:Application xmlns:fx="http://ns.adobe.com/mxml/2009"
               xmlns:s="library://ns.adobe.com/flex/spark"
               xmlns:mx="library://ns.adobe.com/flex/mx"
               xmlns:controls="com.f4ia.view.components.controls.*"
               minWidth="1024" minHeight="768">
  <fx:Script>
    <![CDATA[
      import mx.collections.ArrayCollection;          Import
      [Bindable]                                      ArrayCollection
      public var collection:ArrayCollection  =        Declare Bindable tag
          new ArrayCollection([                       above variable
      {label:"First Item", elementType:"Category"},
      {label:"Second Item", elementType:"Category"},  Build
      {label:"Last Item", elementType:"Category"}]);  ArrayCollection
      ]]>
  </fx:Script>
  <controls:TreeSelector id="tree"                    Bind property to
      treeDataCollection="{collection}"/>             corresponding variable
</mx:Application>
```

When you create a binding, Flex sets an event listener (dataChange is the default unless you override it by specifying and dispatching your own event from the setter function), and when the model changes (properties and variables that you're binding to), the Flex framework handles the update of the view. Binding is one of the fundamental principles of working with the Flex framework; use it wisely because it can save you a lot of time.

Now that you've learned how to get information to a custom component using binding, the next logical step is to get information *from* the custom component. This is where events come in particularly handy because you can use an event to pass data to whomever may be listening for that event.

17.6.3 Use events to pass data

The cool thing about what I'm about to show you is that it can be applied to almost any Flex situation. No matter what the architecture is, or how tightly or loosely coupled the components are with the application and with each other, this method is usually a reliable method of getting data to where you need it. You'll even learn how to expand on it in the next chapter, when we talk about design patterns and architecture.

Staying objective

Notice that I chose my words carefully by stating that "this method is *usually* a reliable method" in regard to passing data with events. You might notice that I do this often because I've seen developers break things that in my mind were unbreakable at the time. I'm convinced that there's some inevitable force that exists solely to prove us wrong about the things that we subconsciously think will "always work." The moral of the story here is to always take an objective approach to every bit of code that you read and the code that you write. By staying objective and understanding that there is no "always" in programming, you'll maximize your ability to troubleshoot errors and fix bugs in large and complex code bases.

DEFINING THE PROBLEM

The `TreeSelector` component that you've been working with now has to notify interested parties when one of the check boxes that belong to its children has been selected, as well as the name of the node that was selected. Similarly, it must also communicate if the check box has been unselected and the name of the node that was unselected.

One of the simplest and most reliable ways to accomplish this task is to dispatch a custom event and pass the data through a property that you create in the event class. Being the savvy Flex developer that you are, you know that this is your preferred method of attack because this isn't an especially large application where a lot of abstraction is required (more on that in the next two chapters).

IMPLEMENTING THE SOLUTION

To implement your solution, you start by creating your custom `Event` class. The code for your custom event is shown in the following listing.

Listing 17.14   TreeSelectorEvent.as: passing data through an event

```
package com.f4ia.events.TreeSelectorEvent
{
    import flash.events.Event;

    public class TreeSelectorEvent extends Event          ◁── Must extend Flex Event class
    {
        public static const CHILD_STATE_CHANGED:String = "childStateChanged";     Static constants for strong event typing
        public static const CHILD_ADDED:String = "childAdded";          ◁──
        public static const CHILD_REMOVED:String = "childRemoved";
```

```
public function TreeSelectorEvent(type:String,
    data:TreeSelectorDataObject=null,
    bubbles:Boolean=true,                        ◁─── ❶ data object passed
    cancelable:Boolean=false)                         through constructor
{
    super(type, bubbles, cancelable);      ❷ Public property set
    nodeData = data;                       ◁┘   to data value
}
                                               ❸ Strongly typed
public var nodeData:TreeSelectorDataObject;  ◁─   data property
override public function clone():Event       Override
{                                            ◁┘  clone method
    return new TreeSelectorEvent( type, nodeData, bubbles, cancelable );
}

    }
}
```

As you've learned, the key ingredient to the custom-built event object shown in listing 17.14 is the data object, which is passed into the constructor when the event is created ❶. Notice the public variable nodeData that's declared under the constructor method ❸. This acts as a proxy to store the data object when it's set in the body of the constructor ❷. Being the conscientious developers that we are, we use our knowledge of best practices and strongly type this variable that will hold the data object as Tree-SelectorDataObject because it makes our code more conducive to proper unit testing. The respective unit tests would likely include a test to ensure that the object being passed with the event has the correct information, and if someone decided to change the information that gets passed through our event, the unit test would then fail, triggering the alarms you have in place to protect your project from such disasters (such as automated email notifications that let you know that one of your tests just failed). Joel Hooks, our resident unit-testing guru, will step in for the final chapters of the book to give you the complete lowdown on unit testing with FlexUnit 4 and test-driven development (TDD).

Now that you have your event class for passing data, it's time to put it to use. The following code snippet is a function from the TreeSelector component that creates a data object, passes it into the event, and dispatches the event:

```
private function onSendData(data:TreeSelectorDataObject):void
{
    dispatchEvent(new TreeSelectorEvent("childStateChanged", data);
}
```

Firing the event with the data passed into it isn't going to do you any good if you don't have something listening for it, right? Listing 17.15 demonstrates how to get your new code to start working for you.

Listing 17.15   Getting the data out of the event

```
<?xml version="1.0" encoding="utf-8"?>
<s:Application xmlns:fx="http://ns.adobe.com/mxml/2009"
               xmlns:s="library://ns.adobe.com/flex/spark"
               xmlns:mx="library://ns.adobe.com/flex/mx"
               xmlns:controls="com.f4ia.view.components.controls.*"
               creationComplete="creationCompleteHandler(event)"        ◁┐
               minWidth="1024" minHeight="768">              Method scheduled to run on
  <fx:Script>                                                  creationComplete
    <![CDATA[
      import com.f4ia.events.TreeSelectorEvent;
      import mx.collections.ArrayCollection;
      import mx.events.FlexEvent;

      [Bindable]
      public var collection:ArrayCollection;

      [Bindable]
      private var                                              Variable
          selectedObject:TreeSelectorDataObject;       ◁┘  selectedObject

      protected function creationCompleteHandler(event:FlexEvent):void
      {
        tree.addEventListener(TreeSelectorEvent.CHILD_STATE_CHANGED,
                      onChildStateChange);        ◁┐  Event listener set on
      }                                                TreeSelector
      private function onChildStateChange(event:TreeSelectorEvent):void
      {
        selectedObject = event.nodeData;        ◁┐
      }                             data object extracted and set to
    ]]>                                  selectedObject
  </fx:Script>

  <controls:TreeSelector id="tree"
                 treeDataCollection="{collection}"
                 selectedItem="{selectedObject}" />        ◁┐
</s:Application>                   Binding TreeSelector.selectedItem
                                           to selectedObject
```

Hopefully by now the code in listing 17.15 is fairly straightforward. It illustrates how the application housing a component (TreeSelector) listens for a custom event (TreeSelectorEvent) to be fired from the component, then extracts the data from the event in the event handler function and sets the value to a bindable variable, which in this case is bound to the selectedItem property of the TreeSelector. Congratulations, you now know how to create advanced custom components in Flex 4!

17.7   Summary

You'll spend a good portion of your time making custom components as you scale your Flex applications, so it's worth gathering as much information as you can on the subject from trustworthy resources so you can gain as solid a foundation as possible in this area.

As you've learned, all visual components are subclasses of the base `UIComponent` class. Remember that you get all the events, styles, properties, and functions that come with the parent you're inheriting from, and the key to making powerful custom components is tapping into and seamlessly integrating directly into the Flex component lifecycle.

Focus on encapsulation, and try to make your components reusable by keeping them decoupled and independent of the applications that you build them for. As you continue to become a Flex master, your reusable components will lead you to an exponentially faster workflow. Chapter 18 takes what you've learned here and continues on the path of reducing duplication by exploring the power of reusability in greater detail.

18

Creating
reusable components

This chapter covers

- Reusable components
- Leveraging Spark
- Code separation
- Skinnable components
- Runtime shared libraries
- Shared reusability

In the last chapter, you got an in-depth look at the Spark component architecture. Now you'll put this newfound knowledge to work by building your own reusable component.

What is *reusability*? The concept of reusability isn't unique to Flex; each language provides mechanisms to achieve it. Words like *encapsulation*, *abstraction*, and *polymorphism* are OOP words that describe methods for creating code that can be easily reused. The more code you're able to reuse, the faster you can develop new applications by leveraging existing code. From a maintenance perspective, you can achieve faster turnaround time when implementing changes too, because you only have to implement the fix in one spot, and anything that accesses that code will be updated because it's all accessing the same source.

The first thing you'll do in this chapter is look at a scenario where you must create a component that reveals content, but in many different ways, yet without having to write a separate component for each implementation. This example dives deeper into the realm of custom component development in Flex 4 than what you were exposed to in the last chapter, with our focus here narrowed specifically to code reuse.

There's no difference between the way you learned to build custom components in chapter 17 compared to what you'll build here. This chapter takes what you learned in chapter 17 and applies it to a real-world scenario, so let's get started!

18.1 Putting reusability into action

At the 2009 Adobe MAX conference, lead architect of the Flex SDK Ely Greenfield did an excellent session involving Spark component architecture. He created an example for the presentation, which I liked a lot, and so I asked his permission to refactor it (the Flex 4 SDK was a lot different then) for use with this book. I'm delighted to have the opportunity to walk you through building your own custom component, dubbed `Reveal` by a highly respected individual in the Flash platform community, Ely Greenfield.

18.1.1 Reveal component background

Ely's demonstration comprised a single component with nine different skins and four different implementations. His purpose was not to dig into the code line by line but rather to demonstrate one of the ways we'd benefit by the movement toward architectural design best practices for the Flex SDK. He accomplished this by showing off some crafty skin swapping and how easily he could drastically manipulate and change the display of a component without having to even touch the component class. Needless to say, Ely's example was a perfect fit for this chapter.

I should point out that I made a good number of changes to Ely's original `Reveal`. The nature of my changes were twofold: First, I had to make sure I kept the code up to date as the Flex framework continued to change through the development of version 4. My second objective was to maximize simplicity so that I could make this as easy for you to understand as possible.

Now it's almost time to start putting Spark into action and build your `Reveal` component; first we'll have a brief discussion on the underlying concepts of Spark component reusability.

18.1.2 Theory and concepts in Spark reusability

In order for your components to be reusable, there must be a many-to-one relationship between the component and the skins that are responsible for styling it. The view must be independent of the component's model. Figure 18.1 illustrates this relationship.

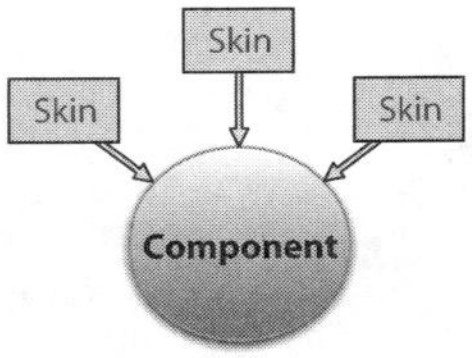

The `Reveal` component is a content container that has the special functionality of being able to reveal its content in a way

Figure 18.1 The Spark component model shows a many-to-one relationship between skins and a component.

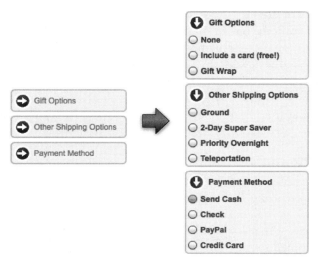

Figure 18.2 Drop-down and reveal: The component on the left shows the state of all three `Reveal` drop-downs in a closed state, whereas the version on the right shows them in their respective open states.

that's specified by the skin. It's made up of a single class (`Reveal.as`) that extends the Spark `SkinnableContainer`. You're about to see this same component with two very different implementations. Notice as you step through the code that the only thing that changes between the two implementations is the skin class. You can refer back to chapter 17 if you get confused at any point. The second thing to make note of as we step through the code is how all of the display logic is held in a different MXML skin for each implementation, and the code that's specific to the application is held elsewhere.

Let's see the component in action before we look at the code. The first implementation is what I call "drop-down and reveal" and is demonstrated in figure 18.2.

In the "drop-down and reveal" implementation (figure 18.2), the default state of the component is shown on the left side, whereas the image on the right shows the component after all three arrow buttons have been clicked, toggling their respective drop-down menus.

The implementation shown in figure 18.3 is the same component but with a different skin.

The "slide open and reveal" version of the component shown in figure 18.3 has the default state shown on the right side. When you click the arrow button, the component slides open and reveals its contents, as shown in the image on the left side of the figure.

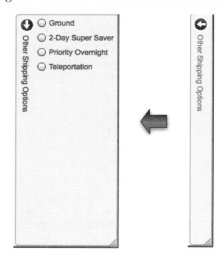

Figure 18.3 Slide open and reveal: The component on the right shows `Reveal` in its closed state, whereas the version on the left shows `Reveal` in its open state. As you can see, this appears as a completely different implementation of the `Reveal` component compared to the drop-down version.

As you can see from the file structure shown in figure 18.4, the Reveal component is only a single class, with various implementations contained elsewhere in the project structure.

Without viewing any code yet, you can probably tell by the organizational structure that the code is loosely coupled and free of any direct dependencies. Now that you have a clear idea of what we're trying to accomplish here, it's time to look at some code!

18.1.3 *Creating the Reveal component*

You're probably wondering how what you just saw was accomplished, so let's take a look at the code for the Reveal component, which I've broken up into

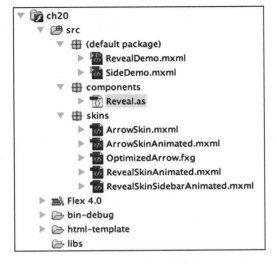

Figure 18.4 Package structure for the Reveal component

three bite-sized chunks to make it a little more palatable. The first part is provided in listing 18.1, where you see the identification of the component's skin states and skin parts.

> **Listing 18.1 Reveal.as, part 1—skin states and skin parts**

```
package components
{
  import flash.events.Event;
  import spark.components.SkinnableContainer;
  import spark.components.ToggleButton;
  import spark.components.supportClasses.TextBase;

  [SkinState("open")]                        ❶ State
  [SkinState("closed")]                        declaration

  public class Reveal extends SkinnableContainer
  {
    [SkinPart(required="false")]                        skinPart
    public var labelDisplay:TextBase;          ❷ metadata with
                                      Reference to  required property
    [SkinPart]                        skinPart
    public var openButton:ToggleButton;
(...)
```

The first set of code in the Reveal.as class identifies the states that the components will use above the class declaration ❶ and identifies the skin parts of the component ❷. This is part of the *contract* that's set between the component and its skin.

Listing 18.2 demonstrates how properties are set on the elements of the skin, but from the component class.

Listing 18.2   `Reveal.as`, part 2 - component properties

```
(...)
    private var _open:Boolean = false;
    private var _label:String;                        Value proxies

    public function set open(value:Boolean):void                    ❶ Sets state of
    {                                                                   component
      _open = value;
      invalidateSkinState();                          ❷ Invalidation
      invalidateProperties();                            routines to trigger
    }

    public function get open():Boolean
    {
      return _open;
    }
                                                                ❸ Sets value for
    public function set label(value:String):void                   labelDisplay
    {
      if(_label == value)
        return;
      _label = value;
      if(labelDisplay != null)
        labelDisplay.text = value;
    }

    public function get label():String
    {
      return _label;
    }
(...)
```

In the `Reveal` component, an `open` property is used to set the state of the component using a boolean value ❶. The state can be set this way because there are only two states. Otherwise, we'd pass the state name as a string into the setter function. The `invalidateSkinState()` and `invalidateProperties()` method calls are then made after the state is set to tell the display list to redraw the component because its properties have changed ❷. The `label` property is the string that's used for the text on the `labelDisplay` skin part ❸.

The third and final section of the code for the `Reveal.as` component class contains the necessary method overrides, as shown in the following listing.

Listing 18.3   `Reveal.as`, part 3 - method overrides

```
(...)
    override protected function getCurrentSkinState():String
    {
      if(_open)
        return "open";                    ❶ Check value proxy,
      else                                   return state
        return "closed";
    }

    override protected function partAdded(name:String,instance:Object):void
```

```
    {
      super.partAdded(name,instance);
                                              ➋  Check
      if(instance == openButton)                 object type
      {
        openButton.addEventListener(Event.CHANGE,
                                    toggleButtonChangeHandler);
        openButton.selected = _open;
      }
      else if (instance == labelDisplay)
      {
        labelDisplay.text = label;
      }
    }
    override protected function partRemoved(name:String,
                                            instance:Object):void
    {
       super.partRemoved(name,instance);
                                              ➌  Remove
      if(instance == openButton)                 listener
      {
        openButton.removeEventListener(Event.CHANGE,
                                       toggleButtonChangeHandler);
        openButton.selected = _open;
      }
      else if (instance == labelDisplay)
      {                                        ➍  Clear
        labelDisplay.text = "";                   label text
      }
    }
    private function toggleButtonChangeHandler(e:Event):void
    {
      open = openButton.selected;
    }

  }
}
```

We want to override three methods here. The first is getCurrentSkinState(), where
we find out if the value of the private _open variable is true or false and send back the
state name accordingly ➊. In the partAdded() override, a conditional checks to see if
the part being added is openButton ➋, and if so, it adds the respective event listener to
it. If the part being added is the labelDisplay, then it sets the respective text value.

The third override is partRemoved(), where garbage collection is the name of the
game. Similar to partAdded(), a conditional is inserted to first check to see if the part
being removed is openButton, and this time we remove the event listener that was set
on the object when it was added ➌. If the part is the labelDisplay, however, we clear
out the text field so the old value isn't held in memory ➍, which will cause it to briefly
display the previously displayed text whenever the part gets added.

Now that we've finished our analysis of the component code, we'll do a similar
code analysis in the next section, but this time on the component skins.

18.1.4 Skinning the first Reveal

I broke up the first skin into three code sections, as I did with the component class, in order to make things more palatable by taking it in a little bit at a time. The beginning of the first skin is shown in this next listing.

Listing 18.4 RevealSkinAnimated.mxml, section 1

```xml
<?xml version="1.0" encoding="utf-8"?>
<s:Skin xmlns:fx="http://ns.adobe.com/mxml/2009"
        xmlns:mx="library://ns.adobe.com/flex/mx"
        xmlns:s="library://ns.adobe.com/flex/spark">

  <s:states>
    <s:State name="closed" />                       Declaring states
    <s:State name="open" />
  </s:states>
                                                                     Draw background   ❶
                                                                           rectangle
  <s:Rect radiusX="5" top="0" left="0" right="0" bottom="0" alpha=".9"
    <s:fill>                                            ❷  Fill background
      <s:SolidColor color="#E1FFBB" />                      with lime green
    </s:fill>
    <s:stroke>
      <s:SolidColorStroke color="#BAD47F" weight="2" />         Outline the
    </s:stroke>                                          ❸   container
  </s:Rect>
(...)
```

The code sample in listing 18.4 does a good job of demonstrating the drawing and styling capabilities of Spark. Beginning with the opening `<Rect/>` tag, we use MXML syntax to tap into the ActionScript graphics API by creating a rectangle to be used as the background of the container ❶. Then we fill the rectangle with a lime green color ❷ and give it a thin outline ❸.

Upon reviewing the code in listing 18.5 and comparing it with the code contained in the `Reveal.as` class, you should be starting to understand how it all fits together. Let's look at the code in the following listing.

Listing 18.5 RevealSkinAnimated.mxml, section 2

```xml
(...)
  <s:Group left="0" top="0" right="0" bottom="5">           ❶  openButton
                                                                component part
    <s:ToggleButton id="openButton"                            declaration
                    skinClass="skins.ArrowSkin"
                    left="5" top="5" />                       Skin declared
  </s:Group>                                               ❷  within a skin

  <s:Label id="labelDisplay"
           left="35" top="13" right="15"                      labelDisplay
           lineBreak="explicit" />                            component part
                                                           ❸  declaration
  <s:Group id="contentGroup"
           top="35" bottom="5"                                Content holder for
           left="5" right="5"                              ❹  implementation
           includeIn="open" >
```

```
    <s:layout>
      <s:VerticalLayout />
    </s:layout>
  </s:Group>
(...)
```
◁ **Configure layout**
⑤ for content

First, we declare the `ToggleButton` display object that corresponds to the skin part that you saw declared as a variable in the `Reveal` component class and give it the `id` of `openButton` ❶. Note that the `id` is identical to the variable name used for that skin part in the component class. This is important because it's another part of the contract that the component has with the skin. If the contract is broken, the skin is no longer compatible with the component it was created for.

The next line is interesting because it points out the fact that a skin can be declared as a property on any display object within another skin ❷. This is pretty cool when you think about it because you can develop, skin, and group composite components within composite components for extremely large applications, making them far easier to manage.

Next, we declare the `labelDisplay` component ❸. Notice that it's typed to a `Label` object even though the corresponding skin part in the component class is typed to `TextBase`. This is okay to do because `Label` subclasses `TextBase`. Typing skin parts to an abstract base class or interface while in the component class gives you more flexibility when creating skins for that component because you can declare and make use of the functionality of any object that extends or implements that base class or interface. Be careful that you don't end up with code that can't be unit tested. We'll discuss that in detail in chapter 24.

After the `labelDisplay`, you see a `Group` container with an `id` of `contentGroup` ❹. The space contained in the `contentGroup` `Group` is where we'll place the content in the implementation of the component, which you'll see shortly. Notice that the `includeIn` property is used here and set to the `open` state. This tells the application that this particular skin part should be added to the stage only when the component is in its `open` state. It's also important to point out that the layout rules that specify how the content will be laid out in the `contentGroup` space are defined within the respective `<Group/>` MXML tag ❺.

Before I show you how this component is implemented, we'll take a quick look at the final section of this skin's code, as shown in the next listing.

Listing 18.6   RevealSkinAnimated.mxml, section 3

```
(...)
  <s:transitions>
    <s:Transition fromState="closed" toState="open">
      <s:Sequence>
        <s:Resize target="{this}" duration="150" />
        <s:AddAction target="{contentGroup}" />
        <s:Fade target="{contentGroup}"
                alphaFrom="0" alphaTo="1"
                duration="150"/>
```
◁ **Transition for**
❶ closed to open state

```
        </s:Sequence>
      </s:Transition>
      <s:Transition fromState="open" toState="closed">
        <s:Sequence>
          <s:Fade target="{contentGroup}"
                  alphaFrom="1" alphaTo="0"
                  duration="150" />
          <s:RemoveAction target="{contentGroup}" />
          <s:Resize target="{this}" duration="150"  />
        </s:Sequence>
      </s:Transition>
    </s:transitions>
</s:Skin>
```

❶⤳ **Transition for**
❷ open to closed state

It's obvious that the last bit of code in the Reveal skin (listing 18.6) is for defining transition effects between states. The first transition does a Resize and Fade from the closed to the open state, as well as making the content that's held within the content-Group area of the component visible ❶. The transition from the open to closed state does the same thing as the first transition in reverse ❷. This concludes our analysis of the first skin.

The next section is what we've been leading up to, and it makes the purpose of the last ten pages clear. You'll now look at the code of a new skin, which we'll use with the same Reveal component. The point here is to recognize how the layout and display of the component change dramatically, and yet they're both still the same component. Now that's great code reusability!

18.2 Reveal gets a new look

The second skin is provided as a single code listing because you already saw the first skin broken into chunks. This gives you an opportunity to see a skin class from start to finish. Most important, listing 18.7 demonstrates how a completely different use case can be applied to the same component by attaching a different skin.

Listing 18.7 "Slide open and reveal" skin

```
<?xml version="1.0" encoding="utf-8"?>
<s:Skin xmlns:fx="http://ns.adobe.com/mxml/2009"
        xmlns:mx="library://ns.adobe.com/flex/mx"
        xmlns:s="library://ns.adobe.com/flex/spark">

    <s:states>
        <s:State name="closed" />
        <s:State name="open" />
    </s:states>

    <s:Rect radiusX="5" top="0" left="0" right="-10" bottom="0" alpha=".9">
        <s:fill>
            <s:SolidColor color="#E1FFBB" />
        </s:fill>
        <s:stroke>
            <s:SolidColorStroke color="#BAD47F" weight="2" />
        </s:stroke>
    </s:Rect>
```

```
<s:Group left="0" right="5" top="0" bottom="0">
   <s:ToggleButton id="openButton"
                   skinClass="skins.ArrowSkinAnimated"
                   left="5" top="5" scaleX="-1"/>
   <s:Label id="labelDisplay" rotation="90"
            left="9" top="35" bottom="5" />
</s:Group>

<s:Group id="contentGroup" top="5" left="35"
         bottom="5" right="5" includeIn="open" />

<s:transitions>
   <s:Transition fromState="closed" toState="open">
      <s:Sequence>
         <s:Resize target="{this}" duration="300" />
      </s:Sequence>
   </s:Transition>
   <s:Transition fromState="open" toState="closed">
      <s:Sequence>
         <s:Resize target="{this}" duration="300"  />
         <s:RemoveAction target="{contentGroup}" />
      </s:Sequence>
   </s:Transition>
</s:transitions>
```

Label moved to first group

Transitions for improved user experience

```
</s:Skin>
```

At first glance, the skin in listing 18.7 may not look much different from the first (shown in listings 18.4, 18.5, and 18.6), but if you take a closer look, you'll see that the layout has changed as well as the transition effects, giving the component a very different way of displaying content (shown in figure 18.3).

18.2.1 *Implementation of the Reveal controls*

Now it's time to see the component implemented in an application. We'll use this opportunity to also learn another way of attaching a skin to a component: with CSS! Listing 18.8 is the application file for the drop-down version of the Reveal component. Notice what's happening within the <fx:Style/> tag because we'll come back to that in a moment.

Listing 18.8 Drop-down Reveal implementation

```
<?xml version="1.0" encoding="utf-8"?>
<s:Application xmlns:fx="http://ns.adobe.com/mxml/2009"
               xmlns:s="library://ns.adobe.com/flex/spark"
               xmlns:mx="library://ns.adobe.com/flex/mx"
               xmlns:components="components.*" >
  <fx:Style>
    @namespace components "components.*";
    @namespace mx "library://ns.adobe.com/flex/mx";
    @namespace s "library://ns.adobe.com/flex/spark";

    components|Reveal {
      skinClass: ClassReference("skins.RevealSkinAnimated");
      color: #849C23;
```

❶ CSS namespace for Reveal

❷ CSS Reveal declaration

Component skin attachment using CSS ❸

```
  }
  components|Reveal:open {
    color: #52533F;
    font-weight: bold;
  }
</fx:Style>
<s:VGroup horizontalAlign="contentJustify" left="40" top="40">
  <components:Reveal label="Gift Options" >
    <s:RadioButton label="None" />
    <s:RadioButton label="Include a card (free!)" />
    <s:RadioButton label="Gift Wrap" />
  </components:Reveal>
  <components:Reveal label="Other Shipping Options" >
    <s:RadioButton label="Ground" />
    <s:RadioButton label="2-Day Super Saver" />
    <s:RadioButton label="Priority Overnight" />
    <s:RadioButton label="Teleportation" />
  </components:Reveal>
  <components:Reveal label="Payment Method" >
    <s:RadioButton label="Send Cash" />
    <s:RadioButton label="Check" />
    <s:RadioButton label="PayPal" />
    <s:RadioButton label="Credit Card" />
  </components:Reveal>
</s:VGroup>
</s:Application>
```

◁─┐ **CSS `Reveal` state**
❹ **pseudo-selector**

◁──── **First `Reveal`**

◁──── **Second `Reveal`**

◁──── **Third `Reveal`**

I did something a little unexpected to make sure you're paying close attention. We're building three different instances of the Reveal component in listing 18.8 and stacking them in a VGroup container, which is similar to the VBox in Flex 3. In this kind of situation, it's usually easiest to use CSS to attach the skin, as demonstrated in listing 18.8. But beware that in Flex 4 you have to declare your CSS namespaces right after the <fx:Style/> tag if the CSS is being used in an MXML file, or at the top if it's a standalone CSS file.

In this case, you want to tell Flex about the components package so that you can set selectors on the Reveal component ❶. Now you can create a global selector for Reveal by using the components prefix ❷. Now that you've selected the Reveal component at the application level (as opposed to an instance of Reveal), you can attach a skin to it ❸.

You might decide that you want some of the styling to be different based on the state of the component as well, but it might not be something you want to place in the skin, such as a small change in text formatting. If that's the case, you can easily accomplish this using a *pseudo-selector*, which allows you to select and apply styles to a component, but only when it's in the specified state ❹. Don't worry; we'll talk about CSS and styling more in chapter 20. For now I want to show you how to attach skins to components using CSS because it's a handy little feature in Flex 4.

Each of the three Reveal instances gets its own label and a set of radio buttons for the user to select an option for each of the components. Now you may be thinking to yourself, How does Reveal know where to put the radio buttons? The Spark

`SkinnableContainer` object that `Reveal` subclasses has a built-in public property called `contentGroup`, which is typed to a `Group` object. The built-in functionality of the `SkinnableContainer` is to push any valid display objects that are inserted within the component's tag (in this case, `<Reveal/>`) into its respective `contentGroup`. How cool is that!

SLIDE-OPEN IMPLEMENTATION

As you've seen, the similarities between these two different implementations of the same `Reveal` component are interesting. Listing 18.9 shows the implementation of the slide-open version of the `Reveal` component.

Listing 18.9 Sliding `Reveal` implementation

```xml
<?xml version="1.0" encoding="utf-8"?>
<s:Application xmlns:fx="http://ns.adobe.com/mxml/2009"
               xmlns:s="library://ns.adobe.com/flex/spark"
               xmlns:mx="library://ns.adobe.com/flex/mx"
               xmlns:components="components.*" >

    <fx:Style>
        @namespace components "components.*";
        @namespace mx "library://ns.adobe.com/flex/mx";
        @namespace s "library://ns.adobe.com/flex/spark";

        components|Reveal {
            skinClass: ClassReference("skins.RevealSkinSidebarAnimated");
        }
        components|Reveal:closed {
            color: #849C23;
        }
        components|Reveal:open {
            color: #52533F;
        }
    </fx:Style>

    <components:Reveal label="Other Shipping Options"      ❶ Declare instance
                    top="0" right="0" bottom="0">            of Reveal

        <components:layout>                                ❷ Set layout
            <s:VerticalLayout />                              property
        </components:layout>

        <s:RadioButton label="Ground" />
        <s:RadioButton label="2-Day Super Saver" />        Content for
        <s:RadioButton label="Priority Overnight" />       contentGroup
        <s:RadioButton label="Teleportation" />
    </components:Reveal>

</s:Application>
```

In the slide-open implementation of Reveal, the only thing you're doing differently is instantiating one instance of the `Reveal` component ❶ and setting its layout property using MXML syntax ❷. The difference in the transition effects is handled in the skin, so there isn't much else to do here other than add the necessary content within the

MXML tag that instantiates the Reveal container, which will automatically be pushed into the contentGroup Group container of the component.

Once you've built up a collection of reusable Spark components, it's convenient to package them into a portable SWC file that you can use for future projects. You can also use SWC files as *runtime shared libraries*, which we'll explore next.

18.3 Runtime shared libraries

Runtime shared libraries are useful for large applications, frameworks, and code libraries. Think of an RSL as allowing classes to be loaded on demand during runtime as opposed to compiling everything into the application. If you've ever done any basic Windows programming, you should be familiar with what a DLL file is. Runtime shared libraries are based on the same concept as DLLs. In this section, we'll discuss how you can reuse your code libraries through SWCs and RSLs.

18.3.1 Understanding SWC files

An SWC file acts in the same way as a zip file. When you create a zip, you're compressing a number of individual files into a single file that can later be decompressed, or unarchived, to expose all of the files within it. Most of the time, third-party components and libraries that you'll include in your Flex application development come in the form of a single SWC file because of the ease of distribution that they offer.

DISSECTING AN SWC

If you open an SWC file with WinZip, you'll find a file called library.swf and one called catalog.xml. The SWF file contains all your code and assets, and catalog.xml tells the compiler what and where everything is in the SWF file (class paths using dot notation and asset names).

Most often, SWC files are used for themes and code that's compiled directly into an application. But the most efficient use of SWC files is sharing code during runtime. Let's look at how to use SWC files for runtime shared libraries.

18.3.2 Types of RSLs

RSLs are code that's compiled into a SWC and can be loaded during runtime by multiple applications and domains by using namespaces. An excellent example of this is the Flex framework, which is made up of several RSLs. Suppose you create a new class that you'll use in 20 applications. Instead of having this class be compiled in all 20 applications and take up an extra 300 KB in each of them, you can trim them down by having the applications load the class during runtime.

To understand how to use an RSL, you'll create a simple class and turn it into an RSL for use in other applications from the same domain. The first step is to create a new Flex library project:

1 In Flash Builder, create a new Flex library project by choosing File > New > Flex Library Project.
2 Name the project MyRSL.
3 Click Finish.

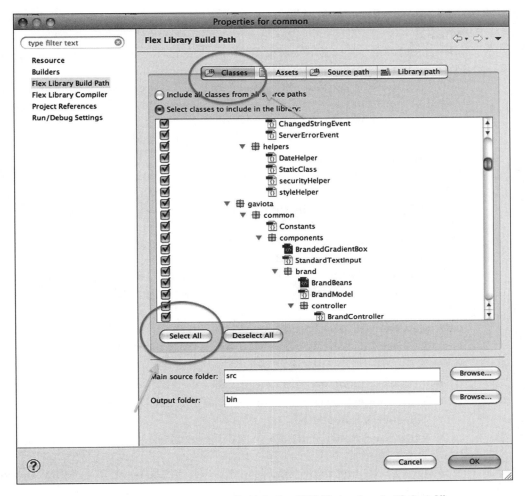

Figure 18.5   Make sure all classes are compiled into the SWC file by choosing Select All.

You now have an empty library project. If you already have classes that you want to convert into an SWC file, all you have to do is drag them into the library folder, navigate to Project > Properties > Flex Library Build Path, select the tab labeled Classes, and then click the button labeled Select All, as shown in figure 18.5.

Flash Builder will now compile all classes into an SWC file for you as long as there are no compiler errors.

At this point, you've successfully compiled an SWC library file, but you haven't told an application to use it yet, which is what you'll do next.

18.3.3 *Making your Flex application use the RSL*

What we've done so far is create and compile a SWC file. This now gives us the convenience of being able to access the SWC and the classes inside it from the application we're building, provided that we've included it in the libs directory.

When working on multiple projects that use shared classes like these, it can be useful to store the SWCs in a centralized folder such as C:\Flex\SWC\ on Windows or /Users/<username>/Documents/SWC on Mac. This would include not only SWCs that you've made but also others that you've downloaded.

STATIC VERSUS DYNAMIC LINKAGE

When an SWC is used as a shared library, it can be linked either statically or dynamically. In the static approach, you're embedding everything for the SWC into the final SWF (or AIR file if it's an AIR application). But this can often result in a large SWF or AIR file.

When the SWF file is too large to compile into the application, dynamic linkage is what makes an SWC an RSL in that it's loading the classes as needed during runtime. This way, you avoid the large file size that's output by the compiler because the SWC file(s) are now being loaded on demand. Let's leave our SWC file and create a project that can use it.

CREATING A PROJECT TO USE THE RSL

For now, leave the SWC file where it is. We'll create a Flex project and then configure it to use the RSL. Follow these steps:

1   In Flash Builder, create a new project called RSLTest.
2   In the project navigator, right-click the RSLTest project and select Properties.
3   Select Flex Build Path.
4   Click the Library Path tab to see the external libraries loaded into the Flex application.
5   One of the first things you should always do when you want to use an RSL is to make sure the Flex framework is running as an RSL. If it isn't, change the Framework Linkage option in the Properties for RSLTest dialog box to Runtime Shared Library.

Doing so creates an SWZ file and an SWF file containing the Flex framework. An SWZ file is a digitally signed Adobe SWF file that can be cached by Flash Player. The next time the user views your Flex application, the load time will be drastically shorter because Flash Player won't have to reload the Flex framework.

But why does Flash Builder create an SWF file when it already has an SWZ file? Framework caching became available in version 9 of Flash Player. By the time you read this, Flash Player 9 or above will be installed on 98.7% of all computers and version 10.1 will have already penetrated an estimated 80% of the online population. But Flex also creates the SWF file so that if the end user doesn't have version 9 or above, the SWF file will be cached in the browser and will act like an RSL. One thing to be aware of is that the browser cache is easily cleared by the user, which would require caching the framework again.

Next up is turning the `myRSL` project into an RSL.

CREATING THE RSL

Now that you've made your Flex framework an RSL, you have to also make `MyRSL` an RSL. First, you must import it into the library:

1 Click Add SWC in the Properties for RSLTest dialog box.
2 Browse to the path of your SWC file.
3 Click OK.

You'll see the `MyRSL` SWC file added to the application library. But you still haven't made it an RSL. If you expand the `MyRSL` tree node, you'll see that the link type is merged to code. Merged to code isn't what you want, because it's the same thing as having `MyRSL` compiled in the application (via static linkage).

Instead, you want to make the SWC an RSL by dynamically linking to it. To do so, continue from the last step and follow these steps:

1 Click the link type, and click Edit.
2 In the resulting Edit dialog box, select the Use Same Linkage as Framework check box. This option gives `MyRSL` the same linkage as the Flex framework, which we've made dynamic and thus would make `MyRSL` dynamic as well and therefore an RSL.
3 The Deployment Path/URL is now MyRSL.swf. This file will be cached by the browser and shared by all applications that use this class.
4 Click OK.
5 Click OK in the Library dialog box. Flash Builder will compile the application with the new properties.

You've linked your custom class and configured it so that it will be cached by the browser and used in all applications that use this class in your domain.

You'll need to perform these steps for every application that you want to be able to share this class. But when you upload your application to your domain, you'll need only these files:

- One MyRSL.swf file
- One Framework.swz file
- One Framework.swf file per domain

Make sure the path of the RSL is the same throughout your applications, so Flash Player knows where to check whether the file is cached in order to load it. You'll see a significant difference in application load times, because Flash Player won't have to load the 200–300KB Flex framework or your custom classes each time you view the application.

18.4   *Summary*

The more Flex applications you develop, the more you'll appreciate the value of code reuse. Flex 4 allows you to reuse code with ease thanks to the new Spark component architecture. You can also reduce the size of your SWF file and make your code much more reusable in other applications by using runtime shared libraries.

You've learned how to reuse your code and make your application perform at its best. But even with increased speed and reusable code, you'll need to know how to implement a proper architecture into your applications, especially if it's a big one. The next chapter will broaden your knowledge of Flex from an architectural standpoint.

19

Architectural design patterns

This chapter covers

- Introduction to architectural frameworks
- Flex and the Model-View-Controller pattern
- How to roll your own architecture
- Mate, Cairngorm, Parsley, Robotlegs, and Swiz
- Principles of the Robotlegs framework
- How to build an application using the Robotlegs framework

So far, you've learned the basics of OOP and how to make custom classes. We've also looked at how to develop cool components that encapsulate and abstract functionality so they can be reused.

Once you've mastered the content of this chapter, you'll feel as though your Flex development skills have reached the next level, so to speak, and rightfully so. You'll start by taking a deep look into Flex-driven design patterns and the thought process behind the core Flex architecture. Then, with that as your foundation, you'll get into the good stuff when you learn how to roll your own Flex application architecture. Many books claim to empower the reader to be able to do this, but most fail in this regard. The reason for this is that most books that attempt to teach

Finding reliable information

It's worth mentioning that although published material specific to the Flash Platform that goes in depth on the subject of application architecture is almost nonexistent (with the exception of some pretty good developer blog sites), there is a plethora of books based on C#.NET that get deep into developing scalable, real-world architectures for the enterprise. Although you may not be a .NET or C# developer, that doesn't mean you can't learn a lot from these books. Once I got past my personal reservations about developing software for Windows, this turned out to be a huge lifesaver for me in terms of sharpening my skills as a Flash Platform developer. Through these books, I learned how to architect applications regardless of their platform or language. I still can't write a lick of C#.NET code though, but that's probably because my objective wasn't to learn C# or the .NET framework by reading these books.

this skill get atrociously and unnecessarily overcomplicated, staying solely in the conceptual and theoretical domains, and fail to bring the concepts to reality by going through the process of designing architectures for enterprise applications.

We're going to give you exactly what you need to be a Flex-master in this chapter, and then we're even going to show you how to develop an enterprise Flex application using the Robotlegs framework. If you consider yourself more of a developer than an architect, then prepare to venture into the world of the abstract, dynamic, and highly conceptual thinking of architectural design patterns and practices!

19.1   *Flex-driven design patterns*

The first thing I'll point out before we begin our journey into the world of architectures and frameworks is that this is not about one design pattern, architecture, or framework being better or worse than another. Unlike many IT professionals who specialize in enterprise-level development, I learned programming by teaching myself, mostly by reading books like the one that you're reading right now. I also had the advantage of being mentored by Clifford Hoelz, a respected individual in the IT community. The first lesson that he taught me was this:

> *If you focus on the business, the tool will present itself.*

There is not currently—nor will there ever be—a single best programming language, platform, architecture, design pattern, framework, microarchitecture, operating system, or anything else related to technology for that matter. If there's one thing that you learn from this chapter, let it be this: When designing architectural solutions to solve complex business problems, your decisions are based on a combination of the knowledge from experiences that have led you to where you are today, combined with nothing more than *best judgment* and exceptional *logical reasoning* skills. Most important, *best judgment and logical reasoning are relative to the context in which the decision is made at that moment.* With that in mind, when making architectural decisions, such as whether to use a framework or what framework to use, always start by asking the simple question, what am I trying to accomplish? For example, slapping together a proof of concept for a company that's raising capital for the production version of that application is a lot different than determining the architecture of Amazon's next major web service.

As Flex continues to mature, we continue to learn from the mistakes that we make in regard to design patterns, just as with any application development technology. One of the things we've learned, as obvious as this may seem, is that when building Flex applications, the most effective architectures and design patterns are those that are consistent with the core design patterns that were used to build the Flex framework. More specifically, patterns that use event-driven design, object binding, the Model-View-Controller (MVC) pattern, as well as the *presentation model* design pattern are particularly useful for working with large-scale Flex applications.

In this section, you'll look at the ingredients that make up the MVC pattern, and then you'll learn how to create your own architectural foundation for an enterprise Flex application.

19.1.1 *The Model-View-Controller pattern*

The Flex framework is based on the Model-View-Controller architecture. MVC became popular in 1995, when SmallTalk was the language of choice for a large portion of client-side applications.

The major characteristic of a framework based on MVC is *separation of concerns*. More specifically, the code is organized into three encapsulated layers: the data (model), user-facing display logic (view), and a third layer that acts as a sort of mediator between parts (controller). This pattern is ideal for event-driven languages and frameworks like Flex. It can be reasonably asserted that the two most distinct and defining facets of the Flex framework are binding and events. This is why the MVC pattern was chosen for Flex, and it's also why you should strive to maintain consistency with the MVC pattern in your application development.

VISUALIZING THE MODEL-VIEW-CONTROLLER

Generally speaking, the view often has the ability to directly impact the model, but the model must go through the controller in order to have an effect on the view. For this reason the MVC pattern is usually shown in the form of a triangle with arrows, as demonstrated by figure 19.1.

The arrows displayed in the diagram in figure 19.1 imply that the flow of control moves from model to controller, then controller to view, and then view back to model. This sounds great in theory, but figure 19.2 provides a more accurate depiction of what this looks like in practice.

The purpose of the diagram in figure 19.2 is to point out that chaotic implementations of MVC that don't have clearly defined

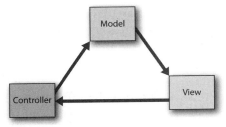

Figure 19.1   MVC is usually diagrammed in the form of a triangle.

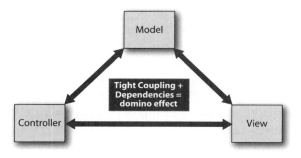

Figure 19.2   Chaotic implementations of MVC architecture lead to a domino effect of regressions caused by minor code changes.

architectural conventions throughout a project cause dependencies between unrelated elements, resulting in a domino effect of regressions whenever there's a minor code change. It's impossible to add or modify functionality within the application without introducing bugs in unexpected places of the application. This alone gives you good reason to learn how to roll your own architecture, which is what you'll be doing in the next section.

19.1.2 Roll your own architecture

It's common to create the initial iterations of an enterprise application around a basic MVC architecture that can easily be refactored to support the introduction of new design patterns and perhaps a microarchitecture. The reason for this is to keep complexity down while you focus on the business requirements.

As the application grows, so will its level of complexity, allowing for an informed decision to be made with regard to architecture and/or framework implementation. The architectural diagram shown in figure 19.3 provides an example of a makeshift MVC implementation for a prototype application that would typically be refactored after the first iteration with the full implementation of a microarchitecture such as Robotlegs.

You can see the clear separation of the three layers (model: bottom right; view: top; controller: bottom left). In order to understand how this implementation works, you must understand how the pieces are wired together. Before we get into the code, though, there are a few things you must know about what you're about to look at.

CONTEXT IS CRITICAL

There are definite use cases for the singleton design pattern, but they're few and far between, and it's more common to see them used improperly than it is to see singletons used in a way that's conducive to best practices. But in the context of prototype applications with hardly a lick of budget, it can be a powerful solution that can get a smoke-and-mirrors proof of concept up and running quickly.

It's true that a large population of developers (particularly those who hail from the world of Java) consider the use of singletons to be one of the seven deadly sins. In this regard, I emphasize the point of using best judgment to give the business what it needs at that moment. I've thrown together a lot of prototypes on the fly—probably

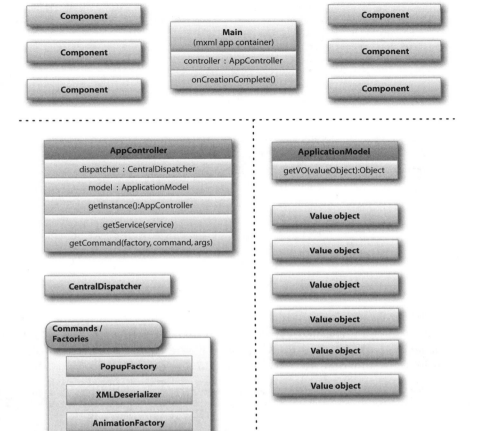

Figure 19.3 A simple MVC architectural diagram to show the separation between the model, view, and controller.

just as many as I have full-blown applications. The reason is that there's nothing more effective than an impressive proof-of-concept application to communicate an idea to a group of investors, a potential partner, or even a high-profile client.

Keep in mind as you move through the rest of this section that *context is critical*, and this first solution is meant to be used with caution because it's hardly scalable and prone to many types of problems if used in a production setting. *The cardinal rule in regard to best practices with design patterns is that singleton classes, static methods, and constants should not be used if they affect application state.* Don't worry, though; you'll see a number of scalable and production-ready solutions later in the chapter when we dive into the Robotlegs framework.

First, take a look at the code for our prototype's main application file in listing 19.1 to see how the business logic is initialized at runtime.

Listing 19.1   Custom architecture main application file

```
<?xml version="1.0" encoding="utf-8"?>
<s:Application xmlns:fx="http://ns.adobe.com/mxml/2009"
               xmlns:s="library://ns.adobe.com/flex/spark"
               xmlns:mx="library://ns.adobe.com/flex/halo"
               creationComplete="ccHandler(event)"            ◁─┐ Listen for
               minWidth="1024" minHeight="768">                  │ creationComplete
  <fx:Script>                                                  ❶ event
    <![CDATA[
      import com.f4ia.controller.AppController;
      import mx.events.FlexEvent;

      private var _controller:AppController;

      protected function              ❷ creationComplete
          ccHandler(event:FlexEvent):void  ◁─ handler method
      {
        _controller = AppController.getInstance();   ◁─┐ Get the
      }                                             ❸ controller
    ]]>
  </fx:Script>

</s:Application>
```

When the application's `creationComplete` event is dispatched ❶, the `onCreation-Complete()` method is called ❷, which then makes the first call to `AppController.getInstance()` ❸. Because the controller has not been yet been initialized, this results in its instantiation, as shown in the following listing.

Listing 19.2   Custom application controller example

```
package com.f4ia.controller
{
  import com.f4ia.model.ApplicationModel;
  import mx.core.IFactory;

  public class AppController
  {                                              ┌ Enforces the
    private static var lock : Boolean = false;  ◁┘ singleton
    private static var instance:AppController;
    private var _dispatcher:CentralDispatcher;  ┌❶ Private accessors
    private var _appModel:ApplicationModel;      │
    private var _services:Services;

    public function AppController()
    {                              ┌ Enforces the
      if(!lock)                   ◁┘ singleton
      {
        throw new Error("Error: Attempt to re-init");
      }
      initialize();
    }                                              ┌ Accessor to
                                                   │ singleton
    public static function getInstance():AppController ◁┘ instance
    {
```

```
      if (instance == null)
      {
        lock = true;
        instance = new AppController();
        lock = false;
      }
      return instance;
    }
    private function initialize():void                          ❷ Business layer
    {                                                              initialize() initialization
      _dispatcher = new CentralDispatcher();
      _services = new Services();
      _appModel = new ApplicationModel();
    }

    public function get appModel():ApplicationModel
    {
        return _appModel;                                       ❸ Read-only
    }                                                             public
                                                                  accessors
    public function get dispatcher():CentralDispatcher
    {
        return _dispatcher;
    }

    public function callService(name:String,
        args:*):void
    {
      _services.call(name, args);
    }                                                           ❹ Hooks into
                                                                  business layer
    public function callFactoryMethod(factory:IFactory,
        method:Function,
        args:*=null):Object
    {
        factory.method(args);
    }

  }
}
```

The AppController is the center point by which the application revolves. The App-
Controller is a singleton class, which means that there will only ever be one instance
of it. The first time the controller class is called, the getInstance() method creates a
new instance of AppController. After that, anytime a call is made to App-
Controller.getInstance(), the same object instance is returned. There will never be
more than one AppController during the lifespan of the program, which is the whole
purpose of the singleton design pattern.

In addition to its being a singleton class, four other facets of the application controller class are important here.

INTERNAL (PRIVATE) ACCESSORS

First is a set of private accessors for the controller to talk to the *business layer* of the
application ❶. When we speak of the business layer, we're talking about code that's

not directly involved with the user interface (view) of the application. This is most commonly referred to as the domain model and is most easily characterized by containing the application's value objects (VOs), also known as data transfer objects (DTOs) in the worlds of Java and .NET programming.

INITIALIZING THE BUSINESS LAYER

The second important element is the instantiation of the main business classes, which in this case are the `CentralDispatcher`, `Services`, and `ApplicationModel` classes **2**. These objects are instantiated in the `initialize()` function of the `AppController`, which is called only once in the application's lifecycle. We ensure that this method is called only once by calling it in the singleton's constructor (remember, the constructor is called only once, because it's a singleton).

I should note that this is also a major violation of best-practice conventions; nothing should ever run in a class's constructor because it's nearly impossible to unit test.

> ## Learn from others' mistakes!
>
> There's great value in learning how to spot the most common mistakes and knowing the potential repercussions of decisions made during development. The reason these mistakes are so prominent is largely because a lot of the beginner-level Flex 2 and Flex 3 books that were published focused on the simplest way to make something work, without mention of best practices and potential repercussions. As a result, many of us had to learn the hard way the inherent flaws with the patterns that were taught in these books. No one is to blame; it's just that no one knew because Flex was such a baby in the enterprise. We hadn't yet seen how many different ways we could make our applications break down. It's reassuring to know that the Flex SDK team was always heavily involved in many enterprise application development projects, and so many of the changes in Flex 4 are in the interest of progressing toward standards and best practices for Flex development. I'm proud to say that comparatively speaking, the Flex framework is maturing at an incredibly fast rate.

After the first time the `getInstance()` function is called, these classes are accessed only through the controller. This provides predictability and allows the controller to do its job as a mediator between the model and the view.

The `CentralDispatcher` acts as the application's *event bus*. All events are dispatched from the application controller's dispatcher, and all listeners are placed on that dispatcher. The `CentralDispatcher` class implements `IEventDispatcher`.

PUBLIC ACCESSORS

The third element is the public accessors to the primary business layer classes **3**. This is how presentation-layer objects outside the controller gain access to the domain model.

CONVENIENCE METHODS TO PROMOTE ABSTRACTION

The fourth major facet of our controller class is convenience methods that make calls into business classes that the view layer isn't allowed to access directly **4**. For example, the `callService()` method does nothing more than make the specified service call (provided as an argument) to the services class, along with any parameters that were passed along with it.

Now give yourself a pat on the back because you just learned how to create your own mini-microarchitecture (pun intended). You've also learned about a few different design patterns that are used within the Flex framework, and you learned about the underlying Model-View-Controller architecture that's the foundation of the Flex framework. Remember that the primary objective for the first iteration of an application is to ensure that it's in alignment with the business requirements. After that's been solidified, the next objective is to protect future iterations by taking actions that promote scalability and best practices, which is what you'll learn to do in the next section.

19.2 Introduction to microarchitectures

This is where the fun begins! Now it's time for us to review and discuss the architectural frameworks that are available for your enterprise Flex applications so you can make them robust, loosely coupled, and scalable. Before we dive in headfirst, though, we'll answer the question of why you'd even want to use a Flex microarchitecture in your application.

> **TIP** Don't succumb to the false authority of tools or models. There's no substitute for creativity, intuition, and inventiveness. Keep in mind that the context of the application is critical. *There comes a point where architectural rules become counterproductive by diminishing creativity.*

19.2.1 What is a microarchitecture?

There's a significant difference between an application framework and a microarchitecture. Flex is an application framework based on ActionScript 3.0, whereas Cairngorm, for example, is a microarchitecture for the Flex framework. The reason for mentioning this first is that a microarchitecture is most often a framework too, which can make things confusing at first. The term *microarchitecture* refers to an architecture within a much larger architecture. For example, the Flex framework has a large architecture. One could reasonably suggest that multiple architectures make up the global framework. The important thing to recognize is that it provides a certain level of flexibility in terms of how Flex is used for application development. As the Flex SDK team often points out, their objective is to enforce only a small number of general conventions and not limit developers to strict architectural policies. This is why they have remained, for the most part, unbiased in terms of particular microarchitectures. The Flex product managers state that the goal is to support the development of any and all future microarchitectures for Flex and to make sure that the Flex framework caters to such progressive development without bias.

In short, a microarchitecture is a framework that takes the extra step of establishing a more specific set of design pattern guidelines and architectural policies for a Flex application.

For the sake of illustration, let's compare this notion to music. The rules of what define a piece of music aren't specific. For example, must there be sound in order for there to be music? Many great composers would passionately argue that the answer is no, and technically speaking, they'd be correct. This was proven by American avant-garde composer John Cage, who wrote the infamous piece titled "4'33"" (pronounced as *Four minutes, thirty-three seconds*), which consisted of—you guessed it—4 minutes and 33 seconds of nothing but silence. This is why we have symbols in music that represent points in time where there's no sound. With that said, we can assert that one of the rules of music is that there does *or does not* have to be audible sound. Pretty general, right?

Now let's consider the role that a genre of music plays and how a musical genre relates to music in general. Every genre of music has a more specific set of characteristics that define it. In this respect, a song is like an application. For example, the songs "Who Dat" by artist Young Jeezy and "Click Clack" by Slim Thug fall into the category of hip hop and the subcategory (or genre) of gangsta rap, because they possess specific patterns and characteristics that are consistent with other songs that fall under that genre or category. Similarly, if application A and application B were both built using the Swiz microarchitecture, they're computer applications (music), that use the Flex framework (hip hop), and are built on top of the Swiz microarchitecture (gangsta rap).

> ### Are all frameworks Flex-ible?
> The purpose of a framework is to provide a means of speedier application development with a particular language. At Universal Mind, we do a lot of ActionScript framework development for code reuse across applications that are similar in nature. We use these together with the Flex and AIR frameworks when developing RIA applications. Sometimes our own frameworks are extensions of the Flex framework or a framework built with the Flex framework (ack!). The point is, it isn't uncommon to find a framework that extends (builds upon) another framework, which extends (builds upon) Flex. In the end, it all boils down to the goal of providing the client with the advantage of having a faster time to market.

19.2.2 Why use a microarchitecture?

Using a microarchitecture has many benefits, but also a certain amount of risk is introduced. A simple cost-benefit analysis is illustrated in table 19.1 to help you weigh the pros and cons of using a microarchitecture.

As you can see from the cost-benefit analysis in table 19.1, using a microarchitecture is usually most beneficial when developing large applications, which is the focus of the rest of the chapter. Let's look at some specific microarchitectures.

19.2.3 First-generation microarchitecture

Around the time version 1.5 of the Flex framework was released, two initial architectural frameworks surfaced for managing larger Flex applications: PureMVC and

Table 19.1   Costs and benefits of using a microarchitecture for Flex development

Costs	Benefits
– Adds a layer of complexity in most cases. – Effects are disastrous when not properly implemented (for example, developers who have not learned how to use the framework work on the project). – Creates a learning curve for developers who step into the project and have never used or learned the framework. – If the framework becomes obsolete, so do the developers who know how to maintain projects that implement it.	– Enforces a set of guidelines for consistent design patterns. – Provides guidelines for organization and naming conventions. – Provides application scalability. – Code is easier to maintain. – Code can be maintained by different programmers over time. – Usually provides advantages such as decreased dependencies, loose coupling between components, enhanced performance, and code reusability.

Cairngorm. We refer to these as *first-generation microarchitectures* because they were the first attempts at creating architectural standards for enterprise Flex applications. Let's take a deeper look into these two microarchitectures, starting with PureMVC.

PUREMVC

The PureMVC microarchitecture focuses on maintaining strict adherence to the MVC patterns and practices. PureMVC started as an enterprise architecture for ActionScript 3.0, including Flex, Flash, and AIR. The architects soon realized that their architecture could apply to a number of other languages as well. Since then, versions of PureMVC have been created for C#, ActionScript 2.0, ColdFusion, haXe, Java, JavaScript, Objective-C, PHP, Python, and Ruby.

The most obvious characteristic of PureMVC is that it relies heavily on the singleton design pattern, in that there exists a singleton class that holds all references for each of the three MVC layers. In addition, whereas Cairngorm relies on value objects for data transfer (also known as DTOs, or data transfer objects, in Java), PureMVC uses proxies to manage data objects. Other design patterns used in PureMVC include Façade, Mediator, and Command.

The biggest argument against PureMVC is the lack of abstraction and encapsulation due to the fact that pretty much any object or class can access any other object or class. The singleton design pattern is probably the most controversial of design patterns among architects because that singletons and multitons aren't necessarily meant to be used liberally and should exist only for certain specific instances. It's therefore argued whether PureMVC is truly using what is considered to be best practices in the world of software architecture and design patterns.

CAIRNGORM

Cairngorm is a microarchitecture for enterprise Flex applications initially created by a company known as Iteration II, which was bought by Adobe Systems and merged with Adobe Consulting. Since then, Adobe Consulting has made strong efforts at focusing the continued development and maintenance of Cairngorm on that of Flex. For this reason Cairngorm is worth more than just a look when considering a microarchitecture for your enterprise Flex application. Like many microarchitectures, Cairngorm is a moving target. For example, in the recent release of version 3, Cairngorm is touted as a set of standard patterns and practices that happens to include a code base that comes from the Parsley microarchitecture.

Furthermore, if you've already commenced development on an enterprise-level Flex or AIR application and you don't have any microarchitecture implemented, all of the frameworks mentioned here include documentation that explains how to integrate them into existing projects, including Cairngorm.

Iteration II was a firm that did much of its development in J2EE. As a result, Cairngorm implements a number of design patterns that are most popular in J2EE development. With that in mind, Flex developers who come from an enterprise Java background should be able to get used to Cairngorm fairly quickly and easily. Even if you don't have an enterprise Java background, Cairngorm is still an easy platform to understand as long as you're familiar with basic object-oriented programming concepts and design patterns.

Some distinguishing factors of Cairngorm include the use of a central event and central event dispatcher and the use of business delegates. Cairngorm is centered largely on the use of the observer and command design patterns as well.

The strongest criticism against Cairngorm has been that it forces the developer to use J2EE design patterns even if those patterns aren't suitable for the application. Previous versions of Cairngorm have a history of suffering from scalability breakdown, which is why almost the entire version 2 code base was retired in favor of using Parsley for version 3.

Because first-generation microarchitectures are rapidly becoming obsolete, this is where our discussion of first-generation frameworks comes to a close. As you'll see in the next section, second-generation microarchitectures implement more efficient design patterns for greater enterprise scalability and don't force developers into specific architectural impementations.

19.2.4 *Second-generation microarchitectures*

One of the primary reasons we have microarchitectures and design patterns in the first place is to maximize simplicity in application code. The problem is that not every architect understands this. Often we find architectures and design patterns being used in ways that do nothing more than increase complexity, which is counterintuitive. This is why it's important to understand the framework that you're working with before you begin development on a production project that uses it. Now let's do a short analysis of the three major second-generation microarchitectures: Swiz, Mate, and Robotlegs.

SWIZ, MATE, AND ROBOTLEGS

A common characteristic among second-generation microarchitectures is that they're built to *empower* the developer rather than *overpower.* Currently the most popular and

Interesting fact

One of my fellow authors for this book and a colleague whom I work with at Universal Mind, Joel Hooks, has been instrumental in the rapid development and support of the Robotlegs framework. The quality of a framework or code library of any kind can often be judged by taking a look at the people behind it. With names like Joel Hooks and Jesse Warden backing Robotlegs, rest assured that the same meticulous approach is taken to the framework's code and documentation as these individuals are known for taking to all of their work.

developer friendly of the second-generation microarchitectures are *Mate* (French, pronounced: Mah-tey), the *Swiz* framework, and one that has recently seen exponential growth in popularity, *Robotlegs*. Among these frameworks, Mate has gained the reputation for being the easiest to get up and running quickly, although it's a bit limited in terms of flexibility. Swiz is the more complex of the three, but it's also flexible. Robotlegs has gained a large following in a relatively short period of time because of its ability to be both highly customizable and easy to get up and running quickly.

Don't worry; we'll spend some time with Robotlegs in this chapter to help you familiarize yourself with it.

One thing that all of these second-generation microarchitectures have in common is that they use some form of Inversion of Control (IoC) and dependency injection, as defined by Martin Fowler in his book *Patterns of Enterprise Application Architecture* (Addison Wesley, 2002). With that in mind, you'll first learn a bit about how these design patterns work from a conceptual standpoint before you get your hands dirty.

19.2.5 *Inversion of Control and dependency injection*

Generally speaking, a good microarchitecture should allow the developer to decide how to implement an effective model based on the unique characteristics of the application. As previously stated, it should *never* force the developer into a specific model implementation. The Flex framework is largely based on principles of Inversion of Control. This is true for most event-driven user interface development toolkits and frameworks such as Java Spring, EJB 3, Spring.NET, the ColdSpring framework for ColdFusion, Needle for Ruby, and FLOW3 for PHP 5.

The *Inversion of Control pattern* originally comes from another pattern described in a important book published in 1995 that's often referred to as the "Gang of Four" or "GoF" book, titled *Design Patterns: Elements of Reusable Object-Oriented Software* (Addison-Wesley). If you don't have this book already, I strongly suggest you add it to your collection because it's universally considered a staple in the world of computer programming. One of the 22 design patterns described in this book is the *factory method* design pattern. IoC is a derivative of this pattern.

As you've learned, the ActionScript language is an object-oriented programming language, as opposed to being a *procedural* scripting language. In OOP languages, objects are created by *instantiating* or *declaring* the object and assigning the instance of that object to a variable. In most declarative languages, this is done with the new keyword:

```
private var thisObject:ThisObject = new ThisObject(params...);
```

In contrast, IoC instantiates and registers a specific set of predefined objects at runtime and injects them into each other using a concept known as *dependency injection*. By injecting these dependencies at runtime, the dependencies can be quickly and easily modified because the objects remain *loosely coupled*. The objects are loosely coupled because their dependencies aren't hardcoded into the classes. This makes managing large code bases much easier.

Objects and object properties can then be wired up through binding. That means that all of your views and components can have what they need before anything ever even shows up on the stage!

With other implementations like Java Spring, an application's objects and implementations can be declared in an XML document. This eliminates dependencies and increases loose coupling because the implementation is created dynamically based on the contents of the XML document. But this particular method isn't possible with Flex because of the order of operations that happen at application startup. More specifically, an application isn't ready to parse an XML document until *after* its objects have already been instantiated, defeating the whole purpose of dependency injection. Robotlegs, Swiz, and Parsley all handle this with metadata instead, whereas Mate uses MXML mapping files to tell the framework what to do on startup.

19.3   *Using the Robotlegs framework*

Robotlegs caters specifically to enterprise-level Flex and pure AS3 development by providing a solid architectural foundation. A framework like Robotlegs provides this foundation through the use of proven enterprise design patterns, including the following:

- Optimizing dependencies to promote loose coupling through "component wiring"
- Inverting the typical control flow of object-oriented design through context-managed dependency injection
- Dynamic mediation of components to reduce the amount of boilerplate code that must be written
- Centralized context-level event bus for efficient communication between application tiers

One of the goals of Robotlegs is simplicity, which allows you to write applications without the framework getting in your way. There's a narrow focus with Robotlegs: wiring your application together. Because it's a dependency injection–based framework, it's important to understand how exactly to use dependency injection within Robotlegs. Let's look at how to provide your classes with their dependencies.

19.3.1 Injecting dependencies with Robotlegs

We're now going to look at the standard Robotlegs dependency injection setup. The use of dependency injection with Robotlegs will provide your application's objects their dependencies in a quick and painless manner.

Supplying an object with its dependencies is accomplished by marking a property with the [Inject] metadata; the injector will provide that property with a value that you've mapped for injection. This principle is also applied to setter and constructor injection, where you'd have arguments whose values would be mapped and provided via injection. Let's look at property injection:

```
[Inject]
public var myDependency:Depedency; //unnamed injection
```

This declares simple property injection. You'll have mapped a class of type Dependency, and the injector will inject that value into the myDependency property based on the rules you defined when configuring the mapping. Don't worry right now about the mapping and rules; we'll get to that soon.

```
[Inject(name="myNamedDependency")]
public var myNamedDependency:NamedDepedency; //named injection
```

Property injection will also allow you to configure named injections. This is useful when you have multiple rules that use the same object type. When this is the case, it's necessary to name the injection so that the injector understands which rule you want to use.

You should note that this injection doesn't take place automatically. You must first map your objects to let Robotlegs know that they need to be injected into. In section 19.3.2 we'll be taking a close look at the utilities available to accomplish this mapping.

ROBOTLEGS DEPENDENCY INJECTION ADAPTERS

Robotlegs doesn't perform dependency injection natively. The framework is equipped with adapters for—and by default uses—the SwiftSuspenders dependency injection tool. SwiftSuspenders is a performance-tuned DI solution written specifically for use with Robotlegs. Through the use of the pluggable adapter model, Robotlegs can use other DI solutions such as SmartyPants-IoC or Spring ActionScript. When you're just starting out, it's highly recommended to use SwiftSuspenders unless you have a specific need for another DI toolkit. It's nice to have options, though, and Robotlegs doesn't want to hold you back.

SwiftSuspenders makes use of two standard metadata tags for providing your objects with injection points. These are [Inject] and [PostConstruct]. Using these tags you're able to mark properties and methods within your classes, and Swift-Suspenders will recognize these and perform work on them for you. The [Inject] tag is the most commonly used because it specifies injection points, as you saw previously. [PostConstruct] is used to mark methods for execution after your class has been constructed and all of its injections have been satisfied.

For a complete discussion of all of the injection types, as well as other options that are available through SwiftSuspenders, you can visit the project's home page at http://github.com/tschneidereit/SwiftSuspenders.

That's all there is to defining your injection points in your classes. Where does Robotlegs come into the picture beyond being an adapter for a DI solution? What Robotlegs does for you is provide a convenient mechanism for configuring these injections through a series of mapping utilities. This may seem like a lot to take in before we start looking at some code, but we're almost there. Let's look at these utilities and how to use them to configure dependency injection in your application.

19.3.2 Configuring dependency injection with the Robotlegs mapping utilities

Robotlegs has four base mapping utilities for configuring dependency injection in your application. Each of these utilities provides convenient methods for supplying dependencies to your application. These maps are made available throughout Robotlegs and are typically accessed through the Context and Command classes. We'll take a closer look at when and where to access these utilities in section 19.4. Table 19.2 describes these mapping utilities.

Table 19.2   The Robotlegs MVCS classes

Name	Description
Injector	The injector is the direct adaptor to SwiftSuspenders (or the DI provider you have chosen) and implements the IInjector interface.
MediatorMap	The MediatorMap is used for defining the relationship between view components and their mediators.
CommandMap	The CommandMap is used for configuring commands that are triggered by events dispatched through the context.
ViewMap	The ViewMap is used to define view component classes that will be injected with dependencies when they're added to the stage.

Let's take a detailed look at each of these utilities starting with the Injector.

THE INJECTOR

The Injector is a direct adaptor to the DI solution your application is using. Although these examples use the default SwiftSuspenders adaptor, any adaptor that implements the IInjector interface can be used. For common development, Swift-Suspenders will prove to be sufficient, but in flexibility lies power. The IInjector interface provides four methods for configuring dependency injections.

- `mapSingleton` is used to map a single instance of a class.
- `mapSingletonOf` is used to map a single instance of a base class or interface.
- `mapValue` is used to map a specific instance of a class.
- `mapClass` is used to map many unique instances of class.

Figure 19.4 illustrates how the `Injector` class maps your injections and provides your objects with their dependencies.

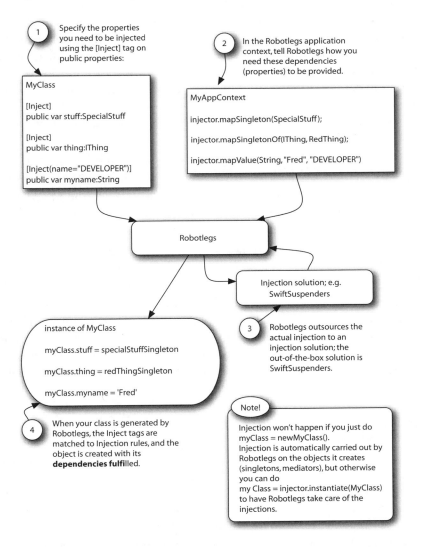

Figure 19.4 Robotlegs uses an injector to provide your objects with their dependencies. Injections are defined by rules (mappings), and Robotlegs matches the rules to properties marked with the [Inject] metadata tag.

The `mapSingleton` method takes a class as an argument and maps one instance of that class to all of your defined injection points:

```
//someplace in your application where mapping/configuration occurs
injector.mapSingleton(MyClass);
```

It's important to note that this singleton isn't a class-enforced Singleton (capital *S*). You aren't restricted from creating several instances of a mapped singleton within your application. Your injection points will be injected with the same instance of the object for every request. This instance will be instantiated lazily when the first request is made. The injector will do the work of creating the instance for you. With all of these mappings it's worth noting that the injector will also apply injections to the mapped class. This means that if you use `mapSingleton` as shown previously and have injection points defined in `MyClass`, the injector will apply any applicable rules to those injection points.

The `mapSingletonOf` method is similar to `mapSingleton`, but it allows you to define a base type of interface:

```
//someplace in your application where mapping/configuration occurs
injector.mapSingletonOf(IMyClass, MyClass); //MyClass implements IMyClass
```

In this case `MyClass` implements the `IMyClass` interface. When the injector encounters an injection point that's asking for a class that implements `IMyClass`, it will inject a `MyClass` object. You can also use this for supplying instances of a base class:

```
//someplace in your application where mapping/configuration occurs
injector.mapSingletonOf(MyClassBase, MyClass); //MyClass extends MyClassBase
```

This can provide your application a lot of flexibility, allowing you to make substitutions and take full advantage of polymorphism. This approach is extremely useful when you want to supply your injected classes with a stub version of a class during testing and development and quickly replace that with another version of the class in production.

The `mapValue` method maps a single object instance of a class. This means that any injection points you've defined that request a particular class will be provided with the instance you've created:

```
//some place in your application where mapping/configuration occurs
var myClassInstance:MyClass = new MyClass();
injector.mapValue(MyClass, myClassInstance);
```

This will map the new `MyClass` object you created, `myClassInstance`, to any injection points that ask for `MyClass`. Using `mapValue` gives you control of the instantiation of the object that will be mapped. The remaining three methods of the injector use lazy instantiation. No object is created until the first time it's requested. If you don't need to control the creation of the object manually, lazy instantiation can benefit your application. If an object isn't specifically requested it won't be created, and the application won't waste any resources on it.

The `mapClass` method provides a new instance of the mapped class for each injection point that you've defined:

```
//some place in your application where mapping/configuration occurs
injector.mapClass(MyClass);
```

Using `mapClass` doesn't require that you create a new instance of `MyClass`. You provide the class that you wish to have injected, and each time it's requested in your application, a brand-new instance of the class will be created and injected into the requesting class.

The injector provides an all-purpose mechanism for mapping your injections. The remaining three mapping utilities are specifically targeted to areas of your application controlled by Robotlegs. Let's look at the `MediatorMap` utility and how you'll use it to define the relationship between your view components and their mediators.

THE MEDIATORMAP

The `MediatorMap` class is used to define the relationship between your view components and the mediators that connect them to the rest of your application. Don't worry; we'll be discussing mediators is depth in the next section. For now you just need to know that a mediator is an object that serves as a bridge between your view components and the rest of your application. The mediator has default injection points that will be satisfied through dependency injection. Because of its targeted purpose, the `MediatorMap` has a single method for defining this relationship: `mapView`.

```
//someplace in your application where mapping/configuration occurs
mediatorMap.mapView(MyAwesomeWidget, MyAwesomeWidgetMediator);
```

Using `mapView` in this way will define a relationship between the view component class `MyAwesomeWidget` and the mediator `MyAwesomeWidgetMediator`. The `MediatorMap` is behind the scenes watching your application for an instance of `MyAwesomeWidget` to be added to the stage. When you add `MyAwesomeWidget` to the stage, an instance of `MyAwesomeWidgetMediator` will be created and its injection points will be filled with the appropriate values that you've defined. Figure 19.5 illustrates the relationships between view components and their mediators as defined by mappings that you create with the `MediatorMap`.

The next mapping utility we'll look at is the `CommandMap`, which allows you to create a relationship between `Command` classes and events.

THE COMMANDMAP

Like the `MediatorMap`, the `CommandMap` has a targeted purpose. You'll use the `CommandMap` to define the relationship between ActionScript events and `Command` classes. The `CommandMap` has a single method that's used to define this relationship:

```
//someplace in your application where mapping/configuration occurs
commandMap.mapEvent(MyAppDataEvent.DATA_WAS_RECEIVED, MyCoolCommand)
```

The `mapEvent` method takes an event type and a command class as required arguments. When Robotlegs hears the event type `MyAppDataEvent.DATA_WAS_RECEIVED` dispatched on its event bus, it creates an instance of `MyCoolCommand`, provides its defined injections, and calls its `execute()` method. Figure 19.6 illustrates the relationship between `Events` and `Commands` that have been associated through mapping via the `CommandMap`.

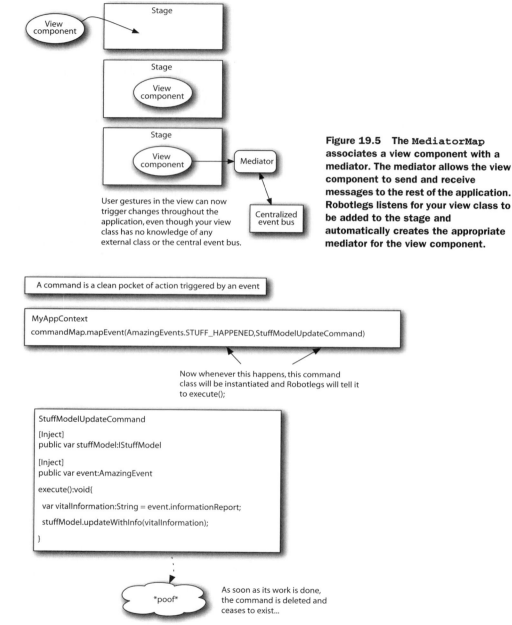

The mediator Map in action

Stage

View
component

Stage

View
component

Stage

View
component

Mediator

Centralized
event bus

User gestures in the view can now
trigger changes throughout the
application, even though your view
class has no knowledge of any
external class or the central event bus.

Figure 19.5   The MediatorMap
associates a view component with a
mediator. The mediator allows the view
component to send and receive
messages to the rest of the application.
Robotlegs listens for your view class to
be added to the stage and
automatically creates the appropriate
mediator for the view component.

A command is a clean pocket of action triggered by an event

MyAppContext
commandMap.mapEvent(AmazingEvents.STUFF_HAPPENED,StuffModelUpdateCommand)

Now whenever this happens, this command
class will be instantiated and Robotlegs will tell it
to execute();

StuffModelUpdateCommand

[Inject]
public var stuffModel:IStuffModel

[Inject]
public var event:AmazingEvent

execute():void{

 var vitalInformation:String = event.informationReport;

 stuffModel.updateWithInfo(vitalInformation);

}

poof

As soon as its work is done,
the command is deleted and
ceases to exist...

Figure 19.6   Mapped commands are executed by the CommandMap when the mapped event is
dispatched through the central event bus. Robotlegs provides the command with all of its injections
prior to running the execute() method. Robotlegs temporarily maps the event that triggered the
command for injection to provide access to any custom event properties/payloads you have provided.

We'll be discussing Commands in depth in the next section that covers the MVCS implementation of Robotlegs. Next, let's discuss the last of the mapping utilities, the ViewMap.

USING THE VIEWMAP

The ViewMap allows you to map view components for injection. Much like the MediatorMap, the ViewMap listens for your view components to be added to the stage. Unlike the MediatorMap, the ViewMap will inject any defined dependencies directly into your view component after it has been added to the stage. The most basic usage of the ViewMap is through its mapType method, as follows:

```
//someplace in your application where mapping/configuration occurs
viewMap.mapType(MyViewComponent);
```

The ViewMap will now monitor your application and supply injected dependencies to any instance of MyViewComponent that's added to the stage. The ViewMap also allows you to map entire packages (and subpackages).

```
//someplace in your application where mapping/configuration occurs
viewMap.mapPackage("com.me.myapp.view.components");
```

Using this method will map every component in the com.me.myapp.view.components package and any subpackages that exist underneath. This provides a convenient mechanism for mapping a lot of view components at once and saves you the trouble of typing the boilerplate for each view component under a package.

> ### MVC and MVCS
>
> It's important to note that *MVCS* stands for Model-View-Controller-Services, and for awhile the term *MVC* was still used to describe an application's architecture, even though there was also a services layer. In essence, it was like a silent and invisible S, until logic eventually kicked in and we began to refer to applications built with Flex as MVCS, officially acknowledging the existence of the services layer in these applications.

The ViewMap is a mechanism for providing flexibility to developers. The example application that we'll create in section 19.4 doesn't use the ViewMap. Don't think this is an attempt to stub the ViewMap. It isn't. The utility can be useful for implementing alternative implementations. The next section focuses on the Model-View-Controller-Service (MVCS) implementation of Robotlegs. Although MVCS isn't by any means the only approach that you can take to build a Robotlegs application, you're limited only by your imagination and the platform in this regard; it provides familiar production-tested approaches to application development.

You're probably ready to see some code. Let's get our hands dirty and look at an application built with the Robotlegs framework.

19.4 Creating an application with Robotlegs MVCS

Now that you have a good understanding of the underlying core framework utilities, you're ready to create your first enterprise-level application with the Robotlegs MVCS implementation. Robotlegs is equipped with this implementation as a lightly prescriptive starting point for your application. It's a common-ground approach to building an application so that you and your team will have a solid architectural structure to build upon. Before we start building the application, let's look at what MVCS is and how it's represented by Robotlegs.

In an MVCS application the model stores data, the view provides a mechanism for the user to interact with, the controller responds to those actions, and the service connects the application to external resources such as a web service or local file system. Robotlegs MVCS was inspired by the structure of PureMVC with the addition of the service tier. Within the MVCS implementation are four main classes, as illustrated in table 19.3.

Table 19.3 The Robotlegs MVCS classes

Name	Description
Context	The `Context` class is a hub. It facilitates the communication between tiers and provides the initial bootstrapping of the framework.
Mediator	`Mediator`s serve as the connectors between the view components your users interact with and the framework, and they represent the view tier.
Command	`Command`s serve as a mechanism to bridge your application's tiers and encapsulate common logic, and they represent the controller tier.
Actor	`Actor`s provide some of the base functionality that's used by classes in both the service and model tiers.

Each of these classes plays an important role in your application. By separating the various concerns into these tiers, you can work effectively even within a large team. You've probably noticed that there are no Model or Service classes. This is because Robotlegs does not provide concrete implementations of these classes. They're tiers of an application used to separate concerns, and both utilize the `Actor` class to create the classes that are used in those tiers.

Now let's start writing some code. You'll need to set up your project, so we'll start there.

19.4.1 Setting up a Robotlegs project

You should be familiar with setting up a Flex project. The only major difference with a Robotlegs project is that you'll need to add the library to your project's lib folder. To do that you'll want to grab a copy of the latest Robotlegs library. It can be found at http://www.robotlegs.org.

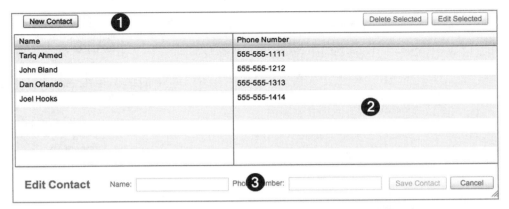

Figure 19.7   The simple contact manager application consists of three main components: (1) the toolbar, (2) the contacts list, and (3) the contact editor.

With the library downloaded, create a new project in Flash Builder called `Robotlegs-ContactManager` with the application type web. Drag the Robotlegs SWC file into the new project's libs folder. Your new project now has access to all of the Robotlegs classes. Figure 19.7 is the simple contact manager that we're building here.

Now that the project is set up, you're ready to begin adding classes to the contact manager starting with the `Context` class.

19.4.2 *Bootstrapping your application with the Context class*

The `Context` class, as shown in table 19.3, can be considered the heart of your Robotlegs application. It's the entry point for the framework and creates instances of the mapping utilities described in the previous section. You aren't limited to a single `Context` within an application, but for many use cases one `Context` will be sufficient. The ability to make use of multiple `Contexts` within an application is essential for modular applications. For the purposes of this discussion, we're going to focus on the use of a single `Context` within a nonmodular application. Listing 19.3 shows the `ContactManagerContext` created in the `com.fx4ia.robotlegs.contacts` package that will serve as the root package for our example.

Listing 19.3 `ContactManagerContext.as`

```
package com.fx4ia.robotlegs.contacts
{
import com.fx4ia.robotlegs.contacts.controller.*;
import com.fx4ia.robotlegs.contacts.events.ContactEvent;
import com.fx4ia.robotlegs.contacts.model.ContactsModel;
import com.fx4ia.robotlegs.contacts.service.*;
import com.fx4ia.robotlegs.contacts.service.events.ContactServiceEvent;
import com.fx4ia.robotlegs.contacts.view.*;

import org.robotlegs.mvcs.Context;

public class ContactManagerContext extends Context
```

`ContactManagerContext extends Context`

```
{
  override public function startup():void
  {
    injector.mapSingleton(ContactsModel);
    injector.mapSingletonOf(IContactService,
        XMLContactService);

    mediatorMap.mapView(ContactsView,
        ContactsViewMediator);
    mediatorMap.mapView(EditContactView,
        EditContactViewMediator);
    mediatorMap.mapView(ContactsToolbarView,
        ContactsToolbarViewMediator);

    commandMap.mapEvent(ContactServiceEvent.LOAD,
        LoadContactsCommand, ContactServiceEvent);
    commandMap.mapEvent(ContactEvent.UPDATE,
        SaveContactCommand, ContactEvent);
    commandMap.mapEvent(ContactEvent.CREATE,
        CreateContactCommand);
    commandMap.mapEvent(ContactEvent.CANCEL_CREATE,
        CreateContactCancelCommand);
    commandMap.mapEvent(ContactEvent.DELETE,
        DeleteContactCommand);
    commandMap.mapEvent(ContactEvent.EDIT,
        EditContactCommand);
    commandMap.mapEvent(ContactEvent.CANCEL_EDIT,
        EditContactCancelCommand);
    commandMap.mapEvent(ContactEvent.SELECT,
        SelectContactCommand);
  }
}
}
```

Mapping `ContactsModel` for injection

Mapping `IContactService` interface for injection

Mapping mediators to view components

Mapping commands to events

When you create your application's Context, you'll override the startup() method of Context. The startup() method is called by Robotlegs when the Context has been fully initialized. At this time you'll have access to the utility maps and can begin mapping your dependency injection configuration. The Context is a convenient place to bootstrap your application. In the ContactManagerContext we're mapping the model, the service, the view components, and their mediators, as well as the various commands to their respective events that trigger them. In larger applications this bootstrapping is often placed in commands to provide separation and prevent the Context's startup method from growing to large. For this example, placing these mappings here will be sufficient. You should quickly recognize the use of the maps discussed in the previous section. We'll discuss the classes being mapped for injection and what they do shortly. Your Context is instantiated within your view component. In general this is the root Application component. Listing 19.4 shows a Robotlegs Context initialized via an MXML tag.

> **Listing 19.4   RobotlegsContactManager.mxml**

```
<?xml version="1.0" encoding="utf-8"?>
<s:Application xmlns:fx="http://ns.adobe.com/mxml/2009"
        xmlns:s="library://ns.adobe.com/flex/spark"
        xmlns:mx="library://ns.adobe.com/flex/mx"
        xmlns:contacts="com.fx4ia.robotlegs.contacts.*"
        xmlns:view="com.fx4ia.robotlegs.contacts.view.*">
  <fx:Declarations>
    <contacts:ContactManagerContext
      contextView="{this}"/>
  </fx:Declarations>
  <s:layout>
    <s:VerticalLayout/>
  </s:layout>
  <view:ContactsToolbarView/>
  <view:ContactsView/>
  <view:EditContactView/>
</s:Application>
```

ContactManagerContext created in **Declarations** tag ❶

❷ Define the **contextView**

The application's views

As with all nonvisual elements in MXML, your Context must be added within the Declarations MXML tag ❶. You can also create the context instance with Action-Script in a lifecycle event such as creation complete, but utilizing the MXML to create the instance is convenient. The Context requires a reference to a view component, provided via the contextView property ❷, and won't automatically start up until one is provided. This view component acts as a scope for the application, and things like automatic mediation, for example, occur only within this scope.

Something you'll notice right away is that the Application definition is extremely small. There is no script block performing any work, and all of the visual elements are contained in component classes. The Application is an entry point and nothing more. The work that your user will do occurs elsewhere in nicely encapsulated components and classes.

That's it. Your application is now using Robotlegs. It isn't doing much for you yet, but you've created a Context upon which to build the rest of your application. For the next step we're going to look at view components and how to mediate them so that they can communicate with other mediators and application tiers.

19.4.3 *Mediating your views*

Mediators are named after the design pattern they represent, the Mediator (Gamma95), as presented in the venerable Gang of Four's *Design Patterns: Elements of Reusable Code.* You could consider a mediator like the post office. Your mother has written you a nice letter. She drops it in the mailbox, and the postal worker picks it up. It's routed around the country until it's delivered to you. You wouldn't want to have to trek halfway across the country to your mom's house to retrieve the letter, and she certainly doesn't have the energy to deliver it by hand to you. In this way the post office has mediated the process of delivering the letter. The Mediator design pattern functions in a similar way by delivering and receiving messages between the classes in your application.

With the Robotlegs MVCS implementation, mediators represent the view tier. Each view component in your application can potentially have a Mediator that serves as its gateway to other view components and to the other tiers within the application. This sort of granular control, having a Mediator for *every* view component in your application, is probably not necessary. Instead, you'll mediate the major components within your application. Take, for example, a form. You wouldn't mediate each TextInput, DropdownList, and Button that makes up the form. Instead, you'd mediate the form as a complete component. Let's look at the ContactsView (see figure 19.7 where the Contacts view is labeled as 2) that contains a DataGrid for displaying the list of Contacts in this next listing.

Listing 19.5   ContactsView.mxml

```
<?xml version="1.0" encoding="utf-8"?>
<s:Group xmlns:fx="http://ns.adobe.com/mxml/2009"
    xmlns:s="library://ns.adobe.com/flex/spark"
    xmlns:mx="library://ns.adobe.com/flex/mx"
    width="100%" height="100%" enabled="{_viewEnabled}">
  <fx:Script>
    <![CDATA[
      import com.fx4ia.robotlegs.contacts.events.ContactEvent;
      import com.fx4ia.robotlegs.contacts.model.vo.Contact;

      import mx.collections.IList;
      import mx.events.ListEvent;

      [Bindable]                              Bindable IList used as
      public var dataProvider:IList;     ◁⌐  DataGrid dataProvider

      [Bindable]
      private var _viewEnabled:Boolean = true;

      public function set viewEnabled(value:Boolean):void
      {
        _viewEnabled = value;
        list.selectedItem = null;
      }

      public function
                                              Method to
      selectContact(contact:Contact):void ◁⌐ select/highlight list item
      {
        list.selectedItem = contact;
      }

      protected function list_changeHandler(event:ListEvent):void
      {
        dispatchEvent(new ContactEvent(ContactEvent.SELECT,
            selected));
      }                                ◁⌐  Dispatching SELECT event

      protected function list_doubleClickHandler(event:MouseEvent):void
```

```
      {
        dispatchEvent(new ContactEvent(ContactEvent.EDIT,
          selected));                          ⟵  Dispatching EDIT event
      }

      protected function get selected():Contact
      {
        return list.selectedItem as Contact;
      }

    ]]>
  </fx:Script>
  <mx:DataGrid id="list" width="100%" height="100%"        ⟵  DataGrid that
      doubleClickEnabled="true"                                displays Contacts
      dataProvider="{dataProvider}"
      change="list_changeHandler(event)"
      doubleClick="list_doubleClickHandler(event)">
    <mx:columns>
      <mx:DataGridColumn id="nameColumn" dataField="name"
                         headerText="Name"/>
      <mx:DataGridColumn id="phoneNumberColumn" dataField="phoneNumber"
                         headerText="Phone Number"/>
    </mx:columns>
  </mx:DataGrid>
</s:Group>
```

The ContactsView is a typical component. It's a Group that wraps a DataGrid. The dataProvider property is bindable, and the DataGrid itself binds its dataProvider property to this value. When an item is selected, the event handler dispatches a ContactEvent.SELECT with the currently selected Contact as its payload. Likewise, as a convenience to our users, when an item is double-clicked, a ContactEvent.EDIT is dispatched. As you'll see shortly, this component's Mediator is listening for these events. Let's look at the Mediator now and find out what sort of work it's doing for us in the following listing.

Listing 19.6 ContactsViewMediator

```
package com.fx4ia.robotlegs.contacts.view
{
import com.fx4ia.robotlegs.contacts.events.ContactEvent;
import com.fx4ia.robotlegs.contacts.model.ContactsModel;
import com.fx4ia.robotlegs.contacts.model.events.ContactsModelEvent;
import com.fx4ia.robotlegs.contacts.service.events.ContactServiceEvent;

import flash.events.Event;

import org.robotlegs.mvcs.Mediator;

public class ContactsViewMediator extends Mediator
{
  [Inject]                                            View component
  public var view:ContactsView;            ⟵           is injected

  [Inject]                                            ContactsModel
  public var model:ContactsModel;          ⟵           singleton is injected
```

```
override public function onRegister():void
{
  eventMap.mapListener( eventDispatcher, ContactServiceEvent.LOADED,
                        handleContactsLoaded );
  eventMap.mapListener( eventDispatcher, ContactServiceEvent.SAVED,
                        handleContactSaved)
  eventMap.mapListener( eventDispatcher, ContactEvent.CREATE,
                        disableViewOnEvent);
  eventMap.mapListener( eventDispatcher, ContactEvent.CANCEL_CREATE,
                        enableViewOnEvent);

  eventMap.mapListener( view, ContactEvent.SELECT,
                        dispatch );
  eventMap.mapListener( view, ContactEvent.EDIT,
                        dispatch );

  dispatch(new
      ContactServiceEvent(ContactServiceEvent.LOAD));
}

protected function handleContactsLoaded(event:ContactServiceEvent):void
{
  view.dataProvider = model.list;
}

protected function handleContactSaved(event:ContactServiceEvent):void
{
  enableViewOnEvent(event);
  view.selectContact(model.editing);
}

protected function disableViewOnEvent(event:Event):void
{
  view.viewEnabled = false;
}

protected function enableViewOnEvent(event:Event):void
{
  view.viewEnabled = true;
}
}
}
```

> **Listen for framework events**

> **Listen for view component events**

> **Dispatch an event to load `Contacts`**

A `Mediator` has a one-to-one relationship with its respective view component. For this reason it's important to inject the view component into the mediator. Don't worry about mapping this injection. The `MediatorMap` did it for you when you created the relationship between the view component and its mediator in the `Context`. In addition to the injection of the view component, you'll notice that the `ContactsModel` is being injected. As we'll discuss in section 19.5.5, the model controls the state of the application and is accessed by the mediator to update it accordingly.

The `onRegister` method will be overridden in almost all cases. This method is your hook into the mediator. When this method is called, you can be assured that the injections have been provided and that the mediator is fully initialized. Within the `onRegister` method you use the `EventMap` to add listeners to both the framework and the view component that your mediator is interested in. This is the primary purpose of the mediator. It listens for events and handles them so that the view component and large application framework don't need to know about one another. It serves as a bridge and provides clean separation of concerns. Your view is there for the user to interact with, and by mediating it the view doesn't have to be overly concerned with the data manipulation and other logic that's occurring within the application. It also promotes reusable component design.

This is the first time you've seen the EventMap. The EventMap is a local object created by MVCS Mediator and Actor classes. It's a utility class used to map events, as the name would suggest. Its primary purpose is to provide a mechanism for cleanly creating and automatically removing event listeners. By using the EventMap you don't need to call removeEventListener for every listener that you've registered. This serves the dual purpose of reducing boilerplate code as well helping to reduce memory leaks that can occur by not removing event listeners properly. The EventMap provides the unmapListeners method to remove all registered listeners at once. A mediator will invoke this function automatically when it's removed.

> ### Use the EventMap for garbage collection friendly event listening
> The EventMap is a real convenience when it comes to mapping event listeners within Robotlegs MVCS classes. It provides a concise syntax and also includes the unmapListeners method to remove all event listeners. Leaving event listeners without proper removal can lead to some serious memory leaks in your application. Unremoved listeners hold a reference to the class they're attached to so the class is not eligible for garbage collection by Flash Player.

You'll notice that the eventMap is listening for events of the Mediator's eventDispatcher property. The eventDispatcher is found within all of the MVCS classes and is a centralized event bus that's used by Robotlegs to communicate between classes within your application. Each Context provides a single IEventDispatcher to facilitate this communication. It's not something you'll need to create or provide, the Context does this for you. But it's important to understand that it exists and is busily working for you. Figure 19.8 illustrates how the central event bus facilitates communication between the objects within your application.

In the ContactsView component we dispatch two events, ContactEvent.SELECT and ContactEvent.EDIT. Both of these events have been mapped in the mediator via the EventMap. You'll notice that the handler is a method called dispatch. This is another convenience method provided by MVCS classes to simplify the syntax required to dispatch a framework event through the Context's IEventDispatcher. Instead of typing out the lengthy eventDispatcher.dispatchEvent(event), you're able to type dispatch(event). When used as an event handler, it works as a sort of relay to dispatch the event received from the view component directly to the framework event dispatcher. This isn't required, and you can create a method within the

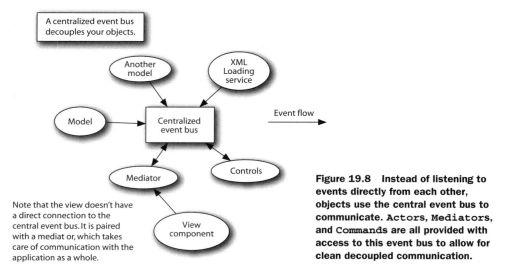

A centralized event bus decouples your objects.

Note that the view doesn't have a direct connection to the central event bus. It is paired with a mediat or, which takes care of communication with the application as a whole.

Figure 19.8 Instead of listening to events directly from each other, objects use the central event bus to communicate. Actors, Mediators, and Commands are all provided with access to this event bus to allow for clean decoupled communication.

mediator to handle the event from the view component, but it's a common pattern to relay the event instead of creating a method to handle the event from the view component. This is a common pattern within Robotlegs. Reduce typing and spare your hands from undue suffering.

In addition to mapping the event interests of the mediator, the onRegister method dispatches an event. The ContactServiceEvent.LOAD is a command trigger that we mapped previously in the Context to execute the LoadContactsCommand. This is dispatched here because we know that the ContactsView is fully initialized and ready to receive and display data. The LoadContactsCommand performs the obvious action of accessing a service and loading our contacts. Let's look at the Controller and the Commands that represent that tier of the application.

19.4.4 *Taking control with Robotlegs commands*

The Command pattern is another classic design pattern that's used to encapsulate a request and perform operations. The Contacts Manager application defines a series of commands that represent actions that a user can do. Each action results in some sort of work that needs to be accomplished by the application. When a user clicks a button labeled New Contact, the new Contact doesn't appear magically. It's a complicated process that requires several of the application's classes to react across all of the tiers. Table 19.4 shows a list of the commands the Contacts Manager has available.

This seems like a lot of commands at first glance, but each command is named distinctly for the exact action (or user gesture) that it executes. The commands are concise and serve a single purpose. By glancing in the controller package, you're quickly able to see everything that the application does. Functionality isn't hidden behind layers of components or deeply nested in a larger multipurpose controller class. Let's look at the SelectContactCommand in listing 19.7 and see what's happening within a command.

Table 19.4 Commands that make up the controller tier in the Contacts Manager example

Name	Description
CreateContactCommand	Creates a new empty Contact for the user to edit
CreateContactCancelCommand	Cancels the creation of a new Contact
DeleteContactCommand	Deletes a Contact
EditContactCommand	Initializes a Contact for editing
EditContactCancelCommand	Cancels the editing of a Contact
LoadContactsCommand	Loads a collection of Contacts from a service
SaveContactCommand	Saves a Contact to a service
SelectContactCommand	Initializes a selected Contact

Listing 19.7 SelectContactCommand.as

```
package com.fx4ia.robotlegs.contacts.controller
{
import com.fx4ia.robotlegs.contacts.events.ContactEvent;
import com.fx4ia.robotlegs.contacts.model.ContactsModel;

import org.robotlegs.mvcs.Command;

public class SelectContactCommand extends Command
{
  [Inject]
  public var event:ContactEvent;          ◁— The triggering event is injected

  [Inject]
  public var model:ContactsModel;         ◁— The model is injected

  override public function execute():void
  {
    model.selected = event.contact;       ◁— Work is performed on the model
  }
}
}
```

The commands in this example are all relatively short. They don't represent a lot of functionality, and most are only a single line of code. This is a product of the relatively simple nature of the example, however, because commands can and do contain more responsibilities. That said, it's a good goal to try to keep the responsibilities of a command at a minimum. In the case of the SelectContactCommand we expect it to do one thing and that's select a Contact.

When you dispatch an event through the Context event dispatcher that's mapped to a command, it's handled by the CommandMap. The CommandMap will answer this event by creating an instance of the Command class mapped to the event type, providing it with any mapped injections, which includes the event instance that triggered the command, and finally it will run the execute method of the command. Refer to figure 19.6, which illustrates this relationship. It's not strictly required to use the MVCS Command class. The only requirement of a command is that it has an execute()

method. The MVCS `Command` provides several other injections that include the Robot-legs mapping utilities, a `dispatch()` method, and access to the `contextView` of the `Context`.

It's important to note that commands are meant to be short-lived, lightweight objects. They're created, do their work, and are then promptly destroyed. Commands are useful for separating the view tier, the mediators and their components, from the model and service tiers. Both the model and service classes can be injected and accessed within mediators, but this practice is highly discouraged because it's not the mediators' job to set data, maintain application state, or make remote requests via a service. When you make use of commands, your application will be infinitely more scalable and easier to manage in the long run.

We've taken a look at the `Mediator` and `Command` classes. Now let's look at the two remaining tiers of an MVCS application, starting with services.

19.4.5 *Services are the gateway to the world*

A service is anything outside our application that we need to access or interact with. The obvious example of a service is a web service that provides remote access to a database. This includes remote applications like LiveCycle Data Services, web APIs from websites such as Google or Flickr, or a host of other remote web applications that provide some sort of method for retrieving data. For our contact manager we're using a mock service. The data resides in an XML file that's embedded into the application, and no remote calls are made. This approach can be handy in the early stages of an application's development, allowing you to work on the client-side portion of the application even before real services exist. It's also an essential approach when it comes to providing your application with unit test coverage because testing applications with remote services is faulty and cumbersome at best. Take a look at the XML data located in the data folder that's being used by the application:

```
<contacts>
    <contact id="1" name="Tariq Ahmed" phoneNumber="555-555-1111"/>
    <contact id="2" name="John Bland" phoneNumber="555-555-1212"/>
    <contact id="3" name="Dan Orlando" phoneNumber="555-555-1313"/>
    <contact id="4" name="Joel Hooks" phoneNumber="555-555-1414"/>
</contacts>
```

This data isn't complex by any stretch of the imagination, but it's a starting point and can easily be expanded upon as the application grows. In a real contact manager you'll likely want more detailed information such as addresses, pictures of your contacts, and other details about your associates. Listing 19.8 is the `Service` class that loads the previous data.

Listing 19.8   XMLContactService

```
package com.fx4ia.robotlegs.contacts.service
{
import com.fx4ia.robotlegs.contacts.model.ContactsModel;
import com.fx4ia.robotlegs.contacts.model.vo.Contact;
```

```
import com.fx4ia.robotlegs.contacts.service.events.ContactServiceEvent;
import com.fx4ia.robotlegs.contacts.service.helpers.ContactXMLParser;

import mx.collections.ArrayCollection;

import org.robotlegs.mvcs.Actor;

public class XMLContactService extends Actor
    implements IContactService
{
    [Embed(source="/data/contacts.xml",mimeType="text/xml")]
    protected var ContactsXML:Class;

    [Inject]
    public var model:ContactsModel;

    public function load():void
    {
        var xml:XML = XML( ContactsXML.data );
        model.list =
          ContactXMLParser.getCollection(xml);
        dispatch(
          new ContactServiceEvent(ContactServiceEvent.LOADED));
    }

    public function save(contact:Contact):void
    {
        if(!model.list.contains(contact))
            model.list.addItem(contact);
            if(contact.id == 0)
            getNextId(contact);
        model.editing = null;
        dispatch(new ContactServiceEvent(ContactServiceEvent.SAVED));
    }

    protected function getNextId(forContact:Contact):void
    {
        var id:int = 0;
        for each(var contact:Contact in model.list)
        {
            if(contact.id > id)
                id = contact.id;
        }
        forContact.id = id++;
    }

    public function remove(contact:Contact):void
    {
        model.remove(contact);
    }
}
}
```

XMLContactService extends `Actor` and implements `IContactService` ⟵

Embedded XML data ⟵

ContactsModel is injected ⟵

Helper class parses the XML ⟵

Service dispatches `ContactServiceEvent` framework events ⟵

Service contains methods ⟵

When we mapped the service within the Context's startup method, we used the map-SingletonOf method of the Injector to map the service instance. Notice that the XMLContactService implements the IContactService interface. This allows us to change a single line, the mapping in the Context, to use another IContactService. When it's time for your application to connect to a live service, you can swap it out in a matter of seconds. This approach is extremely powerful and allows for a lot of flexibility within your application. In addition to implementing IContactService, XMLContactService extends the Robotlegs MVCS Actor class. Actor is a utility class that provides the Context's event dispatcher and the dispatch() method.

When making use of external services it's important to parse and convert the data that you retrieve as soon as possible. In this service's load() method you see that a ContactXMLParser is being utilized. This helper class takes the XML data and creates an ArrayCollection of Contact objects. We don't want to deal with generic XML data when we can use strongly typed value objects specific to our application.

In addition to loading the initial data, this service provides the ability to save and remove Contacts from the service. If this were connecting to a remote service, you'd be performing these actions asynchronously with event handlers or responders listening to an HTTPService, RemoteObject, or NetConnection. Although this example sets the data on the model immediately, the principle is the same. The last tier of MVCS is the model that manages our application's data and the current state of that data. Let's take a look at the model now.

19.4.6 *Using the model to manage data and state*

Models represent your data. Your data represents the state of your application. Selected items, the Contact currently being edited, updates to the list of Contacts, and any other changes that affect the represented state of your application will occur through the model. Like services, models don't have a class that specifically represents them. Extending the Robotlegs MVCS Actor class creates them. Both services and models are conceptual tiers in Robotlegs MVCS. This provides you with a lot of flexibility in terms of how these tiers are implemented within your application. Listing 19.9 is the ContactsModel used by this example.

Listing 19.9 ContactsModel.as

```
package com.fx4ia.robotlegs.contacts.model
{
import com.fx4ia.robotlegs.contacts.events.ContactEvent;
import com.fx4ia.robotlegs.contacts.model.events.ContactsModelEvent;
import com.fx4ia.robotlegs.contacts.model.vo.Contact;
import com.fx4ia.robotlegs.contacts.service.events.ContactServiceEvent;

import mx.collections.ArrayCollection;

import org.robotlegs.mvcs.Actor;                          ContactsModel
                                                          extends Actor
public class ContactsModel extends Actor
{
    private var _list:ArrayCollection;                    Holds collection
                                                          of Contacts
    public function get list():ArrayCollection
    {
        return _list;
    }
```

```
public function set list(value:ArrayCollection):void
{
    _list = value;
}

private var _selected:Contact;

public function get selected():Contact
{
    return _selected;
}

public function set selected(value:Contact):void
{
    _selected = value;
    dispatch(new
        ContactsModelEvent(ContactsModelEvent.SELECTED));
}

private var _editing:Contact;

public function get editing():Contact
{
    return _editing;
}

public function set editing(value:Contact):void
{
    _editing = value;
    dispatch(new ContactsModelEvent(ContactsModelEvent.EDITING));
}

public function create():Contact
{
    var contact:Contact = new Contact();
    editing = contact;
    dispatch(new ContactsModelEvent(ContactsModelEvent.CREATED));
    return contact;
}

public function remove(contact:Contact):void
{
    var contactIndex:int = list.getItemIndex(contact);
    if(contactIndex > -1) list.removeItemAt(contactIndex);
    if(selected == contact) selected = null;
    if(editing == contact) editing = null;;
    dispatch(new ContactsModelEvent(ContactsModelEvent.REMOVED));
}
}
}
```

Annotations in right margin:
- **Currently selected Contact**
- **Dispatches `ContactsModelEvents` to framework**
- **Contact being edited**
- **Method to create new Contact**
- **Method to remove Contact**

When a user performs an action within the application such as selecting a Contact in the list, a command is triggered. The command subsequently accesses the model and sets its selected property. The selected property is set through a setter method, and when the selection changes, the ContactsModel dispatches the ContactsModel-Event.SELECTED event through the framework's event dispatcher. This event is then received by any interested listeners, including mediators, and perhaps triggers another command.

In addition to managing these state-related items, the model handles manipulation of the data. When a `Contact` is created or removed from the list of `Contacts`, it's done within the model. By containing these actions within the model, you encapsulate the manipulation data. It isn't spread out across the entire application. This encapsulation makes it much easier to debug your application and creates clarity during the development process.

Now that you've seen each of the tiers of a Robotlegs MVCS application, you should have a good idea of how it operates. The full source to this example is available, and you'll probably want to review it to see the application running. We didn't look at all of the classes in the application to avoid repetition, but this overview covers all of the basics that you'll need to start writing Robotlegs applications of your own. Using a framework such as Robotlegs will allow you to program complex applications faster and create common patterns and practices for you and your team to follow. If you get stuck, you won't be left out in the cold. Visit http://robotlegs.org for more examples and links to support forums.

19.5   *Summary*

Congratulations, you've now ventured into the realm of enterprise Flex development. But there's one thing you can be certain about: The more you learn in this field, the more you'll realize how much more you have yet to learn. Don't be frustrated by this, though. The world of enterprise development is vast and constantly expanding as more and more intelligent people like you contribute to its evolution. The key is to not be overwhelmed by the size and complexity of the material but rather to use logical reasoning to expand the work of others that you've found to be the most profound in your own research. The references I made to Martin Fowler in this chapter are a good example of this concept.

In this chapter, you took Flex development to the next level and learned about concepts that are used in enterprise development circles so you can begin to implement these concepts into your own work. You learned about the Model-View-Controller architectural foundation that the Flex framework is built upon, how to roll your own architecture, and how to build an application using the Robotlegs framework. You now have the ability to solve complex problems with simple solutions. Armed with this knowledge, projects that once appeared to be overflowing with complexity will seem a lot more manageable.

In the next chapter, you'll take your skills even further and learn how to customize the user experience.

Part 3

The finishing touches

Technically, by the end of part 2 you have what you need to make full-fledged Flex applications. Part 3 takes you beyond making vanilla applications and shows you how to create customized experiences.

For starters, you not only have stylesheets that are similar to HTML's CSS, but also the ability to create themes that package a complete look and feel for a Flex application, including skins that transform the look of any Flex component.

In this part of the book, you'll learn how to add pizzazz with jaw-dropping effects that will wow your users. Enabling these effects is ridiculously simple but has a powerful impact.

It's all about the experience. Although it has a major cool factor, you'll leverage Flex's drag-and-drop feature to add usability to your applications.

Last but not least in the coolness bag, you'll have management eating from the palm of your hand when you give them a dose of Flex's charting abilities, which let you visualize data in a variety of ways.

As part 3 wraps up, your Flex projects are near the end of their development lifecycle. This is the point at which you'll learn how to test, debug, and prepare your applications for prime time.

Customizing the experience

So far, you've learned how to work with the built-in Flex components. You've learned about data binding, transferring data to and from different types of servers, and how to build your own custom components. In the last chapter, you even learned how to use architectural frameworks to make your applications scalable.

Genuine consideration for the audience for which an application is being developed is a consistent trait with highly respected programmers and application architects. In recent years, this has led to more widespread acceptance of user experience design (UXD or UED). In this chapter, we'll focus on the user experience and how you can leverage UXD techniques in Flex to enhance your applications and the ways in which people use them.

20.1   *Principles of user experience design*

User experience design has its roots in human factors and ergonomics, which study the way humans interact with machines in the effort to build better systems. UXD has evolved to become a multidisciplinary field that encompasses aspects of psychology, anthropology, computer science, graphic design, industrial design, and cognitive science. As an application developer who understands the principles of UXD/UED, you'll benefit by being associated with some of the most successful and highly regarded applications. In this section we'll focus on specific principles of UXD related to software programming that you can apply to your Flex applications, starting with the concept of building around user stories.

20.1.1   *Building around user stories*

User stories originated with—and are loosely related to—the concept of *use-case scenarios*. With use-case scenarios, however, a developer attempts to identify the expected use of the application by the user. Eventually people began to realize that this methodology was backwards. Microsoft is probably the software developer that has been best known in the past for using use-case scenarios as the focal point for development. Why doesn't this methodology work? Software programmers don't think the same way that someone from a specific, targeted user demographic does. Figure 20.1 demonstrates how a programmer might think through a particular set of requirements. Notice the number of things that aren't accounted for, such as types of errors that could occur and how each type of error should be handled.

As hard as we try to see through the eyes of the people who use our applications, the fact is that we're incapable of seeing the world through their eyes, just as they're incapable of seeing the world through ours. For this reason a large part of the UXD process must take place prior to commencing development. This begins with the creation of fictional characters who in their daily lives experience some sort of pain that's described in the user story. The following example is a mock user story that I recently wrote to illustrate this:

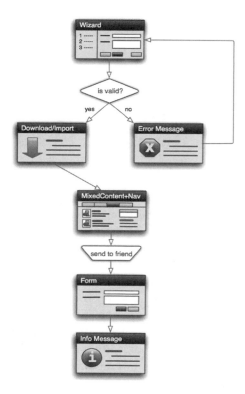

Figure 20.1   Flow diagrams characterize users like robots who follow a predictable path every time. When compared to the effectiveness of user stories, flow diagrams have little value.

User story example

DJ La Bamba has 12 electronic music devices that can all communicate using the MIDI (Musical Instrument Digital Interface) protocol. Currently, musical instruments are forced to run in a master-slave mode when synchronizing beats per minute between music-sequencing devices. Therefore, during live shows and in the studio, DJ La Bamba is forced to set the tempo using a laptop. With so many devices though, his laptop isn't always within reach. Yet, every one of his musical instruments has a Tap Tempo button, where he can change the tempo by tapping the button or pad at the speed at which he wants the song to play. But the Tap Tempo functions on all of the devices are disabled except for one (the laptop) because of this master-slave paradigm that he's stuck in. Nonetheless, DJ La Bamba believes he should be able to set the tempo of the music he's playing using any one of the Tap Tempo functions on his musical instruments, and they should all synchronize automatically to the new beat clock. Reasonable as this may seem, it's surprising to find that such a thing isn't possible with the MIDI communication protocol or any other method of time-clock synchronization between computers and musical instruments.

Notice that the user story is built around a fictional character, which allows the readers to use their imagination, making the story feel more real. This helps in understanding the pain that the proposed product will alleviate for the character in the story. It also infers on the result that will take away the character's current pain.

20.1.2 *Considering context*

When it comes to user experience, *context* plays a vital role in the decisions you make. When creating a mockup for an interface, it's common to create a design similar to the interfaces you may be used to working with. This can be a huge mistake, which is why context is so important.

Three major categories of experience design rely heavily on contextual implications:

- Visual and interaction design
- User feedback
- Responsiveness/performance

Let's look at each of these elements to better understand the role that context plays in the decisions you make about these things.

VISUAL AND INTERACTION DESIGN

The first thing you'll notice about this category is that it consists of more than visual elements such as color scheme, bevels, drop shadows, and the like. It also includes navigation, interactivity, and metaphorical references. For instance, an application's toolbar is arguably the first place the user looks when figuring out where to access certain commands. For example, regardless of the type of application, an individual usually expects to see a familiar set of icons at the upper-left corner of the application's main window. This is demonstrated in figure 20.2.

Right now you might be thinking that this is all obvious, but that's where things get interesting. In the past, this section would have ended at the last paragraph. Until fairly recently, user response to visual stimulus was often treated as a common consistency among all people who use software applications with no regard for the context in which a given application was being used by a specific individual. This mindset is reminiscent of older UML standards, where a user was considered an object.

Figure 20.2   A set of standard icons that use metaphorical references

Ironically, the only other time we refer to people as *users* is when making reference to drug addiction. The implication here is that addicts are viewed as objects until they develop the ability to make decisions based on their own logical reasoning and are therefore no longer controlled by the addiction, suggesting that users don't think for themselves. They're like robots that choose a specific path to completing a task within a software program time and time again as if they're programmed to do it a specific way every time without fail. We call this the *happy path*.

Any developer who has coexisted in the real world, however, will laugh at this type of reasoning and argue adamantly against it, and for good reason. There's no predicting the paths that individuals will take to accomplish their goal, and therefore your job is to require as little thinking as possible on the part of the individual working in the software. That greatly reduces the chances of choosing an obscure path, which could lead to a dead end. Figure 20.3 shows the wireframe for a Flex interface I put together to demonstrate the merging of various social media and RSS-based informational content into a single application.

Although the design in figure 20.3 isn't all that impressive, it scores high in terms of user experience. This is because it employs such features as pagination of large data sets, an automatically updating Facebook feed, and stateful tabbed navigation.

Figure 20.3   This wireframe shines in usability by employing pagination, tabbed navigation that holds the state of the tab when it's switched, and a Facebook feed that updates itself automatically.

These features are valuable, but one of the most critical elements for providing a pleasant experience is feedback.

USER FEEDBACK

Feedback has many implications related to the audience you're building for. For example, unless you're writing an application for IT professionals, it probably wouldn't be considered user friendly if you were to show the corresponding AMF stack trace in an `Alert` control if the application experiences a server error; nor would it make sense to show the server's hexadecimal response because it wasn't what the client application was expecting. Similarly, using generic global notifications such as "An unknown error occurred" will quickly make the user feel helpless and frustrated.

For the sake of best practices, you need to provide an informative error message to the user and give them some direction as to what they should do next. It's usually a good idea to dump stack traces to a log file when an error occurs. That way, if the suggestion is to contact customer support, the helpdesk can help the user locate the log file and send it to the helpdesk for troubleshooting. All this work pays off when it leads to the fixing of a bug and the release of a patch that saves thousands of users from being frustrated by the same bug. This also saves the company money in support calls and what could have been a lot of lost confidence in the product.

RESPONSIVENESS AND PERFORMANCE

A data-driven Flex interface, when combined with animated effects and transitions, can quickly come to a grinding halt, ultimately stalling out or crashing depending on the severity of the situation. Unfortunately, at the time of this writing, the Flash Virtual Machine (FVM) can't take advantage of more than one processor core, and graphics can't be off-loaded to the graphics processor, although this is expected to change in a future version. In highly customized, rich enterprise Flex applications, it's not uncommon to find yourself in a situation where creativity may be required to overcome performance obstacles. This may involve such strategies as caching, or buffering, of data on the client side so it's available immediately upon request.

In a world where we're seeing online applications that run from a web browser competing with the desktop applications of yesteryear, application performance and responsiveness can make or break the application's usefulness. The solution is to adopt a best-practices approach to Flex development, much of which is described throughout this book, and especially as you move into the final chapters.

In order to help shed more light on the things we've discussed so far in this chapter, I created an acronym that I call *the VIBE model* as a way of simplifying the development process of applications that are centered on user stories as opposed to traditional means such as UML modeling and complex flow diagrams. In the next section, you'll learn about what the VIBE model is, and then you'll have the opportunity to see VIBE in action.

20.1.3 *The VIBE model*

I use the VIBE model as a way of measuring the overall user experience of a software product. VIBE is an acronym for

Visual appeal
Interactive experience
Business optimization
Extensibility

Webster's Dictionary defines the word *vibe* as follows:

A person's emotional state or the atmosphere of a place as communicated to and felt by others.

As you can see, the word used for the acronym is fitting. The key phrase that's used in the definition is "emotional state." Any product can be evaluated by first asking the question, "What is the VIBE I am feeling from using this product right now?"

> **TIP** When conducting usability testing and Quality Assurance (QA) analysis, the question should be modified to "What is the vibe *you're* feeling from using this product right now?"

The answer should always be limited to short phrases that describe *feelings and emotions only.* For example, "frustrated and annoyed" qualifies as a legitimate answer to the question, whereas "clunky and slow" expresses an opinion of the software's functionality—or lack thereof—which is the *cause* of an emotional state that the individual failed to describe. Your goal in this first step is to focus on the *effect*, not the cause.

In the second step of evaluation, you can determine the cause of the emotional state by iterating through the four elements of the VIBE model. We'll be doing this in the sections that follow. I'll also show you how you can use the VIBE model in your Flex 4 application development for enhancing the experience. We'll start with the most visual part of the application: themes, skins, CSS, and effects.

20.2 *Visual appeal*

The visual design of a Flex application is created by the use of themes, skins, CSS, and effects. An application can utilize any combination of these four design elements but isn't required to use them in order to function. As rich application developers, we utilize these tools to make these applications rich in their visual appeal. In this section you'll learn how to use each of these elements in Flex 4, starting with themes.

20.2.1 *Using and creating themes*

A theme describes the overall design—often referred to as the look and feel—of components for a specific Flex application. Themes are typically packaged in the form of an SWC file.

> **MIGRATION TIP** The default theme for Flex 3 applications is known as Halo, whereas the default Flex 4 theme (at the time of this writing) is known as Spark. The Spark theme is a combination of styles and programmatic skin classes that make up the appearance and the architecture of the components

that are contained in the spark package. The components that use the Halo theme are located in the mx package. You might be wondering why the Flex 3 default theme was called Halo instead of MX. To address this evident lack of consistency, the release of Flex 4 marks the transition of the components formerly known as Halo over to MX. This includes the change in namespace that you've seen in the code examples contained in this book where halo is replaced by mx.

The alternative is to not compile the assets into an SWC and use the theme as a loose collection of files. Table 20.1 describes the advantages and disadvantages of the two methods.

Table 20.1 Advantages and disadvantages of using an SWC file versus loose assets

	Advantages	**Disadvantages**
Theme compiled as SWC	– Easier to distribute. – Reduces compile time (already precompiled).	– Encapsulation makes design changes somewhat tedious (must recompile). – Harder to debug display issues if the interface doesn't render correctly.
Loose collection of assets	– Design can be easily modified. – Styles can be easily inspected for debugging purposes.	– Extends application compile time. – Risk of missing assets breaking other developers' local workspaces.

In many cases, a precompiled SWC is used when an application's codebase is frozen for that iteration, meaning any further changes will go into the following release. This way, developers don't have to spend time modifying assets and recompiling the theme's SWC separate from the application.

APPLYING A THEME

A theme is applied by using the theme compiler argument. If you're using Flash Builder, you can access the compiler arguments by navigating to Project > Properties > Flex Compiler and locate the field labeled Additional Compiler Arguments, as shown in figure 20.4.

If you aren't using Flash Builder and are instead using the command-line compiler, set the theme using the respective argument at the command line, like so:

```
mxmlc -theme /Users/path/to/Theme.swc /Users/path/Main.mxml
```

Notice that the first argument that follows the theme declaration is the path to the theme SWC, followed by a space, and then the path to the main application file for which the theme should be applied.

CREATING A THEME SWC

A theme SWC contains all of the assets that pertain to your theme and is much like creating a SWC Runtime Shared Library (RSL) or custom component SWC, because you use compc on the command line or build from a library project if you're using Flash Builder. Typically four types of files are compiled into a theme SWC:

- CSS stylesheets
- Media files (images, videos, SWFs)
- Fonts
- Programmatic skin classes (ActionScript files)

The preferred and most manageable method is to build and use a configuration file to compile your theme SWC. This is an XML file that specifies all of the files that you want to include in the SWC. As a matter of convention, this file is often named manifest.xml or catalog.xml, but you could name it kung-pao-chicken.xml and it wouldn't make a difference aside from the fact that it may annoy your coworkers. The important thing is that when you compile, you use the `load-config` compiler argument, followed by the filename, like so:

```
compc -load-config manifest.xml
```

If you're in Flash Builder, you locate the Additional Compiler Arguments field, as shown previously in figure 20.1, and insert

```
-load-config manifest.xml
```

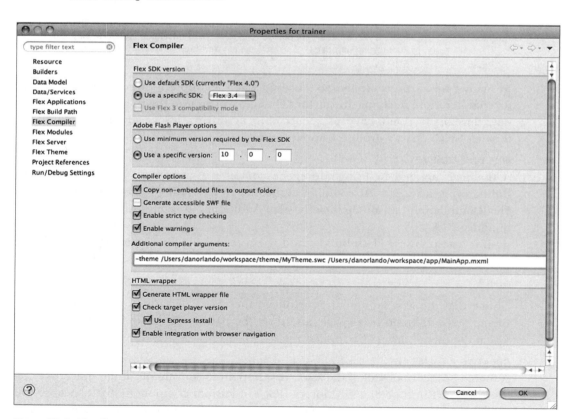

Figure 20.4   The theme argument is used to set the theme in the field labeled Additional Compiler Arguments.

TIP Note that the configuration file should be placed in the application's root directory, which by default is named `src`.

The configuration XML file contains a list of the files that you want to be included in the SWC. The node names are compiler arguments and are used as such when the Flex compiler parses the configuration file. The XML code shown in listing 20.1 demonstrates what a theme SWC build config file might look like.

Listing 20.1   A config file can make the compiler options easier to read and maintain.

```xml
<?xml version="1.0"?>
<flex-config xmlns="http://www.adobe.com/2006/flex-config">     output defines
    <output>MyTheme.swc</output>                                resulting SWC file
    <include-file>                                              For CSS and media files,
        <name>mycss.css</name>                                  use include-file
        <path>c:/myfiles/themes/mycss.css</path>
    </include-file>
    <include-file>
        <name>upIcon.jpg</name>
        <path>c:/myfiles/themes/assets/upIcon.jpg</path>
    </include-file>
    <include-file>
        <name>downIcon.jpg</name>
        <path>c:/myfiles/themes/assets/downIcon.jpg</path>
    </include-file>
    <include-file>
        <name>overIcon.jpg</name>
        <path>c:/myfiles/themes/assets/overIcon.jpg</path>
    </include-file>
    <include-classes>                                           For programmatic skins,
        <class>MyButtonSkin</class>                             use include-classes
        <class>MyAccordionHeaderSkin</class>
        <class>MyControlBarSkin</class>
    </include-classes>                                          Root node must be
</flex-config>                                                  flex-config
```

Now that you've learned how to create and apply themes to your Flex 4 applications, you'll now learn about a broad and popular subject of interest in the development communities: styling and skinning Flex interfaces.

20.2.2 *Styling Flex 4 applications with CSS*

In contrast to Flex 3, the emphasis on using style properties in Flex 4 has been significantly reduced. In contrast, the capabilities of CSS have been greatly expanded in Flex 4 because of popular demand from the community. As you might imagine, this caused some confusion for some of us during our beta testing. What I figured out was that often it came down to a matter of personal preference, and as long as you follow general conventions and best practices, often you can use component skinning or CSS to accomplish the same thing. In some cases it's even advantageous to use both! My only advice there would be to make sure you don't make it hard for other developers to follow your code because you're using both methods.

MIGRATION TIP   When I use CSS with my Flex 4 applications, I've found it to be particularly useful to organize things in such a way that I use CSS specifically for styling and use MXML component skin classes to handle layout (sometimes an additional, preferably reusable layout class is also needed if the layout is complex). My personal preference is usually to write the component classes in pure ActionScript (with the skins in MXML) as well. This leaves me with CSS stylesheets (I usually have one stylesheet per module of an application), MXML skins, and ActionScript component classes. This may sound familiar to web developers who use XHTML to handle page layout and CSS for styling and then JavaScript for behaviors of objects in the page. In other cases, I use FXG instead, and in such cases I find much less use for CSS. We'll talk about FXG later in this chapter.

Flex developers for the most part got used to a certain design workflow with Flex 3, which usually included CSS for styling applications and components. Most Flex 3 applications that I've encountered house most—if not all—styling elements in one or more CSS files, which are usually contained in an assets folder. In Flex 3 applications, the CSS file usually performs double duty, also acting as a repository (or dumping ground, depending on how you look at it) for asset file paths and their respective @Embed statements, which embeds the respective assets at compile time. Although you can continue to do this in Flex 4 projects, you won't be able to take advantage of the advanced skinning features of Flex 4 if you choose to use this method. I anticipate that this will be the toughest thing for Flex designers, who deal primarily with the view layer, to grasp. I started a series of entries on the subject on my blog site (http://danorlando.com) to help Flex developers make a smoother transition, which may be worth a look if you find yourself struggling with it. The chapter on custom component development (chapter 17) of this book, combined with the remaining content in this section, will hopefully give you the ammunition you need to make the transition to Flex 4 as smooth as possible when it comes to styling your applications.

CSS serves a slightly different purpose in Flex 4, although significant enhancements were made to using stylesheets for Flex 4 (even though this isn't necessarily the recommended way of doing things), largely as a result of a heavy amount of requests from the community. These enhancements include

- Global selectors by namespace
- ID selectors
- Descendant selection
- Selection by component state (pseudo selectors)
- Multiple class selectors

Let's look at these items in greater depth, starting with global selectors by namespace.

GLOBAL SELECTORS BY NAMESPACE

The recent release of the CSS 3.0 specification included support for namespaces within CSS stylesheets. When combined with the Flex framework's division between

Spark and MX, it made sense to build in namespace support for Flex 4 CSS. But it's important to understand that the use of namespaces with CSS in Flex 4 isn't an optional feature; it's a requirement. If you forget to declare namespaces before you begin making style declarations, you'll be bombarded with compiler errors when you attempt to build your project. As shown in listing 20.2, namespaces are declared at the beginning of the file. In addition, these namespaces must also be the first thing that's declared after a `<fx:Style/>` tag in MXML. Declaring namespaces is worthless unless they're referenced in the code that follows. With CSS in Flex 4, namespace prefixes are placed in front of your style selectors with a pipe delimiter, as shown in the next listing.

Listing 20.2 Namespace declaration and usage with CSS in Flex 4

```
@namespace s "library://ns.adobe.com/flex/spark";          ◁┐  Declare the
@namespace mx "library://ns.adobe.com/flex/mx";         ◁┘  ❶ Spark namespace

mx|Button {                        ◁┐  Notation for an           Declare the MX
    baseColor:#FFF;                ❸  MX button             ❷  namespace
    color:#000;
}

s|Button {                         ◁┐  Notation for a
    baseColor:#000                 ❹  Spark button
    color:#FFF;
}
```

As you can see from listing 20.2, namespaces are declared in stylesheets using `@namespace` before any styles are written. In the code sample, the Spark namespace is declared first ❶, followed by the MX namespace ❷. Two selectors are then named so that styles can be applied to them, starting with the MX `Button` component ❸ and followed by the Spark `Button` component ❹. Although `Button` is a global selector, it's global only to the respective namespace in Flex 4, as specified on the left side of the pipe delimiter.

ID SELECTORS

Many developers found the CSS functionality in Flex 3 to be rather limiting. One of the biggest complaints was that the Flex 3 CSS implementation didn't allow styles to be assigned by referencing a display object's `id` property.

The problem with cascading

The roots of CSS are found in web design with HTML/XHTML, and CSS stands for Cascading Style Sheet. Referring to the stylesheet implementation in Flex as CSS is inaccurate because the "cascading" part is missing. Put simply, you don't define the specific layout of the components on the stage with CSS. Instead, this is done in either an application's MXML view classes or in a component's MXML skin classes in Flex 4.

For example, let's say you create a Spark button with an `id` of `submitButton` and you want to make the base color of the button black and the text white. To accomplish this, you use the following code:

```
s|#submitButton {
    baseColor: #000000;
        color: #FFFFFF;
}
```

Notice in the code that the hash symbol precedes the `id` selector, which is the same as it is in CSS for HTML/XHTML.

I could take things a step further and limit these styles to being applied only to Spark buttons that have an `id` of `submitButton`, which is useful if, for example, you have a `LinkButton` component in another MXML file with the same `id`. It's a better practice to change the `id` if you have a conflict, but at least now you know what to do if that's not an option. The code for this is as follows:

```
s|Button#submitButton {
    baseColor: #000000;
        color: #FFFFFF;
}
```

ID selectors are a big addition to CSS for Flex and a win for the Flex community, but it doesn't end there. Next we'll take a look at another feature, called *descendant selection*.

DESCENDANT SELECTION

Descendant selection is almost like a conditional within a stylesheet in that it references a particular display object only when that display object exists as a child of a particular container. This is included as part of the selector notation, as you're about to see.

For example, if you wanted all Spark `Button` components that are contained inside a Spark `Panel` container to have red text, you'd use the following code in your stylesheet:

```
s|Panel s|Button {
    color: #FF00000;
}
```

Notice in this code that the `s|Button` selector comes after the parent container selector, separated by only a space.

You could also take things a step further again by adding the condition of applying the style only when a Spark `Button` exists within a Spark `Panel` with an `id` of `myPanel`. In this case, the code would be modified to append the `id` selector to the parent, as shown here:

```
s|Panel#myPanel s|Button {
    color: #FF00000;
}
```

It may seem a bit peculiar that all of these enhancements were made to CSS when the Spark component architecture doesn't exactly promote the use of CSS but rather that of FXG. Nonetheless, there's no denying that the added functionality is a much-needed improvement and is starting to seem a lot closer to what a developer coming from the world of web design would expect to be able to do when working with CSS. The next enhancement I'll describe—called *pseudo selectors*—is an excellent example of this.

SELECTION BY COMPONENT STATE (PSEUDO SELECTORS)

If you're coming from the world of web design, nothing I've described so far should be new to you, and the concept of pseudo selectors is no exception. This specifies the precondition to apply the style only when the specified component is in a particular state. As with the examples we've looked at, Flex 4 follows the same notation as that which is used with CSS in HTML/XHTML, as follows:

```
s|Button:up {
    baseColor: #000000;
    color: #FFFFFF;
}
```

In this code example, a colon separates the selector and the name of the state for which the style should be applied.

There's something interesting about this that's worth mentioning. In HTML/XHTML, states are predefined and limited to up, over, down, selected, and disabled. Flex 4 provides much greater flexibility in this regard. This is because you can use as many states as you want for any selector, and you can name them whatever you want, rather than only being allowed to use the aforementioned state names.

Let's say, for example, that you have a skin class for a `Button` component that includes the following code for specifying the states of the component:

```
<s:states>
    <s:State name="enabled" />
    <s:State name="focus" />
    <s:State name="selected" />
</s:states>
```

As you can see from the style code in listing 20.3, which corresponds to the states specified here, your `Button` still works as you'd expect, even though you're no longer using the default up, over, and down state names.

Listing 20.3 CSS state selector example

```
@namespace s "library://ns.adobe.com/flex/spark";

s|Button:enabled {
    baseColor: #5387B7;
    color: #304F6B;
}
s|Button:focus {
    baseColor: #917541;
    color: #B8A553;
}
s|Button:selected {
```

Corresponds to the enabled state

Corresponds to the focus state

Corresponds to the selected state

```
        baseColor: #B8A553;
        color: #6B5630;
}
```

The last enhancement I'll show you is also available in HTML/XHTML, and as such it's a welcome enhancement to Flex.

MULTIPLE CLASS SELECTORS

At the time of this writing, this enhancement was unknown to the general community because it wasn't included in the documentation (although it probably will be in the full release version). Simple as it may be, it will likely come in handy at some point for you.

This enhancement allows you to specify more than one class selector when setting the styleName property on a component. Let's say, for example, that you built a custom component that you want to utilize two class selectors in your stylesheet rather than copying and pasting the styles from both of them into a new class selector when the styles already exist, albeit in two different class selectors. Instead of using the dreaded copy-and-paste mechanism to accomplish this, you could set the styleName property of the component as follows:

```
styleName="fontStyle headerStyle"
```

I admit that I didn't even know about that feature until I came across a PDF that Flex QA team member Joan Lafferty uploaded from her session at the 2009 MAX conference.

So far, you've learned how to create and implement themes, skins, and CSS in Flex 4, which means you're almost finished with visual appeal, the first part of the VIBE model. In the next section I'll show you how to improve user experience using animation. But this isn't comprehensive by any means. In the next chapter, John C. Bland takes you in depth with Flex 4 effects and animation. For now, we'll concentrate on how effects improve the interactive experience.

20.3 *Interactive experience*

Because we covered the basics of Spark skinning in chapter 17, we'll dive deeper into the abyss of Flex 4 skinning in this chapter. We'll start by covering the land of declarative graphics and animation.

20.3.1 *Declarative design with FXG and Flash Catalyst CS5*

Flash Catalyst CS5 is the major proponent of FXG, a declarative graphics framework that's supported by all of the CS4 and CS5 design-oriented programs, including Photoshop, Illustrator, InDesign, and Fireworks.

Flash Catalyst CS5 deserves an entire book in and of itself, and I suspect that we'll soon see a number of them released. An excellent example of Flex 4 declarative graphics and skinning is provided at the beginning of chapter 18, on code reusability. In this section I'll provide a basic overview of how declarative graphics and Catalyst fit into the product development lifecycle for development that's centered on an enhanced user experience.

OPTIMIZING YOUR WORKFLOW WITH FLASH CATALYST CS5

Flash Catalyst CS5 allows you to import user interface designs built with Photoshop, Illustrator, and Fireworks and add interactivity, states, transitions, and effects through an intuitive user interface that doesn't require any programming.

> **TIP** At the time of this writing, Adobe Illustrator CS5 is the only application capable of "round-tripping" with Flash Catalyst CS5. This means that you could create a file in Illustrator CS5, import it into Catalyst, and then export from Catalyst and reimport into Illustrator if you need to make additional changes from Illustrator. For as long as this is the case (it's not expected to change for awhile), seriously consider designing in Illustrator if you plan to use Catalyst because if you use a program like Photoshop, once you import into Catalyst you can't go back to Photoshop and expect to retain the work you did in Catalyst.

Catalyst is also good for wireframing and prototyping conceptual applications. As shown in the workflow diagram provided in figure 20.5, Adobe is using user experience and Flash Catalyst CS5 to bridge the inherent gap that exists in the workflow between designer and developer.

To fully understand what's going on in figure 20.5, consider the following:

- UXD/UED is a central mediation point by which design and development can be brought together in the application development workflow.
- Flash Catalyst CS5 can open FXG files exported from any of Adobe's CS4 or CS5 design programs so that the user experience elements such as interactivity, transitions, and effects can be implemented.
- Catalyst has the capability of directly exporting a single FXP (Flex Project) file, which can then be seamlessly imported into Flash Builder. Flash Builder uses FXG to read out and display graphics, whereas Spark library declarations, which are brought in when adding interactivity in Flash Catalyst, hold the necessary information regarding states, transitions, user interactions, and other elements that are specific to the display of the user interface.
- The business layer of the application, or behavioral logic, is added to the project in Flash Builder, and then debugging and profiling can be commenced prior to exporting the final build.

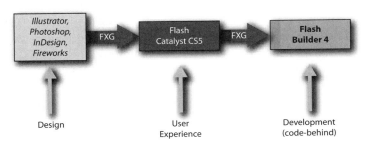

Figure 20.5 Moving from left to right, notice that FXG is used to translate graphics between the Adobe applications.

The application takes many of the things that used to be the responsibility of the developer and brings them into the designer's world. Your first thought after reading that might be along the lines of "Uh-oh, that sounds like it could be dangerous." In my experience, designers fare particularly well (a lot better than developers) when it comes to the inevitability of having to make assumptions about the needs of the target user base for a given application. Although UED is a specialized practice in and of itself, don't be surprised if you notice many designers moving over to this field of study.

Proceed with caution

While writing my chapters of this book, I had the opportunity to oversee development of a few applications that were done using the beta versions of Flash Builder, Flex 4, and Flash Catalyst. The biggest consistency was that designers who came from a strictly Photoshop/Illustrator/Fireworks background (usually with a little bit of Flash timeline experience but no coding) developed nice-looking functional interfaces in Catalyst, which when imported into Flash Builder were described as "useless" by the development team. The reason for the failure in the workflow was merely a lack of basic knowledge in regard to conventions and organizational structure of a Flex project.

At the time of this writing, the Catalyst development team at Adobe was working hard to resolve this, but it will likely become part of the learning curve for designers when using Flash Catalyst. Similarly, incorporating Catalyst into the project lifecycle also means that Flex developers will need to learn the basics of Flash Catalyst CS5. This should come as no surprise, but this is important information for project managers wanting to incorporate Catalyst in order to avoid the aforementioned breakdown.

DEGRAFA: REACHING THE DECLARATIVE GRAPHICS PROMISED LAND

A declarative graphics framework available for Flex has been available for several years now, called Degrafa. This open source framework is active and will continue to be because the purpose and direction of Degrafa are different from that of FXG.

A group of talented individuals from both Universal Mind and EffectiveUI has been instrumental in the continued development of the Degrafa framework. Joe Johnston's blog is an excellent resource for Degrafa tutorials, as well as just about anything and everything having to do with user experience design. You can find it at http://www.merhl.com. Ryan Campbell's blog is also an excellent resource, especially for the Degrafa examples he provides for beginners and experts alike, located at http://www.ryancampbell.com.

Probably the most appealing thing about Degrafa is how easy it is to pick up. Speaking from experience, I used it once to deliver a lightweight and skinnable custom component in two hours that would have otherwise taken at least a day or two of development.

The Degrafa framework is also mature, and the fact that it's open source certainly doesn't hurt. More information on Degrafa can be found at http://www.degrafa.org/. The best thing about Degrafa is that the website is packed with documentation, tutorials, and links to additional resources to help you get started with it as quickly and painlessly as possible. At the time of this writing, support for Flex 4 had not yet been released. Knowing how fast the Degrafa team moves, it won't be long before we see a new version come out with full support for integrating with Flex 4 projects.

You haven't learned about using themes and skins to maximize the visual appeal of your applications. Next, we'll look at how CSS can be leveraged in Flex 4.

20.3.2 *Enhancing the experience with effects*

There's no question that animation is always a fun subject to talk about when building rich internet applications, and Flex 4 doesn't disappoint when it comes to animated transitions and effects. Flex 4 introduces a more sophisticated API for producing effects than that of version 3. The new API takes advantage of features that were included with the release of Flash Player 10, such as simulated 3D rendering.

3D EFFECT PRIMER

Probably the most attention-grabbing, awe-inspiring, and visually pleasing effects are those that simulate the use of 3D space. If you know a lot about the internals of the Flash virtual machine, you already know that true 3D can't be realized with the Flash Player architecture the way it is right now, which doesn't allow you to offload graphics processing to the GPU, among other things. But the release of Flash Player 10 introduced some convincing simulated 3D capabilities by adding a Z-axis to the stage. This is especially intriguing for Flex and AIR developers because of the impact that 3D visualizations can have on user experience, not just as eye candy but for advanced data visualizations and browsing through large amounts of media thumbnails.

Peter Dehaan, a quality assurance engineer on the Flex SDK team, has become well known for the gobs of Flex 4 samples and tutorials he made available to the Flash Platform development community throughout the two years that Flex 4 spent in development. In a moment you'll take a look at an example of the 3D rotation effect that Peter kindly provided, which can also be found on his blog site at http://blog.flexexamples.com. Listing 20.4 demonstrates how easy it is to use the Rotate3D effect in Flex 4.

Listing 20.4 3D Rotation on the X axis with the `Rotate3D` effect

```
<?xml version="1.0" encoding="utf-8"?>
<s:Application name="Spark_Rotate3D_test"
        xmlns:fx="http://ns.adobe.com/mxml/2009"
        xmlns:s="library://ns.adobe.com/flex/spark"
        xmlns:mx="library://ns.adobe.com/flex/mx">
    <s:layout>
        <s:BasicLayout />
    </s:layout>

    <fx:Declarations>
        <s:Rotate3D id="rotate3DX"
            target="{image}"
```

Place effects inside **Declarations** tag

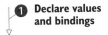 **1** Declare values and bindings

```
                angleXFrom="0"
                angleXTo="360"
                duration="2000"                        ➊ Declare values
                autoCenterTransform="true"                and bindings
    />
    <mx:ApplicationControlBar width="100%" cornerRadius="0">
        <s:Button id="buttonX"
                label="Rotate3D X-axis"
                click="rotate3DX.play();" />            ➋ Effect triggered
    </mx:ApplicationControlBar>                            using play()
    <s:BitmapImage id="image"
            source="@Embed('assets/fx_appicon.jpg')"
            resizeMode="scale"
            smooth="true"
            horizontalCenter="0"
            verticalCenter="0"
            width="100"
            height="100" />

</s:Application>
```

As shown in listing 20.4, you start by declaring an instance of the Spark Rotate3D object inside the <fx:Declarations /> tag ➊. Next, you bind the effect to an object in the display list. Binding the effect to a specific display object is optional. Not binding it allows the effect to be used on more than one object by calling rotate3DX.play (target), where target is any of the objects in the display list that can be animated. In the example, angleXFrom and angleXTo are used to rotate the object. The angleX-From property is used as the starting point of the rotation, whereas angleXTo is used as the end point of the rotation.

The duration property is the length by which the animation should last. In the example, we set duration to 2000 milliseconds, causing the object to take 2 seconds to complete a single rotation. The autoCenterTransform property tells Flex that we want the object to use its center as the registration point for the rotation, rather than using its upper-left pixel point as it normally would.

Most important, the effect is triggered on the click of buttonX as denoted with the code click="rotate3DX.play()". Notice that we didn't have to pass the object into the constructor of the effect's play method because the effect is already bound to a target ➋.

EXPERIENCE VERSUS POINTLESS ANIMATION

The result of the code example above is a neat, simulated 3D rotating effect on the given image, as shown in figure 20.6.

You might be wondering whether this improves the user experience or if it's pointless animation similar to the likes of the infamous website Flash intros that infected the internet for many years.

Luckily, it's not as easy to create such random, pointless animations with Flex because effects are generally aimed at user feedback; they're based on events usually caused by some user interaction. As long as you stick to this model when creating user

**Figure 20.6
Pressing one of the
three buttons
rotates the plane on
the respective axis.**

experiences, you can be confident that your awesome effects will always have purpose. Remember that a good user experience also means that you're not robbing helpless users of their system resources.

This leads nicely into our next topic of discussion. So far we've taken a fine-grained approach to user experience by analyzing visual appeal and user interactivity. It's now time to look at the third element, business optimization.

20.4 *Business optimization*

When I refer to business optimization, I'm specifically referring to application performance. Business development is attained from gaining long-term clients and customers, which is attributed to applications that perform predictably and therefore build trust and confidence.

When the quality of an application directly affects the stability and performance of a business, that means a well-performing application with a strong foundation translates to a well-performing business with a strong foundation. The business depends on you to make good decisions in your development, or that business could ultimately fail if it hits what I refer to as the "scalability wall." In chapters 18 and 19, you learned about ways of organizing your Flex 4 applications in order to avoid hitting this scalability wall. Now let's discuss how this affects user experience.

20.4.1 *Using best practices to improve the experience*

The scalability wall is the point at which no new functionality can be added to an application without breaking it. The most prolific cause of the scalability wall is lack of unit testing. In the perfect world, every application would be built using test-driven development (TDD). Unfortunately, a large portion of development projects don't attempt to implement TDD until they've experienced the scalability wall. The problem with this is that it's hard to implement TDD into a project after development has already commenced.

The benefit of using TDD is that it prevents tight coupling in code, lack of architecture, and bad design in regard to the way the code is written. It's clear when an application has hit the scalability wall for one reason: The only viable solution is to refactor the code. Speaking of refactoring (and I bring this up only because I just finished reading it, so it's fresh on the brain), there's a book written by Martin Fowler (whom I'm sure you're sick of hearing me talk about by now) titled *Refactoring: Improving the Design*

The case for best practices

At Universal Mind, a substantial portion of the projects we take on involves refactoring. One observation I've made over the years is that companies almost always try to save as much money as possible on the development of the application that makes up the core of their business, and exceptions are rare. As backwards as this may seem, it's a reality that costs companies millions of dollars and ensures the job security of many IT professionals (many of whom tend to be offshore). When you factor in the loss in time and the loss of first-to-market opportunity among other things, the loss often runs upwards of hundreds of millions of dollars when all is said and done. That's an expensive lesson to learn, so the smart ones don't make the mistake again. The rest are still clueless as to what went wrong and will probably make the same mistake again. I don't know about you, but I'd much rather be developing cool, bleeding-edge, next-generation applications than refactoring projects and troubleshooting and then fixing other people's mistakes, so I'm a huge advocate of anything and everything that has to do with establishing, learning, and religiously following a universally accepted set of standards and best practices for Flex development.

of Existing Code. If you often find yourself stepping into projects that either have already hit the wall or you anticipate that they will for obvious reasons, this book is an absolute must-have. It will totally change your perspective toward the concept of refactoring.

The good news is that you can easily avoid the scalability wall by following these simple steps:

1   Prior to commencing development, create clearly defined best-practices documentation and post it on an internal private wiki site for application programming specific to your company. This is the reference documentation that every new developer reads before they start writing code. This document should be treated like a contract, and developers should hold each other accountable for sticking to it in a constructive manner that's conducive to learning and quality assurance.

2   Proactively use revision-control software like Atlassian's FishEye, which integrates right into your code repository and tracks all changes, which are easily viewed using a user-friendly browser. Then get the Crucible code review tool (also from Atlassian), which plugs right into FishEye and can be used for team-member-initiated code reviews.

3   Don't develop using an architectural framework unless and until you and all your teammates have learned and feel comfortable writing code that utilizes that framework. Not all second-generation microarchitectures tightly couple the framework deep into the application code base, so if you're seeing code that's framework-specific at a component level, that's a dead giveaway that the developers don't understand how to use the framework.

4   Hold regular brown bag lunches, whether virtually or in a real office, to discuss and brainstorm things like alternative design patterns and ways that the code

can be simplified (refactoring). You'd be amazed at what your team will come up with when everyone puts their heads together. Solving performance problems or optimizing performance is often a candidate for this type of thing.

TIP A great way to avoid many of the common pitfalls that companies typically face during the application development lifecycle is to facilitate continuing education by holding daily one-hour sessions that can be in the form of code reviews or discussion about design patterns and solving common programming problems.

One of the most critical elements of best practices involves unit testing your applications, which you'll get a brief overview of next. For a more involved discussion on unit testing, see chapter 24 of this book.

20.4.2 *Improve the experience by unit testing*

You may be asking yourself right now, how does unit testing have anything to do with user experience? The answer is simple: Good software experiences evolve when programs work as expected. A great example of a bad experience is one in which the client or customer hits a runtime exception while using your program, crashing the application and disrupting their workflow. With test-driven development, you write code that's meant to break things. By artificially breaking your program, you can plan for and write code around such breakages.

Test-driven development revolves around writing unit tests prior to commencing development. In order for this to work, however, it's important that the practice of writing user stories take place prior to commencing development. This makes writing unit tests a lot easier because you're no longer thinking only about coding for "the happy path." Instead, you're thinking about Jane, who never takes the happy path with anything she does and will undoubtedly find a way to break your code. With unit testing, Jane can do as many strange and seemingly messed-up things to your program as she can think of, and the program will always handle it gracefully.

As the application grows, you can rest assured that your code is safe as long as your unit tests pass on each new build (assuming you wrote them all and wrote them properly). Unit testing is covered in the final chapters of this book, but for a comprehensive look into unit testing your Flex applications, I recommend you visit FlexUnit.org. The release of FlexUnit 4 marks a significant milestone for the FlexUnit framework as a robust testing framework for enterprise Flex applications.

20.4.3 *Profiling Flex 4 applications*

It's a fact that only a handful of Flex developers use the built-in profiler, yet thankfully that number is growing as the demand for high-performance Flex applications increases. It's also reassuring to know that Flash Builder 4 includes some great enhancements to the application profiler. The Flex profiler has historically been severely lacking in terms of being useful, which is a major reason why so many Flex developers didn't bother with it. But Adobe took notice and overhauled the profiler

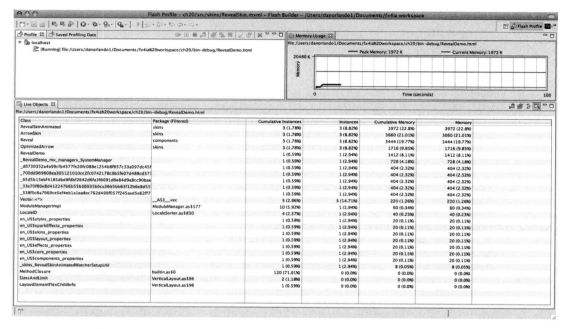

Figure 20.7   At first glance, the Flash Builder 4 profiler looks quite similar to that of Flex Builder 3.

for Flash Builder 4, building in a whole slew of new functionalities that make it a far more useful tool.

As you can see in figure 20.7, the Flash Builder 4 profiler doesn't look much different from the one that shipped with Flex Builder 3. But under the covers it's an entirely different beast.

An excellent article written by Jun Heider is available on the Adobe Developer Connection, and it walks you through the process of profiling in a step-by-step fashion. The article is located at http://www.adobe.com/devnet/flex/articles/flashbuilder4_debugging_profiling_03.html.

In this section, you learned about business optimization in application development and how it relates to user experience design. This leads us to the last of the four facets of the VIBE model, which is extensibility.

20.5 *Extensibility*

When evaluating extensibility, one of the key facets that you're evaluating is the ability to modify or add to an existing code base without causing *regressions*. A regression is the breaking of a seemingly unrelated piece of a given application when code is changed in order to fix a bug, fulfill a functional requirement, or implement a feature request. Unless you're brand new to the world of software development, that probably sounds familiar. If you recall, we discussed this subject and how it relates to application architecture at the beginning of chapter 19. In this section, we'll discuss the implications of extensibility, but this time we'll focus on how it affects user experience.

20.5.1 *Extensibility's indirect relationship to user experience*

The term *extensibility* is mostly synonymous with scalability in computer programming. The Oxford American Dictionary defines it best: "to expand in scope, effect, or meaning." Imagine the following scenario:

You're three-fourths of the way through a big project, and all of a sudden you're handed a new set of wireframes for the entire application user interface. You're told that you must ditch the designs that you've been working on for months now in favor of these new ones. See, while you were coding away, the product team was conducting *usability studies.* The product team concluded from their months of research that people won't respond favorably to the current interface, and the product will ultimately fail unless the new designs are implemented.

THE PROGRAMMER'S CURSE

In terms of logical reasoning, it makes sense that you should be given a chance to rescope the project now and provide a new estimated delivery date, right? After all, the requirements just changed. Well, this story wouldn't represent a real-world example very well if we didn't mention the stakeholders. As far as they're concerned, you were given the target date months ago and you agreed to it. They could care less if product design made a mistake or assumptions were made about the interface that shouldn't have been made. Your job is to get the product delivered on time and under budget. Their primary concern is *time to market opportunity.* After all, they're stakeholders!

As severe a predicament as this may be, it's so common that it happens every single day! This is where the value of extensibility comes into play. All of a sudden, whether or not you'll meet your deadline and with a successful product depends on how well you'll be able to scale this application and modify the code without causing an onslaught of regressions. The bottom line is this: When code is scalable, its parts are interchangeable and implementations can be made quickly and without breaking other parts of the code base. Unfortunately, the demand for highly complex systems produced in shorter periods of time is one constant that you can always depend on being there. The only way to combat this is with extensible, scalable, reusable code.

20.5.2 *The direct relationship between extensibility and user experience*

A more direct type of relationship between extensibility and user experience has to do with bug fixes, feature implementation, and release schedule.

When it comes to squashing bugs, nothing is more frustrating than fixing a problem that was reported, only to have your QA team file four more bug reports because although you may have fixed *that* bug, you caused four others somewhere else in the application along the way!

You'll probably hear the cause of this described as tight coupling or messy code, but at its core it's a lack of established design patterns and principles, which makes a company prone to code chaos, the situation that occurs after a developer has completed a task but destroyed something without knowing it and blocked other developers as a result. This is typically due to dependencies between seemingly unrelated objects, and it typically requires an overhaul of the code base. Obviously this is a no-brainer that doesn't require an astrophysicist to conduct a series of complex scientific studies to figure out that it's a train wreck. *The reason we see such dependency-driven code so often is that most of the people who can tell you why the code breaks can't tell you what needs to be done to prevent it from happening again.* This conundrum has plagued the software industry throughout its existence.

Meanwhile, a number of other software researchers and computer scientists derive theoretical solutions that work conceptually but fail miserably in practice.

The same scenario exists with feature implementation and the release schedule as with bug fixing. When features can be added and the code base can be easily modified and optimized without introducing regression potential, the user experience improves because the end user benefits from getting a much higher-quality application in a much shorter period of time, with regular and dependable iterative releases.

Extensible code begins with a solid foundation, or architecture, as you learned in chapter 19. After that, it's all about programming what's commonly referred to as clean code. Let's take a quick look at what that means before we bring this chapter to a close.

20.5.3 *Write clean code for the sake of usability*

The term *clean code* can easily be misinterpreted as a generic way of describing proper object-oriented coding practices, the definition of which is subjective. In contrast, when I refer to *clean code*, I'm talking about an unofficial standard of coding practices that are universally accepted by community leaders and expert programmers for object-oriented languages such as ActionScript 3. I couldn't possibly do this subject justice in such a short amount of space, so here are a few golden rules of writing clean code, followed by a reference that I've found to be of great value on the subject.

The following clean code tips can also be viewed as a precursor to the section on unit testing in chapter 24, because writing clean code is synonymous with writing testable code.

THE LAW OF DEMETER

The Law of Demeter is simple: It states that although object A can access a property of object B, object A should not reach through object B in order to access a property of object C. This topic tends to remind me of the early days of Flex when Cairngorm was the de facto standard for enterprise application architectures. It wasn't uncommon to see something like this:

```
this.globalAccessors.businessServiceDelegate.objectServiceCommand.objectData.
    userCollection.getItemAt(i).address;
```

This code example is the metaphorical equivalent of following a noodle through grandma's fifteen-gallon tub of spaghetti on Christmas Day (okay, so I grew up in an Italian family!). A better way of accessing the same value might look like this:

```
user.address;
```

I don't know about you, but that second example makes me feel warm and fuzzy inside after viewing the horrifying first example. The beauty of the Law of Demeter is in the simplicity and readability of the code that you write.

DO ONE THING AND ONLY ONE THING

This concept is also simple, despite the fact that it's violated more often than not. When you write a function, that function should have one job and one job only. Here's a nice example:

```
protected function clickHandler(event:MouseEvent):void
{
   if (currentState == 'Register')
      Alert.show(userid.text + " registered!");
   else
      Alert.show(userid.text + " logged in!");
}
```

Nesting `if` statements and `for` loops are the ultimate epitome of violating this golden rule, as shown in the following listing.

Listing 20.5   Nested loops are a direct violation of clean code standards.

```
protected function clickHandler(event:MouseEvent):void
{
   var n:int = event.stateIndex;
   var s:String = event.state

   if (s == 'Register')
   {
      for (i = 0; i < n; i++)
      {
         for (j=0; j < n; j++)
         {
            c[i][j] = 0;
            for (k = 0; k < n; k++)
            {
               c[i][j] += A[k][j] * B[i][k];
            }
         }
      }
   }
   else
      Alert.show("good thing that nested loop didn't run!");
}
```

If you can explain what that function is doing, go out and get a lotto ticket because you're one in a billion. Not only is this an example of dirty code, but it's also impossible to unit test effectively.

USE PRACTICAL NAMING CONVENTIONS

Looking back at listing 20.5, something else is also going on that isn't considered clean code, and that's the naming convention, or lack thereof. How is anyone supposed to know what `c`, `j`, `A`, and `B` are? This is often also referred to as code obfuscation (otherwise known as job security), and it will never fail to be a thorn in your side through the duration of that project's development until it's refactored and split into five separate functions.

I strongly suggest picking up the book titled *Clean Code* by Robert C. Martin (Prentice/Pearson, 2009). I've had 15-year-veteran programmers who thought that book was rudimentary for them. Little did they know that they'd end up both shocked and appalled to find out that they had been using such antipatterns for so many years. Point being, you'll get something out of reading that book whether you're a developer of only one month or 20 years.

20.6 *Summary*

You went on quite a journey in this chapter, beginning with the fundamentals of user experience design. You then ventured deeper into the depths of UXD with Flex 4 as you were introduced to the VIBE model. You then learned how to leverage Flex 4 for enhanced visual appeal as well as how Flash Catalyst CS5 fits into the picture. You then saw how best practices in application development really do have an effect on the end user's experience.

In the coming chapters, you'll be taken through the VIBE model in greater detail as John and Joel bring visual appeal, interactive experience, business optimization, and extensibility into action, starting with the fun stuff: working with effects!

Working with effects

This chapter covers

- Defining effects
- Using effects
- Exploring Flex effects
- Customizing effects

Effects set Flex applications apart. Because Flex is based on the Flash platform, it draws on a long history of delivering engaging animated UIs, which gives it a powerful base on which to create effects.

In the last chapter we showed you how to customize the user experience through CSS, skinning, and a little bit on effects. In this chapter, we'll take you further into effects starting by explaining what they are and how to use them, then describing the types of out-of-the-box effects, and finishing off with customization and font integration. Having conquered some heavy topics up to this point in the book, we're going to keep this chapter light.

21.1 What's an effect?

An *effect* modifies visual properties of a component over a period of time. These properties include a component's position, transparency, size, and more. To picture effects you can look all around you. Think of a pendulum in a grandfather clock swinging left to right, your TV fading in when you turn it on, or a landscape through a camera lens as you zoom in and out. Those are all examples of effects. In the prehistoric days (two years ago in Flex 3), you could animate only display objects (UI components), but Flex 4 lets you target display objects/components, graphic objects (gradient entries and so on), and filters. For example, you can transition the transparency (alpha) up or down over a period of five seconds to create a fade effect.

In this section you'll learn what's available to you as a Flex developer through the different effects and effect combinations. To dig in we need to first look at the default effect capabilities provided in Flex 4.

21.1.1 *Available effects*

Flex comes with an assortment of effects ready to go out of the box. Table 21.1 lists the prebuilt Flex 4 effects.

Table 21.1   Available Flex effects out of the box

Effect	Animates
Fade	alpha property
Move and Move3D	x, y, and/or z properties
Resize	Width and height
Scale and Scale3D	scaleX, scaleY, and/or scaleZ properties
Rotate and Rotate3D	rotation, rotationX, rotationY, and/or rotationZ properties
CrossFade	Two objects or the text of an object between states
Wipe	Two bitmaps

This list covers some of the abilities that are prebuilt and available for you right now. What's that? Not seeing effects you once saw in Flex 3? Things have changed quite a bit. Table 21.1 is purely a list of prebuilt effects, but Flex 4 provides you with base classes for pimping your own effects. Much more advanced animations are possible using MotionPaths, Keyframes, and numerous combinations of effects, filters, and shaders. The effects from table 21.1 extend core effect classes. Table 21.2 shows the core effect classes and what they do.

> **TIP**   If you want to do complex transitions along a path, you can now define multistep animations using Animate, Keyframes, and MotionPaths. Fully explaining these goes beyond the scope of this chapter, but a great example is Chet Haase's "Stretch and Squash in Flex 4" blog post: http://graphics-geek. blogspot.com/2009/07/video-stretch-and-squash-in-flex-4.html.

Along with these prebuilt effects you can also combine effects, creating what's known as composite effects.

Table 21.2 Core effect classes

Effect	Animates
Animate	Base class to all effects; allows granular customizations
AnimateColor	A color over time using interpolation between two colors on a per-channel basis
AnimateFilter	Filters (BlurFilter, GlowFilter, and so on)
AnimateTransformShader	Two bitmaps through a pixel-shaders program (CrossFade and Wipe extend this class.)
AnimateTransform and AnimateTransform3D	A combination of translation, scale, and rotation properties (Move, Scale, Rotate and their 3D counterparts extend this class.)

21.1.2 Composite effects

To do some cool stuff, you can combine effects using either of these approaches:

- *Sequence*—Plays one effect after another
- *Parallel*—Plays all the effects in parallel, at once

Hold onto this knowledge for a little bit. We'll cover composite effects in detail within section 21.3. At this point, you've been introduced to effects at a high level; let's see how to use them.

21.2 Using effects

In the previous section, you were briefly introduced to the available out-of-the-box effects. Let's look at how we can use these effects, starting with effect trigger mechanisms and then jumping into examples of each.

21.2.1 Cause and effect

Effects are played from a trigger. Think of it as cause and effect in normal life. You push a button and your car starts, flip a switch and the lights come on, and so on. The same is true in programming effects. A user does something and you, the developer, respond to that trigger by playing an effect. We'll explore the different triggers used to integrate effects.

There are three effect triggers in Flex 4:

- *Event*—The effect is automatically kicked off when a certain effect-specific event occurs (for example, <s:Button mouseOverEffect="myEffect" />).
- *Programmatically*—You can create an effect declaratively or on the fly and run it as desired (for example, myEffect.play();).
- *State transitions*—The effect runs during a Flex state change (for example, currentState = "newState").

You can use any of these approaches on either out-of-the-box or custom effects. How or when you use them is based on your specific scenario(s). Moving forward, we'll explore each of the different effect triggers and look at examples of how to use them.

21.2.2 *Event-triggered effects*

As we mentioned in the previous section, an event-triggered effect occurs as a result of a specific event firing. All visual components support a set of properties, allowing you to specify which effect you want to automatically play for the corresponding event.

Table 21.3 shows the available effect triggers for native Flex components.

Table 21.3   Effect event triggers

Property	Caused by
addedEffect	The component being added to a container
creationCompleteEffect	Flex finishing creating the component
focusInEffect	The keyboard focusing on the component
focusOutEffect	The keyboard focusing off the component
hideEffect	The component's `visible` property changing to `false`
mouseDownEffect	The mouse button being pressed down on the component
mouseUpEffect	The mouse button going up after being pressed down on the component
moveEffect	The component changing position
removedEffect	The component being removed from the container it was in
resizeEffect	The component being resized
rollOutEffect	The mouse moving off the component
rollOverEffect	The mouse moving over the component

TIP Your own custom components can expose effect triggers as well. This chapter doesn't cover writing your own custom effects, but you can accomplish it through metadata like so: `[Effect(name="eventNameEffect", event="eventName")]`.

Let's use this information in a practical example. A popular effect for photo albums is to make the thumbnail grow in size as you mouse over the item; listing 21.1 does this using a `Resize` effect on a black `Rect` in a `Group`.

Listing 21.1   Using the `Resize` effect to enlarge an image on mouse-over

```
<?xml version="1.0" encoding="utf-8"?>
<s:Application xmlns:fx="http://ns.adobe.com/mxml/2009"
               xmlns:s="library://ns.adobe.com/flex/spark">
  <fx:Declarations>
    <s:Resize id="fxEnlarge" widthTo="300" heightTo="300" />
```

① Define enlarge resize to 300x300

```
      <s:Resize id="fxShrink"  widthTo="100" heightTo="100"/>
   </fx:Declarations>
   <s:Group width="200" height="200"
            rollOverEffect="{fxEnlarge}" rollOutEffect="{fxShrink}">
      <s:Rect id="box" width="100%"
       height="100%">
        <s:fill>
          <s:SolidColor color="black" />
        </s:fill>
      </s:Rect>
   </s:Group>
</s:Application>
```

Define shrink resize to 100x100 ❷

Set the effects ❸

Could it be any easier? The Group applies two effects, rollOverEffect ❸ and roll-OutEffect ❸, when the mouse moves over and off the graphic, as shown in figure 21.1. When the rollover event is dispatched, the fxEnlarge effect ❶ is told to play(), and the same is true for fxShrink ❷ and the rollOutEffect.

> **NOTES** - Effects go in a Declarations block because they aren't visual components.
> - When you match a trigger with an effect, it's referred to as a *behavior*.

Triggered effects are easy to create but are limited to the known triggers supported by components. If you need an effect to occur as a result of business logic, you must programmatically apply the effect.

21.2.3 *Programmatically applying an effect*

You just learned how with triggered events you can leverage canned scenarios, which Flex considers "the usual." This means you take an event and assign an effect to it, custom or built in, and then automagically the effect plays. Your application(s) will include unique scenarios to which you may want to apply an effect at your chosen time and how you choose to apply it. In doing so, you can learn how to play effects programmatically.

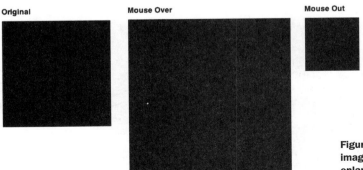

Original   Mouse Over   Mouse Out

Figure 21.1 Mousing over the image triggers the image to enlarge using the Resize effect.

TRIGGERING EFFECTS WITH ACTIONSCRIPT

Suppose you have a reminder feature, and if something becomes overdue you want to make the reminder glow red. Listing 21.2 demonstrates this concept by counting down the seconds; if a threshold is crossed, the message glows repeatedly.

Listing 21.2 Playing an effect when certain business rules kick in

```
<?xml version="1.0" encoding="utf-8"?>
<s:Application xmlns:fx="http://ns.adobe.com/mxml/2009"
               xmlns:s="library://ns.adobe.com/flex/spark"
               applicationComplete="init()">
  <s:layout>
    <s:VerticalLayout paddingLeft="20" paddingTop="20" />
  </s:layout>
  <fx:Script>
    <![CDATA[
      import flash.utils.Timer;

      import spark.effects.animation.RepeatBehavior;

      [Bindable]
      protected var secondsTillDue:int = 5;
      protected var _timer:Timer;

      protected function init():void{
        _timer = new Timer(1000); //tick every 1000ms          ❶ Set and run
        _timer.addEventListener('timer', onTimerTick);            timer every
        _timer.start();                                           1000ms
      }

      protected function onTimerTick(event:TimerEvent):void{
        secondsTillDue = Math.max(secondsTillDue-1, 0);        ◁── Update
        if(secondsTillDue == 0){                                   secondsTillDue
          effect.play();         ❸ If secondsTillDue is 0,      ❷ value
          _timer.stop();            play effect and stop timer
        }
      }
    ]]>
  </fx:Script>
  <fx:Declarations>
    <s:GlowFilter id="filter" color="#4e7800" blurX="20"     ❹ Set up GlowFilter
      blurY="20" />                                              to glow orange
    <s:AnimateFilter id="effect" target="{box}"              ❺ Set up
      bitmapFilter="{filter}"                                    AnimateFilter,
        duration="1000" repeatCount="0"                          the effect we play
        repeatBehavior="{RepeatBehavior.REVERSE}">
      <s:SimpleMotionPath property="alpha" valueFrom="0"      ❻ Set up motion path
        valueTo="1" />                                            to animate alpha
    </s:AnimateFilter>
  </fx:Declarations>
  <s:Label id="labelField" fontWeight="bold" fontSize="14"
        text="Due in {secondsTillDue} seconds" />
  <s:Rect id="box" width="200" height="200">
    <s:fill>
      <s:SolidColor color="black" />
```

```
    </s:fill>
  </s:Rect>
</s:Application>
```

When you run the application, you'll see a message that begins to glow when the countdown gets to 0 seconds, as shown in figure 21.2.

If you used effects in Flex 3, you might have noticed something: We have a reversing effect and didn't have to define two effects! This is different, new, and a welcome change in Flex 4. Previously you'd have two `mx:Glow` effects, one to go up and one to go down, maybe wrapped in a Parallel or Series to run a `glow` and `alpha` change together. In this example we defined one `GlowFilter` ❹ and targeted this filter using the `AnimateFilter` class.

The `AnimateFilter` class allows us to target an object, or array of objects, as well as a filter: `box` and `filter`, respectively. In the `AnimateFilter` we also define our settings to animate over 1000ms, repeat indefinitely (0–indefinite; anything greater than 0 repeats that number of times), and the lovely repeat behavior using the `repeatBehavior` property ❺. I call it *lovely* because this is where you're saved from having to have two animations to get a clean to-and-from effect. You can, as we did, use the `RepeatBehavior` constants `REVERSE` and `LOOP` to change this property, or you can pass in simple text: `reverse` and `loop`, respectively.

Our animation is set up and ready to go, but we also want to fade in the glow. If it just popped in, it wouldn't look as spiffy as if it faded in, so our inner designer took over and we added a `SimpleMotionPath` as a child declaration to `AnimateFilter` ❻. The declaration sets up an animation to occur in tandem with the targeted `bitmapFilter`. In this case we're animating from a 0 (transparent) to 1 (fully opaque).

Now that the effect is set up, you can play it as done in the `onTimerTick` method ❶ ❷ ❸. One of the great things about bitmap filters is that you can interchange them. If you wanted to swap the `color`, change from a `Glow` to `DropShadow` or `Blur` or a `Convolution` filter, or tweak the `duration`, you'd change the `filter` declaration and maybe nix or tweak the `SimpleMotionPath`.

This last example has you up to speed on adding in business logic with declared effects. The same approach can be used purely in ActionScript with no effects declarations, because all of the declarations are purely ActionScript classes anyway. Let's look into how to achieve the same effect using ActionScript.

Due in 2 seconds

Due in 0 seconds

Figure 21.2 On the left the countdown is running, with 2 seconds left, and the right shows the effect after it has triggered.

USING JUST ACTIONSCRIPT

You can accomplish listing 21.3 all in ActionScript. Instead of using declarations, listing 21.3 adapts the previous example to use the class version of an effect (versus the MXML component).

Listing 21.3   Creating an instance of an effect using pure ActionScript

```
<?xml version="1.0" encoding="utf-8"?>
<s:Application xmlns:fx="http://ns.adobe.com/mxml/2009"
               xmlns:s="library://ns.adobe.com/flex/spark"
               applicationComplete="init()">
  <s:layout>
    <s:VerticalLayout paddingLeft="20" paddingTop="20" />
  </s:layout>
  <fx:Script>
    <![CDATA[
      import flash.utils.Timer;

      import spark.effects.AnimateFilter;
      import spark.effects.animation.MotionPath;
      import spark.effects.animation.RepeatBehavior;
      import spark.effects.animation.SimpleMotionPath;
      import spark.filters.GlowFilter;

      [Bindable]
      protected var secondsTillDue:int = 5;
      protected var _timer:Timer;
      protected var _effect:AnimateFilter;

      protected function init():void{
        var filter:GlowFilter =
          new GlowFilter(0xde7800, 1, 20, 20);          ⟵  Set GlowFilter
        _effect = new AnimateFilter(box, filter);           to glow orange
        _effect.duration = 1000;                        ⟵  Create effect
        _effect.repeatCount = 0;                            instance
        _effect.repeatBehavior = RepeatBehavior.REVERSE;
        _effect.motionPaths = new <MotionPath>[         Set up MotionPath
          new SimpleMotionPath("alpha", 0, 1)];         for alpha animation

        _timer = new Timer(1000); //tick every 1000ms   Set timer to tick
        _timer.addEventListener('timer', onTimerTick);  every 1000ms
        _timer.start();
      }

      protected function onTimerTick(event:TimerEvent):void{
        secondsTillDue = Math.max(secondsTillDue-1, 0);    ⟵
        if(secondsTillDue == 0){                         Update
          _effect.play();                                secondsTillDue
          _timer.stop();                                 value
        }
      }
    ]]>
  </fx:Script>
  <s:Label id="labelField" fontWeight="bold" fontSize="14"
           text="Due in {secondsTillDue} seconds" />
  <s:Rect id="box" width="200" height="200">
    <s:fill>
```

```
      <s:SolidColor color="black" />
    </s:fill>
  </s:Rect>
</s:Application>
```

Remember the advantage of the previous example, where it's relatively easy to switch to a different effect? You can also do that using this approach, but the real advantage of creating an effect this way is the ability to create Effect objects dynamically and on the fly. For example, if you wanted to go to town, you could store configuration information about what effect you want to play, based on certain circumstances, in your database or data file (XML and so on) and dynamically choose which one to apply. This can be achieved through declarative effects as well but with a mixture of declarative and programmatic.

Creating one effect is great, but at times you want one effect to trigger only after another one, or you want two effects to play at the same time without having to call play() on 10 different effects. If this is you, composite effects will be your new best friends. If it isn't, you'll still befriend composite effects because they're freaking cool!

21.2.4 *Using state transitions to trigger effects*

The last way to trigger an effect is through a transition from one state to another. A quick glance at chapter 14 wouldn't hurt, if you need to brush up on view states in Flex 4. Listing 21.4 showcases how to implement a state transition.

Listing 21.4 Implementing a state transition

```
<?xml version="1.0" encoding="utf-8"?>
<s:Application xmlns:fx="http://ns.adobe.com/mxml/2009"
               xmlns:s="library://ns.adobe.com/flex/spark"
               xmlns:mx="library://ns.adobe.com/flex/halo">
  <s:layout>
    <s:VerticalLayout />
  </s:layout>
  <s:states>
    <s:State name="orange" />                       ❶ Define states
    <s:State name="black" />
  </s:states>
  <s:transitions>                                   ❷ Define Transition
    <s:Transition fromState="*" toState="*">           for all states
      <s:Resize target="{box}" />                   ❸ Set desired
    </s:Transition>                                     transition effect
  </s:transitions>
  <s:HGroup>
    <s:Button label.orange="Black" label.black="Orange">
      <s:click>
        <![CDATA[
        currentState = (currentState ==            ❹ Change states on
          'orange' ? 'black' : 'orange');             button click
        ]]>
      </s:click>
    </s:Button>
  </s:HGroup>
```

```
<s:Rect id="box" width="200" height="200"
        width.black="150" height.black="150">
  <s:fill>
    <s:SolidColor color.black="#000000"
      color.orange="#de7800" />
  </s:fill>
</s:Rect>
</s:Application>
```

❺ **Set dimensions for each state**

❻ **Set color for each state**

Listing 21.3 comes directly from chapter 14 with one change: the <s:transitions/> code block ❷. This block defines desired transitions for each state ❶. In this case we cover all states with one transition using * but we could have defined specific transitions for specific state changes. The current transition is a Resize ❸. Notice that we don't give any specifics on the resize (such as widthTo or heightTo). This is because the Transition applies those properties ❻ accordingly based on the new state ❹ values for the target object ❺. That's pimp, right? Maybe effects don't excite you as much as they do us, but our boat is floating!

You've seen a few examples of singular effects, but you still have more to learn here regarding composite effects, running multiple effects concurrently or in sequence. More often than not, you'll desire to play two or more effects at the same time or one after the other. This is where composite effects save the day.

21.3 *Creating composite effects*

You were introduced to composite effects in section 21.1.3. Here we'll dive deeper into the why and how of using composite effects.

It's possible to group independent effects into a single effect called a *composite effect*. You can do so in either a parallel or a serial manner. Composite effects are awesome and answer a huge need to emulate timeline animations. Think of a timeline animation where frames 1 to 10 shows a box move from (0,0) to (0,10), speaking in x/y coordinates here; then from frames 10 to 20 the box moves from (0,10) to (10,10). This is a sequence of effects showing a box making a right angle at 10 pixels. What about scattering boxes randomly across the stage at the same time? This would be a parallel effect.

These types of effect combinations are possible in Flex through prebuilt and custom effects, as you'll see in the upcoming sections. To kick things off, we'll dive into sequential effects and parallel effects, finishing off with composite composites, the grouping of composite effects, before diving into each of the Flex 4 effects. Whoa—that's quite a bit of content! No worries; Flex 4 makes it easy and we'll guide you through it all.

21.3.1 *Sequential effects*

Your boss just handed you a requirement to make a box fade in and then zoom. No problem. Sequential effects are your friend. To make one effect come after another, group them using the <s:Sequence> tag, as shown in the following listing.

Listing 21.5   Playing multiple effects in sequence

```
<?xml version="1.0" encoding="utf-8"?>
<s:Application xmlns:fx="http://ns.adobe.com/mxml/2009"
               xmlns:s="library://ns.adobe.com/flex/spark">
  <fx:Declarations>
    <s:Sequence id="effect" target="{boxes}">                    ① Set up
      <s:Fade alphaFrom="{boxes.alpha}" alphaTo="1" />              Sequence effect
      <s:Scale scaleXTo="1" scaleXFrom="{boxes.scaleX}"          ② Set up Fade
              scaleYTo="1" scaleYFrom="{boxes.scaleY}"/>            as first effect
    </s:Sequence>
  </fx:Declarations>                                  Set up Scale
                                                      as second effect ③

  <s:Group id="boxes" alpha=".2" x="20" y="20"                  ④ Initialize
          scaleX=".5" scaleY=".5"                                 boxes Group
          rollOverEffect="{effect}">                      On rollover,
    <s:Rect width="200" height="200">                  ⑤ play effect
      <s:fill>
        <s:SolidColor color="black" />
      </s:fill>
    </s:Rect>
  </s:Group>
</s:Application>
```

When you mouse over the boxes ④ Group ⑤, the Fade effect ② begins. After the Fade is finished, a Scale effect ③ runs. In English, you'd read this sequence as "the box fades in and then zooms in." ① Your job is done, and your boss should give you a $20/hr raise for those few lines of code.

Sequential effects open the doors to all sorts of animations. In this example, the effect is pretty bunk (or boring for those of you not hip to 1993 lingo). It doesn't pop and isn't smooth. Alternatively, if you want to play all the effects at the same time to get a better pop, you can use a Parallel effect.

21.3.2 Parallel effects

To make a group of effects begin at the same time, use the `<s:Parallel>` tag. Listing 21.6 alters the previous example to apply the effects in parallel.

Listing 21.6   Playing multiple effects in parallel

```
<?xml version="1.0" encoding="utf-8"?>
<s:Application xmlns:fx="http://ns.adobe.com/mxml/2009"
               xmlns:s="library://ns.adobe.com/flex/spark">    ① Set up
  <fx:Declarations>                                              Parallel
    <s:Parallel id="effect" target="{boxes}">                    effect
      <s:Fade alphaFrom="{boxes.alpha}" alphaTo="1" />     ⟵ Set up Fade effect
      <s:Scale scaleXTo="1" scaleXFrom="{boxes.scaleX}"
              scaleYTo="1" scaleYFrom="{boxes.scaleY}"/>
    </s:Parallel>                                         Set up
  </fx:Declarations>                                     Scale effect

  <s:Group id="boxes" alpha=".2" x="20" y="20"                  Initialize
          scaleX=".5" scaleY=".5"                                boxes Group
```

```
                 rollOverEffect="{effect}">
    <s:Rect width="200" height="200">
      <s:fill>
        <s:SolidColor color="black" />
      </s:fill>
    </s:Rect>
  </s:Group>
</s:Application>
```

⊲ ⌐ **On rollover,
| play effect**

Wait—listing 21.6 looks the same as listing 21.5. You have an astute eye. They're the exact same except 21.6 uses a `Parallel` ❶ rather than a `Sequence` effect. Running this example will, in English, fade *and* zoom. This provides a smoother experience, for this example.

Both `Sequence` and `Parallel` effects have their place. Neither is flat out better because it depends on your particular need. But what if you want to do a bit of both? Flex lets you combine composites by allowing a `Sequence` to run parallel effects and/ or other sequence effects and vice versa. Are you feeling the effects love yet?

21.3.3 Composite composites

The fun doesn't stop there. You can mix and match these approaches any way you can imagine. For example, you can play two sets of parallel effects one after the other, as shown in this next listing.

Listing 21.7   Nesting two parallel composites in a sequence

```
<?xml version="1.0" encoding="utf-8"?>
<s:Application xmlns:fx="http://ns.adobe.com/mxml/2009"
               xmlns:s="library://ns.adobe.com/flex/spark"
               applicationComplete="effect.play();">
  <fx:Declarations>
    <s:Sequence id="effect" target="{boxes}"
        repeatCount="5">
      <s:Parallel>
        <s:Fade alphaFrom="{boxes.alpha}"
          alphaTo="1" />
        <s:Scale scaleXTo="1"
                 scaleXFrom="{boxes.scaleX}"
                 scaleYTo="1"
                 scaleYFrom="{boxes.scaleY}"/>
      </s:Parallel>
      <s:Parallel>
        <s:Fade alphaFrom="1" alphaTo="0" />
        <s:Scale scaleXTo=".5" scaleXFrom="1"
                 scaleYTo=".5" scaleYFrom="1"/>
      </s:Parallel>
    </s:Sequence>
  </fx:Declarations>

  <s:Group id="boxes" alpha=".2" x="20" y="20" scaleX=".5" scaleY=".5">
    <s:Rect width="200" height="200">
      <s:fill>
        <s:SolidColor color="black" />
```

❶ **Play effect on
application
complete**

❷ **Setup effect to
repeat 5 times**

❸ **Set up fade
and zoom
in effect**

❹ **Set up fade
and zoom
out effect**

```
    </s:fill>
   </s:Rect>
  </s:Group>
</s:Application>
```

Listing 21.7 is a combination of listings 21.5 and 21.6. Instead of being triggered on rollOver of the boxes Group, you tell it to play as soon as your application begins ❶. You also duplicate and reverse the effect after the initial effect is complete ❷. This creates a nice, smooth fade-and-zoom effect ❸ ❹.

> **TIP** If you want to suspend the background processing (measurement, layout, data processing, and so on) while playing composite effects, set the suspendBackgroundProcessing property to true. This also helps with performance. If user input or data updates could occur, set the property to false.

Theoretically, there's no limit to how deep you can nest composite effects, but from a usability perspective, you don't need to go overboard with effects in order to communicate change. Gratuitous effects can lessen the overall effect they have on the user's experience. Always keep the user in mind.

At times you need to pause and reflect on life. With effects there are also times, in a sequence effect, when you want to pause and then continue with other effects. Flex answers with the Pause effect.

THE PAUSE EFFECT

What about starting an effect, waiting a few milliseconds, and then starting another effect? You're more than sure Flex makes you jump into ActionScript for that, right? Wrong! A Pause effect is probably the only non-effect. It doesn't do anything visual except pause the presently running composite effect.

Pause doesn't have any unique properties—you use the common duration property to control the length of the delay. The following snippet shows how to add a two-second pause between Fade and Scale effects in a sequence effect:

```
<s:Sequence id="effect" target="{boxes}" repeatCount="5">
    <s:Fade alphaFrom="{boxes.alpha}" alphaTo="1" />
    <s:Pause duration="2000" />
    <s:Scale scaleXTo="1" scaleXFrom="{boxes.scaleX}"
             scaleYTo="1" scaleYFrom="{boxes.scaleY}"/>
</s:Sequence>
```

> **NOTE** If you try this with a parallel effect, the pause effect won't be noticeable because all the effects run at the same time.

The previous snippet shows you the same effect as listing 21.7. You added a Pause reference and set the duration, and your animation now pauses after the first Parallel sequence. Pretty cool, huh? We think so.

You now know how to create, instantiate, and combine effects. Let's slide into exploring effect specifics to more intimately learn each of the properties and use cases.

21.4 *Exploring effects*

So far you've learned the different ways to trigger effects, the different effects, and how to combine them. At this point you're ready to deep dive into learning how to use each effect, the differences between the types of effects, customizing the effects, and finishing with integrating sound effects.

Each effect has specific properties necessary to create your desired result. They all have certain unique properties but also share (as a result of inheritance) a number of common properties. These properties are listed in table 21.4.

Table 21.4   Properties all effects support

Property	Type	Description
duration	Number	Time, in milliseconds, over which the effect transpires. For example, a value of 5000 results in an effect taking five seconds to complete.
easer	IEaser object	Easing behavior of the effect. Default is to use spark.effects.easing.Sine(.5).
repeatCount	Number	Number of times you want the effect to repeat. Default is 1. To loop indefinitely, use 0.
repeatDelay	Number	If you're repeating the effect, the delay in milliseconds before the effect plays again. Default is 0 (no delay).
repeatBehavior	String	How the effect responds when repeatCount is > 1. (See RepeatBehavior class for constants.)
startDelay	Number	Time, in milliseconds, before the effect begins.
id	String	Name by which the effect will be referenced.

These properties allow you to control the primary configuration of an effect; they focus on runtime changes. Each property is useful, but we won't cover every one of them. In the following sections we'll examine the effects from table 21.1, starting with Animate, and throughout the section you'll see most of them used.

21.4.1 *The Animate effect*

This is a general-purpose effect that lets you change a component property from one value to another. For example, you can use an Animate effect to change the width of something to a specific value or use it to alter a component's alpha property and make the component disappear or change both width and alpha at the same time, similar to Parallel effects.

That sounds like some of the other effects, you say. Yes, some effects are effectively pre-selected property manipulations that use Animate. But if you needed fine-grained control, Animate can do the job. Listing 21.8 alters a button's width and color. Color? Yep! You can now animate RGB values using the interpolator property of a MotionPath.

Listing 21.8 Creating an effect with the Animate class

```
<?xml version="1.0" encoding="utf-8"?>
<s:Application xmlns:fx="http://ns.adobe.com/mxml/2009"
               xmlns:s="library://ns.adobe.com/flex/spark">
  <fx:Script>
    <![CDATA[
      import spark.effects.interpolation.RGBInterpolator;
    ]]>
  </fx:Script>
  <fx:Declarations>
    <s:Animate id="effect" target="{mybutton}">
      <s:SimpleMotionPath property="width"
          valueTo="100" />
      <s:SimpleMotionPath property="color"
          valueTo="#4e7800"
          interpolator="{new RGBInterpolator()}" />
    </s:Animate>
  </fx:Declarations>
  <s:Button id="mybutton" label="Click Me!"
    click="effect.play();" />
</s:Application>
```

❶ Import **RGBInterpolator**

❷ Initialize **Animate** effect

❸ Set up motion path to animate **width**

❹ Set up motion path to animate **color**

❺ On click, play effect

Your goal here is to widen and change the text color of the button. You've seen MotionPath and SimpleMotionPath references from the previous examples. SimpleMotionPath is a subclass of MotionPath, which defines the targeted change in a specific property. If you ever did the bumblebee tutorial in Flash 6 to learn motion path animations, this is close to the same thing but in code.

The first SimpleMotionPath targets the width property ❸ and changes it to 100, whereas the second targets the color property and sets the color to orange (#4e7800) ❹ using the RGBInterpolator ❶ for the interpolator property.

Interpolation allows the SimpleMotionPath to define how the effect will change the values. By default the interpolator uses NumberInterpolator. The great thing is you can write your own interpolator by extending IInterpolator.

When this animation is played ❷❺, the button will enlarge in width and the color will change just as you'd expect ❶. You could encapsulate this animation into your own animation class and use it across components or applications. This is what Flex 4 offers with the many different effects extending Animate.

Before you fade into the next chapter, we'll explore more effects that extend the Animate class starting with the Fade effect.

THE FADE EFFECT

A Fade effect works by transitioning a component's alpha property over a period of time, which makes it identical to using an Animate class with a SimpleMotionPath targeting the alpha. Table 21.5 lists the properties that are specific to the Fade effect. Listing 21.9 uses these properties by fading the image from fully transparent to fully opaque.

Table 21.5   Properties specific to the `Fade` effect

Property	Type	Description
alphaFrom	Number	Starting transparency value. $0.0–1.0$.
alphaTo	Number	Ending transparency value. $1.0–0.0$.

Listing 21.9   Using the `Fade` effect on an image

```
<?xml version="1.0" encoding="utf-8"?>
<s:Application xmlns:fx="http://ns.adobe.com/mxml/2009"
               xmlns:s="library://ns.adobe.com/flex/spark">
  <s:layout>
    <s:VerticalLayout paddingLeft="20" paddingTop="20" />
  </s:layout>
  <fx:Declarations>
    <s:Fade id="effect" alphaFrom="0"
        alphaTo="1" target="{image}" />           ◀── ❶ Initialize fade effect
  </fx:Declarations>
  <s:BitmapImage id="image" alpha="0" source="@Embed('images/flex.jpg')" />
  <s:Button id="mybutton" label="Click Me!"
        click="effect.play()" />                   ◀── ❷ On click, play fade effect
</s:Application>
```

Initially you set the image's `alpha` to 0. This hides the image, visually, to where the only thing showing is the Click Me! button. When the button is clicked ❷, the image progressively fades in from 0 to 1 ❶. This is a simple and subtle effect. When properly used, it can enhance an application's visual effectiveness.

Moving on, we'll look at the `Move` effect. Wow—puns abound when chatting about effects, and they don't stop here!

THE MOVE EFFECT

The `Move` effect lets you transition the position, x and y, of a component from one place to another. All the properties in table 21.6 are in pixels, starting from the upper-left corner relative to the container the component is in.

Table 21.6   Properties specific to the `Move` effect

Property	Type	Description
xFrom	Number	Starting horizontal position. If unspecified, uses the current position as the starting point.
xTo	Number	Ending horizontal position. If unspecified, uses the current position as the ending point.
xBy	Number	Number of pixels to move horizontally. Negative values move to the left, positive to the right.
yFrom	Number	Starting vertical position. If unspecified, uses the current position as the starting point.

Table 21.6   Properties specific to the Move effect (continued)

Property	Type	Description
yTo	Number	Ending vertical position. If unspecified, uses the current position as the ending point.
yBy	Number	Number of pixels to move vertically. Negative values move up, positive down.

Listing 21.10 moves the button diagonally down to the bottom right every time you click it.

Listing 21.10   Using the Move effect to move the button diagonally

```
<?xml version="1.0" encoding="utf-8"?>
<s:Application xmlns:fx="http://ns.adobe.com/mxml/2009"
               xmlns:s="library://ns.adobe.com/flex/spark">
  <s:layout>
    <s:VerticalLayout paddingLeft="20" paddingTop="20" />
  </s:layout>
  <fx:Declarations>
    <s:Move id="effect" target="{image}"          ⎤ Set up the
      xBy="10" yBy="10" />                         ⎦ Move effect
  </fx:Declarations>
  <s:Group width="200" height="200">
    <s:BitmapImage id="image"
      source="@Embed('images/flex.jpg')" />     ◁——— Embed an image
  </s:Group>
  <s:Button id="mybutton" label="Click Me!"
      click="effect.play()" />                   ◁——— On click, play the effect
</s:Application>
```

Figure 21.3 visually showcases listing 21.10's results.

If you're thinking there's no difference between this and manipulating the x and y properties yourself, you're somewhat correct. Flex allows you to manually set the target x and y properties to animate an object, or you can do the inverse: change the property and let the Move handle it. Listing 21.11 shows how you can use a Move effect to respond to x and y value changes.

Figure 21.3   Moving an object using the Move effect

Listing 21.11   Using the `Move` effect in response to `x/y` changes

```
<?xml version="1.0" encoding="utf-8"?>
<s:Application xmlns:fx="http://ns.adobe.com/mxml/2009"
               xmlns:s="library://ns.adobe.com/flex/spark">
  <s:layout>                                                       ❶ Set the
    <s:VerticalLayout paddingLeft="20" paddingTop="20" />            Group's
  </s:layout>                                                        moveEffect
  <s:Group id="mygroup" moveEffect="Move">                           to Move
    <s:BitmapImage id="image" source="@Embed('images/flex.jpg')" />
  </s:Group>
  <s:Button id="mybutton" label="Click Me!">
    <s:click>
      <![CDATA[                                    ❷ Change mygroup's
        mygroup.x += 10;                              x value by 10 pixels
        mygroup.y += 10;                            Change mygroup's y
      ]]>                                           ❸ value by 10 pixels
    </s:click>
  </s:Button>
</s:Application>
```

NOTE   `BitmapImage` doesn't have a `moveEffect` property, so you have to wrap it in a `Group` to showcase this effect.

Listing 21.11 is no different from listing 21.10, in terms of the visual result. The way you get there is a little different, though. All display objects that extend `UIComponent` have default effects. In this case you're telling `mygroup`: Use the `Move` effect ❶ whenever you're moved ❷ ❸. Under the hood Flex is aware of the move and triggers a `Move` effect. You also could have defined a `Move` effect, like listing 21.10, and used that effect, instead of the default one Flex uses, through databinding.

You're definitely growing as an effect guru. More growth is on the way with the `Resize` effect.

THE RESIZE EFFECT

You saw the `Resize` effect in listing 21.1; it lets you control resizing both vertically and horizontally. You can resize from/to a specific size or increase/decrease size by an incremental amount, just as you'd move an object by a specific amount. Table 21.7 lists the properties specific to the `Resize` effect.

Table 21.7   Properties specific to the `Resize` effect

Property	Type	Description
heightFrom	Number	Starting height. If unspecified, uses the current height (for example, if you specify only `heightTo`).
heightTo	Number	Ending height. If unspecified, uses the current height (for example, if you specify only `heightFrom`).
heightBy	Number	Number of pixels by which to change the height. Negative values decrease the height; positive values increase it.

Table 21.7 Properties specific to the `Resize` effect (continued)

Property	Type	Description
widthFrom	Number	Starting width. If unspecified, uses the current width (for example, if you specify only widthTo).
widthTo	Number	Ending width. If unspecified, uses the current width (for example, if you specify only widthFrom).
widthBy	Number	Number of pixels by which to change the width. Negative values decrease the width; positive values increase it.

Listing 21.12 uses a button to resize the image 50 pixels taller than its current height, producing a continuously growing image as the button is clicked repeatedly.

Listing 21.12 Resizing an image by 50 pixels

```
<?xml version="1.0" encoding="utf-8"?>
<s:Application xmlns:fx="http://ns.adobe.com/mxml/2009"
               xmlns:s="library://ns.adobe.com/flex/spark">
  <s:layout>
    <s:VerticalLayout paddingLeft="20" paddingTop="20" />
  </s:layout>
  <fx:Declarations>
    <s:Resize id="effect" target="{image}"          ❶ Set up
      heightBy="50"/>                                     Resize effect
  </fx:Declarations>
  <s:BitmapImage id="image" source="@Embed('images/flex.jpg')" />
  <s:Button id="mybutton" label="Click Me!"
    click="effect.play()" />                        ⬅──❷ On click, play effect
</s:Application>
```

Because you aren't manipulating the width property, the image stretches vertically only ❷ while maintaining the width ❶, as shown in figure 21.4.

Similar to using `Resize`, you can also use a `Scale` effect. Even though it may sound so, no fish were harmed in the writing of this next section.

Initial size

After 1 click

Figure 21.4 Animating the resize of an image's height using the `Resize` effect

THE SCALE EFFECT

A Scale effect is somewhat like a Resize effect but retooled to focus on starting with a small component and zooming in to make the component bigger (as well as the other way around). Extra parameters are available to specify the scale-origin point (by default, it zooms from the center). Table 21.8 lists properties unique to the Scale effect.

Table 21.8   Properties specific to the Scale effect

Property	Type	Description
scaleXFrom	Number	Starting scaleX. Defaults to the current scaleX if unspecified.
scaleXTo	Number	Ending scaleX. Defaults to the current scaleY if unspecified.
scaleXBy	Number	Number by which to change the scaleX. Negative values decrease the scaleX; positive values increase it.
scaleYFrom	Number	Starting scaleY. Defaults to the current scaleY if unspecified.
scaleYTo	Number	Ending scaleY. Defaults to the current scaleY if unspecified.
scaleYBy	Number	Number by which to change the scaleY. Negative values decrease the scaleY; positive values increase it.

In listing 21.13, after you click the button, a Scale effect is used to grow the button's scaleX and scaleY by 2.

Listing 21.13   Using the Scale effect to make the button zoom-in larger

```
<?xml version="1.0" encoding="utf-8"?>
<s:Application xmlns:fx="http://ns.adobe.com/mxml/2009"
               xmlns:s="library://ns.adobe.com/flex/spark">
  <fx:Declarations>
    <s:Scale id="effect" target="{mybutton}"          ❶ Increase
        scaleXBy="2" scaleYBy="2"                        scale by 2
            autoCenterTransform="false" />
  </fx:Declarations>
  <s:Button id="mybutton" label="Click Me!"
        click="effect.play()" />               ⬸——— On click, play effect
</s:Application>
```

The main difference in the Scale and Resize effects is the properties they affect: scaleX/scaleY ❶ and width/height, respectively. They both accomplish the same goal but in different ways with potentially different visual outcomes.

Let's roll on to our next effect: Rotate.

THE ROTATE EFFECT

Make it spin! You can use the Rotate effect to rotate a component around a point of your choice. Table 21.9 lists the properties that are specific to the Rotate effect and a few through extension of the AnimateTransform class.

Listing 21.14 rotates the component 45 degrees clockwise around the center and without affecting the VerticalLayout defined on our Application.

Table 21.9 Properties specific to the `Rotate` effect

Property	Type	Description
angleFrom	Number	Starting angle. If unspecified, starts from the current angle. 0–360.
angleTo	Number	Ending angle. If unspecified, ends at the current angle. 0–360.
applyChangesPostLayout	Boolean	Controls how to apply the layout changes, before or after the rotation.
autoCenterTransform	Boolean	Controls whether the rotation occurs around the middle of the object (width/2, height/2).

Listing 21.14 Rotating the button 45 degrees

```
<?xml version="1.0" encoding="utf-8"?>
<s:Application xmlns:fx="http://ns.adobe.com/mxml/2009"
               xmlns:s="library://ns.adobe.com/flex/spark">
  <s:layout>
    <s:VerticalLayout paddingLeft="20" paddingTop="20" />
  </s:layout>
  <fx:Declarations>
    <s:Rotate id="effect" target="{image}" angleBy="45"
          applyChangesPostLayout="true"
          autoCenterTransform="true" />          ❶ Initialize the
  </fx:Declarations>                                 rotate effect
  <s:BitmapImage id="image" source="@Embed('images/flex.jpg')" />
  <s:Button id="mybutton" label="Click Me!"
      click="effect.play()" />                   ❷ On click, play effect
</s:Application>
```

Listing 21.14 does a simple rotate on the image ❷, but we made a couple modifications. To start with, we wanted to rotate around the center of the image so we set `auto-CenterTransform` to `true`. You can explicitly tell the effect what point to rotate around using the `transformX`, `transformY`, and `transformZ` properties. We have the correct transform point, the center, now, but we also don't want our layout to adjust to the rotation of the image. Notice that we're using a `VerticalLayout`. This means "measure every child, then vertically align each one after the other with a gap." When the image rotates, the width/height of the image doesn't change but the space it takes up does. This forces the layout to change accordingly. This may be exactly what you want. It can be a pretty cool effect, but if you don't want the image rotation to mess with the layout, set the `applyChangesPostLayout` property to `true`, as we did here ❶. Figure 21.5 shows the rotation based on listing 21.14.

Figure 21.5 Rotating an image around the center without affecting the layout

On the flip side of figure 21.5, we want you to see how it looks with `applyChangesPostLayout` set to `false`, as shown in figure 21.6.

It's possible to use ActionScript to apply your own algorithm to manipulate the button's properties to achieve the rotation, but using this effect is so much easier.

Flex animates not only properties but also filters.

21.4.2 *Animating filters with AnimateFilter*

Filters are a big part of Flash Player in general. They provide a way to change the appearance of white text on a bright background with filters like a drop shadow or a

Figure 21.6   Rotating an image around the center while maintaining the layout

glow. There are countless possibilities, and Flex 4 now gives you a super-easy way of animating those filters using `AnimateFilter`.

Unlike the `Animate` class, `AnimateFilter` class is required to use filter animations. For clarity, `Animate` is extended by `Fade`, `Move`, and so on, and `AnimateFilter` is instantiated and passed a reference to a filter, as shown in the following snippet:

```
//some effect with id="myfilter" here
<s:AnimateFilter bitmapFilter="{myfilter}" ... />
```

It's time to dig in. Flex 3 blurred the line between animating filters versus properties, but things definitely changed, for the better, in Flex 4. To start, we'll look at the `BlurFilter`.

THE BLURFILTER

Animating a filter is similar to using the `Animate` class. Instead of targeting a specific property, you target a specific filter. A blur effect uses a `BlurFilter` and does what you'd expect: It make things blurry. You have control over two directions: horizontal (x) and vertical (y). Table 21.10 lists the properties used to manipulate the blur.

Listing 21.15 uses a blur filter to blur an image of Flex Alexander, the actor. We figured his name was fitting to the subject...go figure.

Table 21.10   Properties specific to the `Blur` effect

Property	Type	Description
blurX	Number	Value for the horizontal blur. `0–255`.
blurY	Number	Value for the vertical blur. `0–255`.
quality	Number	Number of times to apply the blur (see `BitmapFilterQuality` for constants `LOW`, `MEDIUM`, and `HIGH`.)

Listing 21.15   Using a `Blur` effect on a `BitmapImage`

```
<?xml version="1.0" encoding="utf-8"?>
<s:Application xmlns:fx="http://ns.adobe.com/mxml/2009"
               xmlns:s="library://ns.adobe.com/flex/spark">
```

```
<s:layout>
  <s:VerticalLayout paddingLeft="20" paddingTop="20" />
</s:layout>
<fx:Declarations>
  <s:BlurFilter id="blur" blurX="10" blurY="10" />
  <s:AnimateFilter id="effect" target="{image}" bitmapFilter="{blur}" />
</fx:Declarations>
<s:BitmapImage id="image" source="@Embed('images/flex.jpg')" />
<s:Button id="mybutton" label="Click Me!" click="effect.play()" />
</s:Application>
```

When you click the button, as shown in figure 21.7, the image becomes blurred for the duration of the animation and then returns to normal.

Hrmm...that was pretty easy. There has to be more you can do with filter effects, right? Absolutely! You're probably glowing with excitement awaiting the next effect. Wait no more. Let's glow it up like a glowworm!

THE GLOWFILTER

Implementing a `GlowFilter` effect is similar to creating a border around a component while at the same time blurring and fading the border. Listing 21.3 showed an example of using the `GlowFilter` effect. This effect shares the properties of a `BlurFilter`. Table 21.11 lists the properties unique to the `GlowFilter` effect.

Table 21.11 Properties specific to the `GlowFilter` effect

Property	Type	Description
blurX	Number	Starting value for the horizontal blur. 0–255.
blurY	Number	Starting value for the vertical blur. 0–255.
alpha	Number	Starting transparency value. 0.0–1.0.
color	Color	Color of the glow.
inner	Boolean	true or false (default). Lets you control whether it's an inner or outer glow (the default).
knockout	Boolean	true or false (default). If true, the inner part of the component is transparent.
strength	Number	Strength of the glow. 0–255.
quality	Number	Number of times to apply the blur (see BitmapFilterQuality for constants LOW, MEDIUM, and HIGH).

Before

After

Figure 21.7 The result of animating the blur on an image

Listing 21.16 creates a glow effect using the color orange around the image.

Listing 21.16   Using a `Glow` effect on the button

```
<?xml version="1.0" encoding="utf-8"?>
<s:Application xmlns:fx="http://ns.adobe.com/mxml/2009"
               xmlns:s="library://ns.adobe.com/flex/spark">
  <s:layout>
    <s:VerticalLayout paddingLeft="20" paddingTop="20" />
  </s:layout>
  <fx:Declarations>
    <s:GlowFilter id="glow" blurX="20"
       blurY="20" color="#4e7800" />
    <s:AnimateFilter id="effect" target="{image}"
       bitmapFilter="{glow}" />
  </fx:Declarations>
  <s:BitmapImage id="image" source="@Embed('images/flex.jpg')" />
  <s:Button id="mybutton" label="Click Me!"
     click="effect.play()" />
</s:Application>
```

❶ Set up glow effect

❷ Set AnimateFilter to use GlowFilter

❸ On click, play effect

NOTE   On click ❸, the resulting effect purely adds a glow to the image ❶ ❷ and then takes it away. There is no default fading in and out of the glow. If you want to animate the `alpha` property of the glow, see listing 21.3 and the use of the `SimpleMotionPath`.

You have seen a glow and a blur, so the logical next step is a drop shadow, right? Absolutely!

THE DROPSHADOWFILTER

Sticking with the same approach, you can also utilize a `DropShadowFilter`, as shown in the following listing.

Listing 21.17   Using a `DropShadowFilter` on a `BitmapImage`

```
<?xml version="1.0" encoding="utf-8"?>
<s:Application xmlns:fx="http://ns.adobe.com/mxml/2009"
               xmlns:s="library://ns.adobe.com/flex/spark">
  <s:layout>
    <s:VerticalLayout paddingLeft="20" paddingTop="20" />
  </s:layout>
  <fx:Declarations>
    <s:DropShadowFilter id="dropShadow" />
    <s:AnimateFilter id="effect" target="{image}"
                     bitmapFilter="{dropShadow}" />
  </fx:Declarations>
  <s:BitmapImage id="image" source="@Embed('images/flex.jpg')" />
  <s:Button id="mybutton" label="Click Me!" click="effect.play()" />
</s:Application>
```

Listing 21.17 pulls from listing 21.16 by not blurring but adding a drop shadow to the image.

We could go on like this covering all of the different filters, but we believe you get the point. Aside from the aforementioned filters, Flex also has the following filters: `BevelFilter`, `ColorMatrixFilter`, `ConvolutionFilter`, `DisplacementMapFilter`, `GradientBevelFilter`, `GradientGlowFilter`, and `ShaderFilter`. You can also create your own filters by extending `IBitmapFilter` and passing them `AnimateFilter`'s `customFilter` property.

The beautiful thing about Flex 4 is that just when you think you're stuck in a hot, sunny corner, there's a shade tree nearby to help you relax. In this case, your shade is provided by pixel shaders, which allow you to write your own custom effects using the Adobe Pixel Bender Toolkit and the `AnimateTransitionShader` class.

21.4.3 *Animating pixel shaders with AnimateTransitionShader*

Pixel Bender was introduced with a ton of potential for creating complex effects with optimized code, created outside of ActionScript. Pixel shaders are external PBJ files known as pixel-shader programs, not to be mistaken for peanut-butter-jelly files.

Flex 4 ships with two types of pixel shaders: `CrossFade` and `Wipe`. You can also write your own shaders and animate those just like the default Flex pixel shaders using Pixel Bender.

> **TIP** You can view the Pixel Bender Shader source code in [Flash Builder directory]/sdks/4.0.0/frameworks/projects/spark/src/spark/effects/.
> Open the *.pbk files to view the source in the Adobe Pixel Bender Toolkit.

You first saw the `Transition` class in section 21.2.4. Let's expand on section 21.2.4 by learning how to implement the pixel-shader programs with transitions. Our first dive into pixel shaders showcases the `CrossFade` effect.

THE CROSSFADE EFFECT

A `CrossFade` effect is similar to a `Fade`, but it's implemented differently. You already saw the `AnimateFilter` class used earlier. To animate shaders you use the `Animate-TransformShader` class, to which the `CrossFade` effect extends. Listing 21.18 applies a `CrossFade` effect transitioning from the `flex` state to the `flash` state, fading one in and fading the other out.

Listing 21.18   Using a `CrossFade` effect in a transition

```xml
<?xml version="1.0" encoding="utf-8"?>
<s:Application xmlns:fx="http://ns.adobe.com/mxml/2009"
               xmlns:s="library://ns.adobe.com/flex/spark">
  <s:layout>
    <s:VerticalLayout paddingLeft="20" paddingTop="20" />
  </s:layout>
  <s:states>
    <s:State name="flex" />                      ❶ Initialize states
    <s:State name="flash" />
  </s:states>
  <fx:Declarations>
```

```
<s:CrossFade id="crossfade"                          ❷ Define
    targets="{[image, mybutton]}" />                    CrossFade
</fx:Declarations>
<s:transitions>                                      ❸ Define
  <s:Transition effect="{crossfade}" />                 Transition
</s:transitions>
<s:Group>
  <s:BitmapImage id="image"
    source="@Embed('images/flex.jpg')"               ❹ Initialize
      source.flash="@Embed('images/flash.jpg')" />       BitmapImage
</s:Group>
<s:Button id="mybutton" label="Go Flash!"
    label.flash="Go Flex!"                           ❺ Set up button to
        click.flash="currentState='flex'"               change states
        click.flex="currentState='flash'"/>
</s:Application>
```

Most of listing 21.18 should look familiar. You initialize the two states (flex and flash) ❶ and the CrossFade effect ❷. Notice that the effect targets the BitmapImage instance ❹ and the mybutton Button instance. That might look weird, but it's pretty sweet. We'll cover this in a moment. mybutton has two different labels and click states to correspond with each state and to toggle the states ❺, respectively.

There's something new here, though. We're introducing the transitions property of Application. Here you define an array of transitions to use across different states or all states. The Transition ❸ targets the effect you want to play and occurs automatically when the states change. As previously noted, you could explicitly state which effects this transition affects.

When you run listing 21.18, you'll notice two things: 1) the image source cross-fades from flex.jpg to flash.jpg, and 2) the mybutton label cross-fades from Go Flash! to Go Flex! Yep, you read right. The CrossFade effect targets image and mybutton so the label change fades as well. It's difficult to show this type of effect in a book, but you can try to visualize it through figure 21.8.

The first section of figure 21.8 shows the flex state, the middle shows the button and the images transitioning, and the last shows the final view while in the flash state. Pretty sweet, huh?

That's sweet for sure, but wipe your brow and dig in for another effect. Building on this example you can showcase how to transition with a Wipe effect.

'flex' State

Transition

'flash' state

Figure 21.8
CrossFade
between two
images and two
button labels

THE WIPE EFFECT

Wipes progressively show or hide a component by sliding the top component off while revealing the second. You can use four types of `Wipe` effects, all controlled through the `direction` property:

- `Left`
- `Right`
- `Up`
- `Down`

Listing 21.19 is a simple application to show the different `Wipe` effects on the previously shown flash.jpg and flex.jpg.

Listing 21.19 Using a `Wipe` effect to transition between images

```
<?xml version="1.0" encoding="utf-8"?>
<s:Application xmlns:fx="http://ns.adobe.com/mxml/2009"
               xmlns:s="library://ns.adobe.com/flex/spark">
  <s:layout>
    <s:VerticalLayout paddingLeft="20" paddingTop="20" />
  </s:layout>
  <fx:Script>
    <![CDATA[
      import spark.effects.WipeDirection;
    ]]>
  </fx:Script>
  <s:states>
    <s:State name="flex" />
    <s:State name="flash" />
  </s:states>
  <fx:Declarations>
    <s:Wipe id="wipe" targets="{[image, mybutton]}"              ┌─  ❶ Set up
            direction="{directions.selectedItem                     Wipe effect
            as String}" />                                       └─
  </fx:Declarations>
  <s:transitions>
    <s:Transition effect="{wipe}" />                             ┌─  Target transition
  </s:transitions>                                               ❷ to wipe
  <s:Group>
    <s:BitmapImage id="image" source="@Embed('images/flex.jpg')"
                source.flash="@Embed('images/flash.jpg')" />
  </s:Group>
  <s:DropDownList id="directions" selectedIndex="0">
    <s:dataProvider>
      <s:ArrayList>
        <fx:String>{WipeDirection.LEFT}</fx:String>             ❸ Set up drop-
        <fx:String>{WipeDirection.RIGHT}</fx:String>               down to select
        <fx:String>{WipeDirection.UP}</fx:String>                 wipe direction
        <fx:String>{WipeDirection.DOWN}</fx:String>
      </s:ArrayList>
    </s:dataProvider>
  </s:DropDownList>
  <s:Button id="mybutton" label="Go Flash!" label.flash="Go Flex!"
```

```
            click.flash="currentState='flex'"
            click.flex="currentState='flash'"/>
</s:Application>
```

Our simple application shown in figure 21.9 is a direct rip from listing 21.18 except it uses a Wipe effect ❶ ❷ and allows you to specify which direction you want to wipe by selecting a direction from the drop-down list ❸, using data binding. You could have set the direction explicitly, but it's more fun to play with each one independently.

Figure 21.9   Shows a wipe right

Transition shaders are amazing because Pixel Bender shaders are wildly small, by lines of code, and purely up to your imagination and shader skills. If you can and want to write a shader to split an image into four pieces, rotate them, and then reorder them, go ahead. Flex will let you use that shader directly in your application. You can also use shaders in other Adobe products such as Photoshop. We point this out to note that the communities capable of and willing to create shaders are vast. Always remember that shaders aren't Flex specific but can be used across multiple Adobe products, so you can most likely find your desired effect online before attempting to write it.

You're doing great and have learned the different types of effects and how to use each of them. The lion's share of the work is done, so stick with us as we move forward.

Continuing on our journey, our next stop is in customizing effect easing. So far, all of our animations have used the default easers, mathematical functions used to apply easing. Flex makes it easy like a Sunday morning to create your own or use any of the built-in easers.

21.4.4   *Customizing effect easing*

By default, when Flex plays an effect, it spaces the changes evenly over time. In this section, we'll look at the default easing classes as well as how to write our own easing classes.

As an example, a Move effect moving a component 100 pixels over 100 seconds is moving the component at a rate of 1 pixel per second. You can control the number of pixels per second using common math. For instance, you could add a little spice and choose to do the first 10 pixels at 5 pixels per second, moving fast, and then finish off the other 90 pixels at 2.5 pixels per second. These are examples of easing.

Prior to Flex 4, you'd define a function to handle the transition, called an easing function. In Flex 4, you have easers. They're classes implementing the IEaser interface and the ease function. This function is akin to the easing functions of old, just wrapped in a class.

To begin, we'll look into the out-of-the-box easers and then move into writing our own easer.

OUT-OF-THE-BOX EASERS

Out of the box, Flex provides an easing package (spark.effects.easing) including a number of classes with ease functions. Table 21.12 lists these classes and functions.

Table 21.12   Available easers out of the box

Class	Descriptions
Bounce	Simulates gravity pulling on and bouncing the target.
Elastic	Target object movement is defined by an exponentially decaying sine wave.
Linear	Defines an easing with three phases: acceleration, uniform motion, and deceleration.
Power	Defines the easing functionality using a polynomial expression.
Sine	Defines easing functionality using a Sine function.

That's quite a few options! Fortunately, using them is simple, as this next listing shows.

Listing 21.20   Using easing functions with the Move effect to make motion less linear

```
<?xml version="1.0" encoding="utf-8"?>
<s:Application xmlns:fx="http://ns.adobe.com/mxml/2009"
               xmlns:s="library://ns.adobe.com/flex/spark">
  <s:layout>
    <s:VerticalLayout paddingLeft="20" paddingTop="20" />
  </s:layout>
  <fx:Declarations>
    <s:Elastic id="easer" />
    <s:Move id="effect" target="{image}" xFrom="0" xTo="500"
            easer="{easer}"/>
  </fx:Declarations>
  <s:Group width="200" height="200">
    <s:BitmapImage id="image" source="@Embed('images/flex.jpg')" />
  </s:Group>
  <s:Button id="mybutton" label="Click Me!"
    click="effect.play()" />
</s:Application>
```

❶ Define Elastic easer

❷ Set Move effects easer

❸ On click, play effect

This example makes the image ❸ slingshot to the right ❷, as if being catapulted by an elastic band, then bounce against the edge until it comes to a stop, sort of like bungee jumping ❶.

As previously mentioned, you can use any of the out-of-the-box easers or create your own easers using your chosen math formula(s).

MAKING YOUR OWN EASERS

You can make your own easers by creating custom classes that implement IEaser. In your ease function, you do the math you desire and return another fraction. That's it!

Flex will keep calling your ease function for each time interval to find out what the current position of the object should be (the number you return). Listing 21.21 shows a rudimentary example using the following custom easer:

```
package easing{
  import spark.effects.easing.IEaser;

  public class MyEaser implements IEaser{
    public function ease(fraction:Number):Number{
      return Math.cos(fraction * Math.PI/2);
    }
  }
}
```

Listing 21.21   Using a custom easer

```
<?xml version="1.0" encoding="utf-8"?>
<s:Application xmlns:fx="http://ns.adobe.com/mxml/2009"
               xmlns:s="library://ns.adobe.com/flex/spark"
               xmlns:easing="easing.*">
  <s:layout>
    <s:VerticalLayout paddingLeft="20" paddingTop="20" />
  </s:layout>
  <fx:Declarations>                                      ❶ Set up MyEaser
    <easing:MyEaser id="easer" />                          instance
    <s:Move id="effect" target="{image}" xFrom="0" xTo="500"
          easer="{easer}"/>                              Target MyEaser
  </fx:Declarations>                                      instance
  <s:Group width="200" height="200">
    <s:BitmapImage id="image" source="@Embed('images/flex.jpg')" />
  </s:Group>
  <s:Button id="mybutton" label="Click Me!" click="effect.play()" />
</s:Application>
```

MyEaser ❶ is a simple ease, the inverse of a Sine ease by using Math.cos instead of Math.sin. The same ease occurs except MyEaser starts at the ending value, xTo, and returns to the starting value, xFrom. Granted, you could just swap the xTo and xFrom values.

You're now an expert at creating your own easer. It takes only a little math ingenuity, a small amount of ActionScript, and you're finished! Knowing how to animate and customize animations is sweet until you attempt to animate text.

Flash designers and developers have always had a black art skill for animating text to achieve visible text while animating. This isn't lost on Flex 4 either, but things are a bit easier, if you're using the Flash Text Engine. Let's dive in and see how Flex 4 handles fonts and animations.

21.4.5   *Maintaining fonts while animating*

If you've been experimenting with various effects, you may have noticed that sometimes the text inside components doesn't seem to be affected by the effect. What's up with that?

By default, Flex uses system fonts—as a result, it's limited in its ability to manipulate them. This is particularly true with the effects where the text changes position, alpha, and so on. But there are workarounds: embedding the font or using a Flash Text Engine (FTE) supported component. All Spark components support FTE, and some support Halo but not all of them. Halo components with FTE support like Date-Field, Label, DataGrid, and so on allow you to set the `textInputClass`, via CSS, to an FTE equivalent. For more information on FTE in Halo components, read more here: http://blogs.adobe.com/flexdoc/fonts.pdf. In the case where a component doesn't support FTE, you must embed the font.

You can do this by using styles, as shown in the following listing.

Listing 21.22 Embedding fonts to ensure that effects work on text

```
<?xml version="1.0" encoding="utf-8"?>
<s:Application xmlns:fx="http://ns.adobe.com/mxml/2009"
               xmlns:s="library://ns.adobe.com/flex/spark"
               xmlns:mx="library://ns.adobe.com/flex/mx">
  <s:layout>
    <s:VerticalLayout paddingLeft="20" paddingTop="20" />
  </s:layout>
  <fx:Style>
    @font-face{                                           ❶ Embed font with
      src: url("fonts/Feel Script.otf");                    embedAsCFF
      font-family: myfont;                                  false
      advancedAntiAliasing: true;
      embedAsCFF: false;
    }

    .haloFont{                                            ❷ Set up CSS
      fontFamily: myfont;                                   class to
      fontSize: 30;                                         use font
    }
  </fx:Style>
  <fx:Declarations>
    <s:Rotate id="effect" targets="{[spark, halo]}" angleBy="45"
              applyChangesPostLayout="false" autoCenterTransform="true" />
  </fx:Declarations>
  <s:Button id="spark" label="spark" click="effect.play()" />
  <mx:Button id="halo" styleName="haloFont"
             label="halo"                    ⟵  Set the halo button's
             click="effect.play()" />            stylename to
</s:Application>                              ❸ haloFont CSS class
```

Listing 21.22, effect-wise, isn't anything new. The only thing you did differently was embed a font ❶ ❷ and add a halo button (`mx:Button`) to the application. When you click either button, the effect will play, and both buttons will rotate, showing the fonts properly embedded. The halo button is the only one with the embedded font ❸, though. This shows the rotation working in the Spark component with no font changes needed.

NOTE The drawback of embedding fonts is that the file size of your application will grow with the size of the font. Be careful not to go overboard and embed too many fonts or include the entire font range.

Figure 21.10 shows the Spark and Halo components both rotated with fonts properly showing in both.

If you're still using Halo components, fall back to your normal expectation of embedding fonts. For those of you using the FTE, you see how easy it is to work with fonts and animations. FTE removes all of the pain of fooling with fonts, making animating that much easier.

You're now ready to tackle visual effects in Flex. Keep in mind that there's no way we could cover every effect in this chapter. The information we've covered thus far is great, but the knowledge train doesn't stop here. Look into the effects documentation, watch the CodeDependent video series on Adobe TV (http://tv.adobe.com/show/codedependent/), and start playing with the different effect classes and individual effect properties. You'll be surprised at what you can build in a short amount of time.

Figure 21.10 Spark and halo buttons rotated with fonts intact

The simplicity of Flex 4 effects sounds great, right? Well, you haven't heard anything yet. Flex provides not only display effects but also the ability to add effects with sound by giving you an easy mechanism for adding sound to your application using the SoundEffect class.

21.4.6 *Creating sound effects*

Flex doesn't stop with visual effects but dives into auditory effects. Using the Sound-Effect effect, you can add an element of usability to your applications by communicating without the user having to read anything.

The SoundEffect employs a concept called *panning*, which lets you control the volume from left to right (if you wish). Table 21.13 lists the properties that are specific to the SoundEffect effect.

Table 21.13   Properties of the SoundEffect effect

Property	Type	Description
autoLoad	Boolean	Whether the MP3 is loaded automatically. true (default) or false.
bufferTime	Number	Number of milliseconds to buffer. Default is 1000.
loops	Number	Number of times to repeat a loop. 0 (default) plays once.
panEasingFunction	Function	Easing function to use when panning.
panFrom	Number	Starting pan value. Default is 0 (center). -1.0 (full left) to 1.0 (full right).
panTo	Number	Ending pan value. Default is 0 (center). -1.0 (full left) to 1.0 (full right).
source	Object	Reference to an MP3 sound file.
startTime	Number	Milliseconds into the sound file to start. Default is 0.
useDuration	Boolean	Whether to respect the duration property. true (default) or false.

Table 21.13 Properties of the `SoundEffect` **effect** *(continued)*

Property	Type	Description
volumeEasingFunction	Boolean	Easing function to use on volume changes.
volumeFrom	Number	Starting volume. 0.0-1.0 (default).
volumeTo	Number	Ending volume. 0.0-1.0 (default).

The example in listing 21.23 plays a sound #1 when the button is clicked #2.

Listing 21.23 Playing a sound when the button is clicked

```
<?xml version="1.0" encoding="utf-8"?>
<s:Application xmlns:fx="http://ns.adobe.com/mxml/2009"
               xmlns:s="library://ns.adobe.com/flex/spark"
               xmlns:mx="library://ns.adobe.com/flex/mx">
  <fx:Declarations>
    <mx:SoundEffect id="effect"
        source="@Embed(source='sounds/ding.mp3')"/>
  </fx:Declarations>
  <s:Button label="Click Me!"
        mouseDownEffect="{effect}" />
</s:Application>
```

❶ Set up `SoundEffect` and embed source

❷ On mouse down, play effect

Unfortunately, sound is a dimension that isn't often utilized in RIAs, largely because developers who come from traditional web applications aren't used to leveraging sound. We encourage you to try adding this element to your applications. This effect isn't native to Flex 4. It's a Flex 3 effect, so the mx namespace is required.

What an amazing set of effects features! Flex 4 is a rock star upgrade, topping off the visual effects with a splash of sound.

21.5 Summary

We covered the basics of what effects are, how to implement/use effects, the core set of effects classes, plus out-of-the-box effects, pixel shaders, customizing easing, fonts, and animations, and then we finished off with sound. You're ready to start sprucing up your applications. Take what you've learned here and apply it to your projects. Don't limit yourself to thinking that effects are only good for the "wow" factor, though. They also play a role in adding to the user experience by drawing attention to things going on in your application as well as providing a motion-driven vehicle for communication.

Effects can take your applications to new levels. They can definitely get a "wow" reaction from an audience—particularly management folks whom you're trying to impress as you sell them on the idea of using Flex—but mainly effects provide a visual, or auditory, gateway for users to interact with your application. Knowing how to use effects, as you've learned in this chapter, is great, but knowing when and how to use them is most important, as you learned in the previous chapter.

Another "wow" topic raising a lot of eyebrows is Flex's drag-and-drop abilities. We'll look at these in the next chapter.

Drag-and-drop

When Flex first came out, drag-and-drop (D&D) set the tone as a key feature, showcasing what Flex-based RIAs were capable of providing with minimal integration effort. From a developer's perspective, Flex's D&D feature is easy to implement because many native components provide a built-in mechanism to support it. At the same time, you can hook into and override any of the default behavior throughout the stages of the process.

In this book, we want to show you not just how to do something but also *why* to do something. We don't want you doing D&D just for the sake of it, or because it's cool, but because it adds usability.

In traditional web applications, you rely on boatloads of links and buttons to move data—web developers not using modern JavaScript frameworks (like jQuery) tend to forget the D&D concept (in the web context), even though they use it every day on the desktop side of life. And because D&D is so uncommon on the web, even users forget the concept.

We urge you to consider D&D from a usability point of view rather than just because you can or because of the coolness factor. The challenge isn't so much the programming effort (you'll see in this chapter how easy it is) but rather the mindset. You'll want to provide the typical data-management paradigms common in web applications, because that's what your users look for by default, but you should also train them to use your application's D&D capabilities.

Ultimately, the level at which your users are successful is the level at which your application is successful. We get the ball rolling for your success by reviewing the overall D&D process.

22.1 The drag-and-drop process

You love events, right? Well, the D&D process is nothing but events being fired off at various stages in the lifecycle of dragging and dropping.

Let's first get some definitions out of the way:

- *Drag initiator*—The component from which the drag starts.
- *Drag proxy*—The mouse icon displayed to the user during the D&D process.
- *Drag source*—The data being transferred between the drag initiator and the drop target. The name is somewhat misleading because it sounds like it's the source of the drag operation; that's the drag initiator.
- *Drop target*—The component receiving the drop.

Which one is in play at certain points can be confusing, so let's go through the D&D process. It includes a number of steps, depending on what the user does. We go over each step in moderate detail so you can understand what the user is doing, which events are fired, and what the user experiences at each step.

1 Drag is initiated.
- The user clicks an item in a drag-enabled component (by setting the drag-Enabled property to true).
- Event fired: mouseDown.
- While holding down the mouse button on the item, the user begins the drag process. The starting component is now the drag initiator. Events fired: mouseMove and dragStart.

2 Drag source object is created.
- It contains all the data associated with the item being dragged.

    MORE DETAILS For example, if you're dragging a row from a List component, it may show only the label although the record includes 10 fields. When you drag, you're dragging the entire record consisting of all 10 fields.

3 An initial visual drag proxy is shown.
- A red (x) icon ⊗ indicates that the component the mouse is over won't accept the current drop.
- A green (+) icon ⊕ is used when the current drop is allowed.

4 A destination drag proxy is shown as the user mouses over components.

- A red (x) icon ⊗ indicates that the component the mouse is over won't accept the current drop.
- A green (+) icon ⊕ is used when the current drop is allowed.
- Events fired: `dragEnter` and `dragOver`.

> **MORE DETAILS** The destination is a potential drop target, and the destination component examines the drag source to see if it likes what it sees (Is the data of compatible type? Are certain business rules in place? and so on).
>
> In figure 22.1, the drop target's acceptance or denial is visibly communicated to the user by the showing of the green (+), known as the drag proxy.

5 User mouses out of a potential drop target.

- The drag proxy is updated.
- Event fired: `dragExit`.

6 User drops the item on a target.

- Drag is completed or cancelled.
  - If the component accepted the drop, the drag is completed.
  - If the component rejected the drop, the drag is cancelled and the item returns (animates back) to the source.
- Events fired: `dragDrop` and `dragComplete`.

Figure 22.1 shows an example of the drag proxy with a + icon to show the drag operation can be completed.

This is a high level of detail, but don't worry about remembering all of it. We'll walk you through the steps in this chapter to help you better grasp each concept.

As you can see, events keep coming up—Flex is an event-driven system. If there's ever a place for events, it's definitely in D&D, and in the next section we'll cover and clear up each of the D&D events.

22.1.1 Drag-and-drop events

Previously, we mentioned that a lot of events are fired during the D&D process. Let's flesh these out so you know what they imply. The Recipient column in table 22.1 tells which component gets the event.

So far, we've defined the process and the associated events. Next, we discuss how to implement D&D in Flex components.

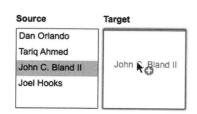

Figure 22.1 The drag proxy provides a visual indicator to the user about whether the operation is allowed.

Table 22.1   Drag-and-drop events

Event	Recipient	Description
mouseDown	Drag initiator	Occurs when the user mouses down on the draggable item. This is the point at which you can add business logic to determine whether you want to allow the start of a drag operation.
mouseMove	Drag initiator	User begins to move the draggable item.
dragStart	Drag initiator	Drag initiator fires an event to itself.
dragEnter	Drop target	Drag proxy initially moves over a potential drop target. The drop target can use this as an opportunity to examine data and determine whether it will accept or deny the drop. This event is triggered multiple times, for each mouse move over the target. **CAVEAT** If you're developing for Adobe AIR, this event will fire only once.
dragOver .	Drop target	Occurs immediately after dragEnter and is dispatched only if the target accepts the drop. Can be used to visually update the target to show it's ready for acceptance. **CAVEAT** If you're developing for Adobe AIR, this event will fire regardless of the acceptance or denial of the item.
dragDrop	Drop target	Result of the user releasing the mouse button. This is where you commit the data and finalize the operation.
dragExit	Drop target	Occurs if the user doesn't release the mouse button and moves off the drop target; you go from dragOver to dragExit. This is where you undo/reset things you did in the dragOver process.
dragComplete	Drag initiator	Sent to the drag initiator when the D&D process ends for whatever reason (the user drops the item or cancels the operation by letting go of the mouse button while not over an accepting component).

22.2   *Implementing drag-and-drop in Flex components*

You now have a familiarity with the D&D process. It may seem like a lot to remember or keep track of, but Flex makes it super simple with a set of native D&D capable components. We cover which components have D&D, how to add D&D support, and the different D&D operations (copy, move, internal sorting, multiple-item D&D, and two-way D&D) before moving on to implementing D&D on your own custom components.

Starting our journey, we look at native D&D components.

22.2.1   *Components with native drag-and-drop support*

The obvious usage candidates for D&D operations are data list components. In Flex, those are the List-based components, particularly the following, shown in table 22.2.

You may have noticed the depth of Halo components versus Spark components. Remember, Spark isn't yet 1:1 with Halo, in terms of available components. Also

Component	Namespace
List	Spark, Halo
TileList	Halo
HorizontalList	Halo
Tree	Halo
DataGrid	Halo
AdvancedDataGrid	Halo
PrintDataGrid	Halo

Table 22.2   Available D&D components

remember that List is a powerful component. You can build a TileList or HorizontalList in Spark by setting the layout to TileLayout or HorizontalLayout, respectively. As the Spark component set continues to grow, more native D&D Spark components will become available. In the upcoming sections we're going to focus purely on List to keep our minds on Flex 4. Later in the chapter we'll cover how to D&D between Spark and Halo components.

Knowing which components to use is great, but learning how to use them is another thing. Let's eagerly jump in and learn how to enable D&D on a List component.

22.2.2 *Enabling D&D on Lists*

The List component natively supports D&D with the setting of specific properties. Enabling D&D is easy—almost too easy. The List component supports two properties to make this happen (see table 22.3).

Table 22.3   Drag-and-drop properties of the List component

Property	Type	Description
dragEnabled	Boolean	Indicates whether the component is allowed to serve as a drag initiator. true or false (default).
dropEnabled	Boolean	Indicates whether the component is allowed to serve as a drop target. true or false (default).

NOTE   There's a third property, dragMoveEnabled, but you don't need to worry about it until section 22.2.3.

Using those two properties, listing 22.1 shows the code used in figure 22.1 (D&D process).

Listing 22.1   List accepting dragging and dropping from another List

```
<?xml version="1.0" encoding="utf-8"?>
<s:Application xmlns:fx="http://ns.adobe.com/mxml/2009"
               xmlns:s="library://ns.adobe.com/flex/spark">
  <s:layout>
    <s:HorizontalLayout paddingLeft="20" paddingTop="20" />
```

```
    </s:layout>
    <fx:Declarations>
      <s:ArrayCollection id="authors">
        <fx:Object label="Dan Orlando"
                   telephone="555-0000" />
        <fx:Object label="Tariq Ahmed"
                   telephone="555-0001" />
        <fx:Object label="John C. Bland II"
telephone="555-0010" />
        <fx:Object label="Joel Hooks"
                   telephone="555-0011" />
      </s:ArrayCollection>
    </fx:Declarations>
    <s:VGroup>
      <s:Label fontWeight="bold" text="Source" />
      <s:List dragEnabled="true" dataProvider="{authors}" />
    </s:VGroup>
    <s:VGroup>
      <s:Label fontWeight="bold" text="Target" />
      <s:List dropEnabled="true"
dataProvider="{new ArrayCollection()}" />
    </s:VGroup>
</s:Application>
```

> **Define author data**

> Set source's **dragEnabled** `to true`

> Set target's **dropEnabled** to true

Figure 22.1 shows the result of a D&D operation using listing 22.1. Notice that the only thing special about listing 22.1 is the use of dragEnabled and dropEnabled in the two Lists, respectively. Refer to table 22.3 to recall their use. This chapter will talk more about customization and control, but this listing is real-world application material wrapped in a simple example.

> **TIP** Flex will not restrict duplicate items from being dropped on the list. You can add this functionality by intercepting the dragEnter event and accepting or denying the item based on your own data requirement (such as no duplicates).

By default, the D&D operation will perform a copy. A copy is purely taking a copy of the drag item and adding it to another component without affecting the source component. Flex also allows you to easily move the item, remove the item from the source, and add it to the destination.

22.2.3 *Moving versus copying*

You may have noticed that listing 22.1 results in a copy operation instead of moving the data from one List to another. If you want to make it a move operation instead of a copy, the change is simple.

List-based components support a dragMoveEnabled property, which by default is set to false and causes the default behavior of copying the data item.

> **HALO TIP** There's one exception: The Tree component has the opposite default.

All you need to do is set `dragMoveEnabled` to `true`, and the D&D performs a move instead of a copy. The following snippet builds on listing 22.1, but for brevity we show only the changes to enable a move operation:

```
<s:List dragEnabled="true" dragMoveEnabled="true"
        dataProvider="{authors}" />
```

Yes, we're serious. That's all it takes to enable moving. Notice that `dragMoveEnabled` was added to the `List`, which tells the source list, "when the dragComplete event occurs, delete the drag item from my `dataProvider`." Figure 22.2 shows the result of two D&D operations based on listing 22.1 plus the previous snippet changes.

This workflow is probably something you're quite familiar with, and it works well for moving a single item. Think about your favorite desktop email client (Microsoft Outlook or Mail on OS X). When you drag an email from your inbox and drop it into another folder, you're doing a move operation. The same is true for dragging items to your Recycle Bin (Windows) or Trash (OS X); the item is moved to the receptacle.

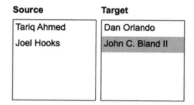

Figure 22.2   Notice that the target now has two of the source's items.

> **TIP** You can still do a copy with `dragMoveEnabled` set to `true`; to do so, hold down the Ctrl (Command on Mac) key during the dragging process. The inverse isn't true when `dragMoveEnabled` is `false`; holding Ctrl or Command doesn't invoke a move.

`dragMoveEnabled` allows for moving to targets, but what if you want to sort a list of items within the same list? No worries. Using all three drag properties lets you easily accomplish this, as shown in the next section.

22.2.4 *Using D&D for user-controlled sorting*

D&D doesn't have to be about moving or copying data from one component to another. You can also use it to reposition data within the same component. Envision an application where you take the best four authors you know on earth, writing a Flex 4 book, with the collective initials of DOTAJCBIIJH, and you want to sort the list by your favorite. Okay, maybe that isn't real world, but it will help us drive the point home.

From a usability perspective, it becomes progressively more time consuming without D&D to manage the ordering of content in a list as the amount of content grows. This kind of antiquated sorting mechanism is heavily used throughout the web today. Using D&D, you can save yourself and your users a lot of time.

Set the following properties on a component to allow dragging and dropping from and to the component itself:

- `dragEnabled="true"`
- `dropEnabled="true"`
- `dragMoveEnabled="true"`

The example in listing 22.2 demonstrates by using an updated version of listing 22.1's `List` enabling both drag and drop.

Listing 22.2 Dragging and dropping within a component, to allow ordering

```
<?xml version="1.0" encoding="utf-8"?>
<s:Application xmlns:fx="http://ns.adobe.com/mxml/2009"
               xmlns:s="library://ns.adobe.com/flex/spark">
  <s:layout>
    <s:VerticalLayout paddingLeft="20" paddingTop="20" />
  </s:layout>
  <fx:Declarations>
    <s:ArrayCollection id="authors">
      <fx:Object label="Dan Orlando" telephone="555-0000" />
      <fx:Object label="Tariq Ahmed" telephone="555-0001" />
      <fx:Object label="John C. Bland II" telephone="555-0010" />
      <fx:Object label="Joel Hooks" telephone="555-0011" />
    </s:ArrayCollection>
  </fx:Declarations>
  <s:Label fontWeight="bold" text="My Favorite Authors" />
  <s:List dragEnabled="true" dropEnabled="true"
          dragMoveEnabled="true"
          dataProvider="{authors}" />
</s:Application>
```

> **Set drag properties accordingly**

After running listing 22.2, you can do something similar to figure 22.3 and control the order of your favorite authors. We promise the sort was purely random, after the selected item, and nothing is implied by the sort order (*wink wink*).

You now know how to enable a `List` to allow copy, move, and sort. This is awesome, but what about really long lists? Moving one item at a time would be super tedious, right? We're overjoyed you asked that question.

The next section shows you how to enable multi-item D&D between lists. Surprisingly, or maybe not so much so now, it's incredibly easy.

My Favorite Authors

John C. Bland II
Tariq Ahmed
Joel Hooks
Dan Orlando

Figure 22.3 Using D&D on itself, the `List` lets the user easily control the position of items.

22.2.5 *Multi-item drag-and-drop*

You saw how moving and copying items works well when you're dealing with simple data lists, but what happens when you want to remove 10 items? 20 items? How about 5 nonconsecutive items? Flex answers the call by allowing multi-item D&D.

If you want to let the user move many items at once, check out the `allowMultiple-Selection` property. Setting it to `true` enables this ability (see the following listing).

Listing 22.3 Enabling the user to move many items at once

```
<?xml version="1.0" encoding="utf-8"?>
<s:Application xmlns:fx="http://ns.adobe.com/mxml/2009"
               xmlns:s="library://ns.adobe.com/flex/spark">
  <s:layout>
```

```
        <s:HorizontalLayout paddingLeft="20" paddingTop="20" />
    </s:layout>
    <fx:Declarations>
        <s:ArrayCollection id="authors">
            <fx:Object label="Dan Orlando" telephone="555-0000" />
            <fx:Object label="Tariq Ahmed" telephone="555-0001" />
            <fx:Object label="John C. Bland II" telephone="555-0010" />
            <fx:Object label="Joel Hooks" telephone="555-0011" />
        </s:ArrayCollection>
    </fx:Declarations>
    <s:VGroup>
        <s:Label fontWeight="bold" text="Source" />
        <s:List dragEnabled="true" dragMoveEnabled="true"          ◁┐ Set the
                allowMultipleSelection="true"                         │ List's D&D
                dataProvider="{authors}" />                        ◁┘ properties
    </s:VGroup>
    <s:VGroup>
        <s:Label fontWeight="bold" text="Target" />
        <s:List dropEnabled="true" dataProvider="{new ArrayCollection()}" />
    </s:VGroup>
</s:Application>
```

The user can select multiple items in either of two ways: using individual selections or using a range of selections.

To select items one by one, follow the steps in table 22.4.

Table 22.4   Available ways to select items in a `List`

Type	Steps
Individual selections	**1** Hold down the Ctrl key (Command on Mac) and use the mouse to select each item you want to drag. **2** Once all the items are selected, release the Ctrl key.
Range of selections	**3** Click the first item in the range. **4** Press and hold down the Shift key. **5** Select the last item in the range.

Either way you choose results in a selected set of multiple items. Once you have the items selected, you click any one of the selected items and drag it to the target or, if moving within the same component, to the target position in the data list.

Figure 22.4 shows what this looks like by moving every other row to the target.

This UI behavior isn't unique to Flex, and it's something you've most likely experienced in a Windows application. Think back to your desktop email application we spoke of earlier. In the previous example we talked about moving one item, but email clients allow you to take multiple items (range or nonconsecutive) and move them at will. You now have the power to provide such functionality in your Flex applications.

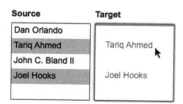

Figure 22.4   Use the Ctrl/ Command key to select multiple items to drag.

What we've shown so far is a one-way D&D operation, where you have a source and destination. There are times when you need to move an item from one component to another and then back to the other component. This is two-way D&D, which Flex also supports.

22.2.6 *Two-way drag-and-drop*

To this point, you've seen how to move or copy items from one List to another. This is great but we're talking D&D here, so forget about an undo button, and let's allow the user to drag the items back to the source target. In Flex, that's not a problem, and here's how you do it.

Set the dragEnabled and dropEnabled properties to true for all components involved. Don't forget to set dragMoveEnabled to true as well, if you want the default behavior to be moving instead of copying, which we do in this case.

Listing 22.4 shows the same example application from previous listings but with both Lists set up for D&D, enabling two-way communication. You can move the items back and forth across the lists.

> **Listing 22.4 Two-way dragging and dropping between two List components**

```
<?xml version="1.0" encoding="utf-8"?>
<s:Application xmlns:fx="http://ns.adobe.com/mxml/2009"
               xmlns:s="library://ns.adobe.com/flex/spark">
  <s:layout>
    <s:HorizontalLayout paddingLeft="20" paddingTop="20" />
  </s:layout>
  <fx:Declarations>
    <s:ArrayCollection id="authors">
      <fx:Object label="Dan Orlando" telephone="555-0000" />
      <fx:Object label="Tariq Ahmed" telephone="555-0001" />
      <fx:Object label="John C. Bland II" telephone="555-0010" />
      <fx:Object label="Joel Hooks" telephone="555-0011" />
    </s:ArrayCollection>
  </fx:Declarations>
  <s:VGroup>
    <s:Label fontWeight="bold" text="Source" />
    <s:List dropEnabled="true" dragEnabled="true" dragMoveEnabled="true"
        allowMultipleSelection="true" dataProvider="{authors}" />
  </s:VGroup>
  <s:VGroup>
    <s:Label fontWeight="bold" text="Target" />
    <s:List dropEnabled="true" dragEnabled="true" dragMoveEnabled="true"
        allowMultipleSelection="true"
        dataProvider="{new ArrayCollection()}" />
  </s:VGroup>
</s:Application>
```

As you move an item from one List to another, it's removed from the source location. You can always move it back using D&D. Figure 22.5 shows dragging from the source List to the target List and vice versa.

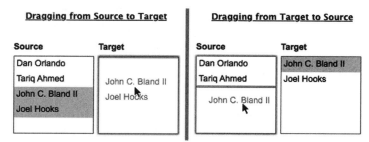

Figure 22.5   The left side shows dragging from source to target, and the right is vice versa.

So far, you've been able to add D&D in an autonomous manner: Components employ their built-in D&D behavior. If only life were that easy! With Flex 4 skinning you can, most of the time, get away with utilizing the built-in components without having to write your own D&D logic. In a real-world application, you'll need to enter business logic and business rules for your custom components.

Adding drag-and-drop to custom components is far from as simple as setting one or more of three properties, but it isn't close to pulling teeth, if that helps any. In the next section we fully explore adding D&D to custom components.

22.3   *Enter the DragManager*

The DragManager is a class of static methods—it does all the work behind the scenes to make D&D possible. Whenever you need to handle objects in play, you can employ the DragManager to help. You can use it to implement custom D&D, as you'll see in the upcoming sections, or circumvent the D&D process between native Flex 4 components.

In this section we'll cover the specifics of the DragManager properties and methods as well as how to circumvent the process when using native components. Before we get into those specifics, it's worth summarizing a few key properties.

22.3.1   *DragManager properties and methods*

The DragManager has four static values (also called *constants*, which are variables whose value can't change at runtime) available to evaluate the user's action(s), such as a move or a copy, and communicate back to the user visually. Those values are listed in table 22.5.

Table 22.5   Constants defined in the DragManager

Value	Description
COPY	Current action is copying the dragged item. – List-based components assume, when you're holding down the Ctrl key, you're doing a copy (if dragMoveEnabled="true").
LINK	Current action is linking; like a copy, but instead of making a duplicate, you have multiple items linking to a single source. – This action occurs when the Shift key is held down.
MOVE	Current action is moving the dragged item from one place to another.
NONE	No action allowed. Operation is denied.

These constant values are typically used for comparison sake. You'll see this later, but the following snippet shows how to tell if the current action is a copy:

```
protected function onDragEnter(event:DragEvent):void{
  if(event.action == DragManager.COPY){
    //do something
  }
}
```

This snippet is a simple method to catch a drag enter event. In the event you check to see if the `event.action` is `DragManager.COPY`, which has a value of `copy`; if so, then you'd do something within your application.

These constants are useful, but the `DragManager` has more. You can take advantage of its static methods to gain even more control over the D&D process. You can take advantage of three important methods in order to perform custom D&D work:

- `doDrag()`—Kicks off the D&D process. Usually initiated in a `mouseDown` event handler.
- `acceptDragDrop()`—Lets the `DragManager` know whether it's allowed to continue the D&D process.
  - Called in a `dragEnter` event handler.
  - `showFeedback()`—Communicates to the user about the current operational value (`COPY`, `LINK`, `MOVE`, or `NONE`).

Using a combination of the `DragManager`'s constants and its supporting methods, you have the pieces necessary to implement your own accept or deny logic. To further the point, the next section covers how to circumvent the D&D process with your own logic.

22.3.2 *Accepting or denying a drop*

All of what we've discussed is fine and dandy if you're allowing D&D in an uncontrolled manner, but in the real world, the next logical step is to add business logic to determine whether to allow a drop on a given component. A common case includes doing a check to prevent duplicates, so the user can't add another item if there's already a copy.

LIMITING WHO GETS INTO THE PARTY

The key event to facilitate adding a gatekeeper—business logic determining whether to allow a drop—is the `dragEnter` event. This event fires whenever the mouse moves into a potential drop target.

Let's use an example where the drop target lets the drop take place only after inspecting the item to see if the record appears to be active. Here's the game plan for the code in listing 22.5:

1 Add a `dragEnter` event handler to the `List` to accept or deny a drop.
2 The event handler looks at the `DragEvent` event to see what data is being dragged.

The data is in the form of a vector of objects. Even though you may be dragging only one item, the `DragManager` supports multi-item drags—it's possible to receive more than one item (as you learned in section 22.3.6 using allow-MultipleSelection="true").

3 Examine the data to see whether any of the items are active (via isActive being false).

4 If all is well, tell the DragManager to continue; otherwise, take a pass and update the visual feedback.

NOTE   isActive is a custom data property. It's not part of the Flex 4 SDK or native to a D&D operation.

Listing 22.5   Allowing a drop only for items that are active

```xml
<?xml version="1.0" encoding="utf-8"?>
<s:Application xmlns:fx="http://ns.adobe.com/mxml/2009"
               xmlns:s="library://ns.adobe.com/flex/spark">
  <s:layout>
    <s:HorizontalLayout paddingLeft="20" paddingTop="20" />
  </s:layout>
  <fx:Script>
    <![CDATA[
      import mx.core.UIComponent;
      import mx.events.DragEvent;
      import mx.managers.DragManager;

      protected function onDragEnter(event:DragEvent):void{
        var items:Vector.<Object> =
          event.dragSource.dataForFormat("itemsByIndex")
                as Vector.<Object>;
        if(items[0].isActive)
          DragManager.acceptDragDrop(event.target
                as UIComponent);
        else{
          DragManager.showFeedback(DragManager.NONE);
          event.preventDefault();
        }
      }
    ]]>
  </fx:Script>
  <fx:Declarations>
    <s:ArrayCollection id="authors">
      <fx:Object label="Dan Orlando" telephone="555-0000"
                isActive="false" />
      <fx:Object label="Tariq Ahmed" telephone="555-0001"
                isActive="false" />
      <fx:Object label="John C. Bland II" telephone="555-0010"
                isActive="true" />
      <fx:Object label="Joel Hooks" telephone="555-0011"
                isActive="true" />
    </s:ArrayCollection>
  </fx:Declarations>
  <s:VGroup>
    <s:Label fontWeight="bold" text="Source" />
    <s:List dragEnabled="true" dragMoveEnabled="true"
```

Annotations:
- Access dragged item(s) data
- Check isActive property
- Accept drop
- Update visual feedback
- Prevent default event functionality

```
            dataProvider="{authors}" />
  </s:VGroup>
  <s:VGroup>
    <s:Label fontWeight="bold" text="Target" />
    <s:List dropEnabled="true" dataProvider="{new ArrayCollection()}"
            dragEnter="onDragEnter(event)" />         ◁┐ Add dragEnter
  </s:VGroup>                                             │ event handler
</s:Application>
```

> **NOTE** Vector is an array whose elements are all of the same data type. This means you're guaranteed only to insert and retrieve the expected type of elements. For more information on Vector, see the ActionScript 3.0 Reference (http://help.adobe.com/en_US/FlashPlatform/reference/actionscript/3/Vector.html).

When you try this example, if you drag the author "Tariq Ahmed," the List will refuse to allow the drop to occur. A crucial part of this working is the event.preventDefault(). Without stopping the event from occurring, the List component will, internally, see the call and accept the drop. By preventing the default, you kill the event from being handled within the target List component. You can revisit chapter 12 to get a refresher on event propogation.

You may wonder how exactly you're denying the drop without explicitly saying so. The way the DragManager works is that if it never sees that acceptDragDrop call, the D&D is considered denied, which prevents the dragOver and dragDrop events from firing. Figure 22.6 shows the results of dragging an active versus inactive author to the target component.

Listing 22.5 doesn't allow multiple drag items, but if you did allow them, it's important to know the data is in index order from the source component. This means the first dragged item in the list of items will be the one with the lowest index value on the source dataProvider. Looking at figure 22.6, you see the order is Dan, Tariq, John, then Joel, which results in indexes of 0, 1, 2, and 3. If you were dragging Dan and John, you'd receive indexes 0 and 2.

With that said, your code only verifies whether index 0 is active: if(items[0].isActive). This means you can't drag a list of elements where the first item is inactive. If you did, the entire drag would be denied. But what if you wanted to allow the drop and filter only the inactive ones but allow the active ones? This is where you can use the dragDrop event to manually manage the dropped items.

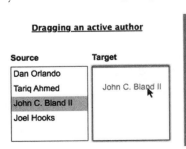

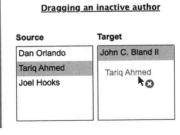

Figure 22.6 Notice the visual feedback when dragging an active author (left) and an inactive author (right).

MIGRATION TIP Halo drag-and-drop components use a different way of obtaining the dragged items and a different type. To access the dragged items from an mx:DataGrid, you'd use the following:

```
//halo
  var items:Array = event.dragSource.dataForFormat("items") as Array;
  //spark
  var items:Vector.<Object> =
  event.dragSource.dataForFormat("itemsByIndex") as Vector.<Object>;
```

The difference is in the format available within the dragSource. Spark components don't provide an items format, whereas Halo components do. This is a subtle change but will bite you if you're not careful.

22.3.3 *Applying your own drop*

The next need you're likely to encounter is to apply the drop yourself. You could circumvent the default functionality, as we did in listing 22.5 for accepting a drop, to filter the dragged items, or you may want to store information in a database on the backend as it's dropped.

To do this you'll add a dragDrop event handler to take the data being moved and copy it to the component's dataProvider. Because we're implementing our own move functionality, we're going to turn off dragMoveEnabled on the source component.

TIP By default, the target component's dataProvider isn't set to anything, so it defaults to null. We're setting the dataProvider in MXML, but you could gracefully handle setting the default dataProvider within the dragDrop, as shown in listing 22.6.

Listing 22.6 shows our new app with item filtering on the dragDrop rather than the dragEnter.

Listing 22.6 Creating a function to directly add data to a component

```
<?xml version="1.0" encoding="utf-8"?>
<s:Application xmlns:fx="http://ns.adobe.com/mxml/2009"
               xmlns:s="library://ns.adobe.com/flex/spark">
  <s:layout>
    <s:HorizontalLayout paddingLeft="20" paddingTop="20" />
  </s:layout>
  <fx:Script>
    <![CDATA[
      import mx.core.UIComponent;
      import mx.events.DragEvent;
      import mx.managers.DragManager;

      protected function onDragDrop(event:DragEvent):void{
        var target:List = event.target as List;
        if(!target.dataProvider)
          target.dataProvider = new ArrayCollection();

        var items:Vector.<Object> =
         event.dragSource.dataForFormat("itemsByIndex") as Vector.<Object>;
        var sourceIndex:int;
```

```
        var source:List = event.dragInitiator as List;
        var sourceData:ArrayCollection = source.dataProvider
                                                as ArrayCollection;

        for each(var item:Object in items){
          if(item.isActive){
            target.dataProvider.addItem(item);
            sourceIndex = source.dataProvider.getItemIndex(item);
            source.dataProvider.removeItemAt(sourceIndex);
          }
        }
        event.preventDefault();
      }
    ]]>
  </fx:Script>
  <fx:Declarations>
    <s:ArrayCollection id="authors">
      <fx:Object label="Dan Orlando" telephone="555-0000"
                isActive="false" />
      <fx:Object label="Tariq Ahmed" telephone="555-0001"
                isActive="false" />
      <fx:Object label="John C. Bland II" telephone="555-0010"
                isActive="true" />
      <fx:Object label="Joel Hooks" telephone="555-0011"
                isActive="true" />
    </s:ArrayCollection>
  </fx:Declarations>
  <s:VGroup>
    <s:Label fontWeight="bold" text="Source" />
    <s:List dragEnabled="true" allowMultipleSelection="true"
          dataProvider="{authors}" />
  </s:VGroup>
  <s:VGroup>
    <s:Label fontWeight="bold" text="Target" />
    <s:List dropEnabled="true" dragDrop="onDragDrop(event)" />
  </s:VGroup>
</s:Application>
```

Listing 22.6 is similar to 22.5 but provides much more control over the filtering. Remember in 22.5 the whole set of dragged items was denied if the first item was inactive. You could have looped over the list and allowed the drop if there was an active item, but this would have allowed inactive elements through as well. To prevent this we turned off `allowMultipleSelection` and forced only one element dragging at a time. This worked but isn't ideal by any means.

In listing 22.6 we allow multiple selection, don't bother with the `dragEnter` event, and filter the items in the `dragDrop` handler. By doing this we're able to ascertain each element's state (active or inactive) and then decide whether we want to add the item or not. We also set the target's `dataProvider` if it isn't already set. Figure 22.7 shows dragging all of the source items and the result of the drag.

As noted previously, you may want to save this data to the database. You could easily do this in the `dragDrop` handler by storing a list of items and then sending only those valid ones, as shown in the following snippet:

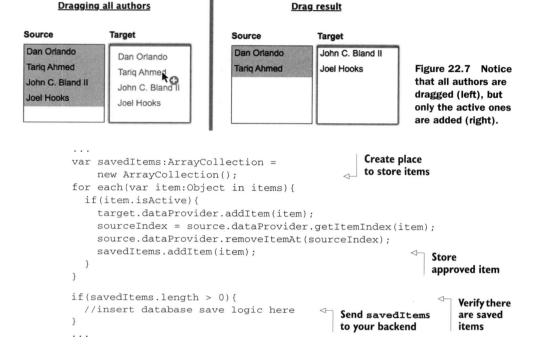

Figure 22.7 Notice that all authors are dragged (left), but only the active ones are added (right).

```
...
var savedItems:ArrayCollection =        ⟵ Create place
    new ArrayCollection();                  to store items
for each(var item:Object in items){
  if(item.isActive){
    target.dataProvider.addItem(item);
    sourceIndex = source.dataProvider.getItemIndex(item);
    source.dataProvider.removeItemAt(sourceIndex);
    savedItems.addItem(item);             ⟵ Store
  }                                           approved item
}

if(savedItems.length > 0){                ⟵ Verify there
  //insert database save logic here          are saved
}                        ⟵ Send savedItems   items
...                         to your backend
```

The previous snippet is a tweak to listing 22.6. The only change is the use of the `savedItems ArrayCollection` to store a reference to the saved items. We then check to see if any items were stored for save, and if so, we send those items to our backend. The database logic is for you to implement. We're just providing the building block here.

Using what you know about the `DragManager`, you can take this one step further and add D&D capabilities to components without native D&D support.

22.4   Adding D&D to non-List components

The `List`-based components do all the work when it comes to D&D. If you want to add D&D to a non-`List`-based component, you're pretty much on an island with the `Drag-Manager` and a volleyball named Wilson.

To do this, you'll leverage the events from the previous sections (`dragEnter` and `dragDrop`), but you need to use a few more events as well—particularly `mouseMove` and `dragComplete`. We're going to step through creating a custom component with D&D capabilities as well as a container to catch the items. This will be a dumbed-down version of a shopping cart, but it's more to illustrate the point than to focus on e-commerce.

22.4.1   Setting up the example

This example uses a rudimentary shopping-cart concept, where you choose things to buy by dragging and dropping them into a shopping cart (see figure 22.8).

This example is *really* rudimentary, but you get the point. In the real world, you'd query a database for all the details of your catalog (price, title, description, thumbnail image, and so on) and build a list containing those details.

You'll use completely custom components to build this application. Using what you know about the process, let's begin by initiating the drag operation.

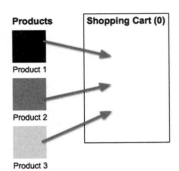

Figure 22.8   A quick look at how the sample shopping cart will function

22.4.2   *Initiating the drag*

Our products are represented by a `ProductItem` class, extending `SkinnableComponent`, and encapsulate the drag functionality. We don't care for the products to have drop functionality because nothing will drop on them; they will only drag. This class also leans on the knowledge gained from chapter 17 on custom components.

To kick off the D&D process, you'll listen for the `mouseMove` event and create an event handler to utilize the `DragManager`. This drag-initiator function performs three major tasks:

- Creates a reference to the drag initiator
- Creates a drag-source object containing all the data that needs to be passed along by the `DragManager`
- Calls the `DragManager`'s `doDrag()` function and passes along the reference to the drag initiator, the drag-source object, and the `mouseMove` event object created by the user

Listing 22.7 shows the complete component, including expected skin parts.

Listing 22.7   Custom `ProductItem` class

```
package components{
   import assets.graphics.DragProxyGraphic;

   import flash.events.MouseEvent;

   import mx.core.DragSource;
   import mx.managers.DragManager;

   import spark.components.Label;
   import spark.components.supportClasses.SkinnableComponent;
   import spark.primitives.supportClasses.FilledElement;

   public class ProductItem extends SkinnableComponent{
      [SkinPart(required="true")]
      public var imageElement:FilledElement;

      [SkinPart(required="true")]
      public var titleElement:Label;
```

```
    [Bindable]
    public var title:String;

    [Bindable]
    public var color:uint;

    public function ProductItem(){
      super();
      addEventListener(MouseEvent.MOUSE_DOWN,
        onMouseDown, false, 0, true);
    }

    protected function onMouseDown(event:MouseEvent):void{
      var ds:DragSource = new DragSource();
      ds.addData(this, "product");
      DragManager.doDrag(this, ds, event);
    }
  }
}
```

❶ Create
   DragSource
   instance

   Add custom data
❷ **to DragSource**

❸ **Start dragging**

Listing 22.7 should look familiar. It's a basic component with a couple skin parts and a couple properties. The key point to see here is that the onMouseDown function holds the only code necessary to add D&D to a custom component. This means that with four lines of code, you'd update your current applications to allow your components to start dragging.

The first thing you do in the onMouseDown handler is create the DragSource ❶. Remember listing 22.5 where you pulled the data from event.dragSource? This is how the data made it there, through a DragSource. In this case you're creating a custom format named "product" and setting the value to this ❷. You could take a bitmap snapshot, pass the title and color properties for adding it to a list, or any other combination you can think of or need to have. The drag data is completely in your control. Because you're keeping it simple and want to move the entire component, versus a copy, you use this.

The final step is to start dragging ❸ the component. To do this you use Drag-Manager.doDrag and pass in the dragInitiator (which started this process) and then drag data and the event used to start the drag. You could use other arguments, and will later, but at this point dragging integration is complete.

To test the dragging, you created three instances of the ProductItem class and set them to a custom skin. The skin is shown in the following snippet:

```
<?xml version="1.0" encoding="utf-8"?>
<s:Skin xmlns:fx="http://ns.adobe.com/mxml/2009"
        xmlns:s="library://ns.adobe.com/flex/spark">
  <fx:Metadata>[HostComponent("components.ProductItem")]</fx:Metadata>
  <s:layout><s:VerticalLayout /></s:layout>
  <s:Rect id="imageElement" width="50" height="50">
    <s:fill><s:SolidColor color="{hostComponent.color}" /></s:fill>
  </s:Rect>
  <s:Label id="titleElement" text="{hostComponent.title}" />
</s:Skin>
```

With your skin in place, you only need an application to test. Listing 22.8 shows our initial application with the `ProductItem` instances in place.

Listing 22.8   An initial application to test the D&D process

```xml
<?xml version="1.0" encoding="utf-8"?>
<s:Application xmlns:fx="http://ns.adobe.com/mxml/2009"
               xmlns:s="library://ns.adobe.com/flex/spark"
               xmlns:components="components.*">
  <s:layout>
    <s:HorizontalLayout paddingLeft="20" paddingTop="20" />
  </s:layout>

  <fx:Script>
    <![CDATA[
      import assets.skins.ProductItemSkin;
    ]]>
  </fx:Script>

  <s:VGroup width="100">
    <s:Label text="Products" fontWeight="bold" fontSize="14"
           paddingTop="5"/>
    <components:ProductItem title="Product 1"
           color="0x333333"
           skinClass="assets.skins.ProductItemSkin" />
    <components:ProductItem title="Product 2"
           color="0xFF6666"
           skinClass="assets.skins.ProductItemSkin" />
    <components:ProductItem title="Product 3"
           color="0x66FF66"
           skinClass="assets.skins.ProductItemSkin" />
  </s:VGroup>
</s:Application>
```

Create three instances of `ProductItem`

Figure 22.9 shows how the application looks in its current state while dragging Product 1.

Now you're in business! Halfway, anyway: The other half is to add the logic for the drop operation. Before we dive into handling the drop operation, let's improve figure 22.9 by creating a custom drag proxy instead of using the default, boring rectangle.

22.4.3   Using a custom drag proxy

By default Flex draws a simple box to illustrate a custom item it's dragging, called the drag proxy. The great thing is you have control over how this proxy looks. It's super simple to add a custom drag proxy. The following snippet shows your custom proxy:

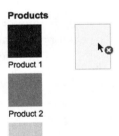

Figure 22.9   Showcases our drag process from listing 22.7

```xml
<?xml version="1.0" encoding="utf-8"?>
<s:Graphic xmlns:fx="http://ns.adobe.com/mxml/2009"
           xmlns:s="library://ns.adobe.com/flex/spark" >
```

```
  <s:Path data="M 119,0 L 148,86 238,86 166,140 192,226 119,175 46,226
          72,140 0,86 90,86 Z" y="2" scaleX="0.3361345" scaleY="0.3361345">
    <s:fill><s:SolidColor color="#333333" /></s:fill>
    <s:stroke><s:SolidColorStroke color="white" /></s:stroke>
  </s:Path>
</s:Graphic>
```

This is nothing more than an MXML component with a `Path` drawing a star. Again, rudimentary, my dear Watson. You'd do a better graphic than this one. To use this custom proxy, you need to update your `DragManager.doDrag` method from listing 22.8 and pass in an instance of the proxy:

```
DragManager.doDrag(this, ds, event, new DragProxyGraphic());
```

The only change from listing 22.7 is the passing of a `DragProxyGraphic` instance, which is the filename of the previous snippet. Figure 22.10 shows the new drag proxy graphic in use.

In this case you're still only using a static graphic. You could also expose a property in your component allowing the proxy to be set dynamically. For a real shipping cart you'd probably want to use the product's graphic as the drag proxy. The following snippet shows how you could pass an image to accurately represent which product is being dragged:

```
  protected function onMouseDown(event:MouseEvent):void{
    var screenshot:BitmapData = new BitmapData(width, height);
    screenshot.draw(this);
    var proxy:Image = new Image();
    proxy.source = new Bitmap(screenshot.clone());
    var ds:DragSource = new DragSource();
    ds.addData(this, "product");
    DragManager.doDrag(this, ds, event, proxy);
  }
```

This snippet shows how to "screenshot" the dragging component and use the screenshot as the drag proxy. Figure 22.11 shows the results of the previous snippet.

Your dragging is solid, so you need only a shopping cart in which to place the products.

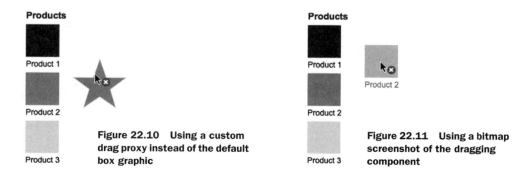

Figure 22.10   Using a custom drag proxy instead of the default box graphic

Figure 22.11   Using a bitmap screenshot of the dragging component

22.4.4 Handling the drop

The products are now dragging and have a custom drag proxy. This is great, but without a place to drop the products, your e-commerce store will never make a dime! To illustrate the droppable shopping cart, you're going to build another custom component. In this component, you're going to look for the dragEnter, dragExit, and dragDrop events. You're also going to track the total number of items added to the shopping cart and then use states to visually update the display to show that items are in the cart. Listing 22.9 shows the ShoppingCart class.

Listing 22.9 The `ShoppingCart` class used to handle dropping

```
package components{
  import flash.events.Event;

  import mx.events.DragEvent;
  import mx.managers.DragManager;

  import spark.components.Group;
  import spark.components.Label;
  import spark.components.supportClasses.SkinnableComponent;
  import spark.filters.BlurFilter;

  [SkinState("noitems")]
  [SkinState("items")]

  public class ShoppingCart extends SkinnableComponent{
    [SkinPart(required="true")]
    public var titleElement:Label;

    [SkinPart(required="true")]
    public var contentGroup:Group;

    [Bindable]
    public var title:String;

    protected var _itemCount:uint = 0;
    [Bindable(event="itemCountchanged")]
    public function get itemCount():uint{ return _itemCount; }

    public function ShoppingCart(){
      super();
      addEventListener(DragEvent.DRAG_ENTER,
        onDragEnter, false, 0, true);
      addEventListener(DragEvent.DRAG_DROP,
        onDragDrop, false, 0, true);
      addEventListener(DragEvent.DRAG_EXIT,
        onDragExit, false, 0, true);
    }

    protected function onDragEnter(event:DragEvent):void{
      if(event.dragSource.dataForFormat("product")          ❶ Verify dragSource
        is ProductItem){                                       has ProductItem
        DragManager.acceptDragDrop(this);      ⬅─❷ Accept the drop
        filters = [new BlurFilter()];
      }                                                      Add a blur for
    }                                                     ❸ visual feedback
```

```
    protected function onDragExit(event:DragEvent):void{
      filters = [];
    }

    protected function onDragDrop(event:DragEvent):void{
      var element:ProductItem =
        event.dragSource.dataForFormat("product")
          as ProductItem;
      contentGroup.addElement(element);
      _itemCount = contentGro.numElements;
      dispatchEvent(new Event("itemCountChanged"));
      invalidateSkinState();
      filters = [];
    }

    override protected function getCurrentSkinState():String{
      return _itemCount == 0 ? "noitems" : "items";
    }
  }
}
```

❹ Remove all visual filters

❺ Get drag data

❻ Add element to display

❼ Update the item count

This covers the bulk of what needs to be done. Everything in listing 22.9 should look familiar. You first add event listeners in the constructor for each of the relevant drop events. When an element is dragged over this component, you check to make sure the data is in the proper format ❶, and if it is, accept the drop ❷ and then add blur to the cart ❸. The blur is a way to illustrate to the user that a drop can occur, as shown in figure 22.12.

Subsequently, when the user mouses out of the cart, you remove the blur ❹. Granted, a blur probably isn't the best way to illustrate the acceptance, but it works for demonstration purposes.

The remaining meat of the D&D process is to take the dropped item and add it to the display. You do this in the onDragDrop event handler. Because the ProductItem class adds itself as the dragged data ❺, you take the dragged data and add it to your contentGroup list ❻. Because the number of items in the cart has changed, you update the _itemsCount property with the total number of child elements in the contentGroup ❼ and then dispatch a custom event to update any data bindings on

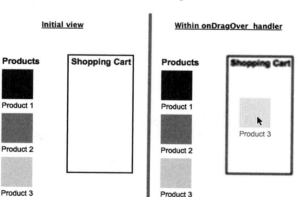

Figure 22.12 Notice the initial view versus the look when an item is over the cart.

the `itemCount` getter. You're also using custom states to update the UI, so you invalidate the skin state, forcing the component to get the current skin state. The drop operation is now complete but the component is still blurred, so you remove all filters.

You can now add your `ShoppingCart` class to your application. To customize the cart, you create a custom skin, as shown in the following listing.

Listing 22.10 Custom skin for the `ShoppingCart` class

```
<?xml version="1.0" encoding="utf-8"?>
<s:Skin xmlns:fx="http://ns.adobe.com/mxml/2009"
        xmlns:s="library://ns.adobe.com/flex/spark">
  <fx:Metadata>[HostComponent("components.ShoppingCart")]</fx:Metadata>

  <s:states>
    <s:State name="noitems" />
    <s:State name="items" />
  </s:states>

  <s:Rect width="100%" height="100%">
    <s:fill>
      <s:SolidColor color="white" />
    </s:fill>
    <s:stroke>
      <s:SolidColorStroke color.noitems="black" color.items="#de7800"
                          weight="2"/>
    </s:stroke>
  </s:Rect>

  <s:VGroup left="5" right="5" top="5" bottom="5">
    <s:Label id="titleElement" width="100%"
             color="black"
             fontSize="14" fontWeight="bold"
             text.items="{hostComponent.title} ({hostComponent.itemCount})"
             text.noitems="{hostComponent.title}"/>

    <s:Group id="contentGroup" width="100%" height="100%">
      <s:layout>
        <s:VerticalLayout/>
      </s:layout>
    </s:Group>
  </s:VGroup>
</s:Skin>
```

Listing 22.11 shows your application with the shopping cart integrated.

Listing 22.11 The final application with the shopping cart and products

```
<?xml version="1.0" encoding="utf-8"?>
<s:Application xmlns:fx="http://ns.adobe.com/mxml/2009"
               xmlns:s="library://ns.adobe.com/flex/spark"
               xmlns:components="components.*">
  <s:layout>
    <s:HorizontalLayout paddingLeft="20" paddingTop="20" />
  </s:layout>
```

```
<fx:Script>
  <![CDATA[
    import assets.skins.ProductItemSkin;
  ]]>
</fx:Script>

<s:VGroup width="100">
  <s:Label text="Products" fontWeight="bold" fontSize="14"
        paddingTop="5"/>
  <components:ProductItem title="Product 1" color="0x333333"
                    skinClass="assets.skins.ProductItemSkin" />
  <components:ProductItem title="Product 2" color="0xFF6666"
                    skinClass="assets.skins.ProductItemSkin" />
  <components:ProductItem title="Product 3" color="0x66FF66"
                skinClass="assets.skins.ProductItemSkin" />
</s:VGroup>
<s:VGroup>
  <components:ShoppingCart title="Shopping Cart"
                    minHeight="200"
                    skinClass="assets.skins.ShoppingCartSkin" />

</s:VGroup>
</s:Application>
```

Figure 22.13 shows the result of a couple drag-and-drop operations.

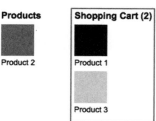

You're finished! Great job. The drag-and-drop experience is fully integrated into your application using 100% custom code. Taking what you learned from implementing D&D with List-based components and custom components, you're ready to customize the D&D experience.

Figure 22.13   Notice the border change and the item count after dragging two products into the cart.

22.5   *Customizing the drag-and-drop experience*

Before we wrap up this chapter, we'll shift to the creative aspect of D&D. This means you can swap in your own icons for the various UI gestures to the user. You already saw how to change the drag proxy. Beyond the drag proxy, the icons are fair game as well.

22.5.1 *Changing the drag proxy icons*

As we mentioned earlier, the drag proxy is the visual feedback communicated to the user during the D&D process. The easiest way to change it is to use CSS/styles (see chapter 20 for more information).

From a code perspective, the following snippet shows how using CSS declarations you can define which images are used by the drag proxy for each D&D scenario plus how to globally set the drag proxy itself:

```
<fx:Style>
  @namespace mx "library://ns.adobe.com/flex/mx";
```

```
mx|DragManager{
  copy-cursor: Embed(source="/assets/images/copy.png");
  link-cursor: Embed(source="/assets/images/link.png");
  move-cursor: Embed(source="/assets/images/move.png");
  reject-cursor: Embed(source="/assets/images/reject.png");
  default-drag-image-skin:
    ClassReference("assets.skins.DefaultDragImageSkin");
}
</fx:Style>
```

This is obviously a lot easier than changing the drag image, and it lets you leverage your CSS skills. Keep in mind that the `default-drag-image-skin` is used only when the drag proxy isn't explicitly set.

This is great for the icons, but what about skinning the `List` components to show a custom drop indicator? Skinning provides a perfect avenue for this as well.

22.5.2 *List component skinning for drag-and-drop*

In our early examples, we show dragging elements from one `List` to another. In doing so, the dragged item was a copy of the text for that row. What if you wanted to spruce up the drag item and show a different text color? How about customizing the drop indicator on the target `List` to show an orange line to indicate the drop location? All are possible. The next small sections show simple ways to customize both the drag item and the drop indicator.

CONTROLLING THE DRAG ITEM

The drag item typically is a simple `Label` field with the same color as the `List` itself. We're rebels, so we're going to use a custom item renderer to change the dragging font color to orange, as shown in the following snippet:

```
<?xml version="1.0" encoding="utf-8"?>
<s:ItemRenderer xmlns:fx="http://ns.adobe.com/mxml/2009"
                xmlns:s="library://ns.adobe.com/flex/spark"
                xmlns:mx="library://ns.adobe.com/flex/mx"
                autoDrawBackground="true" minHeight="15">
  <s:states>
    <s:State name="normal"/>
    <s:State name="dragging"/>
  </s:states>
  <s:Label id="labelDisplay" fontWeight.dragging="bold"
           color.dragging="0xde7800" />
</s:ItemRenderer>
```

To use this renderer, you reference it in the source `List` like so:

```
<s:List dragEnabled="true" dataProvider="{authors}"
        itemRenderer="assets.renderers.ListItemRenderer" />
```

This handles the source `List`, but we also want to tweak the target `List`.

CONTROLLING THE DROP INDICATOR

A drop indicator shows the location of the dragged item once it's dropped. It's a precursor to the drop and is purely for a visual reference to the user. Create a copy of the default List skin and replace the dropIndicator component with the following snippet:

```
<fx:Component id="dropIndicator">
    <s:Group minWidth="3" minHeight="3">
        <s:Rect left="0" right="0" top="0" bottom="0">
            <s:fill><s:SolidColor color="0xde7800" /></s:fill>
            <s:stroke>
                <s:SolidColorStroke color="0xde7800" weight="5"/>
            </s:stroke>
        </s:Rect>
    </s:Group>
</fx:Component>
```

To use the new skin, set the skinClass property on the target List:

```
<s:List dropEnabled="true" dataProvider="{new ArrayCollection()}"
        skinClass="assets.skins.ListSkin"/>
```

Your drag-and-drop skills have just expanded to knowing how to customize the experience. You can, and should, take the customization further than we've discussed here. With so many customization avenues, we purely want to give you the keys and let you fly around.

So far, we've discussed only Spark components, to an extent. It's worth looking into how to integrate drag-and-drop between Spark and Halo components.

22.5.3 *Mixing drag-and-drop between Spark and Halo*

At the time of this publication, not all Halo components have Spark equivalents. This means, as mentioned in previous chapters, that if you want to use a DataGrid you'll be using the Halo DataGrid. That's perfectly fine, for now. The concern is whether you can use drag-and-drop between the two, and the answer is yes!

Listing 22.12 shows how D&D works between a Halo DataGrid and a Spark List component.

Listing 22.12 Exchanging data between Spark and Halo using drag-and-drop

```
<?xml version="1.0" encoding="utf-8"?>
<s:Application xmlns:fx="http://ns.adobe.com/mxml/2009"
               xmlns:s="library://ns.adobe.com/flex/spark"
               xmlns:mx="library://ns.adobe.com/flex/mx">
  <s:layout>
    <s:HorizontalLayout paddingLeft="20" paddingTop="20" />
  </s:layout>
  <fx:Declarations>
    <s:ArrayCollection id="authors">
      <fx:Object label="Dan Orlando" telephone="555-0000" />
      <fx:Object label="Tariq Ahmed" telephone="555-0001" />
      <fx:Object label="John C. Bland II" telephone="555-0010" />
      <fx:Object label="Joel Hooks" telephone="555-0011" />
    </s:ArrayCollection>
  </fx:Declarations>
```

```
    <s:VGroup>
      <s:Label fontWeight="bold" text="Source" />
      <mx:DataGrid dragEnabled="true" dragMoveEnabled="true"
                   dataProvider="{authors}" />
    </s:VGroup>
    <s:VGroup>
      <s:Label fontWeight="bold" text="Target" />
      <s:List dropEnabled="true" dataProvider="{new ArrayCollection()}" />
    </s:VGroup>
</s:Application>
```

Hrmm…the only thing changed from listing 22.1 is that the source component is an mx:DataGrid rather than an s:List. This is 100% correct and 200% awesome! There are no issues or quirks when moving data from a Halo drag-and-drop component to a Spark drag-and-drop component. Figure 22.14 adds visual proof of this Flex sweetness.

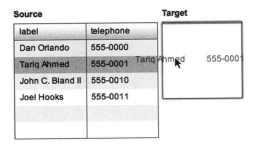

Figure 22.14 Dragging data from an mx:DataGrid to an s:List

Your drag-and-drop journey is complete, and you can now rock your application with some sweet drag-and-drop.

22.6 *Summary*

Drag-and-drop is interesting because it can be as involved as you want it to be. For the most part, Flex does all the hard work for you; you just need to intercept the points at which you want to interject custom business logic.

List-based components come with built-in support for doing most of the work, but you can trap none, some, or all of the D&D events. For non-List-based components, leverage the DragManager as your workhorse. Flex calls your drag-related event handlers and passes you the DragEvent object each time, giving you the information you need to work with.

Don't forget to make your application fun by customizing the user experience. Keep usability the primary reason you're using D&D, and take advantage of its ability to save your users time.

In the next chapter, we'll shift gears to a different subject: charting. Continuing the theme of usability, just as D&D adds interface usability, charting adds usability to information.

Exploring Flex charting

This chapter covers

- Understanding the parts of a chart
- Using chart series
- Types of charts
- Customizing charts

Charting is the visual display of data using graphical elements called charts. If you ever need a way to sell Flex to your organization, charting will help you do it. Management loves charting; give the bosses a taste of Flex's charts, and you'll soon have them addicted and begging for more.

Flex charts are so compelling because, unlike using static charts (and even some animated ones), with Flex you can create interactive and engaging dashboard experiences. This is especially true if you combine charting with effects to seal the deal.

In this chapter, we'll explore what makes up a chart, the charts that come with Flex, and how to customize them. Let's start with an introduction to charting.

23.1   Introduction to charting

Flex's charting feature comes as part of the Professional Edition. But even if you haven't paid for that version, you can still build charts—they'll just have a Flex Charting Trial watermark superimposed on the image.

Flex's charting engine is incredibly flexible from a developer's point of view. You can control what each specific data point looks like, build powerful dashboards, employ multiple axes, and support various forms of user interaction.

For example, you can handle the event when a user clicks a particular data point and use that information to drive another chart or pull up data related to that data point. Your charts can be programmed to support drag-and-drop operations and let the user draw selections around a collection of data points.

In Flex, all charts are derived from either the `Cartesian` charting class or the `PolarChart` class. Cartesian charting is premised on the Cartesian coordinate system of using x and y coordinates to define data points on horizontal and vertical axes. The `PolarChart` class is used to define regions within a circular or radial space, although the only chart derived from this is the pie chart. Let's look at the parts of typical Flex chart and the types of charts you can create.

23.1.1 Chart parts

Charts comprise various pieces that make them work; those parts exist as MXML components and ActionScript class equivalents. The parts of a chart are listed in table 23.1.

Table 23.1 Parts of a chart

Chart part	Description
Chart	The chart itself, the framework to which all other parts are connected.
Series	A collection of related data points.
Axis/axes	Horizontal and vertical axes. Flex's charts are two-dimensional only, but you can have multiple axes.
Axis renderers	A powerful mechanism to control how lines and labels are displayed.
Elements	Anything else that needs to be displayed in the chart area. For example, you can display special icons at certain points, grid lines, annotations, and so on.
Labels	Textual information about the chart's axes and series.

They may not sound like much, but with those pieces you can produce an enormous variety of charting experiences for your users. Several types of charts are available in Flex. Let's have a look at those now.

23.1.2 Chart types overview

You want charts? We've got charts—nine types of charts, as listed in table 23.2.

We know you're anxious to start using these. Before you do so, let's prepare by discussing a hypothetical FlexMoto exotic car company for which you'll build a sales dashboard. A dashboard is a quick way for a user to get a high-level overview of a large amount of data. Charts make this data easily digestible with a graphical representation.

Type	MXML component and class	Series component and class
Area	AreaChart	AreaSeries
Bar	BarChart	BarSeries
Bubble	BubbleChart	BubbleSeries
Candlestick	CandleStick	CandlestickSeries
Column	ColumnChart	ColumnSeries
HLOC	HLOCChart	HLOCSeries
Line	LineChart	LineSeries
Pie	PieChart	PieSeries
Plot	PlotChart	PlotSeries

**Table 23.2
Types of charts in Flex 4**

Underlying every chart is the data being represented, so let's look at how charts use data in a series.

23.2 *Setting the stage with series and data*

We'll set the stage by talking about how charts display data in the first place and how you'll facilitate that display in the examples.

Charts display collections of related data in what's called a *series*, and each chart has at least one series. A ubiquitous usage of a series is to display financial information broken into periodic time internals—for example, sales by month or quarterly revenues.

The series is the heart of a chart, and each chart type has a corresponding series component/class to go along with it. Figure 23.1 illustrates a line chart that has a single series with a data point at each quarter in the year.

A series is nothing without its data, and that information traditionally is in tabular form. In the FlexMoto example, let's assume the data is as shown in table 23.3.

In the real world, you'd retrieve this data from a database using a backend data service such as a web service or a remote object (see chapter 14) and assign that to an

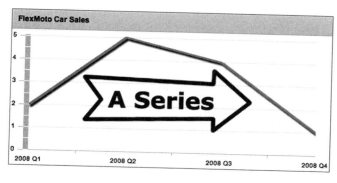

Figure 23.1   This chart has one series representing the number of cars sold per quarter.

Table 23.3 FlexMoto data that will be used for the examples

Interval	FerrariUnits	FerrariSales	PorscheUnits	PorscheSales
2008 Q1	2	2.32	2	0.180
2008 Q2	5	7.82	3	0.240
2008 Q3	4	6.92	7	0.420
2008 Q4	1	1.80	12	1.180

`ArrayCollection`. The result would be an `ArrayCollection` similar to the hardcoded example in listing 23.1 (just to give you an idea).

Listing 23.1 FlexMoto's data in the form of an `ArrayCollection`

```
salesAC:ArrayCollection = new ArrayCollection( [
{interval: "2008 Q1", ferrariUnits:2, ferrariSales:2.32, porscheUnits:2,
    porscheSales: 0.180},
{interval: "2008 Q2", ferrariUnits:5, ferrariSales:7.82, porscheUnits:3,
    porscheSales: 0.240},
{interval: "2008 Q3", ferrariUnits:4, ferrariSales:6.92, porscheUnits:7,
    porscheSales: 0.420},
{interval: "2008 Q4", ferrariUnits:1, ferrariSales:1.80, porscheUnits:12,
    porscheSales: 1.180}
] );
```

Alternatively, data in the form of XML is always a popular choice, and you'll use this form in the examples. Listing 23.2 contains the XML version of the data.

Listing 23.2 data.xml: FlexMoto's sales data in XML form

```
<salesdata>
  <all>
    <data interval="2008 Q1" ferrariUnits="2" ferrariSales="2.32"
                    porscheUnits="2" porscheSales="0.180"/>

    <data interval="2008 Q2" ferrariUnits="5" ferrariSales="7.82"
                    porscheUnits="3" porscheSales="0.240" />
    <data interval="2008 Q3" ferrariUnits="4" ferrariSales="6.92"
                    porscheUnits="7" porscheSales="0.420"/>
    <data interval="2008 Q4" ferrariUnits="1" ferrariSales="1.80"
                    porscheUnits="12" porscheSales="1.180"/>
  </all>
</salesdata>
```

Now that you have your data, you can move forward to create charts.

23.3 Creating charts

A convenient feature of charting is that you can create a chart, and if you don't like it, you can change it to a different type of chart with minimal effort. In this section, we'll show you how to create a chart and progressively add pieces to it to build it out.

23.3.1 *Invoking a chart*

Creating a chart involves picking the chart type you want, using its corresponding series component to plot the data points, and providing at least a horizontal axis.

TIP   The chart is the foundation upon which a series and other pieces build.

Using the FlexMoto sales data, let's start by using a line chart to display how many Ferraris and Porsches have been sold quarter by quarter (see the following listing).

Listing 23.3   Line chart displaying the number of units sold by car type

```
<?xml version="1.0" encoding="utf-8"?>
<s:Application xmlns:fx="http://ns.adobe.com/mxml/2009"
  xmlns:s="library://ns.adobe.com/flex/spark"
  xmlns:mx="library://ns.adobe.com/flex/mx" >
  <fx:Declarations>
    <fx:XML id="salesDataXML" source="data.xml"/>
    <s:XMLListCollection id="salesData"
      source="{salesDataXML.all.data}"/>
  </fx:Declarations>
  <s:Panel title="FlexMoto Car Sales" width="500" height="250">
    <s:layout><s:VerticalLayout/></s:layout>
    <ns:LineChart id="salesChart" dataProvider="{salesData}"
      height="100%" width="100%">
      <ns:horizontalAxis>
        <ns:CategoryAxis categoryField="@interval"/>
      </ns:horizontalAxis>
      <ns:series>
        <ns:LineSeries yField="@ferrariUnits"/>
        <ns:LineSeries yField="@porscheUnits"/>
      </ns:series>
    </ns:LineChart>
  </s:Panel>
</s:Application>
```

Annotations:
- **Nonvisual MXML must be in declarations tag**
- **Spark containers must have layout assigned**
- **Retrieve and set up data**
- **Set up horizontal axis to display quarters**
- **Set up series for each car manufacturer**

Compiling and running the application gives you a chart with two line series on it, resembling figure 23.2.

Note a few things in this example:

- The Y axis represents the value in the series. It's sometimes called the value axis.
- The Y axis by default starts at 0 and goes to the largest value found in the entire series.
- The X axis represents the category and is known as the category axis.
- The X axis labels by default are spread evenly across the width of the chart.

That was fairly painless, considering you created a chart in only nine lines of code. But you're missing something: How is a user to know what each line color represents? This is where a *legend* comes in.

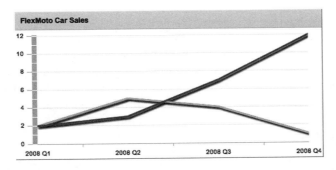

Figure 23.2 FlexMoto's car sales by units sold for each type of car, displayed using a line chart. The two lines, or series, clearly show the sales for each brand.

23.3.2 Adding a legend

A legend is a visual guide whose purpose is to map each series to a context. We could have said that a legend is used to map a color to a series, which is true to an extent, but a series can be differentiated by more than just a color. For example, a series may plot itself with a different transparency level, pattern (such as dashed lines), or texture (such as gradient colors).

Let's add a legend using the code in the next listing.

Listing 23.4 Adding a legend so users know what each line means

```
<mx:Legend dataProvider="{salesChart}"/>        Uses chart as
<mx:LineChart id="salesChart"                   data source
            dataProvider="{salesData}"
            height="100%" width="100%">
    <mx:horizontalAxis>
        <mx:CategoryAxis
            categoryField="@interval"/>
    </mx:horizontalAxis>
    <mx:series>
        <mx:LineSeries
            yField="@ferrariUnits"
            displayName="Ferrari Count"/>
        <mx:LineSeries                          Tells legend to
            yField="@porscheUnits"              label each series
            displayName="Porsche Count"/>
    </mx:series>
</mx:LineChart>
```

This code produces an application that has a Legend component at the top. You should observe a few things:

- The Legend component exists outside of the chart tag.
- The legend uses the chart's id property as the source for its data.
- The legend that has a reference to the chart examines all of the chart's child series and extracts the design of each series (such as its color) as well as the displayName property used for each series.

You have a fully viable chart at this point. But if you need to change to a different type of chart, doing so isn't difficult.

23.3.3 *Changing chart types*

How easy it is to switch from one chart type to another depends on the specifics, but even in the worst case it doesn't require much effort. To cover every permutation wouldn't be of much value; all we want to do here is give you a sense of the process.

Imagine that you've taken your FlexMoto sales dashboard to your boss. He's the kind of guy who's never happy and who has a thing against line charts, and he prefers that you switch to a different type of chart. Not a problem; let's change to an area chart, as shown in the following listing.

Listing 23.5   FlexMoto's sales dashboard switched to an area chart

```
<mx:AreaChart id="salesChart"
        dataProvider="{salesData}"
        height="100%" width="100%">
<mx:horizontalAxis>
    <mx:CategoryAxis categoryField="@interval"/>
</mx:horizontalAxis>
<mx:series>
    <mx:AreaSeries yField="@ferrariUnits"
            displayName="Ferrari Count"             Alpha property
            alpha="0.5"/>                    ◁┘ controls transparency
    <mx:AreaSeries yField="@porscheUnits"
            displayName="Porsche Count"
            alpha="0.5"/>
</mx:series>
</mx:AreaChart>
```

All you've done is to change `line` to `area` in the code and call it a day. Figures 23.3 and 23.4 show how the chart looks now.

One problem, as you can see, is that the Ferrari series is blocked by the Porsche series. Here, you solve that by customizing the chart and controlling the transparency level (using the `alpha` property). We'll get further into customization later in this chapter.

> **TIP**   The examples use the @ character because you're accessing attributes of an XML node. You wouldn't need it if your data came from an `ArrayCollection`.

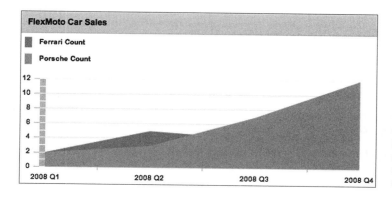

Figure 23.3   Because the area chart defaults to laying one series on top of another, you can see only where one series exceeds the other.

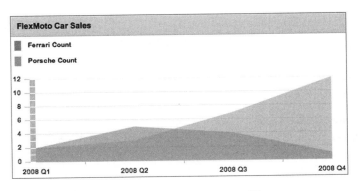

Figure 23.4 Using transparency levels lets you see where one series overlaps the other.

Unfortunately, your boss still isn't happy. He wants you to switch to using a bar chart—which, although still fairly easy, requires a bit more work (see the following listing).

Listing 23.6 A bar chart, which uses a vertical axis

```
<mx:BarChart id="salesChart"
        dataProvider="{salesData}"
        height="100%" width="100%">
  <mx:verticalAxis>
    <mx:CategoryAxis categoryField="@interval"/>
  </mx:verticalAxis>
  <mx:series>
    <mx:BarSeries xField="@ferrariUnits"
          displayName="Ferrari Count"/>
    <mx:BarSeries xField="@porscheUnits"
          displayName="Porsche Count"/>
  </mx:series>
</mx:BarChart>
```

◁── **Required because bar charts use Y axis for categories**

◁

◁

Listing 23.6 uses the same approach of using the `<BarChart>` and `<BarSeries>` where necessary, but a bar chart uses the vertical (Y) axis to display groupings. See figure 23.5.

Charts can be supplied with data from a variety of sources. Many times you'll want to apply filters to the data to clean the data or prevent null values from appearing in the dataset.

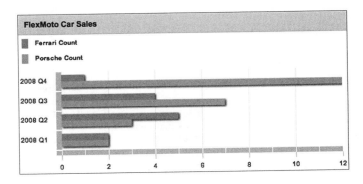

Figure 23.5 Switching to a bar chart also requires switching to using a vertical axis for the category axis.

23.3.4 *Filtering chart data*

Flex 4 provides three ways to filter the data in your chart series:

- filterData
- filterDataValues
- filterFunction

filterData is the most basic of the three filtering options. It can be set to either true or false. When set to true, filterData will remove invalid values from your dataset, including null, NAN, undefined, and values that are out of the predefined ranges set for your chart axes. Filtering takes a toll on the performance of your charts. If you know for certain that your data is clean and free of invalid values, this property should be set to false (which is the default). If you've set the filterFunction or filter-DataValues properties of your Series, the filterData value will be ignored.

filterDataValues provides a finer grain of control over what values are filtered from your dataset. Like filterData, filterDataValues gives you the ability to filter null, NAN, undefined, and out-of-range values from your dataset. The three possible values for the filterDataValues property are none, nulls, or outsideRange. For optimum performance when you know your data is clean, choose none. To filter out null, NAN, and undefined values, choose the nulls value. To filter null, NAN, undefined, and out-of-range values, choose outsideRange. If your Series has a filterFunction set, this property will be ignored.

By far the most powerful way to filter a chart Series is by setting the filter-Function property. This allows you to supply a function that can perform complex custom checks on your data. Listing 23.7 shows an example of a filter function applied to an AreaSeries.

Listing 23.7 filterFunction supplied to an AreaSeries

```
<fx:Script>
  <![CDATA[
    import mx.charts.series.items.ColumnSeriesItem;
    private function filterValues(data:Array):Array
    {
      var cache:Array = [];
      for(var i:int = 0;i<data.length;i++)
      {
        var item:ColumnSeriesItem = data[i] as ColumnSeriesItem;
        if(item.yNumber > 0 && item.yNumber < 60)
          cache.push(item)                              ◁⎤ Adds item
      }                                                   ⎟ that meets
      return cache;                    ◁⎤ Returns Array of ⎦ requirements
    }                                    ⎟ items that met
  ]]>                                    ⎦ requirements
</fx:Script>
```

A filterFunction takes an Array that contains all of the items in the Series and returns an Array of items that have met the criteria you've defined in the function.

Listing 23.7 checks the data on the items in a `ColumnSeries` and filters out those items that have a `yNumber` value less than 0 and greater than 60.

The charts used in these examples all support a capability called *stacking*, but there are different ways charts can stack or cluster their display.

23.4 *Stacking charts*

A number of charts support the ability to stack their series; stacking is useful when you need to show an accumulative visualization of data. The following charts support stacking:

- Area chart
- Bar chart
- Column chart

They support stacking through the use of their `type` property. The possible stacking options for this field are as follows:

- `clustered`—Clusters the data points in the series by category. This is the default for the bar chart and column chart, which you saw in figure 23.4. Note that this type isn't available for the area chart.
- `overlaid`—Layers one series over another (think onion skin) in the order in which the series are defined in the code. This is the default for the area chart (figure 23.3). It's used to contrast one series from another.
- `stacked`—Stacks one series on top of another (think Lego blocks). It's used to demonstrate how each series makes up a whole (via the cumulative effect). Each series accumulates toward the total value.
- `100%`—The same as `stacked`, but each series accumulates to 100% (similar to how a pie chart works).

Listing 23.5 used an area chart to show sales volume, but its default behavior was to use an `overlaid` display to layer one series over the other. To show how the sales of each car accumulate to a total, you can switch the `type` property to `stacked`:

```
<mx:AreaChart id="salesChart"
        type="stacked"
        dataProvider="{salesData}"
        height="100%" width="100%">
...
</mx:AreaChart>
```

Figure 23.6 shows how the display provides a different perspective than figure 23.3, even though they're both area charts of the same data.

Similarly, if you switch the type to other values, you get different visual perspectives. Each perspective tells part of the story.

Now that you have a feel for creating charts, let's take a closer look at the types of charts that come with Flex.

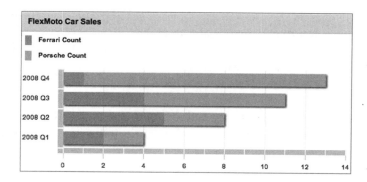

Figure 23.6   Changing the area chart to a stacked mode accumulates each series toward a whole.

23.5   Exploring chart types

From what you've seen so far, there's not a drastic difference (codewise) between using one chart or another. But you also saw a case (the bar chart) where the difference was significant enough to require additional details.

In this section, we discuss each of the charting types and how to create them, as well as provide tips on the business cases for which they're most useful.

23.5.1   Area charts

Area charts are like line charts, except the area under the line is filled in. By controlling transparency levels, you can make your charts appear either *layered*, where you can visually see the differences and overlap, or *stacked*, where one series appears to be stacked on top of another. Although line charts and area charts are similar, they differ in that an area chart is particularly good at representing volume trends.

Using the `AreaSeries` component, you can use a number of parameters to control the display of the series.

To show you something interesting, let's look at the `minField` property. Area charts are used to represent volume, and that volume can have a specific range of values.

NOTE   The area chart supports stacking; see section 23.3.

Suppose you have temperature data specifying daily high and low values for each day. You can use an `AreaSeries` defined as follows:

```
<mx:AreaSeries yField="@max" minField="@min" displayName="Temperature" />
```

This results in figure 23.7, where the temperate range is filled in between the low and high values.

This is an interesting way to look at data: Changes to the shape tell a story without users having to look at the numbers. Where the width expands, you're able to determine that differences emerge, and as the width becomes thinner, the variance converges.

Using the area chart's stacking abilities, you can display many types of stories that the data can tell. The `overlaid` type can highlight and contrast differences and

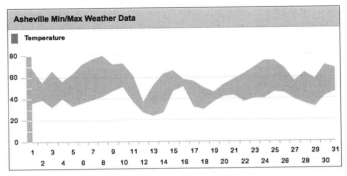

Figure 23.7 Using the `minField` property, you can start each data point from an arbitrary value.

commonalities in data, and `stacked` and `100%` show you the cumulative effect of all the series combined.

Although the area chart supports these stacking modes, it doesn't support clustered series—this is something supported by bar charts and column charts.

23.5.2 Bar charts and column charts

Bar charts and column charts are the same thing; the only difference is that a bar chart draws horizontally, whereas a column chart is vertical. Oddly enough, if you say "bar chart" to someone, the first thing they think of is what Flex calls a column chart.

Although these charts can be used to display trending information (information that changes over time), they're particularly strong displaying *clustered* information—data clumped together by some category.

NOTE Bar charts and column charts support stacking; see section 23.3.

In figure 23.5, you saw a bar chart used to show how many cars by type were sold over each given quarter. Bar charts are perfectly useful for showing this time-bound information, but consider the data in this next listing.

Listing 23.8 data.xml: political party affiliation by age demographics

```
<enrollment>
  <all>
    <data category="18-29" republican="25" democrat="30" other="45"/>
    <data category="30-49" republican="29" democrat="32" other="39"/>
    <data category="50-64" republican="28" democrat="35" other="37"/>
    <data category="65+" republican="30" democrat="40" other="30"/>
  </all>
</enrollment>
```

Listing 23.8 shows statistical information broken down by age groups (the category); the percentage of support from that demographic bracket is listed for each political party. To visualize this information, you can employ a bar chart, as shown in the following listing.

Listing 23.9   Using a bar chart to show clustered information

```
<mx:Legend dataProvider="{partyChart}"/>
<mx:BarChart id="partyChart"
        dataProvider="{partyData}"
        height="100%" width="100%">
  <mx:verticalAxis>
    <mx:CategoryAxis categoryField="@category" title="Age Group"/>
  </mx:verticalAxis>
  <mx:horizontalAxis>
    <mx:LinearAxis title="Party Identification"/>
  </mx:horizontalAxis>
  <mx:series>
    <mx:BarSeries xField="@republican"
            displayName="Republican"/>                    ◁┐
    <mx:BarSeries xField="@democrat                        ◁─  Uses xField
            displayName="Democrat" />                           because chart
    <mx:BarSeries xField="@other"                               is horizontal
            displayName="Independent, Other or Do Not Know "/>  ◁┘
  </mx:series>
</mx:BarChart>
```

After compiling and running the application, you get the chart shown in figure 23.8.

No time intervals here—figure 23.8 shows the statistical breakdown for each age cluster. Bar charts and column charts support stacking, and their default mode, as previously shown, is to cluster each series by category.

You can change the type to use the other stacking values. To demonstrate, let's switch to a column chart and set the `type` property to `stacked` (see the next listing).

Listing 23.10   Using a stacked column chart

```
<s:Panel title="Political Party Identification"
     width="500" height="250">
  <s:layout><s:VerticalLayout/></s:layout>
  <mx:Legend dataProvider="{partyChart}"/>
  <mx:BarChart id="partyChart" type="stacked"
        dataProvider="{partyData}"
        height="100%" width="100%">
    <mx:verticalAxis>
      <mx:CategoryAxis categoryField="@category"           Defines categories
            title="Age Group"/>              ◁┘            on X axis
    </mx:verticalAxis>
    <mx:horizontalAxis>
      <mx:LinearAxis title="Party Identification"/>    ◁───  Defines values
    </mx:horizontalAxis>
    <mx:series>
      <mx:BarSeries xField="@republican"
            displayName="Republican"/>
      <mx:BarSeries xField="@democrat"
            displayName="Democrat" />
      <mx:BarSeries xField="@other"
            displayName="Independent, Other or Do Not Know "/>
    </mx:series>
  </mx:BarChart>
</s:Panel>
```

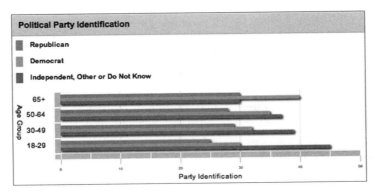

Figure 23.8 This bar chart shows statistics clustered by an age-range category. Ages make up the vertical axis, and party affiliation makes up the horizontal axis.

Note that you have to switch to using yField because column charts are vertical in nature: The height of each data point requires a Y-axis value. Similarly, because the horizontal axis displays each category, you switch back to the horizontalAxis.

The values now accumulate to 100—this is because the data represents percentages. But suppose the data represented the number of votes that each party has acquired; you could set type to 100% to achieve the same result (Flex would automatically calculate the percentages for you).

Bar charts and column charts can show time series with no problem, and a unique advantage comes into play when you need to show clustered information using some arbitrary grouping. But if trending against time is what you're after, you want a line chart.

23.5.3 Line charts

Line charts are the classic way to display data points that represent a trend over time. Because you used a line chart back in listings 23.3 and 23.4, we've covered the primary ground already.

We have something new to show you: the interpolateValues property. This property lets Flex fill in the gaps for missing data points if needed.

In this example, let's purposely take out one of the data points. Flex can then only draw lines from the spot at which it has contiguous data points, as shown in figure 23.9.

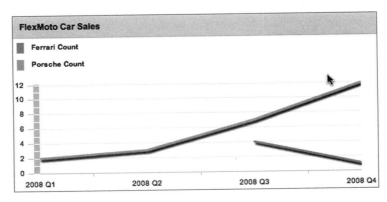

Figure 23.9 Without contiguous data points, the Ferrari series is broken.

You can fix this by setting `interpolateValues` to true:

```
<mx:LineSeries interpolateValues="true" yField="@ferrariUnits"
    displayName="Ferrari Count" />
```

After rerunning the application with this setting, the line is able to continue as Flex fills in the gaps.

Odds are that you're likely to use line charts in your career as a Flex developer; they're versatile and great for historical trending. The other value of line charts, along with bar/column charts, is that people are familiar with them and are able to digest what they display. If you want to get away from the traditional charts, look no further than the bubble chart.

23.5.4 Bubble charts

Bubble charts have been around for awhile, and you've probably seen examples, but have you seen one actively used in your workplace? They've been slowly gaining traction in the business intelligence space, but some argue that their usefulness is limited.

Bubble charts let you add a third dimension by not only plotting X and Y coordinates but also using the size of a bubble as a way of communicating scale (for example, volume, intensity, weight, or size). Flex supports only two-dimensional charts, so this type of chart allows you to get around that limitation.

The `BubbleChart` component supports some unique properties you'll want to be aware of (see table 23.4).

Table 23.4   Additional properties of bubble charts

Property	Type	Description
minRadius*	Number	Minimum value for a data point; defaults to 0
maxRadius*	Number	Maximum value for a data point; defaults to 50

* These values are used to calculate how to scale the bubbles.

Next, to complement the `BubbleChart` component, the `BubbleSeries` component has a unique property among the list in table 23.5.

Table 23.5   `BubbleSeries` properties

Property	Type	Description
xField	String	Optional. Field that contains the related category value. If not specified, the series looks for the category specified in the `CategoryAxis` component.
yField	String	Field that contains the category/value field.
radiusField	String	Field that contains the value for the size of the bubble.

So far, you've been plotting the number of units sold in FlexMoto's sales data (see listing 23.2). To add an extra dimension, you can include sales revenues. Listing 23.11 does so by using a `BubbleChart` component to plot units sold and using the sales revenues as a basis for the size of the bubbles.

Listing 23.11 Bubble chart that visually demonstrates sales revenue

```
<mx:Legend dataProvider="{salesChart}"/>
<mx:BubbleChart id="salesChart" maxRadius="20"
                dataProvider="{salesData}"
                height="100%" width="100%">
    <mx:horizontalAxis>
        <mx:CategoryAxis categoryField="@interval"/>
    </mx:horizontalAxis>
    <mx:series>
        <mx:BubbleSeries
            yField="@ferrariUnits" radiusField="@ferrariSales"
            displayName="Ferrari Count"/>
        <mx:BubbleSeries
            yField="@porscheUnits" radiusField="@porscheSales"
            displayName="Porsche Count"/>
    </mx:series>
</mx:BubbleChart>
```

Look at how the data is visually communicated in figure 23.10.

Adding that third dimension helps put a different perspective on the same data. In a line chart it may look like management should focus on selling Porsches, but on a bubble chart (figure 23.10) Porsche revenues are overshadowed by the larger Ferrari sales revenues.

In going back to the question of whether bubble charts are useful, our opinion is that they definitely are, thanks to that third dimension of information. The key to business intelligence is being able to communicate the story behind the numbers, and the more dimensions you're able to leverage, the more rounded the picture.

The only real issue with bubble charts is that because they're not common, people aren't used to them and aren't immediately sure how to interpret what they're seeing. If you use a bubble chart, be sure to provide thorough training or help information for the end user.

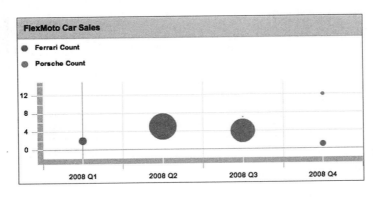

Figure 23.10 A bubble chart tells a different story by adding a third dimension.

The bubble chart isn't alone in its learning challenge for users. Candlestick and HLOC charts share some of that challenge.

23.5.5 *Candlestick and HLOC charts*

You may have seen a candlestick and/or high-low-open-close (HLOC) chart in your walks through life—they're heavily used in the financial industry to illustrate granular levels of information. Without this type of chart, you'd need to use many individual charts, which would clutter the screen and be difficult to assimilate.

Candlesticks and HLOC charts are four charts in one. A user of financial information can easily interpret these four sets of data as well as examine the relationships between them.

Here's how candlesticks work:

- A vertical line represents the high and low (the top is the high, and the bottom is the low). For financial data, this line indicates the range of prices for that day (or whatever the time interval is).
- A rectangular box (a.k.a. the *body*) floats on top of the line.
- If the box is hollow, then the top of the box is the closing price and the bottom of the box is the opening price: The closing price is higher than the opening, meaning that the financial vehicle (such as a stock) appreciated.
- If the box is filled in, then the top of the box is the opening price and the bottom is the closing price: The financial vehicle depreciated.

Figure 23.11 illustrates.

The varying size of the body (the rectangle) tells the user different perspectives. For example, a longer body indicates increased buying or selling pressure; a shorter body represents consolidation. Long, hollow candlesticks indicate strong buying pressure (due to aggressive buyers); long, solid candlesticks indicate strong selling pressure (a bearish market).

HLOC charts work the same way, except that they use left and right sticks to indicate the opening and closing prices. Here's how they work:

- A vertical line represents the high and low (the top is the high, and the bottom is the low). This line indicates the range of prices for that day (or whatever the time interval is).
- A left tick indicates the opening price.
- A right tick indicates the closing price.

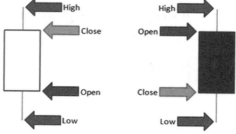

Figure 23.11 Candlestick charts have a "wick" on either end that shows the high/low points for the data. Unfilled blocks have close at the top, and filled blocks have open at the top.

One key difference is that candlesticks require all four data points. Despite the HLOC's name, the open value is optional. Figure 23.12 shows how to interpret an HLOC chart.

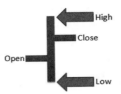

Figure 23.12 HLOC charts display the high and low of data with a horizontal bar on the left showing the open and another horizontal bar on the right showing the close.

To use these charts, you need the four data points to create the `Candlestick-Series` and `HLOCSeries`, as listed in table 23.6.

Table 23.6 `CandlestickSeries` and `HLOCSeries` properties

Property	Type	Description
highField	String	Field that contains the high value
lowField	String	Field that contains the low value
openField	String	Field that contains the open value; optional for `HLOCSeries`
closeField	String	Field that contains the close value
xField	String	Field that contains the category value for the X axis; optional

Imagine that the CEO of FlexMoto wants to chart the stock price using a candlestick chart. Assume that listing 23.12 contains the historical stock price data.

Listing 23.12 hloc.xml: FlexMoto's stock-price history

```
<stockdata>
  <ticker>
    <data interval="09/01/2008" high="54" low="40" open="53" close="43"/>
    <data interval="09/02/2008" high="69" low="37" open="62" close="40"/>
    <data interval="09/03/2008" high="62" low="52" open="55" close="60"/>
    <data interval="09/04/2008" high="65" low="30" open="60" close="52"/>
    <data interval="09/05/2008" high="60" low="20" open="42" close="48"/>
  </ticker>
</stockdata>
```

You can use a `CandlestickChart` as shown in listing 23.13 to plot the data.

Listing 23.13 Candlestick chart displaying stock prices

```
<fx:Declarations>
  <fx:XML id="stockDataXML" source="data.xml"/>
  <s:XMLListCollection id="stockData"
          source="{stockDataXML.ticker.data}"/>
</fx:Declarations>
<s:Panel title="FlexMoto Stock Price"
    width="500" height="250">
  <s:layout><s:VerticalLayout/></s:layout>
  <mx:CandlestickChart id="stockChart"
              dataProvider="{stockData}"
              height="100%" width="100%">
```

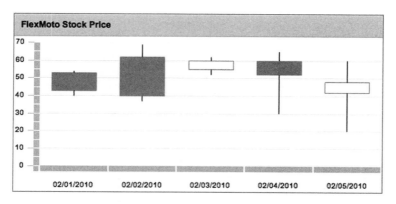

Figure 23.13 Candlestick chart used to display stock price information. The price of the stock is on the vertical axis, and the date is on the horizontal axis.

```
    <mx:horizontalAxis>
      <mx:CategoryAxis
        categoryField="@interval"/>
    </mx:horizontalAxis>
    <mx:series>
      <mx:CandlestickSeries
        highField="@high" lowField="@low"
        openField="@open" closeField="@close"/>
    </mx:series>
  </mx:CandlestickChart>
</s:Panel>
```

The results of this application are shown in figure 23.13.

Similarly, if you switch from `<mx:CandlestickChart>` to `<mx:HLOCChart>` (and its related series), the result is the chart shown in figure 23.14.

The financial context is the most prevalent for these types of charts, although if you're creative with your data you can supply business and management folks with nonfinancial data as well.

Unless you're in the financial industry dealing with stock prices, candlestick and HLOC charts, although interesting, aren't going to be of much use. Let's move back into more common charts that you'll likely be using.

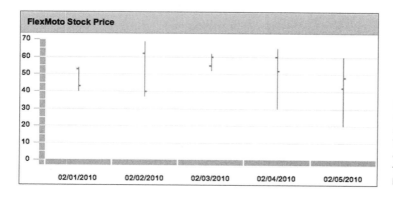

Figure 23.14 HLOC chart used to display stock price information. The price of the stock is on the vertical axis and the date is on the horizontal axis.

23.5.6 *Pie charts*

This type of chart is one that everyone is familiar with—we're used to partitioned segments that make up a whole. The size of each slice is an indicator of weight, importance, or impact.

Because a pie chart represents components that make up a whole, you need data that's representative of that whole (trending data isn't much use for a pie chart). In this case, you'll use a pie chart to display the annual revenues of FlexMoto, broken down by brand sold. Here's the raw sales data:

```
<salesdata>
  <revenues>
    <data brand="Ferrari" rev="987265"/>
    <data brand="Porsche" rev="678293"/>
    <data brand="BMW" rev="567987"/>
    <data brand="Mercedes" rev="210697"/>
  </revenues>
</salesdata>
```

Using this data, you can use a `PieChart` component with a single `PieSeries` component that looks at the brand and revenue fields (see the following listing).

> **Listing 23.14 Pie chart displaying annual revenues by brand**

```
<mx:Legend dataProvider="{salesChart}"/>
<mx:PieChart id="salesChart"
        dataProvider="{salesData}"
        height="100%" width="100%">
  <mx:series>
    <mx:PieSeries field="@rev" nameField="@brand"
           labelPosition="outside"/>

  </mx:series>
</mx:PieChart>
```

The result is a pie chart that slices up each brand by revenue and provides a legend; see figure 23.15.

Here's something neat you can do. Normally, a pie chart has a single series (as shown in figure 23.15). But what if you try more than one pie series? Let's find out.

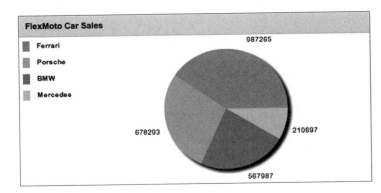

Figure 23.15 Annual revenues by brand, displayed using a pie chart. Each piece of the pie represents a particular brand's sales.

You'll add another set of data to represent profits; pie.xml is now as shown in the following listing.

Listing 23.15   pie.xml: updated to include both revenue and profit data

```
<salesdata>
  <revenues>
    <data brand="Ferrari" rev="987265"/>
    <data brand="Porsche" rev="678293"/>
    <data brand="BMW" rev="567987"/>
    <data brand="Mercedes" rev="210697"/>
  </revenues>
  <profits>
    <data brand="Ferrari" profit="87265"/>
    <data brand="Porsche" profit="78293"/>
    <data brand="BMW" profit="67987"/>
    <data brand="Mercedes" profit="10697"/>
  </profits>
</salesdata>
```

Now, let's modify listing 23.14 to include both sets of data and create a PieSeries component for each one (see the next listing).

Listing 23.16   Code extended to create a pie chart with two series

```
<fx:Declarations>
  <fx:XML id="salesDataXML" source="data.xml"/>
  <s:XMLListCollection id="salesData"
          source="{salesDataXML.revenues.data}"/>
  <s:XMLListCollection id="profitData"              ⊲  Creates second
          source="{salesDataXML.profits.data}"/>         set of data
</fx:Declarations>
<s:Panel title="FlexMoto Car Sales"
    width="500" height="250">
  <s:layout><s:HorizontalLayout/></s:layout>
  <mx:Legend dataProvider="{salesChart}"/>
  <mx:PieChart id="salesChart"
        dataProvider="{salesData}"
        height="100%" width="100%">
    <mx:series>
      <mx:PieSeries field="@rev" nameField="@brand"
            labelPosition="callout" calloutGap="50"/>      Creates second
      <mx:PieSeries                                         PieSeries (note
      dataProvider="{profitData}"                        ⊲ its dataProvider)
            field="@profit" nameField="@brand"
            labelPosition="inside"/>
    </mx:series>
  </mx:PieChart>
</s:Panel>
```

Note how the second pie series specifies a dataProvider; it does this because otherwise it will default to the data that the pie chart is using.

There's always more than one way to do something, and listing 23.16 demonstrates how you can handle two complete sets of data. You could instead structure your data as follows:

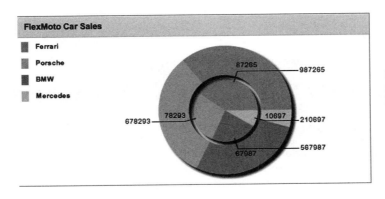

Figure 23.16 Annual revenues and profits by brand, displayed using nested pie charts. Each piece of the inner pie represents a particular brand's sales. Each piece of the outer pie represents a brand's profits.

```
<data brand="ferrari" rev="987265" profit="23424"/>
<data brand="porsche" rev="678293" profit="42323"/>
```

Then you wouldn't need to bother specifying the `dataProvider`, and the code would be as simple as this:

```
<mx:PieSeries field="@rev" nameField="@brand"
    labelPosition="callout" calloutGap="50"/>
<mx:PieSeries field="@profit" nameField="@brand"
    labelPosition="inside"/>
```

The output is a pie chart within a pie chart, as shown in figure 23.16.

The biggest advantage is that you're able to save desktop space by combining pie series—and you could argue that it provides a business use case in which you're able to compare the relative portions of related data sets.

You've almost finished learning about chart types. The last one is the plot chart.

23.5.7 *Plot charts*

The plot chart is simple. Other charts calculate where to draw data points by examining the data and determining how to translate it onto the chart. A plot is just a grid—you tell it specifically where each data point goes. In this example, you'll use x and y coordinate data to plot two different sets of data, as shown in the next listing.

Listing 23.17   plot.xml: data to be plotted

```
<plotdata>
  <one>
    <data x="1" y="5"/>
    <data x="3" y="8"/>
    <data x="3" y="9"/>
    <data x="5" y="9"/>
  </one>
  <two>
    <data x="2" y="1"/>
    <data x="2" y="3"/>
    <data x="4" y="7"/>
```

```
        <data x="4" y="4"/>
    </two>
</plotdata>
```

This data is consumed by a plot chart with two plot series in the following listing.

Listing 23.18   Plot chart used to display two series

```
<fx:Declarations>
    <fx:XML id="plotDataXML" source="data.xml"/>
    <s:XMLListCollection id="plotOneData"
            source="{plotDataXML.one.data}"/>
    <s:XMLListCollection id="plotTwoData"
            source="{plotDataXML.two.data}"/>
</fx:Declarations>
<s:Panel title="FlexMoto Car plotOne"
        width="500" height="250">
    <s:layout><s:HorizontalLayout/></s:layout>
    <mx:Legend dataProvider="{plotChart}"/>
    <mx:PlotChart id="plotChart"
            height="100%" width="100%">
        <mx:series>
            <mx:PlotSeries dataProvider="{plotOneData}"
                    displayName="One"
                    xField="@x" yField="@y"/>
            <mx:PlotSeries dataProvider="{plotTwoData}"
                    displayName="Two"
                    xField="@x" yField="@y"/>
        </mx:series>
    </mx:PlotChart>
</s:Panel>
```

❶ Creates two sets of data

❷ Each series points to related data set

First, you separate the data in the XML file into two separate variables ❶. Each plot series ❷ points to one of those variables. Look at the results in figure 23.17; you can see how each series is assigned a color and shape.

What's a plot chart good for? Because you can control the exact positioning by x and y coordinates, you're inherently using the X axis and Y axis as a way to measure the relationship between the two. For example, if the X axis represented people's ages and the *Y* axis represented the average number of car accidents, you could visually see how those two related to each other.

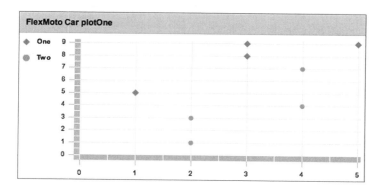

Figure 23.17   Plot chart used to plot two sets of data. Plot charts are useful for spotting data clumps.

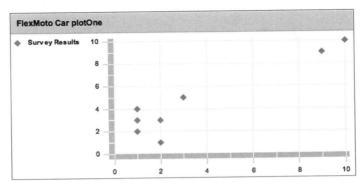

Figure 23.18 Clustering these data points reveals more than the average of their value.

From a statistical point of view, if you have a collection of independent data points and you're able to see how the data points clump together, this may reveal something interesting that averaging those numbers may not tell you. For example, figure 23.18 shows a clustering of data points, from the Y axis perspective, around the 3 mark—yet if you were to average all the values, you'd get a result of 5. Knowing this perspective gives you a better interpretation of the information.

That covers the main chart types that you have access to in Flex. You should now have enough knowledge to put these charts to use and begin customizing them to your own style to fit your application. In the next section, we explore how you can customize your charts.

23.6   *Customizing charts*

It would be boring if everyone's charts looked the same. More important, getting the right look and feel to plug into your application's overall theme is necessary for consistency. In this section, we give you a high-level overview of how you go about customizing your charts.

Many charts support their own unique characteristics, and we'll show you how to find out what those are by using the Flex API Reference, but we'll also introduce a few common customization features. First, let's take a look at series strokes, or the lines displayed on a chart.

23.6.1   *Series strokes*

A *stroke* augments the display of the line or the perimeter of the series. To use a stroke, you need to find out which property to use for a given series. Let's take an area chart as an example by following these steps:

1   Pull up the related series in the Flex API Reference—in this case, the AreaSeries component. The quickest way is to click <mx:AreaSeries> in the code and then press Shift+F2.

2   Scroll down to the Styles section.

3   Look for the style that has stroke in it. In this case, you'll find AreaStroke.

Putting this into practice, define a stroke by declaring an instance of the SolidColor-
Stroke class in the <fx:Declarations> tag:

```
<s:SolidColorStroke id="areaStroke" color="#6600CC" weight="4" alpha="0.8"/>
```

With the stroke defined, bind the stroke-related property to a particular instance:

```
<mx:AreaSeries yField="@ferrariUnits" displayName="Ferrari Count"
            areaStroke="{areaStroke}"/>
```

This changes things by drawing a predominantly thick line over the area.

A stroke has no impact on the area under the line; this is where fills come into play.

23.6.2 *Series fills*

Fills tackle adding background color to a series. You can use them a couple of ways;
the easiest way to demonstrate is to go straight into examples.

SINGLE-COLOR FILL

First, you follow the same steps you use with strokes and identify which property of the
series you're using supports fills:

1   Pull up the related series in the Flex API Reference—in this case, the Area-
    Series component. The quickest way is to click <mx:AreaSeries> in the code
    and then press Shift+F2.
2   Scroll down to the Styles section.
3   Look for the style that has fill in it. In this case, you'll find areaFill.

> **TIP**   Most charting series include fill and fills properties, but these are
> ignored by AreaSeries and LineSeries.

First, create a solid fill by declaring an instance of a SolidColor component in the
<fx:Declarations> tag, and then bind the fill property of the series to that Solid-
Color. Here's an example:

```
<s:SolidColor id="areaFill" color="#33FF66" alpha="0.5"/>
```

Then in the AreaSeries component, you bind the areaFill to it as follows:

```
<mx:AreaSeries yField="@ferrariUnits" displayName="Ferrari Count"
        areaStroke="{areaStroke}" areaFill="{areaFill}"/>
```

This creates a semitransparent greenish fill.

This example works well for charts that show trends. But charts whose data points
aren't linked together (visually) support an array of colors.

COLOR ARRAY FILLS

Charts whose behavior is to segregate each data point as if it's a series (such as bar and
pie charts) use a property called fills that accepts an array of colors. This lets you
color-code all the data items (because they're contained in one series).

For example, if you don't want to use a pie chart's default colors, you can override
them as shown in the next listing.

Listing 23.19 Specifying a color for each slice in a pie chart

```
<?xml version="1.0" encoding="utf-8"?>
<s:Application xmlns:fx="http://ns.adobe.com/mxml/2009"
        xmlns:s="library://ns.adobe.com/flex/spark"
        xmlns:mx="library://ns.adobe.com/flex/mx"
        xmlns:ns="library://ns.adobe.com/flex/mx">
  <fx:Declarations>
    <fx:XML id="salesDataXML" source="data.xml"/>
    <s:XMLListCollection id="salesData"
             source="{salesDataXML.revenues.data}"/>              Creates array of
    <fx:Array id="colorArray">                                    SolidColors
      <s:SolidColor color="#6666CC" alpha="0.5"/>
      <s:SolidColor color="#CC6666" alpha="0.5"/>
      <s:SolidColor color="#66CC66" alpha="0.5"/>
      <s:SolidColor color="#B8B83D" alpha="0.5"/>
    </fx:Array>
  </fx:Declarations>
  <s:Panel title="FlexMoto Car Sales"
       width="500" height="250">
    <s:layout><s:HorizontalLayout/></s:layout>
    <mx:Legend dataProvider="{salesChart}"/>
    <mx:PieChart id="salesChart"
         dataProvider="{salesData}"
         height="100%" width="100%">                              Binds fills
      <mx:series>                                                  property to array
        <mx:PieSeries field="@rev" nameField="@brand"
              labelPosition="callout" fills="{colorArray}"/>
      </mx:series>
    </mx:PieChart>
  </s:Panel>
</s:Application>
```

The result is that each slice of the pie chart adopts those colors (figure 23.19). If there are more slices (data points) than there are colors defined, Flex uses default colors for those additional items.

The amount of customization you can do in Flex is amazing, but customizing the series with strokes and fills is the primary thing to do.

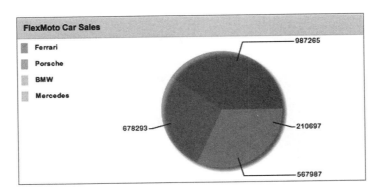

Figure 23.19 Replacing the default colors in a chart is as easy as providing it with an array of colors.

23.7 *Summary*

Charting in Flex is such a powerful and popular feature that it's not uncommon to find teams that use Flex only for this purpose (particularly to build dashboards). Charts are made up of many parts; they have series, labels, axes, elements, and the charts themselves.

Flex comes with nine out-of-the-box charts that cater to the common needs of most businesses. Some charts, like line and area charts, are premised on trending information; others, like bar charts, focus on category comparisons.

Although we've only scratched the surface of customizing charts, it boils down to checking the API Reference for the styles that are available and leveraging them as needed. The stroke and fills features are by far the most popular form of chart customization.

This chapter is the last one that involves coding. We've covered all the programming bases. From here on out, it's all about wrapping up the development lifecycle; testing and debugging are up next.

Debugging and testing

This chapter covers

- Debugging applications using the Flex debugger
- Using the Flash Builder profiler
- Unit and functional testing of your applications

In previous chapters you got a solid foundation for creating your rich internet applications with Flex. This chapter focuses on tuning your application. From the powerful out-of-the-box Flash Builder toolset to third-party debugging and profiling tools, you'll add an arsenal of weaponry to hunt down bugs and improve the performance of your Flex apps.

Flash Builder is equipped with a powerful debugger that allows you to step through code, add breakpoints, watch variables change in real time, and—new to Flash Builder 4—set conditional breakpoints that stop only when variables contain specific values. In addition to the debugger, Flash Builder Professional provides a much-improved profiler for analyzing resource consumption. Flash Builder also provides a network monitoring utility for analyzing data to and from your application and the server-side data source.

Beyond what comes out of the box, the Flex and Flash ecosystem provides a host of tools. From low-cost and free open-source solutions to full-blown enterprise-grade test-automation packages, Flex has a mature selection of tools available for debugging and testing applications. Depending on your needs, it may be awhile before you need that level of advanced tooling, but it's critical to know what's available as your needs expand. To get started, let's look at debugging Flex applications.

24.1 Debugging

Debugging applications is the process of hunting down errors and eliminating them. When your application produces output that's unexpected or crashes, it's time to debug. Debugging is a process that's employed throughout the lifespan of your application.

There are several approaches to debugging Flex applications. At the most basic is writing to the Flash Builder console for analysis of `trace()` statements. These text statements are useful early in your application's life, but as complexity grows, so will your debugging needs. Beyond simple tracing, Flash Builder offers a powerful debugger that allows you to halt the execution of your application at specific lines of code. This feature lets you step through the execution of the application from the breakpoint and analyze the values of variables contained in the objects that make up the application.

Another common debugging task is peering into the results of remote service calls. Flex applications don't really come to life until they connect to a data source and present the data received from that source in a useful manner to your users. The problem arises when the data returned from these services isn't exactly what you expect it to be. Flash Builder is equipped with a powerful monitoring tool to view both what you're sending to remote services and the data that they return in response.

The first step in the debugging process is to install Flash Debug Player. Let's do that now.

24.1.1 Setting up the Flash Debug Player

Flash Player comes in two versions: the debugger version and the standard version. For normal users of the internet, the standard player is the default. As a developer, you need access to additional information to analyze your application during the development process. The Flash Debug Player provides this. Upon installation, Flash Builder installs the version of the Flash Debug Player that it ships with for you; this Player allows for diagnostic logging as well as provides a connection to some external tools for debugging purposes.

It's a good idea to make use of the latest Flash Debug Player, which can be downloaded from http://www.adobe.com/support/flashplayer/downloads.html in the Debugger Versions section of the page.

You can test which version of the Player is currently installed by your browser by visiting http://kb2.adobe.com/cps/155/tn_15507.html. Be sure that the Debug Player area is labeled Yes.

The Debug Player should already be installed if you're using Flash Builder, but there are circumstances where other applications might override the installation. Don't worry; you aren't the first person this has happened to. Be sure you have the

Debug Player installed, and all will be well. Once you've confirmed that you're running the Debug Player, you'll be ready to use the `trace()` function to output text statements to the Flash Builder console.

24.1.2 *Using the trace() function*

`trace()` is a simple global function that's available from anywhere in your code. It lets you record text to the Flash Builder console output panel. To see `trace` in action, enter the following:

```
<s:Application xmlns:fx="http://ns.adobe.com/mxml/2009"
        xmlns:s="library://ns.adobe.com/flex/spark"
        xmlns:mx="library://ns.adobe.com/flex/mx">
  <s:VGroup>
    <s:TextInput id="aMessage"/>
    <s:Button label="Log It!"
        click="trace('Your message is:                  Button's click handler
                    ' + aMessage.text);"/>       <---   traces message
  </s:VGroup>
</s:Application>
```

When you type something and click the Log It! button, the text you type shows up in the Flash Builder console panel.

```
Your message is: Hi flashlog.txt
```

This is an effective mechanism if you want to record the value of various variables and components. Tracing simple strings is extremely handy, but you'll also want to inspect your objects in greater detail. Flex is equipped with the tools to get detailed string representations of objects. Next, we look at two methods for creating these detailed string descriptions of objects.

CONVERTING OBJECTS TO STRINGS

In order to trace objects to the console window, you must transform them into text. Flex makes this easy: most objects support a `toString()` function that will do the conversion for you. Here's an example:

```
var myNumber:Number = 32;
trace(myNumber.toString()); //outputs 32 to the console
```

But for more complex objects like `ArrayCollections`, the Flex framework utility class `ObjectUtil` has a `toString()` function that takes a reference of any other object and converts it to a string.

In listing 24.1, the `ObjectUtil` class is used to display all the items in an `ArrayCollection`.

Listing 24.1 Using `ObjectUtil` to dump an object's properties

```
<?xml version="1.0" encoding="utf-8"?>
<s:Application xmlns:fx="http://ns.adobe.com/mxml/2009"
        xmlns:s="library://ns.adobe.com/flex/spark"
        xmlns:mx="library://ns.adobe.com/flex/mx"
        creationComplete="trace(ObjectUtil.toString(ac))">
```

```
<fx:Script>
  <![CDATA[
    import mx.collections.ArrayCollection;
    import mx.utils.ObjectUtil;
    private var ac:ArrayCollection = new ArrayCollection([
      {label:"Tariq Ahmed", data:"tahmed"},
      {label:"Dan Orlando", data:"dorlando"},
      {label:"John Bland", data:"jbland"},
      {label:"Joel Hooks", data:"jhooks"}
    ]);
  ]]>
</fx:Script>
</s:Application>
```

This code produces something like the log file shown in the following listing.

Listing 24.2 Sample output from `ObjectUtil`

```
(mx.collections::ArrayCollection)
  filterFunction = (null)
  length = 4
  list = (mx.collections::ArrayList)
    length = 4
    source = (Array)#2
      [0] (Object)#3
        data = "tahmed"
        label = "Tariq Ahmed"
      [1] (Object)#4
        data = "dorlando"
        label = "Dan Orlando"
      [2] (Object)#5
        data = "jbland"
        label = "John Bland"
      [3] (Object)#6
        data = "jhooks"
        label = "Joel Hooks"
    uid = "3876E34F-5754-6FEF-C0B1-7FC8C99AC8D5"
  sort = (null)
  source = (Array)
```

As you can see, this approach can give detailed insight into your objects. The odds are that you'll want more advanced tooling to gain even greater control of the debugging process. Moving on to the heavyweight tool of debugging, let's look at the integrated Flash Builder debugger.

24.1.3 *Using the Flash Builder debugger*

If you've reached a point where you need to see how things are changing and you also need fine-grained control, the debugger that's built into Flash Builder is going to quickly become your best friend. It helps you isolate where issues are by allowing you to step through your code in a controlled manner and see how variables change as the code executes.

Figure 24.1 Launching the Flash Builder debugger

The tool works by launching in Debug mode, setting breakpoints to pause execution, and then taking a look at your application's variables as you step through the execution of the code.

LAUNCHING DEBUG MODE

Enabling the debugger is similar to how you've been launching your applications thus far, except in this case you use the Debug button, as shown in figure 24.1.

Notice that along with the bin folder, there's also bin-debug—this is the folder to which Flash Builder publishes a debug version of your application. When you click the Debug button, this version is launched.

If Flash Builder hasn't done so already, switch to the debugging perspective in Flash Builder by choosing Window > Perspective > Flex Debugging. You'll see the view shown in figure 24.2 above your code window.

Now you're ready to take the reins of the debugger and see what it can do. First, let's look at the workhorse of debugging a Flex application, the breakpoint. Breakpoints allow you to control the playback of the application, stopping and starting on any line of code you want to dig into the values of the variables that are available at that line of code.

ADDING/REMOVING A BREAKPOINT

The ability to add breakpoints to your code is a powerful debugging tool. Halting the execution of the application and looking at the current state of objects and their properties can save hours of tedious tracing and guesswork. Breakpoints can be set on any executable line of code. This means that if your line of code isn't a comment you can add a breakpoint. Breakpoints aren't limited strictly to ActionScript files. You can also place breakpoints on lines of MXML files that contain ActionScript:

```
<s:Button click="myVar=myText.text"/>
```

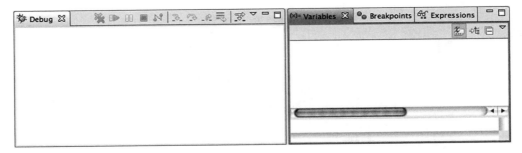

Figure 24.2 Flash Builder debugging perspective panels

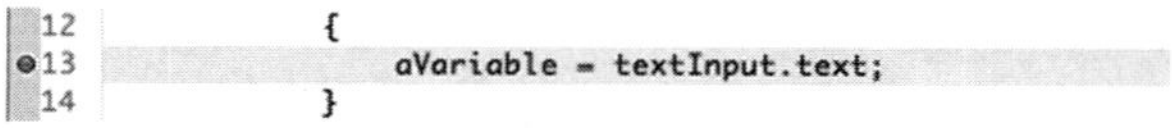

```
12              {
13                      aVariable = textInput.text;
14              }
```

Figure 24.3   Setting a breakpoint places a circle next to the line of code that will halt.

You can also place a breakpoint inside an `<mx:Script>` block or in an ActionScript (.as) file.

To do this, follow these steps:

1   Using Flash Builder, locate a line of code on which you want to halt execution.
2   Double-click the line number to create a breakpoint.

To remove the breakpoint, double-click the breakpoint.

If all goes well, you should see your breakpoint next to the line number, as shown in figure 24.3.

With the debugger launched and breakpoints set, you can control the execution of your application with the debugger.

CONTROLLING EXECUTION

You'll find yourself controlling the execution of your program with breakpoints in many circumstances. If your application isn't behaving as expected or you're seeing values that don't make sense, the first question you'll want to answer is "why?" By stopping the playback of the application, you'll be able to view the values of your object's properties and step through one line at a time to observe what your application is doing. After you've set your breakpoints, launch your application in Debug mode. As soon as you hit the line that has a breakpoint, execution will stop and Flash Builder will want your attention.

You can use Debug view to control what happens next by using the functions outlined in table 24.1.

Table 24.1   Flash Builder's debugger functions

Icon	Function	Description
	Resume	Resumes execution of the application
	Suspend	Pauses the application
	Terminate	Terminates the application
	Disconnect	Disconnects the debugger from the application
	Step into	Steps into the next line of code
	Step over	Skips over the next line of code
	Step return	Continues the current function until it's done

Now that you can control execution, the feature that people generally use the debugger for is watching variables.

WATCHING VARIABLES

There are times in the life of your application when something just isn't right. Everything appears right, you've searched through the code looking for where things might be going wrong, and you still can't pinpoint where things have gone bad. Watching a variable lets you track the value that the variable is assigned in real time. You can also manipulate the value if you want to experiment with how the application would behave using another value. Let's give it a try by setting a breakpoint in this simple application in the listing shown here.

Listing 24.3   Using a breakpoint on the line that sets the variable

```
<?xml version="1.0" encoding="utf-8"?>
<s:Application xmlns:fx="http://ns.adobe.com/mxml/2009"
         xmlns:s="library://ns.adobe.com/flex/spark"
         xmlns:mx="library://ns.adobe.com/flex/mx" minWidth="955"
                      minHeight="600">
  <s:layout>
    <s:VerticalLayout/>
  </s:layout>
  <fx:Script>
    <![CDATA[
      public var aVariable:String;
      public function updateVariable():void        Put a breakpoint
      {                                            at this line
        aVariable = textInput.text;
      }
    ]]>
  </fx:Script>
  <s:TextInput id="textInput"/>
  <s:Button click="updateVariable();"/>
</s:Application>
```

Follow these steps:

1 Set a breakpoint on the line indicated in listing 24.3.

2 Launch your application in Debug mode.

3 Type something in the text box, and click the button. The application will suspend execution.

4 Switch to Flash Builder; you should see the variables listed (see figure 24.4).

Debugging is both a science and an art. With practice you'll find that you're able to use the tools at your disposal to quickly and effectively track down the bugs that scurry around the dark corners of your application. You'll be able to quickly see areas of your applications that need to be thoroughly examined and stepped through with the debugger and zero in on those elusive programming errors. To help you along that path, there are several additional tools for debugging, including conditional breakpoints.

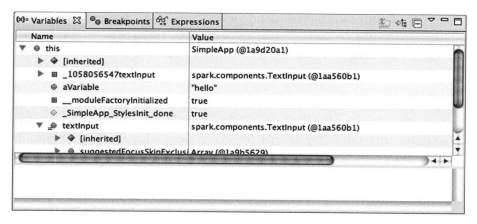

Figure 24.4   Breakpoints allow you to set a stop point in your application and view variables and their values.

CONDITIONAL BREAKPOINTS

New to Flash Builder 4 are conditional breakpoints. You're able to specify conditions to be met for the debugger to stop execution. This allows for fine-grained control of your breakpoint. This is useful in situations where you're performing loops over large sets of objects and want to stop only when a particular value occurs. Conditional breakpoints can be configured to stop under these conditions:

- The expression evaluates to `true`.
- The value of the expression changes.
- A specific hit count has been reached.

To set up the conditions of the breakpoint, you can right-click either the breakpoint next to the line number or the breakpoint in the Breakpoints dialog box. This will display the Breakpoint Properties dialog box, as shown in figure 24.5. From this window you get several options for the breakpoint.

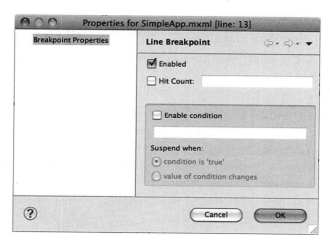

Figure 24.5   Breakpoint Properties dialog box

Setting a hit count on the breakpoint will specify how many times the code can pass over the breakpoint before execution is halted. This option can be useful for debugging loops. In a for loop, you might want to have execution halt on the 13th pass through the loop. In the Breakpoint Properties dialog box, select the check box next Hit Count and enter 13 in the text input area. This breakpoint will now stop the 13th time it has been passed.

By selecting the check box for Enable Condition, you have much-finer-grained control over the breakpoint via expressions. An expression is a piece of code that returns a result. For example, 1 + 1 is a valid expression. Simple arithmetic isn't useful in the context of conditional breakpoints. Flash Builder understands much more complex expressions, and to be useful, the expression needs to have a value that can evaluate to true or potentially change. Table 24.2 is a small sample of some of the expressions that you might use.

Table 24.2 Small sample of available expressions for conditional breakpoints

Expression	Description
myValue + 2	Tracks the current value of a variable plus 2.
myValue == 10	Tracks if the variable is equal to 10 and returns a Boolean result.
myMethod()	Tracks the output of a method if the method is available.
Math.max(x,y,z)	Math functions can be used in expressions.
myXML.property.@value	XML values can be tracked and analyzed.

This isn't an exhaustive list of available expression values, but it should give you an idea of what's available with the powerful conditional breakpoints. Conditional breakpoints can watch for two cases on a given expression: Is the condition of the expression true, or has the value of the condition changed?

The debugger focuses on the objects currently in memory in our application. Another common debugging task is analyzing network traffic as your application communicates with a remote server. Several tools are available to help accomplish this task, including the network-monitoring tool added in Flash Builder 4. Let's take a look at these tools and how they can help you debug your applications.

24.1.4 *Monitoring network activity*

One of the most challenging things you'll encounter when developing Flex applications is trying to figure out why communications with a backend data service (such as a web service or remote object) don't seem to be working. Yes, you can specify fault handlers to handle exceptions, but that may not be enough.

Using the debug tools to stop the playback and analyze the results from remote services is a quick and easy way to see what's being delivered to your application and can provide useful information. New to Flash Builder 4 is the powerful Network Monitor tool. This tool is a full-fledged remote debug proxy built into the IDE. It provides detailed information about the network activity your application is participating in.

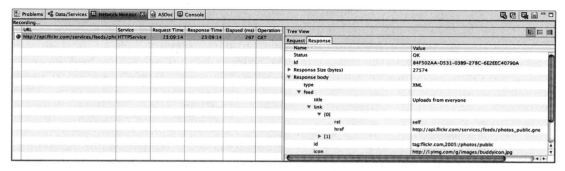

Figure 24.6   Flash Builder 4 Network Monitor displaying the results of a remote service call

Network Monitor shows detailed results of all service calls made within your application. As shown in figure 24.6, the results are presented in an easy-to-understand hierarchical format. The Flickr uploads RSS feed has been accessed, and the XML result is displayed.

As part of the debugging process, it's often necessary to identify and fix memory leaks that can occur through the normal course of developing an application. Flash Builder 4 provides an improved memory profiler to make this task possible.

24.2   *Flex profiler*

Profiling adds the ability to see where resource bottlenecks (processing and memory utilization) in your application occur so you can isolate and address the issues. Like debugging, profiling an application should occur at all stages of development. "Profile early, profile often" is a mantra that will help you succeed in developing applications that run as efficiently as possible and give your users the best experience. The sooner you start profiling, the better off you'll be. It can be painful to wait until the end of the development cycle only to discover a performance issue that will requires days of profiling, debugging, and optimizing your code. By actively monitoring the performance of your application from start to finish, you'll catch performance issues early and prevent them from becoming serious problems later.

The profiler works by periodically sampling what's going on in your application. Kind of like time-lapse photography, it takes a snapshot of what things look like at given intervals. In doing so, it's able to determine how many objects currently exist, how much memory they're using, how many functions are being called, and how much time those functions are consuming.

Here's what you should look for:

- *Function call frequency*—How often are you calling functions? Are you making unnecessary calls? See if you can minimize how often heavy-duty functions are called or if they can be broken into smaller pieces, only a portion of which are called frequently.

- *Duration of functions*—How long are functions taking to run? Hand in hand with the previous item, you can investigate particular functions to determine the average amount of time a particular function takes to run.
- *Who's calling whom*—Observing this *call stack* and observing the chain of functions calling functions may reveal interesting information.
- *Object count/object allocation*—How many objects have been instantiated? What if you have many instances of the same object? For example, if you can use fewer instances, you'll save on overhead.
- *Object size*—How big are these objects? For objects that have many instances, is their combined size a concern?
- *Garbage collection*—By default, Flex takes care of destroying objects when they're no longer needed. *Garbage collection* is the process of recovering the memory that they once held. It's possible that objects may linger for awhile before this process occurs (which causes memory leaks), so you may want to add logic in these cases to explicitly destroy them.

Using the profiler is similar to using the debugger: You launch the tool from Flash Builder.

LAUNCHING THE PROFILER

You'll find the Profile button on the toolbar in Flash Builder, beside the Debug icon, as shown in figure 24.7.

If you click it, the window shown in figure 24.8 opens, where you can select what you want to watch.

Figure 24.7 The profiler is launched by clicking the Profile button on the toolbar.

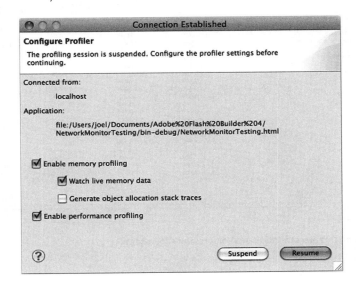

Figure 24.8 Launching the profiler prompts you with configuration options.

The settings in the dialog box are as follows:

- *Connected From*—The server you're connected to (or localhost, if it's the same computer).
- *Application*—Path to the Flex application's SWF file.
- *Enable Memory Profiling*—Enables the tracking of memory usage.
- *Watch Live Memory Data*—Memory tracking will occur if Enable Memory Profiling is selected. Watch Live Memory Data indicates whether you want to watch it in the Live Objects view.
- *Generate Object Allocation Stack Traces*—Lets you track how objects are created.
- *Enable Performance Profiling*—Lets you watch where processing time is spent.

You could use all of these options all the time; the only difference is how much profiling data is generated and the performance impact while profiling is running.

Launch the profiler to see it in action, as shown in figure 24.9.

The profiler functions similarly to the debugger. After you've launched it, switch back to Flash Builder to control the application's execution.

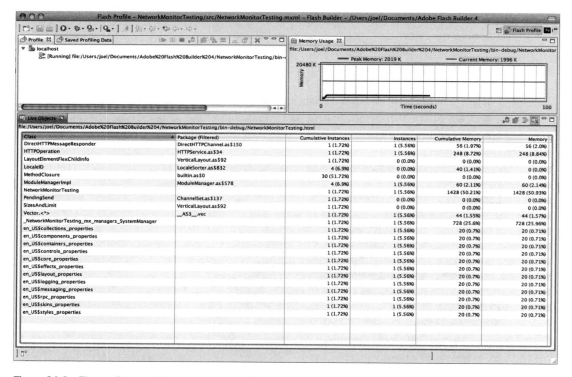

Figure 24.9   The profiler provides aggregate statistics on memory and CPU usage.

CONTROLLING EXECUTION

Once the profiler is running, you'll see your application listed in the Profile view. Select the application, and a bunch of icons will light up and give you options. Table 24.3 describes these options, which are execution-control functionality.

Table 24.3 Flash Builder's profiler functions

Icon	Function	Description
	Resume	Resumes execution of the application.
	Suspend	Pauses the application.
	Terminate	Terminates the application.
	Run Garbage Collection	Forces garbage collection to run now versus waiting for it to happen. This recovers memory from objects that are no longer in use.
	Take Memory Snapshot	Takes a snapshot of your memory usage and breaks it down by how that memory is used. Use this feature to take snapshots whenever you suspect major memory operations occur and later evaluate these snapshots.
	Find Loitering Objects	Goes hand in hand with Take Memory Snapshot in that this feature can compare the differences between snapshots.
	View Allocation Trace	Available after selecting two memory snapshots. Shows which functions were called from one snapshot to another and how much memory was utilized in the process.
	Reset Performance Data	Resets the recorded information.
	Capture Performance Profile	Used in conjunction with Reset Performance Data. After clicking Reset Performance Data, click this button to snapshot a number of function calls and how long they took to run. You can repeat this process as often as you like.
	Delete	Deletes an item you've selected (for example, a memory snapshot).

The profiler is the only tool available for Flex that allows this kind of testing, and it does a great job. It gives you deep insight into how much memory and resources are being consumed and where that consumption occurs.

Next we discuss the various forms of automated testing available for us to use while developing applications.

24.3   *Testing your applications with automation*

When do you test your applications? Every time you run them. The act of launching your application and providing it with input is a form of testing. The problem with this form of testing is that it's slow, somewhat tedious, and prone to error. This is where automation steps in to give you a hand. You can think of automated testing as programming an army of robots that will do your bidding and rigorously test your application as commanded.

We're going to look at two of the major types of automated testing:

- *Unit testing*—Automated testing that breaks down individual units of an application into their simplest parts to test in isolation.

- *Functional testing*—Another form of automated testing that involves recording actions that are played back and checked for certain conditions.

24.3.1   *Unit testing*

If the best defense is a good offense, then unit testing should be in your tool arsenal. If there's something users don't like, it's bugs in applications they're trying to use. At best they interrupt their workflow and can kill the user experience. At the worst bugs can cause serious issues with data loss or the breakdown of larger systems. To minimize the impact of bugs on your application it's important to rigorously test the application throughout its lifecycle.

Testing occurs during all phases of development. Through the process of test-driven development (TDD) programmers rigorously write automated tests before writing the code that the tests exercise. Drawing on agile development processes such as extreme programming (XP) and SCRUM, the test-up-front approach is rapidly gaining popularity in the Flash/Flex universe.

This approach is rigorous and requires significant discipline. Even if you don't apply this sort of regiment to your development, it's still important to consider the various forms of testing that are available to you. By testing your applications you can significantly minimize, fix, and even prevent bugs from appearing in the final application that your users are provided. In a perfect world your software would be perfectly bug free. Unfortunately perfection is rarely the case, and you can only try your best to eliminate the majority of bugs in your software.

You're in luck. Flex is maturing and the tools are maturing along with it. Flash Builder 4 is equipped with integrated unit-testing tools. Let's explore these tools for testing your application in detail.

WHAT IS UNIT TESTING?

Unit testing is the act of isolating your components and rigorously testing their public properties and methods to ensure they act as expected. Through a series of automated programmatic tests, you poke at a class, providing it with varied inputs, and assert that the outputs are as they should be. By isolating your classes you're able to ensure that they stand on their own and function correctly. Unit tests allow you to code with confidence and refactor your code as the need arises without the sense of dread that your changes will break other areas of the application.

Unit tests can be defined as developer tests. They're written by developers for developers to act as low-level verification of the code you write. If you've ever spent countless hours trying to track down an elusive bug in your code, you've been in a situation where unit tests would have been a huge benefit.

Unit tests can be considered the "first user" of an application. They're robots that do our bidding as developers and help to identify the mistakes we humans are prone to make. As the first user of the application, unit tests give us a chance to take a look at the design of our code. Is the code hard to test? If so, it's a good sign that we need to stop and think about the design of the code we're testing. This is one reason TDD has been adopted by so many developers in recent years. By writing tests before you write the code, you're forced to think about how the class or method will act. By utilizing the unit tests as a design tool, you're able to write concise code that's easier to read and manage. The time spent writing the unit tests will save you from writing useless code that serves only to clutter up your application and make it difficult to understand.

Tooling is important when you start to unit test. Without the proper tools the process can be slow and painful. FlexUnit 4 is a mature unit-testing framework that provides most of the tools you'll need to get a solid foundation of unit tests under your application. Flash Builder 4 is equipped with FlexUnit integration that helps speed up the process of unit testing and reduces much of the tedious labor involved with the process. Let's take a look at how to use FlexUnit 4 and the features that Flash Builder brings to the table to help build a solid suite of unit tests for your applications.

UNIT TESTING WITH FLEXUNIT 4

Flash Builder has built-in FlexUnit 4 integration that provides a handy mechanism for creating, executing, and maintaining your unit tests. In addition to the built-in FlexUnit, you can get the latest releases and find community resources at http://www.flexunit.org.

FlexUnit 4 is driven by metadata. The most basic part of a unit test suite is the test method. Test methods in FlexUnit are denoted with the `[Test]` metadata tag. FlexUnit parses the files you designate and searches for public methods that are marked `[Test]`. When it finds such a method, it executes it. Test methods can't require arguments because FlexUnit doesn't have the ability to pass in any parameters. A test method passes if it doesn't throw any errors during execution. Listing 24.4 shows a simple test method.

Listing 24.4 A simple test method

```
[Test]
public function simple_addition_test():void
{
    Assert.assertEquals("Should equal 2", 2, 1 + 1);
}
```

A test method contains one or more assertions. An assertion is an expression that's evaluated. In listing 24.4 we're asserting that 1 + 1 = 2. Flex unit provides the `Assert` class with numerous static methods that provide a convenient way to make assertions within test methods. If an assertion fails, it will throw an error and the test method will fail, as in the next listing.

Listing 24.5 A simple test method that will fail

```
[Test]
public function simple_addition_test():void
{
    Assert.assertEquals("Should equal 2", 2, 1 + 2); //3 does not equal 2!
}
```

Test methods don't require any special syntax outside of the metadata tag. They can be named anything, and the only requirement is that there are no required arguments. Because of the nature of FlexUnit, a test method without an expression will pass because it throws no errors. Your test methods are generally part of a class that contains many test methods. This is referred to as a test case, as shown in this listing.

Listing 24.6 A basic test case

```
public class SimpleTestCase
{
  private var aMathClass:MathClass;

  [Before]
  public function setUp():void
  {
    aMathClass = new MathClass()
  }

  [After]
  public function tearDown():void
  {
    aMathClass = null;
  }

  [Test]
  public function simple_addition_test():void
  {
    Assert.assertEquals("Should equal 2", 2, aMathClass.add(1,1));
  }
}
```

With FlexUnit 4 a test case does require extending a special base class to function. Although you can supply test methods in a class that extends another class, as a general rule your test cases will be simple objects. In addition to the [Test] metadata tag, your cases will often have the [Before] and [After] tags. These two tags denote methods that will run before and after each test method. They're used to reset classes and values so that each test method starts with a clean slate. You can use as many [Before] and [After] tags as you need, and you can run them in a particular order by setting their order property [Before(order="1")].

As mentioned, FlexUnit will fail in a test method if an error is thrown. This is how the Assert class assertions function. They throw an error if the expected result isn't correct. Many times you'll want to test if your code throws a particular error. The

[Test] metadata is equipped with a property to expect a particular error. If the error doesn't occur, the test will fail. For example, [Test(expects="Error")] expects a simple error to be thrown. The test method in listing 24.7 will pass.

Listing 24.7 A test method that expects an Error to be thrown

```
[Test(expects="Error")]
public function test_that_an_error_is_thrown():void
{
    throw new Error("This is the Error you were looking for");
}
```

By the nature of the Flash Platform and rich internet applications, you'll quickly find the need to test for asynchronous actions within your classes. A simple test method isn't sufficient to capture asynchronous events. FlexUnit provides this functionality with the async property of the [Test(async)] metadata. Listing 24.8 shows an example of an asynchronous test method. The example shows several variations of asynchronous tests.

Listing 24.8 An asynchronous test method and the various handlers

```
[Test(async)]
public function test_some_asynchronous_stuff():void
{
    //Async.asyncHandler( this, handleAnEvent, 2000 );
    //Async.asyncResponder( this, aResponder, 2000 );
    //Async.failOnEvent( this, targer, SomeEvent.FAIL, 2000 );
    //Async.handleEvent( this, target, SomeEvent.MAKE_IT_GO,
                        handleEvent, 2000 );
    //Async.proceedOnEvent( this, target, SomeEvent.STUFF_HAPPENS, 2000 );
}
```

These Async methods are also handy for your [Before(async)] and [After(async)] methods. Async.proceedOnEvent is especially handy for watching when events occur before running the test methods or when an asynchronous event needs to occur after a test method has run.

It's common practice to have a test case class for each class that you wish to test. As your test cases grow in number, you'll soon need to pack them into a suite so that they can be easily run. A test suite is much like a test case in that it's not a special class. It's a simple class with public variables that represent your test cases. Listing 24.9 is a simple test suite example.

Listing 24.9 A simple test suite to hold your test cases

```
[Suite]
[RunWith("org.flexunit.runners.Suite")]
public class SimpleTestSuite
{
    public var testOne:TestCaseOne;
    public var testTwo:TestCaseTwo;
}
```

A test suite class must be marked with the [Suite] metadata tag as well as the [Run-With] tag that designates which FlexUnit runner to use for the test cases it contains. The previous listing utilizes the default FlexUnit 4 runner, but it's possible to create or use any number of custom runners for various use cases.

You'll want to run your tests often, and Flash Builder provides a convenient mechanism for doing so. Right-click a test suite or test case class and choose Execute Flex-Unit Tests. The tests will compile and run, and the results will be displayed in the FlexUnit Results panel, as shown in figure 24.10.

This panel provides many features that make unit testing in Flash Builder easier than ever before. You can double-click any of the test methods, and it will jump to the code. You can filter the methods to show only failing tests. You can easily rerun the tests or rerun only the failing tests. With this level of integration, the excuses for not testing quickly fade away.

Flash Builder makes running tests easy. It also adds some significant features for creating tests. It's as easy as File > New > Test Case Class, which presents you with a dialog box for creating a new test case, as shown in figure 24.11.

This dialog box is similar to the dialog box used to create a new class. You can name your test case and supply its superclass. In addition, you can supply a class to test. When you provide a class to test, you're presented with another dialog box that allows you to select methods from that class to create test methods for. With a few clicks you have the beginnings of a unit test suite for your application. Similar functionality is available for creating test suites that allows you to select all of the test case classes to include in the suite. This, coupled with the ease of running tests, takes away a lot of the tedious boilerplate typing that was necessary prior to Flash Builder for creating your test cases and suites. We've just scratched the surface of Flex Unit 4 and unit testing in this section. It's a subject with great depth and one that would benefit you greatly as a developer to pursue more thoroughly.

WHERE TO GO FROM HERE

Unit testing is a vast and interesting topic, with dozens of books devoted entirely to the subject. It takes time and dedication to properly implement and understand the

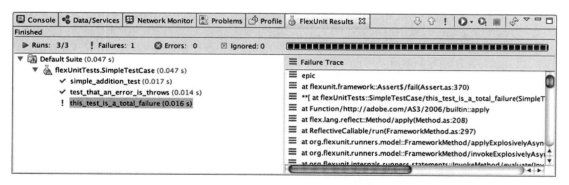

Figure 24.10   Flash Builder integrated FlexUnit results

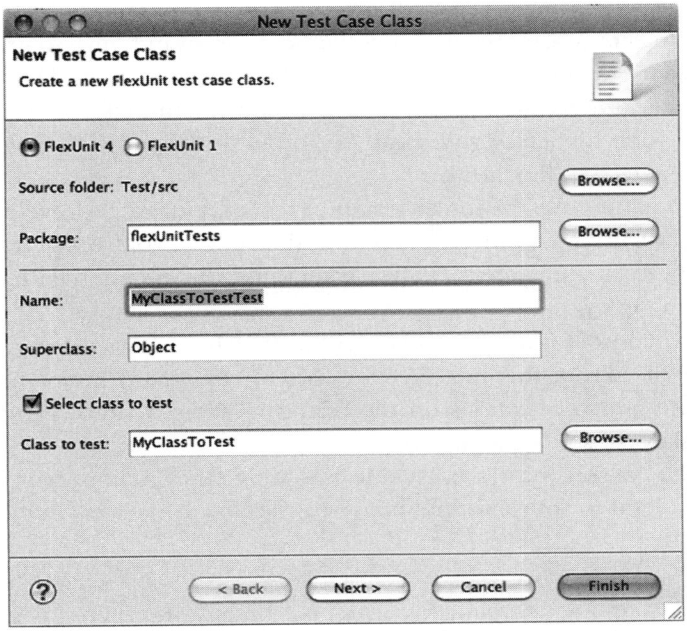

Figure 24.11 The New Test Case Class dialog box makes it easy to create a test case.

concepts. Unit testing will provide you with deep insight into your code-writing practices and give you a front-line defense against the bugs that are bound to appear in your applications. The time saved in time-consuming debugging and frustrating hours of deciphering untested code will more than make up for the time spent writing some simple unit tests. It's certainly extra work, but the rewards are worth the effort.

Unit tests are developer tests providing that low-level exercising of the code that makes a coder feel comfortable. You also want to test you application at a higher level to make sure everything works as expected from a user point of view. One approach to this would be to manually click through your application and its features. This is boring and not fun. We're developers! There has to be a way to automate this sort of tedious testing. There is, and it's commonly referred to as functional testing. Let's take a look at what functional testing is and the tools that are available to help achieve this additional layer of test coverage.

24.3.2 Functional testing

Functional testing is the high-level testing of an application. Sometimes referred to as black box testing, functional testing puts your application through its paces from the top-level user perspective. At the most basic, this means that you or a tester would click through each button or interaction in the application to make sure that it responds as expected. That gets tedious in short order, and in order for this level of testing to be as effective as possible, you'll want to automate the process on any application of significant size. Several tools are available to help you with this process, ranging from the free and open-source FlexMonkey to robust, enterprise-class functional testing suites.

FLEXMONKEY

The FlexMonkey project was originated at Gorilla Logic as an in-house solution. Seeing that the tool was useful and that there was a need for the tool in the Flex community, they donated the software and its source code to the community. Downloads and links to the source code for FlexMonkey can be found at the project's home page: http://www.gorillalogic.com/flexmonkey.

The open-source nature of FlexMonkey can be a real advantage. It provides a high-quality solution out of the box, but with access to the source, you're able to update and modify the tool to fit your needs. This is something the commercial functional testing offerings don't offer.

The FlexMonkey console is an AIR-based application that makes a connection to your running SWF file. From this interface you're able to record interactions with your application and add verifications on the results of those actions. Figure 24.12 shows the FlexMonkey console's user interface.

In addition to the console interface, FlexMonkey will export ActionScript unit-test classes that can be added to your existing unit-test suites for use in a continuous integration environment.

RIATEST

Considering the competition, whose prices are in the thousands, RIATest is a low-cost solution that can save you a lot of time in your QA cycle. The product works by embedding an agent during compile time or by using a runtime loader. It costs $499 U.S. and is available at http:// www.riatest.com.

We like its simple and straightforward approach:

- Compile your application with the RIATest module embedded in it, or use its loader feature to dynamically wrap the agent around your application.

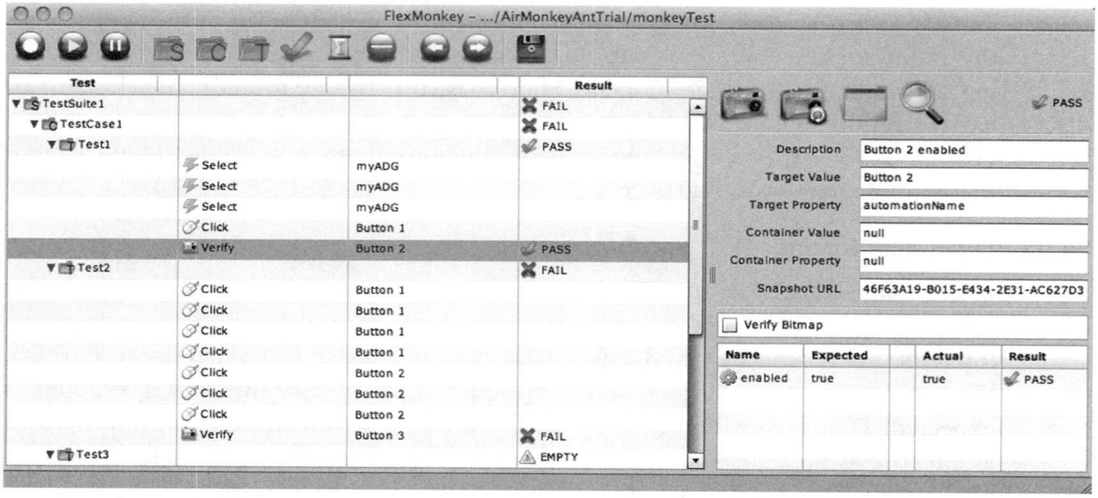

Figure 24.12 The FlexMonkey user interface allows recording of interactions with your application.

- Record your dry runs through the application (optionally, you can hand-write the test scripts).
- Play back your scripts to verify the results.

Key features include the following:

- An Action Recorder simplifies the process of recording actions into a human-readable script.
- Syntax highlighting makes those human-readable scripts even easier to read via color-coding.
- The engine comes with its own scripting language, which is modeled after ActionScript. This gives you a lot of control while using a language you already know.
- A Component Inspector allows you to mouse over a UI component and inspect its properties.
- Built-in script debugging helps you figure out problems with your test scripts.

RIATest has a lot of momentum behind it. What's interesting is that it has a public mechanism for submitting enhancement requests and bug reports—making it community driven.

HP QUICKTEST PRO

QuickTest Pro (QTP) is an industrial-strength product from HP (via acquisition of Mercury Interactive). It's powerful and versatile, hence the price tag: $6,000–$9,000 U.S. (pricing may vary depending on licensing options). Go to http://www.hp.com and search for QuickTest Professional. QTP was the first functional-testing tool available for Flex, and for a long time it was the only choice.

Some key features are these:

- Defect replication
- Keyword-driven test case development
- The ability to update multiple test scripts quickly using a shared object repository
- Easy to use, with minimal training required
- Simple interface

Test cases are in the context of business workflows (versus a purely technical perspective), which makes QTP easy for QA users to relate to.

Test-case creation is advanced. For example, contextual and conditional test cases can go down various branches depending on the results; you can query your database to find data that's in a current state, then perform tests on that data, and so on.

IBM RATIONAL FUNCTIONAL TESTER

Not many Flex developers are aware that Rational Functional Tester exists and in particular that it supports Flex. This enterprise-class product is specifically aimed at the Java and .NET communities, and it supports testing of all sorts of applications from standalone to the web-based variety. It costs $5,400–$10,500 (pricing may vary depending on licensing options) and is available at http://www-306.ibm.com/software/awdtools/tester/functional/index.html.

Some key features are as follows:

- Data-driven as well as keyword-driven test cases
- Supports test scripts written in many languages, including Java and Visual Basic
- Version control
- Dynamic data validation

The Rational Functional Tester is a world-class product that has a world-class price. It's an extremely robust piece of software that even allows for test automation of dumb terminal clients, all the way to Siebel and SAP application testing.

24.4 *Summary*

Flex's testing and debugging tools have matured rapidly. You have access to a host of debugging, profiling, and testing tools to help you tune your applications and provide your application's users with a cleaner user experience.

When it comes to debugging, you can do simple things to get insight into what's going on. In addition, the Flex Debugger is a robust tool that gives you tactile control over isolating issues.

Ancillary to debugging is profiling, and the Flex profiler (new to Flex 4) gives you an advanced tool for understanding the internals of your application. Use it to find out how your application is consuming memory and processing resources.

Making sure new bugs aren't introduced in the first place is what testing is all about. Testing tools range from free, open-source projects to pricey, enterprise-strength tools from commercial vendors.

After you've tested and debugged your software, the last stage in the development process is polishing and wrapping up the project. The next chapter teaches you how to prepare for deployment.

Wrapping up a project

This chapter covers

- Loading applications with wrappers
- Deploying applications

Look at you, Mr./Mrs./Ms. fancy Flex developer: You've come a long way in a short time. You've conquered things like using data services to hook into databases, you know how to lay out an application, you can address usability with up-front validation, and you can deliver an engaging user experience with effects.

You have the power to have managers beg you for cool business intelligence charts, and your AJAX friends are secretly jealous of you. Now it's just a matter of tying up loose ends and getting the project out the door by customizing the HTML wrapper and deploying it to a production server.

25.1 Customizing the HTML wrapper

Your beautiful new application needs just a bit more work to get it ready for presentation to the world. Most browsers will load an SWF file directly, but this approach can have unusual results and lacks the control you'll want when deploying your applications. This is where the HTML wrapper comes in. The internet is HTML's kingdom, and to get along in HTML's world you need to play by its rules. With Flash

Builder 4, Adobe has standardized on the excellent standards-based SWFObject 2 JavaScript library for the loading and placement of SWFs in HTML pages.

As you've probably noticed by now, when you create a new Flex project in Flash Builder, a folder called html-template is created for you with all of the essentials to load and display your application in a browser.

The default wrapper that Flash Builder generates does the following:

- Loads in JavaScript to support backward/forward JavaScript history functionality as well as the ability to bookmark a view of your application (known as *deep linking*)
- Checks to make sure the user has a minimum level of Flash Player
- Creates the HTML to load the Flex application
- Supports Express Install, which is a mechanism that helps users stay up to date on the minimum level of Flash Player required by making upgrades simple and painless

A wrapper is the perfect place to introduce a few things:

- Pass external parameters (`flashvars`) to your Flex application
- Embed JavaScript functions that your Flex application can interact with

Let's look at where these wrapper files are located and what they look like.

25.1.1 Wrapper files

When Flash Builder compiles your project, it takes the index.template.html file from the html-template folder, applies some string replacement on variables in the file, and moves it into the bin-debug folder as YourApplication.html. In addition to the HTML wrapper, Flash Builder moves any other files in the html-template folder: your compiled SWF and any non-embedded assets contained in your project. We're going to take a closer look at the files in the html-template folder and find out what they're doing for you. Table 25.1 shows the default contents of the html-template folder in a Flash Builder project.

Table 25.1 Default contents of the Flash Builder html-template folder

File	Description
index.template.html	The main wrapper file. All the action goes on in here.
swfobject.js	This is the workhorse of the process. It provides clear variables for you to use in your wrapper template and load your SWF cleanly.
playerProductInstall.swf	Invoked when the user's Flash Player version is less than the minimum. Has a simple mechanism of prompting the user to install the latest version.
history/*	This folder contains files necessary to support history functionality in Flex.

These files provide an excellent base and are generally all you need for basic development. For a full-screen Flex application, this template may take you all the way through production and deployment. Let's look at the anatomy of the standard HTML template and what part these components play inside it before we look at customizing it to suit your specific needs.

25.1.2 The HTML template

When you first open index.template.html, you'll see a well-commented and logically laid-out HTML file. Each section of the file describes in detail what it does and why it's in the template. Throughout the file you'll notice variables that are referred to as *tokens*. These can be quickly identified by the `${variable}` syntax:

```
<title>${title}</title>
```

Flash Builder replaces these tokens with values that reflect your application's variables. Table 25.2 lists the tokens that are used, and replaced by, Flash Builder inside the default HTML wrapper.

Table 25.2 Flash Builder HTML template replacement tokens

Token	Description
`${application}`	The identity of the compiled SWF application so that it may be referenced by JavaScript within the page.
`${bgcolor}`	The background color of the page.
`${height}`	The height of your compiled SWF file on the page.
`${width}`	The width of your compiled SWF file on the page.
`${swf}`	The location of the compiled SWF file.
`${title}`	The title of the HTML page as it appears in the browser. Flash Builder replaces this value with the name of your Flex application.
`${version_major}`	The major version of Flash Player required by the compiled SWF application.
`${version_minor}`	The minor "dot release" of Flash Player required by the compiled SWF application.
`${version_revision}`	The revision number of Flash Player required by the compiled SWF application.

A major improvement with HTML templates in Flex 4 is the inclusion of SWFObject 2 to manage the cross-browser embedding of your SWF in the HTML wrapper. Let's dig into SWFObject 2 and see how it works.

25.1.3 *SWFObject 2*

SWFObject 2 is a lightweight, standards-based JavaScript library used to generate the more-verbose HTML required by browsers to load SWFs. SWFObject takes care of a lot of the tedium that was required in the past to properly load SWFs across all major browsers. It takes care of the necessary logic to determine what HTML tags the browser requires to display your SWF. Listing 25.1 is the JavaScript from the default HTML template that loads your application in the browser.

Listing 25.1   JavaScript used to load a compiled SWF with SWFObject 2

```
var swfVersionStr = "${version_major}.${version_minor}.${version_revision}"     ◁─┐
var xiSwfUrlStr = "${expressInstallSwf}";                    ◁─┐              Set Flash Player
var flashvars = {};                           Set Express                         version
var params = {};                          Install location
params.quality = "high";
params.bgcolor = "${bgcolor}";
params.allowscriptaccess = "sameDomain";
params.allowfullscreen = "true";
var attributes = {};
attributes.id = "${application}";
attributes.name = "${application}";
attributes.align = "middle";
swfobject.embedSWF(                              Set location of
    "${swf}.swf", "flashContent",           ◁─┘ application SWF
    "${width}", "${height}",
    swfVersionStr, xiSwfUrlStr,
    flashvars, params, attributes);
```

When Flash Builder assembles your application and places the final HTML wrapper in the bin-debug folder, all of the tokens in the SWFObject JavaScript block are replaced with your application's specified values. SWFObject replaces a specified HTML container element with your SWF movie and the appropriate HTML to display it in the browser:

```
<div id="flashContent">
  <p>
  To view this page ensure that Adobe Flash Player version
  ${version_major}.${version_minor}.${version_revision} or greater
      is installed.
  </p>
  <script type="text/javascript">
  var pageHost = ((document.location.protocol == "https:") ? "https://"
      :"http://");
  document.write("<a href='http://www.adobe.com/go/getflashplayer'><img
      src='" + pageHost +
      "www.adobe.com/images/shared/download_buttons/get_flash_player.gif'
  alt='Get Adobe Flash player' /></a>" );
  </script>
</div>
```

SWFObject refers to this replacement as *dynamic* publishing. If the appropriate version of Flash Player isn't found, this HTML content is displayed. If an acceptable version of Flash Player exists, the HTML content is replaced with the HTML that will load your SWF.

PASSING VARIABLE PARAMETERS TO YOUR APPLICATION WITH SWFOBJECT

You'll often run into situations where you need to pass variables into your application from the HTML that it resides in. This information could range from user identification to variables that are specific to the environment that your Flex application is deployed to. SWFObject makes the creation and passing along of these variables easy through the use of flashvars.

Flashvars can be used to

- Pass in dynamic variables such as build numbers from the web server to the Flex application
- Provide the Flex application with information regarding the user who is logged in to the website
- Provide customization based on variables

Flashvars, as the name suggests, are variables that are used by Flash. These variables are created and passed to the SWF at runtime. In listing 25.1 you may have noticed the following line:

```
var flashvars = {};
```

This line of JavaScript defines a variable object. In listing 25.1 this object is empty. No flashvars are being created or passed to the application. Adding flashvars is as simple as replacing the empty object with a generic key/value pair object such as the following:

```
var flashvars = {username:"bob", phoneNumber:"555-555-1212"};
```

The flashvars variable now contains two properties: username and phoneNumber. These properties will be passed into the application SWF file when it is launched and will be made immediately available to you.

```
swfobject.embedSWF(
    "${swf}.swf", "flashContent",
    "${width}", "${height}",
    swfVersionStr, xiSwfUrlStr,
    flashvars, params, attributes);
```

Pass flashvars object to SWFObject

Accessing flashvars from within your application is simple. Let's look at how to go about that in the following listing.

Listing 25.2 Accessing flashvars from within a Flex application

```
<s:Application xmlns:fx="http://ns.adobe.com/mxml/2009"
        xmlns:s="library://ns.adobe.com/flex/spark"
        xmlns:mx="library://ns.adobe.com/flex/mx"
        creationComplete="creationCompleteHandler(event)">
  <fx:Script>
    <![CDATA[
      import mx.core.FlexGlobals;
      import mx.events.FlexEvent;
```

```
protected function creationCompleteHandler(event:FlexEvent):void
{
    var flashvars:Object =
        FlexGlobals.topLevelApplication.parameters;
    trace(flashvars.username, flashvars.phoneNumber);
}
    ]]>
    </fx:Script>
</s:Application>
```

Access the flashvars object ❶

The flashvars object that was defined in JavaScript and passed into your Flex application is accessed through FlexGlobals.topLevelapplication.parameters ❶. The syntax for accessing the parameters is new to Flex 4. The parameters object *is* the flashvars object that you created in JavaScript, or, more correctly, it's an ActionScript object with the properties and values that match the object created in JavaScript. This object is available globally throughout your Flex application.

This section has covered the basics of creating your HTML wrapper and using SWFObject 2 to make the process easier. Full documentation for SWFObject, as well as examples, can be found on the SWFObject project's documentation page: http://code.google.com/p/swfobject/wiki/documentation.

Now your application is complete. It has a killer UI, the effects are mind blowing, you've debugged it, and the HTML wrapper is good to go. The last step in sharing your application with the world is deployment. Let's look at the basics of deployment so you can let the rest of the world enjoy your creation.

25.2 Deployment

This is the last piece to wrapping up your project—getting it out the door! At this point, the application has been tested, and it passes QA and user acceptance; the next step is to push it into a production environment.

Because applications can vary drastically in implementation, there's no one-size-fits-all approach. But we'll give you general pointers and procedures.

25.2.1 Creating a production build

Throughout the course of building your Flex applications, you'll have noticed that by default they're built into a bin-debug folder. Care to guess what kind of file it is?

Even though it's fairly obvious, if you said "debug," you get a prize. The debug version of your Flex application allows for the memory profiling, step debugger, and so on. These additional options increase the file size of your SWF considerably.

For a production release build, you don't want that overhead. To create the production version of your application, follow these steps:

1 Select Project > Export Release Build. Doing so brings up a dialog box that allows you to do a production build of any of your applications.

2 Select the desired application.

3 Choose the output folder (by default, it creates a bin-release folder, as shown in figure 25.1), and click Finish.

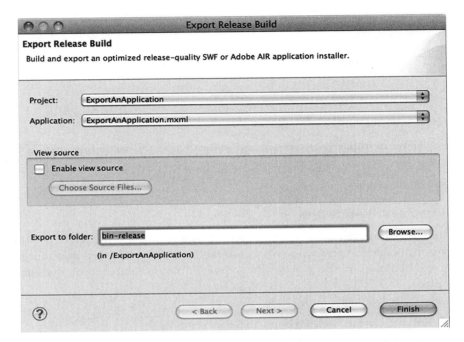

Figure 25.1 The Export Release Build dialog box lets you build production versions of your applications.

You should notice that the export folder has been created and is populated with your application's various files.

NOTE Selecting the Enable View Source option allows users to view the source code of your application.

You're almost there, and now that you have a production build of your application, you need to deploy all the client files.

25.2.2 Positioning client-side files

The next stage involves copying all the client-side Flex files into place. The list of things to move is application specific, but here's a good starting point:

- Everything generated by the release build process:
  - HTML wrapper file
  - JavaScript files (such as swfobject.js)
  - history folder
  - playerProductInstall.swf
  - Your application SWF file(s)
- External assets (things you didn't embed in the application):
  - Graphics and icons
  - Audio/MP3 files

- Video files
- Stylesheets
- Configuration:
    - XML files
- Libraries:
    - RSLs
    - SWCs
    - SWF modules

With the frontend pieces in place, next you need to deal with the backend pieces that reside on the server.

25.2.3 *Positioning server-side files*

If your application relies on backend pieces being in place, you need to position them into your production environment. This is technology specific, but don't forget that if you created a custom wrapper in your web technology of choice, you need to move it into place.

Other server-side pieces include

- Remote objects, web services, and data services
- Database changes
- Server-side configuration
- Web server configuration

Now all you need to do is make sure it works.

25.2.4 *Testing your application*

This may go without saying, but whether you're deploying to a staging environment or directly to production, these environments won't be the same as your local development environment. In particular, you're accessing the application via a web server, whereas locally you may have loaded it directly. For example, your URL may go from /Volume/MyDisk/users/me/projects/MyCoolFlexProject/bin-release/MyApp.html to an HTTP-based URL: http://www.mydomain.com/MyApp.html. Because you're going over the wire, some things may get in the way that you should be aware of:

- Network access
- Firewalls
- Web server configuration/authentication

Network access is a critical component of any rich internet application. If your users don't have network access or have only limited bandwidth available, it can affect the performance and usability of the application. This problem is largely out of your control as a developer. You can take steps to keep down file size throughout development to assist the bandwidth challenged. If users don't have network access, unfortunately there's little you can do to help them.

Firewalls can be a real problem. For most standard Flex applications, you'll be accessing data across standard HTTP ports (80/8080), and there shouldn't be significant issues. If you have complicated backend solutions or use remoting that requires the use of an alternative port, you might have issues with firewalls. Try to stick to the standard HTTP ports when possible, and if you really need to use alternative ports, investigate whether your server-side solution allows for HTTP failover in the event of a firewall. Many solutions, including LCDS and BlazeDS, allow you to fall back to HTTP when a firewall situation is detected. This can be a real lifesaver.

Configuring your web server is a book in and of itself. It can certainly be a fun and rewarding experience, but many variables are at play. If you work in a team environment, you'll likely have skilled teammates who are devoted to managing the server-side configuration. If this isn't the case, then you'll likely spend significant amounts of time and effort learning how your server needs to be configured. Find your technology's user groups, forums, or email lists, and be prepared to ask informed questions. People appreciate it when you've obviously done some research before presenting your questions.

If your application is relatively simple, it should be up and running quickly. If your application is complex and requires many components to run, it may take some trial and error to get it running in production. In either case, you'll soon have your Flex application live and ready to provide a service to your users. Congratulations! It's an app.

25.3 *Summary*

That's a wrap! You know all the things you need to know to be a productive Flex developer. There's always more to learn, and that can come in time; don't sweat it. The more you get comfortable with the technology, the more you'll naturally learn and expand your knowledge.

The next steps are to put your newfound Flex knowledge to work and focus on making real applications. You'll encounter hurdles, and you'll overcome them, but you're never alone.

One of the best things about being a Flex developer is the supportive community you'll be part of. See the resources that follow this chapter, be sure to join your local Flex user group, and attend Flex-based conferences.

As you become proficient, you can help grow the strength of the community by participating in discussion forums, sharing on Twitter, starting a blog, and writing articles. We hope this book has given you a solid foundation to build on, and we look forward to seeing you out in the Flex ecosystem.

index